MATTHEW

Interpreted by
Early Christian Commentators

THE CHURCH'S BIBLE

General Editor

Robert Louis Wilken

• •

The Song of Songs
Richard A. Norris Jr.

Isaiah
Robert Louis Wilken

Matthew
D. H. Williams

John
Bryan A. Stewart & Michael A. Thomas

Romans
J. Patout Burns Jr.

1 Corinthians
Judith L. Kovacs

MATTHEW

Interpreted by
Early Christian Commentators

Translated and Edited by

D. H. Williams

William B. Eerdmans Publishing Company
Grand Rapids, Michigan

Wm. B. Eerdmans Publishing Co.
2140 Oak Industrial Drive NE, Grand Rapids, Michigan 49505
www.eerdmans.com

Published 2018
Printed in the United States of America

27 26 25 24 23 22 21 20 19 18   1 2 3 4 5 6 7 8 9 10

ISBN 978-0-8028-2578-0

Library of Congress Cataloging-in-Publication Data

Names: Williams, Daniel H., translator, editor.
Title: Matthew / interpreted by early Christian commentators ; translated and edited by D. H. Williams.
Description: Grand Rapids : Eerdmans Publishing Co., 2018. | Series: The church's bible | Includes bibliographical references and index.
Identifiers: LCCN 2017027352 | ISBN 9780802825780 (hardcover : alk. paper)
Subjects: LCSH: Bible. Matthew—Commentaries.
Classification: LCC BS2575.53 .M378 2018 | DDC 226.2/0609—dc23
LC record available at https://lccn.loc.gov/2017027352

Special funding for the final preparation of this book was provided by the College of Arts and Sciences, Baylor University 2016.

In grateful and affectionate memory of Fred Norris,
who often reminded me not to lose sight of God in the midst of all our efforts
in studying the ancient Fathers.

Contents

Series Preface

The volumes in The Church's Bible are designed to present the Holy Scriptures as understood and interpreted during the first millennium of Christian history. The Christian Church has a long tradition of commentary on the Bible. In the early Church all discussion of theological topics, of moral issues, and of Christian practice took the biblical text as the starting point. The recitation of the psalms and meditation on books of the Bible, particularly in the context of the liturgy or of private prayer, nurtured the spiritual life. For most of the Church's history theology and scriptural interpretation were one. Theology was called *sacra pagina* (the sacred page), and the task of interpreting the Bible was a spiritual enterprise.

During the first two centuries interpretation of the Bible took the form of exposition of select passages on particular issues. For example, Irenaeus, bishop of Lyons, discussed many passages from the Old and New Testaments in his defense of the apostolic faith against the Gnostics. By the beginning of the third century Christian bishops and scholars had begun to preach regular series of sermons that followed the biblical books verse by verse. Some wrote more scholarly commentaries that examined in greater detail grammatical, literary, and historical questions as well as theological ideas and spiritual teachings found in the texts. From Origen of Alexandria, the first great biblical commentator in the Church's history, we have, among others, a large verse-by-verse commentary on the Gospel of John, a series of homilies on Genesis and Exodus, and a large part of his *Commentary on the Epistle to the Romans*. In the course of the first eight hundred years of Christian history Christian teachers produced a library of biblical commentaries and homilies on the Bible.

Today this ancient tradition of biblical interpretation is known only in bits and pieces, and even where it still shapes our understanding of the Bible, for example, in the selection of readings for Christian worship (e.g., Isaiah 7 and Isaiah 9 read at Christmas), or the interpretation of the Psalms in daily prayer, the spiritual world that gave it birth remains shadowy and indistinct. It is the purpose of this series to make available the richness of the Church's classical tradition of interpretation for clergy, Sunday school and Bible class teachers, men and women living in religious communities, and all serious readers of the Bible.

Anyone who reads the ancient commentaries realizes at once that they are deeply spiritual, insightful, edifying, and, shall we say, "biblical." Early Christian thinkers moved in the world of the Bible, understood its idiom, loved its teaching, and were filled with awe before its mysteries. They believed in the maxim "Scripture interprets Scripture." They knew something that has largely been forgotten by biblical scholars, and their commentaries are an untapped resource for understanding the Bible as a book about Christ.

The distinctive mark of The Church's Bible is that it draws extensively on the ancient commentaries, not only on random comments drawn from theological treatises, sermons, or devotional works. Its volumes will, in the main, offer fairly lengthy excerpts from the ancient commentaries and from series of sermons on specific books. For example, in the first volume on the Song of Songs, there are long passages from Origen of Alexandria's *Commentary on the Song of Songs*, from Gregory of Nyssa's *Homilies on the Song*, and from Bernard of Clairvaux's sermons on the Song. Some passages will be as brief as a paragraph, but many will be several pages in length, and some longer. We believe that only through a deeper immersion in the ancient sources can contemporary readers enter into the inexhaustible spiritual and theological world of the early Church and hence of the Bible.

It is also hoped that longer passages will be suitable for private devotional reading and for spiritual reading in religious communities, in Bible study groups, and in prayer circles.

ROBERT LOUIS WILKEN
General Editor

Acknowledgments

Coming to the end of such a long period in which many were involved, I must first express my gratefulness to Dr. Yelena Borisova, who assisted me in translation as well as other editorial responsibilities. Special thanks are due to Richard Brumback; Jeffrey Cross; Derek S. Dodson; Daniel Eady; Eric Gilchrest; †Robert C. Hill; Justin King; Kevin B. McCruden; †Frederick W. Norris; David L. Riggs; Andrew Selby; Thomas Smith; Kevin J. Symonds; David J. White; Robert Louis Wilken; and Nicholas Zola.

Interpreting the New Testament

The traditional greeting on Easter morning is "Christ is risen!" To which the response is: "He is risen indeed. Alleluia!" This ancient phrase echoes the greeting of the angel to Mary Magdalene and Mary the mother of James and Joseph as they arrived at the sepulchre to anoint the body of Jesus: "He is not here; for he has risen, as he said" (Matt 28:6). After the two disciples recognized Christ in the breaking of bread on the road to Emmaus, they immediately rose and returned to the others gathered in Jerusalem, announcing: "The Lord has risen indeed, and has appeared to Simon!" (Luke 24:34).

The resurrection of Christ is the ground of Christian belief and the wellspring from which the books of the New Testament flow. The Gospels culminate in the resurrection, at the beginning of the Epistle to the Romans Paul invokes the resurrection as warrant for his apostleship, and he brings 1 Corinthians to a close with a magnificent peroration on the resurrected body. In places 1 Peter reads like an Easter baptismal sermon ("we have been born anew to a living hope through the resurrection of Jesus Christ from the dead" [1 Pet 1:3]), and in the Acts of the Apostles the disciples of Christ are portrayed again and again as "witnesses" to the resurrection (1:22; 2:32; 3:15, et al.).

The New Testament is a collection of books whose authors bore witness in their lives (and some in their deaths) to the living Christ. "It is no longer I who live," writes St. Paul in Galatians, "but Christ who lives in me" (Gal 2:20). Before there was a book, there were persons who handed on Christ's sayings and told of the marvelous things God had worked in him. First came Christ, then the witnesses, then the books. This ordering of things is at the heart of the early interpretation of the New Testament. The goal was to delve more deeply into the mystery of God revealed in Christ, to whom the writings bear witness. In introducing the volumes on the New Testament in this series, it may be helpful to say a few things about how the early Christians approached this task.

We are inclined to begin with the book, with historical context and social setting, words and idioms, grammar and literary forms, religious and theological vocabulary, and the many other topics that command our attention. But the early Christians began with the risen Christ, and long before there was a book the faith was handed on orally. Although St. Paul said that he had received his commission "through a revelation of Jesus Christ" (Gal 1:12), not from a human intermediary, he associated himself with traditions that he had received from others. "For I *delivered* to you as of first importance what I also *received*, that Christ died for our sins in accordance with the scriptures, that he was buried, that he was raised on the third day in accordance with the scriptures, and that he appeared to Cephas, then to the twelve. Then he appeared to more than five hundred brethren at one time, most of whom are still alive, though some have fallen asleep. Then he appeared to James, then to all the apostles. Last of all, as to one untimely born, he appeared to me" (1 Cor 15:3-8).

The memory of Christ centered on his death and resurrection, and the brief narrative of his birth, suffering, death, burial, and resurrection formed the core of early Christian tradition. It was complemented by "sayings" of Jesus, but the sayings were understood in light of the events, as the structure of the Gospels makes plain. The setting of the early confessions of faith was almost certainly Christian worship, and they reflect local catechetical instruction. The details varied from place to place, but the central narrative remained constant. Here, for example, is a somewhat freer (and idiosyncratic) form that appears in 1 Peter: "For Christ also *died for sins once for all*, the righteous for the unrighteous, that he might bring us to God, *being put to death in the flesh but made alive in the spirit*; in which he went and preached to the spirits in prison, who formerly did not obey when God's patience waited in the days of Noah, during the building of the ark, in which few, that is, eight persons, were saved through water. Baptism, which corresponds to this, now saves you, not as a removal of dirt from the body but as an appeal to God for a clear conscience, through the *resurrection of Jesus Christ, who has gone into heaven and is at the right hand of God*, with angels, authorities, and powers subject to him" (1 Pet 3:18-22).

The mention of Baptism indicates that the early tradition also included how one was to understand Christian practices. In 1 Corinthians Paul's language about the Lord's Supper is similar to what he had used about the resurrection: "For I *received* from the Lord what I also *delivered* to you, that the Lord Jesus on the night when he was betrayed took bread, and when he had given thanks, he broke it, and said, 'This is my body which is for you. Do this in remembrance of me.' In the same way also the cup, after supper, saying, 'This cup is the new covenant in my blood. Do this, as often as you drink it, in remembrance of me.' For as often as you eat this bread and drink this cup, you proclaim the Lord's death until he comes" (1 Cor 11:23-26). Though Paul says that he had received the account about the Last Supper directly from the Lord, the terms "received" and "delivered" are the customary words for handing on tradition. Paul is repeating word for word what he has received from others.

Early in the Church's history, then, the living Christ was identified by verbal formulas and practices, notably Baptism and the Eucharist. The purpose of the creedlike summaries of faith was primarily catechetical, but they served as guarantors of the truth of what had taken place during Christ's lifetime and unlocked the Jewish scriptures, what Christians would later call the Old Testament. This is evident in an illuminating testimony from Ignatius, bishop of Antioch, at the end of the first century. The Christians in Philadelphia in western Asia Minor were divided over some aspects of Christian teaching, and Ignatius exhorted them to abandon their contentiousness. Apparently some had argued that the only way the matter could be settled was by appeal to what they called "the archives," that is, the Old Testament. "If I do not find it in the archives, I do not believe it to be in the gospel," they said. Ignatius, however, demurred. "For me," he writes, "the archives are

Jesus Christ, the inviolable archives are his cross and death and his resurrection and faith through him. . . ."[1] Although most, if not all, of the books of the New Testament had been written by the time he became bishop, Ignatius makes no mention of Christian writings to settle the dispute. He appeals only to the person of Christ and the brief narrative of his saving deeds, not to written documents.

The time was fast approaching, however, when oral tradition would be complemented by written documents. But not replaced! Even after the writings of the apostles formed the "canon" of writings we call the New Testament, the oral witness of the apostles remained alive. Irenaeus, bishop of Lyons, at the end of the second century still conceived of apostolic tradition in terms of persons first, books second. "The Lord of all gave to his apostles the power of the gospel, and through them we have learned the truth, that is, the teaching of the Son of God. . . . We have not learned the plan of our salvation from any others than those through whom the gospel came to us. They first proclaimed it, and then later by the will of God handed it down to us in writings. . . ."[2] For St. Irenaeus the most authentic tradition was oral, what "the elders, the disciples of the apostles, have handed on to us."[3]

At the same time Irenaeus is the first writer to draw on the apostolic writings as part of an authoritative collection. He does not use the term "New Testament" but its basic structure of Gospels, the Acts of the Apostles, and epistles is clearly visible in his works. In fact, a large part of his work against the Gnostics is given over to the exegesis of specific passages from the New Testament that were in dispute. But the books did not stand on their own. They needed to be explained and individual passages fitted into the pattern of God's saving work in Christ. For this task the oral tradition confessed in the rule of faith and explained by teachers whose lineage could be traced back to the apostles was indispensable. Without a grasp of the plot that holds the books together, said Irenaeus, the Bible is as vacuous as a mosaic in which the tiny colored stones have been arbitrarily rearranged without reference to the original design. Even the apostolic writings, the Christian scriptures, required a framework of interpretation, a canopy of beliefs and practices to envelop the texts.

The oral tradition took form in a tripartite, that is, trinitarian, rule of faith that identified God by narrating key events recorded in the Scriptures, the creation of the world, the inspiration of the prophets, the coming of Christ in the flesh, his death and resurrection, the outpouring of the Holy Spirit. Though drawn from the New Testament, the rule was distinct from the apostolic writings; it was a brief confession handed on at Baptism that provided a key to the Scriptures. In other words, the Scriptures were read and interpreted in light of the Church's tradition. Or, to put it more precisely, the tradition embodied in the apostolic writings, that is, the New Testament, was complemented by the tradition, equally apostolic, that had been handed on orally (primarily in Christian worship) from one generation to another. The New Testament was the book of the Church, and interpretation took place within a context of shared beliefs and practices.

For example, during the great debate over the relation of the Son to the Father in the fourth century, Athanasius, bishop of Alexandria, used Irenaeus's principle of interpreta-

1. *Philadelphians* 8.
2. *Against Heresies* 3, preface.
3. *Demonstration of the Apostolic Preaching* 3.

tion to marshall scriptural support for the decrees of the Council of Nicaea. Arius, whose teaching had been condemned at the council, had called attention to the word "therefore" in Phil 2:9, "*Therefore* God has highly exalted him [Christ] and bestowed on him the name which is above every name." In his view the "therefore" implied that the Son had "become" God and was not God from eternity. Athanasius showed that this was an idiosyncratic and "private" interpretation contrary to the "Church's sense of the Scripture" handed on orally and expressed in other texts in the New Testament, for example, John 1:1, "and the Word was God," or Heb 1:6, "Let all God's angels worship him." For good measure he points out that three verses earlier St. Paul had said that Christ, who was "in the form of God, did not count equality with God a thing to be grasped" (Phil 2:6).[4]

By the third century the canon of the New Testament was universally recognized, though certain books remained in dispute, for example, the Apocalypse. Writers such as Tertullian in North Africa and Clement and Origen in Alexandria had at their disposal a Christian Bible composed of two parts, Old Testament and New Testament. But the written Scripture never replaced the living tradition, and its interpretation was guided by the rule of faith and Christian practice. The engine that drove interpretation was the Church's faith in the triune God confessed in the baptismal creed, made present through Christ in the consecrated bread and wine of the Eucharist, whose power and love were confirmed in the lives of the faithful by the searing flame of the Holy Spirit. Once there was a written Scripture, interpretation inevitably entered a new phase. The church fathers did not doubt that the apostolic writings bore witness to the one God, creator of all things, to the Son Jesus Christ the Lord, and to the outpouring of the Holy Spirit to call into one fellowship a new people. But interpretation not only has to do with the big picture but is most decidedly an exercise in particularity, how specific words and passages are to be understood and related to the faith delivered to the apostles. This was a demanding assigment that could be accomplished only through study, prayer, and, let it not be forgotten, argument and debate. Even in the early centuries the New Testament required interpretation, and its readers no less than we had to train their minds and tutor their affections to discern its meaning. All this took time and hard labor, and the number and variety of commentaries and homilies on books and passages of the New Testament during the early centuries of the Church's history is astonishing. Yet the purpose of commentary was always kept in sight. Interpretation was a spiritual voyage of discovery, a way of exploring the luminous world revealed in the coming of Christ.

A good illustration is Gregory of Nyssa's interpretation of the word "righteousness" or "justice" (either a possible translation of a single Greek word), which occurs twice in the Beatitudes: "Blessed are those who hunger and thirst for righteousness (or justice), for they shall be satisfied." And: "Blessed are those who are persecuted for the sake of justice [or righteousness], for theirs is the kingdom of heaven" (Matt 5:6, 10). The same term occurs in the writings of St. Paul, and Gregory of Nyssa, a fourth-century Greek commentator, noted in particular its use in 1 Corinthians: "[God] is the source of your life in Christ Jesus, whom God made our wisdom, our *righteousness* [or justice] and sanctification and redemption" (1 Cor 1:30).

4. *Against the Arians* 1.37-44.

In a homily on the fourth beatitude Gregory asks: "What is justice?" to which he gives a traditional philosophical answer: justice is to give to each according to his worth. But then he observes that there is a higher form of justice, not based on merit. This is the justice we are to desire; hence the beatitude speaks of those who "hunger and thirst for justice." Here the homily takes a surprising turn as Gregory offers what he calls a "bolder interpretation": in the beatitude the Lord proposes to his followers that he himself is what they desire, "for he became for us wisdom from God, justice, sanctification, and redemption" (1 Cor 1:30).

By appealing to 1 Corinthians Gregory opens the beatitude to a christological interpretation. In his view it is speaking about hungering and thirsting for the living God, as David said in the psalm, "My soul thirsts for the living God" (Ps 42:2). By interpreting the words of Jesus with the help of St. Paul, a procedure, one might observe, that would be shunned by a modern interpreter, Gregory is able to transform the beatitude into an invitation to seek not only "justice" but the living God, or, better, to find justice by knowing Christ. The one who tastes the Lord "has received God into himself and is filled with him for whom he has thirsted and hungered. He acknowledges that he has been filled with the one he desires when he says, 'Christ lives in me' (Gal 2:20)."[5]

Some texts posed perplexing theological problems, as, for example, the passage at the beginning of the Gospel of John: "No one has ever seen God" (John 1:18). The text is straightforward enough: God has never been seen. 1 Tim 6:16 went further: "no one has ever seen or can see [God]."[6] Yet the prophet Isaiah said explicitly that he had seen God: "In the year that King Uzziah died I *saw* the Lord sitting upon a throne, high and lifted up" (Isa 6:1). How was one to reconcile these passages and relate the words of John to other texts, for example, the report in the book of Genesis that Jacob saw God "face to face" (Gen 32:30)?

For many modern interpreters theological questions—for example, what it means to see God—are quite secondary to the task of interpretation and the unity of the Bible; that is, how one book in the Scriptures is to be understood in relation to other parts of the Bible is peripheral to their exegesis. Isaiah is Isaiah, and John is John. But early Christian commentators believed that the Bible spoke with a single (though nuanced) voice, and they took apparent inconsistencies between biblical authors as an invitation to probe beneath the surface of the inspired words, that is, to penetrate the spiritual reality about which the text spoke, in this case to grasp what it means to see God. "Seeing," they explained, was a form of knowledge, and they claimed that when all the relevant passages are considered, the Scriptures teach that God can be known, although the fullness of his divinity, his ineffable nature or essence, is beyond our comprehension. "It is one thing to see," writes Augustine, "it is another to grasp the whole by seeing."[7] One writer said that in the Scriptures "see" means the same as "possess," citing the words of the psalmist: "May you see the good things of Jerusalem" (Ps 128:5), where "see" means "to find." Hence he concludes that one who sees God "possesses all that is good."[8] By drawing on the many uses of the word "see" in the Scriptures (including the beatitude, "Blessed are the pure in heart, for they shall see

5. *Homily 4 on the Beatitudes* (Gregorii Nysseni Opera VII/II.122-23).

6. 1 John 4:12, "No man has ever seen God," was also cited.

7. *Letter* 147.8.21. This letter, a little treatise "on seeing God," discusses the relevant biblical texts.

8. Gregory of Nyssa, *Homily on the Beatitudes* (Gregorii Nysseni Opera VII/II.138).

God" [Matt 5:8]) Christian thinkers were able to explore the place of the vision of God in Christian life and hope.[9]

At times a single biblical word could inspire a preacher to lyrical heights. In a memorable sermon on the phrase "that God may be all in all" (1 Cor 15:28), Augustine asked, "What is the meaning of 'all'? [God] will be for you whatever you desired here on earth, whatever you valued. What did you want here, what did you love? To eat and drink? He himself will be food for you, he himself will be drink. What did you want here? A fragile and transient bodily health? He himself will be immortality for you. What did you look for here? Wealth? Greedy man, what is it that will satisfy you if God himself does not? Well, what did you love? Glory, honors? God will be your glory."[10]

When they listened to the Scriptures read in divine worship or pondered its words in prayer, the early Christians heard the Word of God spoken to their communities and to their lives. In his *Commentary on the Gospel of John* Origen of Alexandria, the first and greatest biblical scholar in the early Church, explained that "a gospel" is a "discourse containing an account of things that have happened which, because of the good they bring, are a source of joy to the hearer." The gospel is a "word that makes present something good for the believer or a word that the promised good is present." Its subject, continues Origen, is the "presence of Jesus Christ, the firstborn of all creation (Col 1:15), among men for their salvation." Accordingly, the Gospels are the "firstfruits" of the Scriptures, and the "firstfruits" of the Gospels is the Gospel according to John, "whose meaning cannot be understood unless one reclines on Jesus's breast (John 13:23) and accepts Mary from Jesus as his own mother."[11]

Anyone who wrote a commentary on the Gospels in this spirit would discover much in the biblical text that a strictly historical approach would miss. And the reader of Origen's *Commentary on John* will not be disappointed. Not only was Origen engaged with the spiritual and theological meaning of the text, but he also assumed that to understand the Gospel one must know Christ, in his words "recline on Jesus's breast." But his commentary is also a work of great scholarship and learning. In the first book he devotes many pages to a single word, "beginning," in the opening sentence, "In the beginning was the Word." Because "beginning" is the first significant term to appear in the Gospel, it sends him off on a discussion of the many uses of "beginning" in the Scriptures. And this in turn allows him to explain why Christ is identified with "beginning." Christ, writes Origen, is the beginning of those "made in the image of God" because he is the "firstborn of all creation" (Col 1:15); he is the beginning of knowledge because he is called "Wisdom" (1 Cor 1:24); he is the beginning of life because he is the "firstborn from the dead" (Col 1:18); the beginning of creation, that is, the agent of creation, because he is "the beginning of [God's] ways for his work" (Prov 8:22).[12]

Origen is interpreting Scripture by Scripture, an axiom accepted by all early Christian writers. "The entire Scripture is one book and was spoken by the one Holy Spirit," wrote Cyril of Alexandria, another prolific biblical commentator.[13] Accordingly, it was presumed

9. Jerome, *Commentary on Isaiah* 6:1 (Corpus Christianorum 73:84-85); Gregory the Great, *Moralia* 18.88.

10. *Sermon* 158.9.

11. *Commentary on John* 1.27.

12. *Commentary on John* 1.90-108.

13. *Commentary on Isaiah 29:11-12* (Patrologia Graeca 70:655a).

that the interpreter would draw on passages from the entire Bible to illuminate and explain the text under discussion. The technique most often used was word association, seeking words or images that are the same or similar to what is found in the text, as Origen did when he explained "beginning" in his *Commentary on John*. The term could be "life," or "water," or "rock," or "rain," or "man," or "mountain," or a myriad of other words or images. As the expositors sought appropriate texts, they were led to yet more passages, and the commentaries and homilies often read like a pastiche of biblical verses. Yet there was method in their exegetical artistry. As words and phrases were invested with meanings drawn from elsewhere in the Scriptures, they acquired a theological clarity and sonority that only the Bible could give. In effect the words of the Gospel of John become "biblical" rather than simply Johannine; that is, the context of understanding was formed by the Bible as a whole, not just the Gospel of John.

We are so accustomed to think of context as literary or historical that we forget that the words of the Bible have a life that transcends their original setting. Think how a verse from the New Testament can sound when read in Christian worship. It is traditional to read from the book of Titus on Christmas Eve: "For the grace of God has appeared for the salvation of all men, training us to renounce irreligion and worldly passions, and to live sober, upright, and godly lives in this world . . ." (Tit 2:11-13). When this passage is read in the Liturgy for the Nativity of Christ, the word "appear" rings out clearly like the peal of a single bell announcing the birth of Christ, the Incarnation of the divine Word. While this understanding of the verse is certainly implicit within the text, the liturgical setting gives the word "appear" a concreteness and directness that it does not have in the context of the epistle, and the Liturgy, in turn, acquires a word so fitting and right that Tit 2:11 seems composed primarily for the occasion.

Under the tutelage of the church fathers, one learns to read the Bible very closely and to pay particular attention to the subtlety and resonance of its words. As Augustine once remarked: "My heart is exercised by the pounding of the *words* of your Holy Scripture."[14] One also learns to see things whole, to interpret individual texts in light of the central biblical narrative and the Christ confessed in the creeds and celebrated in the Church's worship.

But there is something else to keep in mind while reading the volumes in this series. For the church fathers biblical interpretation had to do with the bearing of the text on the present. The interpreter is not a disinterested observer, a voyeur; rather, he is a participant in the mystery about which he speaks. This can be illustrated by a story told about St. Antony, the monk of the Egyptian desert.

> Once some visitors came to Antony and asked him for a good word. He told them that they should heed the Scriptures. When they pressed him for specifics, he said they should follow the word of Jesus in Matthew: "If anyone strikes you on one cheek, turn to him the other also" (Matt 5:39). But they objected, "We can't do that!" So Antony tempered the exhortation: "If you can't do that, at least allow one cheek to be struck." Again they replied, "We cannot do that." So Antony revised the saying another time: "If you are not able to do that, at least do not return evil for evil." But again they protested.

14. *Confessions* 12.1.

> Realizing that it was futile to try to teach such folk how to understand the Bible, he instructed his disciples to "Take a little porridge" to them because "they are ill." And to the visitors he said, "If you cannot do this, or that, what can I do for you? What you need is prayers."[15]

The Bible is a book about how to live in the knowledge of God and of oneself. God's Word is not something to be looked at but something to be acted on. St. Bernard said it well: the interpreter must see himself in that which is said. It is not enough, observes Origen, to say, "'Christ was crucified'; one must say with St. Paul, 'I am crucified with Christ' (Gal 2:19). Likewise it is not enough to say, 'Christ is raised'; one who knows Christ says, 'We shall also live with him' (Rom 6:8)."[16] This is why St. Augustine said that anyone who "thinks he has understood the divine scriptures . . . but does not build up the double love of God and neighbor, has not succeeded in understanding them."[17]

The first major commentaries on the New Testament were written by Origen of Alexandria in the early third century. Like many of the biblical commentaries from the early Church, they have come down to us in fragmentary condition. Fortunately, we still possess large sections of his massive *Commentary on the Gospel of John*. It is not certain whether he completed it, but it took him six books just to reach John 1:29. In addition, he authored a *Commentary on the Gospel of Matthew* and delivered series of homilies on the Gospel of Luke. Others followed his example—some writing commentaries, others delivering homilies that went through a book chapter by chapter. For the Fourth Gospel we have homilies by John Chrysostom and Augustine as well as commentaries by Theodore of Mopsuestia and Cyril of Alexandria. On Matthew there are commentaries by Jerome and Cyril and homilies by Ambrose and John Chrysostom, to mention some of the more important. The Gospel of Mark did not receive a commentary until the Venerable Bede in the eighth century.

Origen also expounded the Pauline epistles. From his commentary on Romans we have only fragments in Greek, but a Latin translation of it was made in the early Church. Homilies on the letters to the Corinthians and commentaries on Paul's minor epistles exist only in fragments. The Latin commentator Ambrosiaster wrote a complete commentary on the Pauline epistles, and Jerome also commented on a number of the letters, including Galatians and Ephesians. Theodore of Mopsuestia wrote a commentary on the minor Pauline epistles, John Chrysostom preached homilies on all of Paul's letters (including Hebrews), and Theodoret of Cyrrhus also commented on the entire corpus. Only fragments of Cyril of Alexandria's commentaries on St. Paul remain. John Chrysostom is one of the few who have preached an entire series of homilies on the Acts of the Apostles. Augustine delivered a series of sermons on 1 John, and Victorinus and Jerome wrote on the Apocalypse.

Even this partial survey gives some idea of the extent to which the church fathers devoted their energies to expounding the New Testament. Commentaries and homilies, however, are only a small part of the exegetical harvest of the early Church. There are sermons and lengthy letters on particular texts, for example, Gregory of Nyssa on 1 Cor 15:28

15. Patrologia Graeca 65:84c.

16. *Against Celsus* 2.69.

17. *On Christian Doctrine* 1.86.

and Augustine on Jas 2:10, and homilies on sections of books, for example, the Beatitudes or the Lord's Prayer.[18] In the new English translation of Augustine's sermons, three volumes are devoted to sermons on passages from the New Testament,[19] and Gregory the Great has a series of forty homilies dealing with select texts from the New Testament.[20] There are also works dealing specifically with the infancy narratives of the Gospels and essays that attempt to harmonize the Gospels. Finally, there are wide-ranging discussions of many texts from the New Testament in theological essays, spiritual tracts, and the like.

Given this vast, diffuse, and often formless body of material, it is often difficult to learn how early Christian thinkers interpreted specific passages in the New Testament. In recent years some of the commentaries from the early Church on the New Testament have been translated into English for the first time. For example, Origen's commentaries on the Gospel of John and Romans and his homilies on Luke are now available,[21] as are Ambrose's homilies on Luke,[22] Theodoret of Cyrrhus on the Pauline epistles,[23] and Origen and Jerome on Ephesians.[24] Nevertheless, the great body of commentaries and homilies remain untranslated in English, and may never be translated.

The Church's Bible will provide commentaries on select books of the New Testament drawn from the writings of the church fathers, and in some cases from medieval authors. We have made a selection of passages from the ancient commentaries and homilies that treat books chapter by chapter. In addition, we have included occasional comments on particular verses drawn from theological writings, sermons, and other early Christian writings. Our aim is not a comprehensive survey of early Christian exegesis of the books of the New Testament, but commentaries that we hope will be interesting, theologically significant, and spiritually uplifting to readers of the New Testament today.

In the excerpts the specific text under discussion is printed in bold. When a passage is cited from elsewhere in the Scriptures, it is printed in italics. In the chapter introductions, quotations from Matthew are in roman type.

The authors and works from which the selections are taken are given in the appendixes.

ROBERT LOUIS WILKEN

18. *St. Gregory of Nyssa: The Lord's Prayer; The Beatitudes*, trans. Hilda C. Graef (New York: Newman, 1954).

19. *The Works of Saint Augustine: A Translation for the 21st Century*, III.3-5, trans. Edmund Hill, O.P. (Brooklyn and New Rochelle, N.Y.: New City Press, 1990-92), 3:3-5.

20. *Gregory the Great: Forty Gospel Homilies*, trans. Dom David Hurst (Kalamazoo: Cistercian Publications, 1990).

21. *Origen: Commentary on the Gospel according to John*, trans. Ronald E. Heine, 2 vols. (Washington, D.C.: Catholic University of America Press, 1989, 1993); *Origen: Homilies on Luke; Fragments on Luke*, trans. Joseph T. Lienhard, S.J. (Washington, D.C.: Catholic University of America Press, 1996); *Origen: Commentary on the Epistle to the Romans*, trans. Thomas P. Schreck, 2 vols. (Washington, D.C.: Catholic University of America Press, 2001, 2002).

22. *Exposition of the Holy Gospel according to Saint Luke: Saint Ambrose of Milan*, trans. Theodosia Tomkinson (Etna, Calif.: Center for Traditionalist Studies, 2003).

23. *Commentary on the Letters of St. Paul by Theodoret of Cyrus*, trans. Robert C. Hill (Brookline, Mass.: Holy Cross Orthodox Press, 2002).

24. Robert E. Heine, *The Commentaries of Origen and Jerome on St. Paul's Epistle to the Ephesians* (New York: Oxford University Press, 2002).

An Introduction to Matthew

In the early Church, the Gospel according to St. Matthew received more commentary and sermons than any of the other three Gospels. At least twenty-five patristic writings deal with Matthew at length, and some forty other writers give it extensive attention. There is no existing canonical collection or listing of the four Gospels that does not put Matthew first. From the unique details of Christ's birth to his post-resurrection appearances, Matthew offers the fullest account of his life. Its popularity was in part because it was the Gospel of fulfillment. "This was to fulfill what was spoken by the prophet" is a common refrain, making Matthew a fitting prologue at the point where the old covenant ended and the new covenant began.

On the basis of the Gospel of Matthew, early Christian interpreters showed that the Christian present and future could not be comprehended without its Hebrew past. In the late fourth century, Chromatius of Aquileia shrewdly observed that "the new" can never stand "without the old, nor does the old have any permanence without the new."[1] What was "foretold by the prophet" in the Old Testament is fulfilled in the new. According to Augustine, the long Jewish genealogy at the beginning of the Gospel demonstrates Christ's humanity as well as his mission.[2] When Jesus sent his disciples to preach the Gospel, he said: "I was sent only to the lost sheep of the house of Israel" (Matt 15:24). Matthew helped Christians understand how the Church emerged out of the people of Israel.

Patristic exposition paid close attention to how the revelation of God was made known. Every word of the text had meaning, and interpretation always began by looking closely at the literal meaning of each word in the text. "For the ancient interpreters, the transparency of the sacred text was as much part of the *divine* nature of Scripture, as was its more obscure revelation. With that in mind they paid special attention to the biblical *littera*."[3] Since God was the primary author of the gospel message and of its particular expression in Matthew, the reader could always presume that there existed a scheme or *ordo* within or "behind" the text. Each word and its placement in the text held a clue for determining the purpose of revelatory events or words. This is why Origen of Alexandria,

1. Prologus, *Tractatus lxi in euangelium Matthei* 1, 3–4, 9, 11; CCSL 9A:185–87, 189–91.

2. *De consensu evangelistarum* II. prol.–4.13.

3. *Handbook on Patristic Exegesis*, ed. C. Kannengiesser (Leiden: Brill, 2006), 168.

the first major biblical commentator in the patristic age, says: "The man who is capable of being taught by 'searching out' and devoting himself to the 'deep things of God' (1 Cor 2:10) can receive the spiritual meaning of the words [of Scripture] and become a partaker of all the doctrines of the Spirit's counsel."[4]

At the same time, there was great elasticity about how broadly the text could be understood and applied, especially when it came to figurative or "spiritual" exegesis. Interpretation was governed by what the church fathers called the *skopos*, "aim," pointing to the central meaning of the Bible. In the words of Cyril of Alexandria: "The *skopos* (aim) of the inspired Scripture is the mystery of Christ signified to us through a myriad of different kinds of things. Some might liken it to a glittering and magnificent city, having not one image of the king, but many, and publicly displayed in every corner of the city."[5]

Among Latin or Greek writers, there is a working assumption that it was possible and preferable to follow the apostles' practice of scriptural exegesis. In fact, the ancient commentators would have been puzzled by the judgment of modern scholars who think it is not possible or even feasible for later Christians to emulate the New Testament.[6] Without question, methods of apostolic interpretation were meant to be followed as models for expounding Christ in Scripture, even if patristic writers would never claim the same degree of spiritual insight as the apostles. Origen wrote: "The Apostle Paul, 'teacher of the Gentiles in faith and truth,' taught the Church . . . how it ought to interpret the books of the Law."[7]

Because Matthew's account itself emphasizes the way Christ fulfilled the Jewish Scriptures, it was natural for later writers to follow the lead and demonstrate the abundance of figurative (or "spiritual") interpretation found in the text. In practice, Matthean commentaries revealed how broadly the text could be rendered in figurative or typological terms. The church fathers follow no one method of interpretation. A good example is the story of the two blind men who called out to Jesus in Matthew 20. Hilary takes them to signify the pagan nations who stemmed from Ham and Japheth,[8] whereas the crowd, which demanded they be silent, was the Jews. Jerome acknowledges that there are several possible interpretations, but he prefers to argue that the two represent the Jews, and the crowd the Gentiles.[9] Augustine claims that one is the Jews and the other Gentiles, and their blindness is the wall (crowd) that separates them.[10] In each case, the narrative in the Gospel is used to convey spiritual truths. So Peter Chrysologus put it this way in the early fifth century:

4. *On First Principles* 4.2.7 (trans. G. W. Butterworth in *Origen: On First Principles* [Gloucester, MA: Peter Smith, 1973], 282).

5. PG 69:308c.

6. The problems are discussed by Richard Longenecker, "Can We Reproduce the Exegesis of the New Testament?" *Tyndale Bulletin* 21 (1970): 3–38, and more recently, Thomas Scheck, *St. Jerome: Commentary on Matthew*, FOC 117 (Washington, DC: Catholic University of America Press, 2008), 24–25.

7. *Homily* 5 (on Exodus 5:1). *Origen: Homilies on Genesis and Exodus*, trans. R. Heine (Washington, DC: Catholic University of America Press, 1982), 275.

8. Cf. Gen 9:20–28; descended from Ham (who was cursed by his father Noah), from whom came the Egyptians and the Canaanites (Gen 10:6), eventual enemies of Israel, and Japheth, from whom originated the "people of the coastlands," which is a phrase used in the Old Testament for the Gentiles. Abram was a descendent of Shem.

9. *Commentary on St. Matthew* 3.20.29–31.

10. *Sermon* 88.10, 13; WSA III/3:425–28.

> The historical narrative of Scripture should always be raised to a higher meaning, and the mysteries of the future should become known through figures of the present. Therefore, we should unfold by allegorical explanation what mystical teaching is contained beneath the outward appearance of the text.[11]

The parables required an allegorical interpretation, but allegory was not limited to parables. They were simply the most obvious cases. According to Ambrosiaster, allegorical interpretation was necessary because Scripture "deliberately keeps many things implicit, to avoid that the meaning gained from the words does not oppose sound piety."[12]

The ancients' approach to the text had to do with their certainty of finding a great deal in them, regardless of exegetical method. They sought to bring the believers into the presence of the divine reality, God's manifestation in history, presented in the text and in that way to deepen their spiritual lives. Put another way, there are no mere historical narratives in Matthew; every part of the text is a divinely punctuated chronicle of revelation, and every verse was a part of God's intention to disclose his salvific purposes.

Even obscure texts or apparent contradictions within the Bible offered an opportunity for the Holy Spirit to work in the Christian's heart. An incongruous or improbable sequence of events was a sign that a figurative interpretation was called for. Contradictions or inconsistencies were not obstacles to be overcome, but open doors by which the believer could perceive the power of God in ways not obvious to the uninitiated.

Augustine explained to his congregation that obscure or conflicting passages in Scripture are not there to conceal mysteries. By means of them, God wants to open the heart of "those who are prepared for them." Such texts lead us on, "heart and soul, to the search."[13] This is what Jesus meant, we are told, when he said, "do not throw what is holy to the dogs, nor toss your pearls in front of pigs" (Matt 7:6).

Allegory, however, had its limits when it came to exegesis. The ancient commentators give close attention to Matthew's simple recounting of the facts of Jesus's life, death, and resurrection. The Beatitudes, for instance, are reckoned according to their plain wording, accepting *prima facie* each precept about the poor in spirit, those who mourn, etc. Most miracle stories are also treated in a straightforward way with minimal commentary. The best example, however, is Jesus's passion and resurrection narrative (Matt 27–28), where the fathers are interested chiefly in elucidating the events as they are recorded. Leo the Great interprets Jesus's final words on the cross about being forsaken in very literal terms:

> **Jesus was crying out with a great voice, Why have you forsaken me?** [He said this] in order to make known to all how it was right that he neither be rescued nor protected, but that he be abandoned to the hands of savage men. . . . [I]t was as much the will of the Father as it was his own will for the Lord to be given over to his passion. As a result, not only did the Father abandon him, but also the Lord even deserted himself in a certain way, not by a timorous withdrawal, but by an intentional surrender.

11. *Sermon* 36 and 96.
12. *Quaestio* 26.1.
13. *Sermon* 60A.1.

Unlike modern scholarly exegesis practiced in academic circles, patristic exegesis took place within the Church and for the Church. In this setting, the catholic character of the gospel was most apparent. Admittedly, sometimes the unpredictable nature of spiritual interpretation can be disconcerting; but the aim is always to display on the basis of the biblical text God's plan of salvation in Christ.[14] Because exegesis was intended for the body of believers, interpretation was closely linked to the Church's faith and practice. For that reason, interpretation was not governed by the supposed original intention of the biblical author, nor could the word of God be comprehended by imposing on biblical texts a single meaning. The Bible was the Church's book, and its meaning was shaped by the Church's teaching, liturgy, and practice.[15]

The principle that Scripture interpreted Scripture rested on the conviction that the Bible was a unified book. Christ was the interpretive key to unlock its meaning and to link the two Testaments. We, therefore, discover that identity of David's Son (9:27; 15:22; 21:9), the Passover lamb (26:26–28), the message of the prophets (23:34–37), the ancient temple (26:61), Jonah in the whale for three days (12:40), etc. These all point to a larger christological pattern that guides the reader in what to look for. Typology linked the remnant of ancient Israel and the Church through similarities between the Exodus and the holy family's escape to Egypt (2:13–15), and also between Elijah and John (11:13–14).

Events in the Gospel are also related to the life of faith. Christ's baptism is a model for the baptism of the Christian: "He was baptized for our baptism because it was his to give; because it was a type of his death and of his resurrection. And just as he died and rose and became the firstfruits from the dead (1 Cor 15:20), so he was baptized in a sacred way for our baptism and immediately gave it to us."[16] The children that came to Jesus are a type of the kingdom of heaven;[17] Christ's tomb becomes a new womb,[18] and the mustard seed represents Christ's faith that grows because it is sown in all believers.[19] Throughout the Gospel, the direct fulfilment of prophecies in the Old Testament are carefully indicated (1:22–23; 2:17–18; 2:23; 4:14–16; 13:14–15; 26:54–56; 27:9–10).

The early Christian commentaries sometimes include harsh criticism of the Jews and Jewish practices. In the ancient world, Christians were challenged by Jewish communities, which possessed the books that Christians claimed as their own in their original Hebrew, whereas Christians (usually) read them only in translation. Pagan critics of Christianity used the Jews to make arguments against the Christians. Why, they asked, do you revere the Jewish books (the Old Testament) but do not, like the Jews, keep the laws written in them? In response, Christian writers drew on their rhetorical skills, charging the Jews with not understanding their own books. These passages make painful reading for Christians today, and it is tempting to omit all such passages. But they are a part of the inheritance from the early Church, and I have tried to respect the integrity of the ancient books.[20]

14. Robert Wilken, "In Defense of Allegory," *Modern Theology* 14 (1998): 201–3.

15. "[T]he question as to who are the rightful possessors of the Scriptures must be uncovered so as to prevent their use by someone who has no right (*competit*) to them" (Tertullian, *De praescriptione haereticorum* 15.4).

16. In Matt 3, Philoxenus of Hierapolis, *Fragment* 13.

17. In Matt 19, Hilary, *On Matthew* 19:3.

18. As Chrysologus (*Sermon* 74.3–5) puts it in Matt 28.

19. In Matt 13, Ephrem, *Exposition of the Gospel* 29.

20. Some of the more confrontational texts have not been included in the course of choosing selections.

Even in our age of sophisticated "search engines," there is no substitute for diligently digging through patristic and medieval sources to determine which texts should be translated. In the Middle Ages, several authors made compilations of texts from the Gospels: the Venerable Bede,[21] Rabanus Maurus,[22] and the *Catena Aurea* by Aquinas. Other anthologies included the *Evangelium secundum Matthaeum* by Nicholas of Lyra and the *Glossa Ordinaria*. As helpful as these are for learning which patristic writers wrote on Matthew, they were dependent on which manuscripts were available at the time they were collected. Since there were no edited collections of patristic writers until the early sixteenth century, annotated volumes filled with excerpted passages from the fathers was the primary means for instruction.

Among patristic authors, we possess commentaries by Hilary, Jerome, and Origen (though not in full). There were also *commentarioli*, that is, brief or short commentaries, usually on select portions of the Gospel. For example: Cyprian's treatment of the Lord's Prayer; Victorinus of Poetovio, *On the Ten Virgins* (Matt 24);[23] and Arnobius the Younger, *Sermonettes* on texts in John, Matthew, and Luke.[24] Then there are collections of sermons on Matthew: John Chrysostom, Chromatius of Aquileia,[25] Augustine,[26] Leo the Great,[27] Caesarius of Arles,[28] Peter Chrysologus,[29] Eusebius of Emesa,[30] Philoxenus of Hierapolis,[31] Gregory the Great,[32] and an otherwise unknown writer dubbed Epiphanius, the Latin, being from the late fifth or early sixth century.[33] Besides there is a collection of fifty-four homilies, formerly attributed to Chrysostom, though now considered to be authored by an anonymous writer of the fifth century. Known as the *Opus imperfectum in Matthaeum*,[34] the commentary has Arian and Pelagian tendencies.

21. *In Matthaei Evangelium Expositio* (PL 92:39–132).

22. *Commentariorum in Matthaeum Libri Octo* (PL 107:788–856). See the preface for the ancient writers that were used (107:727C–30C).

23. PLS 1:174, "*Incipit de matheo evange.*"

24. Arnobius the Younger, *Expositiunculae in Evangelium Iohannis Evangelistae Matthei et Lucae*, CCSL 25A.

25. There are several texts by Chromatius (CCSL 9): *Seventeen Tractates on the Gospel of Matthew*, *Praefatio Orationis Dominicae*, *Preface to the Lord's Prayer*, *Sermon on the Eight Beatitudes*, and *Tractatus* lxi (CCSL 9A).

26. Augustine, *Sermons on the New Testament* (51–94, 148–83) and *On the Lord's Prayer*.

27. Leo of Rome, *Sermons*, ed. Chavasse, CCSL 138. The collection consists of ninety-seven sermons delivered over the course of the church of Rome's liturgical year.

28. PL 67:468–542.

29. PL 52:380–450.

30. E. M. Buytaert, ed., *Eusèbe d'Émèse, Discours conservés en Latin*, I–II (Louvain: Spicilegium Sacrum Lovaniense, 1957).

31. *Philoxenus of Mabbug: Fragments of the Commentary on Matthew and Luke*, trans., J. W. Watt, CSCO 393 (Louvain: Secrétariat du CorpusSCO, 1978).

32. *Grégoire le Grand: Homélies sur L'Évangile*, vol. I, ed. R. Était, C. Morel, and B. Judic, SC 485 (Paris: Les Éditions du Cerf, 2005).

33. G. Morin, "Le Commentaire inédit de l'évêque latin Epiphanius sur les Évangiles," *Revue Bénédictine* 22 (1904): 336–59.

34. PG 56:611–948, and translated into Latin by Erasmus, who determined the homilies were not by Chrysostom. The popularity of the *Opus* during the Middle Ages may have been because it provided a theological antidote to anti-Pelagianism. It presents a view of free-will that placed greater value on the human initiative to respond to God.

In the process of selecting texts for this volume, a few rules of thumb were followed. The overall intent was to select those texts that illustrate patristic interpretation and are also edifying to contemporary readers. In cases where there was much overlap, I have chosen those that most clearly reflect patristic interpretation of the Gospel. I have also included different interpretations of the same text. In many cases, I have drawn from doctrinal or homiletical writings, not only from commentaries. In those cases where there was little or no existing commentary, I simply followed suit. The reader will notice that a few parts of the Matthean text may possess only one or even no remark, whereas there may be an abundance for another. It will quickly become obvious that the ancients had not established a common format on biblical exposition.[35] Divisions in the text do not always reflect modern translations of the Bible, because the commentaries were written before the Bible was divided into chapters and verses. The reader should also note that early Christian authors use different versions of the Bible, depending on whether they were reading the Scripture in Greek, Latin, or Syriac. Quoted passages will sometimes differ from modern English versions. And in some cases, the commentators cite from memory.

Learning about the early fathers' treatment of Matthew through excerpts has its limitations, but it does provide an overview of the patristic sources. Since many commentaries are now translated into English, it is hoped that these will prompt the reader to discover the works of ancients in their entirety and rediscover the ancient wellsprings of the Church's faith.

D. H. Williams

35. For our part, we have divided the various remarks according to Matthew's chapters.

Preface to Matthew

(1) John Chrysostom

When Matthew wrote his account he was filled with the Spirit. Matthew was a tax collector and I am not ashamed to name his profession, nor am I ashamed to call the other apostles by their professions. After all, it is through such limitations that the Spirit's grace and the virtues of these men become evident. Matthew was right to refer to his work as a Gospel, that is, the Good News. For Jesus went about announcing the abolition of punishment, forgiveness of sins, righteousness, holiness, redemption, sonship, inheriting heaven, and kinship with the Son of God to everyone—to hostile people, to ungrateful people, to people sitting in darkness (Isa 9:1). What can equal such glad news as this? God on earth, man in heaven, everything brought together: angels formed a choir with human beings, human beings joined with angels and other heavenly powers. A long-drawn-out conflict was then brought to a close: God and our nature were reconciled, the devil confounded, demons put to flight, death abolished, paradise opened, the curse now annulled, sin expelled, error driven out, truth returned, the word of godliness was sown (Matt 13:3) in every direction and flourished, the heavenly way of life was transplanted to earth, the heavenly powers communed with us without hesitation, angels often appeared on earth, and we enjoy the hope of future benefits in great abundance. For these reasons Matthew calls his account Good News. Every other story in comparison is but mere words.

With God's help we are about to enter a golden city, a city more precious than any gold. So let us explore her foundations and her gates of sapphire and pearls. In Matthew, we have an excellent guide, and as we enter through his gate we must give full attention. . . . What a magnificent and stately city it is; unlike our cities which are made up of market places and palaces. Here in this city all dwelling places are palaces. Let us therefore throw open the gates of our mind, open wide our ears, prepare to enter its doors with fear and trembling, and bow low before the King within.

As we approach this city we are completely amazed. The gates are closed at first but when they are opened wide, so that we can see the object of our search, we shall behold an awesome sight. Guided by the eyes of the Spirit, our tax collector promises to show us everything: where the King is seated, where the heavenly host attends to him, where there are angels, where there are archangels, what dwellings are given to the new citizens in this city, which way leads to the city, what kind of benefit was given to those who first became citizens, what benefits were given to those who come later, what kind of ranking there is of those citizens, how many belong to the senate, and how many grades of ranking.[1] Let us enter, therefore, not with noise and confusion, but in a mystical silence, for we will hear a reading of the text, not from an earthly person, but from the Lord of Hosts.

(2) Irenaeus of Lyons

The number of the Gospels is neither greater nor fewer than what they are. Seeing that there are four regions of the world in which we also have four primary winds,[2] the Church is spread across the entire earth, its *pillar and foundation* (1 Tim 3:15), being the Gospel and the Spirit of Life. It follows that the Church has four pillars as it breathes out incorruptibility everywhere and brings life to humanity. From this it is clear that the Word, is the maker of everything (Col 1:16), who sits upon the Cherubim and preserves everything, who revealed himself to humanity, and who gave to us the four-fold Gospel which is preserved by one Spirit. So David, also referring to his [the Word's] advent, says, *You who sit between the cherubim, show yourself* (Ps 80 [79]:1).

For the Cherubim have a four-fold appearance and their forms are presented as images of the Son of God: the first living-creature, it states,[3] is like a Lion, signifying his effective activity, his dominance, and his royalty; the second was like a calf, signifying his role as sacrifice and priest; the third, *having the facing of a man* (Rev. 4:7), which clearly describes him coming as a man; *and the fourth is like a flying eagle* (Rev 4:7), which indicates the gift of the Spirit who flies within the Church. And thus the Gospels are in agreement with these four images on which Christ Jesus is seated.

(3) Origen

There were more Gospels written than the four Gospels. The ones that we possess were chosen and handed down in the churches. From the preface in Luke we learn: *For as much as many have taken in hand to compose a narrative* (Luke 1:1). The expression *they have taken in hand* involves an implicit charge that there were some who rashly and without the grace of the Holy Spirit set about writing Gospels.

Certainly Matthew, Mark, John, and Luke did not take *in hand* to write, but wrote their Gospels filled with the Holy Spirit. *Many have taken in hand to compose a narrative of the events that are certainly familiar among us.* The Church possesses four Gospels, but the heretics have many, one of which is entitled *The Gospel according to the Egyptians*[4]

1. Chrysostom follows the social order of his time. Senatorial and descending ranks are employed as a metaphor for heavenly ones.

2. Lit., "spirits."

3. The passage indicated is Rev 4:7, which describes each beast. Irenaeus is implying that each represents one of the Gospels: Mark (lion), Luke (calf), Matthew (face of a man), and John (eagle).

4. Known as an apocryphal Gospel, this text survives only in a few small fragments.

and another *The Gospel according to the Twelve Apostles.*[5] Basilides[6] also presumed to write a Gospel and to call it by his own name. Though *many have taken in hand* to write, only four Gospels are recognized. The doctrines concerning the person of our Lord and Savior should be derived only from these four. I know a certain Gospel called *The Gospel according to Thomas* and another entitled *Gospel according to Matthias*, and I have read others. I am saying this to show my awareness of these other books, in order to nullify anyone's argument that he possesses a special knowledge because he is acquainted with these writings.[7] We, however, approve what the Church has recognized by accepting only the four Gospels.

Thus, we say that there are four Gospels. These four provide the fundamentals of the Church's faith from which the whole world is *reconciled to God* in Christ (Col 1:20). . . .

A Gospel is either a word that implies the actual presence of something good for the believer, or a word promising the arrival of a good thing that is expected. Each of the Gospels represents a collection of proclamations that are useful to the one who believes and understands them rightly. The Gospel brings about a benefit for the reader and naturally makes him glad, since it tells how the first-born of all creation (Col 1:15) lived among men, for the sake of all people, and for their salvation.

We have learned by tradition that the four Gospels alone are authoritative in the Church of God under heaven and that the first was written according to Matthew. He was once a tax collector, but afterward he became an apostle of Jesus Christ; he then composed and published his Gospel in the Hebrew language for believers who came from Judaism.

(4) Eusebius of Caesarea

The apostle Matthew did not begin his former way of life with an honorable occupation, since he was among those devoted to tax collection and greed. Yet none of the rest of the evangelists has made this clear to us—neither his fellow apostle John, nor even Luke, nor Mark, his fellow writers of the other Gospels. But Matthew himself exposes his own way of life and becomes his own accuser. Listen, then, to how he has explicitly recalled himself by name in his own composition. He depicts it in this way: **And passing on from there, Jesus saw a man sitting at the tax collector's booth, by the name of Matthew, and he said to him, Follow me. And rising, he followed him. And when Jesus was reclining at the table in the house, there were many tax collectors and sinners reclining with him and his disciples** (9:9–10). And again, when Matthew moves next to enumerate the list of the remaining disciples, he adds the label "the tax collector" to himself. So he says, **These are the names of the twelve apostles: First Simon, who is called Peter, and Andrew, his brother; James, the son of Zebedee, and John, his brother; Philip and Bartholomew; Thomas and Matthew, the tax collector** (10:2–3a).

5. Also known as the *Gospel of the Twelve*, this text does not survive.

6. A well-known teacher of Gnosticism that Origen refutes in other of his writings.

7. The essential feature of Gnostic claims to possess other Gospels was the assertion that they provided a spiritual knowledge inaccessible to other Christians.

Thus Matthew, on account of his exceeding humility, reveals his love for the truth in his own way and labels himself a tax collector. He does not conceal his former way of life, but counts himself together with the sinners and lists himself as second to his fellow apostle, Thomas. For he is paired with Thomas, as Peter is paired with Andrew, James with John, and Philip with Bartholomew. But he places Thomas before himself, honoring his fellow apostle as greater, contrary to what the other evangelists have done. Listen, then, to how Luke refers to Matthew. He does not call him a tax collector, nor does he place him after Thomas, but, recognizing him as greater, Luke lists Matthew first, introducing Thomas second, just as Mark has also done (cf. Mark 3:18). Luke's text runs this way: *And when it was day, he called his disciples and chose twelve of them, whom he also named apostles: Simon, whom he also called Peter, and Andrew, his brother; James, and John, and Philip, and Bartholomew, and Matthew, and Thomas* (Luke 6:13–15a). Thus Luke honors Matthew, according to what those *who were eyewitnesses and servants of the word from the beginning* (Luke 1:2) handed on to him.

(5) Chromatius of Aquileia

The sacrament of our salvation and faith found within the whole of divine Scripture is contained especially in the preaching of the gospel. Here the secret of the heavenly mystery is revealed to us, that is, the mystery of the Lord's passion and resurrection. The transcribers of the gospel are divided into four books: Matthew, Mark, Luke, and John, who were prefigured and predestined in times past to the task of this divine work, as the blessed Luke reported: *Inasmuch as many have undertaken to compose a narrative of the things that have been fulfilled among us* (Luke 1:1).

Matthew is appointed by the divine authority and grace of the Holy Spirit to be the first one who writes down the gospel, then Mark and Luke, most recently of all John. . . . Of course, Matthew and John belong to the number of the twelve apostles, who not only were with the Lord before his passion, but also kept company with him after the resurrection for forty days. They carefully narrated everything they saw and heard just as John testified in his epistle, saying: *we have heard and saw with our eyes and by our hand have been examined, these things we declare to you* (1 John 1:1–3).

The authority of these four evangelists, therefore, is fixed and unwavering because they all composed according to a single principle. Of course, they taught different ideas according to the certainty of their foundation, yet they do not disagree among themselves on anything, because each one of them perceived the same thing by faith concerning the Lord's incarnation, nativity, passion, resurrection, and also his double advent. Because we endeavor to make some comments about the Gospels, the responsibility and gravity of doing so causes us to test also the truth of the Gospels, which were prefigured in the law of the Old Testament, as the Apostle clearly states: *the law was a shadow of things to come* (Heb 10:1). Neither can the new stand without the old, nor does the old have any permanence without the new. It is rightly said that everything recorded is more fully understood when the message comes from the two testaments.

Both the figure and the number of the four Gospels are plainly described in the law and the prophets, exemplified by the four rivers that flow from one source in Eden, or in the four rows of stones that Aaron wore woven into his priestly garment, or in the fourfold row of twelve calves that Solomon set up under the bronze sea in the temple. With even greater distinction and specificity we find that Ezekiel the prophet depicted the four Gospels as four living things whose appearance and shape are described: *Their likeness,* he says, *is the appearance of a human and the appearance of a lion and the appearance of a calf and the appearance of a flying eagle* (Ezek 1:10). It is clear that the evangelists are figured here. Although they are shown in different appearances according to the unique meaning of each, the preaching of the Gospels is the same. In fact, when that prophet stated that their four appearances were distinguished yet related to each other in a heavenly understanding, he meant that each living thing shares these four appearances. The reason for this description is not obscure, because it means that they all are one, both individually and collectively. While the prophet clearly differentiates and separates them in connection with their appearances or number, the unity of preaching still makes them inseparable and whole, because you will find the whole in each one and in each one the whole.

We must understand and become better acquainted with the different descriptions of their appearances. *The appearance,* he says, *of a human, and the appearance of a lion and the appearance of a calf and the appearance of a flying eagle.* The appearance of a human is understood as the Gospel according to Matthew; *a human* since this Gospel begins with the physical birth of the Lord, introducing it by saying: **The book of the generation of Jesus Christ, son of David, son of Abraham** (1:1), etc.

Although there are said to be four Gospels because of the number of the evangelists, there is only one gospel between them all, as the Lord said: **And this gospel will be preached through the whole world** (24:14). He did not say "Gospels" but **gospel**. The Apostle described this too when he says: *If anyone has preached to you a gospel other than what you have received, let them be [sic] accursed* (Gal 1:9). There are certainly four books of the gospel, but one gospel is counted in these four books. For this reason, we must not be confused if sometimes we hear someone say "Gospels" simply because of the number of evangelists or name given to the Gospels, as the most important books do, or because it is the usual custom of most churches[8] to designate the number of the evangelists. Indeed, we both confess and believe that there is one true gospel according to the authority of the Lord or the Apostle.

(6) Augustine

Among all the divine authorities contained in the sacred writings, the Gospel [of Matthew] is rightly foremost. What the law and the prophets foretold of things to come is shown in this Gospel as it was presented and fulfilled. The first preachers of this Gospel were the apostles, who witnessed our Lord and Savior, Jesus Christ, in person while he was yet present in the flesh. Not only did they remember the words heard from his lips and the deeds performed by him before their eyes, but also those things (before they were confirmed in

8. Lit., "majority."

their discipleship)[9] that they were able to discover and learn from the memory of divine and worthy deeds from the Lord himself or from his parents or from any other reliable records and most faithful testimonies concerning his nativity, infancy, and boyhood. Since the task of preaching the gospel was bequeathed to them, they were careful to make these matters known to the human race. Certain members of the disciples, that is, Matthew and John, related in their individual books a written account of those things that should be recorded about him.

Of these four [evangelists] only Matthew is considered to have written in the Hebrew tongue, while the others in Greek. And although each writer seems to have preserved a particular order of his story, we discover nonetheless that each one did not want to be ignorant of what others before him had written or to bypass points that had been disregarded. But since each one was so inspired, there was no need to have a superfluous joint endeavor. For Matthew undertook an account of the Lord's incarnation according to his royal lineage and of the Lord's life generally as a human being according to his deeds and words.

9. That is, before their apostolic calling.

Matthew 1

Since Matthew's Gospel is devoted to demonstrating that Jesus is the messianic fulfillment of the Old Testament prophets, the account begins with a genealogy that ties Jesus to David and as far back to Abraham. Jesus is shown as a continuator of God's covenant promises to his people, as found especially in Gen 12–18; 2 Sam 7 and Ps 110. This act of continuation is therefore the ultimate revelation of God's plan revealing itself "at the right time" (Rom 5:6). Jesus is the Emmanuel, *the one who* will save his people from their sins. *What had been prepared since the time of Abraham was now coming to fruition with the birth of the one whom Joseph was told to name Jesus, the hellenized version of the Hebrew, Joshua, or the Aramaic contracted form, Yeshua. The entire Gospel will be predicated along these lines through signs and testimonies presented in every chapter.*

Chapter one is divided into two parts: the genealogical line by which the Christ descended from Abraham through David to Joseph (vv. 1–17) and the narration of his birth (vv. 18–25). Both parts supply the details showing how All this took place to fulfill what the Lord had spoken by the prophet *(v. 22).*

The discrepancies between Matthew's and Luke's (3:23–38) genealogies were recognized by the early fathers from the first. They took these inconsistencies seriously, because they took the history and the wording of the biblical text seriously. However, they did not perceive these differences as the kind of problems that vitiated the historical value of Matthew's (or Luke's) account. The distinctions unique to each Gospel represented the providential working of God, whose meaning could be discerned by the conscientious believer. The Holy Spirit, who is the ground of unity, allows the reader to discover a unified working of the various scriptural accounts. For this reason, there may be more than one explanation of a given text. Eusebius of Caesarea cites a lengthy passage from an earlier writer, Julius Africanus, who deals with the most glaring difference between the genealogies, most notably, the identification of the father of Joseph. According to Matthew it was Jacob, and Luke says Heli (or Eli). But these were, as Eusebius explains it, brothers. Matthan is the first who traced his family from Solomon and begat Jacob. Then, on the death of Matthan, Melchi traced his descent back to Nathan, married Matthan's widow, and had from her a son named Heli. The difference is that Melchi, according to the Jewish law of levirate marriage, preserved the family name of Matthan for his son, Jacob. Augustine likewise acknowledges this explanation, though he adds that the reader should not be overly vexed about these problems, since the Holy Spirit was the true father of Christ.

Both Matthew's and Luke's genealogies frame the line of descent according to Joseph's family line, not Mary's. Since it was standard in Jewish law that a man should marry only within his tribe, it was understood that Mary must also be from the tribe of Judah.

Hilary's approach to the same issue is different. He believed that Matthew and Luke were using different "models": Matthew construes Jesus's family line according to his kingly lineage, that is, he focuses on the line of Judah; whereas Luke traces the priestly side of the line by stating that some in Jesus's line were from the tribe of Levi. The differences in detail do not trouble Hilary, because he is seeking not to solve the problem of the inconsistencies as much as he is seeking to discern the motive behind each writer's account. Rather than try to harmonize the genealogies, Hilary is satisfied that Joseph and Mary come from the same line, namely, the line of Abraham.

Hilary also notes that while Matthew declares there are from David to the deportation to Babylon fourteen generations, *the Old Testament records there are seventeen (1 Chr 3:10–15). The difference according to Hilary is that three negligible generations, those that derived from a pagan ancestry, should not be counted.*

Augustine also focuses on the differences within the Matthean account, but as he saw it, the problem was that the actual number of the generations listed by Matthew is forty-one, whereas the last verse of the genealogy states: So all the generations from Abraham to David were fourteen generations, and from David to the deportation to Babylon fourteen generations, and from the deportation to Babylon to the Christ fourteen generations, *which equals forty-two. The issue is a simple one, says Augustine. The genealogy counts Jechoniah twice (vv. 11–12) since he ends one line and starts the next. This same principle doesn't apply to the two other generational lines, because the exile in Babylon took place under Josiah, whose father was Jechoniah. Because Josiah lived under Jechoniah's reign, he is mentioned twice.*

The narrative of Christ's birth, beginning with v. 18, is centered on the prophecy fulfilled through the angel's announcement to Joseph about the birth and name of Jesus. Ancient writers understood this passage to be filled with christological meaning, interpreted both allegorically (Chrysologus, viz., "the historical narrative of Scripture should always be raised to a higher meaning," Sermon 36), as a demonstration of the prophetic nature of Christ's birth, and historically (Leo), which showed that Christ's human birth in no way undermined his full divinity.

In Matthew, the description of Christ's birth and Mary's pregnancy is seen from Joseph's perspective (unlike Luke's Gospel). Once her pregnancy became apparent, we are told of Joseph's moral and emotional turmoil. An angelic message comes to him via a dream. Chrysologus asks how Joseph remained both just and good upon learning of Mary's condition. The heaviness of his shame is well expressed, "He thought about sending her away, and he told the whole matter to God, for he could not confide in humans." In response to another angelic message in a dream, Joseph is the one who takes action by moving the family to Egypt and back to Israel. Yet a third angelic admonition provides him with directions to a safe location far from the king's persecution.

Overall, the ancient commentators wished to make three points about Christ's birth. Jesus's birth from Mary was in fact a second birth. The first birth, which reveals his true nature, is his eternal generation from the Father. The second was the physical birth of the Son's divine nature as Jesus, which was a joining of the divine to the humanity, a true incarnation. Both Leo and Augustine emphasize that in assuming our humanity Christ did not acquire our sin.

Third, Mary is the second Eve, in that both were givers of life.[1] *In Augustine's view, it was only fitting that a woman be the bearer of our salvation since it was a woman who convinced her husband to eat of the forbidden fruit. Whereas a woman was first seduced by sin, she becomes the chosen sex to bring the means and the message of salvation from sin. Hilary (and Jerome) reinforces Mary's true virginity by refuting any view that claims she was already married to Joseph and that Jesus was the offspring of their union.*

Matthew 1:1–17

1 The book of the genealogy of Jesus Christ, the son of David, the son of Abraham.
2 Abraham was the father of Isaac, and Isaac the father of Jacob, and Jacob the
father of Judah and his brothers, 3 and Judah the father of Perez and Zerah by Tamar,
and Perez the father of Hezron, and Hezron the father of Ram, 4 and Ram the father
of Ammin'adab, and Ammin'adab the father of Nahshon, and Nahshon the father of
Salmon, 5 and Salmon the father of Bo'az by Rahab, and Bo'az the father of Obed by
Ruth, and Obed the father of Jesse, 6 and Jesse the father of David the king.
And David was the father of Solomon by the wife of Uri'ah, 7 and Solomon the
father of Rehobo'am, and Rehobo'am the father of Abi'jah, and Abi'jah the father of
Asa, 8 and Asa the father of Jehosh'aphat, and Jehosh'aphat the father of Joram, and
Joram the father of Uzzi'ah, 9 and Uzzi'ah the father of Jotham, and Jotham the father of
Ahaz, and Ahaz the father of Hezeki'ah, 10 and Hezeki'ah the father of Manas'seh, and
Manas'seh the father of Amos, and Amos the father of Josi'ah, 11 and Josi'ah the father
of Jechoni'ah and his brothers, at the time of the deportation to Babylon.
12 And after the deportation to Babylon: Jechoni'ah was the father of She-al'ti-el,
and She-al'ti-el the father of Zerub'babel, 13 and Zerub'babel the father of Abi'ud, and
Abi'ud the father of Eli'akim, and Eli'akim the father of Azor, 14 and Azor the father
of Zadok, and Zadok the father of Achim, and Achim the father of Eli'ud, 15 and Eli'ud
the father of Elea'zar, and Elea'zar the father of Matthan, and Matthan the father of
Jacob, 16 and Jacob the father of Joseph the husband of Mary, of whom Jesus was born,
who is called Christ.
17 So all the generations from Abraham to David were fourteen generations, and
from David to the deportation to Babylon fourteen generations, and from the depor-
tation to Babylon to the Christ fourteen generations.

(1) Eusebius of Caesarea

Since Matthew and Luke in writing their Gospels have presented us with a genealogy of Christ in different forms, most people imagine that the two are in conflict.[2] And since

1. Cf. Irenaeus, *Against the Heresies* 5.19.1.

2. This discrepancy was pointed out by critics of Christianity. Jerome claims that the "apostate" Emperor Julian (reigned 361–63) highlighted this text as an instance of contradiction between the evangelists.

every believer through ignorance of the truth has been eager to talk at length about these passages, we must quote the account that has come down to us, which Africanus[3] mentions in a letter he wrote to Aristides on the harmony of the genealogy in the Gospels:

> The names of the families in Israel used to be numbered either by natural means or by law—by natural means, when there was actual offspring to succeed, but by law, when another begat a son in the name of his brother who had died childless.[4] Because no clear hope of a resurrection had as yet been given, they represented the future promise under the figure of a mortal resurrection, so that the name of the one departed might live on. In this genealogy we see that some succeeded by natural descent, the son to the father, while others, though born to one father, were assigned by [a different] name to another. Both are mentioned; those who had actually begotten sons, as well as those who were regarded as having begotten them. Neither account of the Gospels is untrue, since there is a rationale provided both by natural means and by law. As families descended from Solomon and from Nathan became so intermingled, by the resurrection of childless men[5] and through second marriages and resurrection (i.e., the birth of offspring who rightly belonged to one family as well as to another; in one sense they belonged to their reputed fathers and in another sense to their actual fathers). So both accounts of Matthew and Luke are in accordance with the exact truth and descend to Joseph in a complex, yet accurate, manner.
>
> To make clear what has been said, I shall give an account of the interchange of the families. If we proceed with the generations from David through Solomon, the third from the end is found to be **Matthan**, who **begat Jacob**, the father of Joseph. But if it was from *Nathan the son of David* according to Luke,[6] the third from the end was Melchi. For *Joseph was the son of Heli, the son of Melchi.*[7] Since Joseph is the subject of our discussion, we must show how each of the two is recorded to be his father. In other words, Jacob traces his descent from Solomon, and Heli from Nathan; and, before that, how these same persons, namely, Jacob and Heli, were two brothers; and, before that again, how their fathers, Matthan and Melchi, though of different families, are declared both to be Joseph's grandfathers. Both Matthan and Melchi married in turn the same wife, begat children who were brothers by the same mother. For the law does not prevent a widow marrying another, whether she be divorced or her husband be dead. So then from Estha (for tradition asserts that this was the woman's name[8]) Matthan is the first who traced his family from Solomon, and he begat Jacob. Then, on the death of Matthan, Melchi,

3. Eusebius is citing Julius Africanus, a Christian theologian of the second century who wrote to a certain Aristides (now lost).

4. Cf. Gen 38:8; Deut 25:6; Luke 20:28.

5. "Resurrection" here refers to the above "figure of a mortal resurrection," that is, raising up of the name of the dead by assuming the dead man's name. See Ruth 4:1–10.

6. Luke 3:31.

7. Luke 3:23, 24.

8. By "tradition" Africanus may mean that he received his information from an itinerant group called the Desposyni, who claimed to know facts about Christ's birth because they shared a connection with the lineage of Joseph. See Eusebius, *Ecclesiastical History* 1.7.14.

who traced his descent back to Nathan, married the widow, being of the same tribe but another family, as I said before, begat with her a son named Heli. We shall find Jacob and Heli were brothers with the same mother, though of two different families. Jacob, on the death of his brother Heli, who had no natural heir, took his wife and from her in the third place begat Joseph, who according to natural means was his own son (and also according to Scripture: for it is written, **and Jacob begat Joseph**). But according to law, he was also the son of Heli. For Jacob, being his brother, *raised up the seed*[9] to Heli. Therefore the genealogy traced through him will not be rendered void, even though Matthew the evangelist describes the family line **that Jacob begat Joseph**; whereas Luke says, *as was supposed* (for indeed he adds this), the son of Joseph, the son of Heli, the son of Melchi.[10] For Luke could not express more clearly the descent according to law, and he abstains from using the word "begat" with reference to this kind of procreation right up to the end as he traces backward the genealogy up to *Adam, the son of God*.[11]

Matthan, who traced his decent from Solomon, begat Jacob. On the death of Matthan, Melchi, who traced his descent from Nathan, of the same wife, begat Heli. Therefore Heli and Jacob were brothers with the same mother. Heli having died childless, Jacob raised up his seed to him in begetting Joseph, who was by nature his own son, but by law Heli's. Thus Joseph was the son of both.

Now that the genealogy of Joseph has been traced, Mary also has been shown no less to belong to the same tribe as Joseph, since according to the law of Moses intermarrying between different tribes was not permitted. For there was a command to join in wedlock *with one of those from the* same *town* and the same *clan*, so that *the inheritance* of the family *should not remove from tribe to tribe*.[12]

(2) Hilary of Poitiers

Whereas Matthew followed the order of royal succession, Luke reckons it according to priestly origin. Each writer uses a [different] criterion, one tracing the Lord's bloodline, the other by means of his tribe. It is quite right to present the sequence of the Lord's generation in this way since the association of the priestly and royal ancestry inaugurated by David in his marriage is later confirmed through the lineage of Shealtiel to Zerubbabel.[13]

And so while Matthew established his paternal origin that stemmed from Judah, Luke teaches that the lineage proceeded through Nathan from the tribe of Levi.[14] Each writer in his way has demonstrated the glory of the double genealogy of our Lord Jesus Christ, who is the eternal King and priest, even in his fleshly birth. That his nativity is traced from Joseph rather than Mary does not matter, for there is one and the same bloodline for the entire ancestry.

9. Gen 38:8.
10. Luke 3:38.
11. Jdt 5:5; 14:10.
12. Mic 5:2 (Matt 2:6).
13. Cf. Jer 27:20; 28:4; 1 Chr 3:17.
14. Luke 3:23–38. Cf. 1 Chr 3:5; Zech 12:12.

Moreover, Matthew and Luke have likewise given us a model, describing each of the fathers not as much according to lineage as by a race of people who originated from one ancestor and who are encompassed within a family of one succession and origin. For although he must be revealed as the son of David and Abraham, just as Matthew begins: **The book of the generations of Jesus Christ, son of David, son of Abraham** (1:1), there is no difference whether someone is classified by an account of one's origin and lineage provided it is understood that the families of the world began from one man.[15] Thus, as Joseph and Mary are from the same ancestry, so Joseph is shown to have proceeded from the lineage of Abraham, and the same is true of Mary.

Then there is the issue that (as we said, given the reliability of the facts) the sequence of the Lord's generation agrees neither with the [Old Testament] method of enumeration nor its order of succession so that a rationale of the [present] narrative might be sought. There is a reason why the narration makes one kind of emphasis, and the facts say another, and yet another [reason] that is related to the whole, and then another is connected with their enumeration. In fact, **from Abraham to David fourteen generations** are counted and **from David to the deportation to Babylon fourteen generations**, whereas in the books of the Kings seventeen generations are detected (1 Chr 3:10–15; 1–2 Chr offer another version of 1–2 Kgs). But there is not a problem here of falsehood or fault from an oversight. For three generations have been bypassed according to an underlying principle. Joram begot Ahaziah, then Ahaziah begot Joash, after Joash, Amaziah, and from Amaziah, Azariah. But in Matthew, it is written that **Joram begot Azariah**, although the latter is fourth after him. It was done in this way because Joram begot Ahaziah from a pagan woman, that is, from the household of Ahab (2 Kgs 8:18, 25–27), and it was declared by the prophet that not until the fourth generation would anyone from the household of Ahab sit on the throne of the kingdom of Israel (2 Kgs 10:30; 15:12). By removing the disgrace of a pagan family and bypassing its ancestry, the royal origin of those to follow in the fourth generation is then counted. And although it is written that there are fourteen generations until Mary,[16] and thirteen are found in counting them, there can be no mistake for those who know that our Lord Jesus Christ has an origin not only from Mary, but in the procreation of his bodily nativity, his eternal significance is discovered.

(3) Augustine

When Matthew counts the generations, he says from Abraham to David there were fourteen, and from David to the migration to Babylon fourteen, and from the migration to Babylonia to Christ fourteen. Multiply fourteen by three; you get forty-two. But some people[17] count the actual number and they find forty-one generations. And so they bring their charge, making fun and taunting us by saying: "So what does it mean, when it says in the Gospel that there are three fourteens, and yet when we count them all up we don't find

15. That is, Adam (Luke 3:38).

16. Matt 1:17.

17. Critics, perhaps the Manichees, of the conflicting accounts.

forty-two but forty-one?" Without a doubt there is a deep meaning latent here. And we are delighted, and we give thanks to God that these critics give us the opportunity to discover something. For the more difficult something is hidden, so finding it is more pleasurable.

So then, from Abraham to David there are fourteen. From there we begin counting with Solomon, because David begot Solomon. If the count begins with Solomon and reaches Jechoniah, in whose lifetime the migration to Babylonia took place, and then you have another fourteen generations—counting Solomon at the top of this second division, and also counting Jechoniah, with whom this count ends—the result is fourteen. The third division, however, begins with the same Jechoniah.

Beginning the count of the third division from Jechoniah up to the Lord Jesus Christ, there are fourteen. Because this Jechoniah, being the last of the previous division and the first of the following division, is counted twice, someone will say, "Why is Jechoniah counted twice?" Nothing took place in the past among the people of Israel that was not a mysterious representation of things to come. It is not at all unreasonable to count Jechoniah twice; after all, if there's a boundary between two fields, whether a stone or a dividing wall, the one on this side is measured up to the wall, and the one on the other is measured from it as a starting point.

But then why wasn't this done in the first connection between divisions, where from Abraham we count fourteen generations up to David, and then another fourteen, not repeating David, but beginning to count from Solomon? There must be a deep reason for this.

The migration to Babylon took place when Jechoniah had just been installed as king in the place of his deceased father. The kingdom was taken away from him, and another man was put in his place. But all the same, it was during the life of Jechoniah that the migration to live among the nations took place. No fault of Jechoniah's is mentioned as the reason why he lost his kingdom; everything is blamed on those who succeeded him. So the captivity follows and they go off to Babylonia. It's not only the wicked who go, but holy people also go with them. In captivity there we also find the prophet Ezekiel, we find Daniel there, and the three youngsters who became famous amid the flames. They all went off to captivity in accordance with the prophecy of the prophet Jeremiah.

Here we can add that there was another explanation, peculiar to the Jews, by which someone could become the son of a man even if he was not sprung from him in the flesh. Kinsmen used to marry the wives of their kinsmen who had died childless, to raise up seed for the deceased. So the one who was born would be the son both of the man he was born of, and of the man he was born to succeed.

I have said all this in case anyone should insist that you cannot rightly list two fathers of one and the same person, and then go on to bring a sacrilegious charge of lying against one or other of the evangelists who relate the genealogy of the Lord. This is especially so because it is implied by their own words. Thus, Matthew, who mentions the father Joseph was begotten by, lists the generations in this way: "So-and-so begot So-and-so," until he reaches the point where he says at the end, Jacob begot Joseph (1:16). Luke on the other hand—because a son by adoption is not properly said to be begotten, and neither is one begotten who succeeds a dead man by being born of the woman who had been his wife—Luke did not say "Eli begot Joseph," or "Joseph whom Eli begot," but "the son of Eli" (Luke 3:23), whether by adoption, or by being begotten by a kinsman to be the dead man's heir.

Enough has been said to show why it shouldn't bother us that the ancestry of Christ is reckoned through Joseph and not through Mary. Just as she was a mother without carnal desire, so Joseph was a father without carnal intercourse. So the generations come down through him, and they go up through him.

But why did Matthew count the generations downward, and Luke count them upward? Listen then, as attentively as the Lord enables you to, that your minds may be quite serene and free from the trouble of knotty and hostile objections. Matthew goes down through the generations to signify that our Lord Jesus Christ came down from heaven to bear the burden of our sins that all nations might be blessed in the seed of Abraham. That's why he didn't begin with Adam—the whole human race comes from him, nor with Noah, because again the whole human race sprang from his family after the flood. The fulfillment of prophecy is not connected to the way that the man Christ Jesus was from Adam, from whom all human beings spring; nor that he is from Noah, who again is the ancestor of all. But the point is that his descent is from Abraham, who was chosen at a time when the earth was already full of nations, that all nations might be blessed in his seed.

Luke, on the other hand, proceeds backward, since he doesn't begin to list the generations from his account of the Lord's birth, but from the place where he tells the story of his baptism by John. In his incarnation, the Lord undertook to bear the burden of the sins of the human race; so too in his baptismal consecration he undertook the task of expiating them. So Matthew signifies Christ coming down to bear our sins by counting the generations downward; Luke signifies Christ going up to expiate sins by counting the generations upward—our sins, of course, not his own. The former, though, comes down the list through Solomon, with whose mother David sinned; the latter goes up the list through Nathan, another of David's sons, through whom he was purged of his sin. For we read that Nathan was sent to him to rebuke him, so that he might be healed by repentance. Both lines meet in David, one coming down, the other going up; and from there as far as Abraham—or from Abraham as far as David—they don't vary from each other in any generation. In this way, Christ, the son of David and the son of Abraham, goes back to God; and back to God, of course, we have to be led by the deletion of our sins and our renewal in baptism.

(4) Jerome

The book of the generation of Jesus Christ. In Isaiah we read, *Who will tell of his generation?* (Isa 53:1). We do not think that the Gospel contradicts the prophet even though the Gospel here attempts to describe what the prophet considers inexpressible. For the prophet is concerned with the generation of divinity, whereas the Gospel is talking about the incarnation. In other words, it begins with bodily matters, so that we may begin to know God through a man.

Judah begat Perez and Zerah from Tamar. It should be noted that the women mentioned in the Savior's genealogy are not holy women, but the kind whom Scripture disapproves. Nonetheless, he came for the sake of sinners, himself being born from sinful women, so that all sin should be put to an end. For this reason, Ruth the Moabite (1:5) and Bathsheba the wife of Uriah (1:6) are also put into the narrative.

The diligent reader might ask, "Since Joseph is not the father of the Lord Savior, what does the order of births leading up to Joseph have to do with the Lord?" To this we will first answer that it is not customary in Scripture for women to be included in the order of generations. Second, Joseph and Mary were from one tribe, which means that she is regarded as a relative under the law, and that they would be counted together in Bethlehem, being born from one stock.

Matthew 1:18

18Now the birth of Jesus Christ took place in this way. When his mother Mary had been betrothed to Joseph, before they came together she was found to be with child of the Holy Spirit;

(5) Peter Chrysologus

Christ's birth, the Gospel writer says, **was like this.** Notice he did not say "*came about* like this," but rather, "*was* like this." Why? Because prior to his birth by his mother, he had already come into being from his Father. What he "was," therefore, he had always been; what "came about," on the other hand, was given to him at his birth. He *was* God; he *was given* a human nature—that is, he received the same type of nature from the womb that was molded into us from the mud (Gen 2:7).

Nothing in the holy Gospels—not people, not names, not words, syllables, letters, not even the slightest vowel marks—is devoid of a figurative interpretation. A woman engaged to be married, for instance, was sought in order to prefigure the Church, the bride of Christ, just as Hosea predicted: *I will take you as my wife in judgment and justice; you will become my wife in mercy and compassion, and I will wed you in faith* (Hos 2:19–20). John, too, tells us that *he who weds the bride is the bridegroom* (John 3:29), and Saint Paul says, *I have engaged you to man, so that I may present you as a pure virgin to Christ* (2 Cor 11:2). And the Church *is* a true bride in the manner of Mary—after all, she too "rebirths" the infant Christ in a virgin birth.[18]

Or Joseph, as the bridegroom, he became Mary's protector in order to alert us to the fact that Christ's passion was foreshadowed in the actions of the *patriarch* Joseph. Think about it: the former Joseph was denounced by his brothers, just as Christ was accused by false witnesses. Joseph's prophetic dreams aroused jealousy, just as Christ's prophetic visions provoked hatred. Joseph was thrown into a pit of death and emerged from it alive (Gen 37:24), just as Christ was given over to the grave and returned from the grave, alive! Joseph was sold as a slave; Christ too was valued at a price. Joseph was taken to Egypt, and to Egypt Christ fled (2:13–15). Joseph supplied his starving people with an abundance of bread, Christ satisfies the nations of the world with bread from heaven. Truly Joseph shimmers as a model and foreshadowing of the heavenly bridegroom: he bears his image, he walks in his likeness.

18. That is, through baptism.

(6) Leo the Great

Moreover, beloved, this very fact—that Christ chose to be born from a virgin—does it not appear to be of deepest design? Clearly, it was so that the devil would be ignorant of the salvation born for the human race. And, because Christ hid the spiritual conception, the devil would not believe that this child, whom he did not perceive as being different from others, was born in a way different from the rest. For the devil observed that his nature was just like everyone else's; he believed that he had an origin in common with all of them, but he did not understand that he was free from the fetters of transgression, although he did not find him to be a stranger to the infirmity of the mortal state.

Indeed, *the mercy* of God *is truthful* (cf. Ps 85 [86]:15). Although many options were available for him to renew the human race in an ineffable way, he chose chiefly this manner of considering it so that he might use the reasonableness of his justice, not the strength of his power, to destroy the work of the devil (1 John 3:8). For this to come to pass, Christ was begotten without the seed of a man, from a virgin whom no human union but rather the Holy Spirit had made fruitful. And although conception in all mothers occurs accompanied by sin's filth, this mother acquired its cleansing from the one with whom she conceived. For where the transfusion of the father's seed does not reach, there the beginning of sin does not assert itself.

Because her inviolate virginity did not know concupiscence, it provided the substance of the flesh. This nature, not its defect, was received from the Lord's mother. He was begotten in the *form of a servant* (Phil 2:7) but without its slavish condition. And in this way, the new man was tempered with the old so that he might take on the reality of the human race, but shuck off the vice of its antiquity.

Matthew 1:19

19 and her husband Joseph, being a just man and unwilling to put her to shame, resolved to divorce her quietly.

(7) Peter Chrysologus

But how can we call Joseph a just man when he refused to inquire into the cause of his betrothed's pregnancy, when he failed to unravel the circumstances surrounding her alleged shame, and when he spurned even the opportunity to clear the rumors about his marriage?

He wished to send her away privately. His response seems more kind than just, but that would be to judge him by human, not divine, standards. In God's eyes, kindness does not exist without justice, nor justice without kindness; by heavenly standards, fairness cannot exist in the absence of tenderness, nor tenderness without fairness. Such virtues are inextricably connected; if separated, they each fall to pieces. For fairness without tenderness is savage, justice without kindness is cruel.

Joseph, therefore, may rightly be called "just" precisely because he was kind, and "kind" precisely because he was just. In short, as long as he remained kind, cruelty could find no place in him; as long as he placed his own rights to one side, he remained clear-headed. By waiving his right to vengeance, he avoided committing a crime; by refusing to find fault, he escaped condemnation.

This righteous man's mind burned with pain, stricken by the strangeness of the situation. His wife was pregnant, yet a virgin; nearly ready to give birth, yet devoid of shame! There she stood, concerned for her child, yet secure in her chastity, clothed in the garments of a mother, but somehow still bearing the honor of a virgin. What could he do in such a case? Accuse her of a crime? But he himself was a witness to her innocence. Proclaim her unfaithfulness? But he himself was the guarantee of her purity. Perhaps he should threaten her with adultery proceedings? But he himself was the champion of her virginity. What to do with her? He thought about sending her away, for he could neither talk about the matter openly nor, as it turned out, could he keep it to himself. He thought about sending her away, and he told the whole matter to God, for he could not confide in humans.

Matthew 1:20–21

20 But as he considered this, behold, an angel of the Lord appeared to him in a dream, saying, "Joseph, son of David, do not fear to take Mary your wife, for that which is conceived in her is of the Holy Spirit; 21 she will bear a son, and you shall call his name Jesus, for he will save his people from their sins."

(8) Ephrem of Nisibis

The Only-Begotten journeyed from the Godhead[19] and resided in a virgin, so that through physical birth the Only-Begotten would become a brother to many (cf. Rom 8:29). He journeyed from Sheol[20] and resided in the kingdom with the result that he forged a path from Sheol to the kingdom. For our Lord gave his resurrection as a guarantee to mortals that he would lead them out of Sheol, which takes the departed as equal in the kingdom; which welcomes guests with discrimination, so that we might journey from where everyone's bodies are treated the same; where everyone's efforts are treated unequally (cf. Luke 7:36–50).

The Firstborn, who was begotten according to his nature, underwent yet another birth outside his nature, so that we too would understand that after our natural birth, we must undergo another birth outside our nature. As a spiritual being, he was unable to become physical until the time of physical birth. And so too, physical beings, unless they undergo another birth, cannot become spiritual. The Son, whose birth is beyond comprehension, underwent another birth about which we can speak. So by the one we learn that his majesty is limitless, and by the other we realize that his goodness is boundless. For the

19. In Syriac *ituta*, literally "Being," which Ephrem connects with the Hebrew YHWH (cf. Exod 3:14) and sometimes uses the same word as an epithet for the Father.

20. The grave or place of the dead.

majesty of him whose first birth cannot be imagined by any mind increases infinitely and the goodness of him whose other birth is proclaimed by every mouth overflows without limit.

(9) John Chrysostom

Can you see from the introduction what the Gospels are like? If, on the other hand, you have any doubts about your own humanity, have faith in it because of his. It is far more difficult for human reason to conceive of God becoming man than for a man to be called son of God. So when you hear that the Son of God is son of David and of Abraham, have no further doubts that you too, the son of Adam, will be a son of God. I mean, it was not without purpose that he humbled himself. His intention was to exalt us. He was born in the flesh so that you might be born in the spirit; he was born of a woman so that you might be more than the son of a woman. Hence the twofold birth, like ours and also surpassing ours: being born of a woman was our lot, but being born *not of blood or of the will of flesh or man but of the Holy Spirit* (John 1:13) proclaims a birth that surpasses ours. This birth he promises as a gift from the Spirit. Everything else followed from this. Take his baptism for example. It had something of the Old and something of the New: being baptized by the prophet [John] was a mark of the Old, the descent of the Spirit foreshadowed the New. It was as though someone was standing in the gap between two persons at a distance from each other, bringing them together as one and uniting them by taking their hands. This is what he did, linking the Old to the New, the divine nature to the human nature, his condition to ours.

(10) Augustine

Our Lord Jesus Christ became a Son of Man *by being born of a woman.*[21] But supposing he hadn't been born of the virgin Mary, would he have been any the less a man? Someone may say, "He wanted to be a man; he would have been a man, even though he hadn't been born of a woman. After all, God did not make the first man from a woman." Let's see how to answer this. You say, "Why should he choose a woman in order to be born?" The answer you get is, "Why should he avoid a woman in order to be born?" Even if I am not able to show why he should choose to be born of a woman, you must still show me why he should have avoided being born of a woman.

If Christ had avoided a woman's womb, it might have indicated that he could be defiled by it. But in fact, the more undefiled he was in his own proper being, the less reason he had to shrink from a bodily womb, as though he could be defiled by it. On the other hand, by being born of a woman, he would bring home to us a point of great significance.

I too am perfectly ready to admit that if the Lord had wanted to become man without being born of woman, it would have been quite easy for his sovereign majesty to achieve

21. Gal 4:4b.

it. Just as he was able to be born of a woman without a man, so he could have been born without a woman. But what he is showing us here is that in neither sex does humanity need to despair of itself. Human beings, of course, are divided by sex into males and females. So if, while appearing as a man—and I agree he had to be that—had he not been born of a woman, women would have despaired of themselves, remembering their first sin, how it was through a woman that the first man was ensnared, and would have thought that there was absolutely no hope for them in Christ.

Man was ensnared through a woman administering poison; let man be restored through a woman administering salvation. Let woman compensate for the sin of the man ensnared through her by giving birth to the Christ. That too is why women were the first to tell the apostles about God rising from the dead. A woman brought the news of death to her husband in paradise; and women too brought the news of salvation to men in the Church. The apostles were to carry the news of Christ's resurrection to the nations; the news was brought to the apostles by women. Nobody, therefore, should belittle Christ for being born of a woman. For the female sex that could not defile him as liberator is the sex by which the Creator was created.

Observe that Matthew calls him the Son of David: whom he had, he says, from the seed of David, according to the flesh (Rom 1:3). As a matter of fact, the Lord himself put this problem to the Jews, and the Apostle solves it here in these very words. After saying whom he had from the seed of David, he adds according to the flesh in order precisely to have us understand that according to the divinity he is not the Son of David, but the Son of God, the Lord of David. This is how the Apostle speaks somewhere else, when he wanted to speak in favor of the Jewish stock: whose are the fathers, he says, of whom is Christ according to the flesh, who is God above all things, blessed forever (Rom 9:5). According to the flesh means "Son of David"; God above all things, blessed forever means "Lord of David."

So the Lord says to the Jews, Whose son do you say the Christ is? They answered, David's. They knew that perfectly well, they could gather it easily enough from the preaching of the prophets. And indeed he was from the seed of David, but according to the flesh, through the Virgin Mary, married to Joseph. So when they answered that Christ was the Son of David, Jesus said to them, **So how does David in the spirit call him Lord, saying: The Lord said to my lord, Sit at my right hand until I place your enemies under your feet? So if David in the spirit calls him Lord, how is he his son?** (22:42–45; Ps 110:1). And the Jews couldn't answer. That's what we have in the Gospel. He did not deny he was the Son of David, even though they were unaware that he was the Lord of David. What they held to about the Christ was that he came to be in time; what they did not understand about him was that he is in eternity. So, therefore, wishing to teach them about his divinity, he put a problem to them about his humanity, as though to say, "You know that the Christ is the Son of David; answer and tell me how he can also be the Lord of David." But to prevent them saying "He isn't David's Lord," he quoted David himself as a witness. And what does he say? He says the truth, of course. On the one hand, you have that place in the Psalms where he says to David, *I will place the fruit of your body upon your throne* (Ps 132:11). There you have "Son of David." And how is the one who is the Son of David also "Lord of David"? *The Lord said to my lord*, he says, *Sit at my right* (Ps 110:1). Are you surprised at David having his son as his Lord, when you see Mary has given birth to her Lord? David's Lord, because he's God; David's Lord, because he's everyone's; but David's son, on the other hand, because he's the Son of Man. One and the same person who's Lord and who's son: David's Lord, because *since he was in the form of God, he did not think it robbery to be equal to God*; David's son, because *he emptied himself taking the form of a slave* (Phil 2:6–7).

Matthew 1:22–25

22All this took place to fulfill what the Lord had spoken by the prophet:
23"Behold, a virgin shall conceive and bear a son,
and his name shall be called Emman'u-el"
(which means, God with us). 24When Joseph woke from sleep, he did as the angel of the Lord commanded him; he took his wife, 25but knew her not until she had borne a son; and he called his name Jesus.

(11) Hilary of Poitiers

The explanation of his generation is simple. That he was "conceived by the Holy Spirit, born of the Virgin Mary"[22] is the message of all the prophets. But many irreligious people and those who are complete strangers to spiritual teachings seize an opportunity in dealing with this matter of entertaining disgraceful notions concerning Mary because it is written: **Before they came together, she was found with child** (1:18), and again: **Do not be afraid to take your spouse** (1:20), and again: **He did not know her until she gave birth** (1:25). They do not remember that she was engaged to be married and that this was spoken to Joseph who wanted to cast her out because he was a righteous man and did not want her to be judged by the law. So that there would be no uncertainty about her offspring, Joseph therefore becomes a witness to Christ, who was "conceived by the Holy Spirit." It is thereafter, because she had been engaged, that she was taken in marriage, and thus he knew her after the birth. That is, the term **marriage** applies to their relations, for she has been known by Joseph, not merely in terms of being legally related. Finally, when Joseph was warned to cross over into Egypt, it was said: **Take the child and his mother** (2:13), and **Return with the child and his mother** (2:20), and again in Luke, *And there were Joseph and his [the child's] mother*. However often reference is made to one or the other, she is properly the mother of Christ, for it was not the case that she was called the wife of Joseph, because she was not. But this also is the reason why the angel, who, indicating that she was engaged to Joseph, a righteous man (1:19), called her espoused. For as he said: **Joseph, son of David, do not be afraid to take Mary as your spouse** (2:20). The name "fiancée" acquired the name of "spouse," and while she was recognized to be engaged *post partum*, she was revealed solely as the mother of Jesus.

22. Very probably a citation from a local creedal statement.

(12) Jerome

When his mother Mary was betrothed. . . . Why was Jesus conceived, not from one who was simply a virgin, but from one who was betrothed? First, so that through Joseph's ancestry Mary's origin could be demonstrated. Second, so that she would not be stoned by the Jews as an adulteress. Third, so that when she fled to Egypt she might have the support [of a husband]. The martyr Ignatius added a fourth reason why he should have been born of a betrothed woman: that his birth might be concealed from the devil, who thought that he would be born not from a virgin but from a wife.[23]

(13) John Chrysostom

You shall see how the tyrant was bound, how the multitude of the captives following him were set free, and how the capital from which that unholy demon ruled over all things in time past is broken up and laid open. For even there, our King was present (See 1 Pet 3:19–20; 4:6).

So don't be wearied, beloved, by such a struggle. If anyone were describing a visible war, and trophies, and victories, you would not be satisfied till you knew the ending. Neither meat nor drink can compare to that kind of history. But if you readily welcome that kind of fare, how much more should you accept this one. For consider what pleasure it is to hear, how on the one hand God from heaven, rising out *of the royal thrones, leaped down*[24] to the earth, and even to hell itself, and stood there in battle array. See how the devil, on the other hand, sets himself in array against him, who appears not as unveiled, but as God hidden in man's nature.

And what is more marvelous than to see death destroyed by death, curse extinguished by curse, and the dominion of the devil put down by those very things by which he prevailed. Let us therefore rouse ourselves fully from sleep. For I see the gates open before us. Let us enter in an orderly fashion, with trembling, and set foot straightway on the threshold itself.

But what is this threshold? **The book of the generation of Jesus Christ, Son of David, Son of Abraham.**

(14) Augustine

What the Holy Spirit achieved, he achieved in both of them. **Since he was a just man** (1:19), it says. So, **a just man,** a just woman. The Holy Spirit came to rest in the justice of both of them and gave both of them a son. But through the sex whose function it was to give birth he brought this about in such a way that the son would also be born to the husband. So

23. The reference is to the epistle of Ignatius (Antioch) to Mary at Neapolis, almost universally regarded by scholars as a pseudo-Ignatian work.

24. Wis 18:15.

the angel tells both of them to give the child a name; this establishes the authority of the parents. For with Zacharias too (Luke 1:59–63), while he was still dumb, it was the mother who gave the newborn son a name; and when those who were present signaled to the father what he wanted him called, he took a writing pad and wrote what she had already said. Mary is told, *Behold, you shall conceive a son, and you shall call his name Jesus.* And Joseph too is told, **Joseph, son of David, do not be afraid to take Mary for your wife. For what is conceived in her is of the Holy Spirit. She will bear a son, and you shall call his name Jesus; he is the one who will save his people from their sins.** It also says, **And she bore him a son** (1:25), which as plainly as can be confirms his position as father, not by the flesh but by love. So he is indeed a father, in his own proper way.

Matthew 2

This chapter offers one of the rare glimpses into Jesus's early childhood. Later apocryphal Gospels will supply many stories and some fanciful moments in Jesus's younger years, though ancient writers do not regard them with the same authority as Matthew's Gospel. By the time the magi reached Bethlehem, Jesus was no longer an infant, and after Jesus's birth, it is said that the family had taken up residence in Bethlehem. This is where the magi found them, as verse 11 says, going into the house they saw the child with Mary his mother.

Of all the characters who make their appearance in the Gospel, none stirred the imagination of the early fathers as much as the magi,[1] *as well as the star that they followed. Matthew alone carries the story of the magi. Since they are said to have come* from the east *with no other information provided, they are a somewhat mysterious addition to the narrative of Christ's birth. Given that Jewish law forbids sorcery, their presence would have been surprising had it not been for the fact that they had been used by God to announce Christ's birth to the world. Origen states emphatically that magi communicate with demons, from which they derive their magic powers, but which was thwarted by the divine effect of the angels' praising God. Unable to perform their usual practices, the magi were prepared to recognize the star as a sign. For early Christian readers, the magi or wise men were regarded as prophetically fulfilling the promise of God's inclusion of the Gentiles or pagans into the covenant plan of salvation.*

Their gifts are essential to the star story, as Hilary says: "then follows the offering of gifts, which represented their awareness of Christ's full identity: the gold proclaims him as King, the incense as God, the myrrh as man." Each gift contains an aspect of the mystery of Christ's purpose. Gold is for his kingship, myrrh for his death as a man, incense for his resurrection as God. The gifts celebrate not only the newborn Christ, but also a new humanity, as Basil of Caesarea observes: "salvation of the world, the birthday of humanity."

1. Magi, normally associated with Persian priesthood, were an upper caste of soothsayers and interpreters of omens and dreams. *It was for this occupation that Daniel and his three friends had been trained in Babylonia.* Amidst the scenes from the New Testament that survive in catacomb art, the most commonly depicted is that of the magi. Though the Gospel never tells how many magi came to Bethlehem, they have been usually portrayed with the star as three men (identified by their Persian caps) with gifts approaching Mary and Jesus (on her lap). See J. Stevenson, *The Catacombs: Rediscovered Monuments of Early Christianity* (London: Thames and Hudson, 1978), 87.

Another instructive feature of the magi is that they left their homeland to follow the star and see the Christ. This was taken to mean that they had to depart from their present situation so that they could enter into another. The Christian must likewise leave his or her former life in order to find a new one. So Chrysostom, "Let us also, then, follow the magi by ridding ourselves of questionable behavior and set ourselves apart from it so that we may see the Christ. Even the magi would not have seen him had they not made that separation." For this reason, also, the magi returned to their country transformed by the majesty of Christ's divinity (Leo), returning by another route.

In sharp contrast to the faith and transparency of the magi is Herod's suspicion and self-deception. With the news of the rising of another king, Herod ordered the death of all young children in order to thwart any challenge to his throne. But more is at stake than a jealous king attempting to rid himself of a rival. In a terse summation, Chrysologus accuses Herod of trying to kill the one who was life and of "wickedly pursuing Goodness itself." Such an attack was self-defeating. Trying to elevate himself to heaven, Herod only ended up by entering hell. The deceiver was, in the end, deceived by thinking he had secured his kingdom, whereas he had ensured his own death.

Patristic writers saw in the killing of the innocents a foreshadowing of the persecution of the Church. For Epiphanius, this loss represented the Church because "from the person of Rachel was shown the Church that will have martyrs."[2] The slain children are prototypes of the "glory of martyrdom" (Hilary) or the "dignity of martyrdom" (Leo), which leads to eternal life.

Of some interest to the ancient writers is Matthew's reference to Jesus as a Nazarene, according to what was spoken by the prophets. *That he would be called a Nazarene on prophetic grounds moved the focus of interpretation from mere identification with a geographical location (Nazareth) to a moral and spiritual status known in the Old Testament as Nazarite (or Nazirite) vows. Only in (Latin) Judges 13:5, 7 and 16:17 is the word "nazareus" actually used. As far as the ancients were concerned,[3] the citation from Judges 13:7c ("for the child will be a nazareus of God from the time of his infancy and from the womb of his mother until the day of his death") was perfectly apropos given Jesus's circumstances as one who was uniquely separated (sanctified) for God from his birth.*

Augustine closes this chapter by commenting on another textual problem: the differences between the birth narrative in Matthew and Luke. His argument is that the omissions (or inclusions) in the two evangelists' narratives are not the same as contradictions between their accounts.

2. *On the Interpretation of the Gospels* 7.

3. Apparently, the evangelist was under the same impression, although the term *nazir(aios)* is used only in Judges 13:5 per the LXX, whereas Matthew uses *Nazōraios*.

Matthew 2:1–2

1Now when Jesus was born in Bethlehem of Judea[4] in the days of Herod the king, behold, wise men from the East came to Jerusalem, saying, 2"Where is he who has been born king of the Jews? For we have seen his star in the East, and have come to worship him."

(1) John Chrysostom

In order to end the ancient curse, and to call the world to worship him, and for him to be venerated in every land and sea, as it was from the very beginning, the Lord opened the door to the Gentiles. God was willing to instruct his own people through strangers. After all, the prophets had been continually proclaiming his advent, and yet the people gave this no great consideration. So it happened that the Lord brought barbarians from a far country, seeking after the King who was "among the Jewish people."

Thus the people first learned from a Persian tongue what they had refused to learn from the prophets. . . . For what could they say once they saw the wise men and the vision of a single star, while neglecting so many prophets and refusing to receive Christ? Through the magi, God acted in much the same ways as he did with the Ninevites when he sent Jonah, as well as with the Samaritan and the Canaanite women (John 4:7; 15:22).

Someone might ask, didn't God reveal this star to all the wise men of the East? Perhaps, but not all of them would have believed. No doubt these who came were better prepared than the rest. Notice how virtuous they were, not only by coming, but also by their boldness of speech. In order to show that they were not impostors, the magi explained what vision had shown them the way and how far they had traveled. And once they arrived, they spoke boldly: **for we are come**, they said, **to worship him**. They feared neither the people's anger, nor the tyranny of the king.

But why did they worship him at all? As it concerned their own situation, what did they expect to receive from a youngster and a poor mother? If it was for future benefits, did they imagine that the child whom they worshiped in swaddling clothes would remember what they had done?

What more shall I say about this mystery? I see a carpenter and a manger, an infant and swaddling clothes, a virgin giving birth without the necessities of life; nothing but poverty and complete destitution. But have you ever seen wealth in the midst of such poverty? How could he who was rich have become so poor for our sake that he had neither bed nor bedding but was laid in a manger? O immeasurable wealth concealed in poverty! He lies in a manger, yet he shakes the whole world. He is bound with strips of swaddling clothes, but he breaks the bonds of sin. Before he could speak, he taught wise men and converted them.

4. Because Micah 5:2 speaks of Bethlehem in the land of Judah, Jerome believed the Matthean account was a copying error and that the alleged Hebrew original read "in Judah" (*Comm. on Matt* 2:5).

(2) Leo the Great

Moreover, beloved, the manifestation of this ineffable mercy occurred when Herod was holding kingly authority among the Jews, when a foreigner had obtained dominion since legitimate succession was absent and the power of the priests was torn down, with the result that the birth of the true King was proven by the speech of that prophet who had said, *A ruler from Judah will not be lacking, nor a leader from his loins, until he for whom it was reserved should arrive, and he himself is the expectation of nations* (Gen 49:10).

Formerly, an endless succession of offspring from these nations had been promised to the most-blessed patriarch Abraham, one fit to be produced not from the seed of his flesh, but from the fruitfulness of his faith. Therefore, this succession was compared even with the multitude of the stars, so that the father of all nations would hope for a progeny not of earth, but of heaven. Therefore, so as to create the promised posterity, the heirs, themselves foretold in the stars, were stirred up by the birth of a new star. This happened so that the obedience of the heavens would serve the one for whom their testimony had been employed.

(3) Epiphanius the Latin

When therefore Jesus had been born in Bethlehem. The Hebrew word "Bethlehem" means "house of bread." Bethlehem is the house of God and also the house of bread. For Jesus, who was born in this city, became the true bread for believers (26:26; John 6:32). He was born in the days of King Herod. Herod was a Sadducee, just as it says elsewhere, *Pharisees with the Herodians* (22:15–16).

Magi from the East came to Jerusalem. The magi are figures for all the nations (i.e., the magi represent the Gentiles), who had come to that court where the law resides, searching for a savior. They said, **We have seen his star in the East and we have come to worship him.** The magi claimed that he is the King of the Jews, but the Jews responded: *We have no king but Caesar* (John 19:15). Pilate said: Are you the King of the Jews? Jesus said to him: **You have said that I am a king** (Matt 27:11). So you can see that the Gentiles, such as the magi and Pilate, understood more easily that he is a king than did the Jews. This was also the case for Nebuchadnezzar: *I see the figure of a fourth, like [that of] the son of God* (Dan 3:25). Could no one else from that crowd see him except Nebuchadnezzar? It was, then, the Gentiles who saw him, adored him, and followed him.

(4) Origen

Magi are in communion with demons and by their formulas invoke them for the ends that they desire; and they succeed in these practices so long as nothing more divine and potent than the demons and the spell that invokes them appears or is pronounced. But if anything more divine were to appear, the powers of the demons would be destroyed, since they would be unable to withstand the light of the divine power. Accordingly, it is probable that at the birth of Jesus when, as Luke records and as I believe, *a multitude of the heavenly host praised God and said, "Glory to God in the highest, and on earth peace, goodwill among men"* (Luke 2:13–14), the effect of this was that the demons lost their strength and became weak; their sorcery was confuted and their power overthrown; they were not only overthrown by the angels who visited the earthly region on account of the birth of Jesus, but also by the soul of Jesus and the divine power in him. Accordingly, when the magi wanted to perform their usual practices, which they had previously effected by certain charms and trickery, they tried to find out the reason why they no longer worked, concluding that it was an important one. Seeing a sign from God in heaven, they wished to see what was indicated by it. I think that they had the prophecies of Balaam recorded by Moses, who was also an expert in this kind of thing. They found there the prophecy of the star and the words: *I will show to him, but not now; I call him blessed, though he is not at hand.* And they guessed that the man foretold as coming with the star had arrived; and as they had already found that he was superior to all demons and the beings that usually appeared to them and caused certain magical effects, they wanted to worship him.

They therefore came to Judea, because they were convinced that some king had been born and because they knew where he would be born, but without understanding over what kingdom he would rule. They brought gifts that they offered to him who was, so to speak, a combination of God and mortal man. These gifts were symbols, the gold being offered as to a king, the myrrh for one who would die, and the frankincense to God; they offered them when they learnt his birthplace. Since, however, the Savior of the human race was God and superior to the angels who help man, an angel rewarded the piety of the magi in worshiping Jesus by warning them not to go to Herod but to return to their own country by another route.

Matthew 2:3–6

3When Herod the king heard this, he was troubled, and all Jerusalem with him; 4and assembling all the chief priests and scribes of the people, he inquired of them where the Christ was to be born. 5They told him, "In Bethlehem of Judea; for so it is written by the prophet:

> **6"And you, O Bethlehem, in the land of Judah,**
> **are by no means least among the rulers of Judah;**
> **for from you shall come a ruler**
> **who will govern my people Israel.'"**

(5) Gregory of Nazianzus

When Christ appeared, earth and heaven were shaken because of his birth. A heavenly choir sent down hymns of praise, while a star from the East guided the magi on their way and the magi brought gifts to worship the new-born King.

Here then is the teaching about the novelty of Christ's birth. There is no shame involved, since only sin is shameful. No shame attaches to him, as the Word formed him, nor was he mortal with a mortal's transience. He came, however, from flesh that the Spirit had previously made holy—that of a noble mother, unwedded—and he, as a self-formed mortal came and underwent purification for our sake. Indeed, he undertook all obligations to the law; a kind of recompense for his nurture, as I see it, offering a parting gift to the law as it withdrew from the scene.

But when he had been heralded by a lamp that shone a great light (Isa 9:2), the lamp that preceded his birth and his teaching proclaimed Christ as God in the midst of the wilderness (Isa 40:3). He was then fully revealed and became a mediator to those peoples who were far off and those who were near (Eph 2:13); he was a cornerstone for joining both (Eph 2:20). He bestowed on mortals the twofold cleansing by the everlasting Spirit who purged our former evil in flesh and purified our own blood. For the blood of Christ my Lord was poured out as a ransom for our primal disease and a healing for the world.

Matthew 2:7–8

7Then Herod summoned the wise men secretly and ascertained from them what time the star appeared; 8and he sent them to Bethlehem, saying, "Go and search diligently for the child, and when you have found him bring me word, that I too may come and worship him."

(6) Leo the Great

Hearing that a ruler of the Jews had been born, Herod became greatly afraid, for he suspected that this was his successor. And having set in motion a murder for the author of salvation, he deceitfully pledged his obedience. How happy he would have been if he had imitated the faith of the wise men and if he had converted to the devotion that he planned to deceive! O the blind impiety of foolish jealousy, which, by its own madness, supposes that the divine purpose must be confounded! The Lord of the universe, who is in charge of an eternal kingdom, does not seek a temporal one. Why do you try to alter the immutable order of established things and anticipate the crime of others?

The death of Christ is not for your time. Beforehand the gospel must be established; beforehand the kingdom of God must be preached; beforehand health must be conferred; beforehand miracles must be performed. . . . He who by his own will was born, by the power of his own authority will die.

(7) Epiphanius the Latin

Then Herod secretly called the magi. When the magi had been summoned, Herod secretly asked where the star would appear. Because he feared a successor, this most wicked man was now thinking about killing Jesus. He believed that he could do it by ordering all infants to be killed who had been born from that time he heard the magi's reply. It is not unimportant that Herod said: **Report back to me, so that I too may come and adore him.** He spoke these words, though he harbored a wicked intent.

Matthew 2:9–10

9When they had heard the king they went their way; and lo, the star which they had seen in the East went before them, till it came to rest over the place where the child was.
10When they saw the star, they rejoiced exceedingly with great joy;

(8) Leo the Great

A star more brilliant than the others spurs on the wise men dwelling in the far-off Orient. And from the brightness of its amazing light these men, not unskilled at observing such things, understand the magnitude of its significance. Clearly a divine inspiration advances this in their hearts, so that the mystery of so great a sight might not be unknown to them and that this extraordinary thing, which was revealed to their eyes, would not be unintelligible to their minds. Thereafter, they array their service with worship and furnish themselves with these gifts so that they might demonstrate that, although about to honor one, they believed that he was threefold, honoring his royal character with gold, his human character with myrrh, his divine character with incense.

And thus they enter the chief city of the Judean kingdom, and in the royal city they request to be shown to the boy whom they had learned was begotten to rule. Herod is disquieted. He is afraid for his own safety, he fears for his power, he demands to know from the priests and teachers of the law what Scripture has predicted concerning the birth of the Christ. What had been prophesied comes to their notice. While truth enlightens the wise men, faithlessness blinds the teachers. Fleshly Israel does not understand what he reads, he does not see what he reveals, he uses writings whose declarations he does not believe. . . .

When the wise men had adored the Lord and completed their whole devotion, according to a warning in a dream they do not return by the same way that they had come. It was proper that now believing in Christ they not walk through the paths of their old way of life, but enter upon a new path and abstain from the wanderings they left behind. It also served, at the time, to make void the plot of Herod, who was arranging an irreverence of deceit against the Lord Jesus through the pretense of kindness.

They saw and adored the Child, small when it came to size, dependent on others for help, unable to speak, and in no way different from the general condition of human infancy. Certainly, the proofs that attributed to him the majesty of an invisible divinity were reliable. Likewise, it ought to have great probative value that the Word made flesh and that the eternal essence of God's Son took up true human nature, preventing the miracles of ineffable works that would follow or the punishments of sufferings he would undertake from disturbing the mystery of faith through contradictory elements. No one could in any way be justified unless they come to believe that the Lord Jesus is both true God and true man.

Matthew 2:11–12

[11]and going into the house they saw the child with Mary his mother, and they fell down and worshiped him. Then, opening their treasures, they offered him gifts, gold and frankincense and myrrh. [12]And being warned in a dream not to return to Herod, they departed to their own country by another way.

(9) Hilary of Poitiers

The appearance of the star that the magi first apprehended reveals that the pagans were soon to profess belief in Christ. Men long opposed to a knowledge of divine understanding were about to understand that light that shone forth the moment it appeared.

There then follows the offering of gifts, which represented their awareness of Christ's full identity: the gold proclaims him as King, the incense as God, the myrrh as man. And so through the magi's veneration [of him], the understanding of every mystery is summed up concerning his death as man, his resurrection as God, about his judgment as King. Just as the magi were prohibited from retracing their route and returning to Herod in Judea, so we ought never to look to Judea for our knowledge and learning. Instead, we are admonished to refrain from following the "route" of our former life by placing all our salvation and hope in Christ.

(10) Basil of Caesarea

Stars run across the sky (2:9), the magi leave their lands (2:1), and the earth receives him in a cave.[5] Let no one be without gift, let no one be without gratitude. And let us exclaim a cry of exultation. Let us give our festival the name *Theophania*.[6] Let us celebrate the salvation of the world, the birthday of humanity. Today the condemnation of Adam was undone.[7] No longer is it, *You are dust and to dust you shall return* (Gen 3:19). No longer is it, *You shall bring forth children in pain* (Gen 3:16), for *blessed is she who painfully brought forth Emmanuel, and blessed are the breasts that nourished him* (cf. Luke 11:27). For this reason, *a child was born to us, and a son was given to us, whose rule is on his shoulder* (Isa 9:6).

(11) John Chrysostom

What further need was there for this star, you may ask, once it located the place? It was necessary to make the child known since there were no obvious signs: the house was not

5. The popular birth narrative of the *Protoevangelium of James* (second century) tells that Christ was born of Mary in a cave.

6. That is, "divine manifestation" or "godly appearance," an early name for Christmas.

7. The idea here being that Christ, as the second Adam, brought about the recapitulation or a new beginning of humanity.

conspicuous; the mother was neither famous nor celebrated. So it was necessary for the star to bring them to the place, which is why it appeared again when they left Jerusalem, not stopping before it settled over the manger. Wonder upon wonder: both events were remarkable—the adoration of the magi and the guidance of the star—enough to bring joy to people made of stone. I mean, if the magi had said that they heard prophets saying one thing, or that angels conversed personally with them, people might have disbelieved them. But because the star appeared from on high, even the most skeptical were reduced to silence. Due to a greater power than belongs to a star, it was able to hide itself at one moment and appear at another, finally seeming to stand still above the child. As a result the magi themselves, too, were encouraged in their faith; and for this reason they rejoiced in finding what they sought. For it proved that they were messengers of truth; not making such a long journey without reason, so great was their longing for the Messiah. Let us also, then, follow the magi by ridding ourselves of questionable behavior and set ourselves apart from it so that we may see the Christ. Even the magi would not have seen him had they not made that separation. Let us keep ourselves from earthly things. Although the magi saw the star was first in Persia, it was only when they left Persia that they perceived the Sun of Justice. In other words, they would not have seen the star had they not eagerly departed from their earthly country.

(12) Gregory the Great

[W]hen the King of heaven was born, a king on earth was alarmed. Earthly pride is undoubtedly shaken when heavenly eminence is made manifest.

But we must ask why it happened that when our Redeemer was born, an angel appeared to the shepherds in Judea, but a star, rather than an angel, guided the magi from the east to worship him. This was the reason: a rational being, namely, an angel, was preached to the Jews as persons capable of using their minds, whereas a sign rather than a voice guided the Gentiles, who did not know how to make use of reason concerning knowledge of the Lord. This is why Paul says: *Prophecy has been given for believers not for unbelievers, but signs have been given for unbelievers and not for believers* (1 Cor 14:22). Prophecy has been given to the Jews as believers and not to unbelievers, whereas signs have been given to the pagans as unbelievers and not to believers. We should note that the apostles preached our Redeemer to these same pagans when the Lord was already a grown man, but it was a star that declared him to the pagans when he was a small child, not yet able to perform the normal human function of speaking. It was surely reasonable, both that the preachers should make the Lord (when he was already speaking) known to us with words, and that the silent elements should preach him when he was not yet speaking.

The magi indicate something important to us by their returning to their own country by another way. By doing what they were advised to do they suggest to us what we should do. Paradise is our country. We are forbidden to return to it, once we have known Jesus, by the way by which he came. Indeed, we left our country by being proud, by being disobedient, by pursuing visible things, by tasting forbidden food. We must return to it by weeping, by being obedient, by rejecting visible things and by curbing our bodily appetites. Thus we return to our country by another way. While pleasure led us away from the joys of paradise, sorrows summon us to return.

So, dearly beloved, we must always be fearful and alert, setting before the eyes of our hearts the sinfulness of our works, on the one hand, and the severity of the final judgment, on the other. Consider how severe a judge is coming. He threatens sinners with terrors, and yet he still bears with them. He puts off coming for this reason: that he may find fewer to condemn. Let us punish our sins with tears, and with the voice of the psalmist, let us anticipate his presence by admitting our guilt (Ps 95 [94]:2). Don't be deceived by beguiling pleasures, don't be led astray by barren joys. The judge who said *Woe to you who laugh now, because you will mourn and weep* (Luke 6:25) is near. Solomon says in this regard: *Laughter will be mingled with sorrow, and mourning follows at the end of joy* (Prov 14:13); and again: *I have accounted laughter as an error and said to joy, Why do you deceive in vain?* (Eccl 2:2); and again: *The heart of the wise is where there is sadness, and the heart of fools where there is happiness* (Eccl 7:4).

Let us fear the commandments of God if we would truly celebrate a feast of God. Distress over sin is a pleasing sacrifice to God, according to the psalmist who says: *An afflicted spirit is a sacrifice to God* (Ps 51:17 [50:19]). Our past sins were forgiven when we received baptism; since baptism we have committed many sins, even though we cannot be cleansed again by the water of baptism. Therefore, because we have defiled our lives even after baptism, let us baptize our conscience with our tears. Since we are seeking our country again by another way, let us who departed from it in frivolity return to it in bitter anger at our sins. Let us do this with the help of our Lord, who lives and reigns with the Father in the unity of the Holy Spirit, God for ever and ever. Amen.

Matthew 2:13–18

[13]Now when they had departed, behold, an angel of the Lord appeared to Joseph in a dream and said, "Rise, take the child and his mother, and flee to Egypt, and remain there till I tell you; for Herod is about to search for the child, to destroy him." [14]And he rose and took the child and his mother by night, and departed to Egypt, [15]and remained there until the death of Herod. This was to fulfill what the Lord had spoken by the prophet, "Out of Egypt have I called my son."

[16]Then Herod, when he saw that he had been tricked by the wise men, was in a furious rage, and he sent and killed all the male children in Bethlehem and in all that region who were two years old or under, according to the time which he had ascertained from the wise men. [17]Then was fulfilled what was spoken by the prophet Jeremiah:

**[18]"A voice was heard in Ramah,
wailing and loud lamentation,
Rachel weeping for her children;
she refused to be consoled,
because they were no more."**

(13) Hilary of Poitiers

But a glorious honor is rendered to the slain through the prophet who said: **A voice was heard in Ramah, weeping and great lamentation, Rachel weeping for her children, and she did not wish to be comforted because they were no more.** Rachel, wife of Jacob, was for a long time barren, but she lost none of those whom she had borne. In fact, she is presented in Genesis as a type of the Church. It is not therefore her voice and weeping that are heard, since she harbored no sorrow over slain children, but it is that of the Church; for a long time barren, yet now fruitful. This kind of weeping over her children is heard, not because she was grieving that they had been slain, but because they were being slain by those whom she had wanted to preserve as her firstborn sons. In this way, she did not wish to be comforted in her grief. For there is no denial of those who died; yet they were appointed, through the glory of martyrdom, for the gain of eternity.

(14) Leo the Great

But when the wise men had returned to their own country and Jesus had been brought into Egypt on account of the divine warning, a frustrated frenzy kindled in Herod's ruminations. He orders all the infants of Bethlehem to be killed, and since he does not know the infant whom he dreads, he extends his general savagery unto those of the suspected age. But those whom this wicked king removes from the world, Christ introduces in heaven, and for those whom he has not yet expended the redemption of his own blood, he already has allotted the dignity of martyrdom.

Therefore, beloved, lift up your faithful hearts unto the shining grace of everlasting light and, revering the sacraments for human salvation, apply your zeal to these things that have occurred for you.

(15) Peter Chrysologus

Seeing that he had been tricked by the magi. Wickedness bewails having been tricked; cruelty raves against the escape. Deception howls over being cheated; fraud is turned back upon itself. Herod gnashes his teeth, falling prey to his own trap. He now unsheathes his barbarity, hitherto carefully concealed. He takes up the weapons of treachery, in which he has full trust, and in terrestrial madness he searches for the one he knows is heaven-born.

Reaching for the highest he sinks from on high; beating on the doors of heaven, he enters the abyss. In his advance against God, he opposes himself. He who seeks to slay the living can only slay himself, for the damned cannot seize salvation. . . . Herod, who rules his earthly kingdom by force of arms, now attacks the heavenly realm. He who covets earthly lands now hurls himself against divine ones, wickedly pursuing Goodness itself.

(16) John Chrysostom

Surely it was a time for fear and awe, not for anger. Herod should have understood that he was attempting to do the impossible, but this does not stop him. When a soul is insensible and incurable, it will not be open to medicine given by God. Notice how this man follows the path of his earlier acts by adding many murders to another as he himself hurtles over the precipice. Driven wild by this anger and envy, as if by some demon, Herod takes account of nothing, raging even against nature herself. He vents his anger against the wise men who had mocked him upon children who did nothing wrong. He performed such a deed in Palestine that was like those done only in Egypt.[8]

Why are you so angry, O Herod? At being mocked by the wise men? Didn't you know that the birth they sought was divine? Didn't you summon the chief priests? Didn't you gather together the scribes? And didn't they, being called upon, bring the prophet also with them into your judgment court, who explained the things that were from long ago? Didn't you see how the old things agreed with the new? Didn't you hear also that a star had guided these men? Didn't you pay homage to the perseverance of these barbarians? Were you not amazed at their boldness? Weren't you horror-struck at the truth of the prophet? Why didn't you, therefore, reason with yourself from all these events that this event was not of the doing of the wise men, but of a divine power, dispensing all matters accordingly?

Someone might reply that although Herod is without excuse and shown to be bloodthirsty, how do you solve the problem about the injustice of what took place? If Herod acted unjustly, why did God permit it? What should we say to this? My answer is one that I have given continually in church, in the marketplace, and everywhere else. You should carefully keep in mind a principle that acts as sort of rule for us, suited to every such difficulty. What is this rule? While there may be many things or people that bring us an injury, we are not truly injured. Without trying to propound a riddle, I mean that whatever we may suffer unjustly from any one, it is meant for eradication of our sins—God putting that wrong to our account—and so suffering unjustly for the blessing of reward (5:11–12).

Now with the same logic we should consider our own sufferings. Whatever we may suffer wrongfully, we are either having our sins mitigated or we are receiving a more glorious crown, provided that the burden of our sins is not too great. Listen to what Paul says concerning the man that had committed fornication, *Deliver such a one to Satan for the destruction of the flesh, that his spirit may be saved* (1 Cor 5:5).

To expand upon my argument we should also remember David, who saw Shimei attacking him by trampling on his affliction and constantly pouring out scorn. David's captains wanted to kill him, but he utterly forbade them, saying, *Let him curse, that the Lord may look upon my humility, and that he may compensate me with good for this cursing this day* (2 Sam 16:11–12). And in the Psalms too, *Consider how my enemies are multiplied, and that they hate me with unjust hatred* (Ps 25:18 [17]), and *forgive all my sins*. Then there's Lazarus, who, for the same reason, enjoyed remission of sin because he suffered in this life innumerable evils. All these who were wronged were not really wronged if they bear nobly all that they suffer. Instead, they gain a greater good, whether they be tried of God or scourged by the devil.

8. That is, the slaying of the firstborn (Exod 11:5).

But it may be said, what sin did these children have that they should be killed? Given those who are of full age and guilty of many abuses, some reason might be shown. But seeing that they endured a premature death, what sort of sins did their sufferings resolve? Didn't you hear me say that though there were no sins, there is a future reward for those that suffer injustice? This is why the Lord prepares for them no small reward beforehand, since their lives were ended for such a cause.

And these are only the reasons we know about, though there are others. There are also others more mysterious than these, which God knows perfectly, who himself orders these things. Let us then leave to him a more perfect understanding of this matter and apply ourselves to what happens. In the trials of others, let us learn to bear all things nobly. It was truly a great tragedy that fell upon Bethlehem as its children were snatched from their mother's breast and dragged to this unjust slaughter.

Finally, let us learn the end of him who dared to do all this. Herod was quickly overtaken by punishment for these acts; he paid the penalty deserved for such an abomination by ending his own life, which was more troubling to him than death itself.

(17) Jerome

From Rachel was born Benjamin, in whose tribe Bethlehem is not a part. It may be asked, why would Rachel lament the sons of Judah, that is, Bethlehem, as her own? I will answer briefly that she may have been buried near Bethlehem in Ephrathah (it received its name from a corpse dwelling inside the tomb). Or perhaps, since Judah and Benjamin were two tribes joined together, Herod would have to kill infants not only in Bethlehem but in all its surrounding area. In this case, we understand by "Bethlehem" that many from Benjamin would also have been slain.

Matthew 2:19–20

19 But when Herod died, behold, an angel of the Lord appeared in a dream to Joseph in Egypt, saying, 20 "Rise, take the child and his mother, and go to the land of Israel, for those who sought the child's life are dead."

(18) Jerome

Many fall into error because of their ignorance of history, since they think this passage refers to the same Herod who mocked the Lord in his passion and who is now dead. That Herod, who had a friendship with Pilate, is the son of this Herod, the brother of Archelaus, and the very same whose brother Herod Tiberius Caesar (of Lyons, a city of Gaul) was made successor of his kingdom. Read the history of Josephus.[9]

9. Viz., *Antiquities of the Jews* 18.2.1–3.

(19) Gregory of Nazianzus

Christ is born, give glory to him;
Christ comes from the heavens, gather to meet him;
Christ comes upon the earth, be filled with rejoicing.
Sing to the Lord, all the earth (Ps 96:1)
and, that both heaven and earth are drawn together I say, *Let the heavens be glad and the earth rejoice* (Ps 96:11).
Through the heavenly and then the earthly spheres Christ is in the flesh;
exalt with trembling and with joy—
with trembling, because of sin,
with joy, because of hope.
Christ is come of a virgin.
First without a mother.
Second without a father.
The laws of nature are abrogated
that the cosmos above he brought to perfection.
Christ urges us, let us not resist;
All you nations clap your hands (Ps. 47:1)
because a child is born to us, a son is given to us.
Sovereignty is upon his shoulder (for he was raised up by the cross),
and his name is called Mighty Counselor (of the Father), [and] Angel (Isa 9:6).
Let John cry out, **Prepare the way of the Lord** (3:3).
I, too, shall proclaim the power of the day.
The one without flesh has assumed flesh;
The Word has taken on materiality;
The Invisible had become visible;
The Impalpable is able to be touched;
The Timeless takes on a beginning;
The Son of God becomes Son of Man, Jesus Christ,
He who is *yesterday, today, and forever* (Heb 13:8).
Hasten after the star, and offer gifts with the magi,
gold, incense, and myrrh; offer them to Christ
as King, the gold; as him who died for you, the myrrh.
With the shepherds give glory, with the angels hymn praise, join the choir of the archangels.
May there be common celebration in the powers of heaven and earth.
I am convinced that the latter will join in the rejoicing
and the festive making today if indeed they are of good will toward God and humankind, like
those whom David conducts after the passion of Christ.
They mount upward, encouraging
one another to lift up their gates (cf. Ps 24:7–9).
You are to detest only one aspect of the birth of Christ,
the massacre of the infants ordered by Herod.

Deplore this, the sacrifice of the children of the same age as Christ;
they were sacrificed on behalf of the victim of the new age.
And when Christ flees to Egypt, call him out of Egypt,
rightly adoring him in that place.
As the disciple of Christ,
Pass blamelessly through all the stages of the life
and growing strength of Christ.

Matthew 2:21–23

**21And he rose and took the child and his mother, and went to the land of Israel. 22But
when he heard that Archela'us reigned over Judea in place of his father Herod, he was
afraid to go there, and being warned in a dream he withdrew to the district of Galilee.
23And he went and dwelt in a city called Nazareth, that what was spoken by the prophets
might be fulfilled, "He shall be called a Nazarene."**

(20) Hilary of Poitiers

Once Herod was dead, Joseph was later instructed by the angel to return to Judea with the boy and his mother. And as he was returning, he learned that the son of Herod, Archelaus, was ruling, so feared to enter there and is warned by the angel to cross over into Galilee and to live in Nazareth, a town of that region. So [we learn that] Joseph is instructed to return to Judea, and having returned, he is afraid; then being admonished in a dream, he is told to cross over into the land of pagans. But it is strange that he should be afraid once he was encouraged to go, or that the initial instructions conveyed by an angel should be changed so readily.

In this case, however, a figurative principle[10] has been observed here. Joseph provides an image of the apostles to whom [the gospel of] Christ was entrusted for dissemination far and wide. These men were commanded to preach to the Jews, because even as Herod was being overtaken by death, his people were becoming lost as to the meaning of the Lord's passion. The apostles had been sent to **the lost sheep of the house of Israel,**[11] but because the domination of a hereditary infidelity persisted, they were afraid and drew back. Joseph was warned in a dream, by which we understand how the gift of the Holy Spirit was directed to the pagans. The apostles now have announced life and salvation for the pagans, introducing them to Christ, who was sent to the Jews.

10. Latin *typica ratio*.
11. Matt 15:24.

(21) Epiphanius the Latin

He will be called a Nazaraean. Nazaraeans are holy men, on whose head a blade has not been used. For they are not shaved. As a figure of the Savior, Samson the Nazaraean, was a man of great strength. His hair was cut off by his wife. He lost seven locks of hair, in which all his strength was held, which reveals the head of the man is Christ. Without doubt all strength is held in him. Where the text refers to the locks of hair, it means the sevenfold Spirit (cf. Judg 16:13; 1 Sam 2:5). Samson was shorn by his wife and the Lord is nailed to the Cross . . . but he did not lose the sevenfold Spirit on account of his passion. And immediately there was light shining upon the things below[12] with the whole strength of divinity, by the one who is called the King of glory.

(22) Jerome

And he came and lived in a town called Nazareth so that what was spoken through the prophets might be fulfilled: **For he shall be called a Nazarene.** Were he to set forth a firm example from the Scriptures, he would never have said **what was spoken through the prophets**, but simply what was spoken through the prophet. By mentioning several prophets here, he shows that he has taken an interest not in the words of Scripture but in the meaning. Nazareus means "holy." All of Scripture bears witness that the Lord who is to come will be holy. Alternatively, we might say that even in the exact words according to the truth of the Hebrew it is written in Isaiah, *A shoot springs from the root of Jesse, and a scion (or Nazarene) blossoms up from the root* (Isa 11:1).

(23) Augustine

From this account, we may rightly inquire both into the events that Matthew omits but Luke mentions, as well as those that Luke omits but Matthew mentions. Once the magi, who had come from the East, returned to their own region, Matthew observes and relates [how] Joseph was warned by the angel to flee into Egypt with the infant lest Herod should kill him; then, when Herod could not find the child, how he put to death boys who were two years and under; how Joseph returned from Egypt after Herod's death, and upon hearing that Archelaus reigned over Judea in place of his father Herod, had lived with the child in the city of Nazareth, within the region of Galilee. Luke is silent about all these things, but Matthew and Luke do not appear to contradict [one another] because of what the former said or what the other left out, or because one recalled what the other does not say.

Yet we must inquire when these events occurred with which Matthew deals, namely, Joseph's departure into Egypt, and his return following Herod's death to live in the city

12. A liturgical reference to Christ's so-called "harrowing of hell," in which Ps 24:7–10 comprises the heavenly chorus.

of Nazareth to which Luke records they returned after having performed in the temple everything concerning the child according to the law of the Lord.

From instances such as this we need to understand how these differences[13] affect other such instances [i.e., passages] so that similar cases will not disrupt or agitate our thought. For each one of the evangelists composes his narrative in such a way that nothing, as it were, seems to be omitted in the sequence of events. He is thus silent [about those events] that he doesn't wish to mention, whereas on matters he wishes to mention, he makes connection with those things so that it seems as if the narrative follows along without any gap. But when one writer speaks about something of which the other is silent—once we have diligently considered the order indicated by the context—it is apparent something was omitted, as if the author intended to speak about such matters but instead joined his account with things mentioned earlier, whereas the former inserted nothing and followed the sequence of the account.

Accordingly, we understand that Matthew, when he tells how the magi were warned in a dream not to return to Herod and go back to their land by another way, at this point had omitted things that Luke relates about the events concerning the Lord in the temple and the words spoken by Simeon and Anna. In contrast, Luke has omitted [Joseph's] departure for Egypt, which Matthew relates just as if he connected their return to the city of Nazareth without interruption.

It could again be in this case that someone is troubled because Matthew reported that Joseph had feared returning to Judea with his child because the son of Herod, Archelaus, ruled there in his father's stead. How could Joseph go into Galilee when there was another son of Herod, that is, Herod the Tetrarch. Did not Luke testify likewise? But as there were those times in which Joseph then feared for the child, Luke recalled these events in his time, times that were continuously in the process of change, such that Archelaus was no longer the king at that time in Judea. Pontius Pilate, however, was not a king of the Jews, but he was a governor in whose times the sons of the elder Herod held no kingdom except as functionaries under Tiberius Caesar. The Tetrarchy, in any case, did not yet exist when Joseph, fearing Archelaus then ruling over Judea, took flight with the child into Galilee where there was also his city of Nazareth.

Or perhaps this disruption (v. 22) is the reason why Matthew says the parents had gone to Galilee with the boy Jesus because they did not want to go to Judea out of fear of Archelaus, although it seemed more the case, however, that they went to Galilee because their city was Nazareth of Galilee, about which Luke also is not silent.

It must be understood that when the angel spoke to Joseph in his dreams while in Egypt, **Arise, and take the young child and his mother, and go into the land,**[14] he initially understood this as a command that he should go to Judea—this is the first way of understanding **the land of Israel**—however, Joseph also learned afterward that Archelaus, the son of Herod, was reigning there and he did not want to put himself in danger. Whereas **the land of Israel** can be understood here, it can also refer to Galilee, since the people of Israel live there (Judea). However, this issue can be resolved in another way. Because it may have

13. For example, the evident differences between the two Gospel narratives.

14. Augustine cites 2:20 but leaves off "Israel" at the end of the verse for purposes of his argument.

seemed to Christ's parents, about whom they had learned through the angel's remarkable response,[15] that they should live nowhere except in Jerusalem with the child where there was the temple of the Lord. For this reason, upon returning from Egypt they were ready to go to Jerusalem and live there except that they were frightened by the presence of Archelaus. In any case, they were not commanded by heaven to live there as if they were supposed to disregard their fear of Archelaus.

15. To Joseph's doubts about Mary (1:20–21).

Matthew 3

Ancient commentators highlight the role of John the Baptist as prophet. John's birth was an integral part of God's revelation of the Christ, and his place in history was unique as the bridge between the former times and the future. He was both the last representative of the old covenant and the herald of the new. As a prophet, his preaching pointed to the fulfilment that was about to come. He baptized with water but not with the Spirit; he called for repentance but not for the remission of sins.

Commentators drew a sharp line between the baptism of John and the baptism of the one who will baptize you with the Holy Spirit and with fire. *Since Christians were baptized with water in the power of the Holy Spirit, the baptism of John was only a preparation for the fiery and potent baptism to come, first exemplified by the tongues of fire that came upon the disciples at Pentecost (Acts 2). Theodore observes that this divine fire is nothing to be trifled with, because fire has a double-sided character: it both destroys and creates new growth. Christian baptism is the calling down of that life-giving fire of the Spirit, but it also "burns" what is not true and good from the believer. Such power also has the effect of separating the wheat from the chaff (Epiphanius), for "God is a consuming fire" (Heb 12:29).*

What was the reason Jesus came to be baptized by John? Jesus said, to fulfill all righteousness, *but that could have different interpretations. Gregory of Nazianzus sees the baptism as having a reversed blessing. Christ is baptized, thus sanctifying John, our Adamic nature, and even the waters of the Jordan. Chromatius likewise declares that Jesus wasn't merely offering an example of humility, but the entire event was the bestowal of a "new baptism" upon humanity. Theodore elaborates on this point when he explains that Jesus's baptism was not a matter of receiving grace for him but grace for us. He had to fulfill all the good things that come through grace to us, that is,* to fulfill all righteousness.

The emergence of Jesus from the Jordan immediately takes commentators in a new direction. The descent of the Spirit like a dove and the voice from heaven anoint the Son, an action that shows who he truly is, and so presents a glimpse of the holy Trinity that secures our salvation (Hilary). There can be no doubt now that Jesus is the Son of God. The appearance of the Spirit and the voice of the Father are themselves testimonies, not only to the Son, but to what the Son, in concert with the Father and the Spirit, is doing on our behalf. As Philoxenus puts it so clearly, "all those born of baptism, that is, born of the Trinity, will return to the Trinity."

Matthew 3:1–4

1 In those days came John the Baptist, preaching in the wilderness of Judea, 2 "Repent, for the kingdom of heaven is at hand." 3 For this is he who was spoken of by the prophet Isaiah when he said,

> **"The voice of one crying in the wilderness:**
> **Prepare the way of the Lord,**
> **make his paths straight."**

4 Now John wore a garment of camel's hair, and a leather girdle around his waist; and his food was locusts and wild honey.

(1) John Chrysostom

How extraordinary it must have been to see a man who had lived in the mountains for thirty years, and who was son of a chief priest, and who had never known the common wants of men, and who was in every way honorable. Drawing on Isaiah, the Lord said of him, *This is he who I said would come proclaiming and preaching throughout the whole wilderness with a clear voice* (cf. Isa 35:6). The witness of the prophets concerning this event was so powerful that we recall what they proclaimed long ago. They mention not only John, but the place where he would live, the manner of his teaching upon his arrival, and the beneficial effects he produced. At the very least, we should see how both the Old Testament prophet and the Baptist operate with the same ideas, even if not in the same words.

But there was more to it than this. Luke states, *he came into the country about Jordan, preaching the baptism of repentance for the remission of sin* (Luke 3:3). In actuality, the effect of John's baptism was not for remission of sins since such a gift pertained only to the baptism that was given later. Only in this way *we are buried with him* (Col 2:12; Rom 6:4), and our old man was then crucified with him; before the cross there was no full remission. And Paul also says, *But you are washed, but you are sanctified*, not by the baptism of John, but *in the name of our Lord Jesus Christ, and by the Spirit of our God* (1 Cor 6:11). And elsewhere Paul said, *John truly preached a baptism of repentance* (he did not say "of remission"), *that they should believe on him that should come after him* (Acts 19:4). For until the sacrifice was offered, the Spirit had not yet come down, nor had sin been put away, nor the enmity removed, nor the curse destroyed. How then could remission take place?

Then what is meant by *for the remission of sins*? In the case of the Jews, for example, Paul himself charged them by saying, *that they being ignorant of God's righteousness, and going about to establish their own, had not submitted themselves unto the righteousness of God* (Rom 10:3). And again: *What shall we say about the Gentiles, who did not follow after righteousness. . . . Because both of them sought righteousness not by faith, but by works* (Rom 9:30–32).

John brought them an awareness of the sinful things they had done. Among other things, his very clothing declared repentance and confession. This was clear in what he preached. For he said nothing else but *bring forth fruits fitting for repentance.* Since they would not condemn their own sins . . . coming to an awareness of sin would enable them to seek after their Redeemer and to desire remission. This is what John brought about; persuading them to repent, not so that they might be punished, but that having been humbled by repentance through self-condemnation, they would be ready to receive remission.

John's baptism led the way for the remission of sins because he also said that *they should believe on him which should come after him* (Acts 19:4). It would have done little good for him to pay a visit to their homes, introducing them to Christ, saying, "Believe in This Man." It was far better for that blessed voice (of Christ) to be heard, in addition to all those other things he did in the presence and sight of all.

In response to John's appearance, they came to baptism. John's reputation and his baptism were attracting the whole city to the Jordan, where the event became a great spectacle.

(2) Hilary of Poitiers

Surely there was a more suitable location for [John's] preaching, as well as more practical clothing and more appropriate food. A pattern, however, underlies these events as they occurred, and in this [pattern] there is a deliberate operation at work, which gives a deeper sense of what is recorded.

So it was that John came to a deserted Judea: deserted by the visitations of God, though not of the people; emptied of the Holy Spirit's dwelling, though not of men. The place where John preached bore witness to the barrenness of those to whom it was directed. John also called for repentance in light of the approaching kingdom of heaven by which one is turned from error, restored from guilt, and, due to the shamefulness of sins, decides to give them up. . . . Moreover, a garment woven of camel hair indicates the strange clothing of John's prophetic preaching. With the garments of unclean animals (cf. Lev 11:4; Acts 10:12–15)—to which we bear a resemblance—the preacher of Christ is clothed. Whatever emptiness or filth there once was in us has become sanctified by the clothing of the prophet. The girding around of John's belt, which is effective in every good work (cf. Eph 6:14), has been provided so that we may be prepared in our desire to serve Christ in every way.

Locusts were chosen as food, for they flee from people and fly off any time we come near them. We too want to flee from every word of the prophets that confronts us and are represented by those same bodies. With a will that wanders, being unprofitable in works, argumentative in words, in a strange place, we are even now the nourishment of the saints and the sufficiency of the prophets. We who have been chosen, just like the *wild honey*, will furnish from ourselves the sweetest food, drawing it not from the beehive of the law but from the trunks of wild trees.

Matthew 3:5–12

5Then went out to him Jerusalem and all Judea and all the region about the Jordan, 6and they were baptized by him in the river Jordan, confessing their sins.

7But when he saw many of the Pharisees and Sad'ducees coming for baptism, he said to them, "You brood of vipers! Who warned you to flee from the wrath to come?

[8]Bear fruit that befits repentance, [9]and do not presume to say to yourselves, 'We have Abraham as our father'; for I tell you, God is able from these stones to raise up children to Abraham. [10]Even now the axe is laid to the root of the trees; every tree therefore that does not bear good fruit is cut down and thrown into the fire.

[11]"I baptize you with water for repentance, but he who is coming after me is mightier than I, whose sandals I am not worthy to carry; he will baptize you with the Holy Spirit and with fire. [12]His winnowing fork is in his hand, and he will clear his threshing floor and gather his wheat into the granary, but the chaff he will burn with unquenchable fire."

(3) Jerome

He will baptize you with the Holy Spirit and with fire. It may be that the Holy Spirit is that fire about which the Acts of the Apostles teaches, and which descended and rested on the tongues of the believers (Acts 2:3). The word of the Lord was fulfilled, saying: *I have come to send fire upon the earth, and how I wish it were blazing*, or it may be that in the present we are baptized in the Spirit, but in the future with fire. This interpretation also concurs with the Apostle's meaning: *The quality of each person's work will be tested by fire* (1 Cor 3:13).

(4) Theodore of Heraclea

The souls of the saints are said to be completely baptized by fire when they have received the mystery of our religion and their souls are perfected in baptism through the Spirit, which first descended upon the disciples with fiery tongues (Acts 2:3). Perhaps the verse means that in the age to come all will be baptized by the coming fire, *for all shall be salted by fire* (Mark 9:49), in order that the fire might test the character of each person's work (1 Cor 3:13). This surpasses our understanding because fire, when applied to any material, is neither evil nor bad, yet it is indeed powerful enough to cleanse away evil. In this case, fire should be understood as a good and strong power that destroys what is inferior and builds up what is better. . . .

When God is called a *consuming fire* (Deut 4:24; 9:3; Heb 12:29), this does not imply wickedness but reveals simply the token and name of the power. For just as fire is stronger than the elements and prevails over everything, so also is God all-powerful; he is able to prevail, able to create, able to accomplish, able to nourish, able to make grow, able to save; it is he who has authority over both body and soul. Just as fire prevails over the elements, so also the all-Powerful prevails over gods, and powers and rulers.

Now the power of fire is twofold. On the one hand, it can serve for creating the species of living things and ripening fruit, of which the sun is an example. Or its power can cause dissolution and destruction, as the sun can do to things on the earth. When God, therefore, is called a *consuming fire* (Isa 33:14), this refers to a power that is both strong and gentle, for which nothing is impossible, and yet can destroy at the same time. Concerning this sort of power the Savior said: *I came to bring fire upon the earth* (Luke 12:49), clearly indicating a power for cleansing the saints of their material bodies as some might say for destruction, but as we perhaps might say for their education. So we see that fire engenders both fear and light.

(5) Epiphanius the Latin

I indeed baptize you in the water of repentance. John has no other mission than to bring about the conversion of the people so that they believe him who baptizes in the Holy Spirit, and whose sandals John confesses he is not worthy to carry. Reference is made to untying the strap of his sandal, of this King, because of the passage, *where you are standing is holy ground* (Exod 3:5). John is commemorating this. Just as Moses said that he was not worthy, so too does John. For John indicates what sort of person is the one for whom he is preparing the way: **He will baptize in the Holy Spirit and fire, having a winnowing-fan** (which is the way chaff is separated from wheat when the wind carries it away). The winnowing fan, therefore, is the power of God, the greatness of the royal word. The day is coming when the chaff, that is, frivolous men, will be separated from the righteous and from others who present the food of doctrine; just as the lambs, which display a wool coat, are separated from the unproductive goats.

When John says *I am not worthy to carry his sandals* (Luke 3:16), he is first indicating that he is not worthy to preach. Each one who does not judge himself worthy shows that he is all the more likely to be chosen, just as Peter was (Luke 5:8; John 13:6). Moses too claimed *I am not worthy* and sought God to provide another man. Such is the form of the saints, therefore, when they do not judge themselves worthy; they are indeed found worthy, just as Solomon says: *In the beginning of his prayer the just man was his own accuser* (cf. Prov 18:17). Now John says that he was not worthy but the Savior himself bears testimony that there is no one born among women greater than John the Baptist (Luke 7:28).

Even today, no one, except the one chosen, should seek ordination in order to aspire to a prominent place out of ambition. This was what happened in the case of the two brothers, James and John, who demanded that one sit at the right hand in the kingdom and one at the left (20:21). To them it was said that the place has been prepared for others.

Matthew 3:13–14

13Then Jesus came from Galilee to the Jordan to John, to be baptized by him. 14John would have prevented him, saying, "I need to be baptized by you, and do you come to me?"

(6) Gregory of Nazianzus

We recently celebrated the feast of the Lord's birth . . . [in which] earth and heaven participated. Together we ran after the star (Matt 2:8, 10); with the magi we fell and worshiped

(Matt 2:11); with the shepherds light shone around us (Luke 2:9), and with the angels we glorified him (Luke 2:13–14). With Simeon we embraced him ourselves (Luke 2:28), and with Anna, the patient old woman, we freely returned thanks to God (Luke 2:38). Thanks be to the one who, as a stranger, is coming to his own (cf. John 1:11), because he glorified the stranger.

But now there is another deed of Christ before us, another mystery. I am unable to control my excitement! I am becoming inspired! Almost like John, I proclaim good news (Matt 3:1), if not as a forerunner, but as a man from the desert![1] Christ is illuminated; let us be enlightened together! Christ is baptized (cf. Matt 3:16); let us descend together, so that we might be raised together!

Jesus is baptized, but is that it? Or must we also pay careful attention to the other details? Who is he? And who baptizes him? And at what time? He is pure. He is baptized by John when he began to do signs (cf. John 2:11). So what is it that we should learn? What should we be taught? [It is] to be purified in advance of baptism, to be humble in our minds, and to proclaim the gospel in the perfection of adulthood, both spiritually and bodily. The first answer challenges those who spontaneously want to be baptized, who are neither being prepared nor graced with the habitual doing of good that assures redemption. For if the gift—and it is a gift!—can remit transgressions, then it is certainly worthy of reverent fear, so we don't fall back into the same vomit (Prov 26:11; 2 Pet 2:22). The second answer challenges those who, if they should become prominent by some sort of fame, become puffed up against the stewards of the mystery (1 Cor 4:1). The third answer challenges those who place confidence in their youth and suppose that any time is the right time for teaching and leading.

Jesus is purified, and do you think little of purification? He is baptized by John, and do you struggle against your messenger? He is thirty years old (Luke 3:23), and do you, before you have a beard, teach those more senior to you? Or do you trust in your teaching having neither from your age nor from your manner of life that which confers respect? You will answer: "What about Daniel (cf. Dan 1:3–6, 17–21) and all of the other young judges?" These are the examples on your lips. And of course, because every unjust man is prepared for a defense! But that is not the Church's practice any more than one swallow makes spring or one pen stroke a geometer or one cruise a sailor!

To return to the point: John baptizes, Jesus comes up to him. Jesus will perhaps sanctify the Baptist, but he makes plain that he buries the whole of the old Adam (1 Cor 15:45) in water. But even prior to these reasons, but including them both, he goes up to sanctify the Jordan River. Just as he was spirit and flesh, so in the Spirit and in the water he brings about completion. The Baptist protests: **I have need to be baptized by you**. The lamp (John 5:35) says this to the sun (cf. Mal 3:20), the voice (Matt 3:3) to the Word, the friend (John 3:29, cf. Matt 9:15) to the bridegroom, he surpassing all men among those born of women (Matt 11:11; Luke 7:28) to the firstborn of all creation (Col 1:15), he who leapt in the womb (Luke 1:41) to the one worshiped in the womb, the forerunner (cf. Matt 11:10) and the one who will forerun Jesus's death to the one who appears and will appear after his resurrection.

1. An allusion to the town in Cappadocia in Asia Minor from which Gregory was called to Constantinople to preach in support of the Nicene faith.

I have need to be baptized by you. For the man who would be baptized by martyrdom or who, like Peter, would not only have his feet washed, recognized the Savior. **And would you come to me?** This is prophetic. For he knew, that just like Herod, Pilate would be murderous (cf. Matt 14:3–5; 27:26); thus Christ follows him who dies before him. But why did Jesus say, **Let it be so now**? Because this is the plan of salvation. For he recognized that after a little while he himself would baptize the Baptist. But what is the **winnowing fan** (3:12)? Purity. But what is **fire** (3:10–12)? Provisions for the spiritual life and the zeal of the Spirit. But what is the **ax** (3:10)? The surgical removal of the unhealed soul, even after it is fertilized (cf. Luke 13:8). But what is the **sword** (10:34)? The sharpness of the word (cf. Heb 4:12), the separating of the worse from the better, and the dividing of the faithful and the unfaithful, and the rising of son and daughter and daughter-in-law against father and mother and mother-in-law (10:35), new and novel things against the old and gray. But what is the *strap of the sandal* that you, the one who baptizes Jesus, *do not loose* (Mark 1:7; Luke 3:16)? You are undernourished in the desert (3:4), the new Elijah (cf. 11:14), the one greater than a prophet (cf. 11:9), because you beheld the one who was prophesied. You are the intermediary between Old and New. What is the *strap*, then? Perhaps the Word dwelling in the flesh, which is the hardest thing to untie, not only for people of the flesh still also infants in Christ (1 Cor 3:1), but even for those as full of the Spirit as John!

Matthew 3:15

15 **But Jesus answered him, "Let it be so now; for thus it is fitting for us to fulfill all righteousness." Then he consented.**

(7) Chromatius of Aquileia

In order to fulfill every sacrament of the law, Jesus went down from Galilee to the Jordan to be baptized by John. But John, when he recognized his God through the Holy Spirit, whose sandal he had professed himself unworthy to unloosen, he excused himself from fulfilling what was commanded. He didn't believe baptism was necessary for the one who he knew had come to him so that by his baptism he might take away the sins of the world. Therefore he affirmed that it was more appropriate that he be baptized by him and said, **I should be baptized by you. And yet you come to me?** It is as if he said, "I am a man; you are God. Because I am human, I am a sinner; and because you are God, you are without sin. Why do you want to be baptized by me? I am not refusing to serve you, but I do not understand this mystery. I myself baptize sinners in repentance. Why do you, who have no cause of sin, wish to be baptized? Even more to the point, why do you, who came to take away sins, want to be baptized as a sinner?" So this is why John said, **I should be baptized by you. And yet you come to me?** It is not a matter of his servant carrying out his service faithfully, but it has to do with the mystery of his dispensation, when Jesus says, **Let it be, for it is fitting in this way to fulfill all righteousness.** He shows that **all righteousness** is this: that the Lord and Master himself should fulfill the sacrament for our salvation.

The Lord, then, did not come to be baptized for his own sake, but for ours so that he might fulfill all righteousness. It is only right that what one teaches another, the other should do first. Since Jesus came as Lord and teacher of the human race, he wanted to teach by his example what had to be done so that the disciples would follow their teacher as servants of their Lord. Because he was about to bestow a new baptism for the salvation of the human race and the forgiveness of sin, he himself was worthy to be baptized, not for his sins to be done away (since he alone had committed no sin), but so that he might sanctify the waters of baptism to wash away the sins of believers. The waters of baptism could certainly not cleanse the sins of the faithful unless they were sanctified by the touch of the Lord's body. He was baptized then so that we might be washed of our sins. He touched the water so that we might be purged of the filth of our faults. He received the washing of regeneration so that we might be reborn by water and the Holy Spirit. For as he himself said elsewhere: *Unless one is born of water and the Holy Spirit, he will not enter the kingdom of heaven* (John 3:5).

John may have baptized our Lord and Savior, but in a larger sense he was baptized by Christ. For Christ sanctifies the water, while John is sanctified by the water; Christ gives grace, while John receives it; John ceases from sins, while Christ forgives them. The one is a man, the other God. Forgiving sins belongs to God, as it is written, *Who can forgive sins, but God alone?* (Luke 5:21). And so John said to Christ, **I should be baptized by you. And yet you come to me?** John had need of baptism because he could not be without sin. Yet Christ did not need baptism, for he had committed no sins. Hence, in his baptism our Lord and Savior first cleansed the sins of John, then those of the whole world. And so he said, **Let it be, for it is fitting that we in this way fulfill all righteousness.** The grace of this baptism was mystically foreshadowed long ago, when the people were led through the river Jordan into the promised land. Just as it was for the people of that time who made their way into the promised land, led through the Jordan, with the Lord going before them, so now, through the very same waters of the river Jordan, the first path of the heavenly way has been opened up, along which we are led to that blessed land of promise, that is, the promise of the kingdom of heaven. Joshua the son of Nun was their leader; but for us, Jesus Christ the Lord stands—through baptism—the leader of eternal salvation, the only-begotten Son of God, who is blessed in ages of ages. Amen.

(8) Theodore of Mopsuestia

Many ask about the meaning of the Lord's baptism. Our Lord and Savior Jesus Christ became human for the salvation of all and intended to reveal himself as the origin of that wonderful life. He summoned Adam so that through him and through the rest of those raised up he might become the origin of that eternal life, making Adam the forerunner of this temporary and mortal life (1 Cor 15:22, 45). Just as he died and rose again, we too are destined for this. Speaking figuratively, in order that we might be transferred through baptism from this course of life to the life to come—which we are destined to gain—the Lord fulfilled this first in himself. And receiving this baptism of adoption first through water and spirit (John 3:5), the Lord showed how the baptism to which he truly submitted himself was significant and honorable.

It was necessary, therefore, that the Lord humble himself as a man among the people, as one who submitted to the Baptist and prophet for the sake of baptism. He did this in order to sanctify the waters and to bestow upon us through the washing regeneration, adoption, and forgiveness of sins (Tit 3:5) along with all the other good things coming from our baptism. Although he fashioned himself in this way, he himself lacked none of these things as God and even takes away the sin of the world (John 1:29).

Christ was baptized by John for these reasons: first, not as one liable to sin, but so that as a man he might fulfill all righteousness. Second, so that he might testify of John that God sent him to baptize (John 1:7). Third, so that through the descent of the Holy Spirit he might sanctify the waters of the Jordan so all might be sanctified who were being baptized in it.

As it concerns the heavens opening and the Spirit sweeping down, and the voice: this all took place so that no one might assume that John was greater than Christ. The one who baptizes is not stronger than the one being baptized, just as Ananias was not stronger than Paul (Acts 9:17–19).

Matthew 3:16–17

16 And when Jesus was baptized, he went up immediately from the water, and behold, the heavens were opened and he saw the Spirit of God descending like a dove, and alighting on him; 17 and lo, a voice from heaven, saying, "This is my beloved Son, with whom I am well pleased."

(9) Hilary of Poitiers

In Jesus Christ there was complete manhood, and so, having assumed a body as a servant of the Spirit, he accomplished in himself the entire mystery of our salvation. In this way, he came to John: born of a woman, fashioned under the law (Gal 4:4), made flesh though the Word (John 1:14). There was no need for him to be washed [baptized] since it was said concerning him: *He committed no sin* (1 Pet 2:22; Isa 53:9), and where there is no sin, remission of it is thereby superfluous. Nevertheless, he had assumed both the body and the name of our created condition. Although it was not necessary for him to be cleansed, the purifying water that cleanses us had to be sanctified by him. He then instructed John, who refused to baptize him as God, that it was necessary for him to be baptized as a man. For **all righteousness** (3:15) had to be fulfilled by him through whom alone the law could be fulfilled. And thus, on the one hand, he has no need for washing according to the prophetic testimony (3:14), though, on the other hand, he perfected the mysteries of human salvation by the precedent of his example, sanctifying humanity by his assumption and washing of it.

Moreover, the plan of the heavenly mystery is portrayed in him. After he was baptized, the entrance of heaven was opened, the Holy Spirit came forth and is visibly recognized in the form of a dove. In this way Christ is imbued by the anointing of the Father's affection. Then a voice from heaven spoke the following words, *You are my Son, today I have begotten you* (Luke 3:22). He is revealed as the Son of God by sound and sight, as the testimony of his Lord by means of both an image and a voice; he is sent to an unfaithful people who were disobedient to their prophets. As these events happened with Christ, we should likewise know that following the waters of baptism, the Holy Spirit comes upon us from the gates of heaven, imbuing us with the anointing of heavenly glory. We become the sons of God by the adoption expressed through the Father's voice. These actual events prefigured an image of the mysteries established for us.

(10) Philoxenus of Hierapolis

At that time no one was able to comprehend these mysteries that commenced at the baptism—and perhaps not even the Baptist himself could see it—since they are hidden from all understanding. These mysteries were known only by the Father and by the Spirit, and they gave testimony to make known the greatness of the service rendered by the Son. The Father revealed that he was satisfied with this event, which happened solely according to his will. And the Spirit, in the likeness of a dove, rested upon the Son, made known that he fulfills the ministry, preserving everything done by the Son without alteration or change. Furthermore, the Spirit did not withdraw from these events, as from the things of the law, but here the Trinity was revealed to show its work of fulfillment. The heavens also opened to teach us that the events that happened created a relationship to the things above. All those born of baptism, that is, born of the Trinity, will return to the Trinity as long as they are not unwilling to come and *enter by the gate* (Luke 13:24) that was opened at that moment.

He was baptized for our baptism because it was his to give, because it was a type of his death and of his resurrection. And just as he died and rose and became the firstfruits from the dead (1 Cor 15:20), so he was baptized in a sacred way sacredly for our baptism, and immediately gave it to us.

(11) Chromatius of Aquileia

When the Lord came up from the waters after baptism, the heavens were opened; the Holy Spirit in the guise of a dove descended in bodily form, introducing the Father's testimony about the Son; the Father's voice is heard from heaven, saying, **this is my beloved son, in whom I am well pleased.**

Concerning this holy voice heard over the waters, David foretold, when he said *The voice of the Lord over the waters, the God of majesty thunders* (Ps 29:3). The majestic voice of the Father that sounded like thunder [was a] majesty that bore witness to the Son.

Why, then, is this passage used by heretics against the faith?[2] There is no room for blasphemy in what the Father proclaims; in fact the event and what is said are a testimony to the mystery of the perfect Trinity. In the mystery of baptism, the Son appears living in the body, and the Holy Spirit comes down in the form of a dove, and the voice of the

2. A reference to an "adoptionist" interpretation that (according to one version) claimed the divinity of Christ's sonship was incomplete until the time of his baptism.

Father is heard from heaven. Thus the unity of the Trinity is declared; for the Father cannot be understood apart from the Son, nor can the Son be known without the Holy Spirit. Notice what kind of testimony the Father gives about the Son when he says, **This is my Son**. He is Son, not by the adoption of grace, nor by his human piety, as the heretics hold, but in his own character. Of course many of the saints are called sons of God, and so they are. But the Son is without comparison, the one only-begotten, true and proper Son to God the Father; born of none other than the Father. To the extent that the Father is a true father, he is also true God, just as to the extent that the Son is a true son, he is also the true Lord.

The perfect faith of the Trinity, therefore, is shown here: the Father testifies that Christ, our Lord and God, is his Son, and the Holy Spirit, that is, the Paraclete, is joined together in a sacrament of faith. So we believe in the true Father, the true Son, and the true Holy Spirit: three persons, but one divinity of the Trinity, and one substance.

In truth, since we recognize that everything the Lord has done for us was made known in the sacrament of our salvation. At the Lord's baptism, the heavens were opened, which demonstrated that the kingdom of heaven lies open to those reborn in baptism. The Lord first opened this to us, when he ascended bodily into heaven. Then comes immediately the passage in which the Spirit descends in the form of a dove, and the Father's voice is heard from heaven, saying, **This is my Son**, a statement in which the heavenly mystery and the order of our salvation are revealed. Through the saving waters of baptism we would come to be both sons of God and recipients of the gifts of the Holy Spirit, by whom is praise and glory to the Father and the Son in ages of ages. Amen.

(12) Augustine

We are looking at a kind of divine tableau being presented to us by the river Jordan, where our God is being shown in three persons. When Jesus came and was baptized by John (that is, the lord by the slave), he was giving us an example of humility. He showed us that this humility was a fulfillment of righteousness when John said to him, **I ought to be baptized by you, and are you coming to me? And he answered, Let it be so now, let all righteousness be fulfilled** (3:14–15)—so when he had been baptized, the skies opened and the Holy Spirit came down upon him in the appearance of a dove; then there followed a voice from above, **This is my beloved Son, in whom I have taken delight** (3:16–17).

So we have the three, somehow or other, clearly distinguished: in the voice the Father, in the man the Son, in the dove the Holy Spirit. There is no need to do more than just remind you of this since it's easy enough to see. Clearly, there's not the slightest shadow of doubt that this triad is being presented to us, when Christ the Lord, coming to John in the form of a servant, is of course the Son. You can't say he's the Father, or the Holy Spirit. Jesus came, as the text says, obviously as the Son of God. Can anyone have any doubts about the dove, or say, "is he the dove?" since the Gospel itself testifies in the clearest terms, **The Holy Spirit came down upon him in the appearance of a dove**? Likewise, there can be no doubt that the voice is the Father's, when it says, *You are my Son* (Mark 1:11). So we have the three clearly distinguished.

If we take account of their places, I venture to say (I say it timidly enough, but I still venture to say it), we have the three apparently separable. Jesus comes to the river, from one place to another place; the dove comes down from the sky to the earth, from one place to another place; the Father's voice is heard neither from the earth nor the water, but from the sky. These three are apparently separated by place, separated by function, separated by action.

Now someone may say to me, "Demonstrate that the three are inseparable. Remember you're speaking as a catholic to other catholics. Our faith—that is to say the true faith, the right faith, the catholic faith—is not a bundle of opinions and prejudices but a summary of biblical testimonies. Our faith is not riddled with heretical rashness, but founded on apostolic truth; our faith insists on this. This is what we know, this is what we believe—even if we don't see it with our eyes, nor even with our hearts as long as we are being purified by faith—this is what we hold with the firmest and most orthodox faith, that Father, Son, and Holy Spirit are one inseparable Trinity or triad; one God, not three gods; one God in the sense that the Son is not the Father, that the Father is not the Son, that the Holy Spirit is neither the Father nor the Son, but the Spirit of the Father and of the Son. It is this ineffable divinity, wholly self-contained, renewing, creating, re-creating all things, sending, reclaiming, judging, liberating, this then that we know to be at once both ineffably a Trinity, triad or three, and inseparable.

The question is . . . "Does the Father do anything that the Son doesn't do, or does the Son do anything that the Father doesn't do?" For the moment, let us talk about the Father and the Son. When the one to whom we say, *Be my helper, do not forsake me* (Ps 27:9), has brought our efforts to a successful conclusion, we will have to understand that the Holy Spirit too is in no way excluded from the activity of the Father and the Son.

So then, brothers, here's a point about the Father and the Son. Does the Father do anything without the Son? We answer, "No." You're not quite sure about it? Well, what can he do without him through whom all things were made? *All things*, it says, *were made through him* (Col 1:16). In order to drum it into the heads of the slow, the obstinate, or the argumentative, he added, *and without him was made nothing* (John 1:3). Thus the Father does nothing without the Son, the Son nothing without the Father.

But someone may say to me, "You have said that the Father does nothing without the Son, nor the Son without the Father; and you have produced evidence from the Scriptures that the Father does nothing without the Son, because all things were made through him; and that what has been made is not governed without the Son, because he is the wisdom of the Father. Now you tell me, apparently contradicting yourself, that the Son—not the Father—was born of the virgin; that the Son, not the Father, suffered; that the Son rose again, not the Father. So either admit that the Son does something without the Father, or else admit that the Father too was born, suffered, died, and rose again. Pick one thing or the other; choose one of the two." "How then," you say, "will you get yourself out of this corner?"

The birth of the Son of Mary was the work of both Father and Son. Of course, the Son, and not the Father, was born of the Virgin Mary. Yet this birth of the Son, and not the Father, from the Virgin Mary was the work of both Father and Son. Of course, it was not the Father, but the Son who suffered, yet the suffering of the Son was the work of both

Father and Son. It wasn't the Father who rose again, but the Son, and yet the resurrection of the Son was the work of both Father and Son.

Hold on to what you have heard. I shall repeat it briefly, and so commend to your thinking for safe keeping something that is in my humble opinion very useful. The Father wasn't born of the virgin, and yet this birth of the Son from the virgin was the work of both Father and Son. The Father did not suffer on the cross, and yet the passion of the Son was the work of both Father and Son. The Father did not rise again from the dead, and yet the resurrection of the Son was the work of both Father and Son. You have the persons quite distinct, and their working inseparable. So let us never say that the Father worked anything without the Son, the Son anything without the Father. Or perhaps you are worried about the miracles Jesus did, in case perhaps he did some that the Father didn't do. Then look at Jesus's words, *But the Father abiding in me does his works* (John 14:10). What I have said is plain enough, it only needed to be said.

There's still something else I want to say, for which I really do require both your complete attention and your intercession with God. It is only bodies that are contained by and occupy local space. The divine nature is quite beyond location in space. No one should go looking for it, so to say, in space. It is present everywhere, invisible and inseparable; not more in one part, less in another, but everywhere whole, nowhere divided. Who can see this, who can grasp it? Let us be modest in our aims. Let us remember who we are that are talking and what we are talking about. Whatever God is, it must be believed with a devout mind, reflected on in a holy manner, and as far as possible as is granted us, it must be understood in a way beyond telling. Let words be stilled, the tongue cease from moving; let the heart be stirred, the heart and mind be lifted up to the mystery.

(13) Gregory of Nazianzus

Trinity comes from unity and unity again from Trinity. It is not a case of an underground fountain, a spring, and a great river, but one current being directed down to the earth in three forms. Nor is the Trinity like a torch from the pyre returning to its point of origin, nor is it like the word proceeding from the mind while yet remaining within it. Nor is the Trinity to be compared to some shimmer from the sun's rays coming off the water, reflected on a wall in its fluctuation, giving the appearance of coming and going. For God's nature is not unstable, in flux, or needing to reassemble itself. Stability belongs to God.

The single nature is firmly established in three lights. It is not a unity unrelated to number, since it consists in three excellent forms. Nor is it a Trinity to be worshiped as plural, since its nature is indivisible. The oneness inheres in divinity; those to whom divinity belongs are three in number. Each of them is the one God, when you mention only one. Again, the one God is uncreated, from which flows the rich quality of the divine nature. When there is any reference to three, it is meant to bring about among mortals a reverent proclamation of the three lights and also that we may glorify the clear-shining unity of rule.

In the Trinity we teach there is one power, one understanding, one glory, one might. That is why the unity is beyond flux, possessing great glory in the single harmony of divinity. So great is the splendor that the Trinity has revealed to our eyes, from the wings of the cherubim and within the veil of the temple, under which the sovereign nature of God is hidden. If there is anything beyond this, it is for choirs of angels. What is beyond us, let us grant it can be known only by the Trinity.

Matthew 4

Now that Jesus has been identified as the Father's beloved Son, *upon whom the Spirit rests, and the one who* will baptize . . . with the Holy Spirit and with fire, *he is* led up by the Spirit *into the desert to have his identity further disclosed and authenticated through testing. Chrysostom observes this chain of events: it is exactly how God works in the testing of the Christian's baptismal vows. We are to imitate Christ as he moved from baptism to the trial of testing, which was the realization of a great and heavenly plan (Hilary). Chrysostom relates how this heavenly plan also pertains to the Christian, "you took up arms at your baptism . . . but to fight."*

Jesus's fasting for forty days placed him in the same pattern as others in the Old Testament: Moses, Elijah,[1] *and others (Hilary). In this case, we are reminded of the connection between the life of Christ and the history of Israel. There is also the issue—of great importance to the ancients—about what this temptation reveals about Jesus's nature as both divine and human. For Hilary, the account shows the Son's unmitigated divinity. Not only was the devil unsuccessful in exploiting his fleshly weakness while he was fasting, but he was also unable to compromise Jesus's character, "whom he regarded as man." This was the reason for the devil's downfall: he suspected Christ was more than human yet treated him as only human.*

It is no less of a mistake to construe Jesus as anything other than truly human. Epiphanius sees Jesus's hunger during fasting as proof that Jesus was indeed a human being. The temptation showed that Jesus was no less human than we are.

In the course of the three temptations, patristic commentators were especially intrigued by the devil's ignorance in the face of such evident proofs of the incarnation. Even when he realized that he was dealing with the divine Son of the Father, the devil sought to lead Christ astray by tempting him to use his power, to prove his self-revelation as God, and to gratify his hunger as a human. Again, the devil is deceived because he did not know that Christ's hunger for the salvation of humanity was fed by the bread of the word of God (Deut 8:3). The devil made the mistake of offering power to the one who is God's Power. The devil's own hunger for glory blinded him from acknowledging Christ's true identity and resulted in his ineffective schemes against this Power.

1. A pattern that will be repeated in Matt 17 with the appearance of Moses and Elijah at Jesus's transfiguration.

At the root of the devil's tactics is the lie that he possesses all things that he can then offer to those he tempts. This is the lie that succeeded with Adam and Eve. In this case, however, Satan could not impress the Lord with his offers, because just as a serpent can leave no marks upon a rock (Prov 30:18–19), so the devil cannot introduce his "hurtful tracks" on the Rock, which is Christ. Taking this as the model for our imitation, Hilary says that we too, "by spurning the glory of human authority and disregarding the ambition of this age, we may remember to worship only the Lord God, because all the honor of this age is the devil's affair."

Following the temptation, Jesus begins his ministry. This too was a fulfillment of the Old Testament, for Isaiah had announced that because Christ came, the people who sat in darkness have seen a great light, and for those who sat in the region and shadow of death light has dawned *(4:16; cf. Isa 9:2). With almost exactly the same words John had used in announcing the kingdom (in 3:2), so Jesus declares,* Repent, for the kingdom of heaven is at hand *(4:17). And yet the subsequent account of Jesus's activities is followed not by acts of contrition on the part of his hearers, but by miracles that meet the needs of the multitudes that flocked to him (4:23–25). These miracles are signs that the kingdom is being realized, though this chapter focuses on the calling of the disciples who will be the Church's future leaders. It is not until chapters 5–7 that the disciples are equipped morally and spiritually to follow the kingdom in which Christ "might free human beings from the death of the world" (Epiphanius).*

Just as Jesus chooses fishermen, Gregory notes, he had to be one himself. To do so, he had to become, as Paul said, "all things to all men" (1 Cor 9:22). Christ's condescension to such a humble state was necessary so that he might cast the "net" and draw up humanity from its sinful depths. Hilary adds that the Lord's purpose in calling the fishermen is that they too would bring humanity "from this age to a higher place, that is, into the light of a heavenly dwelling." But first it was necessary to bring the disciples themselves from the darkness of worldly depths and into the light of God's instruction.

Matthew 4:1–2

[1]Then Jesus was led up by the Spirit into the wilderness to be tempted by the devil. [2]And he fasted forty days and forty nights, and afterward he was hungry.

(1) John Chrysostom

After the descent of the Spirit, a voice sounded from above saying, **This is My Beloved Son, in whom I am well pleased** (3:17). Even more amazing is that the Holy Spirit led him to be tempted. With a view to our instruction, the Lord both participated in and endured all these things. He allowed himself to be led to that place where he wrestled with the devil in order that each of those who are baptized, upon enduring greater temptations after our baptism, may not be troubled as if these were unexpected. Rather, we should endure more nobly because temptations happen in the natural course of life.

Indeed, you took up arms at your baptism, not to be idle, but to fight. For this reason, God doesn't block the temptations; he wants to teach you that as you become stronger, you should remain humble. You should neither exalt yourself on account of your great gifts that have the power of temptation to oppress you. In this way, you will be made stronger and better tempered than any steel.

The devil would not attack you unless he had seen that you were brought to greater honor (i.e., baptism). This is why he attacked Adam in the beginning; he saw him enjoying his great dignity. This is why he arrayed himself against Job, because he saw him crowned and proclaimed by the God of all.

Why else would the Lord say, **Pray that you enter not into temptation** (26:41). This is why Matthew's account doesn't tell us that Jesus was simply proceeding toward temptation, but that he was being **led up** to carry out God's work of salvation. This implicitly signifies that we should not look for temptation; but once being confronted with it, we should stand faithfully.

Notice where the Spirit led him: not into a city or a forum, but into the wilderness. It was Jesus's intention to attract the devil by giving him an opportunity, not only by his hunger, but also by the location. For the devil especially attacks when he sees men left alone and by themselves. This is what he did to the woman in the beginning, having found her apart from her husband (Gen 3:1). Just as when he sees us with others, he is not as confident and makes no attack. We have a great need, therefore, to assemble together continually (cf. Heb 10:25), that we may not be open to the devil's attacks.

(2) Hilary of Poitiers

The passage into the desert, the forty days of fasting, the hunger after fasting, the temptation of Satan, and the response of the Lord have been fulfilled in accordance with a great and heavenly plan. That he was led into the desert indicates the prerogative of the Holy Spirit, who exposed Christ's humanity to the devil by allowing him to be tempted. Obviously, this is an opportunity the Tempter would not have had unless it had been given to him.

The devil, accordingly, had a suspicion generated by fear, not from spiritual insight (4:3). Although the Lord was weakened by fasting for forty days, he also knew that in as many days the waters had erupted from the depths (Gen 7:11–12), that the land of promise had been scouted out (Num 13:25), that the law of Moses was written by God (Exod 24:18), and that the people who dwelt in the wilderness living a life like that of the angels (Ps 78:25) had completed the same number of [forty] years (Exod 16:35; Neh 9:21). Because the devil was afraid of losing the opportunity of tempting him, whom he regarded as man, the devil acted rashly. He had enticed Adam and led him to death by deception. He who begrudged God's blessings to humanity was not able to understand that God was in this man before his temptation. Yet it was fitting, given the devil's wickedness and evil deeds, that he should be overcome by a man since he had rejoiced in death and calamity.

The Lord hungered not for food but for the salvation of humanity. In fact, he was hungry after the forty days, not merely during that forty-day period, just as Moses and Elijah were not hungry while they fasted for the same length of time (Exod 34:28; 1 Kgs 19:8).... It was necessary to defeat the devil, not by God, but by the flesh, for the devil would not have dared to tempt him unless he recognized the weakness that hunger brings to human nature. This is at least what the devil discerned concerning the Lord when the devil began with the words: **If you are the Son of God** (4:3). The devil shows his uncertainty when he asks, **if you are the Son of God**. Even though the devil saw him hungry, he was becoming frightened of him who had fasted for forty days.

(3) Epiphanius the Latin

Then Jesus was led into the desert by the Spirit, that he might be tempted by the devil, and he fasted forty days and nights. The Gospel says this especially for those who say either that the Lord did not assume a body and was a spirit, or for those who assert that he was only a man.[2] If he had been a ghost, he never would have eaten food. Because he did eat, it is reasonable to say that he is said to have fasted. If he had been only a human being, he would not have been able to fast for forty days. And just as a human being who had not eaten for so many days, he would certainly have died from hunger.

Perhaps someone might say that Moses also fasted for forty days and forty nights (Exod 34:28; Deut 9:9), although he was a human being. During these forty days and nights, Moses stood in the sight of the brightness of God, where there is no night. When a human being comes into the light, where he speaks with God and receives the law, he does not go hungry. Everything he was doing on the mountain was being shown to him, whether it was concerning the tabernacle or the vessels of the temple (Exod 25:9–10). Moses himself says that a human being lives not only on bread but on every word of God (Deut 8:3). He who was in the light and was speaking with God could not go hungry. So that the Lord Jesus might show his power—that he was not only a human being, but God—he fasted in his contest with the devil. While he fasted, he was indeed hungry, showing his fragility of a human being.

The one who tempts him approaches, asking whether he was the Son of God. There is no reason that the devil should ask this: **If therefore you are the Son of God, speak, so that the stones might become bread** (4:3). Of course Jesus could make bread from the stones. At the same time, it wasn't right that he do the bidding of Satan. So he answered that a human being **does not live on bread alone** but on the word of God (4:4). He said this so that he might do what Moses had already done, as well as Elijah, who had long ago fasted under King Ahab (1 Kgs 19:8).

(4) Gregory the Great

When the Lord was tempted by the devil, he answered him with commands of sacred Scripture. Being himself the Word, he could have plunged his tempter into the depths. He did not reveal the power of his might, but brought forth the precepts of Scripture. This was to give us an example of his patience so that as often as we suffer something from vicious

2. A reference to the Photinians, who asserted that Jesus was solely a man until God's power imbued him to do mighty works. Even then, the divine power was temporary and not an inherent part of Christ's identity.

persons we will be stirred to teach rather than to exact revenge. Consider how great God's patience is and how great is our impatience.

If we are provoked by injuries or by some attack and influenced by rage, we either take vengeance to the extent of our ability or we threaten to do something we cannot do. The Lord endured the devil's opposition, answering him with nothing except words of meekness. He put up with one he could have punished so that it might all the more redound to his praise. He overcame his enemy not by destroying him but by tolerating him for a while.

Notice that after the devil left, angels ministered to him. What else does this reveal but the two natures of his one person? He is both a human being whom the devil tempted, and God to whom the angels ministered. Let us recognize in him our nature, seeing that the devil would tempt only one who was a human being. Let us venerate in him his divinity since angels would minister only to the God who is above all.

Matthew 4:3–7

3And the tempter came and said to him, "If you are the Son of God, command these stones to become loaves of bread." 4But he answered, "It is written,

'Man shall not live by bread alone,
but by every word that proceeds from the mouth of God.'"

5Then the devil took him to the holy city, and set him on the pinnacle of the temple, 6and said to him, "If you are the Son of God, throw yourself down; for it is written,

'He will give his angels charge of you,'
and
'On their hands they will bear you up,
lest you strike your foot against a stone.'"

7Jesus said to him, "Again it is written, 'You shall not tempt the Lord your God.'"

(5) Hilary of Poitiers

According to the ordering of these events, the Gospel indicates that following his experience of forty days, during which Christ would remain in this world after his passion, he possessed a hunger for the salvation of humanity. In that time, he brought back humanity, which he had assumed, as his appointed service to God the Father.

Now we must consider the matter of how the devil conducted the examination of Christ. He said, **If you are the Son of God, tell these stones to become bread.** The devil, who is deceitful and most cunning in leading people astray, knew that Christ held complete power. Even though the devil realized that his hunger as man stemmed from this period of fasting, he was unaware for what Christ hungered.

By tempting him in this way, the devil was establishing tests by which he might learn the power of Christ's divine authority: as God, by changing stones into bread; as man, by taking advantage of his patience as he fasted from food. But the Lord hungered not for bread but for the salvation of men and said, **Man shall not live by bread alone** because he was not man only, but also God. While he abstained from the earthly food at the time of his temptation, he was nourished by the Spirit of God. The Lord shows us that we must put our hope, not in bread alone, but in the Word of God—the nourishment of eternity.

After this examination, the devil took him up to the top of the temple: **If you are the Son of God, throw yourself down,** etc. He sought to draw the Lord by temptation from the heights down to the depths by placing him on the top of the temple, that is, by placing him high above the law and the prophets in order to confine him among the lowest. For the devil knew the ministrations of angels were ready to serve the Son of God and that the latter could not fall against an offensive stone. On the contrary, the Lord was going to tread upon the asp and cobra and trample on the lion and the serpent (Ps 91:13; LXX Ps 90:12). The devil was silent concerning these things that were said, but as he recalled what happened earlier, he wanted to elicit the Lord's obedience by whatever kind of temptation in order to derive glory [for himself] from this. It was necessary only that the Lord of majesty surrender his trust to him. But no opportunity for such a deception came to pass for the devil, as the Lord testified at a later point, *The ruler of this age is coming and has found nothing in me* (John 14:30). An appropriate response from the Lord is thereby given to this impudence of his: **You shall not tempt your God and Lord.** After foiling the efforts and attempts of the devil, he affirms that he is both God and Lord, teaching us that arrogance (like the devil's) has no place among the faithful. Although **all things are possible for God** (19:26), we still should not provoke temptation such as this.

(6) Jerome

He has given his angels charge over you, to take you into their hands, lest you dash your foot against a stone, as we read in Psalm 91. This prophecy certainly does not pertain to Christ, but to a holy man. We see how poorly the devil interprets the Scriptures. If he had known that this verse was written about the Savior, he ought to have quoted what follows in the same Psalm against himself: *You will tread on the adder and the lion, and you will trample the lion and the dragon* (Ps 91:13). He speaks as if to a sick man in need of the angels' aid, although Christ evasively remains silent about the verse that speaks of his own trampling the devil underfoot. Then the Lord breaks the devil's false arrows about the Scriptures with the true shield[3] of the Scriptures: **You shall not put the Lord your God to a test.**

(7) Peter Chrysologus

Stones are offered to a hungry man: such is the "kindness" of the enemy. This is the food of the author of death, the hater of life. **Command these stones to become bread.** Devil! Your foresight has failed you: if he can change stones into bread, can't he also turn starva-

3. Cf. Eph 6:13–20.

tion into satiation? Why should one whose power is capable of such things pay attention to your suggestions? **Command these stones to become bread**! Devil! You've overextended yourself, and failed to feed your Lord.

Think about it: if he can convert water to wine, can't he make bread out of stones? But the supernatural signs of faith are far superior to trickery; they are there for believers, not tempters; they are given for the salvation of those who ask for them, not for the harm of those who work them. Devil! What do you care about miraculous signs? Nothing will bring you to salvation, while everything counts against you: such signs only further your undoing.

Matthew 4:8–9

8Again, the devil took him to a very high mountain, and showed him all the kingdoms of the world and the glory of them; 9and he said to him, "All these I will give you, if you will fall down and worship me."

(8) Epiphanius the Latin

O the fallacies of Satan! Although he has nothing, he claims that all things are his. If only the Lord would adore him, he would give everything to him. The "giving" of Satan is therefore, according to his custom, always to lie. In this way he deceived Adam through Eve by deceiving and lying. Thereafter, he possessed and wounded the entire race of humans by his deceptive lying.

After Satan had been twice repulsed in his [temptations] of stones and the headlong jump, he looked toward the greed and honor of the world and lied that they were his. He uses that artifice—one that he always uses—but here it rebounds and does not sufficiently work as he wished, as Solomon recalls: *There are three things that I do not know, a fourth that I do not understand: the path of a flying eagle, the track of a serpent upon a rock, and the paths of a ship sailing the sea* (Prov 30:18–19).[4] Here the text shows the path of the eagle flying as a figure of the Holy Spirit, because the eagle has the chief place among all birds. The track of a serpent upon a rock is the fulfilling of prophecy in this temptation: a serpent does not make or create a track upon a rock that can be seen or recognized. Thus we see that Satan, who had formerly impressed his hurtful tracks onto all human beings, could not impress them onto the Savior, since Christ is the Rock. Because the devil saw that Christ was a human being, the devil tried to cause some damage to him. However, Christ was immediately repulsed when the devil said, **If falling down you will adore me, I will give [them] to you.** What could the devil, who possesses nothing, give when he has nothing to give but a lie?

4. Prov 30:15–33 sets forth several (im)moral characteristics, each beginning with the words, *There are three things*, which are common occurrences, and *a fourth thing*, which is unnatural to the moral order of wisdom. The fourth thing not mentioned is in Prov 30:20, the ways of an adulterous woman who does not admit it.

(9) John Chrysostom

How are we supposed to get the better of the devil? In the very way that Christ taught us: fleeing to God for refuge, not being downcast in times of want (believing in God who is able to feed us with a single word), and being content with the glory which is from above. This kind of glory is not concerned with what men do on every occasion or with what is beyond our need.

Since all these things have been done for you, be sure to emulate and imitate his victory. . . . Even if the devil offers you glory and influence and an endless amount of money, and asks for your worship, stand bravely firm. Not only did he do the same to the Lord, but he brings his deceptions against all of the Lord's servants every day—not only on mountains and in deserts, on his own, but also in cities, in market places, in law courts, and through our families. So what do we do? Place no faith in him at all, block your ears, reject his attempts at flattery, and when he makes great promises, ignore him all the more.

In the case of Eve, the very moment the devil lifted up her hopes is when he threw her down and created havoc by waging war against us without a truce. We are less anxious for our salvation than the devil is for our ruin. So let us utterly reject him not in words only but also in our actions; not in mind but also in deeds. Let us do nothing that pleases him, and in this way do everything pleasing to God. Bear in mind that the devil makes many promises, not that he may give, but to take. He promises good through robbery (Gen 3:5) so that he might snatch righteousness and the kingdom from us. He sets treasures on earth like snares, and lures us with the intention of depriving us of them and of the treasures in heaven. He wants us to be rich here below so as not to be rich there.

Matthew 4:10–11

10 Then Jesus said to him, "Begone, Satan! for it is written,
'You shall worship the Lord your God
and him only shall you serve.'"
11 Then the devil left him, and behold, angels came and ministered to him.

(10) Hilary of Poitiers

But now, for the third time, all the ambition of the devil's power was being shaken. When he placed the Lord at the top of a mountain, he offered him all the kingdoms of the world and their glory if only the Lord would worship him (4:8). Now, because of the previous two responses, the devil knew whom he was dealing with.

The devil had seduced Adam by means of food and led him away from the glory of paradise into the place of sin, that is, into the region of the forbidden tree (Gen 3:24). On this third occasion, the devil sought to corrupt the Lord with the expectation of the divine title by promising him that he would become like God. All worldly authority is set before the Lord, and possession of this universe is offered to its Creator. In this instance, the devil did not seduce him with food nor a glorious place, but now—in keeping with the pattern of the ancient deception—he tried to corrupt him with ambition. But the Lord responded in keeping with what he had done earlier, saying, **Be gone Satan, for it is written, you shall worship the Lord your God and him alone shall you serve.** The devil was dealt with in a way appropriate to his great audacity. When he heard his name, *Satan*, as a designation for his crimes, he realized that he would have to worship the Lord his God as a man.

By the force of his responses, the Lord presents us with a wonderful example: by spurning the glory of human authority and disregarding the ambition of this age, we may remember to worship only the Lord God, because all the honor of this age is the devil's affair. Following the flight of the devil, the angels ministered to Christ showing that once we have conquered and trampled upon the head of the devil, the services of angels and aid of heavenly power will not be lacking for us.

(11) Leo the Great

Undoubtedly the omnipotent could turn stones into bread, and it would be easy for a creature of any kind to turn into whatever was commanded at the order of its Creator, just as he transformed water into wine at the wedding banquet when he wished (John 2:1–10). But here it was more fitting for his mission of salvation that the cunning of his wickedest enemy be conquered not by the power of his divinity, but by the mystery of his humility.

And at last, once the devil had been driven off, once the tempter had been frustrated in spite of all his arts, **angels came to the Lord and attended to him.** Therefore, let the children and disciples of the devil be confounded, who, filled with the inspiration of a viper, deceive the simple by denying that both natures are true in Christ as they strip the divinity from the man or the man from his divinity. With the double proof of this single event both falsehoods were extinguished, since his perfect humanity was demonstrated through the hunger of his body and his plain divinity through the service of his angels.

For who would dare to pose these temptations unless he was fearless dealing treacherously with our Lord Jesus Christ? Our Gospel story revealed that when our Savior, who was true God, wished to show himself as true man (and so eliminate all wicked and erroneous opinions), he experienced the hunger of human weakness after fasting forty days and nights. The devil was delighted at having found in him an indication of passible and mortal nature in order to test the power he feared: **If you are the Son of God, command that these stones become bread.** There is no doubt the Almighty could do this. It was easy that a creature of any kind could change at the Creator's command, just as when he willed during the marriage feast that the water be changed into wine (John 2:1–11). In this case, however, it better served his purposes of salvation that the cunning of his haughty foe should be vanquished, not by the power of his divinity but by the mystery of his humiliation.

When the devil had been put to flight and the tempter confounded in all his devices, angels came and ministered to the Lord so that, being true man and true God, his humanity might be unpolluted by those crafty questions, whereas his divinity would be revealed by this holy service (4:11).

Likewise, may the sons and disciples of the devil who are filled with the poison of serpents be confounded, because they deceive the simple by denying that Christ has two true natures. In so doing they undermine either his divinity of humanity, or his humanity of divinity. Both errors are destroyed by a twofold and simultaneous proof: by his bodily hunger his full humanity was displayed, and the attendant angels disclose his perfect divinity.

(12) Gregory the Great

Certain persons are accustomed to question what spirit it was that led Jesus into the desert given the account of what follows: **The devil took him into the holy city**; and again, **He took him to a very high mountain**. We truly and wholly believe he was led by the Holy Spirit into the desert, so that his Spirit might lead him where the evil spirit could find him in order to tempt him.

We should be aware that temptation is carried out in three ways: by suggestion, by delight, and by consent. When we are tempted, we frequently fall through our delight of something, or even through consent. Born in bodily sin we have within ourselves the source of the conflicts we endure. But God, who became human in the womb of the Virgin and came into the world without sin to take to himself a body, endured no inconsistency within himself. He could be tempted by suggestion, but took no delight in sin within his heart. In other words, this whole diabolic temptation took place from without, not from within.

If we look at the progress of his temptation, we see an intense struggle meant to set us free from temptation. Our ancient enemy rose up against the first human being, our ancestor, in three temptations. He tempted him by gluttony, by vainglory and by avarice; he overcame Adam by these temptations because Adam was conquered by his own consent; he tempted him by gluttony when he showed him the forbidden food of the tree and told him: "Taste it"; he tempted him by vainglory when he said, *You will be like gods* (Gen 3:5); he tempted him by adding avarice when he said, *knowing good and evil.* Avarice is concerned not only with money but also with an influential position. We rightly call it avarice when we seek to influence beyond measure. If grasping at honor was not related to avarice, Paul would not have said of God's only-begotten Son: *He did not think that being equal to God was something to be grasped* (Phil 2:6). The devil enticed our ancestor to pride by stirring him up to an avaricious desire for a position of influence.

But the means by which he overcame the first man were just like the second temptation that had caused him to yield. Here the devil tempted the Lord by gluttony when he said, **Tell these stones to become bread**; he was tempted by vainglory when he said, **If you are the Son of God, cast yourself down**; he tempted by an avaricious desire for high position when **he showed him all the kingdoms of the world, saying, I will give you all these if you will fall down and worship me.** And yet the second man overcame the devil by the same means that were used to overcome the first man. Now as a captive, the devil would be forced from our hearts by the same means that had given him access when he once possessed us.

Matthew 4:12–20

**12Now when he heard that John had been arrested, he withdrew into Galilee; 13and
leaving Nazareth he went and dwelt in Caper'na-um by the sea, in the territory of Zeb'-
ulun and Naph'tali, 14that what was spoken by the prophet Isaiah might be fulfilled:**

> **15"The land of Zeb'ulun and the land of Naph'tali,**
> **toward the sea, across the Jordan,**
> **Galilee of the Gentiles—**
> **16the people who sat in darkness**
> **have seen a great light,**
> **and for those who sat in the region and shadow of death**
> **light has dawned."**

**17From that time Jesus began to preach, saying, "Repent, for the kingdom of
heaven is at hand."**

**18As he walked by the Sea of Galilee, he saw two brothers, Simon who is called
Peter and Andrew his brother, casting a net into the sea; for they were fishermen. 19And
he said to them, "Follow me, and I will make you fishers of men." 20Immediately they
left their nets and followed him.**

(13) Epiphanius the Latin

Come after me and I will make you become fishers of men. The centuries have been fulfilled, and the appointed time of years according to the course of the ages has arrived. Based on what the Lord himself had promised through the prophets, he would come to the earth—something that the righteous patriarchs hoped to see but did not (cf. Heb 13:13). In fact, this is just what the Lord himself said to his disciples: **Blessed are the eyes that see the things you see, because many prophets and just men wished to see the things you see and hear and did not see them** (13:16–17). At the eleventh hour of the day, just the right time for the redemption of all the nations and for the salvation of the Jews, the Lord with the counsel of the Father came into the world that he himself had made. He did this not so that he would live in the world, but that he might free human beings from the death of the world. By his mercy and forgiveness of sins, and by the grace of the Holy Spirit, he seeks to call them back to the immortal world.

For when he was walking along the Sea of Galilee, he saw two brothers, Simon, who is called Peter, and his brother Andrew, casting their nets into the sea; for they were fishermen. In walking alongside the Sea of Galilee, therefore, we understand that the sea represents the world. The Lord was not walking in the world, but alongside the world, that is, his association was not mixed with the world.

He was **walking along** the earthly toward the heavenly so that he could show us the heavenly path on earth. He called two brothers, two who were related by blood in the world, with the aim that they might be more closely related in heaven. He called those who were fishermen by trade, accustomed to using flax netting for catching fish from the depths of the sea. These men were sent into the world through the command of the Lord with the net of the preaching of the gospel. They were to draw men up from the sea of the world, from the depths of sins, to the gate of the kingdom of heaven.

(14) Gregory of Nazianzus

Jesus, who chose fishermen ahead of time, both uses the net himself and passes from one place to other places. Why? That he might gain not only a great many lovers of God in his visitation, but, it seems to me, so that he might also make many places holy. He becomes to the Jews a Jew so that he might gain Jews, to those under the law as under the law so that he might redeem those under the law, to those who are sick as a sick one so that he might save the sick. He becomes all things to all people, so that he might gain them all (1 Cor 9:20–22). But why do I say, "[he became] all things to all people," which not even Paul dares to say about himself? Because I find that the Savior suffered more than this. For he not only becomes a Jew and takes upon himself the reputation of strangers and wretches, but what is even worse than these: both sin itself (2 Cor 5:21) and the curse itself (Gal 3:10). He is not sin, to be sure, but he submits to it. For how does the one who sets us free from sin become sin (Rom 6:18, 22)? And how does he who redeems us from the curse of the law become a curse (Gal 3:10, 13)? It was so that he could demonstrate humility, impressing us into the humility that lifts us to the heights (cf. Luke 14:11; 18:14). So this is why I said that he becomes a fisherman: he condescends to all, and he catches all people in his net, so that he might bring from the deep the fish, which is the person swimming in the overwhelming and bitter waves of life.

(15) Gregory the Great

But someone may wonder, "What did the disciples [Peter and Andrew] give up at the Lord's command since these two fishermen had almost nothing?" In this, dearly beloved, we must weigh their natural feelings rather than the amount of things they possessed. Someone who has kept back nothing for himself has left much behind; someone who has abandoned everything, no matter how little it is, has left much behind. Surely we hold on to the things we love. Whatever we don't possess, do we not long for it and seek to possess it? Peter and Andrew gave up much when, along with their possessions, they renounced even their desire to possess.

No one need say to himself, even if he thinks others have left a great deal behind, "I want to imitate those who despise this world, but I have nothing to leave behind." You leave a great deal behind, my friends, if you renounce your desires. Our external possessions, no matter how small, are enough for the Lord: he weighs the heart and not the substance, and does not measure the amount we sacrifice to him but the effort with which we bring it. If we think only about the outward things, we see that our holy traders purchased the everlasting life of angels when they gave up their nets and boat!

Matthew 4:21–25

21 And going on from there he saw two other brothers, James the son of Zeb'edee and John his brother, in the boat with Zeb'edee their father, mending their nets, and he called them. 22 Immediately they left the boat and their father, and followed him.

23 And he went about all Galilee, teaching in their synagogues and preaching the gospel of the kingdom and healing every disease and every infirmity among the people. 24 So his fame spread throughout all Syria, and they brought him all the sick, those afflicted with various diseases and pains, demoniacs, epileptics, and paralytics, and he healed them. 25 And great crowds followed him from Galilee and the Decap'olis and Jerusalem and Judea and from beyond the Jordan.

(16) Hilary of Poitiers

By choosing fishermen (4:18–21), the role of their future service is made clear from their profession: just as they drew fish from the sea, they would draw men one by one from this age to a higher place, that is, into the light of a heavenly dwelling. By their abandonment of their profession, their country and homes, we who will follow Christ are taught not to be bound by concern for life in this world or by attachment to our family's home. In the choice of the first four apostles, apart from the evident veracity of the facts (for this is how it happened), the number of the future evangelists is prefigured. Christ went around Galilee preaching in the synagogues about the gospel of the kingdom and healing the infirmities of all the sick (4:23–24). He revealed himself by these deeds so that he would be recognized as one whom the Jews had long read about in the books of the prophets.

(17) Epiphanius the Latin

When moreover he was passing alongside the Sea of Galilee, he saw two brothers. He called Peter and Andrew, so that they, who were fishers of fish, might become fishers of men. Just as fish are raised from the deep by means of a net, human beings are likewise removed from the errors of the worldly depths and brought up to the light by God's instruction through his preachers. **And going on from there he saw two other brothers, James and John**. Even before these two brothers heard the words, **He who considers his father and mother more than me, is not worthy of me**, they had fulfilled the saying (10:37). They leave their father and nets and follow Jesus. **And they brought to him all who were sick**. Isaiah had said this would happen: *And he sends his hand into the holes of asps* (Isa 11:8). The dens of asps are human beings who were in bondage to demonic possession. Therefore, the Lord cures them and others who were bound by various weaknesses. **Blessed are the poor in spirit** (5:3). He called blessed **the poor in spirit**, since we are blessed only in the spirit of God, rather than the spirit of demons. **Blessed are they who mourn** (Matt 5:4). Whoever lives as if he were in mourning because of persecution in this world, will gain happiness and consolation in the reward. **You are the salt of the**

earth (5:13). These words are especially for the apostles, which then flow down to teachers and all the faithful.

(18) Gregory the Great

Nothing can be offered to God more precious than good will. Good will means to experience fear for the adversities of another as if they were our own, to give thanks for a neighbor's prosperity as for our own advancement, to believe another's loss is our own, to count another's gain our own, to love a friend not in the world but in God, to bear even with an enemy by loving him, to do to no one what you do not wish to suffer yourself, to deny no one what you rightly desire for yourself, to choose to help a neighbor in need not only to the extent of your ability but even to assist him beyond your means. What is richer and more substantial than this whole burnt offering when the soul is offering to God on the altar of its heart a sacrifice of itself?

But this sacrifice of good will is never fully accomplished unless the desire for this world is completely abandoned. Whatever we desire in the world is often envy of what our neighbor has. It appears that we lack what someone else has gained! Envy is always so much opposed to good will that, as soon as it seizes our hearts, good will disappears.

Matthew 5

Unlike Mark or Luke, the Gospel of Matthew puts Jesus's instructions about the kingdom into a single cluster (chapters 5–7). Known as the Sermon on the Mount or the Great Sermon, these sayings of Jesus are a guidebook for life in the kingdom of heaven. Augustine points us to Jesus's words as a key to interpreting the Sermon: Everyone, therefore, who hears these my words and acts on them will be like a wise man who built his house upon a rock *(7:24). Leo and Chromatius note the contrast between the first time God gave his commandments, on Mount Sinai where the clouds and trembling of the mountain terrified the people, and the commandments of the new covenant, in which "the severity of the law would be removed through the gentleness of grace."*

At the same time, the church fathers were conscious of the high demands of the sermon. Gregory suggests that the Beatitudes are like a ladder and can be achieved only step by step. In each stage—being poor in spirit, practicing meekness, mourning for one's sins, seeking righteousness above all else, achieving purity of heart and therefore of vision—the believer is called to live out his citizenship in the kingdom and is being prepared for the stages to come.

No other chapters in the Gospel were more commented on than chapters 5–7, with the exception of chapter 17, which has Matthew's account of the Transfiguration. Jesus's words in the Sermon on the Mount provided the key not only for interpreting the rest of the Gospel, but also set the pattern for Christian belief and practice.

In the previous chapter, Jesus healed physical ailments, but now he addresses the healing of the soul, speaking the nine Beatitudes that have to do with the dispositions of the heart and that are to transform the soul into the likeness of God. For example, Gregory of Nyssa understands blessed are the merciful *as the "voluntary sorrow that joins itself to the sufferings of others."* Peacemakers, *says Origen, are those who know how to "produce the sound of the music of God."*

The eighth beatitude is perhaps the most predictable: those who are persecuted for righteousness's sake. *As Chromatius says, "Once perfected virtue has fulfilled all righteousness, it will suffer for the sake of the truth." Already the prophets, the Lord, and the apostles have shown us the inevitability of suffering in the Christian life.*

The remainder of the chapter expands on these themes. As salt preserves meat, so the spiritual virtues bring seasoning to the world through the transformed life of the believer. In the same way, a believer is to reflect openly the light of Christ and not allow it to be hidden under a bushel.

In the sermon, Jesus gives five examples of how the righteousness of the law works, regarding reconciliation, lust and adultery, swearing oaths, and revenge and loving one's neighbor. Each one begins with a literal application of the law: You have heard. . . . *But in each instance, Jesus addresses the intentions behind the commandment, with the result that intentions as well as the deed are highlighted. This is why Hilary can say, "the cutting off of a member is useful if there is an indictment of the heart."*

Since a life devoted to the Beatitudes is also a life lived in love for one's neighbor, acts of sacrificial generosity become the new norm. Willingly doing good for God's sake is the rule. This means loving someone who hates you, parting with one's possessions for the good of another, or offering prayer for those who persecute. These are the marks of what Augustine called "the greater righteousness of the kingdom of God."

Introduction to 5–7

(1) Augustine

I think that anyone who faithfully and seriously examines the sermon our Lord Jesus Christ preached on the mount, as we read in the Gospel of Matthew, will discover in it a perfect pattern of the Christian life designed after the highest standards of conduct. We are not supposed to speak rashly but draw on the words of the Lord himself. In fact, this very sermon concludes in such a way that every formative precept of human life is found in it. Indeed, Jesus says, **Everyone, therefore, who hears these my words and acts upon them, will be like a wise man, who built his house upon a rock. The rain fell, the floods came, the winds flew, and they beat upon that house, but it did not fall; for it had been founded upon a rock** (7:24–25).

Since he did not only say **who hears my words**, but added **who hears these words I am saying**, he clearly emphasized that the words proclaimed on the mount should inform the conduct of those willing to live according to it in every way. Such a person can rightly be compared to a person building upon a rock.

(2) Gregory of Nyssa

We must first consider what exactly is beatitude. Beatitude, in my opinion, is a possession of all things held to be good, and there is no lack of what a good desire would want. Perhaps the meaning of beatitude may become clearer to us if it is compared with its opposite, such as misery. Misery means being afflicted unwillingly with painful sufferings. The condition of either is therefore diametrically opposed to the other. For it is natural that the man who is called **blessed** should thoroughly delight in the things that are set before him for his enjoyment. On the other hand, the man who is deemed unhappy is one sorely grieved by his present condition. The one thing truly blessed is God himself. Whatever else we may suppose him to be—this pure life, the ineffable and incomprehensible good—he is beatitude. Thus it is beatitude, this inexpressible beauty that is very grace, wisdom, and power; this true light that is the fountain of all goodness, mighty above all else; the one thing lovable that is always the same, rejoicing without end in infinite happiness.

Since he fashioned man in the image of God, man (in a derived sense), he who is called by this name, will be blessed to the degree that he participates in the true beatitude. Just as it is in the case of physical beauty, the original attractiveness is in the face itself, whereas its beauty beheld in the reflection of a mirror is secondary. So also human nature, which is an image of the transcendent beatitude, is marked by the beauty of goodness when its image reflects the blessed features. But since the filth of sin has disfigured the beauty of the image, he came to wash us with his own water, the living water that springs to eternal life. As we put off the shame of sin, we shall be restored once more to the blessed form.

When one climbs up by a ladder, he sets foot on the first step and goes on to the next one above. That second step carries the climber up to the third, and this one to the following, and so on. Thus the person who goes up always ascends from where he is to the step above him until he reaches the top of his ascent. Now why do I begin like this? It seems to me that the Beatitudes are arranged in order like so many steps, so as to facilitate the ascent from one to the next one. Once a man's mind has ascended to the first Beatitude, he will accept what follows as a necessary result of the first, even though the next clause may say something new.

(3) Leo the Great

Beloved, when the Lord Jesus Christ was **preaching the gospel of the kingdom** and curing diverse **illnesses through the whole of Galilee**, the report of his power poured forth into all of **Syria**, and **many crowds from all of Judea** were coming together to the heavenly Healer. For since the faith of human ignorance is slow to believe in what it does not see and to hope for what it does not know, it was right, according to his divine knowledge, that they must be strengthened by physical healings and that they be urged on by visible miracles, so that they would not doubt that the teaching of the one whose beneficent power they were experiencing was wholesome. As a result, therefore, the Lord transformed external healings into internal remedies. After [working for] the health of their bodies, he worked for the cure of their souls.

After separating himself from the surrounding crowds, he went up to the seclusion of a neighboring mountain and, having summoned his apostles, he initiated them into more exalted teachings at the height of this mystic place. From the quality itself of this place and of his action he made it clear that it was he who had once honored Moses in speaking with him there indeed with more terrible justice, but here with more sacred mercy. This was for the fulfillment of what had been promised when Jeremiah the prophet said, *Behold, the days are coming, says the Lord, that I will the set the house of Israel in order. After those days, says the Lord, I will give my laws in their mind and I will write them on their heart* (Heb 8:8; cf. Jer 31:31, 33). Therefore, what he had spoken to Moses he also said to the apostles, and the swift hand of the Lord, writing on the hearts of his disciples, was establishing the principles of the New Testament.

Not as before did the thickness of the cloud surround them, nor were the people put off in fear by lightning and terrible sounds of thunder (cf. Exod 19:16). Instead the calmness of his message was revealed to the ears of those gathered round so that the severity of the law would be removed through the gentleness of grace, and so that the *spirit of adoption* would take away the *dread of servitude* (Gal 4:5).

Matthew 5:1–2

[1]Seeing the crowds, he went up on the mountain, and when he sat down his disciples came to him. [2]And he opened his mouth and taught them, saying:

(1) Jerome

The Lord climbed up the mountain so that the multitude might be drawn up with him to higher things, although the crowd was not able to climb. His disciples followed, and even for them he did not stand tall, but spoke while sitting and crouched. They were therefore unable to perceive him in the brilliance of his majesty.

According to the letter of the text, none of the simpler brethren should think that he taught the Beatitudes and the rest on the Mount of Olives since this is not at all the case. It is clear from what precedes and follows that we should regard the location as being in Galilee, either Tabor or some other high mountain. Further, after he has finished his sermons, this immediately follows: **when he went into Capernaum** (8:5).

(2) Chromatius of Aquileia

As the Lord was about to lead his disciples from earthly, humble matters to high and exalted ones, he climbed a mountain (indeed, the Mount of Olives) so that through the very meaning of the term[1] he might show forth the gift of his divine mercy. Once the Lord went up onto the mountain his disciples left earthly things behind and sought after the things above. Now that they were seated in a high place, he could pass on to them teachings of the heavenly commandments. The Lord bestowed with divine favor the blessings foreseen in past times in accordance with what David had testified long ago: *For indeed he who gave the law will give a blessing*. In order to demonstrate more clearly both the grace of the apostles and the author of this benediction, David added, *They will walk from virtue into virtue; they shall see the God of gods in Zion* (Ps 84:7). In other words, the Son of God will give blessings to the apostles in Zion. So then, he—the same one who long ago handed the law to Moses on Mount Sinai—gave the blessings to the apostles on this mountain, proving himself to be the author of both laws. This is in accordance with what the Lord himself expressed through Jeremiah, saying, *And I will give them a new testament, not of the kind that I once gave their fathers when I led them out of the land of Egypt. But this is the testament I will give them: I will write my laws in their hearts, and in their thoughts will I write them* (Jer 31:31–33). Indeed,

1. That is, mountain or high place.

when long ago the law was given near the mountain, the people were forbidden to follow Moses. But now as the Lord is teaching upon the mountain, no one is prohibited; quite the contrary, all are invited to hear. In the law lies severity; in the gospel grace. In the former, terror is cast upon those who do not believe, while in the latter the gift of the blessings is poured out on those who believe. So then, if you too wish to receive benedictions from the Lord, leave behind earthly ways and seek after life above. Climb up to the heights of faith, like going up a mountain, so that you might be truly worthy to be blessed by the Lord.

(3) John Chrysostom

Notice the lack of ambition and boasting on the Lord's part. He didn't drag the disciples around with him. When there was need of healing, he went about freely visiting cities and towns, and when the crowd proved to be numerous he sat in one place. He was not in the middle of a city or market place, but on a mountain or in a wilderness, his purpose being to teach us to do nothing for display and be wary of public admiration, especially when there is a need to discern right values and speech on vital matters.

Once he had climbed the mountain and sat down, the disciples came to him. Do you see how their growth in virtue had suddenly improved? Although the crowd saw the miracles, these men, in contrast, now wanted to hear something noble and lofty. This both encouraged the Lord to give instruction and convinced him to begin these discourses. He was not, you see, simply interested in healing bodies, but he was also seeking to repair souls. In the opening of the account we see how he passed from care of the latter to healing of the former, mingling action with teaching in the words: **Opening his mouth, he began to teach them**.

Matthew 5:3

3 "Blessed are the poor in spirit, for theirs is the kingdom of heaven."

(4) Chromatius of Aquileia

No doubt that we know of many poor people, though the fact of their being poor does not make them blessed. For it is not the neediness of poverty that makes someone among us blessed, but the faith of devout poverty. We know that many lack worldly resources; nevertheless, they do not cease from sinning and are strangers to faith in God. It is clear therefore that one cannot call these blessed. We need again to ask who these blessed people might be of whom the Lord said, **Blessed are the poor in spirit, for theirs is the kingdom of heaven.** He certainly means that those poor people are blessed who, having scorned the world's riches and spurned worldly power to become rich in God, decide to be paupers in the world. Such people seem poor indeed in this age, but to God they are rich; needy to the world, but wealthy to Christ.

The first apostles themselves afforded us an example of this blessed poverty. After scorning every means of support and immediately following the Lord's voice, they became worthy to be his own disciples. We find these sorts of paupers even in the time of the apostles. Once they first believed and had been separated from all of their possessions, they sought the Lord's riches under the power of this devout poverty. Thus the Apostle shows that heavenly riches lie in such poverty, when he says, *as though having nothing, yet having everything* (2 Cor 6:10). Moreover, when Peter went up to the temple and was asked by a lame man for alms, he said, *Silver and gold I do not have, but what I have, I give you: In the name of the Lord Jesus Christ, rise up and walk* (Acts 3:6). O true blessed poverty! While having nothing from this world, it gains so much from heaven! The Lord teaches that the kingdom of heaven belongs to the kind of poor people who, for the sake of religion and faith, become poor in the world so that they might possess the fullness of the Holy Spirit. He speaks also of the blessed poor as those who are in no way puffed up with the pride of the devil or caught up in secular ambition. Rather, they guard their humility of spirit with the devotion of faith. Hence it is said by David in the psalm, *The sacrifice to God is a contrite spirit; a contrite and humble heart God does not reject* (Ps 51:17). The poor in this sense therefore are blessed in the sight of God.

(5) Gregory of Nyssa

It has been said before and I will now say again that the aim of the virtuous life is to become like God. Yet no one can by whatever means imitate that purity without controlling desires. It is simply impossible that the life enmeshed in desires should become like the nature that subdues desires. If, as the Apostle says, the divine alone is blessed (1 Tim 6:15) and man shares in this blessedness through the likeness with God—and yet it is impossible to imitate God—then the beatitude is out of our reach.

There are things belonging to the divine nature that are established for the imitation of those who wish. Now what are these? It seems to me that through poverty of spirit the Word embraced voluntary humility. As an example of this, the Apostle adduces the poverty of God when he says: *Who for us became poor, being rich, that he through his poverty we might be rich* (2 Cor 8:9). All else that is contemplated in the divine nature surpasses the limits of human nature. Humility, however, is not unnatural and, as it were, a brother to us who walk on the ground; we who are composed of earth and again dissolve into earth. If you imitate God in what is possible according to your nature, you will yourself have put on the blessed form.

What greater poverty is there for God than the form of a servant? What more humble for the King of creation than to share in our poor nature? The Ruler of rulers, the Lord of lords puts on voluntarily the garb of servitude. The judge of all things becomes a subject of governors; the Lord of creation dwells in a cave;[2] he who holds the universe in his hands finds no place in the inn but is cast aside into the manger of irrational beasts; the perfectly Pure accepts the filth of human nature. After enduring all our poverty, he passes on to the

2. That Jesus was born in a cave is part of early Christian tradition.

experience of death. Look at the standard by which voluntary poverty is measured! Life tastes death; the judge is brought to judgment; the Lord of the life of all creatures is sentenced by the judge; the King of all heavenly powers does not push aside the hands of the executioners. Take this, he says, as an example by which to measure your humility.

In any case, how can a person be master of another's life, if he is not even master of his own? For this reason, he ought to be poor in spirit and look upon him who for our sake became poor of his own will. Let us consider that we are all equal in nature and not exalt ourselves within humanity foolishly because of our station in life. Being truly blessed, we will gain the kingdom of heaven in exchange for humility in this life that is fleeting.

(6) John Chrysostom

What does **the poor in spirit** mean? The humble and contrite of heart, and by **spirit** here he refers to the soul and free will. Since many people are humble, not willingly, but forced by the pressure of affairs, the Lord passes them over (it would be no compliment, after all) and bestows the first blessing on those who keep themselves humble and restrained by free will. Why didn't he say the humble instead of **the poor**? Because the latter is more significant than the former: he is speaking of those in fear and trembling at God's command; also, in the prophet Isaiah, God accepted them in the words, *On whom shall I cast an eye if not the gentle and tranquil person who trembles at my word?* (Isa 66:2). . . . It is this that Christ also now pronounces blessed.

The worst evils that bring harm to the whole world had their origins in folly. The devil, before he was the devil, in this way became a devil as Paul comments upon, *Lest he be puffed up with conceit and fall into the condemnation of the devil* (1 Tim 3:6). The first human being was likewise carried away with this by the devil. He came crashing down, thus becoming mortal. While expecting to become God, he lost even what he had. Since this was the capital vice, it was the root and source of all wickedness, and Christ prepared a remedy to match the ailment. Like some strong and secure foundation he laid this beatitude down as the first norm.

Matthew 5:4

4"Blessed are those who mourn, for they shall be comforted."[3]

(7) Augustine

Mourning is the sorrow caused by the loss of the things we love. But those who turn to God thereby lose everything they dearly loved in the world. Since their enjoyment is no longer where it once was, and until the eternal goods become the object of their affection,

3. Several old Latin versions of the Bible switched the order of vv. 4 and 5.

they feel a certain measure of sadness. They, therefore, will be consoled by the Holy Spirit, who, for this very reason, is called the Paraclete, that is, the Comforter. By letting go of the temporal delights they fully enjoy the eternal.

But mourning is really mourning when it is the mourning of the penitent. Every person who sins must surely be a mourner. Whom do we mourn for if not for the dead? And what is quite so dead as wickedness? This is an amazing thing: those who mourn only have to mourn for themselves and they come to life again. Let them mourn by repentance, and they shall be consoled by the remission of the sentence of judgment.

(8) Chromatius of Aquileia

Just as it is impossible to take the second step unless you climb the first, so a person cannot be meek unless he has first become poor in spirit. Therefore, a third step is added: **Blessed are those who mourn, for they shall be comforted.** What sort of mourning should be regarded as advantageous to us? Certainly not the kind that arises from the loss of things, nor from the death of loved ones, nor from the loss of worldly dignity—all things no longer bring sadness to the one who has become poor in spirit. Here is profitable mourning: that which is done for sins out of an awareness of divine judgment. Since the mind was previously set amid innumerable worldly undertakings and difficulties, it was unable to reflect upon itself. But once it is made fearless and meek, it begins to have a sense of its own being, to examine its actions by day and by night, and so the wounds of its previous sins become apparent.

To those who mourn in such a holy manner, the consolation of eternal rejoicing is deservedly promised by the Lord. Indeed, holy David, anticipating this, also soaked his bed with the continuous weeping of tears when he said, *Every night will I wash my bed; with my tears will I soak my bed* (Ps 6:6). And again, *I had no bread but tears day and night, while daily it was said to me, "Where is your God?"* (Ps 42:3). Elsewhere he says, *For I ate ashes as bread, and my drink I temper with tears* (Ps 102:9), and *You have fed us with the bread of tears, and have given us tears to drink in measure* (Ps 80:5).

Do you want to know what the holy mourning of the saints is? Until the day of his death, Samuel the prophet mourned King Saul. Jeremiah likewise said as he lamented the peoples' sins: *My eyes flow as torrents of water over the ruin of my people* (Lam 3:48), and *Who will give water to my head, and a fountain of tears to my eyes, and I will lament over this people day and night?* (Jer 9:1). Daniel too was afflicted with sorrowful mourning for the sins of the people, about which he himself testified: *And I was mourning for three weeks, neither eating bread nor drinking wine* (Dan 10:2–3). And the holy apostle wept for certain of the Corinthians with a similar mourning, saying, *I may come to you to mourn over many of those who sinned before and have not repented of the impurities, fornication and uncleanness they committed* (2 Cor 12:21). The Lord repays this kind of mourning with the consolation of unending joy, to which Isaiah referred, saying, *to give to those who mourn over Zion glory for ashes, the oil of rejoicing for mourning, a garment of glory for the spirit of majesty* (Isa 61:3). David adds, *You have changed my lamentation into joy; you have torn up my sackcloth and have girded me with rejoicing* (Ps 30:11).

Matthew 5:5

5"Blessed are the meek, for they shall inherit the earth." (cf. Ps 37:11)

(9) Gregory of Nyssa

The Word wants to make clear something like the following. There is a great tendency toward evil in nature, which easily turns toward the worse. For example, heavy things never float upward; but if they are flung down from a high mountain ridge, their own weight accelerates the movement, so that they are borne downward with such force that their speed defies description. Since speed in these circumstances is something dangerous, the concept of its opposite would be called blessed. This habit, which surrenders to such downward impulses only slowly and with difficulty, is called meekness. Just as fire tends always to move in the upward direction, so also virtue tends to rise to the things above without slowing its speed and yet is hampered in its movement in the opposite direction. Because our nature very easily turns toward evil, slowness and quiet in these matters are called blessed. Calm in such things proves the presence of the upward movement.

The Lord urges us to be meek immediately after encouraging us toward humility. It seems that the one closely follows the other, and well-established humility, as it were, is the mother of the habit of meekness. If you free a character from pride, the desire for wrath has no chance of springing up. If men are subject to anger, this disease is caused by insult and dishonor. But insult does not affect a man trained in humility. If he has purged his mind from such human deceit, he will look at the lowliness of our nature. He will consider the beginning of his existence, as well as the end, as that which hurries us through this transitory life.

(10) Augustine

This **earth**, I think, is the one of which the psalmist speaks, *You are my hope, my portion in the land of the living* (Ps 142:5). This word truly captures the firmness and stability that characterize our everlasting inheritance. Feeling at home there, our soul finds its place of rest, just as our body does in the ground. Just as this resting body is, in a sense, sustained by the ground, the soul also receives its proper nourishment in this environment. This is how the saints find rest and live on. Then, the meek are those who succumb to injustice and do not resist, but conquer evil with good (Rom 12:21). So, then, those who are not meek quarrel and fight about perishable and temporal things, but **blessed are the meek, for they shall possess the land by inheritance,**[4] from which they cannot be expelled.

Now the one reward, which is the kingdom of heaven, is bestowed variously according

4. This slight rephrasing seems to be Augustine's own doing, since it is found neither in the Latin text nor in his predecessors (Cyprian, *Testimonies* 3.5). The wording of the second Beatitude is based on Ps 37:11: *But the meek shall inherit the earth.*

to these qualities. To the meek, an inheritance is given to those carrying out their Father's will in servant-like spirit. And when things go badly, they don't blame God. Rather they glorify God in their good works and blame themselves for their sins. **They shall inherit possession of the earth**, which is none other than what the psalmist says, *You are my hope and my portion in the land of the living* (Ps 142:5).

(11) Chromatius of Aquileia

There are different kinds of grace in the divine promises, because there are different stages of merit. Thus the Lord says, **Blessed are the meek, for they shall possess the earth.** The meek are gentle people, humble and modest, simple in their faith and patient in the face of any suffering; having learned the Gospel teachings, they imitate the example of gentleness of the Lord, who said in the Gospel, **Learn from me, for I am meek and humble of heart** (11:29). Certainly Moses, long ago, had the greatest grace from God because he was meek. It was written of him, *Moses was the humblest man of all who were on the earth* (Num 12:3). So too David in the psalm said, *Remember, Lord, David and all his humility* (Ps 132:1). The Lord declares the meek to be blessed who, following the gentleness of the Lord's humility, will enjoy as their inheritance the everlasting possession of that blessed land. At the highest level he is speaking of the **earth** as our own body, transfigured in glory with the saints, and (according to the Apostle) it will reign in eternal happiness.

And yet how can a mind set upon wealth, on worldly cares and worries—from which arise business dealings, lawsuits, provocations, anger, and unending complications—become attached to such matters as being meek and gentle, unless it first cuts itself off and renounces every cause of anger and occasion for strife? The sea does not become calm unless the winds cease; a fire is not extinguished unless you take away the twigs and tinder that are being burned. Just so, the mind will not be meek and calm unless the things that arouse and inflame it are taken away. It is appropriate then that one step is connected to the next, because those who are poor in spirit are already beginning to be meek.

Matthew 5:6

6 "Blessed are those who hunger and thirst for righteousness, for they shall be satisfied."

(12) Origen

The one who drinks from the water that Jesus gives will have in himself a spring of water bubbling up into eternal life as the promise is fulfilled: that those **who hunger and thirst for righteousness** will be blessed. For the word says, **Blessed are those who hunger and thirst for righteousness, for they shall be fed.** And perhaps, since one is supposed to hunger and thirst before being fed, we should induce hunger and thirst in order to be satisfied. For this reason we read, *Just as the deer pants for springs of water so my soul pants* *after you, God* (Ps 42:1). My soul has thirsted for the strong, living God; *when shall I come and see the face of God?* (Ps 42:2).

(13) Gregory of Nyssa

None of the things that are coveted in this life for the sake of pleasure will satisfy those who run after them. Rather, as Wisdom says somewhere metaphorically, *A cask full of holes is the occupation with the pleasures of sense* (cf. Prov 23:27). For those who are always anxiously busy in filling it show that their unending labor is fruitless. All the while they are pouring something into the abyss of desire, they add pleasure to pleasure, yet never attain full satisfaction. Who has known avarice to come to an end because the man afflicted with it had got what he wanted? Who has ceased to run after fame because he had attained to his heart's desire? When anyone has indulged to the full what pleases his ears or eyes, his mad craze for the things of the stomach and what comes after the stomach, what has he found to be the result of this enjoyment? Does not every form of pleasure provided by the body vanish almost as soon as it comes, remaining hardly a moment with those who have caught it?

We learn from the Lord this sublime doctrine that the only truly and solidly existing thing is our zeal for virtue. God the Word promises that those who hunger for these things shall be filled, and in being filled, their desire will not be dulled but rather kindled anew.

If we would venture on a bolder interpretation, it seems to me that through the ideas of virtue and justice, the Lord proposes himself to the desire of his hearers. He became for us "wisdom from God, justification, sanctification, and redemption," as well as Bread descending from heaven (John 6:50) and Living Water (John 4:10). Somewhere in the Psalms, David confesses his thirst for this when he offers this blessed yearning to God and says: *My soul has thirsted after the strong, living God. When shall I come and appear before the face of God?* (Ps 42:2). It seems that the power of the Spirit has instructed him beforehand in these lofty teachings of the Lord, since he said also that his desire would be fulfilled. *I will appear before your sight in justice*, he says, *I shall be satisfied when your glory shall appear* (Ps 17:15).

In my view, this glory is the true virtue, the good that is unmixed with evil that comprises every concept concerned with goodness. This is God the Word himself, the virtue that covered the heavens, as Habakkuk explains (cf. Hab 3:3), and rightly are those who hunger for this justice of God called blessed. If, as the psalmist says (cf. Ps 34:8), a man has truly tasted the Lord; that is, if he has received God into himself, he is filled with him for whom he has thirsted and hungered, just as he has promised: *I and my Father will come and will make our abode with him* (John 14:23).

(14) Augustine

The Lord here means those who love the true and the immutable good. They will be filled with the food of which the Lord himself said, *My food is to do the will of my Father*, which is righteousness. He also said that the water from which they are all going to drink *will become in him a well of water springing up to eternal life* (John 4:14).

To the hungry and thirsty, therefore, there is an abundant meal; it is for those who have worked and are trying with all their might for their salvation. **Blessed are they that hunger and thirst after justice, for they shall have their fill.**

Being hungry for justice is proper to this earth of ours. Being satisfied will come at another time, when nobody will sin. It will be the repletion of justice, just as the angels enjoy. In the meantime, we who are hungry and thirsty for righteousness should be saying to God, **Your will be done on earth as it is in heaven** (6:10).

(15) Chromatius of Aquileia

The Lord teaches that we must seek after righteousness, though not by some mere longing or fleeting desire of wanting it. Indeed, he means that the blessed are those who burn with an inward desire to attain that righteousness, just as in the manner of hungering and thirsting. If any of us who hungers and thirsts craves with a longing, we can do nothing but think about righteousness and seek after righteousness. For when one hungers and thirsts, necessarily one craves what is hungered and thirsted after.

He who is the heavenly bread and font of living water rightly promises that those who hunger and thirst in this way will have their fill of that everlasting meal: **Blessed are they who hunger and thirst for righteousness, for they shall be filled.** In other words, the righteousness of faith that comes from God and Christ, to which the Apostle referred, *the righteousness of God that comes from faith in Jesus Christ, in all and upon all who believe in him* (Rom 3:22). The point is that the blessed should always have an overwhelming desire for this kind of hunger and righteousness since our Lord and Savior himself *was made our righteousness, sanctification, and redemption* (1 Cor 1:30). As the Lord himself said through Solomon, speaking in the person of Wisdom, *The one who eats me will still hunger, and the one who drinks me will still thirst* (Sir 24:21). We must therefore always hunger and thirst for this righteousness so that we might be worthy of being filled with the food of the everlasting banquet. Those who hunger, not for righteousness, but for unrighteousness—desiring gold and silver, craving wealth or worldly honors, getting their fill of earthly deeds or fleshly desires—are not blessed, but unhappy, because they have no hope of the promise of glory, but the punishment of damnation.

Matthew 5:7

7 "Blessed are the merciful, for they shall obtain mercy."

(16) Gregory of Nyssa

The obvious meaning of the words calls men to mutual charity and sympathy as demanded by the capricious inequality of the circumstances of life. We do not all live in the same conditions as it concerns reputation, nor physical constitution, nor other assets. Life is, in many ways, divided up into opposites. It may be experienced as slave or as master, in riches or poverty, in fame or dishonor, in bodily infirmity or in good health—in all such things there is diversity. The creature in need should be made equal to the one who has a larger share, and the one who goes with little should be filled by one who has abundance; this is the law of mercy given to men concerning the needy. Unless mercy softens the soul, one will not seek the healing of his neighbor's ills since mercy is defined as the opposite of cruelty. The hard and cruel man is inaccessible to those who would approach him; whereas the merciful person is, as it were, predisposed by his attitude to give the sympathy that is needed. This enables him to be to those afflicted exactly what the distressed mind is looking for. To sum up the explanation in a definition: Mercy is a voluntary sorrow that joins itself to the sufferings of others. We may say that mercy is love intensified. A person of such disposition of the soul is truly blessed because he has reached the summit of virtue.

(17) Augustine

Blessed are the merciful, for they shall obtain mercy. Do whatever action you are going to do and it will be done. Do it with others so that it may be done with you. The reason is that you have plenty and that you are in need. You have plenty of temporal things, yet you are in need of eternal things. You hear a man begging although you yourself are a beggar to God. Something is asked of you and you too are asking for something. The way you treat the one who asks you will be the way God responds, since you are both full and empty. Fill the empty person from your fullness so that your emptiness may be filled from God's fullness.

It is appropriate that this saying follows, *Blessed are those who hunger and thirst after justice.* You are hungry and thirsty for justice. And if you are hungry and thirsty you are a beggar to God. So you are really standing as a beggar at God's door while there's another beggar standing at your door. The way you treat your beggar will be the way God treats his.

(18) Leo the Great

Even though someone is faithful and pure and temperate and adorned with other distinguished habits, nevertheless, if he is not merciful, he does not merit mercy. For the Lord says: **Blessed are the merciful, since God will have mercy on them.** But when the Son of Man will come in his own majesty and sit in the throne of his own glory, with all the nations gathered together, he will separate good deeds and bad deeds. For what will those who stand at his right hand be praised if not for works of benevolence and the observances of the love that Jesus Christ will consider as done for himself (cf. 25:40)? Since he made the nature of man his own, he in no way separated himself from the lowliness of manhood. But what will be cast to the left (cf. 25:33), if not a neglect of love, a hardness of inhumanity, and mercy denied to the poor?

In that great and last judgment, either the benevolence of generosity or the ungodliness of parsimony will be so greatly valued that, in spite of the worst of all crimes, for one good deed some are led into the kingdom and, in spite of the fullness of all the virtues, others are sent into eternal fire for one wicked deed.

Matthew 5:8

[8]"Blessed are the pure in heart, for they shall see God."

(19) Irenaeus of Lyons

The prophets indicated beforehand (i.e., Job 19:26; Ps 52:6) that God would be seen by man, as the Lord also said: **Blessed are the pure in heart, because they will see God.** But because of God's greatness and indescribable glory, *no one will see God and live* (Exod 33:20). For in accordance with his greatness and indescribable glory, the Father is beyond our comprehension. However, in accordance with his love and kindness, and because he is able to do anything, he gives to those who love him to see, as the prophets foretold: *For those things that are impossible for humans are possible for God* (Luke 18:27). Of course we cannot see God by our own power. But when he wishes, he is seen by men, those to whom he wishes, when he wishes, and to the extent that he wishes. For God is capable of anything and was seen prophetically through the Spirit, by the mediation of the Son through adoption, and he will be seen in a fatherly way in the kingdom of heaven. He was preparing humanity for the Son of God by the Spirit, while leading them to the Father by the Son, and bestowing upon them incorruptibility for eternal life by the Father, which happens to each one by seeing God. For just as those who see light are within the light and receive its brightness, so also those who see God are within God, receiving his brightness. The brightness of God gives life: therefore those who see God receive life. And because of this, God, impenetrable and inconceivable and invisible, presents himself as visible, comprehensible, and apprehensible by us, so that he might restore to life those who see and partake of him. Just as his greatness is unsearchable, so his favor is indescribable, and when he is seen, he offers life to those who see him. To live without life is of course impossible, but we find life in fellowship with God; indeed, fellowship with God is to know God and to delight in his favor.

Consequently, we must see God in order to live. By this vision they are made immortal and attain to God. This was foretold by the prophets in figures, since God will appear to those who carry his Spirit and wait patiently on, as Moses said in Deuteronomy: *We will see in that Day, because God will speak to man, and he will live* (Deut 5:24). For some saw the prophetic Spirit, and his works poured out in all manner of gifts; others truly saw the coming of the Lord and the plan that was from the beginning, by which he accomplished the will of the Father in heaven and on earth; others even saw the Father's glories adapted to the times, both those who saw and heard then and those who were later to hear. In this way, God was made known, for God the Father was revealed by all these things: by the Spirit working, by the Son ministering, by the Father sanctioning, and, by humans beings perfected for salvation....

All have learned by his Word that there is one God, the Father, who sustains everything and gives existence to all, as it is written in the Gospel: *No one has ever seen God, unless the only-begotten Son, who is in the bosom of the Father, has revealed it to him* (John 1:18).

Therefore the Son of the Father declared him from the beginning, since the Son was of course with the Father from the beginning. He has revealed to us prophetic visions and diversities of gifts, by his own ministry and the Father's glory. . . . For the glory of God is a living person, the life of man is the vision of God; for if the revelation of God through his work gives life to everything living on earth, how much more does the manifestation of the Father through the Word give life to those who see God!

(20) Gregory of Nyssa

Blessed are the pure of heart for they shall see God. The vision of God lies before those whose heart has been made pure. But *No man has seen God at any time* (John 1:18), as the great John declares. The sublime mind of Paul confirms this verdict when he says, *Whom no man has seen, nor can see* (1 Tim 6:16). This is the slippery sheer rock that provides no foothold for our thoughts. In the same way, Moses in his own teaching on the subject, insisted that it was in no way possible for the human mind to come close to God, for he says that all power of apprehending God is beyond us, when he says, *it is not possible for anyone to see God and live* (Exod 33:20).

Yet to see God is eternal life. On the other hand, John, Paul, and Moses, those pillars of the faith, assert that this is impossible. Do you not perceive how dizzy the soul becomes when drawn to the depths contemplated in these words? If God is life, he who sees him cannot fail to see life itself. Nevertheless, the inspired prophets and apostles are agreed that God cannot be seen. If so, what hope is there for human beings? Still the Lord supports our wavering hope even as he did in the case of Peter, who was in danger of drowning, by setting him safely on the solid surface of the water (cf. Matt 14:28–31). If the hand of the Word comes to us and supports us despite the whirl of our imagination, we shall be freed from fear. As we take a firm hold on the Word that takes us by the hand he says, **Blessed are the pure of heart for they shall see God** (Matt 5:8).

This promise is so great that it completely surpasses the highest rung of blessedness. What could anyone possibly desire after such a good as this since he already has seen everything possible? In scriptural usage, seeing means the same as possessing. So it is that when Scripture says, *May you see the goods of Jerusalem* (Ps 128:5), it means the same thing as "May you find." Similarly, when Scripture says, *Let the wicked be removed so as not to see the glory of the Lord* (Isa 26:10), the prophet means *not seeing* is the same as *not sharing in*. Whoever has seen God has possession through that sight of whatever is contained in the list of good things: life without end, everlasting freedom from corruption, immortal happiness, a kingdom that knows no end, unceasing joy, true light, the spiritual and sweet voice, unapproachable glory, perpetual rejoicing, and the complete good.

However, because our rejoicing depends upon the purity of heart, my mind finds itself again in a state of perplexity if purity of heart is impossible and wholly beyond our reach. If that is the way one sees God, and Moses did not see him and Paul stated that neither he nor anybody else could see him, it seems that it is impossible to achieve this beatitude. What use is it to know how God may be seen if we lack the power to implement this promise?

Is the Lord urging us to do something beyond our nature? Has he gone beyond the limitations of human capacity by the enormity of his command? Not at all. He does not demand wingless creatures to fly, or insist that those who naturally live on dry land dwell underwater. Should we not be at liberty to conclude that the prescription of the beatitude contains the hope of being fulfilled?

It seems like an excellent idea to discuss the matter briefly and be careful that our investigation of this subject proceeds in an orderly manner. The divine nature in and of itself, whatever its essential character, lies beyond our human comprehension. It is unapproachable and inaccessible to human conjecture. There has never been found one with the ability to grasp what is ungraspable with the human intelligence, nor has there ever been found a method of comprehending the incomprehensible. For this reason, the great apostle calls God's ways *unsearchable* (Rom 11:33). By this, he means that the road that leads to the knowledge of the divine essence cannot be found by human reasoning. None of those who have gone before us on the road have provided us with even a trace of how he may be grasped by a knowledge that is above all knowledge. He who by nature is above every nature, he who is both beyond the senses and beyond the mind, must be seen and grasped by some other method.

There are many methods of such understanding. For example, it is possible that he may be seen through wisdom (Ps 104:24) and to have some sort of perception of him who made all things in wisdom. Just as in the case of human achievements, some perception of the artist may be inferred from looking at the creation on the assumption that his work displays his art. But it is not the actual nature of the artist that is revealed, but only the artistry that he has displayed in his work.

The ability to infer something of the nature of the actor from his actions is not the sole purpose of the beatitude. Some perception of the supreme wisdom and power of God might perhaps be available to the wise men of this world by looking at the harmonious order of the universe from a human perception. The nobility of the beatitude seems to indicate something further for those capable of receiving this advice. The idea that occurs to me will be clarified by examples. In human life, bodily health is good. This kind of blessing derives not simply from knowing the nature of health but actually from being healthy. If someone talked about the excellence of health while depending on a sickly and unwholesome diet, what advantages would there be from his praises of health if his own life is worn out by illnesses? So, too, we are to understand the text that lies before us, namely, that the Lord is insistent that blessedness consists not so much in knowing God as in having God within.

Blessed are the pure of heart, for they shall see God. It does not appear that God is offering a face to face vision of himself to those who have purified the *eye of the soul.*[5] Instead the nobility of the saying may mean what is elsewhere stated with greater clarity, that *the kingdom of God is within us* (Luke 17:21). By this we are to learn that whoever has

5. Cf. Plato, *Republic* 533d; Plotinus, *Enneades* 1.6.8; Origen, *On First Principles* 1.1.9.

cleansed his heart from every passionate disposition perceives in his own inner beauty the image of the divine nature.

There are two distinct ideas contained in the promise of seeing God. The first is truly knowing the nature of him who is totally above us; the second is being mingled with him through the purity of our lives. As to the first manner of knowing, the voice of the prophets and apostles makes it clear that it is an impossibility for us. The second, the Lord promises to human nature through his present teaching, when he says: **Blessed are the pure of heart for they shall see God.**

But how this purity may be achieved you can discover by examining the teaching of the Gospel in its entirety. By studying its instructions one by one, you will find a clear account of the meaning of purity of heart. Christ distinguishes two types of vice in words and in actions. First is the evil manifested in our deeds and condemned by the old law. But now he has laid down the law about another type of sin. He does not punish the evil action so much, but tries instead to ensure that the evil shall not occur in the first place. He does this by removing vice from the will and in this way free life from evil actions.

Once we have discovered in what ways vice and virtue are formed, seeing that we possess freedom of choice in both directions, let us run from the image of the devil and assume the likeness of God. Let us become pure of heart that we may be blessed as the divine image is formed in us through the purity of our lives, in Christ Jesus our Lord, to whom be glory for ever and ever. Amen.

(21) Apollinaris of Laodicea

The heart sees God. That which is incorporeal is perceived by what is incorporeal. And when the heart becomes perfected by every possible means of perfection, it shall behold what is perfect. The heart gains this perfection from the cleansing away of impediments, just as once the eye is cleansed of obstructions to sight it sees the light. Therefore, how then does the sacred Scripture say that *no one has ever seen God* (John 1:18), and that no one will see my face and live (Exod 33:20), and that no person has seen him nor is able to see him (1 Tim 6:16)?

Then the Lord says that those who are truly pure have matured in virtue. But then he adds: that they shall see God. How then does it say that no one has ever seen God (John 1:18)? We argue that he is seen and perceived by the Word, just as we see God with the eyes of knowledge from the sacred Scripture, or just as one is capable of seeing from the wisdom that is reflected in everything the one who has created. Take the example of human trade: the craftsman looks over the work set before him because of his intelligence (Rom 1:21). One sees God also in the creation; of course, not his very Being, but the wisdom impressed by him on the things he has created. In truth the Lord said that God would be seen by the pure in heart, and since the Scripture has made this promise, we are confident it speaks the truth when it also says that no one has seen God nor is one able to see God (1 Tim 6:16).

(22) Augustine

Whatever we do, whatever we do well, whatever we strive for, whatever praiseworthy objects we are zealous about—once we attain to the vision of God, we won't seek such things anymore. What after all is there to seek if you have got God? Or what will you be content with if you are not content with God? We want to see God, we are looking for ways to God; we are on fire to see God. Who isn't? But notice what it says: **Blessed are the pure in heart, for they shall see God.**

Provide what you need to see with. To take a material example, why do you long to see the sunrise with bloodshot eyes? Make your eyes healthy, and that light will be a joy; make your eyes unhealthy, and that light will be a torment. You will not be permitted to see with an impure heart what can only be seen with a pure heart. You will be driven back, you'll look away, you won't see it; because **Blessed are the pure in heart, for they shall see God.**

How often has he already called people blessed? What ways to blessedness has he mentioned, what works, what rewards, what merits, what prizes? In no case has it been said, **They shall see God. Blessed are the poor in spirit, for theirs is the kingdom of heaven. Blessed are the meek, they shall inherit possession of the earth. Blessed are the mourners, they shall be consoled. Blessed are those who are hungry and thirsty for justice; they shall be satisfied. Blessed are the merciful; they shall obtain mercy.** Nowhere is it said, **They shall see God.**

Only as it concerns the pure of heart, is the promise made about seeing God. Only when we have the eyes can God be seen with them. The apostle Paul is talking about these eyes when he says, *Having the eyes of your hearts enlightened* (Eph 1:18). So now these eyes, despite their weakness, are being enlightened by faith; afterward, they will be enlightened by sight for their strength. As long as we are in the body we are away from the Lord. *For we are walking by faith not by sight* (2 Cor 5:6–7). And what is said about us, as long as we are in this condition of faith? We see now through a glass in a riddle; but *then it will be face to face* (1 Cor 13:12).

Don't start thinking here about a physical face. If, in your keen desire to see God, you prepare your bodily face ready for seeing, you will want to see that kind of face in God too. If, however, you have at least a spiritual enough idea of God not to think that God is something physical; if in your heart—as in a temple of God—you succeed in smashing the idol of a human form; if now you call the text readily to mind and take it deeply to heart (in which the Apostle denounces those who say they are wise and have become foolish, and have changed round the glory of the incorruptible God and the likeness of the image of corruptible man) [Rom 1:22–23]); if you have also denounced such evil; if you are cleaning out his temple for the Creator, if you want him to come and make his home with you; then think of the Lord with goodness, and seek him with simplicity of heart (Wis 1:1). Give your full attention to the one when you say—and if you say it, say it sincerely—from the heart, *Let me seek your face* (Ps 27:8). Let your heart say it too, and then add, *Your countenance, Lord, will I seek* (1 Cor 1:24). . . .

So be mindful how you receive God. God is spirit; and it is necessary to worship God in spirit and truth (John 4:24). If you agree, let the ark of the covenant enter your heart, while Dagon crashes down (1 Sam 5:1–5). Listen and learn to desire God. Learn to prepare for what you need in order to see God. And why prepare the eyes in your head? If you are going to use them at all, you will be looking at something or some place. The one who is everywhere in his wholeness is not in a place. Nonetheless, purify what you can see with.

If we long to see God, how are these eyes going to be purified? Who wouldn't take pains to look for ways of purifying the instrument with which he can see the one he is longing for with all his heart? Divine authority has given us this clear answer to our question: *purifying their hearts*, it says, *by faith* (Acts 15:9). Faith in God purifies the heart; the pure heart sees God. But faith is sometimes defined by people who wish to deceive themselves; as if it were enough merely to believe—some people, you see, promise themselves the vision of God and the kingdom of heaven for believing while living bad lives. Against these the Apostle James indignantly took umbrage out of spiritual charity, so he says in his letter, *You believe that God is one.* You pat yourself on your back for your faith; you observe that many godless people assume there are many gods, and you congratulate yourself for believing that there is only one God. You think you are doing well. The demons also believe—and shudder (Jas 2:19). Shall they too see God? Those who are pure of heart shall see him. Whoever would say that the unclean spirits are heart-pure? And yet, they believe—and shudder.

So our faith has to be distinguished from the faith of the demons. Our faith purifies the heart, their faith makes them guilty. They act wickedly, and so they say to the Lord, What have you to do with us? When you hear the demons saying this, do you imagine they don't recognize him? *We know who you are*, they say. *You are the Son of God* (Luke 4:34). Peter says this and he is praised for it; the demon says it, and is condemned. The words may be the same, but the heart is very different. So let us distinguish our faith and see that believing is not enough. That's not the sort of faith that purifies the heart. *Purifying their hearts*, it says, *by faith.*

But what sort of faith? It must be the kind that the Apostle Paul defines when he said *Faith that works through love* (Gal 5:6). This faith is different from the faith of demons; different from the morals of dissolute and desperate men. What faith? The one that works through love and hopes for what God promises. You couldn't have a more perfect, a more carefully thought out definition than that.

Matthew 5:9

9 "Blessed are the peacemakers, for they shall be called sons of God."

(23) Origen

As for the person who is in any way a peacemaker, there is nothing in the divine words that appears either confused or knotty since everything is plain for those who have insight (Prov 8:8ff). Because there is nothing crooked or perverse in such a person, he perceives a wealth of peaceful harmony throughout all the Scriptures (Ps 72:7), even in those [passages] that seem to present discrepancies and contradictions when viewed alongside one another.

He also becomes a peacemaker who has demonstrated to others that a seeming discrepancy in the Scriptures is in fact not a discrepancy. Then he proceeds to reveal the harmony and peace that is found in them. Such is the case, whether we are dealing with the relationship between the Old Scriptures and the New, or the Law and the Prophets, or the Gospels and each other, or the Gospels and the Apostolic Letters, or the Apostolic Letters and each other. For according to the Preacher, all of Scripture contains *words of the wise, words that have been planted like goads and nails in proper arrangement by the one shepherd* (Eccl 12:11). And there is nothing excessive in them (Eccl 12:12).

Now the Word is the one shepherd of rational things that, though seemingly discordant to those who do not have ears to hear (Luke 8:8), are really quite harmonious. Take the example of the different chords of the psalter and the lyre. Each of these has a distinctive sound, which is quite unlike the sound of another. Now to the one who lacks musical talent and is thoroughly ignorant of the principles of musical harmony, these sounds appear discordant. In a similar way, those who do not know how to listen to the harmony of God in the Holy Scriptures think that there is a lack of harmony between the New and the Old, between the Law and the Prophets, between the Gospels, between the Apostle and the Gospel, even the Apostle and himself or the other Apostles.

But when a person educated in the music of God appears, a person who is wise both in words and deeds (Luke 7:22), and who for this very reason bears a title like David, which is translated "skilled of hand,"[6] then this person will produce the sound of the music of God. He has learned how to strike the chords at the appropriate time: now the chords of the Law, now the chords of the Gospels in harmony with them, and now the chords of the Prophets. When it is appropriate he strikes also the apostolic chords with them, as well as the apostolic chords with the Gospels. This person recognizes that all of Scripture is the one perfect and harmonious instrument of God that raises a single saving voice from the various sounds for the benefit of everyone who desires to learn.

(24) Epiphanius the Latin

This beatitude is put in the seventh place. God established the construction of the world for six days, and on the seventh day he rested. Likewise, until a spiritual person is inclined toward heavenly aims and has fulfilled the six beatitudes, he will not be able to obtain the seventh. There will be nothing else, where there is a loss of peace and tranquility. What therefore is our course of action, most beloved? Can we have peace with the sinful and godless nations or those acting against God? It should not be so. For this reason the Apostle says: *If it is possible, having peace with all men* (Rom 12:18). It is written if *it is possible*, because it is impossible to have peace with every person.

But there is that peace, which the Lord handed over to his disciples as an inheritance, saying: *My peace I leave to you, my peace I give you, not in the way this world gives it, but which I give to you* (John 14:27). There is one kind of earthly peace, while another is heavenly peace; one carnal, the other spiritual. For adulterers and thieves and plunderers

6. The etymology for the Hebrew word "David" is uncertain though usually rendered "beloved."

and doers of all evils agree with one another; a peace that is in agreement with the earthly, animal, and diabolical.

We have the excellent and blessed peace, having fulfilled all the previous beatitudes so that one might deserve to be made a child of God. Unless someone is first poor in spirit, gentle, mournful, hungering and thirsting for justice, merciful, and with a clean heart, he will not be able to be a peacemaker. To be sure, it is good and holy to have harmony with those who are close to you, and even to have peace with those not wanting peace. However, it is far better that one's flesh and soul and spirit have peace with God. Then we will have perpetual peace with God and we can be children of God. When sin does not prevail over the flesh and the soul does not fall into weakness, the flesh and soul agree with the spirit, as the Apostle says: *so that he may be holy in body and spirit* (1 Cor 7:34).

(25) Chromatius of Aquileia

They are peacemakers who have kept clear from strife and discord, and who keep the affection of brotherly love and the peace of the Church within the unity of the catholic faith. It is in guarding this peace that the Lord in the Gospel especially commends to his disciples when he says, *My peace I give you, peace I leave you* (John 14:27). David earlier testified to the peace that the Lord would give to his Church, saying, *I will hear what the Lord says to me, for he speaks peace to his people and upon his saints, and to those who turn to him* (Ps 85:8). The apostle too warns about the keeping of this peace when he says, *in all things guarding the unity of the Spirit with the bonds of peace* (Eph 4:3). He also says, *The peace of God that passes all understanding guard your hearts and your bodies from evil* (Phil 4:7).

Nothing is so needed by the servants of God, so beneficial for the Church as guarding love and loving peace, without which it is impossible to see God. As the Apostle teaches in the letter to the Hebrews, *Above all, love peace, without which no one may see God* (Heb 12:14). He calls us to guard the peace of the Church with every effort and devotion, possessing a zeal for peace and faith to call back as many as we can to the love of the Church. We have as an example the prophet who said, *Among those who hate peace, I will be a peacemaker; when I speak to them, they fight me for nothing* (Ps 120:6–7). Rightly too in the Gospel, when the angels announce with exultation the birth of the Lord, this holy voice is revealed: *Glory to God in the highest and peace on earth to men of good will* (Luke 2:14). And David refers to this peace: *Great peace for those who love you, and there is no stumbling block for them* (Ps 119:165). Similarly, we find in Isaiah: *I will place your sons in great peace, and you will be founded on equity* (Isa 54:13).

If then the Son of God was worthy to take on flesh and suffer for making peace between us and God through the blood of his cross, then surely we must be peacemakers in every way so that we might truly be worthy to have the very God of peace in us. For this is written: *He made his place in peace, and his dwelling in Zion* (Ps 76:2). In this way, we will be not only sons of God, but heirs of God, coheirs with Christ. This is what the Apostle is referring to: *If sons of God, also heirs of God, and coheirs with Christ* (Rom 8:17).

Matthew 5:10

[10]"Blessed are those who are persecuted for righteousness' sake, for theirs is the kingdom of heaven."

(26) Augustine

We must pay serious attention to the number eight. The first beatitude is one that comes from humility: **Blessed are the poor in spirit**, that is to say, those who are not proud, whose soul is subject to divine authority and fears punishment after death, although it may perhaps be lucky in this life. The soul next acquires the ability to understand the Holy Scriptures. Here, our soul must show humility in godliness, lest we take liberty to dismiss the words of Scripture that appear to be a stumbling block[7] to the ignorant, and thus lose our learning ability hindered by stubborn disputations.

The soul now becomes increasingly aware of the grip the world has on it through habit and sin. Therefore, in the third step, where the soul obtains knowledge, it mourns the loss of the highest good because of its attachment to the lowest. In the fourth step there is work of a zealous effort the soul must diligently perform in order to pull itself away from destructive pleasures holding it captive. At this point the soul hungers and thirsts for righteousness and sorely needs courage, because we do not leave behind without pain that in which we once delighted. On the fifth stage, those who have persevered in work receive an advice how to avoid this pain. Without the help of a higher power, no one has the innate ability to be delivered from the grasp of miseries so great. The advice is perfectly suitable: the one who wants to be helped by a stronger person should help a weaker one in an area where he himself is stronger. And so, **Blessed are the merciful, for mercy will be shown them**. The sixth step is purity of heart resulting from a clear consciousness of good works, a heart thus enabled to contemplate the highest good, which can be perceived only by a pure and serene mind. Finally, the seventh step is wisdom itself, that is, the contemplation of truth. It brings peace to our entire being and makes us like God—the ideas picked up in the conclusion, **Blessed are the peacemakers, for they shall be called the children of God.**

In a sense, the eighth beatitude leads us back to the beginning, because it declares and affirms that which is complete and perfect. For example, both the first and the eighth beatitude mention the kingdom of heaven: **Blessed are the poor in spirit, for theirs is the kingdom of heaven**; and **Blessed are they that suffer persecution for justice's sake, for theirs is the kingdom of heaven.** It is also mentioned in another passage, *Who shall separate us from the love of Christ? Shall tribulation? Or distress? Or persecution? Or hunger? Or nakedness? Or danger? Or the sword?* (Rom 8:35). It follows, then, that the number of the beatitudes that lead us to perfection is seven. On the other hand, the eighth beatitude clarifies and reveals the role of the first seven, thus allowing the others to follow these steps toward perfection—as if starting all over again from the beginning.

7. By "stumbling block" Augustine means a seeming contradiction or inconsistency within the biblical text.

(27) Chromatius of Aquileia

Blessed are they who suffer persecution for the sake of righteousness, for theirs is the kingdom of heaven. With good reason did the Lord earlier call to mind hungering and thirsting for righteousness. We should thirst with such desire and for its own sake that we hold in contempt the world's persecution, bodily punishment, and even death itself. Especially significant in this statement are the martyrs, who, for the sake of righteousness, faith, and the name of Christ, undergo persecutions in the world. For them a great hope is promised, namely, possession of the kingdom of heaven. The apostles stand out as the foremost examples of this blessing, and all the righteous who for the sake of the righteousness of the law have been afflicted with various persecutions will deservedly, through their faith, attain to the kingdom of heaven.

Whatever dreadful and treacherous thing we can imagine being done against the righteous in a time of persecution, the various insults heaped on them, or bodily punishments they bear, we must also bear patiently, even accepting [them] with the joy of exultation because of the glory to come. How glorious is the bearing of such persecution, whose reward the Lord says is stored up in heaven! And considering the prize of glory set before us, let us be prepared with devout faith for complete toleration of suffering, so that we may be worthy to become sharers of the glory of prophets and apostles, through Christ our Lord, who is blessed forever.

(28) Epiphanius the Latin

The one instructed in such heavenly disciplines and beatitudes secures the rewards of the kingdom of heaven, the Lord himself saying: **Blessed are those who suffer persecution for the sake of justice, since theirs is the kingdom of heaven.** For many suffer persecution but it is on account of their evil deeds. There is no blessing in this case, since the death of the sinner is the worst that can happen. But blessed is the one who suffers persecution unjustly for the sake of God and a holy life and justice. This is the last beatitude that completes all the beatitudes: **For so suffered the prophets also, who were before you.**

If the most beloved, namely, the prophets and the righteous who lived before the advent of the Savior fulfilled all those things, how much more do we deserve by receiving such great beatitudes of our Savior, and afterward, the rewards of the kingdom of heaven, and following the example of the apostles and the passion of our Lord himself, we are found more learned and readier to suffer without any excuse or fear.

Matthew 5:11–12

11"Blessed are you when men revile you and persecute you and utter all kinds of evil against you falsely on my account. 12Rejoice and be glad, for your reward is great in heaven, for so men persecuted the prophets who were before you."

(29) Chromatius of Aquileia

Once perfected virtue has fulfilled all righteousness, it will suffer for the sake of the truth from the abuses of others, being afflicted with tortures, even to undergo death. We should not be terrified since we follow the example of prophets who were injured in various ways for the sake of righteousness as they were conformed to Christ's passion and were worthy to be the first ones to suffer. Here is that higher step in which Paul, gazing upon Christ, said, *one thing, forgetting what lies behind and striving for what lies ahead, I run after the prize of the higher calling of God in Christ Jesus* (Phil 3:13–14). He also said quite clearly to Timothy, *I have fought the good fight; I have finished the race* (2 Tim 4:7). As one who ascended each and every step, he added, *I have kept the faith. What remains for me is the crown of righteousness reserved for me* (2 Tim 4:8). When the entire course had been completed, there remained nothing less than this: that Paul, rejoicing through tribulations and suffering, should attain to the even higher step of martyrdom. It is appropriate, then, that the Lord's words urge us: **rejoice and be glad, for your reward is great in heaven**. This evidently shows that persecution will gradually increase, but so does our reward.

(30) John Chrysostom

In case you think that simply being spoken of badly by others makes you blessed, the Lord set two conditions: when it is for his sake, and when what is said is false. If these are not present, the one being badly spoken of—far from being blessed—is even miserable. Let us observe the prize again: **your reward is great in heaven**. On your part, however, even if you do not hear of a kingdom being awarded in each of the blessings, do not lose heart. If he gives different names to the rewards, still he brings everyone into the kingdom. In fact, when he says, they that **mourn will be comforted**, and the merciful will **obtain mercy**, and the pure in heart **will see God**, and the peacemakers **will be called children of God,** with all these, it is nothing other than the kingdom that the Lord makes hints about. Those receiving these blessings will definitely attain them. So do not think that the prize is for the poor in spirit only: it is also for those who hunger for righteousness, for the meek and for all the others without exception.

(31) Augustine

It seems to me that the seven operations of the Holy Spirit of which Isaiah speaks (Isa 11:2) correspond to our Lord's seven stages and principles. But the order is not the same: in Isaiah, you start from the highest; here, you start from the lowest. Isaiah begins with wisdom and ends with the fear of God. Yet, we are told that *the fear of God is the beginning of wisdom* (Ps 111[110]:10), which allows us to work through Isaiah's principles in the reverse, now ascending, order. Thus, the fear of God becomes first; godliness, second; knowledge, third; courage, fourth; prudence, fifth; discernment, sixth; wisdom, seventh.

The fear of God befits the humble, about whom it is said, *Blessed are the poor in spirit*—those who are not puffed up, not arrogant. To them the Apostle says, *Do not be conceited, but fear* (Rom 11:20), that is, do not extol yourself. Godliness befits the meek since the one who studies the Holy Scripture in a godly manner honors it. Such a person does not criticize the content he does not yet understand and therefore does not resist it; and this is what it means to be meek. Hence, the Gospel says about such people, **Blessed are the meek**.

Knowledge befits those who mourn. They already know from the Scriptures what evils once controlled them by turning into an object of their longing, ignorantly mistaken for something useful and good. It is said about them, **Blessed are they who mourn**.

Courage befits those who hunger and thirst, as they toil in order to obtain the enjoyment of the true good and detach their hearts from earthly and material things. It is said of them, **Blessed are they that hunger and thirst after righteousness**.

Counsel befits the merciful because the only way to escape so many evils is to forgive as much as we want to be forgiven, and to help others as much as we can, just as we seek help in matters we cannot handle on our own. It is said about these, **Blessed are the merciful**.

Understanding befits those who are pure in heart, because their "purified eye" can see what the bodily *eye hath not seen, nor ear heard, neither has it entered into the heart of man* (1 Cor 2:9); and it is said to them, **Blessed are the clean of heart**.

Wisdom befits the peacemakers in whom all things have been properly ordered, and there is not a single emotion to rebel against reason. Rather, everything is subject to the spirit of man which itself obeys God. It is said about them, **Blessed are the peacemakers**.

But heaven, the only reward for all, takes different names according to different steps. First in order, as suited, the kingdom of heaven is listed first because it is the sovereign and perfect wisdom of the rational soul. So we said, **Blessed are the poor in spirit, for theirs is the kingdom of heaven**, just as it could be said: *The fear of the Lord is the beginning of wisdom* (Prov 1:7).

An inheritance is reserved for the meek, because they seek the will of the Father in a godly manner. **Blessed are the meek** for they will possess the earth as their inheritance. The consolation is for those who mourn, for they know what they have lost and what evils caused their downfall: **Blessed are they that mourn, for they shall be comforted.** The satisfaction is for those who hunger and thirst, as a necessary repair work in those who fought bravely for their salvation. **Blessed are they that hunger and thirst after justice, for they shall have their fill.**

Mercy is for the merciful, because they exercise the true and the best counsel to get a more powerful person to treat them as they themselves treat a weaker one. **Blessed are the merciful, for they shall obtain mercy.** The ability to see God is for the pure in heart, because this purity enables them to contemplate the eternal things as though their eyesight had been purified. **Blessed are the clean of heart, for they shall see God.**

Likeness to God is for the peacemakers, because they have perfect wisdom and they are conformed to the image of God through the regeneration of the new man. **Blessed are the peacemakers, for they shall be called the children of God.** And all this can be accomplished in this life, as we believe this took place in the apostles. It is certainly impossible to describe in words the all-embracing transformation into the angelic form that is promised to us in the next life.

Matthew 5:13

13 "You are the salt of the earth; but if salt has lost its taste, how shall its saltiness be restored? It is no longer good for anything except to be thrown out and trodden under foot by men."

(32) Chromatius of Aquileia

The Lord calls his apostles the **salt of the earth**. Let us see what the Lord wanted us to understand by comparing his apostles to this phrase. In order for us to grasp it fully, we must ask carefully what this salt is, what is its relation to earth, and how is it supposed to be useful afterward. Let us treat the nature and use of salt itself so that by being aware of this we might more easily comprehend the Lord's words with spiritual understanding.

The nature of salt is constituted by water, by the heat of the sun, and by the blowing of the wind. In this process, it is changed from what it was into another type of material. In the same way, the apostles and all who believe have been reborn by the water of baptism by faith in Christ (who is called the Sun of righteousness), and by the inspiration of the Holy Spirit they pass from earthly things to a heavenly birth. It is not without reason that the holy apostles are called **the salt of the earth** by the Lord. But what about the connection to the earth? One can easily recognize that the term refers to our corporeal self continuing in foolishness and baseness because of its sense of vanity. The apostles are meant to season it with the wisdom of the preaching of the gospel. They are thus made **the salt of the earth** because it is through them that we receive the words of wisdom and are transformed by heavenly birth into a spiritual nature.

Since we have spoken above about the nature or grace of salt according to a spiritual understanding, now let us examine the real virtue of salt. He says, **You are the salt of the earth**. When grains of salt are applied to meat they prevent rot, carry away bad smells, cleanse it of filth, and do not allow worms to be produced. So too, the heavenly grace and faith given by the apostles works in us in a like manner. It carries away the rot of carnal lusts, cleans out the filth of sins, eliminates the odor of evil lifestyles, and doesn't permit the worms of evil deeds to be produced—that is, libidinous and deadly sensual pleasures to rise up from the body. It also guards our bodies from that immortal worm that torments sinners with ceaseless punishment, of which it is written, *Their worm will not die, and their fire will not be extinguished* (Isa 66:24; Mark 9:44).

Just as bits of salt are put on the meat from the outside, and the potency of their nature works to the inside, so heavenly grace penetrates through both the exterior and interior parts of a person. This saves the person entirely, making him incorruptible from sin. The fact that those seasoned with the salt of heavenly wisdom are worthy before God is shown long ago figuratively in the law; every sacrifice offered to God was seasoned with salt. The evangelist calls this very thing to mind when he says: *Every sacrifice will be salted with salt* (see Mark 9:49), showing that the person truly worthy to make sacrifice is infused with the virtue of heavenly wisdom. If indeed anyone will make use of this heavenly salt, he will be seasoned; if he refuses, he will become foolish. With good reason the Apostle reminds us that our speech should always be seasoned with the salt of grace (cf. Col 4:6).

And so it is appropriate that the Lord calls his apostles the salt of the earth, whom he fills from himself with divine and heavenly wisdom. He testifies that they are salt of the earth, just as they are the light of the world. Since he himself is professed to be the light of the world, he desires to call his disciples by this name. This does not detract from the fact that he himself is the light, but they are an extension of it, that true and eternal light (light can be extended without any detriment to its own nature). We know, of course, that many kinds of salt are produced from the earth, but this analogy also agrees with the person of the apostles. For however much they might appear to be born of the human body and thus earthbound, they begin to be something else through faith in Christ. So they exist not just as earth, but as **salt of the earth**, because from their carnal beings they are made spiritual. By faith they are able to season the unsalted hearts of those who believe.

He says, **You are the salt of the earth. But if the salt of the earth has become foolish, it is good for nothing, except to be thrown away and trampled under by men.** He says that those who have become foolish, though they once were wise through faith and heavenly wisdom, must remain faithful and steadfast. Having rather neglected faith and divine wisdom, or fallen into heresy, they have reverted to the stupidity of the pagans. Concerning this he says, **if the salt becomes foolish, in what will it be seasoned?** Those who are foolish in this way, through the devil's fraud and abandoning the grace of faith, simply pass away. Though they had been able to season even unbelievers previously strangers to faith, with the word of divine preaching, they turned out to be useless even to themselves. Indeed, Judas Iscariot was of this kind of salt. After he rejected divine wisdom and was changed from apostle to apostate, not only was he of no benefit to others, but he also became miserable and useless to himself.

(33) Epiphanius the Latin

After our Lord explained the Beatitudes and the rewards of the kingdom of heaven, he turned to his disciples in his position of authority, saying: **You are the salt of the earth.** Salt is wisdom. Just as salt receives its name from that which seasons and flavors, no food will be able to be flavored or even stored for later without this. Likewise, no one, unless he will have been flavored by the wisdom of Christ, will be able to be safe for ever. For wisdom is Christ, just as the Apostle says: *Christ* is *the* power *of God and the wisdom of God* (1 Cor 1:24). He is himself the wisdom of the Father who chose his disciples and filled them with the Holy Spirit, that is, with heavenly wisdom. Then the apostles were sent to preach repentance and the kingdom of heaven and the future judgment, so that they might season the hearts of believers with the fear of God, that is, with the wisdom of God. Whoever has not been seasoned with divine salt cannot be saved forever. This is why he also says, **if salt will have lost its saltiness, with what will it be salted?** Whoever has withdrawn from the true wisdom, that is, from Christ, will succumb either to heresy or live in the manner of the pagans.

If he is not able to become salt, what will he become? He will be cast forth outdoors and will be trodden underfoot. What else is there except that such a teacher should become anathema and be separated from the bond of the Church?

(34) Gregory the Great

If we are salt, we should season the hearts of believers. You who are shepherds, consider that you are pasturing God's living beings. Of them the Psalmist said: *Your creatures shall dwell in it* (Ps 68:10). We often see a block of salt put out for brute animals; they are to lick it and are made better. A priest among his people should be like a block of salt in the midst of brute animals. A priest must be careful about what he says to individuals, to counsel each one in such a way that anyone associated with the priest may be seasoned with the taste of eternal life just as if he had contact with salt.

We are not the salt of the earth if we do not season the hearts of those who hear us. The one who does not withhold his preaching offers this seasoning to his neighbor. We are truly preaching what is right to others, if our words are revealed in our actions, if we ourselves are pierced by divine love, and if we wash away with our tears the stains of the human condition that we daily endure, since we cannot live without sin. We feel true remorse if we diligently ponder the deeds of God's servants; when we consider their renown, our own lives may appear mediocre in our eyes. Then do we truly feel sorrow as we carefully examine God's commandments and strive to advance using the same means as they did for their own advancement.

For what shall we call human souls but the Lord's food? They were created to be transmuted into his body, to enlarge the eternal Church. We were to be the seasoning for this food, as I said earlier in connection with the sending out of preachers: **You are the salt of the earth.** If the people are God's food, the priests are to be its seasoning. If we ceased to practice prayer and offer holy instruction, the salt has lost its taste. It cannot season God's food, and so is not acceptable to our Creator. Because of its uselessness, we will have lost the power to season.

Matthew 5:14–16

14"You are the light of the world. A city set on a hill cannot be hid. 15Nor do men light a lamp and put it under a bushel, but on a stand, and it gives light to all in the house. 16Let your light so shine before men, that they may see your good works and give glory to your Father who is in heaven."

(35) Origen

The Lord said, *While I am in the world, I am the Light of the world* (John 9:5). Yet he said to his disciples, **You are the light of the world** and **Let your light so shine before men**. We understand the Bride or the Church and the disciples to be in a position analogous to the moon and the stars. In both cases, they possess their own particular light acquired from the true sun in order to enlighten those who cannot construct in themselves a source of light. So we call Paul and Peter **the light of the world**, although ordinary people who are called into discipleship by them are enlightened. They cannot, however, enlighten others because they are the *world*, whereas the disciples are **the light of the world**.

Being **the light of the world**, the Savior does not enlighten bodies but, by an incorporeal power, he enlightens the incorporeal mind. We are enabled to see other intelligible things, just as we each see other things enlightened by the sun. When the sun is shining, our ability to see the moon and stars is dimmed. Those illuminated by Christ and receiving his radiance do not require the mission of any apostles or prophets or—one must dare to tell the truth—angels, or, I add, any of the greater powers, since they are trained as disciples by the First-Begotten Light himself. The saints assisting those who do not receive Christ's solar rays[8]—they are scarcely able to accept even that enlightenment and be filled by it—supply that enlightenment, though it is much inferior to Christ's direct enlightenment.

(36) Hilary of Poitiers

You are the light of the world. It is in the nature of light to emit radiance wherever it moves. Once it has been introduced into a house, darkness is dispelled by its overwhelming brightness. In like manner, the world is reckoned outside of the knowledge of God, enshrouded by the darkness of ignorance. Through the apostles, the light of understanding is brought into it and illumined by the knowledge of God. Wherever the tiny particles of light have gone, darkness is dissipated.

A city built upon a hill cannot be hidden, nor do they who light a lamp place it under a bushel, etc. The Lord calls the flesh that he had assumed a **city** because, just as a city that is composed of a variety and multitude of inhabitants, so too there is contained in him, given the nature of his assumed body, a union with the whole human race. Thus he becomes a **city** from our union with him and we, through union with his flesh, are the community of his **city**. He cannot, therefore, be hidden now that he is situated on God's highest of heights. He is raised up in order to be perceived and understood by all in wonder of his good works.

But neither should a lamp, once it is lit, be concealed under a bushel. What benefit is it to possess something that provides light in a confined area? Yet the Lord appropriately compared a bushel to the synagogue, which, as it eagerly welcomed the fruits that were brought, maintained a sure means of measuring all its observances. Despite all the fruit that was brought, it was empty, though not capable of hiding the light.

And thus, the lamp of Christ should not be hidden under a bushel or under the concealing cover of the synagogue. Rather, it is highlighted in his sufferings on the tree, offering eternal light to those who will dwell in the Church. By a similar light the apostles are also admonished to shine so that in admiration of their works, praise may be rendered to God. It isn't appropriate to seek glory from human beings when everything has been done in honor of God. Let our work, even if it is ignored, shine among those with whom we live.

8. That is, pagans.

(37) Augustine

A city seated on a mountain cannot be hid: that is to say, when it is based on a high and prominent justice, a justice as designated by the mountain on which the Lord has spoken his word. **Neither do men light a candle and put it under a bushel**. How are we to interpret these words? When the Lord said to **put it under a bushel**, was he simply talking about hiding a candle, as you might say, "Does one light a candle to hide it?" Or, does the word **bushel** have another meaning there? When one is said to have **put** a candle **under a bushel**, could it mean that this person prefers the benefits of the body to the preaching of the truth, so that he ceases preaching the truth because he fears that he will experience some physical and fleeting inconvenience? In any case, the word **bushel** is rightly chosen. On the one hand, it may refer to the extent to which each will receive the reward of what he has done, according to the testimony of the Apostle, *that there every man may receive what he has done in the body* (2 Cor 5:10).

The idea about personal measurement is found in yet another passage, **With what measure you give, it shall be measured to you again** (Matt 7:2). On the other hand, the bushel measure may also refer to the perishables one accumulates through the efforts of his corporeal existence, delimited by a certain measure of time when they begin and end. Yet, the eternal and spiritual realities are limited by no such curb: *for God does not give the Spirit by measure* (John 3:34). And so, the one who puts a candle under a bushel is the one who covers and hides the light of good doctrine under his temporal advantages.

Many people, dearly beloved, are often upset because after our Lord Jesus Christ had said, in the Sermon on the Mount, **So let your light shine before men, that they may see your good works, and glorify your Father in heaven**, he went on to say later, **Take care not to perform your justice before men, to be seen by them.** Anyone not able to understand matters and yet eager all the same to obey commandments is troubled in mind and torn between contraries and opposites. It is as impossible for anyone to oblige one master who is giving contradictory orders, as it is for anyone to serve two masters, which the Savior himself asserts in the same sermon. So what is the wobbly soul to do, when it reckons it is unable to oblige, and is afraid not to oblige? You see, if he places his good works in the light to be noticed by other people, as a means to carry out the command, **So let your light shine before men, that they may see your good works, and glorify your Father in heaven**, he will consider himself liable to be held guilty of acting against the command that says, **Take care not to perform your justice before men, to be seen by them.** Again, if he's afraid of this and, to avoid doing it, hides good things he does, he will suppose he is not serving the one who bids him: **Let your light shine before men, that they may see your good works.**

As a matter of fact, the words of the Gospel carry their own explanations with them as they feed the minds of those who are knocking (cf. 7:7) and do not stop the mouths of those who are hungry (7:9). What we have to examine is the intention of the human heart, how it is directed, what it has in mind. If anybody wants his good works to be seen by other people because he is parading his glory and his indispensability before their eyes, seeking recognition from other people, then he hasn't fulfilled either of the commands the Lord gave on this point. He has, on the contrary, taken care to perform his justice before other people to be seen by them and his light has failed to shine before men, that they should see his good works for the purpose of glorifying the Father in heaven. It's himself that he wants to glorify, not God; and it was his own profit he was looking for, not the will of the Lord. Of such people the Apostle says, *They are all looking after their own interests, not those of Jesus Christ* (Phil 2:21).

That's why the sentence didn't end there, when the Lord said, **So let your light shine before men that they may see your good works**. Immediately he added why this should be done: **that they may glorify**, he said, **your Father in heaven.** So when a person is seen by people to do good, his conscience should be prompted by the intention to do good, rather than by any intention of becoming well known about it. The benefit he receives is from being delighted with God, who has enabled him to do the good. He need not give up hope that such a capacity for doing good will be granted to him as well.

(38) Chromatius of Aquileia

The Lord called his disciples the salt of the earth because they seasoned the heart of the human race with heavenly wisdom, but their heart had been rendered insipid by the devil. Now he also calls them the light of the world, since, having been illuminated by the very one who is the true and eternal light, they too were made light within the darkness. Since he himself is *the Sun of Righteousness* (Mal 4:2), he fittingly calls his disciples the light of the world. Through them, as through sparkling beams of light, the light of his knowledge fills the whole earth. The darkness of error flees from human hearts once the light of truth has been revealed. For we too, enlightened by them, have become light out of darkness, as the Apostle says: *Once you were darkness; now you are light in the Lord. Walk as sons of light* (Eph 5:8–9). And again, *Do not be sons of night and darkness, but be sons of light and sons of the day* (1 Thess 5:5). Holy John also testifies rightly in his letter when he says, *God is light* (1 John 1:5), and the one who abides in God is in the light, as he himself is in the light. Let us rejoice, then, for we have been freed from the darkness of error; let us, as sons of light, always walk in the light.

He adds, **A city set upon a hill cannot be hidden.** By **city** here, he means the Church, about which many passages of the Holy Scriptures testify, and about which David spoke most fully, saying: *Glorious things are spoken of you, city of God* (Ps 87:3), and *The flow of the river refreshes the city of God* (Ps 46:4), and *As we have heard, so we have seen in the city of the Lord's virtues, in the city of our God; God has established it forev*er (Ps 48:8).

He shows that the city set upon a hill is the Church, built upon the faith of our Lord and Savior in the glory of heaven. The Church, rising by a spiritual movement above all the lowliness of earthly weakness, becomes evident to the whole world and is glorious. It is no longer hidden by the prediction of the law, but is revealed in clear preaching through the Gospel teaching.

It is appropriate that when the Lord makes mention of a lamp in the present passage, saying, **nor do they light a lamp and put it under a bushel, but on a lampstand, that it may give light to all who are in the house**, he should add, **let your light so shine before men that they may see your good works and glorify your Father who is in heaven.** God is glorified in us before the unbelieving and faithless if we live according to divine teaching—if we shine with good works. So the holy apostle also said: *Glorify and bear God in your body* (1 Cor 6:20). And blessed Peter similarly advises in his epistle, *that while they might disparage you, they will glorify our God for your works of righteousness* (1 Pet 2:12).

It could be understood differently (since the spiritual understanding is many-faceted) that we should take the **lamp** to mean the Lord himself on account of the lowliness of the body he assumed. Indeed, he is called *the Sun of Righteousness* (Mal 4:2) not simply in relation to the glory of his divinity. The **lamp** is made evident to all because of the sacrament of his assumed body. While he is the God of glory and eternal majesty, he appeared in this world with humility, just like a lamp.[9] Not without reason did he appear as a lamp since a lamp customarily shines through the night. He appeared in this world humble as a lamp that he might dispel the darkness of error and the night of ignorance from our hearts, since we were living in this world as if covered in darkness. A lamp of this kind, that is, the incarnation of Christ foretold by the law and the prophets, is no longer hidden in the preaching of the law as if covered by a bushel, nor concealed by the faithlessness of the scribes and Pharisees as a kind of vessel of falsehood. Once he was established on the cross, as if in a lampstand, it illuminates the whole household of the Church. According to the mystery of his incarnation, the Lord is very much a lamp; according to the glory of his divinity he is *the Sun of Righteousness* (Mal 4:2). In the lampstand of the cross he has shone forth as the sun. Through the proclamation of the apostles, as through rays from the sun, as it were, our Lord and Savior cast the clearest light of his knowledge upon the whole world. He is blessed forever.

Matthew 5:17–18

17 "Think not that I have come to abolish the law and the prophets; I have come not to abolish them but to fulfill them. 18 For truly, I say to you, till heaven and earth pass away, not an iota, not a dot, will pass from the law until all is accomplished."

(39) Origen

One stroke means **an iota** not only among the Greeks but also among the Hebrews who call it "yod." It is possible, then, that both **one iota** and **one stroke** stand for "Jesus," since his name is written beginning with a yod not only in the Greek, but also in the Hebrew writers. **One stroke** may also refer to Jesus as the Word of God by law, the one who does not surpass the law until everything comes to pass. As he himself suggests, **an iota** may also signify the ten commandments of the law. Indeed, everything passes away, but these commands do not pass away, and neither does Jesus. Even if he cast himself down to the earth, he did so voluntarily, in order to bring perfect fruit. And so, **one iota** and **one stroke** once again embrace the things of both heaven and earth.

9. That is, a lamp in contrast to the sun.

(40) Hilary of Poitiers

The power and authority of these heavenly words have a lofty meaning. For the law of works was established and encompassed everything pertaining to the faith to be revealed in Christ (Gal 3:23): both his teaching and his suffering, the exalted and profound decision of the Father's will. Moreover, under the veil of spiritual words, the law spoke of the nativity of our Lord Jesus Christ, and of his incarnation, and of his passion, and of his resurrection. It was decreed even before the times of the ages and the time of our age, frequently mentioned by prophetic and apostolic authority. . . .

Lest we should think that there is in his works anything that is not contained in the law, he declared that **he did not come to abolish the law but to fulfill it.** Whereas heaven and earth, the greatest of elements we can imagine, will be destroyed, it is still not possible for the least of the commandments of the law to be left uncompleted since all the law and the prophets are fulfilled in the Lord. During his passion and on the verge of delivering his spirit, he took a drink of sour wine and declared that all was finished (John 19:28–30). Everything that was once spoken by the prophets was summed up in the affirmation of his deeds. So it was established by God that not even the least of the commandments of God should be abolished (except [the statutes] concerning sacrifice). He warned that those who abolish the least of these will be the least, that is, they will be last or of no account at all (Matt 5:19). For no one can be less than those who are the least.

(41) Chromatius of Aquileia

It is not to destroy the law and the prophets that the Son of God—the author of the law and prophets—came. For he himself gave Moses to the people to hand them the law and purified the prophets to proclaim the future by the Holy Spirit, as he says, **I have not come to abolish, but to fulfill.** He fulfilled the law and the prophets in this way: when he himself completed what was written in the law and prophets. Hence when he had drunk the vinegar offered him on the cross, he said, *it is fulfilled* (John 19:30) in order to show clearly that which had been written about him in the law and prophets, including even the drinking of vinegar. He fulfills the law in every way when he fulfilled the mystery of the Pasch or the Lamb, formerly set forth in images in the sacrament of his own passion. So the Apostle said, *for Christ our Passover is sacrificed* (1 Cor 5:7). He fulfills the law when, for the sake of the truth, he completed the sacrifices of the law and all the examples prefigured in them by taking on a body. He fulfills the law when he confirms the precepts of the law that he gave with the addition of the grace of his gospel.

How he came to fulfill the law is shown in the following: **until heaven and earth disappear, not one iota, not one stroke, shall drop from the law, until all things come to pass.** From this we know how true and divine is the preaching of the law that the Lord shows; **not one iota nor one stroke can fall.** Yet even in this **iota** or **stroke** of the law the sacrament of the cross may be understood, since an **iota** and **stroke** in themselves make a sort of image of the cross, which cannot for any reason be omitted from the law and the preaching of the prophets.

Matthew 5:19–20

[19]"Whoever then relaxes one of the least of these commandments and teaches men so, shall be called least in the kingdom of heaven; but he who does them and teaches them shall be called great in the kingdom of heaven. [20]For I tell you, unless your righteousness exceeds that of the scribes and Pharisees, you will never enter the kingdom of heaven."

(42) Jerome

This section goes with the testimony above in which it is said, **not one iota or one stroke will pass from the law until all things come to pass.** It attacks the Pharisees, who, scorning God's commandments, established their own traditions. Their teaching among the people would be useless if they destroyed even the least of what is written in the law. Likewise, we can also understand that a teacher's learning, even if he were guilty of a minor sin, would pull him down from the highest step. It does no good to teach the nature of righteousness that the smallest sin would destroy. Perfect beatitude is to fulfill in deeds what you teach in words.

(43) Hilary of Poitiers

I say to you that unless your righteousness surpasses that of the scribes and the Pharisees, you will not enter the kingdom of heaven. Providing a marvelous introduction to the subject, he begins to surpass the role of the law, not in order to abolish it, but to rise above it through the steps of a higher advancement. He warns that the apostles will not be admitted to heaven unless they should surpass the righteousness of the Pharisees with equity. Once he established those things that were prescribed by the law, he surpassed it by advancement, not by abolition.

Matthew 5:21–22

[21]"You have heard that it was said to the men of old, 'You shall not kill; and whoever kills shall be liable to judgment.' [22]But I say to you that every one who is angry with his brother shall be liable to judgment; whoever insults his brother shall be liable to the council, and whoever says, 'You fool!' (lit., "Raka") shall be liable to the hell of fire."

(44) Augustine

To be "greater" and thus fit for the kingdom, we should act and teach as Christ teaches here. This means that our righteousness should **abound more than that of the scribes and Pharisees**. While the righteousness of the Pharisees demands of them not to kill, the righteousness of those who will enter the kingdom of heaven demands of them not to get angry without reason. Not to kill is thus the least requirement, and the one who violates it is "the least" in the kingdom of heaven. On the other hand, the one who satisfies the requirement not to kill does not immediately become "the greatest" and deserving to enter the kingdom of heaven, even though he makes progress step by step. He will excel, however, if he does not get angry without reason. When a person accomplishes this, he will move even farther away from murder. On this account, one who teaches that we should not be angry does not violate the law that forbids to kill, but rather realizes it more fully. This way we stay away from doing harm, both outwardly, by keeping from killing, and inwardly, in our heart, by keeping from anger.

Who wouldn't be afraid of the Word that states and declares, **Whoever says to his brother, Fool, shall be liable to the Gehenna of fire**? Yet no person can tame the tongue (Jas 3:8). Human beings can tame wild animals; they can't tame the tongue. They may tame lions, but they don't bridle their speech. And while they are good at taming all kinds of creatures, they don't tame themselves. They tame whatever they used to fear, but they are not afraid of what they should fear: the necessity of taming themselves. This is the situation as it stands. It's a true saying, and it proceeds from the mouthpiece of Truth. But no person can tame the tongue.

So we should realize, beloved, that if no person can tame the tongue, we must flee to God for refuge, for him to tame our tongues. If you yourself want to tame it, you can't, because you are a human being, aren't you? No person can tame the tongue. Compare the case of the animals that we tame. Horses don't tame themselves, camels don't tame themselves, elephants don't tame themselves, snakes don't tame themselves, lions don't tame themselves, so too neither do persons tame themselves. But to tame horses, camels, elephants, lions, snakes, you look for a person. In order to tame human beings you should look for God.

(45) John Chrysostom

Why is it that the commandment seems so demanding? Are you not aware that the majority of punishments and sins have their beginning in words? Bear in mind, blasphemies are expressed in words, as are denials, abuse, insults, perjury, and false witness. So don't consider it a mere word; rather, examine carefully whether it involves great risk. Surely you are not unaware that in a moment of hostility, when anger is inflamed and the soul is enkindled, even the smallest thing appears great and the slightest insult seems unbearable. Many a time these trifling things have given rise to murder and brought down whole cities.

Although grievous matters may seem minor among friends, on other occasions where there is hostility, the most trifling words appear very weighty. Even when they are spoken thoughtlessly, they are perceived as spoken with evil intent. So it is with fire. Where there is a small spark in a pile of logs, it does not easily catch fire. But if the flame is strong and blazing high, not only the logs but even stones and all kinds of material falling into it are caught up, and the fire blazes stronger than what is normally used to extinguish it. This is what happens also in the case of anger: whatever someone says turns immediately into fuel for this evil conflagration. In order to suppress this ahead of time, Christ condemned the person who is angry without reason.

(46) Chromatius of Aquileia

The Lord teaches us to be perfect in all things so that we will not be held accountable at the coming judgment for our thoughtless or empty speech. For this reason, when Solomon through the Holy Spirit spoke about a man of the Gospel, he testified thus: *Blessed is he who is not unrighteous in the words of his mouth, and is not vexed by sorrow for sin* (Sir 14:1). And the same Solomon elsewhere said concerning this, *Fasten a bolt across your mouth, and set a steel beam upon your tongues and words* (Sir 28:25). And again: *Cut off from you a depraved mouth, and cast far from you lying lips* (Prov 4:24). Yet again, *Do not accustom your mouth to disorderliness, for therein is the sorrow of sin* (Sir 23:13). David also said: *Set, Lord, a guard at my mouth, and a doorkeeper at my lips* (Ps 141:3). And in another Psalm: *I said, "Lord, I will guard my ways, that I might not transgress in my tongue"* (Ps 39:1). For as Solomon said, *Imprudent lips will tell of foolish things; the word of a prudent man is weighed* (Sir 21:25). Therefore the Lord testifies in the Gospel that we will be repaid for our careless speech. The apostle equally instructs us about this matter: *Let no evil word escape your mouth, but only what is good for the edification of the faith* (Eph 4:29). And again, *Let your speech be always in grace, seasoned with salt, that you might know how to respond fittingly to each one* (Col 4:6). Concerning this matter, it is well for us to be careful in all things, so that our familiarity with detrimental words does not acquire damnation for us instead of salvation.

Matthew 5:23–24

23"So if you are offering your gift at the altar, and there remember that your brother has something against you, 24leave your gift there before the altar and go; first be reconciled to your brother, and then come and offer your gift."

(47) Augustine

In a spiritual sense, we can think of genuine faith as an altar in God's temple within us, the sign of which is the visible altar. Whatever our offering to God might be—be it a prophecy, or a doctrine, or a prayer, or a hymn, or a psalm, or any other spiritual gift of this sort that one might offer—it cannot be accepted by God unless it is backed up by sincere faith and rests upon it as if being firmly attached to it, so that our verbal offering may be perfect and untarnished.

But numerous heretics who have no altar, that is, no true faith, proclaim blasphemies instead of praise, being burdened by ungodly beliefs, as if they were casting their prayers downward onto the ground. The disposition of our mind must be sound when we prepare to offer a gift, just as we prepare to make an offering in our hearts, that is, inside of our divine temple, *for the temple of God is holy, he said, which you are* (1 Cor 3:17); and *in the inward man Christ dwells by faith in your hearts* (Eph 3:17). If we think of a brother who has anything against us, we should realize that this is a result of some harm we did to him, and this is why he now has something against us. We have something against him if he hurt us, in which case there is no need for reconciliation. You will not seek pardon from a person that injured you, but you will go ahead and forgive him just as you wish your own wrongdoings to be forgiven by the Lord. Therefore, we must seek reconciliation when we think of an instance when we might have hurt our brother. For we must approach this task, not by making steps with our limbs, but rather with the motions of our soul. We should lie down prostrate before that brother with a humble heart, run toward him thinking of him dearly, to come before the eyes of the one to whom you wish to offer a gift.

However, you will be able to make peace with him without pretense only if he is also present, and by asking him to pardon you again with gratitude, as if you were doing it before God first, reaching to him with the swiftness of love rather than reluctantly. Then, from the place where you started, that is, by recalling your initial intentions, you can now offer your gift.

Matthew 5:25–26

25 "Make friends quickly with your accuser, while you are going with him to court, lest your accuser hand you over to the judge, and the judge to the guard, and you be put in prison; 26 truly, I say to you, you will never get out till you have paid the last penny."

(48) Tertullian

Remembering the Lord's instructions paves the way for our prayers unto heaven. One of these particularly is that we not approach God's altar before resolving any conflict or offense that has occurred with our brothers. For what kind of deed is it to beseech God for peace without peace? Can we approach God for the remission of our debts while we retain them? How will it please the Father if we are angry at our brothers, when all anger from the beginning (e.g., Gen 4:6–7) is forbidden to us? For even Joseph, after dismissing his brothers for the sake of bringing his father, said, *do not be angry along the way* (Gen 45:24). In other words, he has admonished us—at the time when our instruction was called the Way (Acts 9:2; 19:9)—that we do not, in the way of prayer, come before the Father with anger. . . . How rash it is, either to pass a day without prayer while you refuse to make satisfaction with your brother, or to lose your prayer by maintaining anger!

(49) Hilary of Poitiers

Binding all people together in a mutual love, [the Lord] allows no one to offer a prayer without the spirit of peace. If one remembers while offering his gifts at the altar that he harbors some grudge against his brothers, he is commanded to make reconciliation with a human peace before returning to divine peace and so cross over from the love of humanity to the love of God.

Because the Lord allows that there should always be opportunity for conciliation, he commands us [at every turn] on every road of our lives to be reconciled quickly with our adversary in goodwill. By making a slow return to favor, we arrive at the moment of death without having made peace and the adversary delivers us to the judge, and the judge to the warden, and we are not released [from prison] until we pay up the last cent. According to the precepts of the Lord's Prayer, we pray for the forgiveness of our sins following his example. After we have granted pardon to our adversaries, we seek his pardon (Matt 6:12). So he will refuse this to us if we will refuse it to others, and we are subject to our own judgment if, at the time of judgment, we should have not renounced our grievances.

(50) Caesarius of Arles

This is your adversary: **Come to terms with him while you are with him on the way**. The **way** is your manner of life; the opponent of all the wicked is the word of God. Is it not important to you that, although truth was remaining in its most blessed and hidden place, it came to be with you on the **way**? It wanted to accompany you, so that when you walk and have it in your power, you may settle and plead your case as you finish your journey. In this way, once you've finished your journey, there will be no one with whom you can rest your case, since **your opponent will quickly deliver you to the judge, and the judge to the officer, and the officer will cast you into prison. You will not come out from it until you have paid the last penny.**

The word of God is with you as an adversary on the way: you have it in your power to come to terms with it. What does that adversary seek from you? That you should live in harmony with it. What is that, except your salvation? It walks with its opponents and tells them to live in harmony with it.

Therefore, as we think about these matters in a positive light, dearest brethren, let us conclude friendship with our adversary while we are on the way with him. In other words, let us consent to the word of God as long as we are still in this life, because afterward, when we have passed out of this world, no agreement or satisfaction will be possible. The judge stands fast, as does the officer, and the prison. For this reason, let us love with our whole heart, not only our friends, but also our enemies, so that with the Lord's help we may be able to fulfill all these commands. Likewise, we may realize what is written: *The whole law is fulfilled in one word: You shall love your neighbor as yourself* (Gal 5:14), and further: *Love covers a multitude of sins* (1 Pet 4:8). May he who is himself true love grant this to us, who lives and reigns with the Father and the Holy Spirit forever and ever. Amen.

Matthew 5:27–30

27"You have heard that it was said, 'You shall not commit adultery.' 28But I say to you that every one who looks at a woman lustfully has already committed adultery with her in his heart. 29If your right eye causes you to sin, pluck it out and throw it away; it is better that you lose one of your members than that your whole body be thrown into hell. 30And if your right hand causes you to sin, cut it off and throw it away; it is better that you lose one of your members than that your whole body go into hell."

(51) Hilary of Poitiers

If your right eye offends you, pluck it out and cast it from you, etc. There is a higher progression to purity here, as faith takes a step forward. Not only are we told to abstain from personal vices, but also from that which assaults us from without. It is not because our bodily members have sinned that their removal is prescribed; for the left eye goes astray no less than the right one. Certainly a foot, which lacks awareness of concupiscence, does not need to be cut off, since the reason for punishment will not fall upon it. Although the members [of the body] are different from one another, we are all nevertheless a single body (cf. 1 Cor 12:12–27; Col 3:15). We are told to eject, or rather pluck out, those intimate things whose names are most dear to us. We should discern in them any sort of way in which they bring us into their wicked company because of our familiarity with them. It is better for us to surrender useful and even necessary things, like an eye or a foot, than to cling with affection to a corrupted complicity with the fellowship of Gehenna. In fact, the cutting off of a member is useful if there is an indictment of the heart.

(52) Chromatius of Aquileia

This **eye** and **hand** aren't references to the human body, but to the eye or hand of the heart. In other words, the Lord teaches that the sentiment of evil, lust or carnal desire, must be cut out from our hearts. The Lord himself makes clear in the Gospel that all evils proceed from here, when he says, **For from the heart come evil thoughts, murder, adultery, blasphemy, false testimony, and the other things that make a person unclean** (Matt 15:19–20). Nothing that incapacitates the body is enough to improve an evil mind in which lies a vast abyss of sins. Certainly we see many people deprived of sight or weakened in body who nevertheless do not cease from sinning. The Lord teaches us instead to cut off these members of sin—evils of the mind and depraved thoughts—for the sake of the kingdom of heaven. This is so that our being is not dominated by sins, both of body and soul, which is the whole person and is liable to eternal fire.

Now some think that this passage [**one of your members**] should be understood as referring to sons or close friends who are as dear and beloved to us as the eyes in our head. If any of these should prove themselves opposed to our faith and hope and cause a scandal, they should be cast away from us and regarded as enemies, lest anyone through association with such faithless and blasphemous people should be condemned to a similar punishment.

Not without reason did holy David say, *You have set forth your precepts to be kept diligently* (Ps 119:4)—so *diligently* that not only adultery, but even lust, is seen as guilty of sin. The law condemns adultery, but the Gospel indeed punishes even lust, which is the root of adultery. Through Solomon the Holy Spirit in many places argues the very same thing, saying, *Do not follow after your lusts, and prohibit your desires. For if you give lust to your soul, it will give you over to the joy of your enemies and those who hate you* (Sir 18:30–31).

Since adultery is a grave sin, let our conscience not be soiled. He also prohibits lust, which is the root of adultery, about which the blessed James speaks in his epistle: *Lust gives birth to sin, and the lust of sin brings death* (Jas 1:15). On this account, the Holy Spirit also spoke about this through David: *Blessed is the one who takes and dashes his babies on a rock* (Ps 137:9). He speaks here of the blessed and true man of the Gospel, who, through faith in Christ (who is our rock), immediately crushes the desires and lusts of the flesh that are born of human weakness before they rise up.

(53) Augustine

The lower righteousness is not to fornicate by way of coupling the bodies, but the greater righteousness of the kingdom of God is not to fornicate in one's heart. One who does not commit adultery in his heart stays away from committing adultery in his body much more easily. Hence, the one who commanded the lesser righteousness also confirmed the greater, because he **came not to destroy the law but to fulfill** (5:17). No doubt, it is very important to reflect on the fact that he did not say "everyone who will desire a woman," but rather, **who looks on a woman to lust after her**, that is, the one who intentionally and consciously pursues sexual union with her. And this does not mean to be tickled by physical pleasure, but to fully succumb to your passion, so that your forbidden desire is not only no longer controlled, but even ready to be satisfied if opportunity should be given.

A sinful act is committed in three steps: stimulus, enjoyment, and consent. The stimulus arises either in the memory or through the senses, when we see, hear, smell, taste, or touch a particular object. Should we notice that our enjoyment of an object has become too alluring, such an illicit enjoyment must be curbed. For example, when we fast, our appetite is aroused in our taste buds at the sight of food, and not without an element of enjoyment. Yet, we do not consent to this enjoyment and put an end to it compelled by reason, our primary driving force. On the contrary, have we yielded to that enjoyment, our sinful act would have been taken to completion. A sin committed in our hearts is known to God, even if it remains unknown to men.

Matthew 5:31–32

31"It was also said, 'Whoever divorces his wife, let him give her a certificate of divorce.'
32But I say to you that every one who divorces his wife, except on the ground of unchastity, makes her an adulteress; and whoever marries a divorced woman commits adultery."

(54) Hilary of Poitiers

Establishing equity for all people, the Lord instructs the spouse to remain above all in marital harmony. By adding many things to the law, no part of it is diminished. Nor can one reasonably find fault with the progress made [by the Gospel]. Whereas the law had granted the freedom to give a certificate of separation on the authority of the document, now the evangelical faith not only announced its intention for harmony with the husband, but also imposed guilt for forcing his wife into adultery. If, out of the necessity of separation, she marries another with no other reason than for ending the first marriage, it is said that she dishonored her [new] husband because of his union with a prostitute wife (cf. 1 Cor 7:11).

(55) Augustine

He who commanded to give the wife a bill of divorce did not command that she should be put away. He said instead: *Whoever shall put her away, let him give her a bill of divorce* (Deut 24:1), hoping that the very idea of such a bill would temper the heedless rage of those trying to get rid of a wife. No doubt, the Lord sought to postpone divorce in order to make it as clear as possible to the obtuse that separation was not his intent.

On another occasion, when the Lord was also asked about divorce, he replied as follows: *Moses by reason of the hardness of your heart said this* (19:8). No matter how obstinate a man trying to divorce his wife, when he realizes that, by rendering the bill of divorce, he would enable her to get married again without any obstacle, this thought could easily calm him down. Thus, the Lord made sure that no man divorces his wife too easily, except for the only reason, adultery. As far as the rest of the problems every married couple probably encounters, the Lord commands that they should faithfully endure in the name of marital fidelity and chastity. The Lord also states that a man who marries a woman separated from her husband is an adulterer.

(56) Chromatius of Aquileia

In all things, our Lord and Savior reforms the precepts of the ancient law for the better. For a long time, the Jewish people were given through Moses an indulgence that allowed certificates of dismissal where leniency was shown. It was not the logic of the law that demanded this, but the unbridled desires of a carnal people who were unable to preserve the law's righteousness according to the strictness of its discipline. It was for that reason this possibility was permitted, at least according to what the Lord himself clarified in another passage for those who were still asking him. When they asked why Moses had allowed a writ of divorce to be given, the Lord answered, **Moses wrote this because of the hardness of your hearts, that a writ of divorce be given; but it was not so from the beginning** (19:8). There is a good reason why our Lord and Savior removed that leniency by restoring the precepts of his ancient ordinance. For he commands that the chaste union of marriage be guarded by an indissoluble law, showing he had instituted the law of marriage from the first. He says, **What God has joined as one, let no one separate** (19:6; Mark 10:9).

He says, **except by reason of fornication** a wife cannot be divorced, clearly demonstrating that one acts against the divine will who presumes to dishonor a marriage joined by God with the separation of an illicit divorce. So let them not be unaware of how grave a crime, worthy of condemnation, they incur who, by divorcing their wives due to the unbridled desire of lust, apart from the cause of fornication, want to move to another marriage. They think they do this with impunity, since it seems to be permitted by human and secular laws. But they do not realize that they are committing a great and serious crime by preferring human laws to the divine laws. What God has established as illicit, they believe is proper since it is freely allowed by humans. Although one must not divorce a wife who lives a pure and chaste life, one is allowed to divorce an adulteress, for she has rendered herself unworthy of the marital union by daring to sin in her own body and so violating the temple of God.

Matthew 5:33–37

**33"Again you have heard that it was said to the men of old, 'You shall not swear falsely,
but shall perform to the Lord what you have sworn.' 34But I say to you, Do not swear at
all, either by heaven, for it is the throne of God, 35or by the earth, for it is his footstool,
or by Jerusalem, for it is the city of the great King. 36And do not swear by your head,
for you cannot make one hair white or black. 37Let what you say be simply 'Yes' or 'No';
anything more than this comes from evil."**

(57) Hilary of Poitiers

The law has established a penalty for making false witness because taking of an oath was supposed to repress a fraudulent conscience. In like manner, simple folk and the inexperienced make frequent mention of their god through habitually swearing an oath. Yet faith removes the habit of oath-taking and establishes the affairs of our lives in the truth. Once we have rejected an inclination toward deceit, a straightforward manner of speaking and hearing is prescribed so that whatever is the case, it is what it is; and whatever is not the case, it is not. Because there exists between **yes and no** a possibility for deceit, whatever is beyond this is a great evil. For whatever is, is always what it is, but whatever is not, is by nature not to be. For those who come in the simplicity of faith, there is no need for the observation of an oath: what is "yes" is always "yes," and what is "no" is always "no." For these reasons, every work and word of theirs is trustworthy.

(58) Augustine

The reading from the Apostle we have mentioned fits this guidance of the Lord's so perfectly that it seems God commanded nothing else but this: the one who said this is none other than the one who said through the Apostle, *Above all, my brothers, says he, do not swear, neither by heaven nor by earth, nor any other kind of oath at all. But let your word be: Yes, yes; No, no* (Jas 5:12). The only thing he added was, *Above all*; he put us on alert by increasing the difficulty of the question. The only thing that makes a guilty tongue is a guilty mind.

We find that of the saints to have sworn, the first is the Lord himself, in whom there is no sin whatsoever. *The Lord has sworn, and will not repent: You are a priest forever, according to the order of Melchizedek* (Ps 110:4). He promised the Son an eternal priesthood with an oath. You also have *By myself I swear it, says the Lord* (Gen 22:16). As a man swears by God, so God swears by himself. But isn't it a sin to swear? It's hard to say so; and since we have said that God has sworn, how blasphemous it seems to say so! God swears, and he has no sin; so it is not a sin to swear, but it's a sin, rather, to swear according to oneself.

Someone may say, perhaps, that we shouldn't bring in the Lord God as an example of swearing oaths. He's God, after all, and perhaps he alone is competent to swear since he cannot perjure himself. People swear falsely, either when they are being deceitful or being deceived. I mean, you either think something's true when it's false, and swear to it rashly; or you know or think it's false, and yet swear it's true, and still swear a criminal oath, regardless. These two sorts of perjury, though, which I have mentioned, are very different. Suppose a person swears who thinks what he's swearing to is true, and yet it is in fact false. He isn't deliberately perjuring himself; he's just mistaken because he regards as true what is in fact false. He doesn't knowingly interpose an oath for something false. Now give me another person who knows what he says is false and says it's true, and swears as though what he knows to be false were true. Can you see what a detestable monster he is, properly to be eliminated from human society? Who would want this sort of thing to be done? All people detest such things.

Take another person; he thinks it's false, and swears to it as if it were true—and it so happens it is true. For example, "Did it rain in that place?" you ask someone, and he thinks it didn't, though it suits his purpose to say "Yes, it did." You say to him, "Did it really rain?" "Yes, really," and he swears it did; and in fact it did rain there. But he really doesn't know it, believing it didn't, which makes him a perjurer. What makes the difference is how the word comes forth from the mind. The only thing that makes a guilty tongue is a guilty mind.

Is there anyone who is never mistaken, even though nobody has ever wanted to be mistaken? Is there anyone who is not sometimes caught in a mistake? And still, swearing doesn't disappear from people's mouths; it's a commonplace. There are often far more oaths than words. If you were to count up how often you swear throughout the day, how often you inflict wounds on yourself, how often you strike and run yourself through with the sword of your tongue, could you find anywhere in yourself that remains unhurt? So because perjury is a grave sin, Scripture has given you a simple formula: Don't swear.

So in order not to swear to a lie, don't swear at all. Swearing is a narrow ledge, perjury a precipice. If you swear, you're near the edge; if you don't swear, you're far away from it. You sin, and gravely, if you swear to what is false; you don't sin, if you swear the truth; but then you don't sin either, if you don't swear at all. But if you don't swear and don't sin, you are a long way away from sin; while if you do swear the truth, you don't sin, but you are near to sin. Suppose you are walking in some place along a narrow path where there is plenty of space on your right, but the ground falls away down a cliff on your left. Where would you prefer to walk: along the borderline, on the edge of the cliff, or far away from it? Far away from it, I think. So too, if you swear, you're walking on the borderline; and you're walking on shaky human, feet. If you stumble, down you go. If you slip, down you go. And what's waiting for you at the bottom: the penalty of perjury. So you were wishing to swear the truth? Listen to God's advice by not swearing at all.

Matthew 5:38–42

38“You have heard that it was said, ‘An eye for an eye and a tooth for a tooth.’ 39But I say
to you, Do not resist one who is evil. But if any one strikes you on the right cheek, turn
to him the other also; 40and if any one would sue you and take your coat, let him have
your cloak as well; 41and if any one forces you to go one mile, go with him two miles.
42Give to him who begs from you, and do not refuse him who would borrow from you.”

(59) Augustine

He who did not come to destroy the law but to fulfill it has perfected this imperfect justice by making it not strict but merciful. He thus leaves to the understanding of his listeners two distinct levels and prefers to speak of the perfection of mercy, because there is still something to do for those who do not meet in every respect the command whose standards are those of the kingdom of heaven. That is, we are not to respond to an assault with an equal assault, but rather with a lesser one, for example, with one punch for two, or a severed ear for the loss of an eye. But a person, who, in his progress, does not render evil at all, approximates the Lord's commandment; however, he is not there yet. It is little in the eyes of the Savior that you do not pay back with evil for evil you receive, if you are not willing to suffer even more. The Lord did not say, “But I say to you not to repay evil for evil,” even though this is in itself an important point. Rather, he said, “Do not resist abuse.” In other words, you are expected to avoid not only paying back with evil for the evil inflicted on you, but also to never resist even greater inflictions.

And if a man will sue you and take away your coat, let him have your garment should be rightly understood as a prescription for your heart's intentions rather than as a suggestion of mere gesture. And yet, what is said of the tunic and mantle does not apply to these objects alone, but rather to all good things that we rightly consider to be our own in this life. And, since this has been said of necessities, how much more worthwhile is it to treat unnecessary things with indifference!

(60) Chromatius of Aquileia

If anyone compels you to go a mile, go with him two more. The Lord teaches us to be diligent and prepared for every work of devotion. He wants our goodness to be not so much a matter of necessity as of our own will. And when we do more than we are requested to do by others, we attain the glory of a greater reward. It is the duty of wholehearted love and perfect devotion to perform voluntarily more than you would ask.

Some people believe there is a spiritual meaning of this text: that the one who has been compelled to go a mile goes two more, that is, if some faithless person or one not following the knowledge of the truth, having begun on the road of the law, should make mention of God the Father, Creator of all things, you should go with him two more. After his profession of the Father, you should lead this person along the way of truth to knowledge of the Son and the Holy Spirit, showing him that he must believe not only in the Father but also in the Son and Spirit.

Then follows: **And give to the one who asks from you.** That is, after knowledge of the Trinity, we should with a willing soul show forth the gift of grace. Or at least we should give as much as we can to those who ask for mercy, so that what we ourselves ask from God we might, by our surpassing merit, obtain more easily from him who says, **Ask, and it shall be given to you** (7:7). Truly, if we despise those who ask of us, by what faithfulness do we believe God will accomplish what we ask of him for ourselves?

Matthew 5:43–48

43"You have heard that it was said, 'You shall love your neighbor and hate your enemy.'
44But I say to you, Love your enemies and pray for those who persecute you, 45so that
you may be sons of your Father who is in heaven; for he makes his sun rise on the evil and on the good, and sends rain on the just and on the unjust. 46For if you love those
who love you, what reward have you? Do not even the tax collectors do the same? 47And
if you salute only your brethren, what more are you doing than others? Do not even the Gentiles do the same? 48You, therefore, must be perfect, as your heavenly Father is
perfect."

(61) Hilary of Poitiers

He has bound all things together perfected by his goodness. The law demanded love of one's neighbor and gave license to the hatred of one's enemy. Faith, however, commands us to love our enemies. The disposition of love toward all people breaks the headstrong activity of the human impulse, not only by quelling the anger of taking revenge but also by mitigating the effect of an insult through love. To love those who love you is characteristic of the pagans, and to esteem those who esteem you is commonplace. Instead, he calls us into God's inheritance, as well as to the imitation of Christ at his coming, both for the good and for the unjust [people], and into the mysteries of baptism and of the Spirit even as he confers on us **the sun and the rain**. Thus the Lord establishes us in a life perfected by this mandate of goodness toward everyone, just as we are to imitate our perfect Father in heaven.

(62) John Chrysostom

Note the absolute pinnacle he set for our good deeds, instructing us not only to put up with a slap in the face or to add a cloak to a coat demanded, but even to travel two miles with the person pressing you to go one. The reason for these is that you will accept with complete ease what is far greater than this. But, you may ask, what is greater than this? That we do not regard as an enemy the one guilty of this, or something even greater than this: He said, "Do not hate, but love"; whereas he didn't say, "Do no wrong," but "Do good." If you examine his words carefully, you will even see an even greater addition: he did not command you simply to love but even to pray. Do you see how many steps he has ascended, and how he has placed us on the very summit of virtue? Take note of it, counting from the beginning.

The first step begins not to respond with injustice to an injustice; the second is not merely to give as good as one can get; the third is not to take action against an abuser on account of what you have suffered; the fourth is to leave oneself open to ill-treatment; the fifth is to give even greater freedom than the guilty person is willing to give; the sixth is not to hate the one guilty of this behavior; the seventh is to love them; the eighth is even to do favors for your persecutors; the ninth is to intercede with God on their behalf. Do you see the loftiness of sound values here? This is the reason for having a reward that is also splendid. In fact, since the command was demanding, requiring a generous soul and great zeal, the Lord assigns this behavior a greater reward not like any of the others.

(63) Jerome

Many people evaluate God's commandments according to their own weakness rather than by the power of the saints and think what is commanded is impossible. They say that not to hate one's enemies is virtuous enough. To go further and love them is to command more than human nature can bear. It must be made known, however, that Christ does not command impossible acts, as demonstrated in the perfect way David acted toward Saul and Absalom (2 Sam 18:5). Stephen the martyr also prayed for his enemies as they stoned him (Acts 7:60), and Paul wished to be accursed for the sake of his persecutors (Rom 9:3). And Jesus both taught and practiced this when he said, *Father, forgive them, for they know not what they do* (Luke 23:34).

Matthew 6

In this section of the Sermon on the Mount, Jesus turns his attention to the practice of piety (6:1). He begins with alms (1–4), moves to prayer (5–15), and ends with fasting (16–18). The accent, according to the ancient writers, was on actions being done with the right intentions. "It is not the ability, but the aim of the ability, that receives a reward before God" (Jerome), and "It is not, then, the giving of alms that is required, but the giving of them as one ought" (Chrysostom).

Concerning prayer, Jesus instructs his disciples in its mechanics and intention. They are to enter their "room" where they can offer their prayers in secret. This passage is usually interpreted figuratively to refer to the "secret things of our heart" that "lie open to him alone." For "God hears the faith that prays, not of the voice" (Chromatius). Therefore, it is the intention that matters; whether it is done publicly or privately, whether with many words or few, God truly knows what we need (Origen). We do not inform God about our needs by a prayer but merely submit ourselves to his knowledge (Jerome).

Jesus's prayer was not only a model for how the disciple should pray in light of the kingdom, but his very words were regarded as the most effective manner of praying according to God's will. If it was true that whatever the believer asked of the Father in Jesus's name would be given (John 16:23b), Cyprian reasoned, then "how much more effectually do we obtain what we ask in Christ's name, if we ask for it using his own prayer?"

Each clause of the "Lord's Prayer" designates some aspect of the believer's relationship to God: we pray to the Father who has made us children. God's holiness is communicated through the holiness of believers. For Origen, heaven *and* earth *are to be understood allegorically. The former is Christ, and the latter is the Church on earth, which strives to resemble the heavenly character of Christ. To ask that* Thy kingdom come *is to seek God's will in one's life: "he who prays for the coming of the kingdom of God rightly prays that the kingdom of God may be established, bear fruit, and be perfected in him." Some writers take* daily bread *to mean seeking God the Word, who is the bread of life and our "spiritual food" (Augustine). Whether translated* debts *or* trespasses, *all writers assert that we need to ask every day for the forgiveness of our sins. As the believer becomes transformed into the divine image (Gregory of Nyssa), it is incumbent upon him to emulate God by forgiving others. The petition,* lead us not into temptation, *is a petition that we do not succumb to temptation and be led into evil (Origen).*

Because the doxology, Yours is the kingdom, the power and the glory, *does not appear in the Matthean version of the Lord's Prayer, it is not discussed in the patristic commentaries on Matthew.*

Discipleship is further defined as having the right intentions for fasting. Like almsgiving and prayer, there should be no ostentation in the act of fasting, since its purpose is to purify the inner self: "we are purified for the clarity of a good conscience and have been anointed with oil for the grace of works of mercy, [so that] our fasting commends us to God" (Hilary).

Finally, a genuinely devout life requires detachment from worldly wealth and possessions. For if one clings to "earthly things" instead of the kingdom of heaven, one will have "nothing on earth or in heaven" (Epiphanius).

Matthew 6:1-4

1 "Beware of practicing your piety before men in order to be seen by them; for then you will have no reward from your Father who is in heaven.

2 "Thus, when you give alms, sound no trumpet before you, as the hypocrites do in the synagogues and in the streets, that they may be praised by men. Truly, I say to you,
they have received their reward. 3 But when you give alms, do not let your left hand know
what your right hand is doing, 4 so that your alms may be in secret; and your Father who
sees in secret will reward you."

(1) Augustine

The purification of the heart is comparable to that of an eye with which we see God; and it is essential to keep it clean to the extent required by the dignity of the object that can be perceived with such an eye. But when this eye is largely purified, it is difficult for it not to catch other impurities that usually accompany even our good actions, such as the praise of men. Certainly it is dangerous to live dishonestly, but to live honestly and without a desire of praise amounts to being an enemy of the human race, which is just as miserable as the honest life is pleasing.

It is therefore proper that one who has a pure eye do good deeds without looking for praise in return for the good he has done. In other words, one should never do good deeds in order to please men. Good deeds can even be faked if attention is paid only to be praised by an individual who, because he cannot see your heart, can also praise hypocrisy. Those who do so, that is to say, those who pretend being good, are double-hearted. A person with a simple, that is, a pure heart, is only the one who rises above human praise, who has the only concern—to live righteously, and who seeks to please him who alone penetrates our consciousness. And everything that comes out of such a person's pure consciousness is the more praiseworthy the less human praise he desires.

(2) Jerome

One who blows his horn while giving alms is a hypocrite; one who prays in the synagogues and street corners in order to be seen by people is a hypocrite; one who contorts his face while fasting to show his stomach's emptiness by his expression is also a hypocrite. Taking all these together, hypocrites are those who do things in order to be glorified by people. And it seems to me that the man who said **let me remove the splinter from your eye** (cf. 7:4) did this for the sake of glory, so that he would appear to be righteous. Hence he is told by the Lord, **Hypocrite! First remove the beam from your eye** (7:5). Then and only then is the power of sight agreeable to God—if it is practiced for God's sake. It is not the ability, but the aim of the ability, that receives a reward before God.

(3) John Chrysostom

The Lord first sought to implant virtue in the disciples, and then to remove the passions that mar its fruit. Notice too how he begins: with fasting, and prayer, and almsgiving. The fruit of virtue will grow especially through these good deeds. The Pharisee, however, was full of pride when he said, *I fast twice a week, I give tithes of my substance* (Luke 18:12). He was no less vainglorious in his own prayer, offering it for display. But since there was no one else present, he pointed out the publican, saying, *I am not as the rest of men, nor even as this publican* (Luke 18:11).

The disciples, however, were told to exalt themselves in the abundance of their giving. For the same reason, he says, **Take heed that you do not give your alms before men**, for they are surely God's alms.

And when he had said not to do it **before men**, he added, **to be seen by them.** It may seem as if the same thing was said for a second time, yet if one pays careful attention, he will see that it is not exactly the same thing. One is different from the other: the one *doing* alms before men should *not* do it to be seen, and the one *not doing* it before men should do it to be seen. The point is that it is not simply the act, but the intent that he both punishes and rewards. And if such exactitude were employed, it would make the giving of alms more awkward, because it is not always possible to do it secretly. For this reason, setting us free from this restraint, he defines both the penalty and the reward, not by the result of the action, but by the intention of the doer.

Having forbidden any form of piety for display, and having taught his disciples the penalty for doing so, he provokes their spirits by focusing them on both the Father and heaven by mentioning shameful reasons. **For you will have no reward**, he says, **with your Father who is in heaven.** But he did not stop here; he proceeded to question other motives. Just as he showed publicans and heathens in a shameful light, as well as their imitators, so he also put the hypocrites in this place. **Therefore when you give your alms**, he says, **do not sound a trumpet as the hypocrites do**. Not that they had trumpets, but the Lord through this figure of speech said in derision that they tried to display greatness by their frantic behavior. He rightly called them **hypocrites** for theirs was a mask of mercy, covering the spirit of cruelty and inhumanity. They gave alms, not because they pity their neighbors, but so they themselves may enjoy credit. This was the utmost cruelty; while others were perishing with hunger, they were seeking recognition, and at the same time not helping those in need. It is not, then, the giving of alms that is required, but the giving of them as one ought.

And when you pray, he says, **do not be as the hypocrites, for they love to pray standing in the synagogues, and in the corners of the streets. Truly I say unto you, they have their reward.** These, too, he properly calls **hypocrites**, because while they are feigning to pray to God, they are really looking around for the acknowledgement of others. They will indeed receive a reward, but it will be from the very people from whom they seek it. But God does not wish this. He would rather grant men the reward that he himself gives. Yet, by seeking that which is from men, they can no longer be justly entitled to receive anything from him for whom they have done nothing.

Instead, the Lord introduces the best manner of prayer, and also the reward: **Enter into your closet**. One might retort, "shouldn't we pray in church?" Indeed, we ought by all means to do so, but in such a spirit as this. In every circumstance, God seeks the intention of what is done. If you enter into your closet and shut the door for display, then shutting the doors is of no avail.

(4) Augustine

There is a question about why the Lord in the sermon that he preached on the mountain said, **Let your works shine before men, so that they may see your good deeds and glorify your Father in heaven** (5:16), but a little later in the same sermon said, **Beware of performing your justice before men, to be seen by them; and also, Let your giving of alms be in secret, and your Father who sees in secret will pay you back.**

Very often when people are doing good they want to follow the advice of both admonitions and wobble between them, not knowing which one to follow. How should our works shine before men, so that they may see our good deeds? And again, how should we give alms in secret? If I want to observe the first one, I seem to violate the other; if I follow the second, I am sinning on the other side. So each place of Scripture has to be treated and tempered in such a way as to show that the divine precepts and admonitions cannot contradict each other. What I mean is this: what seems to be a conflict here in words calls for an agreeable understanding. Only let each of us be in harmony with God's word in our hearts, and there will be no discord in Scripture.

So imagine a person giving alms in such a way that no one whatsoever knows about it (if it is at all possible), not even the one who is receiving the benefits. In order that the recipient may not even see it, the giver might provide something for him to find rather than offer something to him openly. What more could he do to conceal his almsgiving? But would he run afoul of that other saying and not do what the Lord tells us: **Let your works shine before men, so that they may see your good deeds** (5:16)? If nobody sees his good deeds, he is not inviting imitation. As far as he is concerned, others remain barren of good works, thinking that nobody is doing what God commanded.

Now imagine another person, advertising his almsgiving among the people and boasting about it all, wanting to be admired for it since he is letting his works shine before men. Notice that he is not violating that admonition, yet he is offending the other one where the Lord says, **Let your giving of alms be in secret.** This kind of person grows lax in his acts if some godless people turn up and find fault with what he is doing. He depends totally on the tongues of admirers. He is like the virgins who did not take any oil with them (cf. 25:1–13).

You know, of course, about the five foolish virgins who didn't take any oil with them, and the other wise ones who did take oil with them. All of their lamps were shining, though some did not have enough with them to sustain that light. These are called foolish, being distinguished from the others who did bring enough, while the others were called wise (25:2–4). So what's the purpose of bringing oil with you if you do not have the conscious intention of pleasing God with your good works, rather than doing it for the ultimate pleasure of being admired by men who do not know your intentions? Doing a good work so that anyone can see it is one thing. But the issue is with what kind of intention you do it, which only God can see.

So now, let us imagine some people who follow both admonitions, obey each of them. They offer bread to the hungry and offer it in the presence of others whom they wish to encourage to imitate them. In this, they themselves also imitate the Apostle, where he says, *Be imitators of me, as I too am of Christ* (1 Cor 11:1). So they offer their bread to the poor, openly for all to see in their work, devoted to God in their hearts. Whether they are thereby seeking admiration for themselves or glory for God, no human being can see; no human being can judge. Yet any who are prepared to imitate them with an eager good will can believe that the good they see being done is done with a devout and religious intention; and they praise God, at whose command and by whose grace they see such things being done.

So their works are open and public, so that people may see and glorify the Father who is in heaven; but their motives are in the heart, so that their giving of alms may be in secret, and the Father who sees in secret may pay them back. These people have kept the due proportion, ignoring neither admonition, carrying out each one. They take care, you see, that their justice is not performed before men. That is, they do not make it their object to be admired by men, seeing that they wished the praise for their good works to go to God, not themselves. But because this will or intention is inside their consciences, it follows that their giving of alms was done covertly in secret, to be rewarded by the one from whom nothing is hidden. Is there anybody, after all, who can reveal his heart to people when he does something in order to show with what conscious intention he does it?

As a matter of fact, brothers and sisters, the Lord weighed the very words he used carefully enough. Notice how he puts it: **Beware of performing your justice before men, to be seen**, he says, **by them** (6:1). Thus he stated the aim when he said **to be seen by them**; this aim is wrong and reprehensible, to do good just to win people's admiration, and not to look for anything further. Anyone who just does it in order to be seen by men is faulted by the Lord in this judgment of his.

In the place where he bids us to have our deeds seen by men, however, he did not state that this was the aim, so that it would simply be a matter of people seeing us and admiring us. Instead, he went on from there to God's glory, to direct our intention in doing good as far as that. **Let your works**, he said, **shine before men, so that they may see your good deeds**; but that is not what you should be looking for. For what then? He adds something else and says, **and may glorify your Father who is in heaven** (5:16). If that is what you are looking for, that God may be glorified, do not be afraid of being seen by men. Even when you are, your giving of alms is in secret, where he alone, whose glory you seek, can see that that is what you are seeking.

So it is that the Apostle Paul, after the persecutor of the gospel has been laid low and the preacher of it lifted up to his feet, can say, *But I* was *not known personally to the churches of Judea that were in Christ. But they had only been hearing that the one who used to persecute us once, now preaches the good news of the faith that he once used to ravage; and in me,* he says, *they glorified God* (Gal 1:22–24). He was not rejoicing because the man who had received the grace was getting well known, but because God who had given it was being praised.

He himself said, *If I were still pleasing men, I would not be Christ's servant* (Gal 1:10). And yet in another place, he says, *Just as I also try to please everyone in everything* (1 Cor 10:33). Here too we have the same problem. But what does he add? *Not seeking,* he says, *my own interests, but those of the many, that they may be saved* (1 Cor 10:33). That is the same as what he says in the other place, *and in me they glorified God* (Gal 1:24); also as what the Lord says, *that they may glorify your Father who is in heaven.* That, you see, is when they are saved, when in the works that they see done by men, they glorify the one from whom men received the grace to do these things.

Matthew 6:5

5 "And when you pray, you must not be like the hypocrites; for they love to stand and pray in the synagogues and at the street corners, that they may be seen by men. Truly, I say to you, they have received their reward."

(5) Origen

Our Savior often shows himself an opponent of the love of glory because it is a destructive passion. He did so here when he forbade his disciples to do what hypocrites do at the time of prayer. For hypocrites work hard at boasting of their piety or generosity before others. We must remember our Lord's saying, *How can you believe, who receive glory from one another and do not seek the glory that comes from the only God?* (John 5:44). And so we must reject the glory that comes from men, even if it may be supposed a good thing. We must, rather, seek the proper and true glory that comes only from him who glorifies the person worthy of glory. In this way the action is appropriate for God himself. . . . Thus, that very thing that is supposed to be good and praiseworthy is defiled when we act in such a way that we may receive glory from men or that we may be seen by men (cf. 6:2, 5). As a consequence, we receive no reward from God for this.

Every one of Jesus's words is without duplicity and, if pressed, we might say that they are even truer when he speaks with his usual oath.[1] And he says the same thing about those

1. That is, "Truly, I say to you . . ."

who seem to do good to their neighbor for human glory or who pray **in the synagogues and at the street corners that they may be seen by men. Truly, I say to you, they have received their reward** (6:5). For just as the rich man, according to Luke, has received *good things* in his own human *lifetime* and because he always expected to receive them, he is incapable of getting them any longer after the present life (cf. Luke 16:25). So it is the case with the man who receives his *reward* for giving something to someone or prayers for someone. If he has not done these things in the Spirit, but in the flesh, he will reap corruption and not eternal life (Gal 6:8). The man who gives alms **in the synagogues and in the streets** with a trumpet before him so that he is glorified by men reaps a reward for the flesh (6:2). So does the man who loves **to stand and pray in the synagogues and at the street corners**, that he may appear to men supposedly holy and a religious person by those who see him.

(6) Hilary of Poitiers

Beware of practicing your righteousness before the eyes of men, etc. He removes every concern about our offering [physical] things, telling us to be inspired only by a future hope. We are not to pursue the favor of others by a display of our goodness, nor to vaunt our religion by demonstrative prayer before the public. Rather, the fruit of good works must be supported within the conscience of one's faith. When the eager pursuit of human praise strives for that alone which comes from others, it will have its reward. Whereas the expectation of the one who seeks to attain God will obtain the reward of [God's] long patience.

Furthermore, **the left hand** should ignore the action **of the right hand** (6:3). But does the nature of the body permit this? Don't the functions of the hands respond to the direction of our intelligence? In order that our actions may be grounded on knowledge of God, may our understanding, when we perform those actions with our members, be a protection within us and with us.

Matthew 6:6

6"But when you pray, go into your room and shut the door and pray to your Father who is in secret; and your Father who sees in secret will reward you."

(7) Chromatius of Aquileia

When his disciples were asking our Lord and Savior Jesus Christ how they should pray, he gave them this form of prayer, which, you will also recognize, is still being used today. Listen then, beloved, to how he taught his disciples to pray to God the Father Almighty: **But when you pray, go into your private room, and with closed mouth pray to your Father.** What he calls the "private room" does not mean a secret place in a house. Rather, he is calling to mind that the secret things of our heart lie open to him alone. Having to pray with **closed mouth** means that we should with a mystical key close our heart from evil thoughts and with closed lips speak to God with a pure mind. For our God listens not to the voice but to the heart that prays in faith. Close then your heart with the key of faith against the deceits of the devil so that it lies open to God alone, for we are God's temple. He dwells in our hearts so that he may be an advocate in our prayers. The Word of God, therefore, and the Wisdom of God, Christ our Lord, has taught us this prayer that we should pray thus: **Our Father, who art in heaven** (6:9b). This is the voice of one who is freely faithful to God and faithfully free in every way. So you must live to be sons of God and brothers of Christ.

(8) Hilary of Poitiers

We are instructed to pray with the door of our room closed (6:6), and likewise taught to offer our prayer in every place since the prayers of the saints were undertaken in the midst of wild beasts, in prisons, within flames, from the depth of the sea, and from the belly of the monster.[2] We are told to enter the secret places, not of a house, but of the room of our heart. Enclosed within the privacy of our mind, we are to pray to God, not with copious speaking, but with our understanding, because every such prayer is superior to the words of our speech.

(9) Augustine

Even in this case we are not prohibited to be seen, but to act with the purpose of being seen by others. It is unnecessary to repeat the same concepts over and over again (cf. 6:7). A single rule must be observed: what should be feared and avoided is not the other's awareness of what we do, but rather our doing anything with the intention of seeking their approval as our reward. The Lord himself here employs the same expressions, adding, as the first time: **Truly I say to you, they have received their reward** (6:5), showing by this that he condemns the rewards that fools seek in human praise.

And your Father, he says, who sees in secret, will reward you. The argument had come to an end with a similar conclusion. Here, the Lord did not urge us to pray, but rather, to learn how to pray; as above, it was not alms that he recommended, but the spirit in which it should be done. He instructs us that the purity of heart is obtained only through the just and honest longing for eternal life, in a unique and pure love of wisdom.

Matthew 6:7–8

7 "And in praying, do not heap up empty phrases as the Gentiles do; for they think that they will be heard for their many words. 8 Do not be like them, for your Father knows what you need before you ask him."

2. Latin *bestia*, a reference to Jonah praying from the belly of the sea monster (Jonah 2:2).

(10) Origen

We heap up empty phrases when we fail to find fault with ourselves, or when the words we offer in prayer cover over corrupt deeds, or blameworthy words or thoughts. All this is foreign to the incorruptibility of the Lord. Whoever, therefore, heaps up empty phrases in his prayers in private is . . . on a more dangerous road than those who are at the street corners (6:5). Such a person is able to preserve not even a trace of good. According to the text of the Gospel only **the pagans** heap up empty phrases. Because they have no impression of the great and heavenly requests, they offer prayers for bodily and outward things. The person who, so to speak, dwells in the heavens and above the heights of the heavens and yet asks from the Lord for the things here below is like a pagan heaping up empty phrases.

It appears that the man who does much speaking is like one who **heaps up empty phrases**, conveying a multitude of things instead of having one object in mind. . . . Everything we suppose to be definite is split, cut up, and divided into more than one, thus losing its unity. The good is one, but shameful things are many; the truth is one, but lies are plural; true righteousness is one, but there are a host of ways of counterfeiting it; and the wisdom of God is one, but there are many wisdoms (doomed to pass away) of this age and of the rulers of this age (cf. 1 Cor 2:6). Most of all, the word of God is one, whereas a multitude of words are foreign to God.

No one therefore will escape sin when words are many. And no one who thinks he is heard, when words are many, can be heard (cf. Prov 10:19). Consequently, we must not make our prayers like those of the pagans, who heap up empty phrases, or speak with many words, or do anything at all like a serpent (cf. Ps 58:4).

The God of the saints (since he is their Father) knows what his children need (cf. 6:8), because such things are worthy of the Father's knowledge. If someone does not know God, he does not know the things of God and does not really know what he needs from God. He is entirely mistaken about what he supposes he should have. But he who has seen the good and divine things that he needs, the things known to God, such a person will receive what he has seen because it is known to the Father even before he asks for it.

(11) Jerome

This passage has in mind a misguided opinion of the philosophers, namely, that if God knows what we will pray, and before we ask he knows what we need, it is useless for us to express ourselves to the one who already knows it. The short answer to this view is that we are not relating information to God but making a petition. It is one thing to inform someone who is ignorant, and another to ask someone who knows. In the former case, it is passing on information, in the latter case, it is entrusting oneself. In the one, we bring knowledge; in the other, we humbly beg.

Preface to the Lord's Prayer

(12) Origen

I now wish to offer a meditation on this powerful prayer written by the Lord as a model. First of all, it must be observed that Matthew and Luke seem to have written down the same prayer to show us how we ought to pray. But in Matthew, the prayer has the following form: **Our Father in heaven, hallowed be your name, your kingdom come, your will be done, on earth as in heaven. Give us today our daily bread. Forgive us our sins, as we forgive our debtors. And lead us not into temptation, but deliver us from the evil one** (6:9–13). Luke's version reads: *Father, hallowed be your name, your kingdom come. Give us day by day our daily bread. And forgive us our sins, for we ourselves forgive everyone who is indebted to us. And lead us not into temptation* (Luke 11:2–4).

I must first deal with the view that thinks these two texts have a close resemblance to one another, though they are different. Others say that it is impossible that the same prayer should be spoken in two places. The first was on the mountain where, **seeing the crowds, he went up . . . and when he sat down, his disciples came to him. And he opened his mouth and taught** (5:1–2). This first version is found written by Matthew in the context of the proclamation of the Beatitudes and of the commandments that follow. The second is in *a certain place* in which *he was praying*, and *when he ceased*, he spoke the prayer to one of the disciples who asked to be taught to pray *as John taught his disciples* (Luke 11:1). How can it be that the same words were spoken in a long speech without a prior request and at the same time offered at the request of a disciple? Perhaps someone will say in reply that the prayers are essentially the same and were spoken as one prayer; on one occasion in a long address, and at another time in answer to the request of a disciple, who was apparently absent or failed to understand when the Lord first spoke the prayer in Matthew's version. On the whole, it seems preferable to suppose that the prayers are different, even though they have certain parts in common.

(13) Chromatius of Aquileia

Everything that is necessary for our faith and salvation is contained in the brief phrases of the Lord's Prayer. Here we confess that we acknowledge the Father's name; we ask that its holiness dwell in us; we pray that his kingdom come; we pray that his will be done in us; we daily pray for the earthly and heavenly bread that is the hope of our salvation; we beg for the forgiveness of our sins; we pray that serious temptation be taken from us; and lastly, we unceasingly pray to the Lord to be delivered from the evil one, who is the author of every sin. The Holy Spirit predicted through Isaiah long ago that this very thing would come to pass, saying, *For the Lord will make a brief word through the whole orb of the earth* (Isa 10:23).

Our Lord Christ offered this form of prayer (which is in today's reading and which you yourselves know quite well) to his disciples who were asking how they should pray. Listen now how he teaches his disciples to pray to God the Father Almighty: **But you, when**

you pray, go into your private room, and with closed mouth pray to your Father. What he calls the private room does not mean a secret place in a house; rather, he is calling to mind the secret things of our heart that lie open to him alone. Praying with **closed mouth** means that we should, with a mystical key, close off our heart from evil thinking and with "closed lips" speak to God with an uncorrupted mind. Our God hears the faith that prays, not the voice. Our heart, then, should be closed off with the key of faith against the deceits of the devil and lie open to God alone, whose temple we are. Because Christ dwells in our hearts, he may be an advocate in our prayers. For it was the Word of God and the Wisdom of God, Christ our Lord, who taught us that we should pray using this prayer: **Our Father, who art in heaven.**

The voice here is one of freedom and faithfulness. And that is how you should live to be sons of God and brothers of Christ. For how rash is it for someone who falls away from God's will to presume to call God his Father? So, most beloved, show yourselves worthy of divine adoption, for it is written: *Whoever believed, to them he gave the power to become sons of God* (John 1:12).

May your name be sanctified: This does not mean that God, who is always holy, may be sanctified by our prayers. Rather, we pray that his name may be sanctified in us, so that we who are sanctified in his baptism may persevere in what we have begun to be.

May your kingdom come: Does not our God already reign entirely since his reign is immortal? But when we say **May your kingdom come**, we pray for the kingdom to come to us. For it was promised to us by God, and obtained by the blood and passion of Christ.

May your will be done on earth as in heaven: That is, we are seeking that his will may be done in this way, that what God wills in heaven, we on earth may do blamelessly.

Give us today our daily bread: We should understand this to mean spiritual food. Christ, who is our bread, says, *I am the living bread who has come down from heaven* (John 6:51). We say these words daily, because we must always pray for immunity from sin to become worthy of heavenly nourishment.

And forgive us our debts, as we forgive our debtors. This precept means that we do not deserve to be forgiven unless we forgive others who sin against us, as the Lord says in the Gospel: **Unless you forgive the sins of others, your Father will not forgive your sins** (6:15).

And lead us not into temptation: That is, do not allow us to be led by the tempter, who is the author of temptation. For Scripture says, *For God is not the tempter of evil* (Jas 1:13). But the devil is the tempter, and to conquer him the Lord says, **Keep watch and pray, lest you enter into temptation** (26:41; Mark 14:38).

But deliver us from the evil one. He says this because the Apostle said, *You do not know what you are to pray* (Rom 8:26). We pray to Almighty God in such a way that our Jesus Christ himself will graciously grant us the ability, even though we are weak, to be on the watch to avoid the evil one and whatever human weakness is unable to guard against or avoid. To Christ who reigns with God be glory in the unity of the Holy Spirit through all ages of ages. Amen.

Matthew 6:9a–b

9"Pray then like this:
Our Father who art in heaven,"

(14) Tertullian

The prayer begins with a testimony to God and on the value of faith: **Our Father who is in heaven**. For we both pray to God and commend faith, whose reward is found in the very name **Father**. It is written: *To them who believed in him he gave the power, that they should be called the sons of God* (John 1:12). Although the Lord very often proclaimed God as a Father to us, he also declared that we are to call no one on earth "father" except the Father in heaven. And so, by praying in this way we are obeying his instruction. Happy are they who recognize God as their Father!

(15) Cyprian

The Gospel precepts, most beloved brethren, are nothing other than divine teachings, foundations on which hope should be built, supports for strengthening faith, sustenance for cheering the heart, rudders for guiding our way, assistance for obtaining salvation. While these precepts instruct receptive minds of believers on the earth, it leads them to heavenly kingdoms. There are many things God willed to be said and heard by means of his servants, the prophets. But how much greater are those things that the Son speaks, the Word of God who was in the prophets, giving testimony with his own voice. No longer is he commanding us to prepare the way for his coming, but he himself is coming and opening and showing us the way, so that we, who once were wandering in the darkness of death (Isa 9:2) without understanding and formerly blind, have been enlightened by the light of grace, holding to the way of life, with the Lord as our ruler and guide.

These are his beneficial admonitions and divine precepts by which he directs his people for their salvation. He also gave us a model for prayer, advising and instructing us for what we should pray. He who made us alive also taught us to pray with the same kindness that he willed to give [us life].

For what can be a more spiritual prayer than what is given to us by Christ, by whom also the Holy Spirit was given to us? What request to the Father can be more truthful than what the Son delivered to us out of the very mouth of the one who is the truth (John 14:6)?

Since we have an advocate with the Father for our sins (1 John 1:9), let us, as sinners petitioning on behalf of our sins, express the words of our advocate. For since he says that *whatsoever we shall ask of the Father in his name* (John 16:23b) he will give us, how much more effectually do we obtain what we ask in Christ's name, if we ask for it using his own prayer?

Before everything else, our teacher of peace and instructor of unity does not want prayers to be made singly and individually with the result that a person may pray only for himself. For we don't say "My Father, which art in heaven," nor "Give me this day my daily bread." Nor should anyone ask that only his own debt be forgiven him. Nor should anyone request for himself that he alone may not be led into temptation or delivered from evil. Our prayer is public and common; and when we pray, we do not ask for the individual, but for the whole people, because we are all one people. The God of peace and the teacher of harmony, who taught unity, willed that everyone should pray in this way for all, just as he, himself, brought us all into one (cf. John 17:21).

(16) Gregory of Nyssa

When our Lawgiver, the Lord Jesus Christ, brings us to divine grace, he does not do so at Mount Sinai covered with darkness and smoking with fire (cf. Exod 19:16–19; Heb 12:18–24). Nor does he strike fear into us by the meaningless sound of trumpets. He does not purify the soul by three days' chastity and by water that washes away dirt (cf. Exod 19:12–15). Nor does he leave the whole assembly (as Moses did) behind at the foot of the mountain (Exod 19:23–24), allowing only one to make the ascent to its summit, which was hidden by a darkness completely concealing the glory of God.

Instead, he leads us, not to a mountain, but to heaven itself, which the Lord has rendered accessible to men by virtue. Furthermore, he gives us not merely visions of the divine power (cf. Eph 1:19), but a share in that power, bringing us, as it were, to kinship with the divine nature. He does not hide his supernal glory in darkness, making it difficult for those who want to perceive it. Rather, he illumines the darkness by the brilliant light of his teaching and then grants **the pure of heart** (cf. 5:8) the vision of his ineffable glory in shining splendor.

Our Father who art in heaven. The words seem to indicate a deeper meaning, since they remind us of the fatherland from which we have fallen and of the noble birthright that we have lost. In the story of the young man who left his father's home and went away to live after the manner of swine (Luke 15:15–16), the Word shows the misery of humanity in the form of a parable, which tells of the young man's departure and dissolute life. And he does not bring him back to his former happiness until he has become fully conscious of his present plight and entered into himself, rehearsing words of repentance. Now these words agree, as it were, with the words of the prayer, for he said, *Father, I have sinned against heaven and before you* (Luke 15:21). He would not have added to his confession the sin against heaven, if he had not been convinced that the country he had left when he sinned was not heaven. This confession, therefore, gave him easy access to the father who ran toward him and embraced and kissed him (Luke 15:20c). And thus, the return of the young man to his father's home became to him the occasion to know the Father's great love. For this paternal home is the heaven against which, as he says to his father, he has sinned.

In the same way, it seems that if the Lord is teaching us to call upon the Father in heaven, he wants to remind you of our beautiful fatherland. And by putting into your mind stronger things, he sets you on the path toward your original country.

(17) Origen

In light of the words, **Our Father in heaven**, it seems fitting to look at what is said in the Old Testament very carefully and see whether any prayer may be found in it calling God "Father." Up to the present time, I have looked as carefully as I can, though I have not found any instance. I do not mean that God was not ever called Father or that those who believed in God were not called sons of God. But nowhere have I found in a prayer the boldness proclaimed by the Savior in calling God "Father." It is often possible to see God called Father and those who have drawn near to the Word of God as sons. For example, it says in Deuteronomy, *You have deserted God who begot you and have forgotten God who nourishes you* (Deut 32:18) and again, *Is he not your Father who possessed you and made you and created you?* (Deut 32:6), and again, *Sons, in whom there is no faith* (Deut 32:20). And in Isaiah, *I have begotten sons and raised them up, but they have rejected me* (Isa 1:2).

If, therefore, we understand what the verse as written in Luke means, *When you pray, say, Father* (Luke 11:2), we shall hesitate to offer this address to him if we have not become genuine sons, so that we would not be guilty, in addition to our other sins, of the charge of impiety. *Everyone who is born of God* (cf. 1 John 3:9; 4:7) and does not sin because he partakes of God's seed, which turns him away from all sin, through his deeds says **Our Father in heaven**. The Spirit bears witness with their spirit that they are *children of God*, his *heirs*, and *fellow heirs with Christ*, when by suffering with him they hope with good reason to be glorified with him (cf. Rom 8:16–17). Thus they do not say **Our Father** in some partial sense, since such people add their works to their heart, which is the fount and origin of good works and which believes to righteousness, while the mouth joins in harmony and confesses to salvation (cf. Rom 10:10).

Therefore, let us not suppose that the Scriptures teach us to say **Our Father** at any given time of prayer. Rather, if we understand the earlier discussion in terms of *praying always* (1 Thess 5:17), let our whole life be a constant prayer in which we say **Our Father in heaven**, and let us keep our citizenship (Phil 3:20), not on earth at all, but in every way in heaven, the throne of God. For the kingdom of God is established in all those who bear the image of the Man from heaven (cf. 1 Cor 15:49) and have thus become heavenly.

Matthew 6:9c

"Hallowed be thy name."

(18) Origen

In Matthew and Luke, when we are commanded to say **hallowed be your name**, the implication of the text is that the name of the Father has not yet been hallowed. For someone might say, how could anyone think that the name of God could be hallowed as if it had not been already hallowed? Let us consider then the meaning of the **name** of the Father and of its hallowing.

A name is a designation that sums up and describes the particular quality of the one named. For example, Paul the Apostle has a certain quality all his own, of soul by which he is what he is, of mind by which he can perceive certain things, and of body by which he looks a certain way. The special character of these qualities is indicated by the name "Paul" since no one else is exactly like Paul in these respects. In the case of human beings, since their unique qualities are subject to change, it is understandable that in Scripture their names are sometimes changed. When the identity of "Abram" was changed, he was called "Abraham" (Gen 17:5). And "Simon" was changed to "Peter" (Mark 3:16; John 1:42). And when "Saul" stopped persecuting Christ, he was named "Paul" (Acts 13:9). In the case of God, however, who is himself unchangeable and always remains unaltered, there is a single name—the one spoken of him in Exodus, "I AM" (Exod 3:14). From this we learn that our conception of God should be that he is holy. We see his holiness in that he creates, oversees us in his providence, judges, chooses, forsakes, welcomes, turns away, determines who is worthy of reward, and punishes each one according to his deeds.

For in these activities and those like them, it seems to me the unique character of God is found, which is what we suppose the "name" of God means in the Scriptures. For example, in Exodus, *You shall not take the name of the Lord your God in vain* (Exod 20:7). And in Deuteronomy, *Let my speech be expected as rain, and let my words come down as dew, as the gentle rain upon the tender grass, and as the showers upon the herb, for I have called upon the name of the Lord* (Deut 32:2–3). And in Psalms, *They will remember your name in all generations* (Ps 45:17). Whoever connects the idea of God to actions that are not fitting takes *the name of the Lord in vain* (Deut 5:11; Exod 20:7). On the other hand, who is able to utter speech *like rain*, which works together with those who hear it, producing fruits in their souls, and which gives encouraging words *like dew*—bringing extremely profitable *gentle rain* in words resulting in the edification of the hearers, that is, most effectual showers—this person can do all this because of the **name**. For he understands that he needs God to bring all this to perfection and calls God to his side as the true provider of the things I have mentioned. . . .

Just as the one who prays must understand what is being said here and ask that the name of God be hallowed, so also in the Psalms it is said, *Let us exalt his name together* (Ps 34:3). The prophet [i.e., the psalmist] commands us to be in complete harmony with the same mind and to strive for the true and lofty knowledge of the unique character of God. This is what it means to exalt the name of God together. . . .

With regard to the wording **hallowed be your name** and the following petitions, which are in the imperative mood, it must be said that quite frequently the translators used imperatives instead of optatives. For example, in Psalms, *Let* the lying lips *be* dumb, which speak lawlessness against the righteous (Ps 31:18) instead of "may they be." Or, *Let the creditor search out all that he has, let him have no protector*, in Psalm 109 about Judas (Ps 109:11–12). For the entire psalm is a request that certain things may happen to Judas. But some do not realize that the verb "become" in the imperative mood does not always signify a wish, but sometimes must be understood according to its form as a true imperative. And in the case of God, it is foolish for someone to pray for him to become *hallowed*. Thus, the verses in our text are imperatives.

(19) John Chrysostom

Concerning the one who calls God "Father," it is appropriate to ask nothing before one prays for the glory of the Father, and to regard everything else secondary to the work of praising him. For **hallowed** means "glorified." For he is perfect in his own glory, and that remains the same forever. However, he commands us when we pray to seek to give him glory by our lives. This is the very thing he had said before, **Let your light so shine before men, that they may see your good works, and glorify your Father which is in heaven** (5:16). So too, the seraphim give glory to God: *Holy, holy, holy* (Rev 4:8). **Hallowed** then means "glorified." That is, "grant, we beseech you, that we might live lives of such purity, that all may glorify you through us." This is what is meant by *perfect self-control*: to present a life so blameless that every one who sees it may offer to the Lord the praise due to him.

Matthew 6:10

10**"Thy kingdom come.**
Thy will be done,
on earth as it is in heaven."

(20) Tertullian

Next comes **Thy will be done in heaven and on earth.**[3] It is not that there is anything that prevents God's will from being accomplished, and we are praying that he succeed in carrying out his will. No, what we are asking is that his will be done in all things. Using a figurative interpretation of "flesh" and "spirit," we are "earth" and "heaven." Even if the verse should be understood in its plain sense, the point of the prayer is still the same: that his will be done in us **on earth**, as it is able to be done **in heaven**. What does God wish other than that we should walk according to his teaching? We pray, therefore, that he may provide us with the means and opportunity of doing his will, such that we may be saved both in heaven and on the earth. For the whole point of his will is the salvation of those whom he has adopted.

There is also the will of God that the Lord accomplished in preaching, and in the performing of works and in his perseverance. Since he declared that he was doing the will of the Father, not his own will (John 6:38)—without doubt the things he did were the Father's will—by his example we are now urged to preach, perform works, and persevere even unto death. This we can accomplish only through the will of God.

3. In most of the older Latin versions of the Gospel, the comparative "as" is lacking in this verse.

(21) Cyprian

The next words in the prayer are these: **Thy kingdom come**. Here we ask that the kingdom of God may be manifested to us, just as we seek that his name may be sanctified in us. For when does God not reign, or when does the kingdom of the one who has always been and has no ending begin? We pray that our kingdom may come, the kingdom promised to us by God and obtained by the blood and passion of Christ, so that we who are first as his subjects in the world, may hereafter reign with Christ in his rule, as he himself promises and says, **Come, ye blessed of my Father, receive the kingdom that has been prepared for you from the beginning of the world** (25:34).

One should also say that Christ himself can be the kingdom of God, for we desire daily that he will come, that it be manifested to us soon. For since he is himself the resurrection, because in him we rise again, so also the kingdom of God is understood to be himself, because in him we shall reign. So we rightly seek the kingdom of God, that is, the heavenly kingdom, to contrast it with an earthly kingdom. But the one who has already renounced the world is greater than its honors and its kingdom. And the one who declares himself for God and for Christ, desires not earthly, but heavenly kingdoms. Let us be in continual prayer and supplication that we not fall away from the heavenly kingdom.

(22) Origen

It is clear that he who prays for the coming of the kingdom of God rightly prays that the kingdom of God may be established, bear fruit, and be perfected in him (cf. 13:23). Every saint who is ruled by God as his King and obedient to God's spiritual laws, as it were, lives within himself as in a well-ordered city. The Father is present to him, and Christ reigns with the Father in the soul that is perfect according to the words that I mentioned earlier: *We will come to him and will make our dwelling* (John 14:23). And I think that the kingdom of God may be understood as the blessed condition of the governing mind and the right ordering of wise thoughts. By the **kingdom** of Christ, the saving words reach those who hear, and the works of justice and the other virtues are accomplished. For the Son of God is himself the Word and Justice.

Thy will be done on earth as it is in heaven. We might ask how is the will of God done in heaven where there are *spirits of wickedness* (Eph 6:12), on whose account *the sword of God will be stained with blood even in heaven* (Isa 34:5)? If we pray that the will of God be done on earth as it is in heaven, are we not inadvisably praying that there remain on earth hostile spirits that dwell in the heavens? For many places of the earth become wicked because they are conquered by the *spirits of wickedness that are in the heavenly places* (Eph 6:12).

But if we understand **heaven** allegorically and maintain that it stands for Christ and **earth** stands for the Church (for who is worthy to be the throne of the Father except Christ? And what can be compared to the Church as a footstool for the feet of God [cf. Isa 66:1]?), we will easily solve the difficulties raised here. We claim that each member of the Church should pray that he might accomplish the will of the Father and accomplish it perfectly (John 4:34). By being *joined to him we can become one spirit* with him (1 Cor 6:17) and consequently accomplish the will of God so that it will be fulfilled **on earth as it is in heaven.** He who is *joined to the Lord*, according to Paul, is *one spirit* (1 Cor 6:17). This interpretation, if considered carefully, cannot be easily dismissed.

And perhaps when our Savior says we should pray that the will of the Father be done on earth as it is in heaven, he is not telling us to pray that those physically on earth should become like those who are in heaven. Rather, by enjoining this prayer, the Lord wills that all beings on the earth, that is, those of the lower kind or earthly, should become like them whose citizenship is in heaven and have become fully all heavenly. For the sinner, wherever he may be, is on earth. If he does not repent, he will pass somehow to that which he is most alike. But he who does the will of God by obeying his saving and spiritual laws, is in heaven.

(23) Gregory of Nyssa

Thy kingdom come. What is there that is not subject to the power of God, who, as Isaiah says, holds the whole heaven in his palm (Isa 40:12), who compasses the earth, whose hand rules nature, and who embraces what has been created in the world and above the world? But if the name of God is always holy, and nothing escapes his powerful dominion, and, if he rules all things, and nothing can be added to his holiness (since he is in all things absolutely perfect) what does it mean to pray **Hallowed be thy name, thy kingdom come**? Perhaps by using such form of prayer the Word intends to set forth something like this: namely, that human nature is too weak to achieve anything good, and that we can obtain nothing for which we are anxious unless the good be accomplished in us by divine aid. Of all good things the most important is that God's name should be glorified through one's life. But perhaps our meaning will become clearer if we start from the opposite end of the argument. . . .

Now since man's nature was deceitfully led astray from the discernment of the good, the inclination of his free will was directed to the opposite and his life subjected to every base thing. His nature was mixed up with death in a thousand ways, for every form of evil is, as it were, a way of death for him. Since we are hard pressed by such tyranny and become slaves to death through the assaults of the passions, which attack us like executioners and enemies in war, we rightly pray that the kingdom of God may come to us. We cannot escape the wicked dominion of corruption unless the life-giving power overcomes the rule of death that governs us.

So if we ask that the kingdom of God may come to us, the meaning of our request is this: I ought to be a stranger to corruption and liberated from death. I should be freed from the shackles of sin and death should be no more lorded over me. Let us not be tyrannized by evil so that the adversary may prevail against me and make me his captive through sin.

Matthew 6:11

[11]**"Give us this day our daily bread;"**

(24) Tertullian

How gracefully has divine Wisdom constructed the order of this prayer so that after heavenly matters, that is, the name of God, the will of God and the kingdom of God, he should also include a place for prayer about earthly necessities! Indeed, the Lord also had taught us, **Seek first the kingdom, and then these things will be added to you** (6:33; Luke 12:31). Although we say, **Give us today our daily bread,** we understand the phrase in a spiritual way. For Christ is our **bread**, because Christ is our life and the bread of life: *He said I am the bread of life* (John 6:51) and a little above, the bread is the Word of the living God who *comes down from heaven* (John 6:33). Then, too, it is written that his body is esteemed in bread: **This is my body** (26:26; Mark 14:22; Luke 22:19). By praying for **our daily bread** we are seeking that Christ be perpetually in us and we be inseparable from his body. But even when the word "bread" is used in a physical sense, it has a religious meaning and spiritual sense. For the Lord instructs us to pray for bread, for that is all that is necessary for believers, while the nations seek **after all these other things** (6:32). Moreover, he justly added, **Give us this day**, because he had taught earlier, **Do not worry about tomorrow, what you shall eat.**[4]

(25) Origen

Give us today our daily bread or, in Luke's version, *Give us day to day our daily bread.* Since there are some who suppose that we are told to pray for physical bread, we need to refute their false opinion and establish the truth concerning "daily bread." So ask them: How can the one who says we must ask for heavenly and great things say we need to ask for bread to sustain our bodies? It would be as though he had forgotten his own teaching and ordered us to offer supplication to the Father for an earthly and small thing. For the bread given for our body is not heavenly, nor is it a great thing to pray for it.

Now I shall follow the teacher himself and shall bring forward what he certainly teaches about bread. In the Gospel of John, he says to those who came to Capernaum to seek him, *Truly, truly, I say to you, you seek me, not because you saw signs, but because you ate your fill of the loaves* (John 6:26). The one who has eaten of the loaves blessed by Jesus and been filled by them seeks rather to comprehend the Son of God more accurately and seek after him. That is why he rightly gives the command. *Do not labor for the food that perishes, but for the food that endures to eternal life, which the Son of Man will give to you* (John 6:27). . . .

He says, *My Father gives you the true bread from heaven. For the bread of God is he who comes down from heaven and gives life to the world* (John 6:32–33). The true bread is that which nourishes the true Man, *made in the image of God.* And the one who has been

4. The reference seems to be to Matt 6:34 (Luke 12:29), which is later, not earlier, in the text.

nourished by it will come to be *in the likeness of him who created him* (cf. Gen 1:26–27; Col 3:9–10). And what is more nourishing to the soul than the Word, or what is more precious to the mind of him who makes space for it than the Wisdom of God? What more fitting for our rational soul than truth?

Not everyone can be nourished by the solid and vigorous food of divine teaching. That is why, when he wishes to offer food for an athlete, which is suitable for the more perfect, he says, *The bread that I shall give for the life of the world is my flesh* (John 6:51), and a little further on, *Unless you eat the flesh of the Son of Man and drink his blood, you have no life in you; he who eats my flesh and drinks my blood has eternal life, and I will raise him up at the last day. For my flesh is true food, and my blood is true drink. He who eats my flesh and drinks my blood abides in me, and I in him. As the living Father sent me, and I live because of the Father, so he who eats me will live because of me* (John 6:53–57). This is the true food, the flesh of Christ, who existed as the Word and became flesh according to the verse *The Word became flesh* (John 1:14). And when we eat and drink him, he also has dwelt in us (cf. John 1:14). And when he is distributed (cf. John 6:11), the verse is fulfilled: *We have beheld his glory* (John 1:14). *This is the bread that came down from heaven, not such as the fathers ate and died; [he who eats this bread] will live forever* (John 6:58).

In the preceding discussion, we saw that the bread that we should ask for is a spiritual bread. It is therefore necessary to understand Being in the same sense as the bread, since the physical bread distributed to the body of the person nourishes it and goes into his being. So also *the living bread that came down from heaven* (John 6:51) and is distributed to the mind and the soul gives a share of its own power to the person who eats from it. And thus the bread we ask for will be **daily** in the sense that it will be "for our being." Therefore, **daily bread**, that is, "bread for being" (cf. John 6:48), is what corresponds most closely with that rational nature in a person and is most similar to [God's] Being. Since the Word of God is immortal, it shares its own immortality with the one who eats it.

Therefore, the one who partakes of "daily bread for our being" is strengthened in his heart and becomes a son of God (cf. Ps 104:15; Jas 5:8; 1 Thess 3:13). If this is so and there is such a difference between foods, there is one that stands out above all the others mentioned. This is "the daily bread for our being," about which we should pray that we will be made worthy of it. Nourished by God the Word, who was in the beginning with God (cf. John 1:1), we may be made divine.

(26) Augustine

Daily bread means everything that is required to sustain this life. The Lord referred to this daily bread saying, **Do not think about tomorrow** (6:34), and so he added, "Give it to us today." It may also be a reference to the sacrament of the body of Christ, which we receive every day; or to the spiritual nourishment about which the Lord said: *Labor for the food that does not perish* (John 6:27), and again: *I am the bread of life that came down from heaven* (John 6:41). But we can examine which of these three is the most likely meaning.

As far as the sacrament of the Lord's body . . . the Lord has given us a form of prayer, a prayer to which we cannot add anything without transgression; nor can we take anything away. However, who would dare argue that we should recite the Lord's Prayer only once? Or that, in case we recite it two or three times, it may only last until the time we participate in the body of the Lord, and not for the rest of the day? Because then we could not say **Give us this day** in reference to something we have already received, and anyone could require us to receive this sacrament at the end of day.

It remains, therefore, that we understand it as spiritual bread, that is, as the Lord's commandments that every day you should meditate on and observe. The Lord alluded to these when he said: *Do not labor for the food that perishes* (John 6:27). But this food is called daily now, as this mortal life will continue through the succession of days and nights. In fact, the affections of the soul are alternately up and down, that is to say, sometimes as spiritual thoughts, sometimes as carnal inclinations; as if being alternately satiated with food and pressed by hunger, the soul needs a daily bread even more in order to stave off hunger and restore her weakened forces. Just as our body, as it is in this life that precedes its final transformation, rebuilds itself with food when it runs out of energy, so our soul rebuilds itself with the nourishment of God's commandments when, as it were, it depletes its temporary emotional energy in its strife after God. And so, when the Lord said **Give us today**, he meant, while it is still called *today* (cf. Heb 3:7; 4:7), that is to say, for the duration of this finite life. Since in the life to come we will be satisfied with spiritual food for eternity, there will be no reason to speak about our **daily bread**. There, the rapid motion of time happening day to day—and so, we say today—will no longer exist.

Matthew 6:12

12 **"And forgive us our debts,**
as we also have forgiven our debtors."

(27) Cyprian

Following the petition that we be supplied bread, pardon of sin is also sought, so that the one who is fed by God may live in God. This is sought not only for the present and temporal life, but for the eternal life also, which we may enter if our sins are forgiven. These sins the Lord calls "debts," as he says in his Gospel, **I forgave you all that debt, because you asked me** (18:32). How necessarily, how providently and beneficently, we, who are sinners, are admonished! We are compelled to pray for our sins so that, while pardon is sought from God, the soul reminds itself of its sin. No one should flatter himself by thinking he is innocent. For if one exalts himself in this way, he will be all the more ruined. So we are instructed and taught that we sin daily and are told to pray daily for our sins. John, also in his epistle, warns us saying, *If we say that we have no sin, we deceive ourselves, and the truth is not in us; but if we confess our sins, the Lord is faithful and just to forgive us our sins* (1 John 1:8–9). . . . John says the Lord is faithful to forgive sins, keeping faith with his promise. He who taught us to pray that our debts and sins may be forgiven has promised that the Father's mercy and pardon will follow.

(28) Origen

And forgive us our sins, as we forgive our debtors, or in Luke's version, *And forgive us our sins, for we ourselves forgive everyone who is indebted to us.* Now concerning debts, the Apostle says, *Pay everyone their debts, taxes to whom taxes are due, fear to whom fear, revenue to whom revenue, honor to whom honor. Be indebted to no one in anything, except to love one another* (Rom 13:7–8). We are truly indebted, since we have certain responsibilities not only in giving, but also in gentle speech and in certain kinds of disposition toward others. Since we are indebted in these ways, either we pay what is ordered by the divine law, discharging it in full, or we do not pay up because we despise the wholesome Word and so remain in debt. . . .

If we are in debt to so many people, it is inevitable that there are people indebted to us. Some are in our debt as men, others because we are citizens, others because we are fathers or sons. In addition, wives are in debt to us if we are husbands, and friends if we are friends. It is only right, therefore, that whenever any of our many debtors are lax about paying what they owe us, we should act kindly toward them by not holding a grudge. For we remember our own debts and how often we have put them off, not only when they are owed to others, but even when they are owed to God himself. For if we remember the debts we have not paid, but have refused to pay when the time came to do one thing or another to our neighbor, we will be gentler toward those liable to us who have not paid their debt. This will be especially so if we do not forget our transgressions against God or highlight wicked practices in lofty terms (cf. Ps 73:8), whether we do so through ignorance, or the truth, or because of our unhappiness with some set of circumstances.

Those who have sinned against us must be forgiven when they claim to repent, even if our debtor does this many times. For it says, *If your brother sins against you seven times in the day, and turns to you seven times and says, "I repent," you must forgive him* (Luke 17:3–4). And we should not act harshly to those who repent. Rather, such people are evil to themselves, for he who ignores instruction hates himself (Prov 15:32). In the case of such people, healing must be sought in every way possible, even for the person so completely perverted that he is not even conscious of his own evils and is drunk with a drunkenness more deadly than that caused by wine, namely, the drunkenness that comes from the darkness of evil (cf. Prov 20:1; Isa 28:1; Matt 24:49).

(29) Gregory of Nyssa

As our inquiry progresses, it comes to the very peak of virtue; for the words of the prayer outline what sort of person one should be if one would approach God. Such a person is just barely revealed in terms of human nature, but is likened to God himself through virtue. He seems to be divine because he does those things that God alone can do. The forgiving of debts is the special prerogative of God, since it is said, *No man can forgive sins but God alone* (Luke 5:21; Mark 2:7). If a person imitates the characteristics of the divine nature with his own life, he becomes like that which he visibly imitates.

This we are told plainly in the present passage. If we approach the Benefactor, we should ourselves be benefactors, if we go to him who is good and just, we should ourselves be the same. Because he is forbearing and kind, we should also be forbearing and kind, and so with all the other things. For he is benign and gentle, he communicates good things and dispenses mercy to everyone—to all these qualities, and whatever else we may see in the divine Being, we should be assimilated by our free will. Thus a man should obtain the confidence presupposed by the prayer.

(30) Augustine

Perhaps you are going to say in your swollen, puffed-up hearts, "Could we actually say that we are just? Of course we had to say, for the sake of humility, that we are sinners." So for the sake of humility you tell a lie? You [claim that you] are righteous, you are without sin; but out of humility you say you are a sinner. How can I accept your evidence as a Christian in someone else's case, when I have caught you giving false evidence against yourself? You are just, you are without sin, and you say you have sin. So you are bearing false witness against yourself.

God does not accept your lying humility. Examine your life; take a look at your conscience. So you are just, but you cannot do other than say you are a sinner? Listen to John. He will repeat to you what he also said so truly earlier on: *If we say*, he says, *that we have no sin, we deceive ourselves and the truth is not in us* (1 John 1:8). You do not have any sin, and you say that you do have sin; the truth is not in you. Because John did not say, "*If we say we have no sin*, humility is not in us"; but he said, *we deceive ourselves and the truth is not in us*. So we are lying if we say that we have no sin. If John was afraid of lying, are you not afraid of lying, by saying you are a sinner when in fact you are just? So how can I accept you as a witness in anyone else's case, when you lie in your own case? You make the saints guilty, when you give false evidence against yourself. What are you going to do to someone else, if you smear yourself? How can anyone else avoid your false accusations, when you make your own self guilty with your lying tongue?

For the moment, let us leave aside John's words. Here we are in the body of the Church, which you say has no stain nor wrinkle nor any such thing, and is without sin. Here's the hour of prayer coming, the whole Church is going to pray, and you indeed are outside. Come to the Lord's Prayer, come to the scale of virtue, come and say: *Our Father, who are in heaven*. Carry on: *hallowed be your name. Your kingdom come. Your will be done, as in heaven, also on earth. Give us today our daily bread*. Carry on, and say, *Forgive us our debts*. Answer, Mr. Heretic, what are your debts? Did you perhaps receive a loan of money from God? "No," he says.

So I am not questioning you any further about that because the Lord himself is going to explain what the debts are from which we are asking to be released. So let us say what comes next: *As we also forgive our debtors*. Let the Lord explain this: *For if you forgive people their sins*—so your debts are sins—*your Father too will forgive you your sins*. So come back, Mr. Heretic, to the prayer, if you have grown deaf to the true import of the faith. *Forgive us our debts*; do you say it, or do you not? If you do not, then even though you should be present in the body, you are still outside the Church.

This is the Church's prayer; it is the voice coming from the Lord's own magisterial chair. It was he who said, **Pray like this** (6:9–14); he said to the disciples **Pray like this**. He said it to the disciples, said it to the apostles, said it to us—whatever sort of little lambs we are—he said to the rams of the flock, **Pray like this**. Notice who said it, and to whom he said it: Truth to the disciples, the Shepherd of shepherds to the rams: **Pray like this: Forgive us our debts, as we too forgive our debtors**. The King was speaking to his soldiers, the master to his slaves, Christ to his apostles. Truth was speaking to men, the Most High to the humble: "I know what's going on in you; I am weighing you up, I am reading you off from my scales, I can undoubtedly say what is going on in you; I know this much better than you do. Say, **Forgive us our debts, as we too forgive our debtors**.

Matthew 6:13

13 **"And lead us not into temptation,
but deliver us from evil."**

(31) Origen

The petition, **but deliver us from the evil one**, is omitted by Luke. If the Savior orders us to pray for things that are not impossible, it seems worthwhile to ask how we are commanded to pray not to enter into temptation, when all our life on earth we are faced by temptation. We are in temptation because we dwell on earth, surrounded by flesh that rages against the Spirit since the mind of the flesh is hostile to God and can in no way submit to God's law.

Let us pray, therefore, to be delivered from temptation not by avoiding temptation (for that is impossible for those on earth), but by not being defeated when we are tempted. Now I suppose that the person defeated in temptation enters *into* temptation, since he is caught fast in its meshes. The Savior entered those meshes because of those who had been caught in them before.

We must pray not that we be not tempted (for that is impossible), but that we not be overwhelmed with temptation, which is what happens to those who are enmeshed in it and conquered. It is also said apart from this prayer not to enter into temptation (Luke 22:40; Matt 26:41; Mark 14:38). The verse can probably be clearly understood from the previous discussion. And in the prayer we must say to God the Father, **Lead us not into temptation**. So it is worth asking how God should be understood as bringing someone, who has not prayed or who has not been seduced, **into temptation**. Since someone who enters into temptation is conquered, it is absurd to suppose that God leads anyone into temptation as if he were giving him up to be conquered. And the same absurdity remains no matter how we interpret the verse, *Pray that you may not enter into temptation* (Luke 22:40). For if falling into temptation is an evil we pray not to suffer, is it not foolish to think that the good God, who cannot endure evil fruit (7:18), relegates anyone to evil?

Now the use of temptation is something like this. What our soul has received escapes everyone's knowledge but God's—even our own. But a clearer knowledge of oneself becomes evident through temptations. In knowing ourselves, we are also conscious—if we are willing—of our own evils. We give thanks for the good things that have been made evident to us through temptations. The fact that the temptations that come to us are meant to show us who we are, or to acknowledge the secret things in our hearts, is established by a verse in Job spoken by the Lord and by one in Deuteronomy. They read, *Do you think that I have answered you for any other reason than that you may be revealed as righteous?* (Job 40:8 [LXX]). And in Deuteronomy, *he humbled you and let you hunger and fed you with manna, and he led you so that you might know what was in your heart* (Deut 8:2–3, 16).

(32) Chromatius of Aquileia

This petition meant that we should not allow ourselves to be led by the one who tempts, who is the author of temptation. For Scripture says, *For God is not the tempter of evil* (Jas 1:13). But the devil is the tempter. To conquer him, the Lord says, **Keep watch and pray, lest you enter into temptation** (26:41; Mark 14:38).

But deliver us from the evil one. He tells us this because the Apostle said, *You do not know what you are to pray* (Rom 8:26). Hence we must pray to Almighty God in such a way that whatever we are unable to guard against or avoid because of our humanity, our Lord Jesus Christ himself will graciously grant us the ability, who lives and reigns as God, in the unity of the Holy Spirit through all ages of ages. Amen.

(33) John Chrysostom

And lead us not into temptation, but deliver us from the evil one. For yours is the kingdom, the power and the glory, forever. Amen.[5] In this he clearly instructs us that we are unworthy and represses our conceit, teaching us to decline contests and not rush into them so that our victory will be all the more glorious and the devil's defeat more ridiculous. You see, if we are forced into it, we must stand firm. Whereas, if the call does not come, it is time to hold our peace and await the time of engagement so as to give evidence both of freedom from vainglory and of nobility. Now, by **the evil one** here he refers to the devil, bidding us wage a war against him that allows of no truce. And he is bringing out that the devil is not like that by nature, evil being one of the things that comes not from nature, but

5. The earliest and most complete New Testament manuscripts of Matthew do not include **For yours is the kingdom, the power and the glory, forever. Amen.** Luke's version of the Lord's Prayer makes no mention of it, nor do most of the later Greek and Latin writers when citing the prayer. It is quite possible that the doxology was variably added to the original prayer after the fashion of Jewish prayers. This is what we find in the late-first- or early-second-century document known as the *Didache*: "so let your Church be brought together from the ends of the earth into your kingdom. For yours is the glory and the power through Jesus Christ forever" (9.4). There are other variations of the doxology in documents roughly contemporary to the *Didache* (2 Clement 20.12: "to whom be glory and majesty forever and ever. Amen"; 1 Clement 61.3: "Through him be the glory and the majesty to you now and for all generations and forevermore. Amen"). By Chrysostom's time, the doxology was recited after the Lord's Prayer in some liturgies.

from choice. In a particular way, the devil gets this name on account of the excess of his wickedness and because, though in no way wronged by us, he wages war against us with no allowance for a truce. Hence he does not say "Deliver us from the evil ones" but **from the evil one**. Likewise, he instructs us not to be at odds in any way with our neighbors because of the trouble they bring on us, but to redirect our enmity from them to the one who is the source of all our troubles.

Now having put us on battle alert by mention of the foe, and cutting away all our indifference, in turn he encourages us and lifts our spirits by recalling the King under whom we serve, presenting him as more powerful than anyone: **Yours is the kingdom, the power, and the glory.** If his be the kingdom, then, there is no need to fear anyone, there being no opposition capable of dividing his empire.

(34) Augustine

So we see that the three earlier petitions—**Hallowed be thy name; thy kingdom come; thy will be done, as in heaven, also on earth**—are forever. The four that follow, though, belong to this life. **Give us today our daily bread**; are we going to go on asking for our daily bread every day, when we arrive at that total satisfaction? **Forgive us our debts**; will we be saying that in that kingdom, when we will not have any debts? **Bring us not into temptation**; will we be able to say it then, when there will not be any temptation? **Deliver us from evil**; will we say it, when there will not be any to be delivered from?

So these four are necessary because of our daily life, the other three because of eternal life. But let us ask for them all, so that we may reach that life; and here let us beg, in order not to be cut off from it. This prayer is to be said by you every day once you have been baptized. This Lord's Prayer, you see, is said every day in the church at God's altar, and the faithful hear it. So I am not afraid of our not remembering it very exactly; even if some of you cannot keep hold of it very perfectly, you will keep hold of it by hearing it every day.

Matthew 6:14–15

14"For if you forgive men their trespasses, your heavenly Father also will forgive you; 15but if you do not forgive men their trespasses, neither will your Father forgive your trespasses."

(35) Tertullian

In a few brief words, how many statements of the prophets, evangelists, and apostles, how many utterances of the Lord in parables, examples, and discourses, are touched upon! How many obligations are likewise expunged! One finds the honor of God in the Father, the witness of faith in his name, the offering of willing obedience, the remembrance of our hope in the kingdom, the prayer for life in bread, the confession of our debts in earnestness, the concern over temptation by seeking protection. What is so amazing? God alone is able to teach us how he wishes us to pray. By him, therefore, the mode of prayer has been ordained and vivified by his Spirit. Even as it came forth from the divine mouth by his prerogative, it rose unto heaven commending to the Father what the Son taught.

(36) Cyprian

The Lord has clearly conjoined and added the law by which our condition and activity are bound. We too seek the forgiveness of our debts according to the way we ourselves forgive our debtors, knowing that what we seek concerning our sins cannot be obtained unless we ourselves have done the same for those who sin against us. For this reason, he also says in another place, **By whatever measure you have measured, you will be measured by this** (7:2; Mark 4:24). Remember the servant who, after all his debt was forgiven by his lord, would not forgive his fellow servant and was thrown into prison (cf. 18:23–35). Because he would not grant anything to his fellow servant, he lost what had been granted to him by his lord. These are the principles that Christ has established even more strenuously in his teaching by a stern rebuke. *When you stand*, he says, *for prayer, forgive whatever you may have against anyone, so that your Father who is in heaven may also forgive your sins. If you will not forgive, however, neither will your Father who is heaven forgive you of your sins* (Mark 11:25–26). There remains no excuse for you on the day of judgment when you will be judged according to your own sentence. Whatever you have done, you yourself will suffer for it. For God instructs us to be peaceable, and in agreement (cf. 18:19), and of like mind in his house. Just as he brings about our first birth, so he wishes us to continue in our rebirth so that we who have become sons of God may remain in the peace of God. Because we should also have one soul and mind, God does not accept the sacrifice from those who are in discord. He commands us to be reconciled with our brother before returning to the altar (cf. 5:23–24), so that God may be appeased by prayers offered in harmony. Our peace and brotherly concord is more important to God than sacrifice. This is a people united by means of the Father and the Son and the Holy Spirit.

(37) Augustine

The number seven, the number of the Beatitudes, also seems to be consistent with the number seven, out of which the whole speech has originated. If indeed it is the fear of God that makes the poor in spirit blessed **because theirs is the kingdom of heaven**, let us pray that *the name of God may be holy among all people through holy fear, enduring forever and ever* (Ps 19:9).

If it is godliness that makes the meek blessed, because they will inherit the earth, ask that the kingdom of God comes both in ourselves so that we become meek and do not resist him, and from heaven to earth in the splendor of the coming of the Lord, because of which we will rejoice and be glorified, for it says, *Come, you who are blessed of My Father, inherit the kingdom prepared for you from the foundation of the world*

(25:34). *My soul,* says the prophet, *will be glorified in the Lord; may the humble hear and rejoice* (Ps 34:2).

If it is knowledge that makes those who mourn blessed, for they shall be comforted, ask that God's will be done on earth as in heaven. Once the body as the earth is subjected to the spirit as heaven, in full and perfect peace, we will weep no more. In fact, the only reason we mourn here is this inner struggle that forces us to say, *I see a different law in my members, warring against the law of my mind,* and to testify our grief with tearful voice, *Wretched man that I am! Who will set me free from the body of this death?* (Rom 7:23–24).

If it is courage that makes those who hunger and thirst for virtue blessed, becasue they will be satisfied, let us pray that we be given our daily bread this day, so that we could achieve full satiation being sustained and strengthened by it.

If the merciful are blessed because of prudence, because they themselves will have mercy, let us **forgive debts** to our debtors and pray that our debts are forgiven to us. If the pure in heart are blessed because of discernment, for **they shall see God,** pray for not being led into temptation, for fear of having a dual heart striving after the temporal and severed from the eternal, instead of pursuing the true good by which we should measure all our deeds. In fact, the temptations from the things that seem oppressive and harmful to men have no power over us, if we are not overpowered by the results of indulging into those things that are generally considered good and enjoyable.

If the peacemakers are blessed because of wisdom, for they shall be considered **the children of God,** let us ask God to be delivered from evil. Indeed, that deliverance will make us free, that is, it will make us the sons of God, so that we could address him *Abba, Father* (Rom 8:15), by virtue of our adoption in the Spirit.

It must be carefully noted that among these seven forms of prayer taught by the Lord there is one to which he has drawn our attention. This is the prayer that has to do with the forgiveness of sins and his desire to make us merciful, which is the only way to escape our troubles. Indeed, in no other prayer do we pray in such a way as if we were bargaining with God, since we say: "Forgive us just as we ourselves forgive." If we do not observe this condition none of our prayers bears fruit.

Matthew 6:16–18

16"And when you fast, do not look dismal, like the hypocrites, for they disfigure their faces that their fasting may be seen by men. Truly, I say to you, they have received their reward. 17But when you fast, anoint your head and wash your face, 18that your fasting may not be seen by men but by your Father who is in secret; and your Father who sees in secret will reward you."

(38) Hilary of Poitiers

Whenever you fast, do not put on a gloomy face as the hypocrites, for they neglect their appearance in order to be seen fasting by men. He teaches us that the benefit of fasting is gained without the outward display of a weakened body, and that we should not curry the favor of the pagans by a display of deprivation. Instead, every instance of fasting has the beauty of a holy exercise. For oil is the fruit of mercy according to the heavenly and prophetic word.[6] Our head,[7] that is, impurities on our face are washed off so that no one is appalled by its disheveled appearance. There is, however, a greater grace of [his] radiance in our encounter [with God]: once we are purified for the clarity of a good conscience and have been anointed with oil for the grace of works of mercy, our fasting commends us to God. Even when we shun the attention of others by fasting with our heads anointed, we will be more pleasing and be acknowledged.

The impurities on our face are washed off so that no one is appalled by its disheveled appearance. There is, however, a greater grace of [his] radiance in our encounter [with God]: once we are purified for the clarity of a good conscience and have been anointed with oil for the grace of works of mercy, our fasting commends us to God. Even when we shun the attention of others by fasting with our heads anointed, we will be more pleasing and be acknowledged.

(39) Chromatius of Aquileia

But you, when you fast, anoint your head and wash your face so that you do not appear to others to be fasting, but to your Father who is in secret. We should cover the work of fasting, its bodily and spiritual affliction, with an expression of happiness. This we learn from historical examples of the holy past. For the most holy Judith, afflicted with great sorrow for her people, fasted solemnly for three days, then anointing her head and washing her face, covered the sadness of her inner affliction with such that her appearance of joy seemed to her enemies to be rejoicing. By covering her fasting with a face of joy, she won a triumphant victory over the enemy (cf. Jdt 12–13). Likewise, after the most holy Esther confused the king for three days by her fasting, sorrow, and affliction, she then washed her face, washed and anointed her head, putting an end to Haman, that most wicked enemy of her people (cf. Esth 5). What can we say of Daniel and the three youths who abstained, while many youths were fed with royal food, and were found to look more healthy than any of the others (cf. Dan 1:12–15)?

Although we have spoken of the literal meaning of this passage, we ought also to give attention to its spiritual sense signified in the anointing of the head. To anoint the head of your neighbor is to do a work of mercy. Such mercy to the poor refers to the Lord, whom the Apostle calls the head of a man. In the Lord's own words, **Whatever you have done for the least of these, you have done for me** (25:40). In alternative to this mercy as a divine restoration, we are filled, as it were, with a kind of heavenly oil by the one who says, **Blessed are the merciful, for God will show them mercy** (5:7). Holy David also recognizes the anointing of the head with this heavenly oil, when he says, *as oil on the head that goes down into the beard* (Ps 133:2). Washing of the face signifies the cleansing of the body and the purity of a sincere conscience.

6. Cf. Ps 44:8 Vg. (Ps 45:7).
7. The head is the part anointed with oil.

So to wash the face means to show forth the face of our heart and the cleansed conscience itself, free from all the filth of sin and squalor of vice, so that we may inwardly rejoice with heavenly joy and the happiness of the Holy Spirit. It is then, when we fast for God in faith rather than for others, we receive from God, who knows the hidden things, the reward of eternal repayment. The Lord says this: **so that you do not appear to others to be fasting, but to your Father who is in secret. And your Father who is in secret will repay you.** Therefore, if you want to carry about a head that is always anointed, and have the face of your heart clean in accordance with the Lord's saying, persist faithfully in works of mercy, continue dutifully in fasting, so that you may be worthy to please the Lord, to whom is glory in ages of ages. Amen.

(40) Theodore of Heraclea

Now the Lord calls it hypocrisy to make oneself appear gaunt on account of self-conceit. For we should understand that such anointing and washing is not according to the letter, but refers to a cheerful expression by which we attempt to forget that we are, in fact, fasting. His words are an indictment against the love of glory, which clings like filth to the soul and must be washed away. It is necessary, rather, for the one guiding the soul to cleanse it through the practice of virtue, and thereby wash the intelligible eyes of the face and make them keen for higher things. By mentioning the more important members of the body, he indicates the purity of the soul. For the face signifies those senses that the understanding uses for the service of good or evil. The Lord wants us to wash these senses by abstaining from evil and to cleanse by practicing good.

Matthew 6:19–23

19"Do not lay up for yourselves treasures on earth, where moth and rust consume and where thieves break in and steal, 20but lay up for yourselves treasures in heaven, where neither moth nor rust consumes and where thieves do not break in and steal. 21For where your treasure is, there will your heart be also.

22"The eye is the lamp of the body. So, if your eye is sound, your whole body will be full of light; 23but if your eye is not sound, your whole body will be full of darkness. If then the light in you is darkness, how great is the darkness!"

(41) Augustine

This passage is to be interpreted in such a way as to help us understand that any of our actions are honest and pleasing before God only if they are carried out with a heart of integrity, that is, in a supernatural aspiration toward the fulfillment of love, because *love is the fulfillment of the law* (Rom 13:10). The **eye** here means the same intention that directs all our actions. If it is pure and right, and aiming at the goal that is to be reached, then the actions we do with that intention will necessarily be good. These works as a whole are called **the whole body**. The Apostle associates some actions that he disapproves with bodily members, and so he orders us to irradiate these actions: *Put to death therefore your members that are upon the earth: fornication, uncleanness, avarice* (Col 3:5), and the like.

So you should consider not only the action that takes place, but also the intent behind it. And this provision is called **light** in us, because it shows us that we should act with good intentions, *for all that is made manifest is light* (Eph 5:13). Indeed the actions themselves that we do for other humans have an uncertain outcome, and, therefore, the Lord has defined them as darkness. In fact, when I give money to a beggar who asks me for it, I know neither what he will do with it, nor what the results will be for him. It may happen that he puts the money to a poor use or brings something bad upon himself with it, something I neither wanted nor intended when I gave it to him. So, then, if I acted with good intent and with an awareness of my good intent for this action, it is called **light**: my action is illuminated whatever the outcome. And this outcome, precisely because it is uncertain and unknown, has been considered **darkness**. If, however, I acted with bad intent, light itself becomes darkness. Everyone is aware of the intentions behind their actions, even if these intentions are evil; but even light becomes darkness, when your undivided intention is not directed above, but rather it falls down, almost like a shadow of a divided heart. **If then the light that is in you is darkness, how great is the darkness!** That is to say, if the conscious intention of your heart that drives your actions is spoiled and blinded by the desire of the earthly and the transient, how much more vile and obscure is the action itself, even if its result is uncertain! And if what you do with an intention that is neither pure nor right benefits another person, it is not the benefit, but the way you yourself acted that will be imputed to you.

Matthew 6:24

24 "No one can serve two masters; for either he will hate the one and love the other, or he will be devoted to the one and despise the other. You cannot serve God and mammon."

(42) Philoxenus of Hierapolis

While it is possible for those in the world to be made righteous, it isn't possible for anyone to reach perfection because the world, having its own righteousness and the righteousness of the law that operates within it, are obstacles to perfection. No one is able to follow after two different ways and be perfected in two different virtues while he is in the world. For this reason, the commandments were established and set apart for those who journey in the world so that they might obtain their salvation through them. These commandments also defined another path of perfection, a path that is above the world.

It was the will of Christ, the Lawgiver, that ordained all people to progress in the way of the angels and not turn aside from the example of renouncing the world. He thus established the difference between two ways. But because they weren't capable of renouncing the world and he wanted all men to be saved, he gave various commandments for their salvation. The Lord placed steps and degrees within his teaching, not because steps and degrees existed but because of those who would receive them, and because of their need of them, without which they could not be saved. According to the way of the world, the rule of law is applied, whereas in the way apart from the world lies perfection. The way of the world comes to ruin in [things], whereas the way of the perfection begins in the renouncement of everything.

As long as a man possesses worldly wealth, whether it is a little or a lot, he is unable to progress in the way of perfection, because wealth, true to its nature, becomes a chain to the spirit and a weight on the mind, which means they cannot take flight along the way to heaven.

The one who possesses wealth necessarily contemplates on it, and the one who contemplates on wealth cannot contemplate about God. Even if there is an occasion that brings God to his mind, it is not lasting, since it's not possible to keep God in mind when he is fixed on his possessions. Or if he imagines that he is keeping God in mind, it is a feigned remembrance and not true. For it is not possible that these two remembrances should hold together at the same time in the soul. . . .

There is that man who isn't able to serve God worthily while in the world. Because he is rich and wealthy, the word of our Redeemer himself addresses him: **You cannot serve God and mammon.** To such a person and all who are like him it must seem that the door of righteousness was shut in his face, because they cannot be wholly free from the care of riches. And according to the cutting word of Christ (cf. Heb 4:12), whosoever cares for riches cannot care about God.

I think this word should be understood in reference to those who are mature in faith. It is clear that the man who cares for riches cannot care for God. But there are those who possess wealth who are justified by another measure of the justice worked in the world. This kind of man is not a servant who worships his riches, but a master of the things he possesses. Some men are slaves of their possessions, and some are masters of their wealth, and one man is enhanced by his possessions, and another man worships them. Now the word of our Lord was spoken to the person who is a slave of his possessions and is unable to be a servant of God. So you see that the Lord presented two masters in his discourse, and to explain who these were, he said, **You cannot serve God and mammon.**

Whoever has made mammon his master cannot serve God but will serve that master whom he has chosen of his own freewill. Service to this master is especially dear to him, and that master's dominion over him is beloved because he has become subjected to him of his own freewill. For the children of men tend to love dearly that which they have chosen of their own freewill. And this they will love much more than him who is naturally, and in truth, Master over them. Those few wealthy men who have pleased God, or who please God, do so because they are masters of their wealth. They sent it forth to do everything like a slave and a subject, sometimes to feed the hungry, sometimes to clothe the naked, sometimes to redeem the captive, sometimes to pay vows and offerings to God, and sometimes to free those who were in the bondage of debt. Wherever someone is master of his wealth, he sends it out like a servant, as did Abraham, and Isaac, and Jacob, and Job, and Joseph, and David, and Hezekiah. Of these men, some were rich, some were princes, and some were kings, and as a group they were all owners of great possessions and wealth. They were, however, masters of their riches; they were not ruled by their riches. Their riches worked for them in all the good things they wished to do, and they did not serve these riches according to the wicked demands of mammon.

(43) Chromatius of Aquileia

Whoever loves the Lord God with all his heart will necessarily hate the devil and his deeds. And whoever commits evil works loves mammon or the devil, since he acts by his own will, cannot love God, whose precepts he despises. A person who loves God, and in faith is ruled by heavenly grace, cannot be called a servant of the devil. In the same way too, one who is a slave to sin subjects himself to diabolical domination and is not worthy to have God as Lord. The Lord therefore says, **It is not possible to serve God and mammon**, which shows that we cannot serve both God and the devil, that is, God, the author of mercy, and the devil, the ruler of mammon and greed. The Apostle shows us this as well when he says, *What fellowship has light with darkness?* (2 Cor 6:14). Mammon is the devil and the author of mammon. One calls us to mercy, the other to greed; one calls us to life, the other to death; one to salvation, the other to perdition. To which of these two should we submit? Surely to the one who invites us to life, not to the one who hands us over to death.

Matthew 6:25–26

25"Therefore I tell you, do not be anxious about your life, what you shall eat or what you shall drink, nor about your body, what you shall put on. Is not life more than food, and the body more than clothing? 26Look at the birds of the air: they neither sow nor reap nor gather into barns, and yet your heavenly Father feeds them. Are you not of more value than they?"

(44) Hilary of Poitiers

Is not your life more than food and the body more than clothing? In all the preceding words, Jesus had enjoined contempt for the world and confidence in the future. When he commanded us to be open to insult, and willingly to accept loss, and to be indifferent about taking revenge, and indiscriminate about those we love, and unconcerned for human glory, he was urging us to set our hopes courageously on eternal gain. Both the love of present things and anxiety about things to come foster uncertainty in many people, either captivating them by enticements, or confounding them through their disbelief. He wants us, therefore, to put our hope, without any of the ambiguity of an uncertain will, in the kingdom of heaven, which the prophets announced, John preached, and our Lord declared was found in himself. If faith is doubtful, how can there be justification by faith? Otherwise, there is no justification by faith, if faith itself becomes doubtful. For this reason, the Lord instructs us to have no care about clothing or about food, for life is more valuable than nourishment and the body more valuable than food.

(45) Jerome

Are you not worth much more than they? The Apostle taught that we should not be wiser than we are. For there are some interpreters who are attempting to surpass the limits of the fathers and fly up to the heights, plunge into the depths and say that the birds of the air are the angels and other powers in God's service, who, without any care, are borne up by God's own providence. If they want to understand it in this way, how can what is said after this—**Are you not worth more than they?**—apply to humans? It must, therefore, be taken to mean simply this: if birds, without worry or misfortune are borne up by God's providence—creatures who are here today and gone tomorrow, whose soul is mortal and will cease to exist when they die—how much more will human beings, to whom eternity has been promised, be directed by God's will?

(46) John Chrysostom

For the present, then, let us put aside idle luxury and be content with moderation. Let us learn to acquire by honest labor all that we possess. For the blessed John (the Baptist) told the tax collectors and soldiers to be content with their wages (Luke 3:14). Though he wanted to lead them to higher things, he settled for less because they were not ready for it. If he had mentioned what was more elevated than these, they would not have paid attention and would have not reached the other. Hence learn to apply yourself to lesser things. We realize that at present the burden of voluntary poverty is too heavy for you, and heaven is no more distant from the earth than such a life is from you. So let us lay hold if need be of the lowest commandments, for this is no small encouragement. Some of the pagans have actually achieved it, if not with the proper intention, and have divested themselves of everything. In your case, however, we are content if you give alms generously. If we start in this way we shall quickly move on to better things.

Matthew 6:27–34

27 “And which of you by being anxious can add one cubit to his span of life? 28 And why
are you anxious about clothing? Consider the lilies of the field, how they grow; they
neither toil nor spin; 29 yet I tell you, even Solomon in all his glory was not arrayed like
one of these. 30 But if God so clothes the grass of the field, which today is alive and to-
morrow is thrown into the oven, will he not much more clothe you, O men of little faith?
31 Therefore do not be anxious, saying, 'What shall we eat?' or 'What shall we drink?' or
'What shall we wear?' 32 For the Gentiles seek all these things; and your heavenly Father
knows that you need them all. 33 But seek first his kingdom and his righteousness, and
all these things shall be yours as well.

34 “Therefore do not be anxious about tomorrow, for tomorrow will be anxious for
itself. Let the day's own trouble be sufficient for the day."

(47) Hilary of Poitiers

By the weight of these examples [e.g., lilies and grass], he encourages the unshakeable assurance of our faith. Inasmuch as doubt holds great danger, so the heavy weight of anxiety seizes every occasion of disbelief. Grass is not produced to be thrown into the fire, nor does God have special concern about clothing that will be burned up. Rather, under the name of grass, we find that God frequently designated the pagans (cf. Ps 37:2; Isa 40:6; 1 Pet 1:24). They are like a plant that, after it has lost the blossom of its vitality, withers in the heat of the sun. Thus there will be given no rest to the pagans, nor will the onset of death bring the peace they desire. Instead, their bodies are destined to suffer eternally, for their punishment will be physical. What they undergo, along with everything else destined for eternity, will have no end. If pagans are given a body destined for eternity in order to suffer the fire of judgment, how great is the impiety of those saints who doubt the glory of eternity, since eternal punishment is assured to sinners!

The Lord expects all our hopes will be placed in the certainty of his promises and in the power of his might, in order that, having ceased to worry about what we lack, we should look forward to receiving all things from him, from whom our very life had its beginning. We should seek the kingdom of God through the service of our life. And this is the reward for those who live a righteous and perfect life: to be transformed from the corruptible matter of this body into a new and heavenly substance; for earthly corruption to be changed into heavenly incorruption (1 Cor 15:50–53). It follows that the pagans, in their unbelief, are anxious about their affairs since they are captured by the love of this age and absorbed in the delights of the body. They do not seek nor desire the way to the heavenly kingdom through faith and praise of God.

God forbids us to be anxious about the future. Release from worry through indifference is not negligence, but faith. Why should we be anxious about tomorrow when tomorrow is anxious for itself? Therefore, the anxious day itself dispels our worries for us. But worry, as I think of it, is a sentiment unique to human beings; for worry provokes this feeling on account of concern, fear, or sorrow. But a day's segment is a lapse of time, and only those who have obtained foreknowledge undergo a sense of anxiety. A "day" thereby must be construed as a living creature that is wary, keeps watch, and frets, and its own evil is sufficient to itself without the addition of sin heaped up from elsewhere. And when one is [inwardly] burdened with sin, nothing further need be added to someone so impaired. But the nature of things does not suppose that the state of our mind should be determined by a day. For the day has its own worries, and its own evils suffice for it. Since we are prohibited from being anxious about tomorrow, everything [that concerns us] is contained by the significance of the heavenly words. We are instructed not to have doubt about what is to come. There are enough evils in our life, and the sins in which we live daily are sufficient that all our preoccupation and effort may be engaged with purging of and expiation for these [evils and sins]. If we should lose confidence in future good, we would be guilty of unforgivable disbelief. Once our worry has come to an end, those future things that had preoccupied us will give way to the good things bestowed on us by God's goodness. On that day we will no longer be anxious.

(48) John Chrysostom

For if he is indeed our maker, then he knows perfectly our needs. So you cannot say, "He is indeed our Father, and the things we seek are necessary, but he does not know we need them." He who knows our nature itself, and was the framer of it, and formed it such as it is, should also know its needs better than we do. There is no question that we are needy.

Let us not, therefore, be anxious because we gain nothing by tormenting ourselves. Since he gives us all things whether we think about them or not. But which is the better of the two? What do we gain by anxiety, except to impose on ourselves unnecessary suffering? When we are traveling to a bountiful feast, do we worry about getting necessary food? Or if walking by a fountain are we anxious about getting a drink? Seeing we have a supply more abundant than any fountain or number of banquets, that is, God's providence, let us be neither beggars nor petty minded.

Together with what has been said, the Lord gives us yet another reason for confidence about such matters when he says, **Seek ye the kingdom of heaven, and all these things shall be added unto you.** Once he has set the soul free from anxiety, he mentions heaven. For, in truth, he came to do away with the old things and to call us to a greater country. He is able, therefore, to deliver us from unnecessary things and from our affection for the earth. This is the context of his saying, **the pagans seek after these things**, that is, those who labor solely for the present life, who have no regard for the things to come, nor any thought of heaven. But for you these present things are not the most important. For we were born not for this end, that we should eat and drink and be clothed; our end is to please God, and attain his good things to come. As we recognize that things here are secondary in our labor, let us also act as if they are secondary. For this reason he also said, **Seek the kingdom of heaven, and all these things shall be added unto you.**

Notice that the Lord did not say, "shall be given," but **shall be added**, so that we might learn that present things are not the greatest part of his gifts in comparison with the things to come. Accordingly, he encourages us not to ask so fervently for these things. But when we ask for other things, we can have confidence that these will be added to them. Seek then the things to come, and you will receive the things present also. Do not seek the things that are seen, and you will certainly obtain them. Indeed it is unworthy to approach your Lord for such things. And you, who ought to spend all your effort and care for those unspeakable blessings, greatly disgrace yourself by being consumed with the desire of transitory things.

But you might ask, did he not tell us to ask for bread? And yet, he stated, **daily bread**, and moreover it was only for **this day**, which is the same thing. For he did not say, "To take thought," but, **Take no thought for tomorrow**. Both of these afford us liberty, allowing us to fasten our soul on those things that are most necessary for us.

(49) Augustine

When we seek first the kingdom of God and his righteousness, that is to say, when we put them above everything else to the point of looking at everything as a means to acquire them, then we need not be afraid to miss what is necessary in this life to achieve the kingdom of

God. Earlier the Lord said, **Your Father knows that you need all these things.** So, having said: **Seek first the kingdom of God and his righteousness,** he did not add, "Then seek these things since they are still a necessity." He said instead: **And all these things shall be added unto you.** In other words, these necessities will reach you if you seek them without putting yourself in trouble; provided that, while seeking them, you are neither diverting yourselves from the goal in any way, nor establishing yourselves two goals: first, the kingdom of God for God's own sake, and then these necessary things. Rather, you should seek these necessities more eagerly for the sake of the kingdom of heaven. In this case you will not miss out on these necessities. The reason is that you cannot serve two masters: it is like a person is trying to serve two masters who desires both the kingdom of God and material things, seeing equally great assets in them. You can neither have a pure eye, nor serve God as the sole master if you fail to evaluate all other things, even the necessary ones, exclusively in relation to this one, namely, to the kingdom of God.

Matthew 7

Chapter 7 brings us to the close of Jesus's address to his disciples on the mountain. Jesus now warns against making judgments on others, while explaining at the same time how one should make judgments. The ancient writers saw no contradiction in the first two verses. He is warning against finding fault with another when one commits the same sin, or, against making judgments without knowing the intention of the doer. Some commonsense advice is added, such as waiting for one's anger to abate before taking action (Caesarius), or not judging hastily, because judgments made in haste are often unjust (Augustine). We must realize that when we pray to God in faith, what we receive will be given according to God's wisdom.

The way of the wide gate *and the way of the* narrow gate *are strongly reminiscent of the Jewish tradition of "two ways," found in the Didache and the Epistle of Barnabas: one way leads to death, the other to life. The wide gate is easy and avoids suffering for Christ; the narrow way involves fasting and hardship. The Christian is to see himself on a journey that takes him through this world, but not as a citizen of it. So Caesarius says that, as we live in this earthly pilgrimage, we long for the country of heaven. In the meantime, by living righteous lives, we demonstrate that we are not of this world.*

Through the wide gate also come false prophets. Augustine, remembering his own mistake of spending nine years with the Manichees, who promised him special knowledge and insight, states that we should first of all "beware of those who promise the wisdom and the knowledge of the truth they do not possess." Merely claiming the name of the Lord is not a substitute for the truth and purity of life. False prophets are easily exposed by the way they live. The true prophet knows that whatever gifts of power he exercises are dependent upon God's goodness. We show our gratitude to God when we "avoid every evil, and submit to heavenly instruction with all our heart. . . . By such service we may be known to God and pursue what the Lord desires rather than what brings glory to ourselves" (Hilary of Poitiers). Gregory (the Great) puts it well, "Materials dealing with external or corporeal matters sometimes demonstrate holiness, but they do not create it."

Matthew 7:1–5

**1"Judge not, that you be not judged. 2For with the judgment you pronounce you will
be judged, and the measure you give will be the measure you get. 3Why do you see the
speck that is in your brother's eye, but do not notice the log that is in your own eye? 4Or
how can you say to your brother, 'Let me take the speck out of your eye,' when there is
the log in your own eye? 5You hypocrite, first take the log out of your own eye, and then
you will see clearly to take the speck out of your brother's eye."**

(1) Hilary of Poitiers

God utterly rejects every element of judging, nor does he allow a place for it at all. Yet the latter part of the verse appears to be opposed to the former when it states: **By whatever judgment you have judged, it will judge you**, while it says above: **Do not judge, lest you be judged.** Is it not appropriate to accept the decision of a good judgment? Indeed he declares that we should be judged according to the terms of our judgment and that everyone should be measured by the terms he has used to measure [another]. There will never be a righteous judgment if there is no judging at all. But as it was already acknowledged much earlier, there is nothing in the words of God that is treated lightly or in vain, and in this case too, every word goes beyond the understanding of pagan ears. In effect, God has forbidden that his promises should be judged. Just as judgments among men are founded upon uncertainties, so we must not annul a judgment that is contrary to God on the basis of the doubt of someone's thought or opinion, and that deeply repels us, so that we may be more confident about our [own] faith. If there is sin that corresponds to our having made a wrong judgment, we are surely guilty in this instance for casting judgment upon God.

Why do you notice the speck in your brother's eye and not notice the plank in your eye? In what follows the Lord taught that only blasphemy of the Spirit will be beyond pardon, whereas there will be leniency for all other sins according to the generosity of God. A sin against the Spirit is to deny the fullness of power to God and to abrogate the eternal substance in Christ, through whom God came into man, so man will become as God.

(2) John Chrysostom

The Lord says elsewhere, *Reprove, rebuke, exhort* (2 Tim 4:2) and, *Rebuke those who sin publicly* (1 Tim 5:20). Christ said to Peter, **go and tell him his fault, between you and him alone** (18:15), but if he refuses to hear you, bring another with you, and if he does not yield even then, tell it to the church (18:15–17). Note that he has appointed many to correct us, and not only to correct, but also to punish. The reason is that whoever refuses to listen, the Lord commands him to be regarded **as a pagan and a publican** (18:17). Note too that the Lord gave his disciples the keys (16:19). The reason is that, if they are not supposed to judge, they will have no authority, and they would have received the power to bind and to loose in vain.

Furthermore, Paul did not absolutely command the Corinthians not to judge, but not to judge their superiors, nor to make judgments on unsubstantiated grounds, nor to refrain from correcting those who sin (1 Cor 4:5). The Lord was in no way rebuking everyone without distinction, but any disciple that was doing so to their teachers was the object of his reproof; and they who, being guilty of innumerable sins, bring an evil report upon the guiltless.

Thus we are told, **first take the log out of your own eye**. Notice that he does not forbid judging but commands us first to remove the log out of our own eye before setting right the action of the rest of the world. Obviously, each one of us knows about his own affairs better than those of others. Each of us sees the more important things rather than the less, and loves himself more than his neighbor. Therefore, if you make judgments out of concern for others, I urge you to care for yourself first, since your sin is both more certain and greater. If you overlook yourself, it is quite evident that you are not judging your brother with concern, but you judge out of enmity, hoping to expose his fault. If your brother ought to be judged, it should be done by someone who did not commit the sin in question, not by you.

(3) Augustine

There are two cases in which we must avoid rash judgment: when we are not sure what was the intention behind an action, and when we don't know for sure what kind of person the man who appears good or bad today will become tomorrow. If, for example, a man complains of stomach discomfort in order to avoid fasting, and you do not believe him and attribute his unwillingness to fast to the vice of overeating, you are judging rashly. You are also judging rashly in case you become aware that a man indulges in food and drink habitually and condemn him as if he had no chance of correction and improvement. So let us not criticize the actions when the intention behind them is unknown to us; likewise, let us not criticize the actions whose intentions are obvious, as if we doubted any possibility of an improvement. This way we will avoid the judgment, of which the text says: **Do not judge so that you will not be judged.**

However, you may be surprised by these words: **For in the way you judge, you will be judged; and by your standard of measure, it will be measured to you.** Since "measuring" means "judgment" in this context, does it imply that, if we judged rashly, God would also judge us rashly? Or, if we measured by an unjust measure, does it mean that God would likewise have an unjust measure for an assessment of our action?

Not at all. God neither judges rashly nor gives recompense to anybody unjustly. What this language means is that the same recklessness with which you punish another necessarily becomes your own punishment. One might suppose that injustice damages those against whom it is directed without any harm for the one who executes it. On the contrary, often injustice does no harm to the one who suffers the indignity, while it inevitably hurts those who do it. In fact, what harm was done to the martyrs by the injustice of their persecutors? Instead, this injustice did much harm to the persecutors themselves. Even though some of them were later converted, their wickedness still blinded them while they were persecutors. Similarly, a rash judgment often does no harm at all to the one who is being judged with rashness, but this rashness itself inevitably harms the one who judges rashly. I believe that this is the principle behind these words: **Whoever strikes with the sword will die by the sword** (26:52).

The Lord warns us about rash and unfair judgment in this passage because he wants us to act with honesty in heart and with God alone in mind every time we act. There are many actions accomplished with an unclear intent, and judging them is rash. But most prone to rash judgments about uncertain matters and quick to reprehend are those who love to blame and condemn more than they do to emend and correct.

(4) Caesarius of Arles

Why do you see the mote in the eye of your brother, but do not see the beam in your eye? You have seen a man to be angry suddenly; do not continue to judge him, but wait for a little while; perhaps he may quickly soften as quickly as he gets angry. Let us point out, however, what the mote and beam signify. The mote is sudden anger, and when it is prolonged over a long time (and nursed through hatred by false suspicions), it becomes a beam. The mote, therefore, is for one to get angry but also appeased quickly; anger continually held in the heart is the beam. Therefore, the long-standing anger is converted into the beam. With what arrogance does the man who holds hatred in his heart presume to judge another man, in whose eye he recognizes not a beam but a mote to exist? For the mote destabilizes the eye of the heart, whereas the beam blinds it. What I have said, brothers, I ought to prove from the testimony of the Scriptures. As to how the anger of the heart destabilizes the eye, listen to the psalmist declaring: *My eye is disturbed*, he said, *before my wrath* (cf. Ps 6:7).[1] Concerning how hatred blinds the eye of the heart, John the Evangelist attests: *He who hates his brother*, he says, *is in the darkness, and walks in the darkness, and he does not know where he goes; because the darkness has blinded his eyes* (1 John 2:11). According to these passages, therefore, the eye of the heart is unsettled through sudden irascibility and the light of charity is extinguished through hatred.

Matthew 7:6

6"Do not give dogs what is holy; and do not throw your pearls before swine, lest they trample them under foot and turn to attack you."

(5) Jerome

The pig that rolls about in a mud-hole wears no ornament, and according to the proverb of Solomon, *If she has a golden ring, she shows herself more foul* (Prov 11:22). Some would understand **dogs** to mean those who, after coming to faith in Christ, return to the vomit

1. RSV: "My eye wastes away because of grief."

of their sins, while **swine** are those who have not yet believed in the gospel and wallow in the mud of unbelief and sins. Such people cannot believe the pearl of the gospel immediately because they are likely to despise it, and turn away, and begin to destroy those who are faithful.

(6) John Chrysostom

Do not give dogs what is holy; and do not throw your pearls before swine. Later on in the Gospel, someone will point out that the Lord also commanded, **What you have heard whispered, proclaim upon the housetops** (10:27). But these statements are not contradictory. For in the second passage, he did not command them to tell all men, but only those to whom it should be spoken and to do so with boldness. In the first passage, **dogs** are figuratively described as those who are living in incurable wickedness with no hope of change for the better. And by **swine**, he signifies those whose lives are continually unchaste. Neither group is worthy of hearing such things. Paul also, it may be observed, declared this when he said, *But a natural man receives not the things of the Spirit, for they are foolishness unto him* (1 Cor 2:14). In many other places, he also says that one who lives a corrupt life cannot receive the more perfect teaching. So he commands that doors not be opened to them, since they become more insolent after some learning. The wise and receptive recognize revealed things as holy, but the dull only venerate what is unknown. So Jesus is saying that, because some are unable to learn, let things be hidden from them. For at least out of ignorance they may show reverence. The swine do not know what a pearl is. Therefore there is no point in showing it to them because they only trample underfoot what they do not know.

(7) Augustine

When we address the commandment that forbids us to **give holy things to dogs** and **to cast our pearls before swine**, we should carefully examine what is meant by a **holy** thing, by **pearls**, **dogs**, and **swine**. A holy thing is the one we cannot violate or defile without committing a crime, and this crime is attributed exclusively to our intention and disposition, while the holy thing itself remains inviolable and incorruptible. Pearls are all the great spiritual values that should be held in high regard, because they are both hidden in a recess, and, in a sense, originate from the deep; they are found under the cover of allegories, comparable to open conch shells. This interpretation is, therefore, acceptable. A holy thing and a pearl can be considered one and the same reality: a holy thing is such because it should not be defiled, and a pearl because it should not be trampled. You are trying to defile something when you want to destroy its integrity. On the other hand, you trample something when you consider it vile, and, as it were, inferior to yourself. In this sense, a stepped-on object is a trampled object. Along the same lines, dogs rush to tear into pieces the object they assault, thus tearing apart what they don't want to leave whole. And so the Lord tells us, **Do not give a holy thing to dogs**, because even if you cannot tear and profane a holy thing, and it remains intact and inviolate, it's still important to think about those who resist with bitterness and extreme hostility seeking to destroy it to the best of their abilities.

Any impurity whatsoever has its origin in the attachment to worldly things, that is to say, in the love of this world, which we are commanded to give up in order to be pure. So whoever wants to have a pure and serene heart should not feel guilty keeping a certain truth a secret, in case this truth is beyond comprehension for the person from whom the secret is held. But this is not to say that lying is permissible: keeping the truth hidden does not entail lying. We must therefore first attempt to remove barriers that prevent understanding. If it is uncleanness that prevents understanding, we must purify it by word and deed, as far as we can.

While we find that our Lord said some things that many of his listeners rejected with resentment and contempt, you should not assume that he gave **holy things to dogs or cast pearls before swine**. He did not speak for those listeners who could not understand, but for those who could, and who were right there in the audience.

Matthew 7:7–8

7"Ask, and it will be given you; seek, and you will find; knock, and it will be opened to you. 8For every one who asks receives, and he who seeks finds, and to him who knocks it will be opened."

(8) Augustine

The Lord urges us to ask, to seek, to knock, when he says, **Ask and you shall receive; seek and you shall find; knock and it shall be opened to you. For everyone who asks receives, and who seeks shall find, and to the one who knocks it shall be opened.** These words first and foremost confront us with the following question, which we will solve as best we can. We know that many people ask and don't receive, they seek and don't find, and they knock and are not opened to. So how can it be said that everyone who asks receives? All this, you see, though it seems to be said three times and in three words, boils down to one petition: Ask, seek, knock, it all amounts to asking. We can tell this from the conclusion of the passage, where he says, **If you, bad though you are, know how to give good gifts to your children, how much more will your Father who is in heaven give good things to those who ask him?** (7:11). He doesn't say "to those who seek and knock," but he includes all three in one when he says **to those who ask**.

So why do many people ask and not receive, if **everyone who asks receives**? Or are we wrong in thinking that we ask and don't receive? Apart from the daily examples we all know about, Scripture itself testifies that the Apostle Paul asked that the angel of Satan should depart from him, and he didn't receive his request (cf. 2 Cor 12:7).

Then we discover that the bad have asked and received, while the good asked and didn't receive. What, after all, could be worse than demons? And yet they asked for the pigs and got them (cf. Mark 5:12–13). So it seems God didn't grant the desires of the apostles, and yet did so for the demons. Nonetheless we can be quite certain that the former belong to God and are going to reign in the chief places with Christ (cf. Luke 22:30; Matt 19:28), while the demons are going to burn forever with their chieftain the devil (cf. 25:41). So what can we say, except that *the Lord knows who are his* (2 Tim 2:19), and that of them **everyone who asks receives?**

But we are still left with a nagging difficulty about the Apostle. We may assume that he is not excluded from the number of those *who are his*, seeing that he is the one who made this statement, *The Lord knows who are his*. So all those who are his ask and receive, and not one of them asks and doesn't receive. Now the question I want to ask is, "Receive what?" I mean, the things we request for this temporal life are sometimes good for us and sometimes bad for us. When God knows they are bad for his people, he does not give them to them however much they desire and ask for them. It is like a doctor who does not give his patient whatever he asks for; because he cares for him, he refuses to give him what he would give him if he did not care for him.

So he listens to all those who are his, as far as eternal life is concerned. He does not listen to them all, as far as temporal longings are concerned. I mean, take the patient whom I have just given as an example; when he asks the doctor for something the doctor knows is harmful, what he really wants from the doctor is a return to health. But in order to pay attention to his patient in the matter of his health, the doctor must pay no attention merely to his wishes.

Finally, just ponder the very words of the passage. When Paul had not received what he had three times asked the Lord for, he told him, *My grace is sufficient for you; strength is made perfect in weakness* (2 Cor 12:9). Why do you want me to take away from you the sting in your flesh, which you received to prevent you from getting a swollen head about your enlightenment? Obviously, the reason you are making the request is that you do not know what is good for you. Trust the doctor. What he has prescribed is painful, but useful; it hurts, but it heals.

The first thing that those who ask for such things must do is examine their own hearts to see whether they are asking in faith. All who ask in faith receive for their own good and sometimes do not receive for their own good. When God does not cure the body, he wants to cure the soul. So trust him, and believe that since he has called you to an eternal kingdom, whatever he wishes is to your advantage. After all, what is this thing that you long for as though it mattered so enormously? Eternal life is what he has promised you; to reign with the angels is what he has promised you, rest without end is what he has promised you. How can that compare to what he does not give you here and now? Isn't it true that the health of human beings is futile (Ps 60:11; 108:12)? And isn't it absolutely certain that all those who get cured will eventually die anyway? When death comes, all those past events will vanish like smoke. But when that other life that he has promised us comes, it will of course have no end. By denying you something here and now, he is equipping you, preparing you, training you for that life.

But do not start fancying yourself above someone else, who may have asked and not received, as you say to yourself, "I have more faith than he has." That is why you heard the words in the Gospel just now, **Do not judge, that you be not judged** (7:1). What else does **Do not judge** refer to, but hidden matters? Is anyone forbidden to make judgments about open matters, seeing that Scripture says somewhere else, *Things that are open pertain to you; while things that are hidden pertain to God* (Deut 29:29)? This means we ought to judge open matters, while leaving hidden matters to the judgment of our God.

How do you know whether or not the person who asked and did not receive temporal health is stronger than you are? He asked and he didn't receive. But what did he ask for? Health of body. Perhaps his faith is stronger than yours, and the reason you did receive is that, if you hadn't, you would have given up. I haven't asserted this. I said "perhaps," to stop myself from doing what I am forbidding, because I dare not pass judgment about hidden matters. Sometimes, you see, the reason he didn't receive is that he made his request without faith; sometimes the reason he didn't receive is that he is stronger than you are and can do with some training in fortitude, as we said about the Apostle. He was stronger, and yet he wasn't yet perfect, so that he was told, *Strength is made perfect in weakness* (2 Cor 12:9).

(9) John Chrysostom

Ask, and it shall be given you; seek, and ye shall find; knock, and it shall be opened unto you. He has enjoined great and marvelous things, and has commanded men to rule their passions, and has led them up to heaven itself, and has charged them to strive to resemble not angels and archangels, but as far as possible to be like the very Lord of all. And he has urged his disciples not only to perform all this, but also to correct others, and to distinguish those who are evil and those who are not, the dogs and those who are not dogs, though there is much that is hidden in men. And so let them not say, "these things are grievous and intolerable." For later in the Gospel, Peter did utter some such things, saying, **Who can be saved?** and again, **If such is the case of a man with his wife, it is not expedient to marry** (19:10, 25).[2]

In order then that they might not now say such things, he shows from what has gone before that they are easy, and offers many reasons, one upon another, that are able to persuade men. After everything, he adds what is at the pinnacle, that which gives no ordinary relief to our labors, the help derived from persevering in prayer. He says that we are not to strive alone, relying on ourselves, but to invoke the help from above. For this help will surely come and be present with us, to aid us in our struggles, and to make all things easy. So he commanded us to ask and pledged that he himself would give. He did not, however, simply enjoin us to ask, but to do so zealously and earnestly. For this is the meaning of **seek**. For he that seeks and puts all things out of his mind, is taken up with that alone which is sought, and is oblivious to what is around him. Those who have lost either gold or servants, and seek diligently for them, know what I am talking about. And this which I am saying they know, as many as have lost either gold, or servants, and are seeking diligently after them.

So that is what is meant by **seeking**. When he says **knocking** he means that we seek earnestly, and by **seeking**, then by **knocking**, he indicates that we approach with earnestness and a mind on fire.

2. In the passage cited by Chrysostom, it is the disciples who are speaking.

Do not be despondent then, my friend, nor show less enthusiasm for virtues than those do who desire wealth. For such things you have often sought and not found. Although you know that you are not sure of finding them, you use all your energy in the search. And yet, though you here have a promise that you will surely receive, your searching is lackluster. Remember that even if you do not receive at once, you should not despair. For that is why he said **knock**, indicating that even if he does not open the door at once, we are to continue to knock. For if you continue to ask, though you do not receive something immediately, nevertheless, you will surely receive. It was for this end that the door was shut: so that he may induce you to knock. For this reason he does not assent at once, that you may ask. Continue then to do these things, and you will surely receive.

Matthew 7:9–12

9"Or what man of you, if his son asks him for bread, will give him a stone? 10Or if he asks for a fish, will give him a serpent? 11If you then, who are evil, know how to give good gifts to your children, how much more will your Father who is in heaven give good things to those who ask him! 12So whatever you wish that men would do to you, do so to them; for this is the law and the prophets."

(10) Augustine

The firmness and strength to walk in a path of wisdom resides in morality that leads to the purity and simplicity of heart. Having spoken at length about it, the Lord concludes: **Whatever good you wish that men would do you, do also to them**. In the Greek manuscripts we find: **Whatever good you wish that men would do you, do also to them**. I think that in the Latin manuscripts the word "**good**" has been added to better explain the statement. . . . And if it is missing in the Greek manuscripts, they must also be corrected. But who would dare to do that? We must therefore assume that the thought is complete and entirely accurate without this addition. This expression, "**whatever you wish**," is to be understood in its proper sense, and not according to its ordinary meaning. Indeed, properly speaking, there is no will but for good; as for the bad and criminal actions, we are dealing with passion and not will. Not that the Scriptures always use a word in its proper sense; but where it is necessary they use appropriate terms in order to exclude incorrect interpretations.

Therefore, the eye that is purified and made clear will be proficient and able to see and contemplate the inner light. This is the eye of the heart. He has that eye who, in order to make his actions truly good, does not aim at pleasing men. Even if it happens to him to please men, he uses it for their salvation and for the glory of God and not for his own vainglory. Such a person does not pursue the salvation of others with the intention to obtain from this the necessities of life. Neither does he rashly condemn the intention and disposition behind an act where the intention and disposition are not obvious. He who serves others in every possible way also exhibits an intention that he wants others to exhibit toward him, namely, without expecting any benefit over time. This is the simple and pure heart that seeks God: **Blessed are the pure in heart, for they shall see God** (5:8).

(11) John Chrysostom

For which of you is there, a father, who if his son shall ask bread, will give him a stone? If you do not receive what you asked, it is because you asked for a stone. So that if you do not receive, your asking for a stone is the cause of your not receiving. For though you be a son, that does not mean necessarily that you will receive what you ask. In fact it is because you are a son that you do not receive, for because you are a son you do not receive what is not profitable for you.

If you ask for what is spiritual and not worldly, you will surely receive what you ask. Take the case of Solomon. Because he asked for what he should ask, note how quickly his prayer was answered. Two things are required in prayer: that one prays earnestly and asks for what one ought. For Christ says, "Though you be fathers, wait for your sons to ask: and if they should ask of you anything inexpedient, refuse the gifts; just as, if it is expedient, you consent and grant it." Considering these things, you too should not cease until you receive, nor relax until you have found, nor give up until the door is opened. For if you approach in this way, saying, "If I do not receive I will not leave," you will surely receive, provided, of course, you ask such things as are both suitable for him to grant your request and good for the one who asks. But what are these? To seek only those things that are spiritual; to forgive those who have sinned and so draw near asking forgiveness, *lifting up holy hands without anger or quarreling* (1 Tim 2:8). If we ask in this way, we will surely receive. "But suppose," someone says, "I ask for spiritual things and still did not receive." In that case you did not knock earnestly, or you made yourself unworthy to receive; or you gave up too soon.

"And why," it may be asked, "did he not tell us for what things we ought to ask?" But he has, in everything that precedes, shown us to what things we should draw near. Do not say then, "I drew near and did not receive." For in no case is it because of God that we do not receive. For God's love is greater even than the love of father and surpasses the love of fathers as goodness surpasses evil.

Matthew 7:13–14

13"Enter by the narrow gate; for the gate is wide and the way is easy, that leads to destruction, and those who enter by it are many. 14For the gate is narrow and the way is hard, that leads to life, and those who find it are few."

(12) Jerome

The wide road is the way of the world for which people strive; the narrow road is the way of hardships and fasting. This is the road the Apostle walked, and the one he exhorted Timothy to take. Note how clearly he describes each road. Many walk along the wide road; few find the narrow one. We do not need to seek or strive to find the wide road; it stands open before us and is the path of error. But not all find the narrow road, nor do those who find it follow it at once. For some, even if they find the road, are caught up by the lusts of the world, and turn back in mid-journey.

(13) Valerian of Cimelium

Medicine brings little benefit to those who will soon die. Similarly, the salutary way of salvation seems hard because the way leading to death is easier to travel. As Scripture tells us, How wide and broad is the way that leads to death, and many there are who enter that way. Perhaps some will wonder why the evangelist calls the way of death wide and easy to travel, since every step of the journey through life is difficult. But who ever found the descent to a lower level hard going? If someone is weighed down by the load of his own baggage, he finds himself pulled down that slope by his own weight. Many obstacles obstruct the way to salvation, even though it be desirable.

Narrow and close is the way that leads to life. Therefore, if anyone is wise, let him rid himself at the outset of the encumbrances of the world, and let him make his journey easier by leading a disciplined life. Let him remove by repentance whatever blemishes he has incurred through negligence. If worldly glory has put any burdens on his back, he should not think they are worth carrying with him. For such burdens are by nature heavy, and they grow heavier still through the difficulty of the journey.

(14) Caesarius of Arles

There are two cities, most dear brothers: one is the city of the world, the other is the city of paradise. In the city of the world the good Christian is always on pilgrimage; he is known to be a citizen of the city of paradise. The city of the world is a toilsome city full of labor and misery, whereas the city of paradise is blessed, peaceful and full of rest. He who lives wickedly in the city of the world will not be able to come to paradise. We ought to be pilgrims in this world, so that we may deserve to be citizens in heaven. He who loves the world, and wants to be a citizen in the world, has no part in heaven. In this we prove we are pilgrims, if we desire our fatherland. Let no one deceive himself, dearest brothers, the fatherland of Christians is in heaven, not this world. The city of Christians, their blessedness, their true and eternal happiness, is not this world. He who seeks happiness in the world will not have it in heaven. Our fatherland is paradise, our city is that heavenly Jerusalem; our fellow citizens are the angels, our parents are the patriarchs and prophets, apostles and martyrs. Our King is Christ. Thus, in order that we will be able to desire so great a fatherland, may we reside in this pilgrimage that we are in for a while. He who intends to live badly will not be able to desire that fatherland.

Matthew 7:15–20

[15]"Beware of false prophets, who come to you in sheep's clothing but inwardly are ravenous wolves. [16]You will know them by their fruits. Are grapes gathered from thorns, or figs from thistles? [17]So, every sound tree bears good fruit, but the bad tree bears evil fruit. [18]A sound tree cannot bear evil fruit, nor can a bad tree bear good fruit. [19]Every tree that does not bear good fruit is cut down and thrown into the fire. [20]Thus you will know them by their fruits."

(15) Jerome

If a good tree can never bear evil fruit, how did Moses sin with a "good tree" at the waters of contradiction (cf. Deut 32:51), or how did David seduce Bathsheba after killing Uriah, or Peter give his denial during the Lord's passion, saying, *I do not know the man* (Mark 14:71)? Or why would Jethro, Moses's father-in-law, who was truly a "bad tree" because he did not believe in the God of Israel, give good counsel to Moses, or why did Achior say something beneficial to Holofernes (cf. Jdt 5:5), and then a pagan comedian is approvingly quoted in what the Apostle confirms: *bad friends corrupt good morals* (1 Cor 15:33).[3] And since the heretics will find no way to answer, we for our part would conclude that Judas too was a formerly "good tree" that bore evil fruit after he forsook the Savior, or that Paul was an "evil tree" during the time when he persecuted the Church of Christ. He later bore good fruit when he was transformed from a persecutor into a vessel of election. So as long as a good tree does not bear evil fruit, the zeal for goodness continues. And an evil tree remains in the fruits of sin as long as it is not converted to repentance. No one who remains in what he was begins to be something else.

(16) Augustine

We must especially beware of those who promise the wisdom and the knowledge of the truth they do not possess, who, like the heretics, often argue for their small number. So, having said that few are those who enter through the narrow gate and the narrow way, so that they do not meddle with the pretext of the small number,[4] the Lord immediately added: **Beware of false prophets who come to you in the clothing of sheep, but inwardly they**

3. Paul is quoting a portion of a Greek comedy, *Thais* (frag. 218), written by the fourth-century-BCE poet Menander. Only fragments of the original work survive.

4. That is, their small numbers demonstrate the uniqueness or special quality of their teaching, as Gnostic or Marcionite Christians claimed.

are ravening wolves. But they did not deceive the clear eye that distinguishes the tree by its fruits, for the Lord says, **By their fruits you shall know them.**

It is certainly a very great reason to ask what fruits the Lord wants us to learn to recognize, by which we could **distinguish** the tree. Many ascribe certain properties to the fruits that also belong to the sheep wool, because of which they are deceived by wolves. Such are fasting, prayers, and alms. What if all these acts could not be executed by hypocrites? Then, the Lord would not have said earlier: **Beware of practicing your piety before others in order to be seen by them** (6:1). Proposing this teaching, the Lord explains these three kinds of good works: almsgiving, prayer, fasting. Many give abundantly to the poor, not out of sympathy but for vainglory. Many pray, or, rather, appear to be praying, careless about God and only desiring to please men. Many fast and parade their abstinence arousing wonder in those to whom these efforts seem difficult and worthy of honor. And with such tricks they attract them, and by their false appearances they either deceive or pillage and kill those who cannot see wolves in the sheep's clothing. So these are not the fruits by which the Lord admonishes us to recognize the tree. If these actions are performed with good intention and in truth, they are the true sheep clothing. If they are performed with bad intention and in error, they serve only to cover the wolves. But this does not mean that the sheep have to hate their own sheep wool only because wolves often hide behind them.

The Apostle teaches what are the fruits by which we can recognize the evil tree: *Now the works of the flesh are obvious, which are fornication, impurity, licentiousness, idolatry, sorcery, enmities, strife, jealousy, quarrels, dissensions, factions, envy, drunkenness, carousing, and things like these; I am warning you, as I warned you before: those who do such things will not inherit the kingdom of God* (Gal 5:19–21). Then he teaches the fruits by which we can recognize the good tree: *The fruit of the Spirit is love, joy, peace, patience, kindness, generosity, faithfulness, gentleness, and self-control* (Gal 5:22–23). You should know that the word "joy" is taken in its literal sense. The wicked, on the other hand, rejoice only outwardly, not literally.

As we have said above, the word "will" also has its proper meaning that cannot be applied to the wicked. The following text puts it this way: **Whatsoever you wish that men do to you, do it to them too** (7:12). The prophet also states that the word "joy" cannot be taken literally unless it refers to the righteous: *There is no joy for the wicked, says the Lord* (Isa 48:22 LXX). It is the same with faith that strictly does not include any other faith, except the genuine one. Joy, faith, and other qualities have their counterfeits in evil men and impostors who use them to deceive those who lack the pure and sincere eye to pick up on the deception. It was therefore quite in order to first speak of the need to purify the eye, and then mention those things against which we should be on guard.

Matthew 7:21–23

21"Not every one who says to me, 'Lord, Lord,' shall enter the kingdom of heaven, but he who does the will of my Father who is in heaven. 22On that day many will say to me, 'Lord, Lord, did we not prophesy in your name, and cast out demons in your name, and do many mighty works in your name?' 23And then will I declare to them, 'I never knew you; depart from me, you evildoers.'"

(17) Hilary of Poitiers

Many will say to me on that day, Lord, Lord, did we not prophesy in your name? He again condemns the deceitfulness of the pseudo-prophets and the pretense of hypocrites who attribute glory to themselves because of the power of their words in prophetic teaching, expelling demons and exercising powers of this kind. They promise themselves the kingdom of heaven as if anything which they speak or do is unique, and as if the power of God, when summoned, does not accomplish everything. It is, however, the reading[5] that brings about knowledge of doctrine, and it is the name of Christ that empowers the expulsion of demons. Therefore, we must merit that blessed eternity, and we must offer something of ourselves in order that we should desire the good, avoid every evil, and submit to heavenly instruction with all our heart. By such service we may be known to God and pursue what the Lord desires rather than what brings glory to ourselves. . . .

(18) Jerome

To prophesy, do miracles, and cast out demons has not to do with the merit of the one who does such things. No, it is the invocation of Christ's name that brings about such things. Of course it must be granted that even though those who call on the name deceitfully are to be condemned, nevertheless their mighty actions still do good and they bring honor to God by invoking his name. For Saul (1 Sam 10:10–13) and Balaam (Num 24:3–9) and Caiaphas (26:63) all prophesied without knowing what they were saying; Pharaoh (Gen 41:25–45) and Nebuchadnezzar (Dan 2:26–49) learned of the future through dreams, and in the Acts of the Apostles the sons of Sceva (Acts 19:13–14) seem to have cast out demons, and the Apostle Judas—with the mind of a traitor—is said to have done many signs while among the other apostles (10:1; Luke 9:1–6; John 6:70).

(19) Gregory the Great

Materials dealing with external or corporeal matters sometimes demonstrate holiness, but they do not create it, whereas the spiritual actions performed in the soul do not make the power of life evident to the senses but create it. Even the wicked perform the former; none but the good can perform the latter. Hence Truth said of some people: **Many will say to me on that day, 'Lord, Lord, did we not prophesy in your name, cast out demons in your name, do many mighty deeds in your name?' Then I will declare to them, 'I do not know you; depart from me you workers of iniquity.'** Dearly beloved, do not love signs that the wicked can likewise perform; love those miracles of love and devotion of which I have just now spoken. The more they are hidden, the safer they are; and the less glory that comes from humans, the greater will be our recompense in the eyes of God.

5. "Reading" certainly refers to Scripture, though perhaps also to lives of martyrs or saints.

Matthew 7:24–27

**24“Everyone then who hears these words of mine and does them will be like a wise man
who built his house upon the rock; 25and the rain fell, and the floods came, and the
winds blew and beat upon that house, but it did not fall, because it had been founded
on the rock. 26And everyone who hears these words of mine and does not do them will
be like a foolish man who built his house upon the sand; 27and the rain fell, and the
floods came, and the winds blew and beat against that house, and it fell; and great was
the fall of it.”**

(20) Jerome

Upon this rock the Lord built his Church, and from this rock the Apostle Peter’s name was chosen. Upon this kind of rock there is no vestige of the serpent, as the prophet speaks confidently: *He has set my feet upon the rock* (Ps 40:2), and elsewhere, *The rock is a refuge for hedgehogs* (Ps 104:18). This timid animal hides in the crevices of the rock and protects itself with a covering of a rough skin fully armed with spikes. Hence Moses too, when he was fleeing Egypt, was regarded as the Lord’s little rabbit: *Stand in the cleft of the rock, and you will see the back of me* (Exod 33:22–23). . . . The foundation that the Apostle, as an architect, has established is our one Lord Jesus Christ. On this foundation—stable, firm, and in itself set upon strong rock—the Church of Christ is built. By contrast the entire teaching of the heretics is built on sand that is shifting and does not hold together, nor can it be formed into a solid mass. In consequence the teaching of the heretics comes to ruin.

(21) Hilary of Poitiers

Repudiating the boasts of false prophets and the fabrications of hypocrites, the Lord describes a man who has perfect faith by means of an example of comparison. The man who hears his words and acts on them is built upon a rock and supported on a stable and firm foundation. He cannot be dislodged by the force of the storm when it occurs, since the Lord indicates [with the words] **on a rock** that he himself is a strong foundation of the highest building.

Moreover, this person who has grown to be a towering construction based on the Lord will not be moved by rain nor by flames nor by wind (by **rain** he indicates the enticements of smooth talkers and of those who gradually slip into sensuality, which is how their faith initially becomes “wet” through the open cracks [of their “house”]). Despite the onset of rushing waters (that is, the swirling of deep desire as an aggressive force), and all the force of the wind whipping around and raging furiously—namely, the assault of every spirit of diabolical power—the person established on the foundation of the rock will stand fast and cannot be dislodged.

But the foolish person, ignoring the words that he heard, is similar to a work of construction that rests upon sand. It stands insecurely, to be quickly undermined by the falling rains, to be destroyed by flames, and to be knocked over by the winds. Given the properties of sand on which it was built, it is broken down into a heavy pile of ruins.

And so, by the example of the preceding comparisons, the Lord wants us also to do what he commands, and to believe what he has promised. Once all these things were accomplished, the crowds were amazed at his teaching because he taught them not in the manner of the scribes and Pharisees. For it was in the power of his words that the efficacy of his authority was measured.

(22) Augustine

Do not deceive yourselves, just because you come eagerly to hear the word, if you fail to do what you hear. Just think: if it is lovely *to hear*, how much more so *to do*. If you do not hear it at all, if you neglect the matter of hearing, then you are building nothing. If you hear and do not do, then you are building a ruin. On this matter Christ the Lord gave us an extremely apt comparison: **Whoever hears**, he said, **these words of mine and does them, I will compare him to a sensible man who builds his house upon rock. The rain poured down, the rivers came up, the winds blew and struck that house, and it did not fall**. Why did it not fall? **For it was founded upon rock.**

So to hear and to do is like building upon the rock. Merely to hear is to build. **But whoever**, he says, **hears these words of mine and does not do them, I will compare him to a foolish man who builds**. He too builds. What does he build? Here you are; **he builds his house**; but because he does not do what he hears, even by hearing **he builds upon sand**. So the one who hears and does not do, builds on sand; the one who hears and does, on rock; the one who does not hear at all does not build either on sand or on rock. But notice what follows: **The rain poured down, the rivers came up, the winds blew, and they struck at that house and it fell; and its ruin was complete.** What a sad, sad sight!

Matthew 7:28–29

28 And when Jesus finished these sayings, the crowds were astonished at his teaching,
29 for he taught them as one who had authority, and not as their scribes.

(23) John Chrysostom

It was natural for them to be distressed at his objectionable sayings, as well as to tremble at the loftiness of his commandments. At the same time, the teacher's power was so great that many of them were captured by its authority and affected by great admiration. But they were astonished most of all at his authority. For the Lord didn't speak with reference to the opinion of others, like the prophets and Moses. Rather, he indicated himself to be the person in every occasion that had the power of making final decisions. For this reason, he established his laws with the repeated words: **But I say unto you**.

Notice the variation that the Lord used for approaching and enabling his hearers. After miracles he uses words, and again from his instructive words he uses miracles. Before they went up into the mountain, he healed many, preparing the way for his sayings; and after finishing that long discourse to the people, he returns to miracles, which confirmed what he had said before. Because he taught as **one having authority** and might then be considered as boastful and arrogant, he operates in just the same way through his works, in this case, having authority to heal.

As another example of his authority, we read elsewhere that **when he was come down from the mountain, there came a leper, saying, Lord, if you will, you can make me clean** (8:1–2). This one who approached Jesus had great understanding and faith: he did not interrupt the Lord's teaching, nor cut off his address, but waited for the proper time to draw near **when he is come down**. This was not a random act, but with great fervor as he fell **on his knees, he sought the Lord** (8:2). As another evangelist put it, he had a genuine faith and proper view about him. Neither did the leper say, "If you request it of God," nor, "If you would pray," but, *If you will, you can make me clean* (Mark 1:40–41). Nor did he say, "Lord, cleanse me," but he leaves it all to the Lord by making his recovery dependent on him, a testimony that all authority is his.

At the same time, we know that the Lord came not only to heal bodies, but to lead souls unto self-control. He did not, for example, forbid others to eat with unwashed hands because he introduced a more excellent law that is not pertinent to various foods (cf. Rom 14:17). In this case also, he provides us with instructions for the future that the soul must be our focus, as outward purifications are overlooked. We must wipe that clean, that dread of leprosy, which is sin, whereas there is nothing in being a leper that prevents virtue.

In order that we may gain a good understanding, let us disengage ourselves from all perishable things so that in doing so it may kindle in us a greater flame. Let us be aware of our wickedness by showing humility of mind and self-restraint, that we may obtain those blessings, both present and future, by the grace and love toward man of our Lord Jesus Christ, with whom be glory, might, and honor, to the Father, together with the Holy and Good Spirit, now and ever, and world without end. Amen.

Matthew 8

In his commentary on Matthew's Gospel, Hilary of Poitiers typically connects what Jesus says with what he does. This is evident as the reader moves from the Sermon on the Mount to the present chapter. For here we encounter six "deeds": three stories of healing, followed by three stories of divine power. Jerome sees these events as the authenticating marks of Jesus's earlier preaching.

The first healed was the leper, who represented the law but "took refuge in faith" (Epiphanius). Likewise, the centurion's servant was the second healed. The centurion stood for the idolatry of the pagans and yet "had astonishing faith and humility" (Epiphanius). As verse 11 articulates, both figures, the leper as the law and the centurion as the nations, had prophetic significance. Peter's mother-in-law, the third healed, further stressed the prophetic nature of Christ's ministry: This was to fulfill what was spoken by the prophet Isaiah, "He took our infirmities and bore our diseases" *(8:17; cf. Isa 53:4).*

In between the first three and the second three miraculous events are two affirmations of loyalty: a scribe (vv. 19–20) and an anonymous disciple who wanted to bury his father before following Jesus (vv. 21–22). Jesus's response is meant to demonstrate the radical call of discipleship (Chrysostom). Compared to the urgency of preaching the gospel, earthly responsibilities are minuscule.

The miracle of Jesus's calming the sea (vv. 23–27) is interpreted as a historical event, but it also carries a figural meaning. The reader needs to awaken Christ within, in order to calm the storms of the world. As Chrysologus says, "So now let us awaken Christ sleeping within us. With groans arising from our innermost being . . . let us cry with the apostles." This second set of miracles has its focus on the Lord's power: first over the elements and then over the demons (vv. 28–34). Both the natural and the supernatural obey his will. In the case of the pagans, they are easily manipulated by the demons and are more liable to be thrown headlong into the sea of unbelief, which is death. Chrysostom also sees a deeper meaning in that it shows how easily "the swinish" kind of person is fooled by the work of demons.

Matthew 8:1–4

[1]When he came down from the mountain, great crowds followed him; [2]and behold, a leper came to him and knelt before him, saying, "Lord, if you will, you can make me clean." [3]And he stretched out his hand and touched him, saying, "I will; be clean." And immediately his leprosy was cleansed. [4]And Jesus said to him, "See that you say nothing to any one; but go, show yourself to the priest, and offer the gift that Moses commanded, for a proof to the people."

(1) Jerome

The crowds hurried over to the Lord as he descended from the mountain because they were unable to ascend to higher things. A leper came to him first. Because his leprosy was so severe, he was unable to hear the Lord's sermon on the mountain. And we should notice that this man was the first one singled out for healing; the second was the centurion's servant; the third was Peter's mother-in-law in Capernaum (who had a fever); and in the fourth place were those oppressed by demons, whose spirits he cast out with a word. He healed all who had ailments. It was appropriate that these events should happen after his preaching and teaching. In this way, there would be a sign of powerful miracles to reinforce in the hearers' minds the sermon just preached.

(2) Epiphanius the Latin

When the Savior was coming down from the mountain, after he had instructed his disciples with all the Beatitudes and had spiritually taught them the precepts of the law, saying: **I have not come to undo the law but to fulfill it** (5:17), **many crowds followed him. And behold, in the whole crowd a certain leper came forward adoring him, saying: Lord, if you wish, you can cleanse me** (8:1b–2). How was the leper able to recognize the Lord, unless he had previously heard the Lord preaching the precepts of faith above the law and the rewards of the kingdom of heaven? The leper recognized Jesus through the law, because Jesus himself was the author of the law. The leper took refuge in faith, saying: **Lord, if you can, you can cleanse me** (8:2). For it was written in the law that if someone was covered with leprosy, he should show himself to the priest, not so that he might be cleansed, but that he might leave and live beyond town (cf. Lev 13:2–8). For leprosy signifies sin. It signifies this in the mystery; namely, if someone would not have been purified in this world through grace or holy life, he is cast out of the kingdom of God. For none of them was being cleansed, when the Lord himself said: *There were many lepers in Israel under the prophet Elisha; and none of them was cleansed except Naaman the Syrian* (Luke 4:27). But because the Lord had not come first to the Gentiles, but to the lost sheep of the house of Israel (Matt 10:6), so first the leper was cleansed from the common people of the Jews. The people of the Jews had been inundated with leprosy, as it were, because they served sin instead of keeping the law. But the leper recognized the Lord through faith. He shouted, saying: **Lord, if you will it**. And the Lord, seeing his faith, said: **I will it**, while the leper said to him: **You are able to cleanse me.** This is the speech of one believing, not of one doubting. And Jesus said to him: **I will it, be cleansed.** He commanded the leprosy, and immediately it departed from the man. The leper believed; the Lord granted. The one asked; and the other commanded.

And now if anyone is inundated in the leprosy of sin, let him show himself faithfully to the Lord and let him confess his sins, so that he might be able to depart from this world clean.

Matthew 8:5–9

5As he entered Caper'na-um, a centurion came forward to him, beseeching him 6and
saying, "Lord, my servant is lying paralyzed at home, in terrible distress." 7And he said
to him, "I will come and heal him." 8But the centurion answered him, "Lord, I am not
worthy to have you come under my roof; but only say the word, and my servant will
be healed. 9For I am a man under authority, with soldiers under me; and I say to one,
'Go,' and he goes, and to another, 'Come,' and he comes, and to my slave, 'Do this,' and
he does it."

(3) Augustine

When the Gospel was read, we heard our faith praised in an act of humility. When the Lord Jesus, you remember, promised he would go to the centurion's house to heal his servant, the man replied, **I am not worthy that you should enter under my roof, but only say the word, and he will be healed** (cf. Luke 7:6–7). By calling himself unworthy, he showed he was worthy to have Christ enter, not within his walls, but within his heart. In fact, he wouldn't have said this with such faith and humility, unless he already carried in his heart the one he was afraid of having in his house. There would, after all, have been no great benefit if the Lord Jesus entered within his walls had he not been in the centurion's heart. The teacher of humility by both word and example had, you may remember, sat down in the house of a certain proud Pharisee called Simon (cf. Luke 7:36–50). And though he was sitting in Simon's house, there wasn't anywhere in his heart where the Son of Man might lay his head.

But what made the centurion so confident? **I too,** he said, **am a man set under authority, having soldiers under me, and I say to this one, Go, and he goes, and to another, Come, and he comes, and to my slave, Do this, and he does it.** To some who are set under me I am authority, being myself set under some authority above me. So if I, he says, a man under authority, have authority to command, what can you not do, seeing that all authorities are subject to you? Now this man was a Gentile—he was, after all, a centurion. The Jewish nation already had troops of the Roman Empire among them. This man was in command of troops there, to the extent that a centurion could be in command; he was under authority, and he had authority; as a subordinate, obedient, as having subordinates, commanding.

It was such humility this woman showed when she said, "**Yes, Lord**; I am a dog, I'm eager for the crumbs" (15:27). It was humility that made the centurion acceptable, the one who wanted his servant cured by the Lord, and when the Lord said, **I will come and cure him, he answered, Lord, I am not worthy that you should come under my roof; but only say the word, and my servant will be healed. I am not worthy that you should come under my roof.** He didn't need to receive him under his roof because he had already received him in his heart. The more humble he was, the greater his capacity, the fuller he became.

(4) Epiphanius the Latin

That centurion is the first of the pagans. He believes that pagans receive forgiveness of sins through faith. Just as the entire body is struck by paralysis, so are the pagan people throughout the whole world. They serve idols and the will of the devil, being bound by the vices of the devil. All things were constrained by him. Therefore the centurion, that is, the first of the pagans, faithfully believed all things, whatever he heard from Christ. For it seems that the pagans believed Christ not from sight, but by hearing him.

And because he judged himself unworthy to approach the Savior, the centurion sends elders of the Jews. Then *he sends friends, saying: Lord, don't be upset. For I am not worthy for you to enter under my roof. But say the word, and my servant shall be healed* (Luke 7:6–7). The centurion had astonishing faith and humility. He believed through faith; he asked through the law. For he says: *I too am a man established under authority, having soldiers under me; I say to this one: Go, and he goes; and to another: Come, and he comes; I say to my servant: Do this, and he does it* (Luke 7:8). The centurion had known through faith that Jesus himself was the author of the world, *by* whose *word the heavens were established and every strength of them by the breath [or, spirit] of his mouth* (Ps 33:6). When he had heard this, Jesus was astonished and said to those following him: *Truly, I say to you, I have never found such great faith in Israel* (Luke 7:9).

(5) Gregory the Great

Why is it that when the ruler asked the Lord to come to his son, the Lord refused to go there in person? Rather, he promised to go to the servant in person even though the centurion had not asked him to do so. The Lord did not condescend to be physically present with the ruler's son, but he hurried to the side of the centurion's servant.

Why did he do this except to rein in our pride? We do not respect people as they are made in God's image, but only their riches and reputation. When we consider what is important about people, we rarely regard what they are like on the inside. We pay attention to what is physically displeasing about them and neglect to consider who they are. In order to show us that the things human beings highly regard are displeasing to the saints, and that we are not to be displeased by what humans consider displeasing, instead of going to the ruler's son, our Lord was ready to go to the centurion's servant.

He was rebuking our pride, you see, which does not know how to consider human beings in the right way. As I said, we consider only the external aspects of people, not looking at their interior nature or acknowledging how God's honor is present in people. God's Son does not choose to go to the ruler's son, yet he is ready to come to cure a servant. Certainly, if someone's servant asked us, asking that we should come to him, our pride would immediately come up: "You shouldn't go because you would be lowering yourself," or "you would be risking your reputation and cheapen your position." Yet you see that the one who came from heaven was not reluctant to hurry to a servant on earth, while we of the earth refuse to be humbled on earth. What is of less worth in God's sight, what more displeasing to him, than for us to preserve our reputation before others and not to fear the eyes of our conscience?

See, my friends, what he is saying. If what is highly regarded by human beings is loathsome in God's sight, then the thoughts of our hearts are diminished in his sight the more attention they receive from humans. Moreover, the humility of our hearts is more highly regarded by God, as much as it is diminished in human eyes.

Matthew 8:10–13

**10 When Jesus heard him, he marveled, and said to those who followed him, "Truly, I
say to you, not even in Israel have I found such faith. 11 I tell you, many will come from
east and west and sit at table with Abraham, Isaac, and Jacob in the kingdom of heaven,
12 while the sons of the kingdom will be thrown into the outer darkness; there men will
weep and gnash their teeth." 13 And to the centurion Jesus said, "Go; be it done for you
as you have believed." And the servant was healed at that very moment.**

(6) Hilary of Poitiers

Concerning the tribune, it is enough for me to think of him as the precursor of those pagans who will eventually believe. . . . To us, it is only an account about a servant. Then, after restoring the paralytic in the person of the servant, there follows the salvation of the pagans in the healing of the people who came down from the mountain. The servant was lying in a humble house, dissolute and dying. Even though the house was falling apart and unworthy of the Savior's entry, he was, nevertheless, in need of the Savior's coming. The tribune knows his servant can be healed by a word—the salvation of all pagans is by faith, and life for all people is found in the precepts of the Lord. The pagans should be reckoned as those "bedridden" in the world, dissolute with the sickness of sin, all their limbs completely atrophied and incapable of performing and executing their duty. The sacrament of their salvation is fulfilled in the servant of the tribune, although Christ does not go into the "house." Although he lingered in this world, he did not enter upon worldly vices and sins.

(7) Augustine

What did the Lord reply to the centurion after he had said, *I am not worthy that you should come under my roof*? To those who were around he said, **Truly, I tell you, I have not found such faith in Israel**; that is, in this people to whom I came, **I have not found such faith.** What did he mean by the word **such**? He meant that his faith was so great. What made it great? It became the greatest from the smallest, that is, from humility. **I have not found such faith**; like a grain of mustard seed, which is all the hotter, the more fervent, for being so tiny (cf. 13:31).

Observe that what you are hearing in the Gospel is now actually happening. **Therefore I tell you**, he says, on account of the centurion whose faith he had praised so much, as of a foreigner in the flesh but a member of the household at heart (cf. Eph 2:19): **Therefore,** he says, **many will come from east and west**. Not all, but many, from east and west, the two points of the compass designating the whole world. **Many will come from east and west, and will sit down with Abraham and Isaac and Jacob in the kingdom of heaven, but the children of the kingdom will be cast out into the outer darkness. . . .** Now we see Christians from east and west summoned to a kind of heavenly banquet, to sit down with Abraham and Isaac and Jacob, where the food is justice and the drink wisdom.

(8) Epiphanius the Latin

They will come from the east and from the west, and they will recline with Abraham and Isaac and Jacob in the kingdom of heaven. For not all these who are from Israel, are Israelites; nor are all those who are from Abraham, his sons; but *in Isaac there will be named a seed for you* (Gen 21:12). It is not someone born according to the flesh, but he who was begotten according to the Spirit through believing the faith. And so all nations that are across the whole world that have believed in Christ through faith will come with the fruits of justice and sanctity and will recline with the patriarchs in the kingdom of heaven. Moreover the sons of the kingdom, that is, the Jews, who used to boast that they were sons of Abraham and are not, **will be cast out into the outer darkness** because the just man lives by faith, just as all the patriarchs did.

(9) Augustine

What do you suppose the Lord praised in this man's faith? his humility: **I am not worthy that you should enter under my roof**. That's what he praised; and because he praised that, he entered there. The centurion's humility was the door by which the Lord could enter so that the centurion might gain more fully something he already possessed.

So the Lord gave great hope to the pagans, the nations on this occasion. We did not yet exist, but we were already foreseen, already foreknown, already promised. What did he then say? **Therefore I tell you, that many will come from east and west**. Where will they come from? Wherever it is they believe. . . . They will come from east and west, not to the temple of Jerusalem, not to some central section of the earth, not to climb some mountain. And yet, they are indeed coming to the temple of Jerusalem, and to some central section, and to some mountain. The temple of Jerusalem is now the body of Christ, about which he said, *Pull down this temple, and in three days I shall raise it up* (John 2:19). The central place they are coming to is Christ himself. He is at the center because he is equally related to all. Anything placed in the center is common to all. They are coming to the mountain, of which Isaiah said, *In the last times the mountain of the Lord shall be manifest, prepared on the summit of the mountains, and it shall be lifted up above all the hills, and all the nations shall come to it* (Isa 2:2). This mountain was a small stone, which grew until it filled the world. This is what Daniel says about it (Dan 2:34–35).

Matthew 8:14–17

14 And when Jesus entered Peter's house, he saw his mother-in-law lying sick with a fever;
15 he touched her hand, and the fever left her, and she rose and served him. 16 That eve-
ning they brought to him many who were possessed with demons; and he cast out the
spirits with a word, and healed all who were sick. 17 This was to fulfill what was spoken
by the prophet Isaiah, "He took our infirmities and bore our diseases."

(10) Hilary of Poitiers

When Jesus had come into the house of Peter, he saw his mother-in-law lying down with a fever. We should understand in Peter's mother-in-law a diseased disposition of unbelief that is associated with a freedom of the will, and links us to her in a kind of bonded fellowship. Thus, with the Lord's entry into Peter's house, that is, in his body, he cured the unbelief of those who are burning in the heat of their sins and who are dominated by the illness of their wickedness. Soon afterward, now healed, she performs a servant's role. Peter was the first to believe and has the primary apostolic place. Although faith was formerly weak in him, he grew strong by the ministry of the Word of God because the Word undertook the work of salvation for all. . . .

(11) John Chrysostom

Sometimes he heals by words alone; sometimes he also extends his hand in the healing; and sometimes he does both, making the healing process clear. His intention, you see, was not always to work miracles in an extraordinary fashion. He had to go unnoticed for a while, and especially as far as his disciples were concerned, since they would very gladly have announced everything abroad. This is obvious when, even after their coming to the Mount, he still told them not to tell anyone.

By touching her body the Lord not only quenched the fever, but also restored her to full health. Even though the disease was an ordinary one, he showed his power by the manner of healing, something medical science would not have achieved. That is to say, you know that even after a fever breaks, patients then require much time to return to their former health. But on that occasion it all happened at once, and not only then, but also with the situation on the sea (8:23–27). In that instance he not only caused the winds and the storm to abate, but also immediately settled the swells, which was certainly unusual. For even when a storm ceases, the waves continue to rise up and down for a long time. But not with Christ: it all ceased at once, the same in the case of the woman. The evangelist's saying indicates as much: **She got up and started serving him**; a sign both of Christ's power and of the woman's regard for the Christ.

(12) Chromatius of Aquileia

Our Lord and Savior entered the house of Peter's mother-in-law, who was racked by fever, and he healed her sickness with a single touch of his hand. This shows that the Lord is himself wholly complete, the author of heavenly medicine, who once had spoken to Moses, saying, *I am the Lord who heals you* (Exod 15:26; Isa 60:16). The healing that he granted by the touch of his hand was caused not by a lack of power, but given by grace. If he was previously able to cure a paralytic with only a word (8:13), then he was not only able to dispel a fever easily in this instance with a word, but through the touch of his hand. In doing so, he bestows a gift of his dignity and makes it clear that he is the one concerning whom it was written: *By the touch of his hand he immediately brings healing,*[1] which we understand was fulfilled in this act. In an instant, her fever ceased at the touch of the Lord's hand. Wholeness returns to the one who confidently believes. He who scrutinizes the heart, bestowed the gifts of wholeness upon that one who needed them for service. After she was restored to her former health, she began to serve the Lord. Clearly, the divinity of Christ is revealed through these powerful works.

According to a figural interpretation, Peter's mother-in-law serves as a type for the synagogue that languished in the weight of its sins as if it were oppressed by a fever. But Peter's mother-in-law is [also] understood as the synagogue because it is there where the first "voice" of the Church first occurs through the preaching of the Lord's resurrection, just as we read in the Acts of the Apostles (cf. Acts 2:14–40) where the holy Peter proclaimed his faith. It is in this message that Peter's mother-in-law, freed from the fever by the Lord's touch, began to serve, which itself shows that when anyone from the synagogue believes in the Son of God, he has been freed from the fever of his sins by the grace of divine power.

Matthew 8:18–22

18 Now when Jesus saw great crowds around him, he gave orders to go over to the other side. 19 And a scribe came up and said to him, "Teacher, I will follow you wherever you

1. Not found in the Vulgate or Old Latin Bible; perhaps a paraphrase of Hilary's.

go." [20]And Jesus said to him, "Foxes have holes, and birds of the air have nests; but the Son of man has nowhere to lay his head." [21]Another of the disciples said to him, "Lord, let me first go and bury my father." [22]But Jesus said to him, "Follow me, and leave the dead to bury their own dead."

(13) Hilary of Poitiers

Then a scribe approached him, saying that he was going to follow the teacher wherever he might go. We read that the scribe said or did nothing offensive. The Lord responds that, while there are holes for foxes and nests for the birds of the air for rest, there is no place for the Son of Man to rest his head. When a disciple asked that he be given time in order to bury his father, it was refused because the religion of human piety and service was forbidden. We should clarify two things here: the reason for such important and diverse events contained in the text, as well as the profound causes of its truth, so that an understanding of interior significance may be explained.

Then a disciple who did not ask whether he should follow the Lord (since he already believed that he ought to follow) approached him. Rather, the disciple wanted to be allowed to **bury** his **father**. We have learned from the beginning of the Lord's Prayer that we ought to first pray: **Our Father, who are in heaven** (6:9). Because the disciple represents those persons who believe, he is told to remember that his living Father is in heaven. And he is told to follow the Lord, as he wished to do, in such a way that the dead would bury the dead. But I think that the dead cannot expect this service. In what way will the dead inter the dead? In the first place, it shows that a perfect faith in itself is not obligated by the scruple of rendering service to the one or the other in the world. The prerogative that belongs to the name of father is not upheld when it comes to the difference between a believing son and an unbelieving father. As the Lord refused the man's entreaty to bury his father, he added, **Let the dead bury their own dead** (8:22), encouraging us not to mix the unbelieving dead with remembrances of the saints. In any case, the unbelieving dead are those who live apart from God. For this reason, the duties performed for the dead should be abandoned so that the dead may be buried by the dead, as it were, just as it is necessary for the living to adhere to the living one through faith in God.

(14) Jerome

That scribe of the law, who knew that his kind of learning was passing away, would not have been refused by the Lord if he had said, "Lord, I will follow you wherever you go." But since he regarded Jesus as but one teacher among many, and was himself a grammarian (which is clearly expressed by the Greek term *grammateus*) rather than a spiritual hearer, he had no place for Jesus to lay his head. The repudiation of this scribe also shows us that he wished to follow Jesus when the scribe saw the greatness of Jesus's signs, hoping to gain wealth from miraculous deeds. He desired the very same thing Simon Magus wanted to obtain from Peter (Acts 8:13). Faith of this kind is rightly condemned by the Lord's words, and he says to him, "Why do you want to follow me for the sake of wealth and worldly riches, since I am so poor that I do not even have a little dwelling, and have no use for it?"

(15) John Chrysostom

If you admire the young person for asking Jesus when the matter (about his father) was so pressing, rather than going off by his own decision, then admire him much more also for staying when forbidden. You might object that surely it was a mark of extreme ingratitude for him not to be present at his father's burial. Had he done so out of indifference, it would have been ingratitude. If it was to avoid interruption of an urgent task, leaving would have been a mark of utter negligence. Jesus forbade him, you see, not as a command to undermine the respect due to parents, but to emphasize that nothing should be more pressing for us than heavenly affairs. We are supposed to attend to them with complete dedication and not put them off for the slightest thing, no matter how urgent and demanding our engagements. After all, what could be more pressing than burying one's father? Would it have taken so much time? If, however, we shouldn't spend even the amount of time required for burial of one's father, since it is not safe to neglect spiritual things for so long, consider what we would deserve for constantly abandoning our duties to Christ, preferring quite mundane matters to what is pressing.

In this case, we should also admire the sound principles in the teaching that caused the young man to be fixed to the Lord's word. They relieved him of countless troubles, like mourning and grief and what ensues from it. Besides the burial, he would have then had to busy himself with the will, distribution of the estate, and everything else involved with it. Wave upon wave coming upon him would have carried him far from the harbor of truth. For these reasons, the Lord draws him away and attaches the scribe to himself.

Matthew 8:23–27

**23 And when he got into the boat, his disciples followed him. 24 And behold, there arose
a great storm on the sea, so that the boat was being swamped by the waves; but he was
asleep. 25 And they went and woke him, saying, "Save, Lord; we are perishing." 26 And he
said to them, "Why are you afraid, O men of little faith?" Then he rose and rebuked the
winds and the sea; and there was a great calm. 27 And the men marveled, saying, "What
sort of man is this, that even winds and sea obey him?"**

(16) Hilary of Poitiers

After the disciples entered the ship, a storm arose, the sea was agitated, and the passengers were thrown into commotion. Having fallen into a deep sleep, he was roused by their nervous fearfulness; they begged him to do something. After he once more scolded the disciples because of their small faith, he commanded the wind and the waves to be quiet. To their amazement, the wind and the sea obeyed his orders.

It is evident that churches that have not followed the Word of God will be shipwrecked. This does not happen because Christ is relaxed in sleep, but because he is put fast asleep in us by our own sleep. That happens most often when we put our hope in God chiefly out of fear or worry arising from danger. Even if our hope comes late, there is the assurance that it can evade the danger, because the power of Christ is awake within it! So the Lord leaves for us a perpetual memory of his rebuke when he said: **Why are you fearful, men of little faith?** In other words, when faith in Christ is awake, there is no need to fear the commotion of the world.

Thereafter follows the amazement of these men who said: **What kind of man is this that the wind and the sea obey him?** This statement comes not from the disciples but from the pagans. As it was said earlier that only the disciples boarded the ship and the Lord was awakened only by the disciples, so it indicates that men were amazed, men who spoke in their amazement of *the* man. By this turn of phrase, it is understood that all of Christ's works and all of his powers should be praised as those of God. Pagan sacrilege and the foolishness of their wretched error show how they called him a man corresponding to the humility of his passion, rather than God on account of his powers.

(17) John Chrysostom

The storm was in full swing and the sea was raging when, **They awoke him, saying, Lord, save us. We are dying.** But he scolded them before he calmed the sea. As I said, these things were permitted for instruction. This situation was a foreshadowing of the temptations that would eventually overtake them. Indeed, even after these events, he often caused them to fall into more dangerous storms for their good and stayed with them through it all. Similarly, Paul also said, *I would not, brethren, have you ignorant, that we were pressed out of measure beyond strength, insomuch that we despaired even of life* (2 Cor 1:8, 10), and after this, *Who delivered us from so great deaths*. Therefore, to show that they should be confident even though the waves rise high, and that he orders all things for good, the first thing he does is reprove them. Moreover, the fact that they were frightened was good for them. Which made the miracle seem more important, something that they will remember for a long time.

At the same time, he also sleeps. Had he been awake when it happened, either they would have not feared, or they would have not begged him, or they would not have thought he was able to do such a thing. Therefore, he sleeps to give an opportunity for their timidity, and to make their perception of what was happening more distinct. For a man does not look at a situation in the same way as others. Therefore, since they all benefited from what they saw, even though they did not physically receive a benefit, and were supine (for they were not lame, nor did they have any other such illness), it was good for them to experience his benefits by what they saw. He permits the storm so that, by their deliverance, they might get a clearer picture of what they have gained.

He does not do this in the presence of many people, so that the crowds might not be condemned for little faith. Rather, he has them alone. He corrects them. And right in front of the stormy waters he puts an end to the storms in their soul, rebuking them, saying, **Why are you fearful, O men of little faith?** This question was also meant to instruct them, asserting that men's fear is not produced by being tested, but by the weakness of their minds.

And why should we be amazed that the disciples responded this way, when even after many other miracles their understanding was still incorrect? This is also why the Lord often rebuked; as when he said, **Are ye also yet without understanding** (15:16)? You should not be too amazed. If the disciples understood so little, then one can hardly expect the multitudes to have a clearer perception of him. And so they were amazed, saying, **What manner of man is this, that even the sea and the winds obey him?**

(18) Ephrem of Nisibis

The sea, stretched out, became a spotless plain
On whose sparkling surface the Pure One walked.
The sea intertwined its waves as a crown for God . . .
It escorted him in triumph over its deeps,
Handing him over to its neighbor, the dry land.
The dry land emulated the sea in exalting him.
To you both land and sea are harnessed, and they escort you
Acting as a mighty chariot that is held without a yoke.
The band of demons that roams about on land saw it
And fled into the swine to hide, but they did not escape:
The land rejoiced at their shame,
The sea leapt in joy at their disgrace;
Both height and depth beheld their destruction.

(19) Peter Chrysologus

Let us now turn to the deeper meaning of the event. When Christ boarded the ship of the Church in order to cross the sea of this age, the whole world rose up in a storm against him—from the gales of the Gentiles to the waterspouts of the Jews, the tempests of the persecutors, the storm clouds of the rabble, even the murky mists of demons!

Then the disciples came to the Lord, and the Lord, awakened by them, exerted his control over the sea. He calmed the globe, he softened the kings, he reconciled the rulers, he restrained the waves by putting the masses in their place, and he made Christians out of Romans. Once, they persecuted the Christian name; now, even the executioners themselves have converted to the truth of his words. Christian emperors now protect this peace that the Church preserves, the Christians possess, and the Gentiles mark with wonder.

Indeed, there are people today, children of this age, who stare incredulously at the conversion of the world and its submission to Christ. They're absolutely astounded that the vaunted heights of their temples have come crashing down like the swelling waves, completely flabbergasted by the retreat of their frothing idols and swirling demons, utterly thunderstruck at the depth and magnitude of the peace that the Christian name has restored to the furthest expanses of the globe. Truly, brothers, a **great storm arose** within the Church when Christ fell into the sleep of death—but as it is written, **a great calm** was restored upon his resurrection.

So now let us awaken Christ sleeping within us. With groans arising from our innermost being, with a voice filled with faith, in Christian tears and deepest weeping, let us cry with the apostles: **Save us, Lord, or we shall perish**!

Matthew 8:28–29

28 And when he came to the other side, to the country of the Gadarenes, two demoniacs met him, coming out of the tombs, so fierce that no one could pass that way. 29 And behold, they cried out, "What have you to do with us, O Son of God? Have you come here to torment us before the time?"

(20) John Chrysostom

Then there is an even more awesome miracle. Several men possessed with devils, like wicked runaways at the sight of their master, said: **"What have we to do with you, Jesus, Son of God? Have you come here to torment us before the time?"**

Although the multitudes called him man, the devils came and proclaimed him God. The people may not have heard the sea swelling and subsiding, but they heard from the devils the same cry, loudly speaking out.

Matthew recounts that they said, **Have you come here before the time to torment us?** But the other evangelists have added that they also pleaded and requested him not to cast them into the deep (Mark 5:10; Luke 8:31). For the devils rightly assumed that their punishment was close at hand. They were afraid since they were about to fall into vengeance.

And although Luke says that it was one person who cried out, and Matthew says two, this does not create any discrepancy. I agree that if the Gospel writers had said there were only one, and no other, Luke would seem to conflict with Matthew. However, the statement of one comes not from disagreement, but from a different angle of narration. I think Luke singled out the fiercest one of them for his narrative, which makes his account the more tragic, because he reports on their miserable situation. The one, for instance, would break his bonds and chains and used to wander about the wilderness (Luke 8:29). And Mark says also that he cut himself with the stones (Mark 5:5).

Moreover, their words betray their implacable and shameless nature. For the one asks Jesus, **Have you come here to torment us before the time?** That they had sinned could not be denied, but they did not seek to suffer their punishment before their time. He had caught them in the act of perpetrating those horrors so incurable and lawless: deforming and punishing his creature in every way. And they supposed that he, for the excess of their crimes, would not wait for the time of their punishment. Therefore, they begged and pleaded with him. For those that survived, not even bands of iron can stay bound. Those that run about the mountains are gone forth into the plain. Those who hinder all others from passing, at sight of him blocking up the way, stand still.

(21) Chromatius of Aquileia

David testified to the punishment of the demons, who claimed they were being tortured before the time of their judgment, when he says, *Turn from heaven, Lord, and come down, touch the mountains and they will smoke* (Ps 144:5). He indicates that these very mountains, are the demons, insightfully called "mountains" because of the magnitude of their evil and the enormity of their sin. "Mountains" of this kind do not burn but smoke, showing to what degree they were already burning in that eternal fire before the advent of the Lord's humility.

These things should first be understood according to a literal sense. According to an allegorical meaning, however, the two demoniacs in the land of the Gerasenes (that is, in the land of the Gentiles), who ran to the Lord, represent a figure of two peoples: those who had descended from Ham and Japheth, both sons of Noah, although the Jewish people derive their origin from Shem, the firstborn son of Noah. Those of the nations were being held captive by the devil in the error of idolatry. They were burdened with the chains of their crimes and the shackles of sin, and did not remain in the city, that is, they did not live within in law and divine precepts, but among the tombs. This is the culture of idols, worshiping the memories of kings or the images of dead men. In order to save them, therefore, he went down from Judea in the region of the Gerasenes. This means that by the body he assumed from the Virgin Mary, he came to the land of the Gerasenes (which is what is illustrated as the world), that he might liberate these demoniacs, who were the people in the chains of demonic captivity. That certainly is what David had testified about in the psalm, *The Lord looked out from heaven, that he might hear the groans of those in chains, that he might free the sons of the murderers* (Ps 102:19–20).

Prior to the time of freeing those demoniacs, as was mentioned earlier, the Lord came through the sea and endured the storm and lack of sleep as the disciples were in danger. This demonstrates that deliverance cannot be given to these two people, except the Lord first, coming through this sea of the age, endured the storm of Jewish persecution and delayed the sleep of death, with the disciples being in danger, who in the night of great intensity came to the point of such fear that even holy Peter, foremost of the apostles, was driven to deny the Lord three times.

In the pigs into which the demons were driven, the figure of unfaithful and unclean humans was shown. The pigs feeding by the sea, that is, living according to the sins of the age, were showing themselves to be a fitting habitation for the demons. Therefore in such a way, in the sea of the age, that is, the deep concealing of error, they are suffocated by the demons with the various desires of sins. As a result of the shepherds of the pigs fleeing at the observed sign of divine power and announcing in the city the things that were done (8:33), the Lord was asked to depart from their borders. . . . We understand that this fulfilled that which was spoken in the Psalm: *Your wonders won't be known in the dark places, or your justice in the forgotten land, will they?* (Ps 88:12). Clearly the *forgotten land* was that which, after the divine signs, not only refused to receive the author of salvation, but also compelled him to depart from their borders.

Matthew 8:30–34

30Now a herd of many swine was feeding at some distance from them. 31And the demons begged him, "If you cast us out, send us away into the herd of swine." 32And he said to them, "Go." So they came out and went into the swine; and behold, the whole herd rushed down the steep bank into the sea, and perished in the waters. 33The herdsmen fled, and going into the city they told everything, and what had happened to the demoniacs. 34And behold, all the city came out to meet Jesus; and when they saw him, they begged him to leave their neighborhood.

(22) John Chrysostom

But for what reason did the devils destroy the swine? Everywhere the devils have labored to drive men to dismay, and everywhere they rejoice in destruction. This, for instance, the devil did with respect to Job, although in that case too God allowed it; but not because God was appeasing the devil, but because he was willing to show that his own servant was the more glorious. This prevented the evil spirit from glorying in its shamelessness. What the evil spirit did against the righteous man God also did to the evil spirit. In the same way, given this current situation, contrary to what demons wanted, it is what occurred. For the power of Christ was gloriously proclaimed. The wickedness of the demons, which God had delivered from those possessed by them, was more clearly indicated. Moreover, God indicated how they want power to touch even swine, without permission from the God of all.

And if anyone would interpret these matters in a spiritual sense, there is nothing to stop them. For the history happened as it did. But, we are also supposed to realize that the swinish sort of men are especially liable to the operations of the demons. And as long as there are men that allow for such things, evil spirits are often able to dominate others. But if such men have become altogether swine, they are not only possessed, but are also cast down the precipice. Let no one suppose that what happened was mere acting. We may believe that the devils really fled. The death of the swine makes this evident.

And also notice his meekness together with his power. For when the inhabitants of that country drove him away, he did not resist, but departed, leaving those who had shown themselves unworthy of his teaching. Nevertheless, he gave them teachers that had been freed from the demons, and the swineherds, that they might all learn what had happened. When he left that area, there remained a certain fear in them. For the fame of what had been done was spreading, and the events penetrated their minds. And from many quarters there sounded utterances, proclaiming the strangeness of the miracle from those cured, and from the drowned, from the owners of the swine, and from the men that were feeding them.

Matthew 9

As Jesus continues to exercise the gift of healing, an issue of authority arises. By whose power are these miracles occurring? To show how it could be that the Son of Man was able to forgive sins, Hilary rewords the Gospel text to read: no one is able to forgive sins except God alone. *Chrysostom observes that here, unlike in the earlier chapters, the power of healing is now connected to one's faith. Whenever "they gave evidence of such great faith, Christ also gave evidence of his power." In each case (e.g., the woman with the hemorrhage of blood), Christ's power indicated that the Son is the same status as the one who begot him. Another aspect of Jesus's authority is on display in the calling of Matthew and his reclining with tax collectors and sinners. Chrysostom sees a parallel to the healing of the paralytic. As the paralytic was able to walk once his sins were forgiven, so Matthew became an apostle when his sins were forgiven. Matthew's decision was radical, for he not only left all his earthly vices and desires behind (Hilary), he also would never again return to that deceitful occupation (Gregory).*

Only those made new by the work of the Spirit are capable of becoming the new wine *for new wineskins. For Jerome,* new wine *meant those who put off the law and embraced the gospel; for Philoxenus,* new wine *was the doctrine of Christ that is to be enjoyed only when we put on godliness and put away evil; for Epiphanius,* new wine *referred to those who admitted their unrighteousness when called by the Lord (v. 13): "Therefore hurry to fill your wineskins, all you who are now present and hear the Gospel of the Lord."*

The Lord's power is graphically demonstrated in the healing of the woman, who merely touched the hem of his garment, and in the raising of the daughter of the ruler of the synagogue from the dead (9:18, 23–26). Augustine sees a figural meaning in these two events: The woman stands for the future churches of the Gentiles, "the healing of the Church of the nations," as it were, whereas the daughter of the synagogue president stands for the Jewish people to whom Jesus was sent.

The question of Jesus's authority is raised again in the healing of the two blind men. The first thing the blind men do is call out for his help with the words identifying him: Son of David. *Hilary asserts that their blindness should also be figuratively understood. Though blinded by putting their hope in the law, because of their faith they were able to see Jesus once he spoke to them. By faith in the gospel, they found their sight.*

The power of the gospel also extends to freeing those who are possessed by demons and leading them to give up the worship of fabricated gods: With a "knowledge of God . . . all super-

stition is put to flight" (Hilary). On this occasion, the Pharisees attribute to Jesus an identity, namely, that of exercising his power by the prince of demons *(v. 34). This is obviously foolish, says Chrysostom, and Jesus ignored their comment. He went on to other towns and villages,* preaching the gospel of the kingdom, and healing every disease.

Matthew 9:1–2

[1]And getting into a boat he crossed over and came to his own city. [2]And behold, they brought to him a paralytic, lying on his bed; and when Jesus saw their faith he said to the paralytic, "Take heart, my son; your sins are forgiven."

(1) Jerome

By **his own city** we should understand none other than Nazareth, which is why he is called a Nazarene. They brought a second paralytic to him (cf. 8:6), lying on a bed because he was not strong enough to walk. **When he saw the faith**, not of the one who was brought, but of those who brought him, he said to the paralytic, **Courage, son. Your sins are forgiven you.** O wondrous humility! He calls **son** a man held in disgust—weakened in every part of his body, his joints not working, someone even the priest would not deign to touch. But he was a **son** indeed, for his sins had been forgiven him. According to the spiritual sense, the passage can refer to the soul dwelling in the body with the strength of all its members out of joint and brought by a mature teacher to the Lord for healing. When healed by his mercy [the body receives] such strength that it immediately takes up its "bed."

Matthew 9:3–8

[3]And behold, some of the scribes said to themselves, "This man is blaspheming." [4]But Jesus, knowing their thoughts, said, "Why do you think evil in your hearts? [5]For which is easier, to say, 'Your sins are forgiven,' or to say, 'Rise and walk'? [6]But that you may know that the Son of man has authority on earth to forgive sins"—he then said to the paralytic—"Rise, take up your bed and go home." [7]And he rose and went home. [8]When the crowds saw it, they were afraid, and they glorified God, who had given such authority to men.

(2) John Chrysostom

Matthew says, **They brought him forward**, whereas the other evangelists say that they made a hole in the roof and let him down (cf. Mark 2:1–12; Luke 5:17–26). They set the disabled man in front of Christ, saying nothing, entrusting everything in Christ's hands.

You see, in the beginning, Christ himself went around not requiring such great faith on the part of those who came to him; but in this case, they approach him and faith was expected of them. **He saw *their* faith**, the text says, that is, the faith of those who lowered him down. He doesn't always require faith on the part of the sick. For example, he did not require faith in those who are possessed or in some other way beside themselves from illness. But in this case, the sick person had faith. He would not have allowed himself to be lowered down were he not a believer. And so, because they gave evidence of such great faith, Christ also gave evidence of his power by forgiving the man's sins with authority, demonstrating that in every way Christ is of equal status with the one who begot him. Notice that from the beginning he had indicated as much by teaching with authority: in the case of the leper, when he said, **I will, be cleaned**; in the case of the centurion, when he said, **only say the word, and my servant will be healed**, Christ marveled at him and praised him above all others; in the case of the sea, when he reined it in with a mere word; in the case of the devils, when they acknowledged him as their judge and he expelled them with complete authority. In this instance, in an even greater way, he forces his actual foes to confess his equal status with the Father, and by their own word to make it plain.

To bring out Christ's indifference to honor—there was a great company of people blocking the entrance, which is why they let the disabled man down from above—he did not at once heal the body that could be seen. Instead, he first dealt with what could not be seen, the soul, by forgiving his sins, which saved the man without bringing any glory on himself.

(3) Hilary of Poitiers

It disturbed the scribes that sin was forgiven by a man (for they considered that Jesus Christ was only a man) and that he forgave sin, for which the law was not able to grant absolution, since faith alone justifies (Rom 3:20, 28). When the Lord discerned the murmuring of the scribes, he said that it was easy for the Son of Man to forgive sins on earth. For truly no one is able to forgive sins except God alone. He who forgave, therefore, is God because no one can forgive except God. For the Word of God that abides in that Man offers to a man healing, and there was no difficulty for him to do and speak since it is given to him to perform everything that he said he would do.

So that we might understand that he became Man to forgive men's sins and to obtain the resurrection of their bodies, he said, **"In order that you may know the Son of Man has power on the earth to forgive sins," he said to the paralytic, "Rise, and take up your bed."** It had been enough for him to say **Rise**, but because each thing that was done needed to be explained, he added, **Take up your bed and [go] to your home.** First he granted forgiveness for sins; then he displayed the power of the resurrection. By raising the man from his cot, he taught that sickness and sorrow will affect our bodies no more. Finally, the man returning to his own home showed that the way to paradise will be recovered for believers, from which Adam, the father of all humanity, separated himself and departed through the ruin of sin.

(4) Chromatius of Aquileia

In the healing of this paralytic, our Lord and Savior shows that he is himself, God, both by providing health and by forgiving sins. For not only does he restore soundness of health to the paralytic, but in addition he says, **Your sins are forgiven.** With respect to this, certain of the scribes within hearing began murmuring among themselves saying, **Who is able to forgive sins except God alone?** In order to expose their unfaithfulness, the Lord showed the power of his divine nature by which he perceived the secrets of their hearts and said to them, **Why are you thinking evil things in your hearts?** The wicked scribes at least ought to have understood that no one else was able to perceive the secret thoughts of the heart than the one who had spoken to Samuel earlier by saying, *God will not see as a man. For a man looks on the outward appearance, but God looks on the heart* (1 Sam 16:7); about which it was written in the psalm, *God searches the heart and inner person* (Ps 7:9 [LXX Ps 7:10]); about which Isaiah testifies saying, *Because of your great majesty and the power of your virtue, nothing is hidden from you* (cf. Isa 40:26); and about which Jeremiah also says, *Lord, proving the just things, understanding the inner parts and hearts* (Jer 11:20). So too, the Lord himself testified in the Apocalypse, *and all the churches will know that I am he who searches the inner parts and hearts* (Rev 2:23).

Nevertheless, when the Lord had spoken to the paralytic, **Your sins are forgiven**, the unfaithful scribes charged the Lord with blasphemy, saying: **Who is able to forgive sins except God alone?** To silence their unfaithfulness, the Lord went right to the heart of the matter when he said, **Why are you thinking evil things in your hearts?** He did this to show the power of his divine nature, not only by forgiving sins, but also by clearly describing the secret things of their hearts. It is, after all, characteristic of and unique to God alone to know the thoughts of the heart.

Because these things done by the Lord contain a spiritual meaning, we need to turn our attention to what the paralytic represents. For we know that the pagans are signified by the paralytic. The pagans were being destroyed in spirit by the weight of their sins, as if they were shackled with a kind of incurable infirmity, and were "lying in bed" (the "bed" representing the four corners of the world). We can substitute "the pagans" in place of the paralytic who received salvation because Adam is known to be the progenitor of the human race. . . .

The Lord, who had come for the salvation of the human race, when considering their faith, deemed it fitting that heavenly health be given abundantly to "Adam," even to the pagans. This salvation is shown when the Lord said to the paralytic, **Your sins are forgiven you.** It was shown that the pagans, who were laboring under the heavy illness of sins, received the whole and perfect health of eternal salvation affecting body and spirit with forgiveness given to them through the heavenly medicine.

Matthew 9:9

9 As Jesus passed on from there, he saw a man called Matthew sitting at the tax office; and he said to him, "Follow me." And he rose and followed him.

(5) John Chrysostom

Why did he not call Matthew along with Peter and John and the others? As with the others Christ came on the scene at the time when he knew these people would believe, so too, he called Matthew at the time he knew he would respond. This was actually the reason why he snared Paul after the resurrection. For he knows the heart, and being acquainted with the unspoken thoughts of each one's mind, he knew also when each of the apostles would obey. Hence he did not call Matthew in the beginning when he was still hard-hearted, but only after many miracles and Christ's reputation had been spread abroad and Matthew was more ready to obey. Now, we also have reason to admire the evangelist's wisdom, for he makes no secret of his former life, and even supplies his name. By contrast, the other evangelists concealed their identity under another name. But why is it said that Matthew was **seated at the tax office**? He did this to emphasize the power of the one who called, that it was not when he had given up his evil trade, being in the midst of his evil practices.

In a similar way, Christ also converted blessed Paul when he was ranting and raving and breathing fire. In this way, he gave proof of the one who called. Paul tells the Galatians, *You heard of my former life in Judaism, how I went out of my way to persecute the Church of God* (Gal 1:13). And the fishermen, too, he called while they were hard at work. Theirs was not a trade with a bad reputation, but they were men with a rather rough disposition, without social skills, simple folk. The work of the other [tax collector] was marked by shamelessness and devious, taking unreasonable profits, behaving high-handedly, a form of theft hiding under the guise of law. Yet the one who called was not deterred by any of this. Why be surprised if he who is able to forgive every sin also makes this man an apostle?

(6) Epiphanius the Latin

And when he was passing by, he saw Matthew Levi. The holy Matthew names himself the publican in his Gospel. Now a publican is a sinner. He calls himself a sinner, even after he had become an apostle and saint. He lived his life as though he was in heaven not only on earth. For truly, every person who exalts himself will be humbled in hell, and he who humbles himself will be exalted in heaven, just as Wisdom says, *The just man is the accuser of himself in the beginning of speech* (Prov 18:17 LXX).

When the Lord passed by, he saw Matthew and he said to him, **Follow me.** That is, follow my path that leads to heaven. *And arising, he followed him* (9:9). Immediately he arose at the voice of the Lord; because he was sitting in his earthly sins and vices, oppressed by his hoard of money and desires, he arose. Once he left all these behind, he followed the Lord and thus was fulfilled the prophecy of blessed David saying, *Let the Lord arouse the powerless man from the earth, and let him lift up the poor man from the dung* (Ps 113:7). And again, *This is the transformation of the right hand of the Most High* (Ps 77:10). Thus he went from sinner to saint, publican to apostle, from being a man to an angel, that is, a messenger. He leaves behind earthly things; he possesses heavenly ones. He dismisses temporal things and grasps eternal ones. He has conquered Gehenna and has obtained a crown. O love, O desire, like no earthly love, no love of the world, no terror of judges held him back even for a moment! And he has fulfilled that which Wisdom had preached, *For who is this man and we shall praise him? For he has done wondrous things* (Sir 31:9). And not only did Matthew follow the Savior, but he even received him into his house. And the Lord reclined with his disciples in his house.

In what way did he leave all things behind? Matthew's counting house was the basis of his sin. But he left behind all earthly vices and desires, and was prepared for the Lord to clean the house of his heart. Not only did the Lord recline there; his disciples and many publicans came and reclined with them (9:10). For those men are publicans now having followed the Savior by Matthew's teaching and example. For by following Matthew's teaching and example those who followed the Savior became, as it were, publicans. O spacious and worthy house of holy Matthew, which was able to contain majesty itself! For *heaven is his seat and the earth is the stool of his feet* (cf. Isa 66:1). Thus his great majesty was reclining spaciously and grandeur with the disciples and publicans in the heart of blessed Matthew.

(7) Gregory the Great

The lesson from the holy Gospel which has just been read out in your hearing, dear friends, impels the mind to ask sharp questions, and, in so doing, points us to the importance of discernment. For it can be asked why Peter, who was a fisherman before his conversion, returned to fishing afterward. Since the Truth says, *No one who has set his hand to the plough, and then looks back, is fit for the kingdom of heaven* (Luke 9:62), why did Peter go back to what he had left behind? We might be tempted to criticize him for this, but if the virtue of discernment is brought into play, we quickly make a distinction. We see that any activity in which he was engaged without sin before conversion, can be returned to after conversion, equally without sin. We know that Peter was a fisherman. Matthew, on the other hand, was a tax collector. After his conversion, Peter returned to fishing, but Matthew did not again sit down to receive the payment of customs. It is one thing to seek food to live on by fishing, and quite another to exploit the collection of taxes to increase one's own wealth. There are indeed many occupations that can clearly be shown to be sinful, either in whole or in part. For those occupations that draw one into sin, it is essential that one should not return to them after conversion.

Matthew 9:10–13

10 And as he sat at table in the house, behold, many tax collectors and sinners came and sat down with Jesus and his disciples. 11 And when the Pharisees saw this, they said to his disciples, "Why does your teacher eat with tax collectors and sinners?" 12 But when he heard it, he said, "Those who are well have no need of a physician, but those who are sick. 13 Go and learn what this means, 'I desire mercy, and not sacrifice.' For I came not to call the righteous, but sinners."

(8) Hilary of Poitiers

The name "publican" comes from the life of those who abandoned the works of the law and preferred to comport themselves according to common and public practice. Thus, it is from his house, that is, from the sins of the body, that the Lord called Matthew in order to enter his mind and recline at its "table." This is the same person who wrote this Gospel, and, upon leaving the home of his sin, he accepted the Lord, who illuminated his innermost dwelling place. In this place, a dinner is richly prepared from the food of the Gospel for sinners and publicans. It was then that a spirit of jealousy agitated the Jews because of the Lord's communion with sinners and publicans. He unveiled their talk about keeping the law as but veiled coverings for unfaithfulness, showing that he was bringing aid for them because they were sick, and was providing medicine for them because they needed it, though they thought they were healthy and in no need of treatment. But so that they would understand that none of them were healthy, he warned them to learn the meaning of *I desire mercy, not sacrifice* (Hos 6:6). In other words, he is saying that because the law is bound up with offering sacrifices it is not able to be of help. Salvation for all people is preserved through the gift of mercy.

For I am come not to call the righteous, but sinners to repentance. If Jesus had come for all people, why then did he say that he had not come for the righteous? It was not necessary that he should come for those who had no need of him (Gal 3:11). But no one is made righteous by the law.

(9) Epiphanius the Latin

Salvation is far away from sinners (Ps 119:155). Because *the holy spirit of teaching will flee from that which is false and will remove itself from thoughts which are without understanding* (Wis 1:5). Because *the Lord Most High looks upon lowly things, lofty things he recognizes from afar.* He recognizes the lofty pride of men from far off, because nothing can hide from him; yet he recognizes them from afar, just as he recognized those Pharisees in the present reading. They were saying that they were righteous and were murmuring against the Lord, *because* **he ate with publicans and sinners** (cf. Mark 2:16). For the Lord did not recline nor enter into the house of their heart, because their heart was filled with greed and iniquity, though on the outside they are like whitened tombs (cf. Matt 23:27). In other words, they boasted of their righteousness in the presence of others, although within they were full of dead bones and every foul thing.

The Lord **had not come to call the righteous**. Not because they were righteous—because they were not, only God alone does good—but because they themselves were saying that they were righteous. In contrast, sinners are called to repentance, so that through repentance the vessels, that is, their heart, may be renewed, so that when the vices of the soul have been erased and wiped away and purged, they may now be worthy of receiving new wine, that is the Holy Spirit. New wineskins are like men made new. The old wineskins are the Jews or the pagans or sinful men. Therefore such men are not able to receive the wine, that is, the Holy Spirit, because they are not worthy to hold the Spirit. Therefore hurry to fill your wineskins, all you who are now present and hear the Gospel of the Lord. Purge your hearts and root out every stench of idolatry, every wickedness of sin, every uncleanness of vices, so that you are like new wineskins (cf. Matt 9:17), that is, like men made new. That you may be worthy to hold new wine, that is, the Holy Spirit, put on the new tunic of immortality, so that you may be preserved for eternity.

Matthew 9:14–17

[14]Then the disciples of John came to him, saying, "Why do we and the Pharisees fast, but your disciples do not fast?" [15]And Jesus said to them, "Can the wedding guests mourn as long as the bridegroom is with them? The days will come, when the bridegroom is taken away from them, and then they will fast. [16]And no one puts a piece of unshrunk cloth on an old garment, for the patch tears away from the garment, and a worse tear is made. [17]Neither is new wine put into old wineskins; if it is, the skins burst, and the wine is spilled, and the skins are destroyed; but new wine is put into fresh wineskins, and so both are preserved."

(10) Philoxenus of Hierapolis

The one who is sullied either with thoughts or deeds of sinfulness first must heal his wounds and rub away the blemishes of his soul and body. Then he may come to the festal chamber of divine mysteries, arrayed in the spiritual garments of the feast. For this reason, it is especially appropriate that every one who becomes a disciple of Christ should, from his earliest age, lay a firm foundation of teaching so that he can later grow. In this way, he makes his own godly habits, and the power of soul and body is not worn down by the world. Then he will not come to this service like an old and worn-out vessel, as the Lord said: **Let us put new wine into new bottles. . . .**

In the beginning of our youth, when as yet our foundation is new and we are still strong, and our vigor has not been made old by sin, let us put within ourselves the new wine of the doctrine of Christ. In this way, we may be zealous in our love of Christ's doctrine, and hold fast to it so that we may ourselves be preserved through it from all evil things.

Matthew 9:18–22

[18]While he was thus speaking to them, behold, a ruler came in and knelt before him, saying, "My daughter has just died; but come and lay your hand on her, and she will live." [19]And Jesus rose and followed him, with his disciples. [20]And behold, a woman who had suffered from a hemorrhage for twelve years came up behind him and touched the fringe of his garment; [21]for she said to herself, "If I only touch his garment, I shall be made well." [22]Jesus turned, and seeing her he said, "Take heart, daughter; your faith has made you well." And instantly the woman was made well.

(11) Tertullian

Jesus is touched by a woman with an issue of blood and does not know by whom: *Who touched me*, he asks. Even when the disciples suggest a reason (Luke 8:45), he persists in his expression of ignorance: *Somebody has touched me*, and he confirms this by proof: *For I have perceived that power is gone out of me* (Luke 8:46).

What says the heretic? Did Christ know who it was? Then why did he speak as if he did not know? Surely it was to elicit her confession, and to test her fear. In this way, he had in former times looked for Adam, as if in ignorance: *Adam, where are you* (Gen 3:9)? You also make an excuse for the Creator along with Christ, and Christ you deal with as you dealt with the Creator. But this too, you object to, as an opponent of the law, because the law sets a barrier against contact with a woman with an issue of blood (Lev 15:19–31). For that very reason, he was intent not merely to permit her to touch him, but even to grant her healing. Here is a god,[1] kind not by his own nature but through opposition to another. And yet, if we find that the woman's faith had deserved it so, when he says, **Your faith has saved you**, who are you, that you should discover hostility to the law in that act which the Lord himself indicates was performed as the reward of faith? But you wish to make out that the woman's faith was just this: that she had held the law in contempt.

It was by her faith, in the first place, that she trusted her God would prefer mercy even to sacrifice (Hos 6:6), for by faith she was assured that that God was at work in Christ. She touched him, neither as a holy man nor as a prophet—which she would know because of his human substance capable of defilement—but as God himself, whom she had assumed to be incapable of pollution. In this way, she was not in error in interpreting that law for herself that indicated that those things contracted defilement that were capable of defilement (cf. Lev 15:20): but not God, who she was confident was in Christ. Moreover, she considered that the proscription in the law was concerned with that ordinary and customary flux of blood at menstruation or childbirth that proceeds from natural functions, not what proceeds from illness. She, however, had an issue caused by ill health, for which she knew she had need of, not a period of time in seclusion, but the aid of divine mercy.

(12) Augustine

The daughter of the synagogue president stands for the Jewish people, while this woman stands for the Church of the Gentiles. Christ the Lord, born of the Jews in the flesh, was present among these Jews in the flesh. He sent others to the nations; he did not go himself. He spent his whole bodily and visible life in Judea. That is why the Apostle says, *For I say that Christ was a servant of the circumcision on account of the truth of God to confirm the*

1. The Marcionites sharply differentiated between the just and exacting god of the law and the merciful and charitable god of the gospel. Most of the events that took place in the four Gospels were supposedly the work of the just god, including this woman's healing. Tertullian shows the inconsistency of such an interpretation of the passage.

promises to the fathers—Abraham, in fact, had been told, In your seed shall all the nations be blessed (Gen 22:18)—*but that the nations glorify God for his mercy* (Rom 15:8–9).

So Christ was sent to the Jews. He was on his way to raise up the daughter of the synagogue president. The woman breaks in and is healed. She is first healed by faith and appears to be unknown to the Savior. Why else could he say [*Who touched me?*]. God's ignorance is a guarantee of a significant mystery; it must surely signify something, when the one who cannot be ignorant is ignorant. So what does it signify? The healing of the Church of the nations, which Christ never saw or visited in person. His voice on this point can be heard in the psalm, *A people that I did not know served me, with the obedience of the ear it obeyed me* (Ps 18:43–44). The world heard and believed; the Jewish people saw and first crucified him, but afterward also came to him. The Jews too believe, but at the end of the world (Rom 11:15, 25–26, 31).

Meanwhile, let this woman be healed, let her touch the hem of the garment. Take the garment as being the choir of the apostles. In it there was one who was the last and the least, a kind of hem, the Apostle Paul. He is the one who was sent to the nations and who says, *I indeed am the least of the apostles, who am not fit to be called an apostle* (1 Cor 15:9). Again he says, *I am the last of the apostles* (1 Cor 15:8). This last and least hem, this was what was needed to restore the unhealthy woman to health.

(13) John Chrysostom

Do you observe how the woman was superior to the head of the synagogue? (cf. Luke 8:41). She did not detain the Lord or lay hold of him: she simply touched with her fingertips. Though she was the last to come, she was the first to go off healed. The ruler directed the Physician to his house, whereas the woman was content with a mere touch. In fact, though she was very sick, her faith gave her wings.

Now, consider how he comforts her with the words, **Your faith has made you well.** Admittedly, if he had drawn her into the limelight, he would not have made this additional remark; it was to teach the head of the synagogue to believe that he said it, and to sing the woman's praises, and by these words to give her satisfaction and recognition no less than the bodily cure. . . .

The Lord was certainly to be admired, since miracles were falling like snowflakes around him, and he was working even greater ones, with the greatest to come. Had this not happened, the woman would have gone off unnoticed without such satisfaction. This was the reason he drew her into the limelight and sang her praises. He cast out her fear (since she came forward "trembling," as it is said (Luke 7:47), made her feel confident, and along with physical health gave her provision for the journey with the words *Go in peace* (Luke 7:48).

(14) Eusebius of Caesarea

I do not think it is right to omit a story that is worthy to be recorded for those that come after us. We are told that the woman who had an issue of blood came from Caesarea Philippi, and, as we learn from the sacred Gospels, found liberation from her affliction at the hands of our Savior. Her house was well known in this city, and the marvelous memorial of the Lord's kindness that was bestowed upon her still remains. For we are told that there stood on a high rock at the gates of her house a bronze figure in the relief of a woman, bending on her knee and stretching forth her hands like a supplicant. Opposite to this there was another relief of the same material: an upright figure of a man, clothed in a double-cloak and stretching out his hand to the woman.

The statue, they said, bore the likeness of Jesus. And it was in existence even to our day, so that we saw it with our own eyes when we stayed in that city.

Matthew 9:23–26

23And when Jesus came to the ruler's house, and saw the flute players, and the crowd
making a tumult, 24he said, "Depart; for the girl is not dead but sleeping." And they
laughed at him. 25But when the crowd had been put outside, he went in and took her
by the hand, and the girl arose. 26And the report of this went through all that district.

(15) John Chrysostom

Seeing the cymbals and the throng, he put them all out (cf. Mark 5:40) and worked the miracle with only the parents present. He did not bring someone else into existence, but restored the one who had departed, awakening her as though from sleep. He takes her hand to assure the onlookers, so that when they see her rise, they might have faith in the resurrection. Her father had said, you remember, **Put your hand on her**, but he does something more: instead of putting his hand on her, he took her and raised her up, showing that everything is at his disposal. He did not simply raise her up; he also gave directions that she be fed (Mark 5:43), lest what had happened should seem a figment of the imagination.

Now, for your part, take note not only of the rising to life but also that he ordered them to tell no one (Mark 5:43; Luke 8:56); and learn from this that Christ was without conceit or vainglory. From this you should learn as well that he cast the noisy mourners out of the house, showing them to be unworthy to behold such things. Do not leave with the mourners; stay with Peter, John, and James. . . . So let no one again mourn to excess, or weep and wail, or doubt Christ's achievement; he has vanquished death.

Matthew 9:27–31

27 And as Jesus passed on from there, two blind men followed him, crying aloud, "Have
mercy on us, Son of David." 28 When he entered the house, the blind men came to him;
and Jesus said to them, "Do you believe that I am able to do this?" They said to him,
"Yes, Lord." 29 Then he touched their eyes, saying, "According to your faith be it done to
you." 30 And their eyes were opened. And Jesus sternly charged them, "See that no one
knows it." 31 But they went away and spread his fame through all that district.

(16) Hilary of Poitiers

Then as the Lord went about, he was soon followed by two blind men. But to what degree were the blind men able to know his direction and the name of the Lord? As a matter of fact, they called him the Son of David and asked that they be healed. . . .

Although the blind men did not know from whom they sought salvation, the law indicated and showed them that their Savior would be from the race of David. And because they were blinded by their former sins, they did not see Christ until they were spoken to by him who introduced the light of the mind. By these things, the Lord shows that faith should not be expected from salvation, but salvation should be expected through faith. Because the blind men had believed, they saw—not that because they had seen, they then believed (John 20:29)—which means we must understand that what is sought for has to be gained by faith, not that faith is to be achieved by accomplishments. The Lord promised sight if they believed, and once they believed, he told them to be silent since it was the role of the apostles to preach.

(17) John Chrysostom

Once he had brought them into the house, he puts another question to them. Often he made a point of healing only when asked, lest anyone should suppose he was anxious to perform miracles to gain honor. Not only for this reason did he heal; he also knew that they were in need of healing.

His goodness had a kind of measure, for it depended on the faith of those who are healed. He also required that they have faith, for he asked: **Do you believe that I am able to do this?** So when they called him **Son of David**, he was able to lead them up to what is higher, and to teach them to imagine him as they ought. He did not say, "Do you believe that I am able to implore my Father, so that I might be able *to pray*," but "that I am able *to do this*?" What is their answer? **Yes, Lord.** They no longer call him **Son of David**, but rise to a higher understanding and acknowledge his authority.

And then at last he lays his hand on them saying, **According to your faith be it unto you.** And he does this to confirm their faith, to show that they are participants in the good work, and to witness that their words were not words of flattery. For neither did he say, "Let your eyes be opened," but, **According to your faith be it unto you.** He said this to many that came to him; before healing their bodies, he was eager to proclaim in advance the faith in their soul that they may be honored and others may take things more seriously.

(18) Chromatius of Aquileia

Although those blind men could not see with the eyes of their body, they nevertheless had clear eyes of faith and of heart. For this reason, they were able to see the true and eternal light, the Son of God, that one about whom it was certainly written: *He was the true light that illuminates every person coming into this world* (John 1:9). This was he whom Isaiah had prophesied that the Savior himself was about to come to give sight to the blind, saying, *The Spirit of the Lord is upon me, by which he anointed me, he sent me to proclaim the gospel to the poor, and to restore sight to the blind* (Isa 61:1). This was he about whom the same Isaiah, in another place, testifies: *Behold our God will restore judgment; he himself will come and will make us well. Then the eyes of the blind will be opened and the ears of the deaf will hear* (Isa 35:4–5). This was he about whom David also, through the Holy Spirit, had testified saying: *The Lord raises up those struck down, the Lord will set free those who are bound, the Lord illuminates the blind* (Ps 146:7–8).

Because those blind men discerned by the sight of the mind that the Savior of the human race had come in the flesh according to the proclamation of the prophets, not unreasonably they shout saying, **Have mercy on us, Son of David.** He was called the **Son of David** because he received a body from the seed of David. Not only did those blind men believe Christ the Lord was the Son of David, but what is most significant, they believed he was the Son of God and for that reason were saved. For they would not have expected to receive sight in their eyes from him if they had not believed he was the Son of God. And so when the Lord said, **Do you believe that I am able to do this?** they say, **Certainly, Lord.** Clearly, in these words they acknowledged him as God and man, Son of God and Son of Man; Son of God and our Lord according to the Spirit, **Son of David** because he had a body.

Note also the wonderful grace of the Lord, that he said to those blind men, **Do you believe that I am able to do this?** It is not as if the Lord would have been unable to do this had those men not believed,; rather he wanted to display the working of his power in the service of faith and also as a reward for those who believed. It is right then that he responds to the faith of these men with a gift of divine power, as the text says: **He touched their eyes and he said to them: According to your faith let it happen to you. And the eyes of those men were opened.** Through their faith these blind were able to see, because they earnestly believed that Christ the Lord was not only a man, but also God. When the Lord asked them saying, **Do you believe that I am able to do this?** he who knows the hidden things of the heart surely knew of their faith. Yet he wanted to ask for this reason, so that by confessing with the mouth what they believed with the heart, they would receive the salvation they were seeking, as it is written: *With the heart it is believed for righteousness, with the mouth confession is made to salvation* (Rom 10:10). And again: **Each one will be justified by his own words, or will be condemned by his own words** (Matt 12:37).

According to an allegorical meaning, those two blind men are figures of the two peoples who, after the death of Solomon, were divided into two kingdoms by Rehoboam, the son of Solomon, and by Jeroboam, the servant of the same Solomon (cf. 1 Kgs 12). So if we wished to see in these two blind men an image of the Jewish people and the people of the nations, it would not fit. For who among the people of the nations had heard either the law or the prophets or acknowledged Christ as the Son of David before being enlightened? Therefore, it is more correct to understand here the two peoples as mentioned above. They were among those who were able to recognize from the law and the prophets that Christ was the Son of David. For both of these were blind through their unbelieving mind because they had not yet seen the true light, the only-begotten Son of God prophesied in the law and prophets. They had lost the light of faith, and their eyes were covered by the veil of the law. They were in a kind of fog of blindness, as the Apostle records: *Indeed today, when Moses is read, a veil is over their heart; but when it has been converted to the Lord, the veil will be taken away* (2 Cor 3:15–16). And again: *That very veil remains in the reading of the old covenant, while it is not uncovered, since it is done away with in Christ* (2 Cor 3:14).

Therefore, sight was immediately restored to these blind men when they believed in the Son of God. This event shows which of these two peoples believed and had faith in the Son of God; he had come for the salvation of the human race, and when someone recognizes the true light, all blindness is removed. And so the gift of his divine grace was revealed, not in another time or in another place, but only when the begotten Son of God had taken up a human body. He dwells in his own body, that is, in the Church, in which all who believe, freed from the blindness of the former error, will see the glory of eternal light. And so when these blind men received light in their eyes, they began to declare the power of the Lord everywhere publicly. This indicates that the grace of his divine gift should be preached everywhere by those who have believed; for the grace of such a gift that the Lord performed and performs daily cannot be hidden nor be silenced. He is blessed forever. Amen.

Matthew 9:32–34

32 As they were going away, behold, a dumb demoniac was brought to him. 33 And when the demon had been cast out, the dumb man spoke; and the crowds marveled, saying, "Never was anything like this seen in Israel." 34 But the Pharisees said, "He casts out demons by the prince of demons."

(19) Hilary of Poitiers

[I]t is clear that the pagans are presented in the mute and deaf demoniac as a people who need an all-encompassing salvation. In every way, this man was besieged by every kind of evil, the demoniac was shackled by the entirety of bodily sins. He gave form to the facts. For instance, the demon is at first cast out, and then the rest of the bodily functions came into their own. Through knowledge of God, the insanity of all superstition is put to flight, while the sight and hearing and the word of salvation take its place. In its astonishment at what had been done, the crowd declared: **Nothing like this has ever appeared in Israel** (9:33b). The demoniac, for whom no help at all could come through the law, was saved by the power of the Word; the dumb and deaf man declared everywhere the praises of God (9:31). Now that salvation had been given to the pagans, all cities and villages (9:35) were illuminated by the power and presence of Christ, and they were delivered from every infirmity of their ancient illnesses.

(20) John Chrysostom

The Pharisees were especially displeased at Jesus because the crowds preferred him to everyone else, not only those who lived now, but those who had ever lived. And it was not only for his healing that they preferred him, but also because he healed innumerable and incurable diseases easily and quickly.

At least this was how the crowds felt. As for the Pharisees, they not only disparaged these works, but they said contradictory things among themselves without shame. Is that not proof of their wickedness? For what did they say? **He casts out devils through the prince of the devils.**

What can be more foolish than this? First of all, as he says further on, a devil cannot cast out a devil, for he would want to strengthen what belongs to him, not destroy it. But he not only cast out devils, he also cleansed lepers, raised the dead, curbed the sea, remitted sins, preached the kingdom, and brought men to the Father; things a demon would never choose to do nor be able to bring about. For the devils lead men to idols and lead them away from the truth, convincing them that there is no life to come. The devil does not return kindness for insult, and even when he is not insulted, he still harms the ones who confer kindness when he is insulted; even when he is not insulted, the devil still harms those who venerate and honor him.

Matthew 9:35–38

35 And Jesus went about all the cities and villages, teaching in their synagogues and preaching the gospel of the kingdom, and healing every disease and every infirmity.

36 When he saw the crowds, he had compassion for them, because they were ha-
rassed and helpless, like sheep without a shepherd. 37 Then he said to his disciples, "The
harvest is plentiful, but the laborers are few; 38 pray therefore the Lord of the harvest to
send out laborers into his harvest."

(21) Theodore of Heraclea

The good news of the kingdom is this: the assurance of the kingdom of heaven. For when we are raised from the dead and share in the grace of the Holy Spirit, our souls remain immutable and we live in heaven with an incorruptible body. And he says that the kingdom of heaven has everywhere drawn near, so that through his coming we have in truth obtained the promise of the covenant, and, in terms of a type, we have already gained the first fruits of the Spirit.

(22) Hilary of Poitiers

Why did the Lord have pity on those who were **harassed and helpless**? Clearly, the Lord took pity on the people troubled by the oppressive violence of the unclean spirit and disabled by the weight of the law because they still had no shepherd who would restore to them the guardianship of the Holy Spirit (cf. 1 Pet 2:25). Although the fruit of this gift was most abundant, nothing had yet been harvested. For the Spirit's abundance surpasses the multitude of those who draw on him. If everyone gathers as much as he needs, there is always enough to give generously. It is useful that the Lord ministers through many; he urged nonetheless that we ask the Lord of the harvest **to send forth many workers into the harvest**, that is, that we ask God to grant an abundance of harvesters who utilize the gift of the Holy Spirit that was prepared. Through prayer and supplication, God pours his bounty upon us. In order to indicate that this harvest and the many harvesters would be drawn first from the twelve apostles (10:2–4), he gave to those gathered together the authority for expelling spirits and for healing every kind of sickness. By the powers of this gift, they were able to expel the one who troubled them and to cure illness.

(23) John Chrysostom

When he saw the multitudes, he was moved with compassion on them, because they were troubled, and **scattered abroad, as sheep having no shepherd. Then says he unto his disciples, The harvest truly is plenteous, but the laborers are few; pray ye therefore the Lord of the harvest, that he will send forth laborers into his harvest.**

Notice again that he is free of self-promotion. He does not insist that everyone come to him, rather he sends out his disciples. This was not the only reason. He also wished to teach that after they gained some experience in Palestine as a kind of training-school, they would strip themselves for the conflicts they would have with the world. This is why he makes their exercises more rigorous than the actual conflicts, so that being trained in virtue they might more easily engage in the struggles that were to come. It was as if they were fledglings whom he was finally leading out to fly. At first he made them physicians of bodies, only later giving them the task of curing souls—the principal goal. And notice how satisfying and how necessary what he has in mind. For what does he say? **The harvest truly is plenteous, but the laborers are few**. In other words, it is not for sowing that I send you, he says, but for reaping. Which in John he expressed in this way: *Other men labored, and ye are entered into their labors* (John 4:38). . . .

Who are these laborers he speaks of here? They are the twelve disciples. How can that be? When he said, **But the laborers are few**, didn't he add to their number? He did not, but sent them out alone. Why then did he say, **Pray the Lord of the harvest, that he would send forth laborers into his harvest**; and yet make no addition to their number? Because though they were only twelve, from then on he made them many, not by adding to their number, but by giving them power.

Then to signify how great the gift, he says, **Pray the Lord of the harvest**; and indirectly declares that it is he who has authority. For after saying, **Pray the Lord of the harvest**, even though they had made no request nor prayer, he himself at once commissions them, reminding them also of the sayings of John (3:12) of the threshing floor, of the person winnowing, of the chaff, and of the wheat. These words make it clear that he is himself the husbandman, himself the Lord of the harvest, himself the Master and Lord of the prophets. For if he sent them to reap, it is obvious they were not supposed to reap what belonged to another, but what he himself had sown by the prophets.

Matthew 10

Now that Jesus has revealed his divine authority in several tangible ways, the reader is introduced to those who are endowed with authority to carry the message of the kingdom. Hilary highlights the importance of the mission: "all authority of the Lord's power is transferred to the apostles." This is the first time in the Gospel the twelve are called apostles. Tertullian explains why Jesus chose twelve and not some other number, and Gregory the Great explains that miraculous signs were intended for unbelievers, not those who already knew God's power.

Most of the chapter is given over to instructions as the apostles prepare for their mission. They are sent to the Jews and are not supposed to seek the salvation of the pagans. Their singular goal is to show the power of the gospel: Cure the sick, raise the dead, cleanse lepers, cast out demons (10:8). Only the kingdom of heaven, says Hilary, no human agency, can perform such miracles. Just as the disciples were instructed to bring nothing with them as they went out, so the gift to perform wonders was derived from the Lord (Chrysostom). Because they had no money, extra clothing, or any accessories, the disciples were free to give and expect nothing in return.

The cost of this kind of discipleship was high. Augustine refers to the disciples as "martyrs," whom the Lord sent into the world where they would be hated for my name's sake. *They are like the grain that the Lord is scattering across the field of "the world" filled with tares. But they are to have no fear of those who can kill the body; for only God can bring judgment upon the soul (Philoxenus), that is, either eternal death or eternal life.*

It is said that Christ brought not merely peace but a sword. This refers to the word that cuts the believer from natural ties. Enemies can even be found in his "household" who separate him from the word of God (Hilary). The peace Christ proclaims indicts the world and causes division even between sons and fathers, between daughters-in-law and mothers-in-law (Eusebius of Emesa). Believers are called to choose the higher love for God, not to cling to earthly bonds. "Love all things in the right order so that you yourself may be rightly ordered. Allot to things their own proper weights and importance" (Augustine).

Whoever graciously receives a disciple of Christ receives him and the Father who sent him. Freed of our possessions, we are able to give even to itinerant teachers or prophets, or to those who seem insignificant. If we give a cup of cold water to someone who is thirsty, we have a reward from God. As Clement of Alexandria astutely observes, this is "the only reward" that cannot be lost.

Matthew 10:1–4

[1]And he called to him his twelve disciples and gave them authority over unclean spirits, to cast them out, and to heal every disease and every infirmity. [2]The names of the twelve apostles are these: first, Simon, who is called Peter, and Andrew his brother; James the son of Zeb'edee, and John his brother; [3]Philip and Bartholomew; Thomas and Matthew the tax collector; James the son of Alphaeus, and Thaddaeus; [4]Simon the Cananaean, and Judas Iscariot, who betrayed him.

(1) Tertullian

Why did he choose twelve apostles and not some other number? . . . This number was indicated figuratively in the Creator's Scriptures: the twelve springs at Elim (Exod 15:27), the twelve jewels on Aaron's priestly garment (Exod 28:9–21), and the twelve stones chosen by Joshua out of the Jordan and laid up in the ark of the covenant (Josh 4:8–9). For these were former indications that apostles of that number would irrigate, like fountains and rivers, the world of the Gentiles that had formerly been dried up like a desert without knowledge—as is also said in Isaiah (43:19d), *I will place rivers in a waterless land.* They would be like jewels that shed light upon the holy vesture of the Church, that vesture that Christ as the Father's high priest has put on. They would be firm in the faith like stones that the true Joshua has chosen out of the baptism of Jordan and received in the holy place of his own covenant.

(2) Jerome

The task of determining the order and merits of each of the apostles belonged to the one who searches the secrets of the heart. Simon is mentioned first with the cognomen Peter to distinguish him from the other Simon, called the Cananaean, from the village of Cana in Galilee, where the Lord changed water into wine. James is called son of Zebedee, since there was another James, the son of Alphaeus. He groups the apostles in pairs: Peter and Andrew go together as brothers, not of the flesh, but of the Spirit; James and John, who left behind their natural father and followed the true Father; Philip and Bartholomew; Thomas and Matthew, the tax collector. When the other evangelists give the list of names, they place Matthew first, then Thomas, but they do not use the term tax collector for him, lest by recalling his earlier way of life they might appear to insult the evangelist. But Matthew, as we have noted above, places himself after Thomas and calls himself a tax collector, so that *where sin abounded, grace* might abound still more (cf. Rom 5:20).

(3) John Chrysostom

Earlier the evangelist had mentioned two pairs of apostles, Peter [and Andrew], John [and James] (4:18–21), and also the calling of Matthew. But he had said nothing about the calling of the other disciples nor given their names. So now he lists them, tells us how many there were, gives their names, saying: **Now the names of the twelve apostles are these: first, Simon, who is called Peter**. He says this because there was another Simon, the Cananaean; and there was also Judas Iscariot and Judas the brother of James; and James the son of Alphaeus, as well as James the son of Zebedee.

Mark also lists them according to their distinction (Mark 3:17–19). So after the two leaders, he numbers Andrew. . . . But let us look at the list of them from the beginning.

First, Simon, who is called Peter, and Andrew his brother. This is no small praise. For the one he named from his virtue, the other from his good birth. Then **James the son of Zebedee, and John his brother**. Notice that they are not arranged by their distinction. It seems to me, however, that John is greater, not only than the others, but even than his brother.

After saying **Philip, and Bartholomew**, he added, **Thomas, and Matthew the tax collector**. Luke does not put it in this way but in the opposite order, putting Matthew before Thomas (Luke 6:15). Next, **James the son of Alphaeus**. There was, as I have already said, another James, son of Zebedee. Then . . . Matthew comes to the traitor. He does not describe him as any sort of enemy or foe, but identifies him as one would in a written account. He does not say Judas is "the unholy, the all unholy one," but identifies him by his city, **Judas Iscariot**. For there was also another Judas, Lebbaeus,[1] whose surname was Thaddaeus, who, according to Luke, was the son of James, *Judas the son of James* (Luke 6:16). Therefore to distinguish him from the other man, it is said, **Judas Iscariot, who also betrayed him.** Matthew is not ashamed to say, **who also betrayed him.** The account does not try to hide anything, not even matters of reproach. Note also that the first, the leader of the group, was an *unlearned, the ignorant man* (Acts 4:13).

But let us see where and to whom he sends them. **These twelve**, it is said, **Jesus sent forth**. What kind of men were these? Fishermen and tax collectors; the publicans, indeed, four fishermen and two tax collectors, Matthew and James, and one was a traitor.

Matthew 10:5–13

**5These twelve Jesus sent out, charging them, "Go nowhere among the Gentiles, and enter no town of the Samaritans, 6but go rather to the lost sheep of the house of Israel.
7And preach as you go, saying, 'The kingdom of heaven is at hand.' 8Heal the sick, raise the dead, cleanse lepers, cast out demons. You received without paying, give without pay. 9Take no gold, nor silver, nor copper in your belts, 10no bag for your journey, nor two tunics, nor sandals, nor a staff; for the laborer deserves his food. 11And whatever town or village you enter, find out who is worthy in it, and stay with him until you depart. 12As you enter the house, salute it. 13And if the house is worthy, let your peace come upon it; but if it is not worthy, let your peace return to you."**

1. Some ancient manuscripts have Lebbaeus instead of Thaddaeus.

(4) Hilary of Poitiers

The disciples are told to keep away from the ways of the pagans, not because they were not also sent for the salvation of pagans, but so that they would keep themselves apart from the activities and lifestyle of ignorant pagans. They were also forbidden to enter the cities of the Samaritans. Yet did he not himself heal a Samaritan? But they are told not to enter churches of heretics, for there is no difference between ignorance and perversity. They are sent instead to the lost sheep of the house of Israel.

They are prohibited to keep gold, silver, or copper in their belts, nor allowed to carry a wallet for the journey, nor take two tunics or two pair of shoes or take a staff in hand, for the worker is worthy of his earnings. It is not wrong, I think, to have money in one's belt. Why, then, does he wish to prohibit them from having gold, silver, and copper in their belts? The belt is a piece of equipment for service, and the waistband for practical reasons. By this we are warned not to let anything in our ministry be for sale, nor should we have a need for possessing gold, silver, or copper in the execution of apostolic service. **Nor a wallet for the journey**. Our preoccupation with worldly goods must be left behind. Because all treasure on earth is insidious, our treasure will be stored in our heart (cf. 6:21).

(5) John Chrysostom

Take note that he is concerned for their conduct no less than for their miracles, implying that the miracles by themselves are nothing. With one stroke he subdues their pride by saying, **You have received freely, freely should you give** and steers them clear of covetousness. He did this so that they would not think the signs were their own work and become haughty. He says, **You have freely received**. But don't think you bestowed something on those who received you, for you did not pay for what you received, nor did you work for it. The grace is mine. So you should give to others, for no price can be put on them.

Then, after pulling out the root of evils (1 Tim 6:10), he says **Provide neither gold, nor silver, nor brass in your purses, nor money for your journey, neither two coats, neither shoes, nor yet a staff**. He didn't say, "take nothing with you," but [implied] even if you can obtain these things from others, nevertheless flee the evil disease. The Lord had several purposes by these instructions. First, he was putting his disciples above suspicion; second, he was freeing them from every care so that they devote all their energy to the word; third, he was teaching them about his own power. For these reasons later on he says: *Did you lack anything, when I sent you naked and unshod*? (cf. Luke 22:35).

Perhaps someone might ask why he insisted they should not **take a bag for the journey, neither two coats, nor a staff, nor shoes**. The Lord wished to discipline them by paying close attention to everything, when he told them not to give a thought even for the next day's provisions. Now he was sending them out as teachers to the whole world, and he wished them to be not men but angels (so to speak), freed from all worldly cares, possessed with one care alone, that of their teaching. So he frees them with the words, **Take no thought how or what you shall speak** (10:19).

And so, what may seem to be a very difficult and nerve-racking experience, he shows to be especially light and even easy for them. For nothing makes men as happy as being freed from anxiety and care. This is especially true when, once being freed, they lack nothing because God is present and has become everything to them.

Anticipating they would say, "how are we supposed to obtain our necessary food?" he didn't say to them, "You have heard what I told you before, **Behold the fowls of the air**; (6:26) (for they were not yet able to understand how this commandment related to their actions), but added something much less drastic, saying, **For the workman deserves his food** (10:10). He intimates that they would be supported by their [own] disciples. The point was that they should not be high-minded toward those whom they were teaching as if they were doing all the giving and receiving nothing. . . .

(6) Gregory the Great

It is easy now when we see everything heading for destruction to disengage our minds from love of the world. But then it was very difficult, because the disciples were sent to preach the unseen kingdom of heaven at the very time when everyone could observe the kingdoms of earth flourishing. Miracles were granted to these holy preachers that their obvious power might lend credence to their words, and that those who were preaching something new might perform something new. It is said in this same reading: **Cure the sick, raise the dead, cleanse lepers, cast out demons.**

With the world flourishing, the human race increasing, life expectancies increasing, and riches abounding, who would believe that there was another life when one heard about it? Who would prefer invisible to visible things? And yet, with the sick returning to health, the dead being raised to life, lepers being cleansed, demoniacs being snatched from the power of unclean spirits—when so many visible miracles had been performed—who would not believe what he heard about invisible things? In truth, visible miracles were brought forth to attract the hearts of those who see them so that they may be moved to faith in invisible things. In other words, miracles were done externally so that what is interior and far more wonderful may be realized.

Once the number of believers has grown, there are many within the holy Church who pursue the life of virtue, though they lack the signs of the virtues, because it is useless for a miracle to be shown externally if it brings about nothing within. For this reason, Paul said that signs are for unbelievers, not believers (1 Cor 14:22). For this reason, that outstanding preacher raised up Eutychus by his prayer in the presence of many unbelievers, when he slept during the preaching and fell from the window and died (Acts 20:9–12). But he did not cure Timothy, his companion on his travels and his helper in holy preaching, when he was exhausted from the weakness of his stomach. He could have healed him with a word, but he restored him instead by his healing art, saying: *Use a little wine for the sake of your stomach and your frequent illnesses* (1 Tim 5:23). If he revived a weak unbeliever by one prayer, who was (as we believe) dead, why did he not save his sick companion by a prayer? Undoubtedly because the former who was still dead within had to be healed outwardly by a miracle so that an inner power might bring him to life through what was made manifest by an external act. Conversely, it was not necessary to have a display of outward signs for a sick believer who was completely alive within.

(7) Hilary of Poitiers

At this point all authority of the Lord's power is transferred to the apostles, those who in Adam had been formed in the image and likeness of God, and now shared in the perfect image and likeness of Christ. Their power differs in no way from that of the Lord, since those who were once earthbound are now of heaven (1 Cor 15:48; Col 3:2–4). They preach the coming of the kingdom of heaven; they have now acquired the image and likeness of God in the fellowship of truth—as all the saints, who are called of heaven, may reign with the Lord; they heal the sick, raise the dead, cleanse the lepers, drive out demons; and, whatever Adam's evils incited by Satan are brought against the body, they cleanse again because they share the Lord's authority. So that they will completely realize the likeness of God according to the prophecy of Genesis (Gen 1:26), they are commanded to give freely as they have freely received. In other words, for a gracious gift, let there be a gracious offering of service.

Matthew 10:14–20

14"And if any one will not receive you or listen to your words, shake off the dust from
your feet as you leave that house or town. 15Truly, I say to you, it shall be more tolera-
ble on the day of judgment for the land of Sodom and Gomor'rah than for that town.

16"Behold, I send you out as sheep in the midst of wolves; so be wise as serpents
and innocent as doves. 17Beware of men; for they will deliver you up to councils, and
flog you in their synagogues, 18and you will be dragged before governors and kings for
my sake, to bear testimony before them and the Gentiles. 19When they deliver you up,
do not be anxious how you are to speak or what you are to say; for what you are to say
will be given to you in that hour; 20for it is not you who speak, but the Spirit of your
Father speaking through you."

(8) John Chrysostom

What does it mean, **Shake off the dust of your feet**? It signifies either that the disciples received nothing from those they visited, or it showed to those who witnessed it that they have made a long journey for their sake. But notice how he did not reveal everything to them. For he did not yet grant them foreknowledge so that they could know who was worthy and who was not. Instead, he tells them to make inquiry and await results. If we ask how did he knowingly spend time with one who oversees tax collection, it is because the tax collector had become worthy by his conversion.

Note also how once he had stripped them of everything, he gave them everything, by urging them to live in the houses of those who became disciples. Even though they had nothing to offer, they were supposed to receive hospitality from the houses they entered. As a result, they were themselves freed from anxiety and were able to convince others that they had come simply for their salvation. This was done first by bringing nothing with them, then by asking no more from their hosts than what was necessary, and lastly, by not entering indiscriminately just any house (10:14).

The Lord did not want them to appear notable because of the signs; rather, they were to be known by their virtue even before the signs. For nothing so much characterizes the virtuous way of life than simplicity, and, so far as able, to be free of wants. This even the false apostles recognized.

(9) Tertullian

We are branded "innocent" by them,[2] and for that reason they do not consider us "wise." They imagine that wisdom has nothing in common with innocence, even though the Lord connected both in his saying, **be prudent as serpents and innocent as doves.** Now, however, if we are stupid because we are innocent, are they not "un-innocent" because they are wise? The most vicious individuals are those who are not innocent, just as the most stupid are those who are not wise. As for me, I would prefer to be convicted of the better fault if I have to make a choice; it is better to have a lesser intelligence than be evil; better to err than to deceive. . . .

[T]he dove was used to reveal Christ; the serpent was used to tempt him. The former from the first was the herald of divine love; the latter from the first was the thief of God's image. Therefore, innocence by itself can easily both recognize and exhibit God. Wisdom by itself can rather attack and betray him.

Let the serpent hide himself as much as he can; let him twist his entire "wisdom" into the windings of his lairs. Let him live deep in the ground, push into dark holes, unroll his length coil by coil; let him slither out—but not all of him at once, the light-hating beast. Our dove, however, has a simple home, always in high and open places toward the light since this symbol of the Holy Spirit loves the sunrise, the symbol of Christ. Just so, truth blushes at nothing except at being hidden away. . . .

(10) Augustine

Notice how our Lord Jesus Christ trains his martyrs with the instructions he gives them. **I am sending you, he says, like sheep in the midst of wolves**. Just think what happens if a single wolf gets in among many sheep. However many thousands of sheep there may be, send just one wolf among them, and they panic, and even if they aren't all savaged, they are certainly all terrified. So what an extraordinary idea it was, what a plan, with a weight of divine authority behind it, not to let the wolf in among the sheep, but to send the sheep

2. Gnostic Christians who claimed to possess a special wisdom beyond that of the common Christian.

to the wolves. **I am sending you,** he says, **like sheep in the midst of wolves;** not to the boundaries of the wolves, but right into the midst of the wolves. So there was a pack of wolves, and only a few sheep; so that many wolves kill a few sheep. But then the wolves were converted and became sheep.

Bear in mind that these words are said to everyone: both to those alive then and listening to the Lord, and those who were going to believe in the Lord through them, as well as to generations that would be born to take their place when they died, right up to our time and after us to the end of the world—to absolutely everyone it's said, **You will be hated by all nations for my name's sake** (10:22)

In other words, the Church as it would exist among all nations was being foretold. We read about the promise, and we see it also being kept. Yes, all nations are Christian, and again no nations are Christian. Throughout the whole field there is grain, and throughout the whole field there are also tares (13:26). So when you hear it said by our Lord Jesus Christ, **You will be hated by all people for my name's sake**, take it like grain since it is being said to the grain.

Join me in reflecting why none of us should say to ourselves, "This was said to the Lord's disciples when our Lord Jesus Christ sent them to preach his word among the nations. All nations hated them for his name's sake. But now all nations glorify his name. We mustn't suppose that we are hated by all nations, but rather that we are loved by all nations." All you Christian nations, O grain crops of the Lord, O catholic seed scattered throughout the world, look at yourselves, and recognize that all nations do hate you for the sake of the name of Christ!

But now let's produce a very, very bad man; let's make him a nobleman, very powerful, glittering with honors, at the peak of his power, and have him full of evil intentions and able to carry them out. He too is hated by everyone, but not for the sake of the name of Christ. The same kind of language is used, but in a very different case. The Lord Jesus knew that extremely bad men are also hated by everyone, so that's why, after saying **Everyone will hate you,** he added, **for my name's sake**. He had heeded the plea of those who say, *Judge me, O God, and distinguish my case from an ungodly nation* (Ps 43:1).

It was this cunning of the serpent that the martyrs imitated when they offered to their persecutors whatever they possessed as mortals to protect Christ as their head. Since Christ is the head of man, they were determined not to let die that part of themselves where they were really alive. They followed the instruction of the Lord advising them to be as cunning as serpents, and so when orders were given for them to be beheaded, they didn't suppose that they would then lose their head. On the contrary, when their heads were cut off, they kept Christ, their head, intact. The torturer may ferociously assault different parts of the body with whatever cruelty he may dig up: cut our flanks with lashes, lacerate our entrails, and get at the innermost part of our bodies. But he cannot get at our head, because he is not permitted even to see it. Although he could get at it if he wishes to, not by raging against us, but by believing the same as we do.

But how were women able to imitate this cunning serpent in order to win the prize medal, the crown of martyrdom? Christ, you see, is called the head of the man, while the man is the head of the woman. But these women didn't die for their husbands, seeing that in some cases they had to spurn the appeals even of their husbands who tried to call them back from the brink. No less women share the same faith as members of the Church, and thus Christ, who is head of the whole Church, is the head of all his members.

So you see that the whole Church is called both a woman and a man, just as it is said to be "one virgin." The Apostle says, *I engaged you to one man, to present you to Christ as a chaste virgin* (2 Cor 11:2). The Church is perceived as a man when the same Apostle says, *Until we all attain to the unity of faith, to the recognition of the Son of God, to the perfect man, to the measure of the age of the fullness of Christ* (Eph 4:13). When it's a woman, Christ is her husband; when it's a man, Christ is his head. Thus since the head of the woman is the husband, and Christ is the husband of the Church, when women also suffered for Christ, they fought for their head against the cunning of the serpent. So let us too guard our head against the persecutors, let us imitate the cunning of the serpent, and let us send up our sighs to God for these same persecutors of ours that we hold on also to the innocence of doves.

Matthew 10:21–23

21"Brother will deliver up brother to death, and the father his child, and children will rise against parents and have them put to death; 22and you will be hated by all for my name's sake. But he who endures to the end will be saved. 23When they persecute you in one town, flee to the next; for truly, I say to you, you will not have gone through all the towns of Israel, before the Son of man comes."

(11) Tertullian

We can prove that one must not avoid persecution by flight. If a persecution is initiated by God, then fleeing is certainly not possible since it is precisely God who is responsible for it. This is supported by a twofold defense: on the one hand, we *ought* not avoid what has been produced by God, on the other hand, we will not be able to escape it. We should not attempt to avoid it: if it is good, what seems good to God is necessarily good for all. Genesis states, *And God saw because* [or *that*] *it is good*, not because God was unfamiliar with the concept of goodness until he saw it, but so that by this expression we may learn that it was good because it was seen by God. Of course there are many things that God has inaugurated seemingly to the harm of someone. However, it is good by definition because it comes from God, and hence it is automatically divine and reasonable (for what is divine if not reasonable, if not good? What good is not divine?). Although this does not appear to be the case in the eyes of all humanity, nevertheless, human perception does not get to prejudge the nature of such things. . . .

Persecution, therefore, is good by its own nature because it bears the mark of a divine and reasonable arrangement. Certainly it is unwelcome in the eyes of those to whom it comes as an evil. Even here, however, when one perceives that such an evil ultimately resides in the rationality of God, he cannot simply call persecution an evil thing. For persecution is good even with respect to its evil, provided that it is directed by divine rationality (for example, when someone's salvation is overthrown by persecution), just as goodness is seen to be a product of divine rationality when God accomplishes another's salvation by means of the same persecution (unless we dare to say that one either perishes or is saved by the Lord *irrationally*). And so we may view persecution as good from either angle, because it is good in its own nature. We rightly assert, then, that because it is good, we should not try to evade it (it is, of course, a sin to refuse what is good); for that matter, since persecution is brought about by God, it is really impossible to evade it, as God's will cannot be avoided. In other words, those who contemplate flight in the face of persecution either implicitly reproach God with evil, since they obviously view persecution as an evil (no one, after all, flees a *good*), or they think themselves stronger than God, since they believe that they can escape what God has willed to occur.

"But I have a right," someone says, "to flee, so that I may not die damned if I deny him. God, after all, has the power to drag me back to the authorities if he so wishes." Answer me this first: are you *certain* that you would deny him if you failed to flee? Most likely you're not, for if you are certain that you would deny him, you've already done so. By presupposing your denial you have despaired of staying true. You thus fly in vain, since, if it was inevitable that you would have denied God, it's as if you've already done it. If, on the other hand, you are instead uncertain whether you would deny or not, why not, since your fear is that it could go either way, focus instead on the possibility of your confessing and thus assuring your salvation? Wouldn't it be better to focus on this, having a reason *not* to flee, than to presuppose your own denial, so that you might?

At this present time, therefore, we see two possibilities: the ability to confess or deny is either in our hands, or in God's. If it's up to *us*, why can't we assume that we would take the better course of confessing, rather than denial (unless we're certain of our inability to confess when threatened with torture—but of course, this is the same as active denial already)? If up to *God*, why can't we simply abandon ourselves to his judgment, acknowledging the fact of his strength and power? After all, if he has the power to lead us back to the authorities even as we flee, why can't he defend us if we stay, dwelling even in the midst of the crowds?

"Quite to the contrary," someone says, "the Lord's teaching itself advocates flight from city to city." In this way, "someone" (of course, the fugitive himself) wants to argue, being totally unwilling to comprehend the specific context of this proclamation of his Lord, in order to use it as a cover for his own cowardice. Instead, the proclamation applies to specific persons, times and situations.

When they begin, the Lord says, **to persecute you, flee from city to city** (10:23). We argue that this commandment properly applies only to the persons, times, and situations of the apostles. The following passage illustrates this interpretation, since it can apply to no one but the apostles: **Do not go through the way of the nations, nor enter into a city of the Samaritans, but instead go to the lost sheep of the house of Israel** (10:5–6). But the **way of the nations** is open to us; in it, after all, we were converted and on it we continue to walk until the end. No city, therefore, has been excepted from the message that we proclaim throughout the world, nor ought we to have any special concern for Israel above and beyond our ordinary proclamation to the nations. Furthermore, if we are caught, we will not be brought before *Jewish* councils nor flogged in *Jewish* synagogues, but will instead be thrown before *Roman* magistrates and *Roman* judgment seats (10:17). We conclude, therefore, that it was only the special circumstances of the apostles that gave them the right to flee, since their preaching was first to **the lost sheep of Israel.**

(12) Hilary of Poitiers

Everything the Lord says here concerns the Jews and the heretics: **Brother will betray brother, and a father his son, and children will rise up against their parents**; that is, a family of the same house will be divided among themselves. Whereas the names of the parents and their bloodline signify a former unity, they are now separated by hostility and hatred for one another to the judges and kings of the earth, who will attempt to extort from us either silence or our cooperation.

For we will present ourselves as witnesses before them [the judges and kings] (10:18) as well as before the pagans. Because we bear witness, our persecutors will not be able to claim that they are ignorant of God. The way of faith in Christ preached shall be opened to the pagans by the tenacious voices of the confessors amidst the tortures of cruel men.

So the Lord urges upon us the necessity of being instructed by the wisdom of the serpent. This creature, before he betrayed Adam, was already declared to be wise according to Genesis (Gen 3:1), having a sagacity that is evident through the scheme of its deceitful plan. For at first it attacked the soul of the weaker sex and then seduced her by the hope and promise of sharing in immortality. By these enticements, the serpent accomplished the work of its plan and its will. Once it had scrutinized the character of the man and the woman, its sagacity provided it with the right words at the opportune moment. It spoke about future blessings and presented the heavenly rewards of a perfect faith—a lie of the serpent. But in truth we preach that those who believe will become **like the angels** (22:30) according to the promise of God. Through the promises of the heavenly kingdom, let us obtain the simple and perfect minds of its citizens despite the raging of wolves and heretics. With the simplicity of a dove, let us provide the truth of these matters through the wisdom of a serpent (10:16).

(13) John Chrysostom

Now that the Lord had spoken of those fearful and terrible things that were going to happen, namely, his cross, and resurrection, and ascension—enough to melt the heart of the courageous—he speaks with his disciples about something more tranquil: allowing those whom he is training to recover their breath, and providing for them full security. He did not tell them to engage the enemy further when persecuted, but to flee. This is, however, a beginning and a prelude to the things they will face, so he lowered the levels of expectations. The Lord wishes to speak about those persecutions to come, but as it concerns those that come before the cross and the passion. He showed by saying, **You shall not have gone about the cities of Israel, till the Son of Man comes.** In other words, if they say, "What if we flee when persecution comes and they overtake us and drive us out again?" To eradicate this fear, he says, "You will not yet have gone throughout Palestine before I quickly come upon you." Notice here again that he is not avoiding the threats, but stands by them in their perils. For he said not, "I will snatch you out of the situation and put an end to the persecutions." But what does he say? **You shall not have gone through the cities of Israel, till the Son of Man comes.** Simply to see him was enough, at least, for their consolation.

You should also notice how the Lord didn't leave everything to grace, as it were, but required them to make some contribution. If you're afraid, he says, **flee**. By saying **flee**, he was telling them not to be afraid. Nor did he command them to flee at first, but only when they were persecuted. . . .

Then he prepares them for another phase of his commands; first, by casting out all care for their food: secondly, by rising above their fear of danger; and now, by dealing with oral abuse. Since the time of that first anxiety, he freed them by saying, *The workman is worthy of his hire* (Luke 10:7) and by signifying that there would be many to receive them, he freed them from their distress about their dangers: **Take no thought how or what you shall speak**, and, **he that endures to the end, the same shall be saved.**

Matthew 10:24–25

24"A disciple is not above his teacher, nor a servant above his master; 25it is enough for the disciple to be like his teacher, and the servant like his master. If they have called the master of the house Be-el'zebul, how much more will they malign those of his household."

(14) Tertullian

Even if Christ had intended that all these persecutions only be inflicted on the apostles of that era, we are clearly united with them in terms of the entire sacrament, the offshoot of the name, and the planting of the Holy Spirit. The teaching he gave them regarding meeting persecution applies to us as well, as disciples by inheritance and fruits of their apostolic seed. If indeed it is true that the sayings, **Behold I am sending you as sheep among wolves**, and **beware of men, for they will hand you over to the councils and will flog you in their synagogues, and you will be brought before governors and kings for my sake in witness to them and to the nations**, etc. (10:16–18) apply in a special way to the apostles, the same chapter *also* states a couple verses later that **brother will betray brother and father son unto death, and children will rise up against parents and kill them** (10:21). Clearly, such turmoil was proclaimed for the benefit of others; we do not find examples of this in the apostles' own era. No apostle, after all, suffered betrayal at the hands of brother or father, which very many of us are now able to claim. After this he returns to the apostles: **and you will be hated by all for my name** (10:22). How much more does this apply to us, who are necessarily turned over to the authorities by our parents? Therefore, by blending the meaning of this passage, first to the apostles in their day, now to all who have been appointed, Christ extends its macabre scope to *all* those who bear the name, *wherever* they might be, when they are judged by a law that rests on the hatred of that name.

But those who endure to the end—they will have their salvation. How would one "endure," though, without persecution, without betrayal, without death? To endure is nothing else than to *suffer*, and that to the bitter end. That's the reason behind the saying, **The disciple is not above his teacher**, and its counterpart, **Nor the servant above his lord** (10:24): when the teacher and Lord himself endured persecution and betrayal and death, how much more should his servants and disciples suffer likewise?

(15) Eusebius of Emesa

These words inspired the martyrs of the Lord to meet their passion, kindling a flame within their hearts. Through his teaching, the Lord roused them to the point they could scorn the present and hope for future things. Through this instruction, he armed them for death. But he also was thinking of their duty, for the steadfastness of martyrs precedes their passion. For he who does not proclaim on the **housetops** will not be arrested; he who has not spoken with boldness will not be distressed. Steadfastness precedes suffering. When a soul has sufficient regard for God's nearness, God will certainly be present in the soul. The soul is not able to be silent about its longing for the divine until God occupies its every corner. Thus, the soul knows what it possesses, as much as it is aware of what those fooling themselves with temporal benefits do not possess.

Since steadfastness precedes suffering, the Lord who leads martyrs to their passion first seeks to inspire them. For he says: **what I say to you in the dark, speak out in the light; and what you hear in your ear, proclaim from the rooftops.** Be steadfast, he says; let your words ring out to the ends of the earth; let your confession not be silent.

But someone might say, "if it is good to speak in the light of day, why did he himself speak in the dark? And if we're supposed to proclaim from the rooftops, then why did the Lord speak in secret?" There were, however, times for Jesus to be silent (cf. 16:20; 27:14). He commanded his disciples to speak and shout out these things; not of course because he was afraid for himself—only those ignorant of the authority of the Lord Jesus would say such a thing—but because he was arranging matters so that he could be silent in the present age, while speaking out in another.

(16) John Chrysostom

The disciples were accused everywhere in the world as rebels and innovators and revolutionaries, yet they dispelled this impression and earned the opposite opinion. They were celebrated by everyone as saviors and guardians and benefactors. All this they achieved through their great endurance; hence Paul's remark, *I die daily* (1 Cor 15:31), for he continued to be at risk to the end.

Given these examples, why do we deserve such quiet and luxury? Even when there is no one at war with us we slaughter ourselves;[3] although there is no one pursuing us, we

3. That is, by weaknesses produced by luxurious living.

fall to pieces, and though we are told to save ourselves in times of peace, we cannot do even that. When the world was on fire, and the pyre was lit throughout the whole earth, the disciples went into it and snatched those burning from the midst of the flames, whereas we cannot even save ourselves. What leniency, therefore, will there be for us? What allowance made? We are afflicted by no scourging, no imprisonment, no hostile rulers, no synagogues or anything of the like—quite the contrary: we rule and are in control, the emperors are pious, Christians enjoying much respect, privileges, reputation, concessions—and still we do not prevail.

In contrast, teachers and disciples alike were arrested, suffering countless wounds and constant scourging . . . whereas we for our part suffer no such thing, not even in dreams, and we are as a result softer than wax.

Matthew 10:26–27

26"So have no fear of them; for nothing is covered that will not be revealed, or hidden that will not be known. 27What I tell you in the dark, utter in the light; and what you hear whispered, proclaim upon the housetops."

(17) Eusebius of Emesa

What I say to you in the dark, speak in the light; that is, what is said in secret, shout out loud; and what you have heard in private, proclaim from the rooftops with courage and perseverance. Let us adopt for ourselves such perseverance. Who or what is persecuting us? Do we fear reproach rather than persecution? But the Lord says: **Do not be afraid.** Let us not be afraid, therefore, when we are killed. For the Lord himself says: **Do not be afraid of those who kill the body, but are not able to kill the soul.** He divides fear into two kinds. To human beings he has given power over the body. But this power comes from God. Casting out fear with fear, he has divided the lesser from what is the greater anxiety. If it is necessary to fear, it is not proper to fear a human being because God is greater. Are you afraid of the penalty of death that is against the body?

Rather than this, he says, **fear him who is able to destroy both the body and the soul in Gehenna.**[4] For power over the body has been given to mankind, but only once. To God there is power both over the body that he formed and over the soul that he created, because his power extends not only to this life, but to **Gehenna**. And the fear of **Gehenna** is certainly greater than that of death. Why is it greater? Because the loss is twofold: a loss of soul and of body; the loss that comes with death is only with respect to our corporal nature.

If then the two dangers are distinguished—people with respect to the body, but God with respect to the soul—then the fear is not of equal weight since the soul is more honorable. So the one fear is greater than the other fear. Since also the body, over which mankind may possess power, is in the hands of God. Even if someone wanted to kill the soul, he

4. Or "hell."

could not (for it is in the hands of God); and this latter of the two is said to depart not only to death, but to **Gehenna**, making the fear much greater in number and magnitude. For this reason, then, (one) fear supersedes the other.

(18) Hilary of Poitiers

We read that the Lord was not accustomed to making pronouncements at night or teaching in the dark. In fact, every word of his is darkness to carnal persons, and his word is night to unbelievers. Whatever he has said must be spoken with a freedom of faith and confession by each one. For this reason, he commands that those words spoken in darkness should be proclaimed in the light. Whatever the Lord entrusted to their hearing in secret, let it be heard on the rooftops, and the speaker's declamation may be heard from on high. For the knowledge of God must be faithfully announced, and the teaching of the Gospel's hidden depths must be revealed in the light of the apostolic preaching. We do not fear those who, though they possess bodily abilities, have no law over the soul. Rather, we fear God who has power of destroying both soul and body in Gehenna.

Matthew 10:28–31

28"And do not fear those who kill the body but cannot kill the soul; rather fear him who can destroy both soul and body in hell. 29Are not two sparrows sold for a penny? And not one of them will fall to the ground without your Father's will. 30But even the hairs of your head are all numbered. 31Fear not, therefore; you are of more value than many sparrows."

(19) Philoxenus of Hierapolis

For the only judge who can destroy the soul is God himself, because he whose nature is more mysterious than that of the soul is alone able to be the judge of the soul. The children of men may be judges of the body, and they are able even to kill it, but they have no power to judge the soul, as Christ testifies in these words: **Fear not those who kill the body but who are not able to kill the soul**. The authority of earthly judges extends only to the body, and it is only the body they can torment, and slay. But as for the soul, it is not subject to the harm that those who can slay it can inflict. It cannot burn in their fire, and scourging does not touch its spiritual nature. It cannot be cut in pieces by their swords, nor lacerated by their instruments of torture. For he that judges can only harm the body, and the sentence he passes on evildoers he utters with the tongue of the body, even if the soul is inwardly moved when passing sentence. It is the members of the body that suffer and only the body that is injured. Because of its spiritual nature, the soul is exalted and raised above these things. And however deep the sufferings may penetrate, they sink into the body only; however far in they may pierce, the soul is situated more deeply within, and the death of these members has no power over its life. Because judges are not able to kill the soul, one should not be afraid of their judgment. **But fear him who is able to destroy both the body and the soul in Gehenna.**

The Lord himself alone is judge of the soul, and he who made it a living thing is himself able to end its life with death and torment its spiritual nature by a spiritual sentence of judgment. For the soul knows that the Lord alone is its judge and by nature is fearful of him. Just as awareness of the judgment of the world restrains those who are alive in the body and dead in their souls from evil actions, so also awareness of the judgment of God checks the man who is alive in his soul from doing wicked things. As long as he remembers that he will be judged, he keeps himself from sin.

(20) Augustine

So that's what the Lord was talking about: **the one who has the right to kill both body and soul in the Gehenna of fire.** How does this happen? When a wicked person is thrown into **Gehenna**, the body will burn there, as does the soul. The death of the body is everlasting punishment; the death of the soul is the absence of God. Do you want to know what the death of the soul is? Hear the prophet saying, *Let the wicked be taken away, and not see the glory of the Lord* (Isa 26:10).

So let the soul fear its own death, but not fear the death of its body. Because if the soul, fearing its death yet lives in God—without offending him or driving him out of itself—it will deserve at the end to receive its body back again (not for eternal punishment like the wicked, but for eternal life, like the righteous). That is the death the martyrs feared, and that is the life they loved. Trusting in the promises of God, they ignored the threats of their persecutors and earned the right to be rewarded with their crowns in the presence of God, leaving us the legacy of celebrating their festivals.

(21) Jerome

The Lord's discourse is a unity; what comes later follows from what has gone before. Let the prudent reader always be wary of a capricious interpretation, so that you do not bend the Scripture to fit two meanings, but rather fit your understanding to the Scriptures by understanding their logical sequence. First he said, **Do not fear those who kill the body, but cannot kill the soul**. Then he says, **Are not two sparrows worth a penny? Yet one of them does not fall to the ground without your Father.** The meaning is this: if small, cheap animals do not fall without God's authority since providence governs all of them, and none perishes apart from God's will, you, who are eternal, should not fear that you live without God's providence. This very same meaning was also expressed earlier: **Behold the birds of the sky, how they neither sow nor reap nor gather into their barns, yet your heavenly Father feeds them. Are you not worth much more than they?** (6:26), and further, **Consider the lilies of the field, how they grow** (6:28) and so on. **If God so clothes the grass of the field, which is here today, and tomorrow is thrown into the furnace, how much more**

will he clothe you, you of little faith? (6:30) By a kind of inference, the two sparrows may be understood as the soul and the body. Also, the five sparrows, which according to Luke are worth two pennies, seems to be hinting at the same thing (Luke 12:6).

How this interpretation fits in with the Gospel as a whole is a matter of no small difficulty. **Even the hairs of your head have been counted. Fear not, therefore, you are worth much more than many sparrows.** The sense of our earlier exposition is more clearly expressed here. We should not fear those who can kill the body but not the soul, because if even small animals do not fall without God's knowledge, how much more is this true for the human being who is upheld by apostolic dignity! When the Gospel says, **Even the hairs of your head have been counted**, he shows the immensity of God's providence toward human beings and his boundless love. Nothing about us is hidden from God; even minor, careless remarks do not escape his knowledge.

Matthew 10:32–36

32"So every one who acknowledges me before men, I also will acknowledge before my Father who is in heaven; 33but whoever denies me before men, I also will deny before my Father who is in heaven.

34"Do not think that I have come to bring peace on earth; I have not come to bring peace, but a sword. 35For I have come to set a man against his father, and a daughter against her mother, and a daughter-in-law against her mother-in-law; 36and a man's foes will be those of his own household."

(22) Hilary of Poitiers

The sword is the sharpest weapon of all that serves as the emblem of authority,[5] due to the severity of its judgment and the punishment of evildoers. The very name of this weapon refers, by the prophet's authority (Ps 149:6), to the preaching of the new gospel (Eph 6:17). We remember that the word of God is signified as a sword—the sword that was brought to earth—that is, the Lord's preaching that has penetrated the bodies of men (Heb 4:12). . . .

When we are renewed in the laver of baptism through the power of the word, we are separated from the sins that come from our origin and are separated from its authors (John 8:44). Once we have endured a sort of excision by God's sword, we are cut off from the dispositions of our father and mother. Casting off the "old man" with his sins and unbelief (Col 3:9–10), we are renewed in soul and body by the Spirit, rejecting our inborn habits and former ways (Col 3:5–8). . . .

The result will be serious dissension in one household, and the "new man's" (Col 3:10) enemies will the members of his [own] household. Now separated from the others by the word of God, he will rejoice to remain, both inside and outside, that is, both his soul and body, in the newness of the Spirit.

5. A juridical reference to the Roman expression, *ius gladii* (right of the sword).

(23) Eusebius of Emesa

Jesus is peace, and he came to bring peace to those who are in heaven and on earth. If that is true, as indeed it is, what do we make of the things that were read today? For the Savior himself says in the Gospel: **Do not think that I came to bring peace on the earth**. Can snow generate warmth of fire or make something cold? Does peace not bring peace? How then does Peace himself say: **Do not think that I came to bring peace on the earth?** Admittedly it is said that *he came to bring peace to those who are in heaven and on the earth*, as the Gospel says elsewhere: *he came not so that he may judge the world, but so that the world may be saved through him. He who believes is saved*. And elsewhere, **he did not come except to the lost sheep of the house of Israel.** Yet certainly most of them have perished.

What should we make of these contradictions? Are the statements contradictory and truth inconsistent with itself? If truth departs from itself, it will lose also its nature. It is the nature of a lie to be in dissension, whereas the nature of truth is agreement. How can these things be consistent with themselves?

Jesus is peace, and he says: **Do not think that I came to bring peace on the earth;** but concerning him it is also said: he came to bring peace to those who are in heaven and on earth (cf. Lk 2:14). How are we to understand that he did not come to bring peace on earth and yet that he came to bring peace to those who are in heaven and on earth? And how is it that he came to the lost sheep of the house of Israel and yet many reject him still today? He was not sent to judge, though he is found to condemn. If someone wishes to understand these things, which are of the Lord, he should expel everything else from his heart and strain to see with the pure eyes of the mind.

Certainly the intention of God, who sent his Son, was such that men would be saved; when the Son was sent, his obedience had as its aim the obedience of him who was sent, that there would be peace in heaven and on earth. Why, then, was there no peace? Because in their infirmity many were not able to receive the splendor of the true light. For the Lord proclaims peace, and the Apostle Paul confirms this when he says: *for he is our peace* (Eph 2:14). It is clear that peace is the mark of those who believe and receive him. How then did he not bring peace on earth? A daughter has believed; a father has remained in disbelief. What do a believer and unbeliever have in common? In truth the proclamation of peace causes division: when a son believes and a father does not, discord is inevitable. Though the preaching of peace caused division, what a good division it is! For in peace, we are saved.

But let me try to explain the meaning of this—for there is nothing of this that we ought not to hear. He says: **Do not think that I came to bring peace on the earth;** and then more vehemently adds: **I came not to bring peace, but a sword.** In what sense does he mean no **peace** and in what way a **sword? For I came to incite a man against his father**: I receive his son, and the father is not amused. Notice the active power of these words. Because he spoke of bringing a sword, he adds, **Do not suppose that I came to bring peace to the earth**. The earth did not receive him. I did not come **to bring peace**! Again, listen: **to the earth**. For he says, I proclaim peace, but the earth does not accept it. This is not, then, the intention of the planter: for he has persisted so that there will be a cluster of grapes, but instead they render thorns. And the planter, who did well toward the vines, is not at fault when he says, **I came to set a man against his father, and a daughter-in-law against her mother-in-law.**

Matthew 10:37–39

37 "He who loves father or mother more than me is not worthy of me; and he who loves son or daughter more than me is not worthy of me; 38 and he who does not take his cross and follow me is not worthy of me. 39 He who finds his life will lose it, and he who loses his life for my sake will find it."

(24) Ambrose of Milan

The Lord summed up everything in one grand rule: reverence toward God and the practice of kindness, when he said: *You shall love the Lord your God . . . and you shall love your neighbor* (Luke 10:27). Should we believe that here he has changed this rule, abolished the basis of good relationships, and commanded us to do away with natural ties of affection? Are we to believe that he demands discord among his dear children? And how can he be *our peace, who has made both one* (Eph 2:14)? How can he say: *My peace I give you, My peace I leave you* (John 14:27)? How can he say these words if he has come to divide parents from their children, children from their parents, and so dissolve the bonds that bind a family together? Or again, does not the Scripture say: *"Cursed is he who does not honor his parents"* (Deut 27:16)? Or how can it be a religious duty to abandon one's parents?

The thing to remember is that reverence for God comes before natural affection. If we recognize this, the matter will become clear. Put briefly, that which is human must be regarded as second to that which is divine. For if we have duties to our parents, we have still greater duties to the Father of all parents. Without him, you would in fact have no parents. Now, if parents refuse to recognize him who is the Father of all, how are you to recognize your parents? Christ is not saying that we are to renounce our beloved parents, but that we are to prefer God to all other beings. Note also what is found in another book of the Gospel: **Whoever loves father or mother more than me, is not worthy of me** (10:37). You are not forbidden to love your parents, but you are forbidden to prefer them to God. The bonds of nature are blessings given to us by God, but no one should love the gift more than he loves God. It is God who preserves and safeguards the blessing he has given.

(25) Augustine

When the Lord urges us to love him, he begins by mentioning those persons whom we are rightly obliged to love. **Whoever**, he says, **loves father or mother more than me is not worthy of me**. So if you are not worthy of Christ when you prefer your father to Christ, how can you be worthy of the slightest trace of Christ when you prefer money to Christ? There are, you see, things that are wrongly loved in the world, and when they are wrongly loved in the world, they make their lovers vile. Unlawful love is a serious pollution of the soul, and a heavy weight holding down the soul that is longing to fly. Just as a right and holy love whirls the mind up to the heights, so a wrong and vile love plunges it down to the depths.

The proper weight of everything, which carries it where it ought to go, is its love. Love doesn't carry it where it shouldn't go, but where it ought to go. Those who love rightly will be carried to what they love, and where will that be, except where the good object is what they love? After all, what other reward does Christ the Lord offer when he urges us to love him, but the fulfillment of what he asked the Father for: *I will that where I am, these also may be with me* (John 17:24)? Do you want to be where Christ is? Love Christ, and be taken away to the place of Christ. Something that pulls or carries you upward doesn't allow you to hurtle downward.

Let my father say, "Love me." Let my mother say, "Love me." Am I to say to these voices, "Be quiet"? Aren't they making a just demand? Am I not to pay back what I have received? My father says, "I begot you." My mother says, "I bore you." My father says, "I reared you." My mother says, "I nursed you." Perhaps these voices have every right to say, "You want to be carried on his wings; don't fly as a debtor; pay back the advance we made you." Let us answer our fathers and mothers, when they say to us, with every right, "Love us," let us answer, "I do love you, in Christ; I don't love you instead of Christ. Be with me in him; I won't be with you without him." "But," they say, "we don't want Christ." I say, "yet I want Christ more than you. Am I to attend to my father and lose my Creator?"

Love all things in the right order so that you yourself may be rightly ordered. Allot to things their own proper weights and importance. Love your father and mother, but you have something you should love more than father and mother. So will our parents, mind you, not be spurned but honored in due order, as they step aside a little from the center of the stage.

Oh that we may love like this, to die to oneself, to come to God!

See how wise and thoughtful he wants you to be, the one who said to you, *Take up your cross and follow me* (Mark 8:34). **Whoever finds his life**, he said, **will lose it; and whoever loses it on my account will find it** (10:39). Whoever finds will lose it; whoever loses will find it. In order to lose it, the first thing is to find it; and when you've lost it, the final thing is to find it again. There are two findings: in between there is one losing, by which you pass across. None of us can lose our life for Christ's sake unless we have first found it; and none of us can find our life in Christ unless we have first lost it. Find, in order to lose; lose, in order to find.

How are you going to find it, in order to have something you can lose? When you think of yourself as being in part mortal, when you think of the one who made you and created you by breathing life into you, and realize that you owe it to the one who gave it; that it's to be paid back to the one who lent it; that it is to be kept safe by the one who provided it; then you have found your life, finding it in faith. I mean, you have believed this, and found your soul, your life. After all, you were lost, before you came to believe. You have found your life; you were dead, that is, in your unbelief; now you have come back to life in faith. You are just like the one about whom it can be said, *He was dead, and has come to life again; he was lost and is found* (Luke 15:32).

So you have found your life in the true faith, if you have come back to life from the death of unbelief. That is, you have found your soul. Lose it, and your soul becomes seed for you. That is, I mean the farmer too by threshing and winnowing finds the wheat, and again by sowing it he loses the wheat. What had been lost in the sowing is found on the threshing floor. What is found in the harvest is lost in the sowing. So, **whoever finds his life will lose it**. You work so hard at gathering, why be so slow in the sowing?

Matthew 10:40–42

**40"He who receives you receives me, and he who receives me receives him who sent me.
41He who receives a prophet because he is a prophet shall receive a prophet's reward, and he who receives a righteous man because he is a righteous man shall receive a righteous man's reward. 42And whoever gives to one of these little ones even a cup of cold water because he is a disciple, truly, I say to you, he shall not lose his reward."**

(26) Didache

If any teacher should come and teach you all the things mentioned above, welcome him. But if the teacher himself goes astray and teaches a different teaching that undermines all this, do not listen to him. However, if his teaching contributes to righteousness and knowledge of the Lord, welcome him as you would the Lord.

Now concerning the apostles and prophets,[6] deal with them in accordance with the rule of the gospel. Let every apostle who comes to you be welcomed as if he were the Lord. But he is not to stay for more than one day, unless there is need, in which case he may stay another. But if he stays three days, he is a false prophet. And when the apostle leaves, he is to take nothing except bread until he finds his next night's lodging. But if he asks for money, he is a false prophet.

Everyone **who comes in the name of the Lord** (21:9) is to be welcomed. But then examine him, and you will find out—for you will have insight into what is true and what is false. If the one who comes is merely passing through, assist him as much as you can. But he must not stay with you for more than two or, if necessary, three days. However, if he wishes to settle among you and is a craftsman, let him work for his living. If he is not a craftsman, decide according to your own judgment how he shall live among you as a Christian, yet without being idle. But if he does not wish to cooperate in this way, then he is trading on Christ. Beware of such people.

6. Here "apostles" and "prophets" are being used as roughly equivalent to itinerant preachers. Cf. Acts 15:6.

(27) Clement of Alexandria

Our love for Christ is first, and second is for the one who honors and cares for those who believe in Christ. For whatever anyone does for a disciple, the Lord takes up for himself, and it is all rendered his own: **"Come, you that are blessed by my Father, inherit the kingdom prepared for you from the foundation of the world. For I was hungry and you gave me something to eat, and I was thirsty and you gave me something to drink, and I was a stranger and you welcomed me, I was naked and you clothed me, I was sick and you looked after me, I was in prison and you visited me." Then the righteous will answer him, "Lord, when did we see you hungry and feed you, or thirsty and give you something to drink? When did we see you a stranger and welcome you, or naked and clothe you? Or when did we see you sick and look after you, or in prison and visit you?" And the King will answer them, "Truly I tell you, as much as you did for one of the least of these brothers of mine, you did for me"** (25:34–40). On the other hand, those who did not offer them these benefits he casts into the eternal fire, as if they have not offered the benefits to him (cf. 25:41–46). And elsewhere he says, **The one who receives you receives me.** *The one who does not receive you rejects me* (Luke 10:16).

These who believe in him he calls *children* (cf. Mark 10:24), *young children* (cf. John 21:5), **infants** (cf. 11:25), and *friends* (cf. Luke 12:4); and here he calls them **little ones** in reference to their future greatness above, saying, **Do not despise one of these little ones. For their angels continually see the face of my Father in heaven** (18:10). And elsewhere, *Do not be afraid, little flock, for the Father is pleased to hand over to you the kingdom* of heaven (Luke 12:32). In the same way, he says that **the least in the kingdom of heaven** (that is, his own disciple) **is greater** than John, the greatest **among those born of women** (11:11; Luke 7:28). And again, **The one who receives a righteous person or prophet in the name of a righteous person or prophet will receive the reward of a righteous person or prophet; and the one who has given** a disciple **a cup of cold water to drink in the name of a disciple will not lose the reward.** So then, this is the only reward that is not lost.

And once more, *Make friends for yourselves by means of the wealth of injustice,*[7] *so that when it runs out, they may receive you into the eternal dwelling* (Luke 16:9). Indeed, he declares every possession that you have acquired by yourself for your own use, and that you do not lay down for the common good of those in need (cf. Acts 4:32), to be unjust by nature. But by means of this thing of injustice it is possible to accomplish a just and saving act, namely, to refresh one of those who have an *eternal dwelling* with the Father.

See, first, how he has not commanded you to wait to be asked or pestered, but to seek out personally those worthy disciples of the Savior who will benefit from your giving. Now the Apostle's saying is also good: *For God loves a cheerful giver*, those who rejoice in giving and do not *sow sparingly*, lest they *reap* in the same way (2 Cor 9:6–7); and those who share without grumbling, discrimination, or grief. This indeed is a pure kindness. And stronger than this is what the Lord has spoken in another place: *Give to everyone who asks of you* (Luke 6:30). For such benevolence as this is truly of God. But this saying here (Luke 16:9)

7. The RSV reads, "by means of unrighteous mammon."

is most godly of all so that you should not wait to be asked, but should personally search for whoever is worthy of benefit and thereafter establish the great reward of your sharing: an *eternal dwelling*.

(28) John Chrysostom

Note that he did not simply say, "He that receives a prophet," or "He that receives a righteous man," but specifically, **he that receives a prophet because he is a prophet** or **because he is a righteous man**. In other words, it's not for any worldly gain or for any other temporal thing that a prophet or righteous man is received. On the contrary, one shall receive the reward of a prophet and the reward of a righteous man that is suitable for him to have. This is what Paul also said: *That your abundance may be a supply for their want, that their abundance also may be a supply for your want* (2 Cor 8:14). Even though your gift may be only a cup of cold water and nothing else, even this will become a reward stored up for you.

Notice how effective the Lord is in opening to the disciples the houses of the whole world. Indeed, he indicated that others are their debtors: first, by saying, **The workman is worthy of his hire** (10:10), second, by sending them out having nothing; third, by giving them over to conflicts and fighting with those that receive them (10:34); fourth, by granting them the power of doing miracles; fifth, by allowing their mouths to bring peace—the cause of all blessings—into the houses of whoever receives them; sixth, by threatening things worse than Sodom to those who do not receive them; seventh, by saying that whoever welcomes them receives himself and the Father; eighth, by promising both a prophet's and a righteous man's reward: ninth, by promising great reward even for a cup of cold water.

Matthew 11

In discussing John the Baptist's relation to Jesus, patristic commentators observe that the questions that John's disciples raised about Christ's identity were not for John's sake, but for themselves. John must have known the truth about Jesus, since he was the "forerunner" and prophet of Christ's birth and death. Theodore explains that John sent his disciples to confirm Christ's coming.

After speaking to John's disciples, Jesus turns to the crowd that had gathered and praises John as a prophet. Among all the prophets, no one born of a woman *(11:11) was greater than John the Baptist. He was the herald for another, who was not only "a human being but also God—both God and human of course—God always, human at a point in time" (Augustine). As important as John was, however, his greatness is still less than any believer who is baptized and has become a son of God (Philoxenus).*

Jesus continues to describe John by asking ironic questions. What did the people go out to see in the desert? Certainly not a reed shaken by the wind, *which is a soul that lacks spiritual depth and therefore is blown around by people's praise or blame (Gregory the Great). The admiration of others did not incline John to flattery, nor did slander cause him to suffer dejection. We should, therefore, imitate John so that "the breezes of opinion" do not allow our hearts to sway back and forth like reeds.*

Jesus's word that the kingdom of heaven has suffered violence *(11:12) is taken by ancient writers as a mandate. Ambrose encourages his listeners to "take the kingdom of heaven by storm," by which he means "to be fervent in devotion." For Clement of Alexandria, it signifies a steadfast life of righteousness and unceasing prayer, a kind of violence against our sinful nature that is commended as a means of taking God by force. That John was rejected by many was evidence that he was a genuine prophet. Although he fasted and practiced, he was reported by those jealous of him to have* a demon. *Ironically, Jesus came eating and drinking (v. 19) and was discredited as* a glutton and a drunkard, *though all who spurn the Wisdom of God will receive their just reward. God is righteous in his judgments, says Ambrose. Chrysostom puts an emphasis on the contrast between the past and present: If the mighty works that he had done took place in Sodom, their effects would have remained until this day. The lack of faith of those in the Gospel is made all the more apparent since Sodom and Gomorrah would have accepted the miracles as a sign of God's revelation in Christ and repented.*

No one knows the Son except the Father, and no one knows the Father except the Son and anyone to whom the Son chooses to reveal him *(11:27) received extensive comment in the early Church, since no one "can attain the knowledge of God" except through the Son (Irenaeus), and that knowledge of God is revealed most fully in Christ's suffering (Origen).*

Matthew 11:1–6

1And when Jesus had finished instructing his twelve disciples, he went on from there
to teach and preach in their cities.[1]
2Now when John heard in prison about the deeds of the Christ, he sent word by his
disciples 3and said to him, "Are you he who is to come, or shall we look for another?"
4And Jesus answered them, "Go and tell John what you hear and see: 5the blind receive
their sight and the lame walk, lepers are cleansed and the deaf hear, and the dead are
raised up, and the poor have good news preached to them. 6And blessed is he who takes
no offense at me."

(1) Hilary of Poitiers

As the forerunner, John announced the one who was to come; as the prophet, he acknowledged his [Christ's] existence; as the confessor,[2] he venerated his [Christ's] advent. How could there occur such an error in his knowledge, which was so varied and prodigious? If, however, we follow the Lord's testimony concerning John, we are not allowed to think this way. Clearly it is reasonable to believe that the glory of the Holy Spirit was not absent in John, who was held in prison, since it was the light of the Spirit's power that would minister to the apostles when they were in prison (see Acts 12:7).

But a deeper understanding is revealed in these things that happened concerning John (11:13). As we perceive in John a grace expressed with the effectiveness of reality, he also is the prophet that prophesies according to the manner in which he was the embodiment of the law. For the law announced he was the embodiment of the law. For the law announced Christ and preached the remission of sins, promising the kingdom of heaven (11:12). John completely fulfilled all of the works of the law. Now that the law has become inactive, confined, so to speak, by the sins of the masses and chained as a result of the people's sins, John is restrained in chains and in prison so that Christ may not be understood by them. The law, therefore, points to the gospel so that unbelief may consider the truth of Christ's words in his deeds.

Whatever of the law was bound through the deceit of sins is delivered when one learns the freedom of the gospel (cf. Rom 7:23; 8:2). For this reason, John was not seeking insight as a remedy for his own ignorance, but for that of his disciples, since he himself

1. While it appears that this passage should be the end of the previous chapter, there is no textual attestation confirming this among ancient commentaries.

2. "Confessor" was a title given to those who suffered for their confession of Christ.

had preached about the one who was to come for the remission of sins. So that they should know none other than the one whom John had preached, he sent his disciples to learn about his works. John knew that those works would confer an authority on his words and that no other Christ should be expected than the one to whom his works bore witness.

(2) Theodore of Mopsuestia

Some say John sent his disciples not because he did not recognize him or because John wanted to know of him. It seems more certain that it was the disciples who did not recognize him—especially for one who has entered deeply into the sacred scriptures. John sent the disciples to reveal to them that the Christ had indeed arrived. Moreover, because John was about to die and join those who had already become perfect, he sent the disciples to inquire whether Christ was the one who was going to free those held under the power of death and preach the good news to them (1 Pet 3:19). When he says *Behold the Lamb of God who takes away the sin of the world* (John 1:29), he surely recognizes that Christ's suffering for everyone would be known to God. Moreover, if John believed that Jesus was the Christ, he could hardly be ignorant of things of this sort concerning him. He knew the good that would come to human beings through him.

These things were also spoken for us so that we might see him from what was reported by the evangelists. How could John, who possessed such great knowledge concerning Christ and proclaimed many things about him, be ignorant of things pertaining to Christ? And how could John have to learn something about him? No one would wish to learn of so great an event from others when he himself was a witness and instructing others.

(3) Gregory the Great

After John was put in prison, why did he send his disciples to ask, **Are you he who is to come, or shall we look for another?** (11:3), as if he did not know the one he had pointed out? Surely John knew whether he was the same person he had proclaimed by prophesying, by baptizing, by pointing him out!

We can resolve this question more quickly if we reflect on the time and order of the events. John was at the river Jordan when he declared that Jesus was the Redeemer of the world; when he was cast into prison he asked whether they were to look for another or whether he had come. He did not ask because he doubted that Jesus was the Redeemer of the world, but to know whether he who had come into the world in person would also go down in person to the courts of hell. By dying, John was to precede into hell the one for whom he had been the forerunner, the one whom he had proclaimed to the world. He said, **Are you he who is to come, or shall we look for another?** as if to say, "Just as you were ordained to be born on behalf of human beings, make it clear whether you will also die on our behalf. Then I, who was the forerunner of your birth, may also become the forerunner of your death and may proclaim you in hell as the one who is to come, just as I have already proclaimed to the world that you have come."

When the Lord heard John's question, he related the miracles accomplished by his power and referred to the humility of his death: **The blind see, the lame walk, lepers are cleansed, the deaf hear, the dead are raised, the poor have the gospel preached to them. And blessed is he who takes no offense at me** (11:5–6). No one who had seen so many signs and such power could have taken offense; he could only have been amazed. But unbelievers took serious offense at him when after so many miracles they also saw him dying. And so Paul says: *We preach Christ crucified, an offense to Jews, and foolishness to Gentiles* (1 Cor 1:23). It seemed foolish to people that the author of life should die on behalf of humanity; people therefore saw him as an offense when they should have considered themselves in his debt. We ought to honor God more worthily in proportion to the unworthy things he sustained on our behalf.

What does he mean then by saying, **Blessed is he who takes no offense at me**, except that he is clearly expressing the abject quality and humility of his death? It is as if he was saying, "Indeed I perform marvels, but I do not refuse to suffer abjectly. I am following you in dying. People who honor my miracles must beware lest they despise my death."

Matthew 11:7–11

7 As they went away, Jesus began to speak to the crowds concerning John: "What did you go out into the wilderness to behold? A reed shaken by the wind? 8 Why then did you go out? To see a man clothed in soft raiment? Behold, those who wear soft raiment are in kings' houses. 9 Why then did you go out? To see a prophet? Yes, I tell you, and more than a prophet. 10 This is he of whom it is written,

> **'Behold, I send my messenger before thy face,**
> **who shall prepare thy way before thee.'**

11 Truly, I say to you, among those born of women there has risen no one greater than John the Baptist; yet he who is least in the kingdom of heaven is greater than he."

(4) Ambrose of Milan

What, asks Jesus, **did you go into the desert to see?** Here it seems that the world is being compared to a desert: still uncultivated, still barren, still without fruit. By going into the desert, the Lord tells us clearly: don't act like one inflated with pride of the flesh, lacking inner strength and valor, boastful of high position and fame—things that inevitably lead one to stumble. For such a person is exposed to the storms of this world and to its flux. He is shaken—like the reed, to which he is so justly compared. This kind of person produces no sound fruit of justice. He is full of worldly display and fine speeches, yet tied up in knots and making a lot of empty sounds. He is of no use to anyone, in fact he is downright harmful. On the inside such people are filled with vanity; on the outside they care only for appearances.

We too are reeds without roots, unable either by nature or strength to fix ourselves firmly in the ground. The lightest breeze of success will sway us and knock us against other reeds, hurting our neighbors by our agitated movements. Incapable of resistance we are swift to perish. As reeds love running water, we are charmed by the fleeting things of this world.

Sumptuous clothing is a sign of one who seeks a life of luxury and pleasure. That is why the Apostle tells us to put off the old man and the old way of life and to put on the new (cf. Col 3:9). In our new way of life, we spurn the luxury that makes us soft and shun lustful or unlawful pleasure, seeking only to bring forth the fruits of good work. The court of heaven does not welcome those who have grown soft by excessive care of the body, or by overindulgence and the burning hot pursuit of pleasure. One climbs the steps to heaven by the austere and laborious practice of virtue. The decadent, and those whose limbs have grown flaccid with pleasure, are banished from the kingdom of heaven. They grow old in the dwellings of earth. But the masters of this darkened world—kings whose power rests on temporal rule—welcome such people, for by their deeds they imitate the rulers of darkness.

But what was it you went out to see? A prophet? Yes, indeed, I can assure you; and more than a prophet (Luke 7:26). How, I ask, could they go to the desert to see John who was already shut up in a prison? The answer is that the Lord is putting John before them as a model. John had prepared the way of the Lord, not only by the manner of his birth in the flesh and by his preaching of the faith, but also—in a certain way—by going before the Lord in his glorious passion. Yes, John is **more than a prophet** (11:9), and last of the prophets; **more than a prophet**, because so many people desired to see (cf. 13:17) him who was prophesied, baptized.

(5) Augustine

We receive testimony from the Holy Spirit that John was born, though his father, because he did not believe, was struck dumb. So when John was announced by the angel and he did not believe, the Spirit deprived his father of speech; when John was born, the Spirit loosened his father's tongue. Let us now consider the inner significance and meaning of this great and mysterious set of events.

John was sent before the Lord Christ. Prophets had also been sent beforehand through previous ages; there was no lack of them to proclaim Christ. In fact, from the very origins of the human race Christ did not cease to prophesy himself and foretell his own coming. Last of all was born John, a human being, but the greatest of any to have existed.

The Lord Jesus was going to come, not only as a human being but also God; both God and human of course; God always, human at a point in time; God before all times, human in time; God before the ages, human at the end of time. God, who made man, deemed it necessary to become what he had made for the sake of man. So when the Lord Jesus Christ was about to come, who is more than man, in case he should be thought to be only a man, it was right and necessary that a great man should bear him testimony.

O John, great man, of whom none greater has arisen among those born of women, now you tell me: Who is this? Tell me, great man; who is this who was thought to be only a man?

Hear who he is: **One whose sandals**, he says, **I am not fit to carry** (3:11). Hear who he is: I'm telling you John's words about the Lord Christ: *The one who has the bride*, he says, is *the bridegroom; but the bridegroom's friend—* mentioning himself *—stands and listens to him, and rejoices on account of the bridegroom's voice* (John 3:29). Again, here's another testimony of John's: *We*, he says, *have all received from his fullness* (John 1:16).

(6) Philoxenus of Hierapolis

None of us would confess that he was greater than John the Baptist, at least, not with regard to prophecy, nor honor, nor the grace of the Holy Spirit that he received. By these gifts he fulfilled his mission to preach and to baptize and to do the other things he did for Christ. Nevertheless, though in this life we are lesser than John (that is, by birth from woman) in the kingdom of heaven (11:11), our text makes clear that the believer is greater than John because the former has been baptized. The believer has become like a son to God the Father, a brother to Christ, and a member of his body the Church. John was greater than all who had gone before him, although he was less than those who are born through baptism and whose glory will be revealed in the world to come.

(7) Gregory the Great

Let us listen to what Jesus said to the crowds about John after John's disciples had been sent away. **What did you go out into the wilderness to see? A reed shaken by the wind?** As soon as a slight breeze blows on a reed it bends away. What does the reed represent if not an unspiritual soul? As soon as it is touched by difficulties or slander, it squirms in every direction. Likewise, if a slight breeze of approbation comes from someone's mouth, it is cheerful and proud, bending completely, as it were, toward being pleasant. But if a wind of slander comes from where the breeze of praise was coming, it is quickly turned in the opposite direction, toward raving anger.

John was no reed shaken by the wind. No one's pleasant attitude made him agreeable, and no one's anger made him bitter. Prosperity could not elevate him, nor adversity bring him down. This was no reed shaken by the wind! No change in events bent him from his upright state. Let us learn not to be a reed shaken by the wind, dearly beloved; let us steady our minds before the breezes of opinion; let our hearts remain unbending. No slander should provoke us to anger, and no favor make us revel in foolish pleasure. Prosperity should not make us proud, nor adversity trouble us. We who are firmly established in faith should not be moved at all by the vicissitudes of passing events.

The Lord continues: **But what did you go out into the wilderness to see? A man clothed in soft garments? Behold, those who wear soft garments are in kings' houses!** John is described as wearing a garment of camel's hair (3:4), as you know. What do these words mean? Are they not a clear indication that those who avoid troublesome things for God's sake are not fighting for a heavenly kingdom but for an earthly one, and that those given over solely to external things are seeking the softness and delights of the present life?

That the text says John was not clothed in soft garments can also be taken in another way. He was not clothed in soft garments because he did not flatter the lives of those who were sinning with his charming words; he reproved them with the force of bitter denunciation, saying: **You brood of adders** (3:7; Luke 3:7), **who warned you to flee the wrath to come?** Solomon said that *the words of wise men are like goads, like nails driven deep* (Eccl 12:11). The words of wise men are compared to nails and goads because they do not know how to chide gently the faults of evildoers; they pierce them.

Matthew 11:12–15

12"From the days of John the Baptist until now the kingdom of heaven has suffered violence, and men of violence take it by force. 13For all the prophets and the law prophesied until John; 14and if you are willing to accept it, he is Eli'jah who is to come. 15He who has ears to hear, let him hear."

(8) Ambrose of Milan

The law and the prophets lasted until John (Luke 16:16). This does not mean that the law came to an end then, but rather that the preaching of the gospel began (cf. Rom 8:1). When that which seems greater arrives, that which is lesser has completed its work. So let us take the kingdom of heaven by storm. Those who take a place by storm rush at their object with great vehemence. They don't dawdle along like people half asleep. In the realm of faith, to take by storm means to be fervent in devotion; to be lackadaisical is a grave fault.

In many ways, the law followed nature; it made allowances for natural desires as it encouraged us to love what is just and good. Christ, on the other hand, pruned our nature and cut back our natural pleasures. We now have to do **violence** to our nature, so that it will not drown once more in earthly things, but will lift itself up to the heights.

(9) Clement of Alexandria

Now the Word going forth is the cause of creation; then it also causes itself, when *the Word became flesh* (John 1:14), that it too might be seen. So the righteous will seek that loving discovery, which they obtain if they seek eagerly. As Jesus says, **For the one who knocks, the door will be opened. Ask and it will be given to you** (7:8, 7; Luke 11:10, 9). For the **forceful men** who **seize the kingdom** were spoken of not as forcing by their quarrelsome words, but by the persistency of their upright lives and by their unceasing prayers, expunging the stains of former sins.

And the Lord says, **What is impossible for humans is possible for God** (19:26; Mark 10:27; Luke 18:27). Again this too is full of great wisdom, because those who train and labor for mastery over the passions[3] accomplish nothing by themselves; but if it becomes clear

3. The Greek word is *apatheia*, the lofty philosophical goal of complete freedom from the emotions, a perfect equilibrium.

that they eagerly desire this and do it zealously, they prevail by the addition of the power from God. For God specially inspires those souls that desire; but if they should shrink back from their eagerness, the Spirit given from God is also withdrawn. For to save the unwilling is an act of force, but to save those who choose is one of grace. And the kingdom of God belongs not to those who are sleeping and lazy, but **forceful men seize it.** For this is the only good force: to force God and to seize life from God. And God, who knows those who forcefully—or rather steadfastly—endure, concedes to yield. For God rejoices to be defeated in such matters (cf. Gen 32:24–32).

(10) Tertullian

I suspect that certain heretics use the example of Elijah. They defend the Lord's statement, **Elijah has already come, and they did not know him** (17:12) as if he were manifested in John like metempsychosis. And in another place: **And if you are willing to accept it, he is Elijah who is to come.** Is it really possible that the Jews referred to John in Pythagorean terms when they asked: *Are you Elijah?* (John 1:21)? Or was it not rather based on divine prophecy, *Behold, I will send you Elijah the Tishbite* (Mal 4:5)? The Pythagorean idea of metempsychosis is the recalling of a soul that died long before and returned to another body. But Elijah is coming again, who didn't depart life, but was translated (2 Kgs 2:11); not after being restored to a body after death, but was returned to the world from which he was translated; not after resuming a lost life, but as a fulfillment of prophecy. He (John) was the same person in name and humanity.

But how could John be Elijah? You have the angel's own announcement: *And he will go before the people,* he says, *in the spirit and power of Elijah* (Luke 1:17)—not in his soul or body. These latter things belong to the man's substance, but *the spirit and power* are bestowed outwardly as gifts by the grace of God, and so they are able to be transferred to someone else according to the will of the Almighty, as it once happened with the spirit of Moses (Num 12:2).

Matthew 11:16–19

16"But to what shall I compare this generation? It is like children sitting in the market places and calling to their playmates,

> **17'We piped to you, and you did not dance;**
> **we wailed, and you did not mourn.'**

18For John came neither eating nor drinking, and they say, 'He has a demon'; 19the
Son of man came eating and drinking, and they say, 'Behold, a glutton and a drunkard, a friend of tax collectors and sinners!' Yet wisdom is justified by her deeds."

(11) John Chrysostom

What the Lord means is something like this: John and I lived quite different lives, yet we have done the same things. . . . Note, for example, that the whole human race is astonished at his hard and demanding life of fasting. It was ordained that, from his earliest years, John should be reared in that way, so that what he proclaimed would be received as trustworthy.

But one might ask, why didn't Jesus choose this way of life? Actually, he did fast for forty days, and he went about without having a place to lay his head. In truth, he achieved the same end by another way and showed how much was to be gained by his way. For it was a much better thing to have someone bear testimony in the way of John than actually to follow John's way. Moreover, John had nothing to offer beyond the example of his life. *John worked no sign* (John 10:41), it is said, whereas Jesus had the testimony both of signs and of miracles. So he allowed John to be honored because of his fasting, but he took a quite different route, accepting hospitality from tax collectors and eating and drinking with them.

(12) Cyril of Alexandria

John put to death the desires of the flesh through an ascetic life, whereas Jesus as God put these things to death by teaching with authority not through ascetic deprivation. John, who preached a baptism of repentance, was an example of self-effacement for those who ought to mourn for sins (9:14–15); but Jesus, who preached the kingdom of heaven, displayed the splendor of joy found in himself, assuring the faithful that there will be a life of untroubled joy. . . . As a servant, John put to death the desires of the flesh through a disciplined ascetic life, but Jesus through the unique power of his divinity masterfully put to death the natural desires of the flesh.

(13) Ambrose of Milan

God himself is justified through baptism, whereas men justify themselves by confessing their sins, as it is written. *Recite your iniquities that you may be justified* (Isa 43:26 LXX). He is "**justified**" (11:19) means that, instead of being repulsed by men's obstinacy, his gracious gift is acknowledged in a life of justice. For *The Lord is just and loves justice* (Ps 11:7). God's "justification" consists in this: it is evident that his gifts have not been bestowed on unworthy and guilty recipients, but on those whom baptism has rendered innocent and just. Let us, then, "justify" the Lord, so that we may be "justified" by the Lord.

We need to inquire more fully into what it means for God to be justified. The Apostle says: *But God is true, and every man a liar, as it is written: 'That you may be justified in your words, and may overcome when you are judged'* (Rom 3:4; Ps 116:11). David also says: *Against you alone have I sinned: and done evil in your sight; that you may be justified when you give judgment, and that you may overcome when you are judge* (Ps 51:4). You see that the sinner who confesses his sin to God justifies God. He admits that God is the victor, and he trusts in his grace. It follows that God is justified in baptism, for by being baptized we acknowledge our sins and receive pardon.

What is meant by **Wisdom has been justified by her children** (cf. Luke 7:35). In a sense, wisdom is justified by all of us. I mean those who believe are made welcome, and those who decline to believe are rejected. That is why many Greek manuscripts [of the Bible] have: **Wisdom has been justified by all her works.** It is the work of justice to measure accurately the worth of whatever has been done.

So it is most fitting that Jesus says: **When we sang for you, you did not dance**. For Moses sang, when the Jews passed through the Red Sea (Exod 15:1–18), and the waves of the sea stood up and formed a wall on either side. But the same waves poured over the horses and riders of the Egyptians and drowned them all. Isaiah, too, sang a song to his beloved vineyards (Isa 5:1). In it he foretold that his people, who had once been fertile and whose virtues had once given excellent fruit, were now—by reason of their sins—going to become a bitter, barren wilderness. The Hebrew youths sang (Dan 3:24–68) when their feet were refreshed by heavenly dew that quenched the flame. Though everything else inside and outside the furnace burned with heat, they alone were unharmed and unhurt; the flames caressed them and did not burn them. There also was Habakkuk. He was told to lift the downcast spirits of the people by the sweetness of a song, and so he prophesied to them that the passion of the Lord would indeed be sweet (Hab 3:13).

Matthew 11:20–24

**20 Then he began to upbraid the cities where most of his mighty works had been done,
because they did not repent. 21 "Woe to you, Chora'zin![4] woe to you, Beth-sa'ida! for if
the mighty works done in you had been done in Tyre and Sidon, they would have re-
pented long ago in sackcloth and ashes. 22 But I tell you, it shall be more tolerable on the
day of judgment for Tyre and Sidon than for you. 23 And you, Caper'na-um, will you be
exalted to heaven? You shall be brought down to Hades. For if the mighty works done in
you had been done in Sodom, it would have remained until this day. 24 But I tell you that
it shall be more tolerable on the day of judgment for the land of Sodom than for you."**

(14) John Chrysostom

Now that *wisdom has been justified* (11:19), and he has shown that everything has been fulfilled, he begins to **upbraid the cities** (11:20). In other words, because he has failed to persuade them, he can only lament over them. This is even more terrifying. For the Lord had presented himself by his teaching and by his signs, yet they remained fixed in their unbelief. So now he now **upbraids** them.

4. This place is mentioned in the Bible only here (and in the parallel passage of Luke 10:15). It was nearest town north of Capernaum.

Then, it is said, **Jesus began to reproach the cities, where most of his mighty works were done**, because they did not repent, saying, **Woe unto you, Chorazin! Woe unto you, Bethsaida!** Then to show that it is not the cities as such that he is speaking of, he mentions the name of the city from which five apostles had come. For Philip and those two pairs of the chief apostles were from Bethsaida (John 1:44).[5]

For if, he said, **the mighty works that were done in you had been done in Tyre and Sidon, they would have repented in sackcloth and ashes. But I say unto you, It shall be more tolerable for Tyre and Sidon, at the day of judgment, than for you. And you, Capernaum, which is exalted as high as the sky, will be brought down to hell; for if the mighty works that have been done in you had been done in Sodom, it would have remained until this day. But I say unto you, It shall be more tolerable for the land of Sodom in the day of judgment, than for you.** He mentions Sodom with the others in order to aggravate the charge against his listeners. Indeed, it is a very strong indictment of their wickedness, that not only among those living at the time but even among all who were ever wicked, none is as evil as they were. Elsewhere the Lord compares them to the Ninevites and to the queen of the South (Jon 3:6–9; 2 Chr 9). In these instances, he speaks about those who had done right, but here he speaks about those who had sinned—a far more grievous matter. Ezekiel was acquainted with this same manner of dealing with things. For he said to Jerusalem, *You have made your sister seem righteousness because of all your sins* (Ezek 16:51).

Matthew 11:25–27

25 At that time Jesus declared, "I thank thee, Father, Lord of heaven and earth, that thou hast hidden these things from the wise and understanding and revealed them to babes;
26 yea, Father, for such was thy gracious will. 27 All things have been delivered to me by my Father; and no one knows the Son except the Father, and no one knows the Father except the Son and any one to whom the Son chooses to reveal him."

(15) Irenaeus of Lyons

The one who was known in the flesh was not a different being from him who declared, **No man knows the Father** (11:27). He is one and the same. The Father made all things subject to him, and everyone bore witness that he was true man and true God, from the Father, from the Spirit, from angels, from the creation itself, from men, from apostate spirits and demons, from the enemy, and last of all, from death itself.

In serving the Father, the Son brings all things—from the beginning to the end—to fulfillment, and without him no man can attain the knowledge of God. For the Son is the knowledge of the Father, but the knowledge of the Son is in the Father, who was revealed through the Son. This was why the Lord declared: **No man knows the Son, but the Father;**

5. The first pair were certainly Andrew and Peter (John 1:44; 12:21); and the other were quite likely James and John.

nor the Father, except the Son, and those to whomever the Son shall reveal (cf. Luke 10:22). For the phrase **shall reveal** was said not with reference to the future alone, as though it were only when the Word was born of Mary that he began to reveal the Father. These words, rather, apply without reserve to him throughout all time. For the Son, being present with what he made from the beginning, reveals the Father to all—to whom he wills, when he wills, and as the Father wills. That is why in all things, and through all things, there is one God, the Father, and one Word, and one Son, and one Spirit, and one salvation to all who believe in him.

(16) Origen

It is written, **No one has known the Son, except the Father**, and it is said, **Blessed are you, Simon Bar-Jonah, for flesh and blood have not revealed this to you, but my Father who is heaven** (16:17). In so far as the Son is not known in the world—*He was in the world, and the world was made by him, but the world did not know him* (John 1:10)—he has not yet been glorified in the world. Of course that he was not glorified in the world brings no discredit on the one who had not yet been glorified, only on the world that does not glorify him. When the heavenly Father revealed the knowledge of Jesus to those of the world, the Son of Man was glorified in those who knew him (see John 17:10). He brought glory for those who knew him, for those who with unveiled face reflect the glory of the Lord are transformed into the same image (see 2 Cor 3:18).

Note that it mentions from what glory and to what glory (2 Cor 3:18), that is, from the glory of the one who was glorified to the glory of those who glorify. This is why, in fulfilling God's plan [to suffer], Jesus brought dawn to the world. And because he knew that he would be glorified beyond the glory of those who were glorifying him, he said, *Now the Son of Man has been glorified*, and also, **No one knows the Father except the Son, and him to whom the Son reveals him.** And because the Son was about to reveal the Father by his suffering, he said, *God has been glorified in him.*

(17) Augustine

Listen to the Lord confessing: **I confess to you, Father, Lord of heaven and earth**. What do I confess? What do I praise you for? (this confession, as I have been saying, is also a matter of praising).[6] **Because you have hidden these things from the wise and the knowing, and revealed them to little ones**. What is the meaning of this? Understand it from the opposite view. **You have hidden these things**, he says, **from the wise and the knowing**, and he didn't go on, "You have revealed them to the foolish and ignorant." But he said, **You have hidden these things, indeed, from the wise and the knowing, and revealed them to little ones**. In mockery of the wise and the knowing, the arrogant, those who falsely consider themselves rather grand and are, in fact, merely full of themselves, he put the opposite to them, not the foolish, not the ignorant, but **little ones**. Who are the **little ones**? The humble.

6. One meaning of *confessio* in Latin.

Thus, **You have hidden these things from the wise and the knowing**. By **the wise and the knowing** he has himself explained that the proud are to be understood, when he goes on, **You have revealed them to little ones**. So: "You have hidden them from the not little ones." What's the meaning of "not little ones"? "Not humble." And what does "not humble" mean, but of course "proud"?

What did the Lord exalt over? Because it was revealed to little ones. We must be little ones, because if we want to be big, as though we were wise and knowing, this thing isn't revealed to us. Who are the big ones? The wise and the knowing. *Calling themselves wise, they became foolish* (Rom 1:22). You have a remedy in the opposite procedure. If by calling yourself wise, you have become foolish, call yourself foolish, and you will be wise. But say it; say it, and say it inwardly, because it is just as you say. If you say it, don't say it to men and fail to say it to God.

So, **You have hidden these things from the wise and the knowing, and have revealed them to the little ones**. What little ones? The humble. He says, *Upon whom shall my Spirit rest? Upon one who is humble and quiet and trembles at my words* (Isa 66:2). At these words Peter trembled, Plato didn't; let the fisherman keep what the great and famous philosopher lost. **You have hidden these things from the wise and the knowing, and have revealed them to the little ones**. You have hidden them from the proud and revealed them to the humble.

Matthew 11:28–30

28"Come to me, all who labor and are heavy laden, and I will give you rest. 29Take my yoke upon you, and learn from me; for I am gentle and lowly in heart, and you will find rest for your souls. 30For my yoke is easy, and my burden is light."

(18) John Chrysostom

That the **yoke** of virtue is sweet and light is evident in many ways. So let me turn to the **burdens** of sin. Take, for example, the greedy, the swindlers and dealers in shameful contracts. What could be more burdensome than such dealings? How much grief, how many trials, how many stumbling blocks, how many perils, how many schemes and conflicts are generated daily by profits earned in such a way? How many difficulties and troubles? In fact, just as you can never observe the sea free of waves, one will never see such a soul rid of anxiety and dejection, fear and alarm. For when one passes, another arrives, and the next takes its turn, and before these are finished, others come to a head. . . .[7]

Who is more given to turmoil and panic than those who are conceited? For Jesus said: **Learn from me, for I am gentle and humble in heart, and you will find rest for your souls.** Patience is the mother of all good things. Fear not the yoke that lightens you, and do not put off the yoke that lightens you of all these things; instead, submit to it with enthusiasm, and you will know its sweetness.

7. The image is the way waves constantly succeed one another on a beach and the rising tide.

(19) Augustine

Take my yoke upon you, and learn from me (11:29) not how to construct the world, not how to create all things, visible and invisible (Col 1:16), not how to perform miracles in this world, and raise the dead; but take it upon you **because I am gentle and lowly of heart.** Do you want to be great? Start from the bottom. Are you thinking of constructing a great skyscraper of a building? First give thought to the foundation of humility. And however much anybody may wish to spend on piling story upon story in his building, making the building ever bigger, the deeper he digs the foundation. As the building is being constructed, of course, it rises higher and higher, but the one who is digging the foundations is pushed down lower and lower. So the building has to be humbled before it reaches its loftiest height, and its topmost pinnacle can be erected only after it has been humbled to the depths.

What is the topmost pinnacle of the building we are striving to construct? How far does the top of our skyscraper reach? I'll tell you bluntly: as far as the sight of God himself. You can see how high that is, what a great thing it is, to see God. Any of you who long for this will understand what I am saying and you are hearing. We have been promised the sight of God, of the true God, of the supreme God. This really is a wonderful thing, to see the one who sees (cf. Gen 16:13–14).

(20) Epiphanius the Latin

Let us leave behind the ways of the devil with all our heart and hear the Lord himself inviting us and saying: **Come to me all you who labor, and I will refresh you.** For the pagans labor by following the devil and are burdened with sins. **And I shall refresh you**: he refreshes all who believe in him with faith, justice, holiness, and eternal life. **Take my yoke upon you and learn from me, since I am gentle and humble of heart**: everyone who wants life and desires to see good days, let him put down the yoke of iniquity and wickedness, just as the prophet[8] says: *Let us break apart their chains and cast their yoke from us* (Ps 2:3). Unless one has put behind him the yoke of sinning, that is, the feeding the fire of his vices,[9] he cannot take up the sweet and light yoke of Christ.

But if the yoke of Christ is so sweet and light, how does holy religion appear harsh and bitter to people? If the heart is infected with earthly desires, it can become so bitter that it cannot love heavenly things. For it has not yet come to Christ, taken up his yoke, and learned that he is gentle and humble of heart. And so we learn, most beloved, from the teaching of our Lord himself, that, unless someone has been gentle and humble of heart, he cannot carry the yoke of Christ. Let us root out from our heart the feeding of our vices with all our strength, because our faith is not a *weapon* of the flesh, but its *strength* comes from the power of God (2 Cor 10:4), which is *against spiritual wickedness* (Eph 6:12).

Once these vices have been rejected, the gifts of the Holy Spirit will come into our life.

8. The psalmist is referred to as the prophet, often thought of as David (cf. Acts 2:29–30)

9. The wood of the kindling (for burning) and of the yoke (strong and weight-bearing) is being contrasted.

Thus we will be able to take up the yoke of holiness without labor and remain gentle and humble of heart in his sight all our days. Because *the Lord will receive the gentle, moreover, he will humble sinners to the earth* (Ps 147:6); *for the gentle will inherit the earth*, that is, the kingdom of heaven, *and will dwell on it forever* (Ps 37:29).

(21) Caesarius of Arles

Dearest brothers, what our Lord requires of us is within our means. He does not say to us, "Fast more than you can, and keep vigil more than your powers can endure." He does not say to us: "Abstain from wine or meat." The Lord does not require such from us, but they are considered worthy to enjoin because all men are able to fulfill it with the Lord's grace without great labor. I ask you, brothers, what labor is it to follow humility, to hold love, to love justice, to preserve chastity, to want for all men what each desires for himself? Truly, as the Lord himself has said, **For my yoke is easy and my burden is light** (11:30). But, what is worse, there are many who want to bear with many labors, the hardest and most bitter yoke of avarice, and neglect to put the pleasant yoke of Christ and his light burden on their shoulders. They choose to submit with many sins under the heavy burden than under the yoke of Christ, which can elevate them in heaven. But we, dearest brothers, thinking wisely and faithfully with us, let us cast off the hard or harsh yoke of avarice from our necks and impose on our shoulders the sweetest yoke of Christ. According to the Apostle, let us lift up our conversation in heaven (cf. Phil 3:20), that we might appear with him in glory. May he grant this, who with the Father and the Holy Spirit lives and reigns unto the ages of ages. Amen.

Matthew 12

In a dispute over the proper interpretation of the law, Jesus says that his actions and those of his disciples were done in the spirit of the law and the prophets. Jesus is greater than the temple (12:6) and is Lord of the Sabbath (12:8). In the second conflict over healing on the Sabbath, the withered hand becomes a symbol of the healing found in the Word. Though his actions were opposed, Jesus continues to perform deeds of healing and does not retaliate against his opponents (Chrysostom).

Jesus turns the tables on his opponents by revealing how alienated they are from the truth; their words appear to be protecting what is good, whereas their intentions are evil (Clement). They should take a lesson from nature: a good tree should be able to produce only good fruit, and an evil tree bad fruit. "A bad tree by nature cannot produce what is good, nor can the same tree have good branches if it is bad" (Hilary). Epiphanius encourages us to be "good trees," namely, to act consistently in such a way that bears a righteous fruit.

Jesus's antagonists try a different tactic by asking for a sign as proof of his divinity. In response, the sign of Jonah is offered as a symbol of his death and resurrection. Then Jesus returns to their earlier comments about demonic power. Augustine discusses the characteristics of these seven wicked spirits and contrasts them with the sevenfold gifts of the Spirit.

Matthew 12:1–9

**1 At that time Jesus went through the grainfields on the sabbath; his disciples were hungry,
and they began to pluck heads of grain and to eat. 2 But when the Pharisees saw it, they
said to him, "Look, your disciples are doing what is not lawful to do on the sabbath." 3 He
said to them, "Have you not read what David did, when he was hungry, and those who
were with him: 4 how he entered the house of God and ate the bread of the Presence, which
it was not lawful for him to eat nor for those who were with him, but only for the priests?
5 Or have you not read in the law how on the sabbath the priests in the temple profane the
sabbath, and are guiltless? 6 I tell you, something greater than the temple is here. 7 And if
you had known what this means, 'I desire mercy, and not sacrifice,' you would not have
condemned the guiltless. 8 For the Son of man is lord of the sabbath."**

9 And he went on from there, and entered their synagogue.

(1) Irenaeus of Lyons

But the law did not forbid the hungry from taking food that was close at hand on the Sabbath day, although it did prohibit them from reaping it and gathering it into barns. It was for this reason that the Lord replied to those who criticized his disciples because they were separating ears of grain in order to eat them, **Have you not read what David did when he was hungry, how he went into the house of God, and ate the sacred bread that none were permitted to eat except priests alone, and gave some to those who were with him?** He therefore absolved his disciples by these words from the law and implied that priests were allowed to act freely. After all, David was declared a priest before God despite Saul's persecution of him; we can state, therefore, that every righteous person has been ordained a priest. In fact, all who are disciples of the Lord are priests. They do not inherit fields or buildings in this world, but rather serve the altar and God at all times. Moses was speaking of these people when he blessed Levi in Deuteronomy: *Those who say to their father and mother, "I do not know you," who do not acknowledge their brothers, renouncing their own sons, and instead guard your teachings and watch over your covenant. . . .* (Deut 33:9). But who, save the disciples of the Lord, would forsake father and mother, rejecting all those closest to them, on account of the Word of God and his covenant? Again Moses refers to them: *They have no inheritance*, he says, *because the Lord himself is their inheritance* (Deut 10:9). And once more: *The Levite priests will not have any share in the whole tribe of Levi nor in Israel's inheritance. Instead the fruits offered to the Lord will be their inheritance, of which they will eat* (Deut 18:1). On account of this, Paul says, *I do not look for a gift, but rather for fruit* (Phil 4:17).

So the disciples, by virtue of their Levitical inheritance, were permitted to procure their food from the fields if they were hungry, **for the laborer is worthy of his food** (10:10). Indeed, the priests "defiled" the Sabbath in the temple every week and yet were not considered guilty. Why not? Well, because when they were in the temple, they were performing not a secular but a sacred service. They carried out the requirements of the law while not neglecting the law, unlike that man who for his own gain carried dry wood into the camp of God and was justly stoned to death. **Every tree**, after all, **which does not have good fruit will be cut down and hurled into the fire** (3:10; 7:19), and *Whoever desecrates the temple of God will himself be desecrated by God* (1 Cor 3:17).

For he says **there is one here greater than the temple.** But **greater** and less do not refer to things that have nothing in common with each other, being contrary natures and fighting among themselves, but instead designate things that share the same nature. Such things mutually join together, differing only in number and size, like water from water, light from light, and grace from grace. Therefore the law of liberty is more powerful than that law which was generated in slavery, and on account of this, it is not limited to one nation only, but has expanded to cover the whole world. Moreover, it is one and the same Lord, who is greater than either the temple, or Solomon, or Jonah, who grants to humankind both his presence and the resurrection of the dead. . . .

From these considerations, it is obvious to all that God did not want sacrifices and burnt offerings from them, but the faith, obedience, and righteousness necessary for their salvation. We can see this also in Hosea, where the prophet records that God, seeking to teach them his will, said: *I prefer mercy to sacrifice, the knowledge of God to burnt offerings* (Hos 6:6). But our Lord also warned them in the same way, saying: If you had only inquired into the meaning of the phrase **I prefer mercy and not sacrifice**, you would never have condemned the innocent (cf. 12:7).

(2) Ambrose of Milan

Not only by his words, but also by his actions and example, the Lord Jesus begins to free us from observing old law, and to clothe us in the new robes of grace. And so, on this Sabbath day, he leads us through the cornfields.[1] By this I mean that he leads us to fruitful works. What the Sabbath, the harvest, the ears of wheat mean to him is a great mystery. The field represents the whole world; the harvest of the field is the rich crop of saints that will come from the sowing of the human race; the ears of wheat are the fruits of the Church, which the apostles rub vigorously in their hands—nourishing and feeding themselves on our spiritual progress.

In his wisdom, the Lord points out that the law prefigures what is to come. But he also reproaches the very guardians of the law of being ignorant of the things of the law. He gives the example of how David, when he and his companions were hungry, went into the house of God and took the holy bread. David and those who were with him ate this bread (1 Sam 21:3–6).

Here is a great and prophetic example, in which for the first time we are shown that we must not attach ourselves to what is trivial in the law, but only to what is solid and useful. Moreover, as David and his comrades were fleeing King Saul [when they ate the holy bread], so Christ is prefigured in the law. For Christ and his apostles had to hide from the prince of this world.

But how could David, so zealous a defender of the law, have eaten the bread and given it to his companions when no one but priests (cf. Lev 24:9) were allowed to eat it? It was to show, in a figurative way, that the lay people were to eat the food of priests; it could also mean that we should all imitate the lives of priests or that all the children of the Church are priests. For all of us are anointed to be a holy priesthood, offering spiritual sacrifices to God (cf. 1 Pet 2:5).

From that time on, Christ's teaching was greater than the law. It does not destroy the law but fulfills it (cf. Matt 5:17). Neither does it destroy the Sabbath. The Sabbath was made for man. For if a hungry man who had long been deprived of the fruits of the earth spurns the emptiness of the ancient hungers, surely the law is not destroyed but fulfilled.

(3) Hilary of Poitiers

The Lord also reminded them of another prophecy found in the law that had been fulfilled in him: the priests in the temple violated the Sabbath without guilt. By this he indicates that

1. I.e., wheatfields.

he is himself the temple in which, by means of the apostolic teaching, salvation is brought to the pagans, whereas the people of the law remain in the lassitude of unbelief. Since he himself is greater than the Sabbath, the gospel is at work in Christ, who cannot be blamed for having violated the law.

And in order to show that every one of these events that happened contains an image of a work to come, he added: **If you knew what this meant, 'I desire mercy, not sacrifice,' you would not have condemned the innocent.** The work of our salvation is found not in offering sacrifice, but in mercy, and, now that the law has ceased, we are saved by the goodness of God. If they had understood the reality of this gift, they would never have condemned the innocent, that is, the apostles. On account of jealousy, they were bound to be accused of having broken the law, because it was through them that, once the ancient practice of sacrifices ceased, the reformation of mercy came to the benefit of all people. The Pharisees should not have thought that the Lord of the Sabbath could be bound by the prescriptions of the Sabbath. It was in the grain field that these words and deeds happened.

Matthew 12:10–14

10 And behold, there was a man with a withered hand. And they asked him, "Is it lawful to heal on the sabbath?" so that they might accuse him. 11 He said to them, "What man of you, if he has one sheep and it falls into a pit on the sabbath, will not lay hold of it and lift it out? 12 Of how much more value is a man than a sheep! So it is lawful to do good on the sabbath." 13 Then he said to the man, "Stretch out your hand." And the man stretched it out, and it was restored, whole like the other. 14 But the Pharisees went out and took counsel against him, how to destroy him.

(4) Hilary of Poitiers

[W]hen the Lord entered a synagogue, the Pharisees presented a man with a withered hand, asking him whether it was lawful to heal on the Sabbath. They were seeking an opportunity to accuse him by his own response. But he entrapped them instead by the example of a sheep that falls into a pit: whether those who are concerned with pulling it out on the Sabbath are guilty in doing so. For it is better to heal a man, who **is more valuable than a sheep**, and it is wrongheaded to think that the Sabbath can be violated in the service of saving humanity, since concern for pulling a sheep out of a pit does not violate the Sabbath.

After returning from the grain field, where the apostles had already received the fruit of their harvest, the Lord went to the synagogue to prepare other workers for his harvest. Many of these would later stand together with the apostles. These were healed, as was the man with the crippled hand. The Pharisees did not have the means of granting healing; the man's hand ceased its function and service to the body that it had been able to perform before it had withered. So the Lord told him to extend his hand, and it was restored just as sound as the other. Complete healing is in the Word, and the hand is returned to wholeness just as the other one. Here there is a likeness produced by the service of the apostles in their duty of presenting salvation. The Lord taught that the Pharisees could hardly undertake the task of humanity's salvation as did the apostles. For the Pharisees to serve in the same way, their "hand" would have to be restored—if they would believe.

But the Lord's works incited jealousy among the Pharisees, who **took counsel against him** because they regarded him with the body as a man and did not understand him to be God in his works. Because he knew their designs, he departed from them that he might learn of their malicious plans from a distance. And large crowds followed him; plainly, he was standing in the company of the faithful as he left the unbelievers behind.

(5) Ambrose of Milan

Now the Lord Jesus goes on to other things. Because he had resolved to save the *whole man*, he now deals with individuals one by one. In truth this is why he said: *You are angry with me because I have made a man whole on the Sabbath day* (John 7:23). In the present passage, he heals the hand that Adam had stretched out to seize the forbidden fruit (cf. Gen 3:6) and waters that hand with the health-giving sap of good works. Though withered through Adam's own fault, the hand was healed through good deeds. Jesus sharply rebukes the Jews who violated the precepts of the law by their false interpretations. They thought that on the Sabbath one was to cease doing good works. In this they were wrong, for the law prefigured future events, and, in the future, evil, not good, was supposed to take a rest. Although worldly activities will take a rest, it is not idleness to rest in the praise of God. To repose in God's praise is a good work!

You have heard the Lord's words. He said: *Stretch out your hand* (Luke 6:10). See, here is a remedy for all ills; if you imagine that your hand is healthy, take care that it is not withered by greed or blasphemy. Stretch it out often. Stretch it out to the poor who beg for help. Stretch it out to help your neighbor, to give a helping hand to the widow. Extend it to snatch from an unjust judge some innocent person subjected to foul play. Stretch out your hand to God in sorrow for your sins. This is how to stretch out one's hand. This is how one is healed. Remember that when Jeroboam sacrificed to false gods, his hand became withered, but when he stretched it out to God in prayer it was restored to health (cf. 1 Kgs 13:4, 6).

Matthew 12:15–21

15Jesus, aware of this, withdrew from there. And many followed him, and he healed
them all, 16and ordered them not to make him known. 17This was to fulfil what was
spoken by the prophet Isaiah:

> **18"Behold, my servant whom I have chosen,**
> **my beloved with whom my soul is well pleased.**
> **I will put my Spirit upon him,**
> **and he shall proclaim justice to the Gentiles.**
> **19He will not wrangle or cry aloud,**
> **nor will any one hear his voice in the streets;**

> [20]**he will not break a bruised reed**
> **or quench a smoldering wick,**
> **till he brings justice to victory;**
> [21] **and in his name will the Gentiles hope."**

(6) John Chrysostom

The prophet celebrates the Lord's gentleness and his unspeakable power, and he opens wide the door to Gentiles. He also foretells the difficulties that will come upon the Jews, and he points to Christ's concord with the Father. For **Behold**, God says, **my servant, whom I have chosen, my beloved, in whom my soul is well pleased** (cf. Isa 42:1). Now if God chose him, he could scarcely be God's adversary in setting aside the law. Having the same mind as God, he was hardly an enemy of the lawgiver.

Then the prophet proclaims his gentleness when he says, **He shall not wrangle or cry aloud**. For the Lord's desire was to bring healing among his enemies; but since they drove him away, he did not fight against them.

Intimating both his might and their weakness, he says, **He will not break a bruised reed** (cf. Isa 42:3). For it was easy to break them all to pieces like a reed, indeed one that was bruised. **And quench a smoldering wick** (cf. Isa 42:3). Here the prophet both says that their anger was kindled and speaks of his power to put down their anger, even to **quench** it with ease. In all this he shows his gentleness.

Are things always going to be this way? Will the Lord bear with them always even though they plot and rage against him? Certainly not. When he has done his part, then he will execute his other plans. In other words, **Till he brings justice to victory; and in his name shall the Gentiles hope** (cf. Isa 42:4). As Paul also says, *Having prepared to revenge all disobedience, when your obedience is fulfilled* (2 Cor 10:6).

What is the meaning of **when he sends forth justice unto victory**? Once he has carried out everything he was to do, then he will visit them with a perfect vengeance. They will endure his fearful deeds, and his brilliant trophy of victory will be displayed, his judgments will prevail and there will be nothing to oppose him, no matter how shameless. He is right to call justice **judgment**. For he brings justice about by his **judgment**. But punishment of unbelievers does not exhaust the working out of his will, for he will also win the whole world to himself. This is why it is added, **And in his name shall the Gentiles hope** (cf. Isa 42:4).

Matthew 12:22–27

[22]Then a blind and dumb demoniac was brought to him, and he healed him, so that the
dumb man spoke and saw. [23]And all the people were amazed, and said, "Can this be the
Son of David?" [24]But when the Pharisees heard it they said, "It is only by Beel'zebul,
the prince of demons, that this man casts out demons." [25]Knowing their thoughts, he
said to them, "Every kingdom divided against itself is laid waste, and no city or house

divided against itself will stand; [26]and if Satan casts out Satan, he is divided against himself; how then will his kingdom stand? [27]And if I cast out demons by Beel'zebul, by whom do your sons cast them out? Therefore they shall be your judges."

(7) Chromatius of Aquileia

In order to manifest the power of divinity in this demoniac who was blind and mute, the Lord had exhibited so great a work that the man was immediately freed from the demon. As a result, the man both saw and spoke, amazing and dumbfounding everyone present. The crowd admired the Lord for such a deed because they believed he was only a Son of David in his incarnate form, even though he performed clear signs of divine power.

When the Pharisees heard of it, they said, This man does not cast out demons except by Beelzebub the chief of the demons. What blindness, what faithlessness, or more precisely rather, what foolishness it was of the Pharisees. Not only did they not believe in the divine power, but they likewise falsely accused him! This is what David had predicted by the foreknowledge of the Holy Spirit that those people would do, saying: *Foreign sons have spoken falsely with me, foreign sons have grown old* (Ps 18:45 [Latin Ps 17:46]). And again: *In the multitude of your power your enemies will speak falsely with you* (Ps 66:3 [Latin Ps 65:3]). Surely the Pharisees discerned that these obvious signs of power were done by the Lord, nonetheless they began to say: **This man does not cast out demons except by Beelzebub, the chief of the demons.** Even if they were doctors of the law, how could they allege such a thing according to the authority of the Scriptures, or invent a charge that was so undeserved? The madness of a frenzied mind is always rash, such that it doesn't know what it is saying. So too, the Pharisees were blinded in just this way by their malice and iniquity, such that they didn't know what they were saying. It was against them that the Holy Spirit rightly proclaimed through David: *Let hostile lips be made silent, which speak wickedness against the just in arrogance and contempt* (Ps 31:18 [Latin Ps 30:19]). What arrogance is greater or what contempt so considerable as to blaspheme the author of divine authority with the name of the adversary? The same one testified about these men in another psalm, saying: *They were turned into a bent bow* (Ps 78:57 [Latin Ps 77:57]). Because they took up the arms of their impiety and iniquity against the Son of God, they dared to associate the divine power with devilish ability.

But Jesus, knowing their thoughts, said to them. While our Lord and Savior exposed the thoughts of their hearts, he showed clearly that he was God to these same men—a fact that they refused to believe—because it belongs to God alone to know the thoughts of the heart, about which it is written, we read: *God searching the hearts and inner parts* (Ps 7:9 [Latin Ps 7:10]). And again: *Man looks on the outward appearance, but God on the heart* (1 Sam 16:7). Therefore the Lord speaks to the Pharisees by criticizing their iniquities because they perverted divine power with a false claim: **Every kingdom divided against itself will be desolate, and every city divided against itself will not stand. If indeed Satan casts out Satan, he is divided against himself. Therefore how will his kingdom stand?** The Lord refutes and dismantles the folly of the Pharisees by making a comparison with earthly things. If a kingdom divided against itself is inevitably overthrown, and a city or a house against itself cannot stand, how could Satan cast out Satan, thus destroying his own kingdom? Then the Lord says, **But if I by the Spirit of God cast out demons, certainly the kingdom of God draws near to you.** In other words, if the apostles expelled demons in no other name than the name of Christ, how much more did the Lord perform this act since he was the one who granted this grace, authority and power to his disciples?

Since the very power of the Lord contains a spiritual meaning of things mentioned, we should turn our attention to what is signified in this event according to a figural understanding. In the man who had a demon, being both blind and mute, we recognize an apparent figure of the pagans. These latter had (before the advent of the Lord) sold themselves to the demons through the error of idolatry, making them both mute and blind. So we see the man who was mute because he was not confessing the Son of God or because he was not giving appropriate thanks to the Lord. Every unbeliever and faithless person is regarded as a mute, even when he talks, if he does not confess the Son of God before God. The man was blind because, being blinded by the error of the age and the darkness of ignorance, he had not yet recognized the true and eternal light. After health returned to him whose withered hand had been healed in the synagogue, he was offered to the Lord. Everyone who is freed through the mercy of the Lord from the error of Satan and leaves the culture of idols behind, immediately begins both to see and to speak. In order to see this true light, which he couldn't see previously, he looks with the eyes of faith. Now the one who was mute confesses freely and faithfully that Christ is Lord.

(8) Epiphanius the Latin

The blind man represented the whole people of the pagans, sitting in darkness and the shadow of death. Because he had become blind in the eyes of his heart, he could not see Christ. As a result, he neither knew the law nor could he bless God. Because he was possessed by an evil spirit in the wake of such great idolatry and demonic desires, he was led around like a captive by the unclean spirit.

The man presented was mute. By him, the devil offered to God all nations that he had troubled. But the Lord cured him immediately, **so that he spoke and saw.** He spoke, because he was blessing God through faith. He saw Christ, because he had the eyes of his heart illuminated. He was healed because he left behind the madness of idolatry and the variety of his errors, and now served the Lord.

Moreover the crowds, seeing this, were astounded, saying: Is this the Son of David? The crowds had heard in the law that the Christ would come from the race of David. Once they saw the miracles (which no one had ever seen before), they asked with amazement whether he himself were the Christ. They, too, were ready to believe in him.

The Pharisees kept to the law and should have encouraged the people toward belief. But they were led captive by jealousy, saying: **He casts out demons by Beelzebub, the prince of demons.** O unbelieving Pharisees, you have always manipulated the law in your hands. When reading the law, did you find there that Satan casts out Satan or gives sight to the blind or cures paralytics or makes the deaf hear? He can certainly mortify and kill and make people mute and deaf; however, no one can bring someone back to life or effect a cure except Jesus Christ alone. It is not Christ but the devil who reigns in you, which is why you do not enter into the kingdom of heaven, nor permit others to enter. Rather, you are sons of the devil, and you seek to fulfill the desires of your father (John 8:44), so that, having been separated from the kingdom of Christ, you might die with the devil.

Now that we, O most beloved, have been healed through our Lord from every spirit of unspeakable idolatry and have had the eyes of our heart illuminated, let our ears resound with him day and night, let our lips repeat him without ceasing, and let us show in our actions and our soul that we deserve the mercy of our Defender both now and forever.

(9) Augustine

This passage shows that Jesus wanted to show that by their own admission, through failing to believe in him, they had chosen to belong to the devil's kingdom, which, of course, could not remain standing if it were divided against itself. So let the Pharisees choose whichever they wish: if Satan cannot cast out Satan, then they could find nothing to say against the Lord, but if he can, then they have all the more reason to look to themselves and clear out of his kingdom, which, being divided against itself, cannot remain standing.

How, then, does the Lord Christ cast out demons? To rid themselves of the idea that it was by the prince of demons, they should pay attention to how he goes on: **And if I**, he says, **cast out demons by Beelzebub, by whom do your sons cast them out? Therefore they shall be your judges.** He said this, of course, about his disciples, sons of that people, who, as the disciples of the Lord Jesus Christ, certainly had clear consciences that they had never learned any evil arts from such a good Master, such as how to cast out demons by the prince of demons.

Therefore, he says, **they shall be your judges** . . . they [who are] *the base-born and contemptible things of this world* (1 Cor 1:28), in whom is displayed not the artful malignity, but the holy simplicity of my power, they shall be my witnesses and your judges. Then he adds: **But if I by the Spirit of God cast out demons, then the kingdom of God has caught up with you.** What does this mean? "**If I, by the Spirit of God cast out demons,** your sons would not be casting them out in any other way either, seeing that I have given them a simple faith, not a malignant science. Without a shadow of doubt, **the kingdom of God has caught up with you,** and it is undermining the kingdom of the devil. You too will be undermined along with it, if you don't change your ways."

Matthew 12:28–32

28"But if it is by the Spirit of God that I cast out demons, then the kingdom of God has come upon you. 29Or how can one enter a strong man's house and plunder his goods, unless he first binds the strong man? Then indeed he may plunder his house. 30He who is not with me is against me, and he who does not gather with me scatters. 31Therefore I tell you, every sin and blasphemy will be forgiven men, but the blasphemy against the

Spirit will not be forgiven. [32]And whoever says a word against the Son of man will be forgiven; but whoever speaks against the Holy Spirit will not be forgiven, either in this age or in the age to come."

(10) Hilary of Poitiers

How can anyone enter into a strong man's house and plunder his possessions? Etc. He indicates that all the power of the devil was crushed by the Lord during the time of his initial temptation, since no one may enter the strong man's house and plunder his possessions unless he has bound up the strong man. Then he can plunder his house, for whoever can accomplish that is surely stronger than the strong man. Satan was already tied up at the moment when he was called Satan by the Lord (cf. 4:10). In fact, he was shackled when his own wickedness was named. Once he was bound in chains, the Lord was able to take away his possessions and his house. In other words, the Lord has led us, who were once Satan's weapons and the army of his Satan's kingdom, back to his own rule. Now that he has conquered and bound up the strong man, he has provided for himself an unoccupied and useful house within us.

He shows, at the same time, that he is far from having derived any power from Satan, for whoever is not with him is against him, and whoever does not gather with him is scattered. From this we may understand that it is a matter of great danger to suppose something evil about someone about whom it is said: **whoever is not with him is against him, and whoever does not gather with him scatters.**

(11) Ambrose of Milan

What a shocking blasphemy, what madness! That at the very time the Son of God took flesh to crush the impure spirits and snatch the booty from the prince of this world, and gave men power to destroy the wicked spirits and like a conqueror divide the spoils, some would invoke the power of the devil to drive out diabolical powers. What madness when it is by the finger of God—or, as Matthew puts it, **by the Spirit of God** (12:28) that demons are cast out.

Understand that the kingdom of God is like an indivisible body. Christ is the right hand of God, and the Spirit is like a finger. We are given the picture, so to speak, of a single body within the divinity. And if it is an indivisible body, how could the kingdom not be indivisible? As Scripture says, *In Christ dwells all the fullness of the Godhead* (Col 2:9). Just as you cannot deny this of the Father you cannot deny it of the Spirit.

In making this comparison with the members of a human body, you must not think that there are reasons to believe there is some sort of sharing of power. Certainly not. An indivisible thing cannot be divided. We are using a figure of speech not to distinguish the power of one person from another, but to indicate their unity. By mentioning "finger," I do not suggest division of power, since the right hand of God declares: *My Father and I are one* (John 10:30). Yes, the divinity is indivisible, but the Person is clearly distinguished.

(12) Augustine

Some people are of the opinion that the only ones who sin against the Holy Spirit are those who have been cleansed by the washing of rebirth (Tit 3:5) in the Church and have received the Holy Spirit, and then afterward have shown themselves ungrateful for such a wonderful gift by plunging themselves in some deadly sin, such as adultery or murder or withdrawal from the Christian religion altogether or, at least, from the catholic Church. But I don't see how this view can be allowed, seeing that the Church does not refuse to accept repentance for any kind of crime you can think of. Moreover, the Church seeks to correct the heretics precisely on this point; the Apostle says, *In case God may perhaps grant them repentance to recognize the truth and to sober up from the snares of the devil, by whom they are held captive to his will* (2 Tim 2:25–26). I mean, what good can correction be, if there is no hope of forgiveness?

In any case, the Lord didn't say, "Any believing catholic who speaks a word against the Holy Spirit," but **Whoever speaks**, that is, "Anyone at all who speaks, anyone you care to think of who speaks," **will not be forgiven, neither in this age nor in the age to come.** So whether it's a pagan or a Jew or a Christian, or a heretic among Jews or Christians, or any other kind of error you like to mention, the text doesn't say, "This sort or that sort," but, **Whoever speaks a word against the Holy Spirit** (that is, blasphemes the Holy Spirit) **will not be forgiven, neither in this age nor in the age to come.**

If, as I have already shown, every error that is contrary to the truth and an enemy of catholic peace is **speaking a word against the Holy Spirit**; and if for all that, the Church does not cease to correct and gather in people from every kind of error, to receive both forgiveness of sins and the Holy Spirit they have blasphemed—then I think I have shown the unfathomable depths and extent of this colossal problem. So let us seek from the Lord the light needed to explain and solve it.

The first thing I want to draw to your attention is that the Lord did not say "*No* blaspheming the Spirit will be forgiven," nor did he say "Whoever speaks any word at all against the Holy Spirit will not be forgiven," but simply **Whoever speaks a word**. You see, if he had said the former, there would be nothing at all left for us to argue about, because if people are not going to be forgiven any blasphemy and any word spoken against the Holy Spirit, then the Church couldn't win anybody from any kind of godless error spoken against the gift of Christ and the sanctification of the Church. . . .

But what is this manner of blaspheming—this unmannerly manner, if I may say—what is this blasphemy, what is this word against the Holy Spirit? . . . Now you know, dearly beloved, that in that invisible and inviolable Trinity that the true faith and the catholic Church profess and proclaim, God the Father is not the Father of the Holy Spirit but of the Son; and God the Son is not the Son of the Holy Spirit, but of the Father; and that God the Holy Spirit is not the Spirit only of the Father or only of the Son, but of both Father and Son; and finally that this Trinity, while in it the distinct properties and subsistence of each of the persons is maintained, is nonetheless one God, not three gods, because of the undivided and inseparable essence or nature of its eternity, truth, and goodness. In this way, we are given to understand (according to our limited capacity and as far as we are still permitted to see by mirrors and in a riddle) that the property of the Father is to be the author and origin of the others, the property of the Son is to be born, the property of the Holy Spirit is to be the communion of Father and Son, and the property of all three is to be equal to each other.

That which is common to them both, the Father and the Son, wished us to have communion, both with them and among ourselves. By this gift that they both possess as one, they wished to gather us together and make us one, that is to say, by the Holy Spirit, who is God and the gift of God. By this gift we are reconciled to the Godhead, and by this gift we enjoy the Godhead. After all, what use would it be to us to know any kind of good if we didn't also love it? Just as truth is what we learn by, so charity is what we love by, and it enables us both to know things more thoroughly and to enjoy them when they are known more happily. Thus charity *has been poured into our hearts through the Holy Spirit that has been given to us* (Rom 5:5). It is by sins that we were barred from the possession of those things that are really and truly good; charity has covered a multitude of sins. So the Father is the true and trusty origin of the Son who is, and the Son is truth sprung from the true and trusty Father, and the Holy Spirit is goodness poured out by the Father who is good and the Son who is good; all three, however, enjoy entirely equal divinity and inseparable unity.

So in order for us to receive the eternal life that will be given to us at the end, on the last day, the first gift that came to us from God's goodness, accompanying the beginning of faith, was the forgiveness of sins. As long as these remain, you see, there also remains some sort of hostility toward God, and estrangement from him, which arises from the evil in us, because Scripture is not lying when it says, *Your sins make a rift between you and God* (Isa 59:2). And so he cannot really bring his own good things into us, unless he first takes the bad things out of us; and the former increase to the extent that the latter decrease, nor will the former be perfected until the latter are eliminated. But now, that Christ the Lord forgives sins by the Holy Spirit, just as he casts out demons by the Holy Spirit, can be gathered from what he said to his disciples after he had risen from the dead: after saying, *Receive the Holy Spirit*, he immediately added, *If you forgive anyone's sins, they shall be forgiven; if you retain anyone's, they shall be retained* (John 20:22–23). And then that rebirth, which brings about the forgiveness of all past sins, takes place in the Holy Spirit, according to the Lord's own words, *Unless one is born of water and the Spirit, one cannot enter the kingdom of God* (John 3:5). . . .

And so the first benefit believers receive from the kindness of God is forgiveness of sins in the Holy Spirit. Thus John the Baptist, who was sent as a runner before the face of the Lord, began his preaching with that. This is what the text says: **Now in those days came John the Baptist, preaching in the wilderness of Judea and saying, Repent, for the kingdom of heaven has drawn near** (3:1–2). So too with the Lord himself, of whom we read, **From then on Jesus began to preach and say, Repent, for the kingdom of heaven has drawn near** (4:17). . . . However, perfect love or charity is the final, perfect gift of the Holy Spirit. First, however, comes the gift that consists in the forgiveness of sins, the benefaction by which we are delivered from the power of darkness, and the prince of this world is thrown outside by our faith. He is the one who is at work in the children of unbelief, in light of the obligations and comradeship of sin. For it is by the Holy Spirit, who gathers the people of God together into one, that the unclean spirit is cast out, who is divided against himself.

What speaks against this spontaneous, free gift, against the grace of God, is an unrepentant heart. It is being unrepentant that is blasphemy against the Holy Spirit, which will not be forgiven in this age, nor in the age to come. I mean to say, you are speaking a very evil, utterly graceless word against the Holy Spirit in whom we are baptized and all our sins forgiven; it is against the Holy Spirit that the Church received so that whoever's sins it forgives are truly forgiven (cf. John 20:22–23). When the patience of God is beckoning you to repentance, you harden your impenitent heart (whether you are speaking in thought or out loud), and so store up wrath for yourself on the day of wrath and of the revelation of the just judgment of God, who will render to us all according to our works (Rom 2:4–6).

So this impenitence (that's the name we can use any time, for both the blasphemy and the word against the Holy Spirit that has no forgiveness forever); this impenitence, I say, against which both herald and judge cried out when they said, *Repent, for the kingdom of heaven has drawn near* (3:2; 4:17); against which the Lord opened his mouth to preach the gospel, and against which he foretold that the gospel itself was to be preached in the whole world, as he said to the disciples after rising from the dead, *It was necessary for the Christ to suffer and to rise again from the dead on the third day, and for repentance and the forgiveness of sins to be preached in his name throughout all nations, beginning from Jerusalem* (Luke 24:46–47). This impenitence has absolutely no forgiveness, neither in this age nor in the age to come; because it is by repenting that we obtain in this age a forgiveness that will be valid for the age to come.

But as long as a person lives in the body in this life, it is impossible to judge this impenitence or unrepentant heart. We must not despair of anybody, as long as God's patience is beckoning to repentance. After all, he who doesn't desire the death of the wicked, but rather that they turn again and live, does not snatch the wicked from this life. Someone is a pagan today; how do you know he won't be a Christian tomorrow? What's more, brothers, on this matter you should also follow the Apostle's advice, *Do not pass judgment on anything before the time* (1 Cor 4:5). Because this blasphemy is against the Spirit, for which there is never any forgiveness (and we have said or discovered, or even as I think demonstrated that it is not any and every blasphemy, but a particular, and what's more persistent, hardness of an unrepentant heart), this blasphemy cannot be detected in anybody, as I have said, as long as they are still in this life.

Matthew 12:33–37

**33"Either make the tree good, and its fruit good; or make the tree bad, and its fruit bad;
for the tree is known by its fruit. 34You brood of vipers! how can you speak good, when
you are evil? For out of the abundance of the heart the mouth speaks. 35The good man
out of his good treasure brings forth good, and the evil man out of his evil treasure
brings forth evil. 36I tell you, on the day of judgment men will render account for every
careless word they utter; 37for by your words you will be justified, and by your words
you will be condemned."**

(13) Clement of Alexandria

Now those who carry wealth in their souls and gold or field in their hearts instead of God's Spirit, who constantly acquire countless possessions and always envision more, who have stooped down and been bound by the snares of the world, who *are dust, and to dust will return* (Gen 3:19)—from this position can they long for and care for the kingdom of heaven? Those who constantly bear not their hearts but their fields or mines will necessarily be found among what they have chosen, **for where one's mind is, there one's treasure is also** (6:21; Luke 12:34).

And indeed, the Lord knows two kinds of treasures: one good, for *the good person out of the good treasure of the heart produces good*; but the other bad, for *the evil person out of the evil treasure produces evil, because from the abundance of the heart the mouth speaks* (Luke 6:45; 12:34). Therefore just as there is not one treasure with him or with us (the first treasure giving sudden great profit in the finding [cf. 13:44], but the second being unprofitable, unenviable, disagreeable, and harmful), so also certain wealth is good, but other wealth is evil, if we really understand that wealth and treasure are not different from each other in nature. So certain wealth would be desirable and displayed, but other wealth undesirable and despised.

(14) Origen

Just as all corporeal matter, since it doubtlessly consists of a single nature, displays varied appearances through the qualities within it, whether bodies, trees, or herbs, in a similar way the nature of all rational beings consists of each one's choice, and since each one's particular abilities have equally been endowed, the movements from these abilities of an exercised choice (whether toward virtue or lust), guiding the soul subjected to itself, fashion the soul's appearance either into a good tree or into a bad one. Therefore, it may either be called a good tree if it would have chosen good things by the power of its choice, or it may be called bad if it would have chosen bad things (cf. 7:17). And in the same way, according to the motions of its intention, each one either is a good olive tree, if it should travel on a journey of virtue; or, if it continually follows the contrary, it will be called a wild olive tree. To summarize all this, the Lord was saying in the Gospel: **Either make the tree good and its fruits good; or make the tree bad and its fruits bad** (12:33), in order to show that a bad tree or a good tree is not so by birth but by coming to be that way.

(15) Hilary of Poitiers

Every sin and blasphemy will be forgiven to men, but blasphemy of the Spirit will not be forgiven. With a very grave qualification, he condemns the view of the Pharisees and the perversion of those who also think like them. He promises pardon of all sins but refuses pardon for blasphemy of the Spirit. While other words and deeds are treated with a generous pardon, there is no mercy if it is denied that God is in Christ. And in whatever way one sins without pardon, he is gracious to us and reminds us again that sins of every kind can be completely forgiven, though blasphemy against the Holy Spirit cannot be forgiven. For who is so completely beyond pardon as one who denies that Christ is of God, or repudiates that the substance of the Spirit of the Father resides in him? Since Christ accomplishes every work by the Spirit of God (John 10:25), and the Lord himself is the kingdom of God, and God is reconciling the world to himself (2 Cor 5:19), whatever sacrilege is directed against Christ is directed against God, because God is in Christ and Christ is in God.

Either make the tree good and its fruit good, or make the tree evil and its fruit evil. This saying can be applied to the present as well as the future. In the present, he refutes the Jews who, although they understand that the works of Christ are beyond human power, nevertheless do not wish to confess that these are works of God. As for the future, he denounces the complete perversion of faith, especially of those who, by divesting the Lord of the dignity and communion with the Father's substance, have boiled over into various heretical allegiances. They choose neither to dwell among the pagans who are pardoned for their ignorance (Acts 17:30–31; Eph 4:18), nor do they turn to an acknowledgement of the truth.

By **tree** Jesus refers to himself in his body, since all fertility bears its fruit through the inner fecundity of his power. A good tree inevitably produces good fruit, or the bad tree consistently produces bad fruit, because it is by its fruit that a tree is known. A bad tree by nature cannot produce what is good, nor can the same tree have good branches if it is bad. We should understand from this analogy that Christ either should be abandoned as useless, or retained as good by the usefulness of his good fruits. Either way, words spoken against the Son of Man are pardoned, but there is no pardon for blasphemy against the Spirit.

(16) Epiphanius the Latin

The kingdom of God is among you (Luke 17:21). **And the enemies of a man are those of his household** (10:36). How is this? Hear the Apostle: *For if you have lived according to the flesh, you will die; if, however, you have, through the spirit, mortified the deeds of the flesh, you will live* (Rom 8:13). **Because a good tree makes good fruit, and a bad tree makes bad fruit. For the tree is known from its fruit.** If we are good trees, that is, just, pious, faithful, and merciful, let us produce fruits of justice and sanctity. If we are bad trees, that is, impious, sorrowful, covetous, and sinful, we will be cut off. That is, on the divine day of judgment, we will be cut off with a *sharp two-edged sword* (Rev 1:16) and cast into the eternal fire.

The present passage makes a distinction between good and evil (Heb 5:14), as you heard in the reading: **Everyone, who hears my words and does them, will be like to a wise man, who has built his house upon rock; the rain comes down, the waves come, the winds blow and rush against that house, and it does not fall; for it had been founded upon rock** (7:24–25). Our Lord desires us to be unshakable to the end, and desires us to be saved eternally. This can only happen through labor, not through leisure. After proclaiming the Beatitudes and countless precepts, he concludes with this parable so that one who has persevered to the end may be saved.

Matthew 12:38–41

38Then some of the scribes and Pharisees said to him, "Teacher, we wish to see a sign from you." 39But he answered them, "An evil and adulterous generation seeks for a sign; but no sign shall be given to it except the sign of the prophet Jonah. 40For as Jonah was three days and three nights in the belly of the whale, so will the Son of man be three days and three nights in the heart of the earth. 41The men of Nin'eveh will arise at the judgment with this generation and condemn it; for they repented at the preaching of Jonah, and behold, something greater than Jonah is here."

(17) John Chrysostom

What does he say? **The men of Nineveh will rise up and condemn this generation, because they repented at the proclamation of Jonah, and see, something greater than Jonah is here.** Jesus might have said: Jonah was a servant, I am the Master; he came forth from the sea monster, I rose from the dead; he preached calamity, I proclaimed the good news of the kingdom. And while the Ninevites believed without a sign, I gave evidence with many signs; they heard nothing more than those words (12:41), I have vanquished every kind of philosophy. Jonah appeared as someone in need, but I came as the Master and Lord of all, issuing no threats, calling no one to account, and instead offering pardon. They were barbarians, whereas those to whom he was speaking had been in the company of countless prophets. No one prophesied about Jonah, they all did of me, and what happened confirmed their words. Jonah fled to avoid being mocked, but though I knew I was going to be crucified and mocked, I stayed on course. He could not bear even to be taunted even for those who were to be saved; yet I even underwent death, and death of the most disgraceful kind. He was a stranger and a foreigner, unknown to the Ninevites; I am of the Jews' own flesh and blood, born of the same ancestors. And you could make many other comparisons if you looked further.

(18) Theodore of Heraclea

The Lord says that for three days and nights he would remain under the earth, from the day of preparation until its end on Sunday, the entire Sabbath, from its beginning until his resurrection from among men. For in marking the days after someone dies, we say three days not because there were three full days, but because we consider that day on which one died as a complete day. It is then on another day when he departs from the grave as the first of those who have died to rise. So that is what is meant by **three days and nights.** This is evident because the women came on the third day to do what was customary to do for the dead.

Matthew 12:42–45

42"The queen of the South will arise at the judgment with this generation and condemn it; for she came from the ends of the earth to hear the wisdom of Solomon, and behold, something greater than Solomon is here.

**43"When the unclean spirit has gone out of a man, he passes through waterless
places seeking rest, but he finds none. 44Then he says, 'I will return to my house from
which I came.' And when he comes he finds it empty, swept, and put in order. 45Then
he goes and brings with him seven other spirits more evil than himself, and they enter and dwell there; and the last state of that man becomes worse than the first. So shall it be also with this evil generation."**

(19) Eusebius of Emesa

When the unclean spirit sought rest in deserted and arid places and did not find rest (for he had gone out of the man), it said, **Let me return to my home, from which I went forth.** It calls the man his **house,** since it wanted him to be his abode. But when the unclean spirit went back, the text says, it found that man was prepared for him by sweeping and putting things in order. The evil spirit saw room for evil in him—it no longer wanted to live alone. So it hurried and brought along another **seven spirits even more wicked** or even eight times more wicked. For they were worse spirits from before. But the number is less important than the growth in wickedness. For when someone has chosen to follow an evil course, or has readied his tongue for foul speech, an unclean spirit will find a way to do his work. For evil was already present in what the person was doing. In such cases, the unclean spirit makes things even worse, as is evident from what is said in the text (v. 45). Indeed, there is more here than meets the eye. For there are many more demons than these seven spirits.

(20) Augustine

There are some proud people,[2] who, once their sins have been forgiven, rely solely on the free choices of the human will for living a good life. By that very pride they shut their doors in the Holy Spirit's face, and their house remains apparently cleaned up from the mess of sins, but it is vacant, with nothing positively good in it. Your sins have been forgiven, you have been cleared of evils, although it is only the Holy Spirit who will fill you with good things. And yet he is repelled by pride. You are relying on yourself, he leaves you to yourself; you trust in yourself, you are handed over to yourself. But once that greed, which made you bad, has been driven out from you, that is to say, from your consciousness when your sins were forgiven, it wanders through desert places looking for rest. When it does not find any

2. He is referring to the Pelagians, who denied that men need the grace of the Holy Spirit to enable them to do good. That human beings had a free will was an act of divine grace.

rest, the greed comes back to the house that was cleaned up, and brings with it seven other spirits more wicked than itself. Thus the last state of that person will be worse than the first.

He brings seven others with him. What's the meaning, though, of **seven others**? Does it mean that the unclean spirit too is sevenfold? What is all this about? Well, the number seven signifies totality. The evil spirit had completely left, then it had come back, and if only it had come back alone! What's the meaning of **He takes along with him seven others**? These he didn't have when he was already bad; these he will have now that he is putting on a façade of good. . . .

The Holy Spirit is presented to us as sevenfold in his activity, so that he may be in us *the Spirit of wisdom and understanding, of counsel and courage, of knowledge and piety, and of the fear of God* (Isa 11:2–3). Now set against this sevenfold good the opposite sevenfold evil: the spirit of folly and error, the spirit of rashness and cowardice, the spirit of ignorance and impiety, and the spirit of pride against the fear of God. These are seven wicked spirits; who are the other seven still more wicked?

Another seven even more wicked are found in hypocrisy: worse is the evil spirit of folly, even worse is the spirit of pretended wisdom; worse is the spirit of error, even worse is the pretense of truth; worse is the spirit of rashness, even worse is the pretense of counsel; worse is the spirit of cowardice, an even worse one is the pretense of courage; worse is the spirit of ignorance, even worse is pretentious knowledge; worse is the spirit of impiety, even worse is the pretense of piety; worse is the spirit of arrogance, even worse is pretended reverence. If seven couldn't be confined, who could put up with fourteen? So it necessarily follows that when you add to malice the pretense of truth, the last state of a person is worse than the first.

Matthew 12:46–50

46 While he was still speaking to the people, behold, his mother and his brothers stood outside, asking to speak to him. 47 Someone told him, "Your mother and your brothers are standing outside, asking to speak to you." 48 But he replied to the man who told him, "Who is my mother, and who are my brothers?" 49 And stretching out his hand toward his disciples, he said, "Here are my mother and my brothers! 50 For whoever does the will of my Father in heaven is my brother, and sister, and mother."

(21) Macarius of Magnesia

Who is my mother, and who are my brothers? These words served as a correction to those who regarded Christ as merely a man and not the Only-Begotten. So he asks, "Who is my brother, if I am the Only-Begotten? Who is my mother, if I created all things? What person, with mother and brothers, ever did the miracles I have done? If no one has ever done or will do them, why refer to me as a mere man with brothers? The man born blind saw divinity with the eyes of his soul, but you are blind to the brightness of such power in your very midst. So I say to you as to blind men, **He that does the will of my Father** (which is also my will) **is my mother and brother.** In so doing, he both brings me forth as a mother does, having conceived me by doing the Father's will. And he too is brought forth along with me, not by entering into my nature, but by being made one with me in the grace of will. Whoever does the will of my Father brings me forth in the fellowship of that deed, and is brought forth with me. He that believes that I am the Only-Begotten of God begets me, not as a natural birth, but by faith, being mystically united with the one who is Only-Begotten."

(22) Ambrose of Milan

Like a true teacher, Jesus offers an example to others in his own person. He gives commandments, and he himself does what he commands. Before telling others that unless they are prepared to leave father and mother they are not worthy of the Son of God (cf. 10:37; Luke 14:26), he is the first to follow his admonition. He does not reprove the honor due to a mother, since he himself decreed: *Whoever dishonors his father and mother shall die* (cf. Exod 20:12; Deut 27:16). But he believes that he has a greater obligation to the mysteries of his Father than he does to his natural feelings for his mother. In no sense does he brush aside the rights of parents. Nevertheless, he is teaching us that spiritual bonds are more sacred than blood relations.

There is no slight to the virtue of piety, that is, of tender love of one's parents. Do not think it stands in the way of piety when the commandment of the law is kept. For it is written: *Man shall leave his father and mother and be joined to his wife, and they shall be two in one flesh* (Gen 2:24). This mystery is most exactly fulfilled in Christ and his Church (cf. Eph 5:31–32). Scripture shows here that one must prefer one's own body to one's parents. Certain heretics, who like to spread snares, would like us to think that in this passage Jesus is denying his mother. But this is wrong. Even from the height of the Cross he recognizes her (cf. John 19:26). But he does want to say that heavenly precepts take precedence over bodily things.

(23) Augustine

So Christ is not teaching you to ignore your parents, but to love your parents. You see, you only love your parents properly and devotedly when you do not put your parents before God. **Whoever loves**—they are the Lord's own words —**Whoever loves father or mother more than me is not worthy of me** (10:37). It seems as though he was advising you with these words not to love. Actually, if you pay careful attention, he was advising you to love. He could have said, "Whoever loves father or mother is not worthy of me." But he didn't say that, or he would have been speaking against the law he gave himself. I mean that he himself gave that law through Moses his servant, where it is written, *Honor your father and your mother* (Exod 20:12). He didn't promulgate a contrary law, but he reinforced that one. He taught you to get the order right, without undermining your filial obligations. **Whoever loves father or mother**— yes, but **more than me**. So they should love, but not more than me. God is God, man is man. Love your parents, oblige your parents, honor your parents, but if God calls you to something greater, which could be obstructed by parental affection, get things in the right order; do not turn love upside down.

Matthew 13

In this chapter, Jesus uses parables to instruct the crowds and his disciples about the kingdom of heaven. The reason he uses parables, says Jesus, is that many people cannot understand his teaching without examples and illustrations, because their hearts are hardened. The disciples, unlike the crowds, have been granted the knowledge of the secrets of the kingdom as prophesied by Isaiah (6:9–10).

The chapter begins with a parable about a sower whose seeds fell on four different kinds of ground and produced four different results. Sowing along the path means hearing without understanding, and the fragile growth can be easily snatched away by the evil one, Satan (cf. Mark 4:15; Luke 8:12). Like seeds on a path, people whose minds are rough and compacted are impenetrable, and the divine seeds can be easily plundered by evil spirits (Cyril of Alexandria). Sowing seed on rocky ground signifies accepting the message readily with joy, *although superficially. Those with this empty and rootless piety fall away, incapable of withstanding even a "modest wind" of testing.*

Next, Jesus compares the kingdom of heaven to a man who sowed good wheat seeds in the field, but the enemy sowed weeds among them at night, causing two kinds of plants to grow inseparably until the harvest. For Chrysologus, the man who sowed good seeds is Christ, the Creator of all good things in the world (the field); for Epiphanius, it is the seed that represents Christ, who is himself sown in the field of our hearts.

The fathers are unanimous in interpreting the harvest as the consummation of the age. Augustine urges believers, Christ's grain and ears of wheat, to rid themselves of the weeds and bring good fruit. The weeds are planted everywhere: not only outside, but also inside the Church (Augustine), not only among the wicked, but also among the just (Chrysologus).

As the mustard seed, the smallest of all, swiftly turns into a tall tree where birds hide, so the kingdom of heaven, starting small, will grow large enough to accommodate both Jews and pagans (Eusebius of Emesa), and even the whole earth (Nicetas). Like the medicinal qualities of the mustard seed, the kingdom, sharp and pungent, represses anger and pride (Nicetas).

Just as the grain releases its vigor when ground, says Ambrose, so faith reveals its pungent fragrance under persecution. Like the mustard seed, faith grows in us until it "conquers us completely" (Ephrem).

In the comparison of the kingdom of heaven to yeast, patristic writers see the three equal measures of flour as three parts of Scripture: the Law, the Prophets, and the Gospels, inseparable and sharing the same potency and purpose (Hilary). Because of its potency, the yeast represents Christ. So Ambrose: "the Son of God was hidden in the Law, veiled in the Prophets, and fulfilled in the teachings of the Gospel." According to Ephrem, the kingdom of heaven, through Christ, "draws us, possesses us, and changes all of us into divinity," as "Christ became like us."

Christ is also the treasure hidden in the field. The message about him, previously hidden in the Old Testament, can now be understood in light of his passion. For Origen, this parable speaks about literal and spiritual interpretation: the plain sense (the field) and the hidden (the treasure). Ephrem identifies Christ as "the pearl, and we (are) the merchants who found him."

For most ancient interpreters, the net in the next parable represents the word of God. Like a net thrown into the sea, the kingdom of heaven gathers people from every race, including Gentiles (cf. Rom 11:25). Like fish sorted on the shore, after the net has been drawn, so people at the end of the present age will be separated by the heavenly selection (Chrysologus). This judgment is final: we can change and improve only while we are in the process of being caught, and not after the net is drawn up (Gregory the Great).

At the end of the chapter, Jesus refuses to perform miracles in his hometown, Nazareth, because of people's unbelief. According to Origen, it was not that Jesus was unwilling, but he was unable to manifest his divine power, because faith is naturally drawn to the divine power as a magnet is drawn to iron. Because they knew Jesus as "the son of a carpenter," they had difficulty believing "that God was doing these things in a man" (Hilary).

(1) Gregory of Nyssa

The creation of the world is the foundation of the Church, and according to the voice of the prophet, *God created a new heaven in the church* (Isa 65:17), which is *the firmness of faith in Christ*, as Paul says (Col 2:5). And God founded a new earth that drinks the *rain falling from heaven* (Heb 6:7). When someone is renewed through birth from above, a new kind of person is formed *in the image of the Creator* (Col 3:10). Such a person becomes a different kind of light, about which Christ spoke, **You are the light of the world** (5:14) and *among them you shine as light in the world* (Phil 2:15). Many stars are rising in the *firmness of faith* (Col 2:5). And what a miracle it is that in this new creation *God names and numbers a multitude of stars* (cf. Ps 147:4 ! With their names inscribed in the heavens, such stars say, "Did we not hear the Craftsman of the new creation saying to his own luminaries, '*Your names have been written in the heavens*'?" (Luke 10:20). Not only are the multitude of stars crafted by the Word, but the amazing thing about the new creation is also that he created many suns to illumine the whole world with rays of good works, as the maker of such suns says, **Let your light shine before men** (5:16) and **Then the righteous will shine like suns** (13:43). . . .

Thus, whoever looks on this new world, modeled on the creation of the Church, sees in it the one who is *all in all* (Col 3:11) and the one who came into the finite world, making it his own through our nature, so he could lead us to the knowledge of the infinite.

(2) Peter Chrysologus

In fashioning the sky, the earth, the sea, and the kaleidoscopic variety of creatures that inhabit them, Christ our God has offered a stunning demonstration of his power. Clearly, he wishes to point us toward heavenly realities through terrestrial analogies—granting us a taste of the future through the patterns of the present, foreshadowing the invisible by pairing it with the visible. The Gospel parables we have heard today fairly shout this truth.

Matthew 13:1–9

**1 That same day Jesus went out of the house and sat beside the sea. 2 And great crowds gath-
ered about him, so that he got into a boat and sat there; and the whole crowd stood on
the beach. 3 And he told them many things in parables, saying: "A sower went out to sow.
4 And as he sowed, some seeds fell along the path, and the birds came and devoured them.
5 Other seeds fell on rocky ground, where they had not much soil, and immediately they
sprang up, since they had no depth of soil, 6 but when the sun rose they were scorched; and
since they had no root they withered away. 7 Other seeds fell upon thorns, and the thorns
grew up and choked them. 8 Other seeds fell on good soil and brought forth grain, some
a hundredfold, some sixty, some thirty. 9 He who has ears, let him hear."**

(3) Hilary of Poitiers

As will become clear in what follows, there was a reason the Lord sat in the boat and the crowd stood outside. He spoke in parables, and by using this manner of speech, he indicates that those outside the Church cannot understand the divine Word. The ship is a type of the Church where the Word of Life can be found and proclaimed. Those on the outside, like barren and useless sand, cannot understand.

(4) Jerome

A sower went out to sow. Jesus was inside the house discoursing about holy things. Then he who sows the word of God went out from his house to sow among the crowds. Now this sower who sows signifies the Son of God the Father who sows the word among the people. And at the same time, we should note that this is the first parable that is given with an interpretation. We need to pay special attention whenever the Lord explains his words. When he is questioned by his disciples and then explains the inner meaning of his words, remember that we should not understand anything more or less than what he has explained.

Matthew 13:10–13

**[10]Then the disciples came and said to him, "Why do you speak to them in parables?"
[11]And he answered them, "To you it has been given to know the secrets of the kingdom
of heaven, but to them it has not been given. [12]For to him who has will more be given,
and he will have abundance; but from him who has not, even what he has will be taken
away. [13]This is why I speak to them in parables, because seeing they do not see, and
hearing they do not hear, nor do they understand."**

(5) Augustine

So that we might be able to see, hear, and understand, the apostle bent his knees on our behalf, that understanding might be given to us. There is also the frightening passage of the Gospel: **To you it has been given to know the mystery of the kingdom, but to them it has not been given. For whoever has will be given**. But who does have (as one given), except the one to whom it has been given? **But whoever does not have, even what he has will be taken away from him.** But who doesn't have, except the one to whom it has not been given? So why was it given to this one, and not to the other?

What can I cry out about this unfathomable depth? *How magnificent are your works, O Lord!* (Ps 92:5). The nations are enlightened, the Jews are reduced to blindness. Some babies are washed clean in the sacrament of baptism, but some babies are left in the death of the first man. *How magnificent are your works, O Lord! How deep have become your thoughts!* And it continues, *The thoughtless man does not know this, and the fool does not understand* (Ps 92:5–6). What doesn't the foolish and thoughtless person understand? That there is something deep to be found. But if the fool doesn't understand, and the sage does, the matter can't be too deep. If the sage does understand that it is deep, the fool doesn't understand that it is deep at all.

(6) Cyril of Alexandria

The divine light shines more brightly than previously in those who are enlightened and lovers of knowledge. But for those who have had sparks of the spiritual light yet turn their knowledge into foolishness, even a little flicker will be extinguished as it happened to those who did not believe in Christ. From the law they had a small light guiding them in knowledge to God. But when they turned against Christ, they were deprived of it. However, the Lord is the one who makes what is clear even more clear as he said, **To the one who has, it will be given; but from the one who does not have—even what he has will be taken from him.**

Matthew 13:14–15

14"With them indeed is fulfilled the prophecy of Isaiah which says:
'You shall indeed hear but never understand,
and you shall indeed see but never perceive.
15For this people's heart has grown dull,
and their ears are heavy of hearing,
and their eyes they have closed,
lest they should perceive with their eyes,
and hear with their ears,
and understand with their heart,
and turn for me to heal them.'"

(7) John Chrysostom

Though they heard that Christ was the one who led them to God and showed his singular unity with the Father, yet they said, *This man is not of God* (John 9:16). Since their judgment was contrary to their sight and hearing, the Lord says, I will deprive them of their ability to hear. For it is of no help to them and leads only to greater condemnation. Not only did they not believe and find fault, they made accusations and laid snares. However, he did not throw these actions in their faces or accuse them. Although from the outset he never spoke anything but plain words to them, they distorted what he said. And that is why afterward he spoke in parables.

So that no one should suppose his words amounted to a mere accusation or say that he is our enemy who brings these charges and tells lies against us, the Lord appeals to the prophet who made the same judgment. **For in them is fulfilled, he said, the prophecy of Isaiah, which says, you will hear, but not understand, and you will see, but not perceive** (13:14; Isa 6:9–10).

Notice that the prophet makes a similar accusation. For he didn't say, "You do not see," but **You will see but not perceive**; nor does he say, "You will not hear," but **You will hear but not understand.** And so they first hurt themselves by stopping up their ears and closing their eyes and hardening their heart. For they not only failed to hear, but had also become **hard of hearing**.

(8) Peter Chrysologus

Christ related a parable to them, the Gospel reading says. Sparks lie cold in flint, buried deep in steel—but when flint and steel are struck together, they burst into flame. Similarly, obscure sayings suddenly glow with clarity once the bare words are given an interpretation. But why speak in parables at all? For this reason: if there were no sacred mysteries in the text, both the faithful and the false, the wicked and the righteous would perceive the same meaning. There would be no difference between the devout and the defiant, the indolent and the industrious, the attentive and the apathetic. But when the soul earnestly seeks, the mind bends its will, and the senses strive for the meaning of the parable; when righteousness desires and faith adjudicates between interpretations; when all one's thoughts are focused on meriting the answer—only then will the fruits of one's labor appear. . . . And that is why Christ veiled his teachings in parables, covered them in figures, enclosed them in sacred rites, shrouded them in mystery.

Matthew 13:16–17

16"But blessed are your eyes, for they see, and your ears, for they hear. 17Truly, I say to you, many prophets and righteous men longed to see what you see, and did not see it, and to hear what you hear, and did not hear it."

(9) Philoxenus of Hierapolis

The Scripture makes known what was hidden even from the holy powers,[1] namely, that there is a Son to God by nature and that he was going to be made flesh: *and through the Church the manifold wisdom of God has been revealed to the principalities and authorities in heaven, that which [he had prepared] before the ages and [which] he effected in Jesus Christ* (Eph 3:10–11). What is written in the prophet that God is a holy threeness (cf. Isa 6:3) is not contrary to the word of the Apostle. Though the older testimonies declared him holy, they did not comprehend the mystery, the meaning of what was hidden. And neither did the demons know this mystery, for *if they had known, they would not have crucified the Lord of glory* (1 Cor 2:8) testifies to this.

You will find many words spoken by the Spirit through the prophets about the Trinity and the incarnation that they did not understand. The Spirit made known to them words concerning these matters but not their interpretation. As our Lord said to his disciples, **Many prophets and righteous men longed to see what you see, and they did not see, and to hear what you hear, and they did not hear.** It is clear that he who pleaded to hear and see more sensed there is more. So then, the prophets learned from the Spirit the words concerning the mysteries, but the understanding was not revealed, since God shows everything in its right time and in the right place.

Sometimes the Lord delivers the word, and other times he prompts its remembrance. In other words, on one occasion there is the recitation of the word, and at another time is its understanding, as we also find its interpretation. It is beyond the measure of our thoughts to know how many varieties, distinctions, degrees, ascents, and responses there are to divine teaching, even if wisdom is instilled in our nature. No human being can know all these things; indeed there are not even any among the angels.

Matthew 13:18–23

18"Hear then the parable of the sower. 19When any one hears the word of the kingdom and does not understand it, the evil one comes and snatches away what is sown in his

1. Angelic beings.

heart; this is what was sown along the path. [20]As for what was sown on rocky ground, this is he who hears the word and immediately receives it with joy; [21]yet he has no root in himself, but endures for a while, and when tribulation or persecution arises on account of the word, immediately he falls away. [22]As for what was sown among thorns, this is he who hears the word, but the cares of the world and the delight in riches choke the word, and it proves unfruitful. [23]As for what was sown on good soil, this is he who hears the word and understands it; he indeed bears fruit, and yields, in one case a hundredfold, in another sixty, and in another thirty."

(10) Jerome

But that which is sown among the thorns, this is he who hears the word, and the cares of this age and the deceitfulness of riches choke the word, and it is made fruitless. It seems to me that the words spoken to Adam, *You will eat your bread among thorns and thistles* (Gen 3:18), give us the mystical sense of what we read here. That is, whoever devotes himself to the pleasures of the age and to the cares of this world devours the heavenly bread and the true food along with thorns. And he has rightly added: **the deceitfulness of riches chokes the word**. For riches are alluring. They promise one thing, but they achieve something else. Possessing them is a slippery thing, for they are carried about by someone without sure footing. Either riches will abandon those who have them, or they choke those who do not. This is why the Lord says that the rich enter the kingdom of heaven with difficulty. For their riches choke the word of God and deprive them of the strength to live virtuously.

Just as there were three different kinds of bad earth—that along the path and that on rocky places and that on thorny places—so there are three different kinds of good earth: the fruit of one a hundredfold, one sixtyfold, and one thirtyfold. The difference between them does not have to do with its nature, but the will. In unbelievers and in believers, it is the heart that receives the seed. **The evil one comes**, he says, **and snatches away what was sown in his heart**. With respect to the second and third, he says: **This is he who hears the word**. Also, in speaking of the good earth he says: **he who hears the word**. So then, first we must hear, then we must understand, and after understanding we are to render the fruits of instruction and produce either one hundredfold fruit, or sixtyfold, or thirtyfold.

(11) John Chrysostom

Take note that even the person yielding thirtyfold is saved. The Lord said that to make the way of salvation easy. What that means is this: Are you incapable of practicing virginity? Then live a chaste married life. Are you incapable of giving up all your goods? Then give some of what you own. Are you incapable of carrying that burden? Divide your possessions with Christ. . . . He first gave you a drink from his own cup: can you not share some cold water (10:42)? He gave you to drink of the Holy Spirit: can you not quench another's bodily thirst?

He gave you to drink of the Spirit: do you overlook his thirst, even though it was he who made it possible for you to give to others? Do you not think it a great thing to hold the cup from which Christ is about to drink, and to put it to his lips?

Think about who it is you are giving to drink, and tremble. Think about how you have become a priest of Christ, giving with your own hand, not flesh but bread, not blood but a cup of cold water. He clothed you in a *garment of salvation* (Isa 61:10), and clothed you himself; now at least let your servant clothe him. He made you glorious in heaven, free him from cold and nakedness and shame. He made you a fellow citizen with the angels, share at least your roof with him.

(12) Cyril of Alexandria

The meaning of **along the path** is clear from our experience. How hard and useless is every path when it is constantly trod under foot. Nothing sown upon it will penetrate, for it lies upon the surface ready to be seized by the birds. Such individuals have a hard and closed mind unable to receive the divine seed. They become a path trampled upon by unclean spirits, that is, by *the birds of the sky.*

Now we understand *sky* here as the space in which the spirits of wickedness roam about, by whom the good seed is plundered and destroyed. But who are those upon the rock? They are those who merely have faith in themselves, not directing their mind to grasp the divine mysteries. Their devotion to God is empty and without root. When blown about by a modest wind, they hardly cling to faith in themselves. But when troubled by a heavy storm of testing, as, for example, persecution, their soul cannot bear the onslaught.

Matthew refers to **the evil one**, Mark wrote *Satan* (Mark 4:15), and Luke recorded the *devil* (Luke 8:12). *By the path* (Luke 8:5, 12) and **along the path** (13:19; Mark 4:4) are not the same thing, and we make a distinction in light of *I am the path* (John 14:6).[2] Nevertheless, the three evangelists wrote **by the path**, and the learned Matthew and Mark wrote **on the rocky ground**. They do not say that the word was sown upon the rock. **The one who does not understand** knows only what is alongside the road. **On the good soil** is the one who hears the word and understands. Thus, those upon the rocky ground and those among the thorns are not to be separated between those who do and those who do not understand. Take care that you are open to instruction. For the seed is taken away from the one who thinks he understands but does not. So one must seek understanding by planting the seed in the good ground and remembering what one has heard. Only then will it take root, even when it's exposed and not taken away by wicked spirits.

2. Despite the more common English rendering of John 14:6 ("*I am the way*"), Cyril's association of Matt 13:19–23 with John 14:6 justifies the translation above.

(13) Gregory the Great

The Lord spoke in this parable not simply about riches but about deceptive riches, and with good reason. . . . Riches are deceptive because they cannot stay with us very long; they are deceptive because they are incapable of relieving our spiritual poverty. The only true riches are those that make us rich in virtue. Therefore, beloved, if you want to be rich, love true riches. If you aspire to the heights of real honor, strive to reach the kingdom of heaven.

Good soil brings forth fruit by patience (Luke 8:15). The reason for this is that nothing we do is good unless we also bear with equanimity the injuries done to us by our neighbors. In fact, the more we progress, the more hardships we shall have to endure in this world. As our love for this present world dies, its sufferings increase. This is why we see many people doing good works and at the same time struggling under a heavy burden of afflictions. They now shun earthly desires and yet are tormented by greater sufferings. But, as the Lord said, they bring forth fruit by patience because, since they humbly endure misfortunes, they are welcomed when these are over in a place of rest in heaven.

Matthew 13:24–30

[24]Another parable he put before them, saying, "The kingdom of heaven may be com-
pared to a man who sowed good seed in his field; [25]but while men were sleeping, his
enemy came and sowed weeds among the wheat, and went away. [26]So when the plants
came up and bore grain, then the weeds appeared also. [27]And the servants of the house-
holder came and said to him, 'Sir, did you not sow good seed in your field? How then has
it weeds?' [28]He said to them, 'An enemy has done this.' The servants said to him, 'Then
do you want us to go and gather them?' [29]But he said, 'No; lest in gathering the weeds
you root up the wheat along with them. [30]Let both grow together until the harvest; and
at harvest time I will tell the reapers, Gather the weeds first and bind them in bundles
to be burned, but gather the wheat into my barn.'"

(14) Epiphanius the Latin

Food has flavor for someone who is hungry, and drink is for the one who is thirsty, just as the wisdom of Solomon says: *The soul placed in fullness mocks honeycombs; however the one that is in want, even bitter things produce sweetness* (Prov 27:7). He who sows in a field sows not every day but once, and thus little by little what is cultivated matures until it becomes ripe and renders its fruit to the one who sowed.

And so it is with our ability to love. Christ has been once sown in you until you bring forth eternal fruits, the reward of grace. Because the Lord has sown in the field of the heart, one must always be on the lookout, lest the wicked man (who is the devil) secretly sow tares (which are sins) on top of the good seed (that is, the catholic faith). We must not be sleeping, so that when it comes to the time of ripeness on judgment day, you will find wheat (which is the works of faith) not tares (which are evil works).

(15) Augustine

Listen, Christ's precious ears of wheat; listen, Christ's dearest corn. Take a look at yourselves, go back to your consciences, interrogate your faith, interrogate your love, stir up your consciences. If you discover that you are good grain, let the thought occur to you, **Whoever perseveres to the end will be saved** (10:22). Any of you who upon shaking up their consciences find themselves among the weeds must not be afraid to change. The command hasn't yet been given for the field to be cut, because it isn't the harvest yet. But don't be today what you were yesterday, or at least don't be tomorrow what you are today.

Do you think that there's any place within you where that enemy has not sown weeds? Has he found cornfields anywhere and not scattered weeds in them? Do you imagine he has sown them among the laity, but not among the clergy, or the bishops? Or sown them among married men and not among those who have made profession of celibacy? Or sown them among married women and not among consecrated nuns? Or sown them in the houses of laypeople and not in communities of monks? He's scattered them everywhere, sown them everywhere. Has he left anything unmixed?

But thanks be to God—who will sort things out in due course according to his pleasure—and cannot be mistaken. It will not, I'm sure, have escaped your notice that weeds are to be found in all kinds of harvests, even those in the most exalted and distinguished circles. They are to be found even among professed religious. And you say, "Really, in that place, have bad people been found even there, have bad people been found even in that community?" But of course, bad people have been found everywhere, but the bad will not reign forever with the good. Why be surprised at finding bad people in a holy place?

(16) Peter Chrysologus

The kingdom of heaven is like a man. But which man? Clearly, Christ is he **who planted** the **good seed**, since the Creator does not plant evil seed. He continues: **In his field**. He means the world, as the Lord himself explains later on: **The field is the world** (13:38).

But while the men were sleeping—here, he's referring to the holy fathers of old, like the patriarchs, prophets, apostles, and martyrs who are temporarily slumbering in the deep sleep of death. . . . **an enemy came** (he means the devil).

He planted over the wheat with weeds. Why? Because the devil loves to sow heresies among the faithful, sins among saints, quarrels among the peaceful, treachery among the simple, wickedness among the innocent. He's not doing this because he is interested in the weeds, but so that he may ruin the wheat. He's not trying to honor the guilty, but rather to corrupt the innocent. The enemy slashes at leaders more than soldiers; he doesn't assail the dead, but the living. The devil doesn't care about seizing sinners—they're already his slaves!—but he does take the time to stalk the righteous.

Matthew 13:31–32

[31]Another parable he put before them, saying, "The kingdom of heaven is like a grain of mustard seed which a man took and sowed in his field; [32]it is the smallest of all seeds, but when it has grown it is the greatest of shrubs and becomes a tree, so that the birds of the air come and make nests in its branches."

(17) Eusebius of Emesa

It is proclaimed in church that the mustard seed is both useful in food and profitable for health. Of course that is its nature. The parable, however, does not say this. It says that the mustard seed is very small among seeds, yet it sprouts larger than other shrubs. So too, the holy proclamation begins small, but in a short time, once it has grown, it becomes a tree, so that the birds of the air come and dwell in its branches. This tree is certainly large enough to cover both Jews and pagans. For the Lord said that the mustard seed signified the kingdom of heaven. However, he speaks correctly when he says we should take note of the nature of a mustard seed: a mustard seed nourishes and so brings health to the body. As much as this is true concerning its nature, however, this is not the whole meaning of the parable.

(18) Clement of Alexandria

The Word proclaiming the kingdom of heaven is pungent and sharp like mustard. It stifles bile, that is, anger, and cuts phlegm, that is, arrogance. From this Word come the true health and everlasting good temperament of the soul.

And the Word flowered with such great growth that the tree growing from it (and this would be the Church of Christ, established everywhere on earth) filled everything, **such that the birds of the sky** (clearly divine messengers and heavenly souls) **settled in its branches.**

(19) Ambrose of Milan

"What is the kingdom of God like? To what should I compare it? It is like a grain of mustard seed, which a man took and sowed in his garden. It grew and became a great tree, and the birds of the air settled in its branches" (Luke 13:18–19).

In reading the present passage, we should focus on what the comparison points to, not just the image. Let us see, now, why the kingdom—so lofty, so majestic in the heavens—is compared to *a grain of mustard seed.* I recall meeting this "mustard seed" in another passage, where it is compared to faith: the Lord says, **If you have faith as much as a mustard seed, you shall say to this mountain: "Go, cast yourself into the sea"** (17:20). A faith that can command a mountain to move away is not small but mighty. Indeed, the Lord does not ask his apostles to have an ordinary faith, for he knew they would have to contend against the arrogance of spiritual wickedness (Eph 6:12).

You wonder what I mean? You want to know what great faith looks like? Read the Apostle: *If I should have all faith, so that I could remove mountains. . .* (1 Cor 13:2).

If the kingdom of heaven is like a grain of mustard seed, and if faith is like a grain of mustard seed, it follows that faith is definitely the kingdom of heaven, and the kingdom of heaven is faith. Therefore if you have faith, you have the kingdom of heaven. It is also true that the kingdom is within us, and faith is within us. For we read: *The kingdom of heaven is within you* (Luke 17:21). In another place he says: *Have faith within yourselves* (Mark 11:22). Peter had *all faith* and therefore he was given the keys of the kingdom of heaven so that he could open the kingdom to others (16:19).

Let us now determine from the nature of the mustard seed, the force of this comparison. The grain is, admittedly, very simple and ordinary. But grind it, and you will see what vigor it has. So, too, faith appears at first to be simple and ordinary, but if crushed by its enemies, it spreads everywhere its virtue and grace; its pungent odor fills all those who hear or read it.

Our martyrs, Felix, Nabor, and Victor[3] were a grain of mustard seed. They guarded within their hearts the perfume of the faith, but no one was aware of this. Then the persecutions came. These martyrs laid down their arms, stretched out their necks, were beheaded by the sword, and so spread to the ends of the earth the beauty of their martyrdom. Rightly I may say of them: *Their sound has gone forth through all the earth* (Ps 19:4).

But faith is crushed in one way, ground in another way, sown in another way. The Lord himself is a grain of mustard seed. He was not harmed, but the people who did not know him did not realize he was a grain of mustard seed. He chose to be crushed and ground up so that we might say: *We are the good fragrance of Christ before God* (2 Cor 2:15). He wanted to be crushed and ground, for remember how Peter said to him: *The crowds presses all about you* (Luke 8:45). He wanted to be sown, like the seed that someone takes and sows in his garden. For it was in a garden that he was arrested (cf. John 18:1), and in a garden he was buried (cf. John 19:41). In a garden he grew to a great height, for it was in a garden that he rose from the dead. And he became a tree, for so it is written: *As an apple tree among the trees of the forest, such is my brother, my beloved among the sons* (Song 2:3).

And you, my friends, you too must "sow" Christ in your garden. Make it a garden of delight, a place made beautiful by every variety of flower and fruit. May the beauty of your virtues flourish there, and may the multiple perfumes of every sort of virtue fill the air with their sweetness. There where the fruit is, let Christ be found. When they arrested him, he was a grain of seed. When he rose from the dead, he was a tree—a tree that gives shade to all the world. Buried in the ground, he was a seed; stretching up to heaven, now he is a tree.

And you, too, must press hard with Christ and sow the seed. The faith is ground and it is pressed, when we believe in Jesus crucified. Paul pressed the faith hard when he said: *As for me, brothers, when I came to you it was not in loftiness of speech or of wisdom. That was not how I declared the testimony of Christ. For I judged myself not to know anything among you, but Jesus Christ, and him crucified* (1 Cor 2:1–2). Having learned to press and

3. Martyrs whose remains were brought to Milan and celebrated there.

grind the faith, he also learned how to lift it on high. For he says: If we have known Christ [crucified] according to the flesh, *we know him now no longer* (2 Cor 5:16).

We sow the faith when, after the Gospel and the readings from the apostles and prophets, we believe in the passion of our Lord. We sow the faith when we cover it, in some sense, with soil sifted and softened and drawn from the flesh of the Lord. In this way, warmed and wrapped by the sacred body, the faith sprouts and spreads. Anyone who believes that the Son of God was made man believes that he died for us, and believes that he rose again for us. I sow the faith when I plant it in the midst of his sepulcher.

(20) Ephrem of Nisibis

The faith of our Lord is like a grain of mustard seed that grew and grew larger like a tree. When at first it is sown within us, it is something tiny, and little by little it grows, and as it sets down roots, it is fixed in our minds. At first we desire only to believe in God, but once faith has found a place in us, we separate ourselves from our fathers, depart from our mothers, detach ourselves from our family (10:37–39). We do not intermingle with our friends who are of the world, and we are cut from all their conduct that is of the world, because the faith that we once received as something tiny like a grain of mustard seed conquers us completely. Our Lord himself is the seed, a grain of mustard seed, and his Father sowed him into the world, as in a garden. The world is of the Father, and if the faith of our Lord is compared to a grain of mustard seed, and it was sown in us, we will know that we are truly his, for the sower sowed in his garden.

Matthew 13:33–35

33He told them another parable. "The kingdom of heaven is like leaven which a woman took and hid in three measures of flour, till it was all leavened."

34All this Jesus said to the crowds in parables; indeed he said nothing to them without a parable. 35This was to fulfill what was spoken by the prophet:

"I will open my mouth in parables,
I will utter what has been hidden since the foundation of the world."

(21) Ambrose of Milan

This comparison is so complex that it gives rise to many interpretations and many questions. We can see why it was mentioned earlier that Christ is a grain of wheat, because he is spiritual leaven for us. Many think that the yeast is Christ, because he causes the virtue implanted in us to rise. Because the yeast is more powerful than the flour—not by reason of its size and appearance but by reason of its energy—so too Christ, same in body as his ancestors, far surpassed them by his divinity. Let us then see the holy Church signified this woman in the Gospel, and ourselves as the flour in which this woman buries the yeast that is our Lord Jesus. She mixes in this yeast until the color of heavenly wisdom reaches to the deepest and most secret depths of our soul.

In Matthew we read that the yeast was immersed in three measures of flour. This would suggest that the Son of God was hidden in the Law, veiled in the Prophets, and fulfilled in the teachings of the Gospel. The goal was that we would obtain a faith that is perfected and formed in us (who are his body), through the [use of the] entire collection of the sacred writings. Thus, he would be all and in all since he truly is the Word of God, *the mystery that has been hidden from age to age* (Col 1:26).

We have only begun to attest clearly and to show every advantage to his divine eternity. For he was truly the one: hidden to the sacrilegious, manifested to the saints, predestined before the ages, destined and preserved for glory.

My brothers and sisters, glory consists in this: that we should plumb the depths of the mystery hidden before all ages in God. Whatever is in God is assuredly of God; for God cannot absorb something foreign to his nature.

And yet I know—and am quite sure—that certain people apply the above parable to this world; that the yeast must rise through the Law, the Prophets, the Gospel, until every tongue gives praise to the Lord. But let us look carefully into the whole matter. Let us search very diligently. You cannot find something unless you first search for it. Let us build a tower, let us count up the cost of the Scriptures, let us calculate the total expense, for fear that one day it might also be said of us, *He wanted to put up a building and was unable to finish it* (Luke 14:28).

If you are putting up a building, you must first have a good foundation. The good foundation is faith; the good foundation is that of the apostles and prophets (cf. Eph 2:20). On the two Testaments all our faith is constructed. I think it no exaggeration to say that these two Testaments contain an equal measure of perfect faith. The Lord himself said: *If you had had faith in Moses, you would have had faith in me* (John 5:46). In actuality, it was our Lord who spoke in Moses. So it is true that both the one and the other contain a perfect measure, because in both Testaments Christ is fulfilled; and in both Testaments is perfect faith. For both the oracle and the response to the oracle have the same force and the same meaning.

Personally, I prefer to stand by the teaching of our Lord himself: the **yeast** is the spiritual doctrine of the Church. We know that **yeast** stands for doctrine; we know it from the moment we read: **Be on your guard against the yeast of the Pharisees** (16:6); we know it because the Apostle says: *not with the yeast of malice and wickedness* (1 Cor 5:8). But there are different sorts of yeast: there is yeast that intoxicates, and there is yeast that causes the bread to rise. So I fully agree with those good authors who say that the Church sanctifies, by the spiritual yeast, man who is made up of body, soul, and spirit.

Body and soul are sanctified, and there is an increase of spiritual grace when, through the ministry of the Church—being intoxicated with joy—and through the teaching of Scripture, the whole person becomes (so to speak) a single yeast. It is the whole person that "rises" and grows by the mingling together of the heavenly words and by their richness. These riches are so thoroughly mixed into us, body and soul, that they penetrate our entire being. This indeed is what happens when these three "measures" accord with one another by an equal balance of desires and are animated as though by one mind and one heart.

(22) Ephrem of Nisibis

Leaven is an element that draws out and takes over other things. It always has this power. When it is mixed with the dough, it changes and turns the dough into something new. And the leaven turns back to flour again. In like manner, the kingdom of God was compared to leaven, because it is mixed in the body and soul and spirit in the likeness of the **three measures of flour**. . . . It is formed in us, draws us, possesses us, and changes all of us into divinity, after the fashion of leaven.

Just as leaven, which at first mixes itself with the flour and together they become the dough, the power of the leaven is hidden in the dough invisibly, and it takes captive (so to speak) the dough little by little. The yeast, which in appearance was smaller than the dough, turns it (the dough) to itself, and from that point the dough is no longer separated from the leaven, because it was absorbed. In a similar manner, the divinity of Christ came and was mixed with our humanity; Christ became like us; he was mixed with our dough. There wasn't anything about him that didn't appear mortal, just as leaven is not apparent from the dough when it is mixed. Little by little our dough is imbued by the power of Christ secretly. And as leaven, we were drawn and were mixed with his divinity, as he was also mixed with our humanity. The result is that we are no longer separated from him because we were absorbed into him. This is what the Apostle meant when he spoke, *Death was submerged by life*.[4] It is in this sense that the kingdom of our Lord is likened to leaven.

Matthew 13:36–43

**36Then he left the crowds and went into the house. And his disciples came to him, saying,
"Explain to us the parable of the weeds of the field." 37He answered, "He who sows the
good seed is the Son of man; 38the field is the world, and the good seed means the sons
of the kingdom; the weeds are the sons of the evil one, 39and the enemy who sowed them
is the devil; the harvest is the close of the age, and the reapers are angels. 40Just as the
weeds are gathered and burned with fire, so will it be at the close of the age. 41The Son
of man will send his angels, and they will gather out of his kingdom all causes of sin
and all evildoers, 42and throw them into the furnace of fire; there men will weep and
gnash their teeth. 43Then the righteous will shine like the sun in the kingdom of their
Father. He who has ears, let him hear."**

(23) Origen

He answered and said to them, **He that sows the good seed is the Son of Man**. The question is whether the **good seed** refers to the children of the kingdom. For everything good that blossoms in the human soul was sown by the Word God *who was in the beginning with God* (John 1:2). It follows then, all sound teachings are offspring of the kingdom of God.

4. Cf. 1 Cor 15:54, *Death is swallowed up in victory.*

But whenever people fall so deeply asleep that they no longer adhere to the commandment of Jesus who said, **Stay awake and pray! so that you may not enter into temptation** (26:41), the devil, who delights in ambushing such persons, sows what are called tares—worthless teaching—among what some call natural opinions, as well as among those good seeds that have their origin in the Word. And so the whole world, not only the Church of God, may be called a field. For as the Son of Man planted the good seed, the devil planted the weeds of evil words. Since these latter words have their origin in wickedness, they are sons of the evil one.

Now at the end of things, what we call the **close of the age**, there will certainly be a **harvest**. This harvest is necessary so that the angels of God (appointed for this task) might destroy the evil thoughts that tightly cling to the soul, overthrowing and consigning them all to a burning fire that will destroy them. In this way, then, the angels and servants of the Word will gather together from the entire kingdom of Christ everything that hinders souls from thinking wicked thoughts. By casting them into a burning oven of fire, the angels will destroy them.

(24) Chromatius of Aquileia

After the crowds were sent away, the Lord Jesus departed to the house where he was staying. His disciples approached him saying: **Explain to us the parable of the wheat and the weeds of the field.** Jesus said to them: **The one who sows the good seed is the Son of Man; moreover the field is this world; indeed the good seed is the sons of the kingdom,** etc. The Lord makes it clear that he is the sower of the good seed, and that in the field of the world he does cease sowing the good seed into the hearts of men. His aim is to have each one of us produce heavenly and spiritual fruit in accord with the divinely sown seed.

He also shows that the hostile devil sows other weeds of malice and iniquity in order to choke the word of God in us. For so he says: **But while the men slept, the enemy came and also sowed weeds in the middle of the wheat, and left** (13:25). It is apparent that the devil sows weeds among those who sleep, that is, who are weighed down through neglect and unfaithfulness. For losing sight of the divine precepts is like what happens in the stupor of sleep. As the Apostle said: *For those who sleep, sleep at night, and those who are drunk, are drunk at night. But let us not sleep like the others, but let us be awake and be sober* (1 Thess 5:6–7).

The ones who are overcome with the stupor of sleep and are unfaithful are like the foolish virgins. As we read in the Gospel, they were unable to meet the bridegroom on the way because they had gone to buy oil for their vessels (25:1–12). From this we learn that the aim of the devil, the enemy of the human race, is to sow weeds again and again among the wheat. Only when one shakes off the sleep of unfaithfulness and is vigilant in mind can one be faithful to the Lord and turn away from the nocturnal sower.

Elsewhere it is said: **Therefore, after the crop had sprung up and produced fruit, then the weeds appeared. And the servants of the householder approached and said to him: "Didn't you sow good seed in your field? Then why does it have weeds?" And he said to them: "An enemy has done this." The servants said to him: "Do you want us to**

go and gather them?" He said, "No, lest while plucking out the weeds, by chance you may also pull out the wheat at the same time. But let both grow together, and at harvest time I will say to the reapers: First collect the weeds and make bundles from them for burning; then gather the wheat into my barn" (13:26–30).

The Lord designates the good seed to be children of the kingdom, and the weeds are wicked children. When the servants (who signify the apostles) of the householder asked whether they should separate the weeds from the wheat (vv. 28–29), the householder allowed both to grow side by side until the consummation of the age. Then the Lord will send reapers, that is, angels, to separate the wheat from the weeds. Once the holy ones have been selected from the midst of the sinners, they will place the just ones in the heavenly kingdom as one stores wheat in the barns. But all who are sinful and have done evil will burn in the punishment of Gehenna like weeds in a fire.

There will be perpetual weeping of the eyes and gnashing of the teeth, as he says: **In that place there will be weeping and gnashing of teeth.** Since the Lord affirms that there are weeping and gnashing of teeth in that place, it is certain that he indicates that there will be a future resurrection not only of the soul, as certain heretics hold, but also of the body. For when the body is punished, one weeps with the eyes and gnashes the teeth.

Matthew 13:44–46

44"The kingdom of heaven is like treasure hidden in a field, which a man found and covered up; then in his joy he goes and sells all that he has and buys that field.

45"Again, the kingdom of heaven is like a merchant in search of fine pearls, 46who,
on finding one pearl of great value, went and sold all that he had and bought it."

(25) Irenaeus of Lyons

But if anyone reads the Scriptures closely, he will discover in them rumors of Christ and foreshadowing of a new calling. For this is the **treasure hidden in the field**, that is, in the world—since **the field is the world**—which is actually hidden in the Scriptures under the cover of symbols and allegories. Humanity was simply unable to understand them earlier, because their long-prophesied fulfillment came about only with the arrival of Christ. It was because of this that the prophet Daniel was told: *Guard these words and seal the book until the time of their fulfillment, until many learn and knowledge is perfected. . . . For when the dispersion has been brought about, they will know all these things* (Dan 12:4, 7). Jeremiah confirms this, saying: *In the last days they will understand it* (Jer 23:20). Of course, all prophecy, until it comes into effect, is ambiguous, a riddle to humankind. But when the time comes for its fulfillment, and what has been prophesied indeed occurs, then the prophecies become crystal clear, their meaning firm.

Therefore, when Christians read the Law according to its true intent, it is a **treasure hidden in a field**. For there the cross of Christ is unveiled and plainly described, there human perception is enriched, there the wisdom of God is placed on display. In the Law is the divine purpose for the human race revealed, the rule of Christ foreshadowed, the inheritance of holy Jerusalem presaged. It even predicts that those who love God will in time see God himself, hear his words, and by them be glorified—to the point that others will not be able to stand in the face of their glory. As Daniel said: *Those who perceive will gleam like the splendor of the firmament, and the multitudes of the righteous like the stars never-ending* (Dan 12:3).

Accordingly, if anyone reads the Scriptures just as we have shown, that is, as the Lord himself explained to the disciples after rising from the dead, when he proved to them from the Scriptures themselves that *it was necessary that Christ should suffer and then enter into his glory* (Luke 24:26) and that they must *proclaim the forgiveness of sins in his name throughout the whole world* (Luke 24:47), that person will become a perfect disciple—**like the master of the household who offered up from his treasure things both new and old** (13:52).

(26) Origen

It seems to me that the field is the Scripture, which was planted in the midst of what is plainly visible in the words of the history; the Law and the Prophets and in other works. Like all of Scripture, the words that are planted are rich and many textured. The treasure hidden in the field signifies teachings that are hidden beneath what is visible, namely, thoughts that come from the wisdom hidden in a mystery (1 Cor 2:7) and in Christ, *in whom are hid all the treasures of wisdom and knowledge* (Col 2:3). Now someone could say that the field *that the Lord blessed* (Gen 27:27), the "Christ of God" (Luke 9:20), is completely filled up and that the treasure hidden in it are those things Paul said are hidden in Christ. For he said of Christ that *in him are hid all the treasures of wisdom and knowledge* (Col 2:3).

The words **Seek and you shall find** are applied to one who seeks fine pearls, and also, **Everyone who seeks shall find**. What do you seek? What does one who seeks find? My answer is "pearls," especially the pearl for which one has sacrificed everything to acquire. This is the pearl Paul was speaking about when he said, *I have accepted the loss of everything in order to gain Christ* (Phil 3:8). The "everything" here means beautiful pearls; *to gain Christ* refers to the unique pearl of great price. . . .

Thus everyone beginning to live a spiritual life and growing toward maturity needs a tutor and guardians or trustees *until the fullness of time* (Gal 4:4) is at hand. For at first he was no different from a slave, although he owned the whole estate, but when he reaches maturity and is freed from his tutor, guardians, and trustees, he will receive the precious pearl as an inheritance. Then one is able to do away with that which is *in part* (1 Cor 13:10) and make one's own the *surpassing worth of the knowledge of Christ* (Phil 3:8). After acquiring various forms of knowledge, if we may so call them, which are inferior to the knowledge of Christ, one is able to comprehend the supreme value of knowing Christ.

(27) John Chrysostom

The parables of the leaven and the mustard seed refer to the power of the gospel that will conquer the world. They depict its surpassing value, for while it grows like a mustard seed and works like leaven, it is as precious as a pearl and as abundant as a treasure. We learn here to rid ourselves of everything else and hold fast to the gospel with joy. So when someone gives away his possessions he knows that the result is gain not loss.

Don't you know the gospel lies hidden in the world, and that good things are hidden in it? If you do not sell everything, you cannot buy; if your soul does not seek, it will not find. Two things then are needful, holding back from worldly things and keeping alert. For he says: **Like someone looking for fine pearls, who finds one of great value, sells everything and buys it.** For truth is one, undivided.

(28) Ephrem of Nisibis

Our Lord said, **The kingdom of heaven is likened to a merchant who searches for an excellent pearl; and he found an excellent and costly pearl; he went (and) sold everything he owned and bought it.** He spoke in reference to disciples committed to him because he is himself the pearl, and we (are) the merchants who found him. A precious object brings joy to the heart and lifts up the mind and spirit and body of the one who possesses it. The result is a radiant countenance and a buoyant mind. Similarly, when the Christian possesses the pearl of our Lord, that is, the commandments, it brings joy to his soul and spirit. His heart is filled with happiness, and one can see in his face the beauty of the pearl within him.

Matthew 13:47–50

**47"Again, the kingdom of heaven is like a net which was thrown into the sea and gath-
ered fish of every kind; 48when it was full, men drew it ashore and sat down and sorted
the good into vessels but threw away the bad. 49So it will be at the close of the age. The
angels will come out and separate the evil from the righteous, 50and throw them into
the furnace of fire; there men will weep and gnash their teeth."**

(29) Origen

We should ask why the kingdom of heaven is compared to a net thrown into the sea. The reason is that this net brings in all kinds of men and shows how different are the various deliberate choices made by men. For they are vastly different from one another. By bringing in men of all kinds, it includes those worthy of praise and those worthy of blame, insofar as they incline toward virtue or vice. So too the kingdom of heaven may be compared to the complex weave of a net, inasmuch as the Old and the New Scripture have both been woven from manifold and varied thoughts.

In the case of the fish that swim into the net, some are found in one part of the net and some in another part, each in the section in which it was caught. Among those caught in the net, some are found caught in the prophetic net; for example, that of Isaiah, Jeremiah, or Daniel. Others are found in the net of the Law, and others in the net of the Gospel, and some in the net of the Apostles. When one is first caught by the word or seems to be caught, the section in which he is caught is part of the whole.[5]

This net has been cast into the sea—the waves of life—tossing men about in every part of the world as they swim in the bitter waters of life. Before the advent of our Savior Jesus Christ, this net was not filled completely; for the net of the Law and the Prophets had to be filled by him who says, **Think not that I came to destroy the Law and the Prophets, I came not to destroy but to fulfill.** And the weave of the net was fulfilled in the Gospels and in the words of Christ given through the Apostles. For this reason the kingdom of heaven is like a net that has been thrown into the sea and gathers some from every race.

One might also say that this gathering together of every race may also demonstrate the call of the Gentiles from among every people. Those who tend the net that was cast into the sea are Jesus Christ, who is the Lord of the net, and the angels who came and served him (4:11). No one can lift up the net from the sea or carry it to the beach beyond the seashore, that is, beyond the affairs of this life, unless the net is full, that is, until the fullness of the Gentiles has come into it (Rom 11:25).

(30) Augustine

Comparing the kingdom of heaven to a net cast into the sea,
Which catches up many fish of every kind from different places.
When they have been pulled to the shore, the fishermen separate them,
Placing the good ones in barrels, the bad they throw back in the sea.
Anyone who knows the Gospel will recognize these words and tremble.
He sees that the nets are the Church, he sees that this world is the sea;
The different kinds of fish are the just men mixed with the sinners;
The shore is the end of the world: then is the time for separation.
Those fish that once burst through the nets were all too attached to the sea.
The barrels are where the saints live, places the sinners cannot reach.

The Lord Jesus Christ said that the kingdom of heaven is like a seine, that is to say, nets (since some nets are called a seine). So **the kingdom of heaven, he said, is like a net thrown into the sea, and collecting things of every kind; pulling it out when it was full, and sitting on the shore, they selected the good ones into vessels, while the bad ones they threw away.** Our Lord wished to indicate that the word of God is now being thrown over the peoples and over the nations, in the way a seine is cast into the sea. It is now collecting with the Christian sacraments both good people and bad; but not all whom the seine hauls in are also stored in the vessels. The vessels, you see, are the dwellings of the saints and the

5. The Scripture is a totality; if one knows only a part, he does not understand the whole.

quiet retreats of the life of bliss, where true Christians can come and only those who are called in such a way that they really are so.

Certainly both good and bad are swimming about within the seine, and the good are putting up with the bad until they are separated at the end. It also says somewhere, *You will hide them in the hidden place of your countenance* (Ps 31:20). He was talking about the saints: *You will hide them*, he says, *in the hidden place of your countenance*, that is, where the eyes of men or the thoughts of mortals can't follow them.

(31) Peter Chrysologus

The kingdom of heaven is like a net that was thrown into the sea. It is the sea of this age: a sea tossed by pride, exultant in its swirling eddies and clashing sects, surging with ignorance, an ocean wracked by storms that sink those lost in sin, submerging them under waves of wickedness. It is into this sea that Christ sent his fishermen, skilled sailors like Peter, Andrew, James, and John, when he said: **Follow me, and I will make you fishers of men** (4:19).

Into this sea he sent his fishermen, carrying with them nets woven from the teachings of law and gospel, knotted with exhortations to virtue, pulled taut with the gifts of grace—capable of collecting an endless catch within their evangelistic bounds. Now, yes now, brothers, is the time to fish: for the nets of Christ are being cast around all nations, all people. A great catch is being made; the masses throughout the whole world are being drawn to the faith regardless of person.

Now these fish, recently dredged from the depths, certainly flounder around a little on the shoreline in their confusion. But they are quickly separated: the wicked are cast aside, the good saved. To be sure, this brief and quickly passing period of confusion does not unnerve the good—indeed, it *makes* them good. Then the otherworldly separation that assigns retribution to the wicked rapidly conveys the good to their reward. Casting the wicked into hell, it sends the righteous to the kingdom and compensates the transitory insults endured by the fathers of old, the righteous elders, with everlasting glory. We know this to be true from the parable itself, which assures us that **At the end of the age, the angels of God will come and separate the wicked from the midst of the righteous**.

(32) Gregory the Great

The kingdom of heaven is said to be like a net let down into the sea, gathering all kinds of fish. When full it is brought to shore, and the good fish are sorted into baskets, while the bad ones are thrown away. The holy Church is compared to a net because it has been entrusted to fishermen, and because all people are drawn up into it from the turbulent waters of the present age for the eternal kingdom, so that they do not drown in the depths of eternal death. This net gathers all kinds of fish, for it calls to forgiveness of sins everyone, wise and foolish, free and slave, rich and poor, brave and weak. Hence the psalmist says to God: *Everyone will come to you* (Ps 65:2). This net will be completely filled when it enfolds the entire human race at the end of time. When they bring it in they will sit down on the shore; just as the sea signifies this present age, so the shore signifies its end.

At the end of this present age the good fish are to be sorted into baskets, and the bad ones thrown away. The elect will then be received into eternal dwellings, and the condemned led away into external darkness, for the latter have lost the light of the kingdom within them.

Now the net of the faith holds good and bad all together, like the different kinds of fish; but it is on the shore that the holy Church reveals what she has caught. When the fish are caught they cannot be changed, but we, who are caught while we are wicked, can become good. Let us bear this in mind as we are being caught, lest we be thrown aside on shore.

Matthew 13:51–52

51"Have you understood all this?" They said to him, "Yes." 52And he said to them, "Therefore every scribe who has been trained for the kingdom of heaven is like a householder who brings out of his treasure what is new and what is old."

(33) Irenaeus of Lyons

Therefore all things are derived from one and the same reality, that is, from one and the same God. This is precisely what the Lord said to his disciples: **For this reason, every scribe who has been instructed in the kingdom of heaven is similar to that master of the household who offered up from his treasure-store things both new and old.** Clearly he was not teaching that while one person brought forward "things old," it was another who brought forth "things new," but rather that one and the same Master was responsible for both. For the Master of the household is the Lord, who rules over the universal household of his Father. He mandates fitting laws for his headstrong slaves, but grants proper teachings for his righteous freedmen, justified by faith, and flings open his own inheritance to his children.

Moreover, he declares that his disciples are those **scribes** and teachers of the "kingdom of heaven," as he says somewhere else to the Jews: **Behold, I am sending you learned ones and scribes and teachers, and you will murder them and force them from city to city** (23:34), and he states that those things new and old that are offered from the treasure refer, without question, to the two covenants. Now obviously the "things old" stand for the ancient law, while the "things new" signify the gospel, which reveals the way of life. David spoke of this "second covenant": *Sing to the Lord a new song* (Ps 95:1), as did Isaiah: *Sing to the Lord a new hymn, his sacred rites: his name is worshiped from the ends of the earth, his virtues proclaimed in the islands* (Isa 42:10–12). Thus also Jeremiah: *Behold*, he says, *I will establish a new covenant, not like the one that I established with your fathers* on Mount Horeb (Jer 31:32). It was one and the same "Master of the household," therefore, who brought forth both covenants: the Word of God. It was our Lord Jesus Christ who spoke to Abraham and to Moses and restored liberty to us in all its freshness, multiplying that grace that is his own.

(34) Origen

Jesus, who is the Master of the house, can bring forth from his treasury both new and old things. The new refers to the teaching of the Gospel; while the old refers to the writings of the Law and the Prophets, fulfilled in the Gospel, of which there are many examples. And on the subject of the old and the new, listen to what the spiritual law says in Leviticus: *And you shall eat old things as well as the old of old things. And you shall clear out the old things to make way for the new. And I shall place my tabernacle among you* (Lev 26:10). For we eat the old things—the words of the Prophets—with blessing; and we eat the old of those old things—the words of the Law. When the new things of the Gospel arrived, we live according to the Gospel, the oldness of the letter gives way to the new, and God places his tabernacle among us, fulfilling his promise: that he spoke: *I shall dwell and walk among them* (Lev 26:12).

(35) Gregory the Great

The Lord concluded his discourse as he began it. First, he compared the treasure discovered in a field and the pearl of great value to the kingdom. Then he spoke of the punishments of the lower world, the burning of the wicked; and he ends: **Therefore the scribe who has been instructed in the kingdom of heaven is like a householder who brings forth from his treasure things new and old.** In the Church, the preacher who is instructed knows how to bring forth new things from the joys of the kingdom and old things from the terrors of punishment. Those who are not enticed by rewards may at least be moved by fear of punishment.

Let one hear about the kingdom he loves, and the other about the punishment he fears. Fear may threaten the mind that is slothful and clings tightly to the world, if love does not draw one to the kingdom. Note that in describing hell, it is said **there will be weeping and gnashing of teeth** (cf. 13:42). Because perpetual sorrow follows the joys of the present, flee from vain joys on earth. For one cannot rejoice with the world here and reign there with the Lord.

Matthew 13:53–58

53 And when Jesus had finished these parables, he went away from there, 54 and coming
to his own country he taught them in their synagogue, so that they were astonished,
and said, "Where did this man get this wisdom and these mighty works? 55 Is not this
the carpenter's son? Is not his mother called Mary? And are not his brothers James and
Joseph and Simon and Judas? 56 And are not all his sisters with us? Where then did this
man get all this?" 57 And they took offense at him. But Jesus said to them, "A prophet is

not without honor except in his own country and in his own house." [58]And he did not do many mighty works there, because of their unbelief.

(36) Origen

The time has come to consider the passage: **He did not do any mighty works there because of their unbelief** (13:58). These words teach us that miracles are performed among believers, for **to him who has, more shall be given, and he will have abundance** (13:12). In the case of unbelievers not only were no miracles performed, but as Mark has put it, they could not be done. Take note of the words, *He could do no mighty work there* (Mark 6:5). Notice that Jesus did not say that he was unwilling, but only that he was unable. For there had to be a collaboration between the faith of the one on whom the miracle was worked and the power that worked miracles. But this was impeded due to the lack of faith. Consider then to those who said, **Why could we not cast it out?** he said: **Because of your little faith** (17:19–20). And similarly, he said to Peter as Peter was beginning to drown: **O man of little faith, why did you doubt?** (14:31).

By contrast there is the example of the woman who had the discharge of blood. Although she did not consider herself worthy to be healed, she nevertheless believed that if she were only to touch the hem of his garment she would be healed. She was healed at once (Mark 5:28–34). The Savior recognized how she was healed when he said to her: *Who touched me, for I perceived power coming from me?* (Mark 5:30; Luke 8:46).

It seems to me that both Matthew and Mark wanted to set forth the excellence of the divine power, and to show that it is able to work even with unbelief. However, in that case it is not as great as when it works among those who believe. To put it precisely: it is *not* that he did not perform powerful deeds because of their lack of faith, but that he did not perform *many* powerful deeds there.

(37) Hilary of Poitiers

The Lord was dishonored by his own people. Although they admired the wisdom of his teaching and the power of his acts, their unbelief prevented them from accepting the truth of his claim. They did not believe that God was doing these things in a man. They were able to point to his father, his mother, and his brothers, and they were contemptuous of his father's trade (13:55; cf. John 6:42; 7:15). Plainly he was the son of a carpenter who hammers on iron with fire, he who smelts all the power of this world by his judgment, and who gives form to matter all for the benefit of humanity. In other words, he is the one who molds the formless matter of our bodies so that our members may perform different functions and do every work that leads toward eternal life.

All of them were scandalized by these things. Though he performed many magnificent deeds among them, they were troubled about his corporeality. The Lord responded that a prophet is dishonored in his homeland, just as he would be despised in Judea to the point of being condemned to the cross. He refrained from doing any works of divine power, because of their incredulity. The power of God belongs only to the faithful.

Matthew 14

The tetrarch Herod Antipas[1] heard about the miracles of Jesus though he mistook him for John the Baptist now raised from the dead. Herod himself had executed John the Baptist, granting the wish of Salome, the daughter of Herod's brother's wife with whom he had an unlawful relationship, which was condemned by John. The wish—a diabolic favor (Chrysostom)—was to bring her John's head on a platter. For Hilary and Ambrose, John the Baptist symbolizes the law as well as the prophetic character of the law that predicted the coming of Christ. Thus, John's death stands for the end of the era of the law.

Having learned about the death of John, Jesus withdrew to remote places with the disciples, but the crowds followed him and eventually needed food. Jesus commanded the disciples to feed the crowds. After they complained of not having enough food, he miraculously fed a crowd of five thousand with five loaves of bread and two fish, so that they were satisfied and had twelve baskets of food left over.[2]

For ancient commentators, by providing bodily nourishment for the five thousand, Jesus taught the disciples to nourish people spiritually, that is, to perform the ministry that they will be performing without him. According to Origen, when Jesus told the disciples to feed the people, he also gave them power "to promote the growth of others." Being concerned not only to nourish their bodies but also to instruct the soul (Chrysostom), Christ had the disciples distribute the food in order to help them remember the miracle, as well as teach humility and self-control to the crowds. Eusebius of Emesa remarks that the body can take only a limited amount of food and be nourished for a limited time, while the soul can absorb much more of heavenly food as it expands and experiences long-lasting benefits.

The fathers see much symbolism in the numbers of loaves and fish. Origen sees five loaves as representing the five senses by which we perceive the words of Scripture, and the two fishes as "the Word made manifest and the Word hidden." Interpreting the increase of the amount of food, Hilary sees the progression from five books of the law (five loaves) and the prophets with John (two fishes) into a greater "abundance of power" in the gospel. The twelve baskets of surplus symbolize for him the overabundance of the divine power of the twelve apostles.

Next, Jesus sent the disciples into a boat and went up on the mountain to pray alone.

1. The ruler of one-fourth of Palestine, one of the sons of Herod the Great (Matt 2:16).

2. All four evangelists report this miracle (cf. Mark 6:30–44; Luke 9:10–17; John 6:1–14).

Now the disciples could escape the crowd and reflect on the miracle in which they also participated. In the fourth watch of the night *(v. 25), Jesus returned to them walking on the water (cf. John 6:19), once again manifesting his power over nature. Ancient interpreters see a lesson on faith in this Gospel account, pointing out significance in every detail. For Augustine, the Lord's solitary prayer on the mountain prefigures his post-resurrection ascension into heaven and his intercession for us. His position on high points to his role as the head of the Church. Hilary comments on the significance of* the fourth watch*: "the first watch is that of the law, the second of the prophets, the third of his bodily advent, so the fourth is in his glorious return." Just as Jesus comes to the disciples into the boat during the storm, so he will return to his Church, harassed and tempted by antichrist, and banish her fear, saying:* "It is I" *(cf. Exod 3:14).*

Peter also receives much attention from the ancient commentators. Hilary and Chromatius see Peter's attempted walking on the water, which ended by sinking, in parallel with his future denial of Christ. The Lord will forgive Peter, just as he saved him from drowning. Christ does not let Peter reach him, for the Lord alone will suffer and forgive the sins of all (cf. Gal 1:4). For Macarius, Peter's inability to walk on the water shows his "presumption and lack of faith," leading him to imitate the devil in the wilderness (cf. Matt 4:3, 6) by saying "If you are. . . ." *(v. 28).*

Augustine sees Peter, "the Rock" (cf. Matt 16:18), as representing "the one and only Church." But the man Peter is at the same time a member of this Church, and, as such, he is "the symbolic representative of us all," demonstrating a typical human behavior. The boat also represents the Church in the midst of "storms of temptations and trials," which is, nevertheless, protected and confident of the Lord's rescue: "if God enables seafarers to come safely to port, is he going to leave his Church to her fate, or bring her through to the final haven of rest?" (Augustine).

When Jesus and the disciples crossed the sea and came to the land at Gennesaret, people recognized Jesus and brought their sick to him to be healed by merely touching the end of his garment (vv. 34–36). For Hilary, these events parallel the upcoming birth of the Church (Acts 4:4). Just as five thousand were gathered and fed, so "five thousand men of Israel had been gathered into the Church." The Lord is the source both of the healing power of the garment and of the Holy Spirit that will empower the apostles. This life-giving power extends to us as well, causing Chrysostom to exclaim, "For if they who touched the hem of his garment found so much strength from him, how much more will those who wholly possess him!"

Matthew 14:1–14

[1]At that time Herod the tetrarch heard about the fame of Jesus; [2]and he said to his
servants, "This is John the Baptist, he has been raised from the dead; that is why these
powers are at work in him." [3]For Herod had seized John and bound him and put him in
prison, for the sake of Hero'di-as, his brother Philip's wife; [4]because John said to him,
"It is not lawful for you to have her." [5]And though he wanted to put him to death, he
feared the people, because they held him to be a prophet. [6]But when Herod's birthday
came, the daughter of Hero'di-as danced before the company, and pleased Herod, [7]so
that he promised with an oath to give her whatever she might ask. [8]Prompted by her

mother, she said, "Give me the head of John the Baptist here on a platter." [9]And the king was sorry; but because of his oaths and his guests he commanded it to be given; [10]he sent and had John beheaded in the prison, [11]and his head was brought on a platter and given to the girl, and she brought it to her mother. [12]And his disciples came and took the body and buried it; and they went and told Jesus.

[13]Now when Jesus heard this, he withdrew from there in a boat to a lonely place apart. But when the crowds heard it, they followed him on foot from the towns. [14]As he went ashore he saw a great throng; and he had compassion on them, and healed their sick.

(1) Origen

What is said here teaches us that we should escape those who—plotting against us because of the Word—persecute us. This is truly the thoughtful way to act. When it is possible for us to keep free of dire situations, it is reckless and rash to rush headlong into them. One should not fret over avoiding such things, for Jesus not only withdrew after what happened to John, he even taught us: **If they persecute you in this city, then flee to the other** (10:23).

Therefore, if an occasion of testing suddenly overwhelms us and we cannot avoid it, we must endure such a test with great nobility and courage. But if such a test can be avoided, it would be extremely reckless not to do so.

(2) Hilary of Poitiers

Now Herod was the leader of the people and had announced his marriage to Herodias, the spouse of his brother Philip, by the right of his authority. This Herodias had a daughter, and when her dancing pleased Herod on his birthday, she received from him an oath swearing she could have whatever reward she wished. The girl, prompted by her mother, requested that the head of John, who had been held for a long time in prison, be brought to her and offered on a plate. Although Herod was saddened, he fulfilled his oath, and the girl then presented the reward to her mother. Then his disciples, after having buried John, went to Jesus.

(3) Ambrose of Milan

Why is it that the passion of John the Baptist is recounted, and yet here we are told in the words of Herod that John is already dead? Perhaps it is because after the end of the law symbolized by John, the food of the gospel begins to nourish the famished hearts of the people. You will remember that this event comes after the Church has, figuratively, been healed of the hemorrhage (9:20–22), and after the apostles were sent out on their mission to preach the kingdom of God (10:5–15), the food of heavenly grace is distributed. Notice, however, who receives this: not those who are indifferent, or city-dwellers (11:21–23), or those in the synagogue, or people in grand and worldly places, but those who search for Christ in the wilderness (11:7). It is these people, not the high and mighty, that Christ welcomes. With these Christ communicates, not about worldly affairs but about the kingdom of heaven (cf. Luke 9:11). And if any are ill with cancer or covered with sores, he liberally applies his healing remedies (14:35–36).

(4) Jerome

In Roman history we read about the Roman general Flaminius, who at a dinner was seated next to a prostitute. She said that she had never seen a man decapitated. So he agreed to cut off the head of a man guilty of a capital crime at the banquet. Because he shed blood at a banquet, Flaminius was driven out of the senate by the magistrates. For pleasure of another, he offered up, however guilty, a man to death, and lust and murder were mixed together. How much more despicable are Herod, Herodias, and the girl who danced for the price of blood. She demands the head of the prophet that she might hold silent his tongue that had condemned an illicit marriage. These things actually happened.

(5) Peter Chrysologus

John chose to warn Herod rather than batter him with accusations. Why? Because he wanted to correct him, not destroy him. But Herod preferred to be destroyed rather than repent; those ensnared by sin are horrified at the prospect of being free of it. Virtue and vice are, after all, on opposite sides; the depraved revile the pure; chastity and lewdness are natural enemies. Integrity is a death-sentence to the corrupt, libertines savagely oppose all restraint. The cruel cannot bear mercy, the wicked, righteousness, nor the crooked, justice.

The Gospel writer illustrates this when he says: **John said, "You are not allowed to take your brother Philip's wife as your own."** Notice who then imprisons John: when you warn the wicked, you may expect their wrath. When they are rebuked, they retaliate. John told Herod only what the law, what justice, what his own well-being were telling him. He was not motivated by hatred, but by love. And look at the sort of reward he received for his troubles at the hands of the wicked king!

The Gospel writer continues: **His desire to kill him was checked by his fear of the people**. It's very easy to stray from the path of justice if your eye is on the people rather than God. While it's possible to *delay* sinning out of such a "fear," your desire to do so won't be shaken. And so we can see that those who want to sin will always find a way to do it in the end, however long it takes. Only the fear of God can reform such a mind by driving out sin, preserving one's innocence, and granting the strength to stay on the path.

You've already heard, my brothers, what kind of cruelty arises from perverse pleasures. **And the head of John the Baptist was brought to him on a plate**. A house is transformed into an arena, a meal becomes a spectacle, the guests are made spectators. A party bends toward madness: food is turned to flesh, wine to blood. A funeral is held on a birthday, a feast becomes a slaughter—and the pipes play a tragedy for the ages.

Such pleasure is a terrible thing. A house is transformed into an arena, the table into a theatre, dinner guests become spectators, a banquet becomes a riotous party, a meal becomes a massacre, wine changes to blood, a funeral is held on a birthday . . . and musical instruments ring out a tragedy for the ages.

Matthew 14:15–21

15When it was evening, the disciples came to him and said, "This is a lonely place, and
the day is now over; send the crowds away to go into the villages and buy food for them-
selves." 16Jesus said, "They need not go away; you give them something to eat." 17They
said to him, "We have only five loaves here and two fish." 18And he said, "Bring them
here to me." 19Then he ordered the crowds to sit down on the grass; and taking the five
loaves and the two fish he looked up to heaven, and blessed, and broke and gave the
loaves to the disciples, and the disciples gave them to the crowds. 20And they all ate and
were satisfied. And they took up twelve baskets full of the broken pieces left over. 21And
those who ate were about five thousand men, besides women and children.

(6) Origen

When it was evening, his disciples came to him, that is, at the close of the age. About this we read in the letter of John: *It is the last hour* (1 John 2:18). Because the disciples do not perceive what the Word was about to do, they say that this place is **deserted**. They could see that the people were deprived of God's law and the Word of God. So they say to him: **The hour has already passed**, as if to say that the time had passed of the law and the prophets. Perhaps they spoke in this manner in order to appeal to that reasoning, which thinks that because John was beheaded both the law and the prophets, which were in place until John, had now ceased (Luke 16:16). They therefore say that the hour has passed (14:15) and that there is no food available because its season is no longer at hand, designating that those who followed him in the desert submitted to the law and the prophets.

Then the disciples also said: **Send them away** so that each of them might purchase food, if not from the cities, then from the villages, which are more deprived. Now the disciples said these things because they considered it hopeless that such new and incredible food could be found for the crowds after the letter of the law had been destroyed and prophecy ceased. Notice what Jesus says in response to the disciples' voiced concerns: "Do you suppose that if this great crowd in need of food leaves me, they will find it in villages rather than with me?"

On account of the power he gave to the disciples, even the power to promote the growth of others, Jesus said to them: **You give them something to eat.** The disciples did not deny that they could give them bread. Rather, they supposed that the loaves were too few in number and therefore incapable of nourishing those who had followed after Jesus. And since they did not imagine that when Jesus takes each loaf or word, he spreads each out as far as he desires, making each loaf sufficient for everyone whom he wishes to feed, they say: **We have no more than five loaves and two fish.** In this way they hint that the five loaves are the perceptible words of the Scriptures, and for this reason equal in number to the five senses. Surely the two fish suggest the Word made manifest and the Word hidden, as these happen to be a taste of those perceptible things in the Scriptures.

(7) Hilary of Poitiers

And when the disciples were sending the crowd away into the nearby villages to buy food, the Lord responded, **They do not need to go away**. He wanted to show that those whom he healed had no need of the food of teaching that is for sale, nor was it necessary for them to return to Judea in order to buy food. Instead, he ordered the apostles to give them something to eat. Was the Lord ignorant of the fact that he had nothing to give? Did he, who perceived the inner thoughts of the human mind (12:25), not know about the amount of food in the possession of the apostles? But there is a figurative reason that deserves to be explained.

The apostles were not yet permitted to make and serve heavenly bread that leads to the food of eternal life. Their response to the Lord directs us toward a model of spiritual understanding. For they responded that they had only five loaves of bread and two fish. As for the five loaves, the apostles were upholding the five books of the law; as for the two fish, they were being nourished by the preaching of the prophets and of John. For there was life in the works of the law just as there was in the bread. Likewise, the preaching of John and the prophets fostered the hope of human life by the power of water. The apostles presented the loaves and fish first because they remained in this mode of life. The preaching of the Gospels is shown to have progressed from these beginning stages until it grew into a great abundance of power.

Once he received the loaves and fish, the Lord looked up to heaven, blessed and broke them, giving thanks to the Father that he was changed into the food of the gospel following the era of the law and the prophets. Then he told the people to sit down on the grass. These people are supported not only by lying on the ground but by the law; each one is borne up by the fruit of his works no less than by the grass of the ground. Bread is also given to the apostles because through them the gifts of divine grace were to be offered.

After the people were fed and filled by the five loaves and the two fish, and were satisfied, there was so much bread and fish left over that it filled twelve baskets. So the multitude was satisfied by the word of God coming from the teaching of the law and the prophets, while an overabundance of divine power through the servicing of eternal food (which abounded in the twelve apostles) was preserved for the pagan peoples.

In such matters the subtlety of meaning becomes foggy, and our perception of reality is dulled because of our difficulty in fully comprehending the invisible. When he had taken the five loaves, the Lord looked up to heaven, professing the honor of him from whom he was. It was not necessary that he look upon the Father with eyes of flesh, but he did so for the benefit of those who were present, that they might know from whom he had received the capacity for such power.

Then he gave bread to his disciples. Multiplying five loaves does not amount to much, but pieces came from other pieces, and it escaped the notice of those breaking off the pieces that they, in fact, continued taking these pieces. In that instance, matter came into being; I do not know whether it was on tables, or in the hands of those taking it, or in the mouth of those eating. There is no surprise that the resources flowed forth.

In the case of the wine, it is comprised of grapes, and from the grapes wine is poured out, just as all the resources of the world flow forth every year in an endless rhythm. With this enormous profusion of bread, we see how the author of this universe speeded up the [usual] means of deploying matter in such stages. The activity of what is invisible is administered by the works of what is visible, showing how the Lord of the heavenly mysteries acts within the mystery of present time. This power of the one who acts surpasses all of nature, as his use of power exceeds our understanding of the facts. Only our wonder at his authority remains.

(8) Eusebius of Emesa

To be sure, they who were revived by bread were accustomed to seek after physical food, though we have been nourished by the hearing of the miraculous, just as they were by bread. In fact, whenever we read, hear, or reflect upon this deed, we are nourished by the miraculous, since the soul is fed, though not in the same manner as the body. Indeed, the body, when it is fed, is not refreshed except within its own limits, limits that make a person sick if they were exceeded. You may, however, feed the soul however much its opening can handle, and it expands so that it may be fed with greater amounts. For the body's food can penetrate for a brief duration of time; yet the soul's food, when it is digested, may [continue to] persist.

As the one who lives, the Son consequently originates and gives life. I say "originates" not in the sense of flowing out, since it is not as though he is a vessel that is filled and then emptied out for whoever receives him. In contrast, this one fills up all others, and yet he is not diminished by this action, since life does not flow out when he gives it, nor is he diminished when he bestows its benefit. Because he remains the same as when he was begotten, he is sufficient both to give life to all and not to be weakened. The Son does not operate, for example, in the same manner as an artisan, but rather like wisdom. In his craft, an artisan makes use of nature—not divine nature. An artisan may work with gold that he obtained from natural elements. He blends the particulars of his craft by means of materials that nature has supplied. The artisan who makes bread receives crops from the earth, increases its capacity by virtue of his skill. He too fashions and completes his craft by means of nature. If it is true of bread—by which we mean the bread of this world, it isn't actually the product of a craftsman's skill, but of nature's crops. It might be more proper to say that the character of the craftsman's skill is, in this case, labor.

The Lord Jesus, of course, does not create in this way. For he who creates does not draw from nature and then work on it; he himself is the one who also offers the benefits of nature. He did not make the loaves from stones (4:3–4), though not because he was unable to do so. He can certainly create out of nothing. Which is more difficult: to create heaven, earth, and sea out of nothing, or bread without specific matter? But he is wisdom who sees the future as if it were the present. Undoubtedly he received the five loaves and increased their number by his command, so that he could offer to us the created things he used and then present a miracle by means of augmenting them.

You shall let me now set before your eyes, not five loaves for five thousand men, but instead, every creature that has been created by one and the same command. There has been displayed a table that is never in fact wanting, but always feeding. The arrangements proceed and proclaim themselves unseen. And yet, the earth did indeed expose his glory: five loaves re-created five thousand, and in so doing they increased the glory of him who has been working all along. We should hardly be amazed by this.

The things that happened were indeed a sampling, a kind of taste. There were thus five loaves for five thousand men: a great miracle that was prepared for the needy crowd. This was, however, a modicum of Christ, the bride that was for the glory of the bridegroom. It is not, of course, in this way that we have learned about Christ, nor in this way that we have been instructed concerning his miracles. For this is the one through whom everything has been created, the very one through whom everything all together is governed, through whom every living thing is fed. He is the one who is a Creator without material, that is, he was Wisdom before the advent of material. He is the Lord who works in wombs, not with instruments or devices, but by his will. Indeed, he says, "I am willing, be made clean, I am willing, be born," and it happens. To be sure, "I am willing, be made clean," is a taste of him, just as when he says, "I will that the earth be made, I will that all things be fed."

(9) John Chrysostom

Then, Christ took the bread, broke it, and distributed it, and had the disciples distribute it, honoring them by this, but not for this purpose alone. He did it through them, so that, when the miracle occurs, they would neither disbelieve nor forget what happened, since their own hands are their witnesses.

For the same purpose he first allows the crowds to feel hunger. For the same purpose he waits for the disciples to take the initiative to come forward and ask. Through them he helps the people to sit down, and through them distributes the food, wishing to predispose each one of them in advance to grasp [the miracle] by their own assent and actions. For the same reason he receives the loaves from the disciples, so that there might be many testimonies of the miracle taking place, and so that they had reminders of it. If they had forgotten even with all these provisions, what might have happened to them without them?

The Lord also commands them to recline on the grass, instructing the crowds in godly and humble ways of life. Indeed, he wished not only for their bodies to be fed, but also for their souls to be taught. Likewise, by choosing this location, by giving away nothing more but bread and fish, proposing the same food to everyone and sharing it, and by offering to one no more than to another, the Lord was teaching humility, self-control, and love. He was also teaching to be equally well disposed to one another, and to hold all possessions in common.

Matthew 14:22–27

[22]Then he made the disciples get into the boat and go before him to the other side, while he dismissed the crowds. [23]And after he had dismissed the crowds, he went up on the mountain by himself to pray. When evening came, he was there alone, [24]but the boat by this time was many furlongs distant from the land, beaten by the waves; for the wind was against them. [25]And in the fourth watch of the night he came to them, walking on the sea. [26]But when the disciples saw him walking on the sea, they were terrified, saying, "It is a ghost!" And they cried out for fear. [27]But immediately he spoke to them, saying, "Take heart, it is I; have no fear."

(10) Hilary of Poitiers

As [Jesus prayed on the mountain], the disciples were being buffeted by the wind and waves, by all the agitations of the world, and by the opposition of the unclean sprit. **In the fourth watch of the night**, the Lord came, for it was at that point that he returned to the errant and foundering church. In fact, **in the fourth watch of the night** is an appropriate number that represents his concern. The first watch is that of the law, the second of the prophets, the third of his bodily advent, so the fourth is in his glorious return. But will he find the church exhausted and buffeted about by the spirit of antichrist[3] and by all the world's troubles (cf. Luke 8:18)? For he will come especially to those who are anxious and in anguish. Because it is typical of the antichrist to harass by using every new kind of temptation, they will panic at the Lord's coming, fearful of the false and insidious images of things that deceive the eyes. But the good Lord will immediately speak to them, drive away their fear, and say: **It is I** (cf. Exod 3:14), banishing their fear of a certain shipwreck with faith at his coming.

Out of all those who were on board, Peter dares to respond and asks that he be told to come on the water to the Lord. This indicates the state of his will at the time of the passion. Peter alone, turning away from the others, forsakes the world just as he did the waves of the sea and sets out to follow the Lord's steps. Possessing a power sufficient for scorning death, he accompanies the Lord, but his fear shows his timidity in the face of a future temptation. For, although he had dared to walk out on the water, he began to sink, compelled by the fragility of the flesh and fear of death even in the desperation of having to deny him. But he cries out and asks the Lord to save him. That cry is Peter's sigh of repentance. He then returned to his profession [of confidence] and found grace at the time of his denial, since the Lord had not yet suffered. It was only later that Christ would suffer for the redemption of all people.

There was a reason that the Lord did not grant to Peter's fearfulness the ability of reaching him. He instead extended his hand and caught him and held him up: Peter was

3. The word *antichristus* has a broader meaning than the devil or a wicked spiritual agent. See 1 John 2:18; 4:3; 2 John 7 (false teacher). It can also refer to one who directly opposes the truth of the Christian faith, such as an unfaithful Christian emperor.

not yet worthy of approaching his Lord (he tried to draw near). We see also a typological pattern has been observed in this situation.

The fact that the Lord walked upon the upheavals and storms of the world shows that no one is able to participate in his passion. He alone is going to suffer for all, and it is he who forgives the sins of all (Gal 1:4). Whatever is granted to the whole world is granted by the one who admits no associate. If he himself was the redemption of the entire world, he could also preserve Peter—before he was redeemed—for that faith of redemption, even to the point of becoming a martyr of Christ.

(11) Augustine

As for the Lord leaving the crowds and going up to pray alone on the mountain, that mountain represents the heights of heaven. Leaving the crowds, you see, the Lord alone ascended into heaven after his resurrection, and there *he intercedes for us* (Rom 8:34), as the Apostle says. So there is some meaning in his leaving the crowds and going up the mountain to pray alone. I mean, so far he alone is the *firstborn from the dead* (Col 1:18) at the Father's right hand after the resurrection of the body, our high priest and advocate of our prayers (cf. Heb 7:24–26). The head of the Church is up above, so that the rest of the body may follow at the end. So if he is interceding for us, on the top of the mountain so to say, way above the highest peak of all creation, he is praying alone by himself.

Meanwhile the boat carrying the disciples—the Church—is being tossed about and battered by the storms of temptations and trials. There's no easing up of the contrary wind, that is, of the devil's opposition to her, but he goes on making every effort to prevent her from reaching calm waters. Nonetheless the one who is interceding for us is greater than he is. For in this turbulent situation in which we find ourselves struggling, he gives us confidence by coming to us and reassuring us. The one thing he has to do is stop us from shaking ourselves loose in our own agitation in the boat and hurling ourselves into the sea. Even when the boat is being agitated and tossed about, it is still a boat. It alone carries the disciples and receives Christ on board. Sure, it's in distress and danger in the sea, but without it we all perish immediately.

So keep yourself in the ship, and turn to God with your requests. With sailors, you see, when every other plan fails, when the vessel doesn't answer the helm, and cramming on more sail is more dangerous than useful—when all human efforts and endeavors have been tried and found unavailing—then all they have is the urgent pouring out of their voices to God in prayer. If God enables seafarers to come safely to port, is he going to leave his Church to her fate, or bring her through to the final haven of rest?

(12) Macarius of Magnesia

The inner meaning of the incident must not be overlooked. Having just performed a miracle that showed his power over bread and the wilderness, Christ now reveals his power by another miracle over water and the sea. The very elements join in the proof. The unusual force of the storm reflects what nature feels even when humanity fails to recognize the creative Word. Thus the prophecy was fulfilled concerning him who *walks upon the sea as upon a foundation* . . . terrifying them through his divinity, and he sympathizes with them through his humanity. He says, **It is I**, and brings them light after cloud, meaning "It is I who called you to be fishers of men and feed the five thousand."

Peter's faith wavers when he says, **If it is you, bid me come to you** (14:28). When Christ says **Come**, he means "Come to faith." If Peter had actually been able to walk on the sea it would have falsified the above prophecy by making it apply to more people than one. Adding to his presumption and lack of faith in saying **If**, his failure is explained. Christ saved him just as his [Peter's own] tongue was making him sink (like a ship through its broken rudder), and taught him not to imitate the devil in the wilderness by saying **If you are.**[4]

Christ says, "Come and learn. You need this fourth watch even more than the ship. The darkness, the winds and the waves are all in your lack of faith and your presumption. The four constituents that should be blended in your body are questionable by your doubting speech." Great, indeed, was the fall of this leading apostle. Two shipwrecks were his—of the body and of the soul.

It was rightly said that **in the fourth watch** Christ came to Peter's help, for there were four elements that raged against them, namely, impenetrable atmosphere, rushing wind, moonless night, and roaring sea. There is, however, a yet deeper allegory underlying the story. The sea denotes the brine and bitterness of existence; the night is human life; the boat is the world; those who sailed all night are the human race; the contrary wind is the devil's opposition; the fourth watch is the Savior's coming. Notice this last point: just as there are four watches in the literal night, so there are in human life. In the first watch the [Old Testament] patriarchs helped life by their light; in the second, the law guided the boat of the world; in the third, the prophets contended for those human sailors; and in the fourth, Christ checked their fear and their foes and ended the night by the light of his love for men. So when Paul says, *The night is far spent*, etc. (Rom 13:12), he refers to this dawn of the knowledge of God through Christianity.

(13) Arnobius the Younger

The sea is the world, and ship that the apostles boarded is the church. Just as the Lord spoke of [the ship] **buffeted by the waves**, so the church was tossed around by persecution. The **opposing wind** is the devil who opposes the church. When the text says, **In the fourth watch of the night he came to them walking on the sea**, that is, he brings the four Gospels to us, but in our ignorance we throw them into the darkness. And the text says, Peter was shaken up when he saw the storm, that is, because he was shaken up by Christ's passion such that he began to sink when he denied his faith.

4. Matt 4:3, 6.

Matthew 14:28–33

28And Peter answered him, "Lord, if it is you, bid me come to you on the water." 29He
said, "Come." So Peter got out of the boat and walked on the water and came to Jesus;
30but when he saw the wind, he was afraid, and beginning to sink he cried out, "Lord,
save me." 31Jesus immediately reached out his hand and caught him, saying to him, "O
man of little faith, why did you doubt?" 32And when they got into the boat, the wind
ceased. 33And those in the boat worshiped him, saying, "Truly you are the Son of God."

(14) Eusebius of Emesa

Jesus was walking upon the waves of the sea. His body was certainly not bringing down his power, but his power was bearing his body. For truly the Lord hungers when he hungers and is fatigued when he is fatigued, so that it may not be believed what some have supposed [namely, that the Lord's body wasn't physically real]. For walking upon the waves of the sea was certainly not characteristic of a body. Accordingly, in order that it would not be supposed that he had made many loaves in appearance only, he really hungers, so that he demonstrates that he has a genuine body. So too, he grows tired, which cannot be regarded as a mere appearance.

He got into the boat, which further demonstrates his incarnation. Without the boat, however, he walks upon the sea so that there'd be no mistake that he is merely a man. He wanted to exhibit his true nature and not give a false impression about his incarnation as he was walking upon the crests of waves. Because of this, also, he restrains the waves so that there'd be no mistake that he was merely a man who appeared. The sea was being disturbed, billowing, being tossed by the waves, surging. And yet the sea was afraid, lest she take advantage of the one who created her. Nevertheless the Lord walked, and the sea became firmer than stone: for the crests of the waves were conveying the body because a stronger power possessed them.

Now the Lord steps onto the sea and was walking upon the crests of the waves. The countenance of the sea was truly joyful, because she was kissing, even if not the lips, at least the feet of the Creator. It is not as accurate to say he was *walking* toward the boat as it was that the Lord's *feet were advancing* (John 6:19). Those who truly comprehended were those who had already sailed first and, it says, wanted to take him up into the boat (John 6:21). However, they did not complete their sea voyage, in spite of their efforts, because as soon as Jesus appeared, immediately their boat, as the Gospel says, came upon land (cf. John 6:21). Not only was the miracle that he was walking on the waves, but also that without wind he propelled the boat to land by his command.

(15) Jerome

Lord, if it is you, command me to come to you on the water. In all passages, Peter is found to be a man of an intensely burning faith. When the disciples are asked who others say Jesus is, Peter confesses him to be the Son of God. When the Savior states his intent to go to his passion, Peter is unwilling that he, whom he had confessed to be the Son of God a little earlier, should die. I will grant that Peter was in error on this matter, but the error was not in his affection. Peter goes up on the mountain with the Savior, as first among the first. And in the passion, Peter alone follows. With bitter tears he immediately washed away the sin of denial into which he had fallen due to sudden fear. After the passion, when they were fishing at Lake Gennesaret, while the Lord was standing on the shore, the others were taking their time in sailing back.

But Peter allows for no delay. He wraps himself with his garment and at once plunges headfirst into the waves. Therefore, the same ardor of faith that he always has had, he has now. Although the others are silent, he believes that by the will of his Master he can do what Jesus was able to do by nature. **Command me to come to you on the water.** You give the command, and on the spot the water will grow solid, the body will become light, which in its own right is heavy.

(16) Augustine

This Gospel is advising us to take the sea as meaning the present age and this world, and the Apostle Peter as representing the one and only Church. . . . By observing this apostle of the Church ourselves, let us try to distinguish in our own lives what comes from God's ideas and what from our own. Then we won't stagger, then we shall be founded on the rock, then we shall be solid and steady against the winds, the storms of rain, and the floods; namely, the trials and temptations of this age. Notice that the man Peter, who was the symbolic representative of us all,[5] is sometimes trusting, sometimes tottering; one moment he's acknowledging Christ to be immortal, the next he's afraid of dying.

Lord, if it is you, bid me come to you on the water. "If it's you, tell me to come, because I can't do it on my own, but only in you." He acknowledged the difference between what he could contribute himself and what the Lord could do, by whose will Peter believed that he could supersede any human weakness.

And he got down and began to walk on the water. Peter, "the rock," was able to do it because the Rock had given the order. There you have what Peter could accomplish in the Lord. But what about himself? When he saw the force of the wind, he grew afraid; and as he began to sink, he cried out, **Lord, save me.** He placed his confidence in the Lord; he was enabled to act by the Lord; he tottered as a man; he came back to the Lord.

So what now is the significance of Peter being so bold as to come to him over the water? Peter, you see, often represents the Church. So what else are we to suppose is meant by **Lord, if it is you, order me to come to you over the water** but, "Lord, if you are truthful and never lie at all, let your Church, too, be glorified in this world, as prophecy foretold this about you"? So let her walk over the water and in this way may she come to you, she to whom it was said, *The rich among the people will seek your favor* (Ps 45:12 [Latin 44:13]).

5. That is, all Christians or the Church.

(17) Chromatius of Aquileia

Peter asked that by walking on the sea he might come to the Lord, saying: **Lord, if it is you, command me to come to you**. It was shown here that holy Peter, because he was possessed of an immense love of the Lord, wanted to suffer with the Lord, such as the time when the Lord said that they all were about to suffer in that scandal, Peter said: **Even if it demands that I die, I will not deny you** (26:35).

But when he saw the powerful wind, he was immediately afraid and began to sink. In what way is Peter understood to have feared the sight of the strong wind, just as when he saw the violence of the persecution inflicted on the Son of God by the Jewish leaders? At that time he was truly afraid and was almost in danger when, as he was questioned by the handmaiden he said for a first, a second, and a third time that he did not know Jesus the Nazarene, that is, Christ the Lord (26:74). In this instance Peter had begun to sink [again] because he now denied that he knew the Son of God, whom he had before confessed and for whom Peter declared that he would die.

When Peter had begun to sink in this [first] way, he shouted to the Lord, saying: **Save me. And extending his hand he grabbed him**. Should not that crying out of Peter, once he had begun to sink, be understood in the same way as his denial of the Lord in faith and heart and afterward he wept very bitterly (cf. 26:75; Mark 14:72; Luke 22:62)? And was he not with extended hand grasped by Jesus? We also read in the Gospel that immediately after his denial, Jesus looked back at him and, in a similar fashion, Peter wept very bitterly (cf. Luke 22:61).

The fact that Peter wanted to come to the Lord through the waves of the sea signified that, before the passion, Peter wanted to suffer with the Lord or in place of the Lord. But because he had not yet been strengthened by the passion of Christ and terrified by the fear of death, he had come upon the danger of denial in place of the constancy of faith. Clearly it was not allowed that Peter actually suffer with Christ, since the passion of Christ alone was demanded for the salvation of the world. He alone was considered worthy to die, both for the entire world and for Peter too.

We read that the Lord entered the boat in the middle of the storm, and the wind stopped, and these who were actually in the boat worshiped him. This is understood as a sign that our Lord and Savior, with the storm of persecution driven away, was about to go again to the disciples, even as far as to his Church, in which he established holy Peter himself as the leader of the apostles, and to whom he entrusted his sheep by saying: *Feed my sheep* (John 21:17). When the apostles had observed the glory of the lordly resurrection in the assembly of the believers, just as when they were situated in the small boat, adoring our Lord and Savior, they preached to the human race that he truly was the Son of God, to whom there is praise and glory forever. Amen.

Matthew 14:34–36

34 And when they had crossed over, they came to land at Gennes'aret. 35 And when the men of that place recognized him, they sent round to all that region and brought to

him all that were sick, [36]and besought him that they might only touch the fringe of his garment; and as many as touched it were made well.

(18) Hilary of Poitiers

After the gathering and satisfying of five thousand men, many things happened in the interval, which have delayed us from eagerly mentioning an underlying principle, although our meaning in this passage is the same. Since the era of the law had ended and the five thousand men of Israel had been gathered into the Church (Acts 4:4), those who believed now went out to meet the Lord, being saved from the law through faith. They brought to the Lord those infirm and sick among them. Those who were presented wanted to touch the edge of his garment so that they would be healed through faith. But just as the edges are made manifest from the whole garment, so the power of the Holy Spirit came from our Lord Jesus Christ. That power was given to the apostles, who also came from the same body, as it were, and it granted healing to those who touched it.

(19) John Chrysostom

For the crowds did not approach him as before, pulling him into their homes, seeking a touch of his hand, or directions from his words. Rather, in a more exalted fashion and yet with greater humility and with a more abundant faith, they hoped to gain a cure for themselves. For the woman who had the issue of blood taught them all how to seek wisdom.

The evangelist, implying that the Lord spent long intervals of time in several regions, says, **After the people of that place recognized him, they sent word throughout the region and brought to him those that were sick**. But still, these intervals did not diminish their faith, but made it even stronger and preserved its vitality.

Let us also touch the hem of his garment. . . . Now then, let each of us who is ill draw near to him with faith. For if they who touched the hem of his garment found so much strength from him, how much more will those who wholly possess him?

(20) Eusebius of Emesa

In the passage above, crowns are offered by both land and sea so that all creation was announcing him who was present. Whatever things the Lord touched show the identity of him who has arrived. Notice he didn't manipulate nature with some skill or exact its use by means of a device. If he took advantage of natural things, it was not to abuse them to satisfy his wishes, but to take advantage in commending creation. This is the Lord for us: the unseen offspring of that invisible Father. Who is this? Certainly the one who said, *Remain steadfast, I am he who has overcome the world* (John 16:33).

Again, he says, *I am the bread* (John 6:35). When you hear him saying, *I am*, be careful lest you end up saying that he is not. And even if you still denied that it is true, you should know that it is not true merely because he says so, but because he is by nature, *I am*. Listen to him saying, *I am* (John 8:58). Listen also to the Father saying about him, *This is the bread that comes down from heaven, that a man may eat of it and not die* (John 6:50). Listen also to Peter declaring about him, **You are the Christ, the Son of the living God** (16:16). Listen also to the demon crying out, *I know who you are* (Luke 4:34). Listen also to the sea speaking through her waves, "I know who you are." Listen also to the waters revealing that "he is." For when the water is changed into wine, it shows that *he* is the one who can exalt these things. Listen also to the thieves, who hung on a cross at the same time as he: for one says to him, *Remember me, Lord, in your kingdom* (Luke 23:42). Undoubtedly, he says this to him who is also the one who reigns. It is not good, however, to speak the contrary. This one is for us **his Son** (22:45; Luke 20:44), he who is the offspring of the unborn Father, the only-begotten Son of his Father, he who alone was born as one good, through whom all things have been created for the glory of the Father.

Let there be glory, honor, power, and majesty to the unbegotten Father, through the Son, in the Holy Spirit, now, always and forever, amen.

Matthew 15

In Gennesaret, Jesus disputes with religious leaders who came from Jerusalem to accuse the disciples of transgressing the tradition of the elders *by not washing hands before meals. Unable to dismiss the miracles done by Jesus, the leaders had to resort to excessive fault-finding by looking for a pretext to blame him, so they accused him of breaking a superfluous and useless human custom (Chromatius). Jesus did not oppose ritual cleanliness, but emphasized that it is cleanliness of heart that matters for God, encouraging others "to present to God a soul that is pure," washed "with the virtues as well as water" (Chrysostom).*

Jesus confronts the Pharisees and scribes with the argument that it was they who transgressed God's law by substituting for it traditions of men. In order to bypass God's command to honor parents (Exod 20:12), they invented a practice of "Corban": dedicating an item to God that would be exempt from giving it to the needy (vv. 3–6), including one's own parents. By keeping the gift to God for oneself, one sinned against one's own parents, writes Cyril. This is why Jesus calls them "hypocrites" and convicts them of making human inventions equal to divine teaching (Isa 29:13), thus rendering their worship void.

As Jesus continues to teach the crowds, he explains to them (vv. 10–11), as well as to Peter (vv. 15–20), that food cannot defile a person by merely traveling through the digestive system. Food or unwashed hands have nothing to do with the cleanness of one's heart. Chromatius notes that food, created and blessed by God for human needs, cannot defile. Rather, we are defiled by the depraved thoughts of the spirit that go forth from the heart and have their origin in the devil: evil thoughts, murder, adultery, fornication, theft, false witness, slander.

After the disciples told Jesus that the religious leaders were offended by his words, he said their teaching did not come from God. Origen observed that they "did not receive the true vine that was cultivated by the Father, Jesus Christ" (cf. John 15:1). Clement warns, we need guides who cannot stumble or stray, the Lord, the Word of God who is keen-sighted and scans the recesses of the heart, leading us on the short and straight path to immortality.

Jesus and the disciples withdrew to Tyre and Sidon, seaports of Phoenicia, populated by a Gentile people, the Canaanites. A Canaanite woman approached Jesus, asking him to heal her daughter possessed by demons. She addressed Jesus as Lord and the Son of David, acknowledging that he was the Messiah promised by the law (v. 22). At first, Jesus did not answer her. She continued begging him, and the disciples asked Jesus to send her away. Jesus reminded them that he was sent only to the lost sheep of the house of Israel. *The woman, however, continues pleading to him, but Jesus said that it was not fair to give to dogs the bread that belongs to children. She replied that* even the dogs eat the crumbs that fall from their masters' table *(vv. 26–27). Jesus saw her faith and healed her daughter.*

Hilary comments that the woman from the pagan region figuratively represented the Church made up of proselytes or the Gentiles who had transferred their identity to the Israelites and were under the dominion of the law. The Lord's silence, Hilary explains, "was a matter of timing, not a conflict of his will." According to Augustine, the Lord replied to the Gentile woman after a moment of silence, so the gospel will be eventually preached to the Gentiles, but not until the Lord's passion and resurrection and the hundred and twenty lost sheep of Israel would believe and receive the Holy Spirit at Pentecost (cf. Acts 1:15; 2:1–4).

There is also praise for the woman's perseverance in prayer, which inspires us to follow her example. In the words of Chrysostom, she "lost all shame, noble shamelessness," and, instead of being discouraged by the Lord's silence, she put forward her "very shamelessness" in supplication. Her persistence made her worthy of receiving the gift that the Lord intended to give her (Augustine).

Next, Jesus journeyed to the hills near the Sea of Galilee (v. 29). A crowd, most likely Gentiles, approached him because he was still in non-Jewish territory (cf. Mark 7:31–37). After Jesus healed their sick, they glorified the God of Israel *(Hilary).*

Feeling compassion for the crowd, Jesus commanded the disciples to feed them (v. 32). Hilary explains the differences between the feeding of this Gentile crowd and the feeding of five thousand Jews (Matt 14:13–21). Jesus feeds the pagans with seven loaves of bread, which stand for the sevenfold gift of the Spirit (cf. Isa 11:2) by whose grace the pagans are saved. An indefinite number of fish signifies diversity of grace and different spiritual gifts in reward for the pagans' faith.

Matthew 15:1–9

**1Then Pharisees and scribes came to Jesus from Jerusalem and said, 2"Why do your
disciples transgress the tradition of the elders? For they do not wash their hands when
they eat." 3He answered them, "And why do you transgress the commandment of God
for the sake of your tradition? 4For God commanded, 'Honor your father and your
mother,' and, 'He who speaks evil of father or mother, let him surely die.' 5But you say,
'If any one tells his father or his mother, What you would have gained from me is given
to God, he need not honor his father.' 6So, for the sake of your tradition, you have made
void the word of God. 7You hypocrites! Well did Isaiah prophesy of you, when he said:**

> **8"This people honors me with their lips,**
> **but their heart is far from me;**
> **9in vain do they worship me,**
> **teaching as doctrines the precepts of men.'"**

(1) John Chrysostom

What does it mean, **the scribes and Pharisees, which were of Jerusalem**? They had been scattered everywhere in tribes and divided into twelve parts. However, those in charge of the metropolis, that is, Jerusalem, were worse than the rest, enjoying greater honor but filled with much pride.

Notice how even the question convicts them! For they are not asking, "Why are the disciples transgressing the law of Moses?" but, rather, **the tradition of the elders**. These words reveal that the priests were introducing many innovations, although Moses, with fearful words and threats, prohibited them from either adding to or taking away from the law. In fact, he says, *You shall not add to the word that I command you this day, and you shall not take away from it* (Deut 4:2).

Nonetheless, they had invented new commandments like this one, which prohibited eating with unwashed hands, and required washing of cups and kettles, as well as washing themselves. When the time was finally right to have the people released from religious observances of the past (cf. Rom 13:8–11), the religious leaders tied them up with many more observances, fearing that their authority might be taken away from them. By becoming themselves lawgivers, they wanted to be more awe-inspiring. However, this lawlessness went so far that now *their* commandments were kept, while God's commandments were transgressed. In addition, they became so powerful that this issue finally became the basis for an accusation. For this very reason then the charge against them was twofold: first, for inventing new commandments, and second, for vindicating themselves in this way, having no regard for God.

Without mentioning other commandments—as this one, about cups and kettles, for indeed, it was ridiculous—they publicly express what seemed to them most worthy of attention. In my opinion, they wanted to provoke the Lord to anger. For this reason, they mentioned the elders, so that, by disregarding them, the Lord would give them a pretext for blaming him in turn.

But first the matter deserves a closer examination, such as why the disciples were eating with unwashed hands. Why, in fact, were they eating in this manner? They didn't do this on purpose; rather, they already looked with disdain upon superfluous things and devoted themselves to the necessities of life. They didn't consider it a law to be either washed or unwashed but acted randomly in both ways. How could those who didn't even think about necessary nourishment consider such things worthy of concern? On many occasions when it unintentionally happened that the disciples ate with unwashed hands—as, for instance, when they ate in the wilderness, or plucked ears of corn—there were those who would present an accusation on this very matter, since they always focused upon the superfluous while neglecting the important.

Why do you also transgress the commandment of God for the sake of your tradition? He did not say, "the tradition of the elders," but **your tradition**. Neither did he say, "the elders say," but **you say**, so as to make his words less offensive. When the scribes and the Pharisees wanted to present the disciples as transgressors of the law, the Lord shows that the officials themselves are doing this and that the disciples have been set free from blame. For, certainly, the law imposed by men is no law (on which account he calls it a "tradition"), especially a law imposed by unlawful men.

So then, after the Lord demonstrated that those trampling the law under foot had no right to blame others for transgressing commandments of some elders, he also proves this truth using the words of the prophet. After forcefully convicting them, he proceeds (as he often does) by quoting Scripture, proving in this way that he himself is in agreement with God. What does the prophet say? *This people honor me with their lips, but their heart is far from me. But in vain do they worship me, teaching the commandments of men as doctrines* (Isa 29:13).

Do you see that the prophecy predicting their wickedness from long ago sounds in complete harmony with Christ's words? Indeed, Isaiah pronounced from the beginning the very thing of which Christ accused them now, namely, that they despise God. Truly he says, *But in vain do they worship me*, but reckon highly their own commandments. Indeed, they are *teaching the doctrines of men as commandments*. Surely, then, it is reasonable if the disciples do not observe them.

(2) Cyril of Alexandria

Some of the Jews were coming forward and seeking to devote their lives to God as a symbolic gesture with respect to the law by promising valuables from their own belongings to the priests and to the others who serve God at the altar . . . and when the Pharisees and scribes—these lovers of money—stressed the necessity of maintaining this practice (15:6), they were bringing shame to the parents.[1] While it was undoubtedly true that they were hardly able to provide the necessities of life for themselves and their parents as well, they had the audacity to persuade the people that they should be guided, not by the proper use of money, but by God.

And yet if they complied with the custom of helping their parents, the Pharisees taught them to say to the father or the mother that this gift, which you received from me—or rather, which you took from me—was depriving the votive offering meant for the temple and thus violating holy possessions. For I have dedicated and promised myself as a gift to God. And the parents feared reprisal for robbing the temple and were afraid of the laws against such things. The result was that the parents expressed their devoutness to God as a valid excuse for them to become hungry; and earnestly maintained, by shouting perhaps, how the divine commandment treated them unjustly . . . Quite rightly the Lord said, **You invalidated the commandment of God for the sake of your tradition.** It was not necessary to honor one's parents by destroying devoutness to God for the sake of the law concerning them. We need not neglect the things owed to God because of human commitments, nor should we neglect the things of family because of God. Instead, we demonstrate to the ruler of all things that which is chosen from love.

Though God commands us to honor the parents, there is always a risk that the greedy will command their children not to honor the parents, just in case the children out of love for honor would want to do this. Now if your parents ask you for something, say to them, "Whatever you take from me, this is robbing from God, for I promised to give it for an offering." Of course it is necessary that God be honored before the parents, but it is necessary

1. By offering to the temple the monetary support that normally went to support the parents.

to demand that the honor for parents be observed. Whenever it seems to be an excuse to offer a gift to God they shouldn't sin against their own parents.

Matthew 15:10–20

**[10]And he called the people to him and said to them, "Hear and understand: [11]not what
goes into the mouth defiles a man, but what comes out of the mouth, this defiles a
man." [12]Then the disciples came and said to him, "Do you know that the Pharisees were
offended when they heard this saying?" [13]He answered, "Every plant which my heav-
enly Father has not planted will be rooted up. [14]Let them alone; they are blind guides.
And if a blind man leads a blind man, both will fall into a pit." [15]But Peter said to him,
"Explain the parable to us." [16]And he said, "Are you also still without understanding?
[17]Do you not see that whatever goes into the mouth passes into the stomach, and so
passes on? [18]But what comes out of the mouth proceeds from the heart, and this defiles
a man. [19]For out of the heart come evil thoughts, murder, adultery, fornication, theft,
false witness, slander. [20]These are what defile a man; but to eat with unwashed hands
does not defile a man."**

(3) Clement of Alexandria

It is our duty to love in return the one who lovingly instructs us in virtuous life, living in accordance with the ordinances of his will. We should accomplish this not only by fulfilling the things he commands, or by being on guard against the things he forbids. We should also demonstrate examples of avoiding certain actions, as well as of performing the actions that in the best way imitate the works of the instructor, because they are after his likeness. This should be done in order that the words "*in the image and after the likeness*" (Gen 1:26) could be truly fulfilled.

When we roam through life, as if in a thick darkness, we stand in need of an infallible and a strict guide. But, according to the words of Scripture, the best guide is not some blind person, leading the blind into a pit, but the Word, who is sharp-sighted, and who perceives clearly the depth of the heart. . . .

Therefore, let us love these commandments through the Lord's works. Indeed, even the Word, who has visibly become flesh, himself exemplifies the same goodness both in teaching and in practice. What is more, by assuming the Word as our law, we will discover that his commandments and warnings are the shortest and the swiftest roads to eternity. Truly, these commandments are persuasive, not fearful.

(4) Origen

In many instances, one must recognize the Jews' astonishment at the words of the Savior because they were spoken with authority, so it is also the case with the words in this passage—**After summoning the crowd, Jesus said to them, Hear and understand**, and so forth. He said this because the Pharisees, stumbling over this saying and due to their evil beliefs and worthless interpretation of the law, were not the plant of his Father in heaven that was being rightly uprooted (15:13). They were uprooted because they did not receive the true vine that was cultivated by the Father, Jesus Christ. To be sure, how could those who stumbled over the words of Jesus be the Father's plant, when those words drive people away from the precept, *do not touch, do not taste, and do not handle anything that was to be completely consumed when used, in keeping with the commandments and teaching of people* (Col 2:21–22), and lead the one who hears them with understanding to inquire concerning these things, *the things above* and *not the things of the earth* (Col 3:2), as the Jews do? Because the Pharisees were not the plant of the Father in heaven, on account of their evil beliefs, Jesus speaks to the disciples about the incorrigible ones among them, **Leave them alone**. Jesus said, **Leave them alone** because, being blind, they needed to become aware of their blindness and to seek guides. They profess to guide blind people, not thinking that they would fall into a pit, although they themselves are unaware of their own blindness. Concerning this situation, it is written in the Psalms, *he prepared a pit and he dug it, and he will fall into the hole that he made* (Ps 7:15). It is therefore written elsewhere, **when he saw the crowds, he went up to the mountain. And, after he sat down, his disciples came to him** (5:1). But here, he motions to the crowd, directing and leading it away from a literal interpretation of questions concerning the law, when first he said to them, **Hear and understand**. They did not yet understand the things they heard, and he spoke the rest to them in parables, **What enters into the mouth does not defile a person, but what comes out of the mouth**.

After these things, it is worthwhile to look at the saying that has been distorted by those who claim that the God of the law and the God of the gospel of Jesus Christ are not the same. They say that the heavenly Father of Jesus Christ is not the *vinedresser* (John 15:1) of those who think they worship God according to the law of Moses. Jesus himself said that the Pharisees, who worshiped the God who created the world and the law, were a plant that his heavenly Father did not plant and, therefore, were being uprooted (15:13). But, someone might also say that even if it were the Father of Jesus who brought and planted the people who came out from Egypt *to the mountain of his inheritance, to his own prepared dwelling place* (Exod 15:17), Jesus still would have said regarding the Pharisees, **Every plant my heavenly Father did not plant will be uprooted.** To these things, however, we say that all those who were not the plant of the Father in heaven, because of their evil interpretation of the things in the law, have been blinded in their minds by the one who was made a god by the children of this age, also called by Paul *the god of this age* (2 Cor 4:4). As a result, the blind do not believe the truth but find pleasure in unrighteousness.

(5) John Chrysostom

Let us learn what it is that defiles a person; let us learn and avoid it. Even in church we see such a practice existing among the general run of people, anxious to enter with clean clothes and hands washed, but not concerned to present to God a soul that is pure. I mention this, not to discourage you from washing your hands or mouth, but because I want you to wash in the proper way, not only with water, but with the virtues as well as water.

The mouth's defilement, you see, is slander, blasphemy, abuse, angry words, profanity, mockery, ribaldry. If your conscience says you commit none of this nor incur this defilement, then draw near with confidence. But if you have incurred such blemishes countless times, why waste time washing your tongue with water while carrying around that grime and dismal stain? Tell me now: if you had mud and dung on your hands, would you try to pray? Certainly not. And yet there is really no harm in it, whereas the other kind of grime brings ruin. So why are some pious in matters of no importance, yet indifferent to what is forbidden?

So what about it? Aren't you going to pray? To be sure, at all times, but not if you're defiled and carry this stain. So what if you're caught off guard? Clean yourself up. How? Weep and groan, give alms, make it up to the person you've insulted, be reconciled in this way, wipe your tongue clean so as not to provoke God further. After all, if someone with hands soiled with dung grasped your feet in supplication, would you not only refuse to listen but also kick him away with your foot? So how is it you approach God in this condition?

If you are going to make accusations, make them against yourself. If you're going to grind and sharpen your tongue, let it be against your own sins. Don't talk about what evils someone else has done to you, but what you have done to yourself. No one is really able to injure you, unless you first injure yourself.

In the case of acquiring property, let us see the truth about ourselves. For a sword is to a madman, much the same way wealth is to a covetous man—in fact, it is worse. At least once the madman has taken the sword and thrust it through himself, he is delivered from his madness and free from all abuse. But the lover of money receives ten thousand wounds every day worse than the madman. Nor can he deliver himself from his madness, aggravating it more and more, for the more wounds he receives, the more does he make allowance for more blows.

No one is more foolish than the slave of wealth. He thinks he conquers everyone else when he is one who is conquered. He thinks he is master, when he is a slave, and putting these chains on himself, he rejoices; making the wild beast fiercer, he is pleased; and becoming a captive, he prides himself and leaps for joy. Upon seeing a rabid dog attacking his soul, he ought to chain it and weaken it by hunger, when in fact, he provides it with lots of food, that it may leap upon him more fiercely and be worse than before.

Reflecting on all these things, let us loose our chains, let us slay the monster, let us drive away the disease, let us cast out this madness, that we may enjoy peace and purity of health, having sailed into a calm harbor with great pleasure. Let us attain the eternal blessings, which we may all attain, by the grace and love toward man of our Lord Jesus Christ, to whom be glory and might, now and always, and world without end. Amen.

Matthew 15:21–28

21 And Jesus went away from there and withdrew to the district of Tyre and Sidon.
22 And behold, a Canaanite woman from that region came out and cried, "Have mercy

on me, O Lord, Son of David; my daughter is severely possessed by a demon." [23]But he did not answer her a word. And his disciples came and begged him, saying, "Send her away, for she is crying after us." [24]He answered, "I was sent only to the lost sheep of the house of Israel." [25]But she came and knelt before him, saying, "Lord, help me." [26]And he answered, "It is not fair to take the children's bread and throw it to the dogs." [27]She said, "Yes, Lord, yet even the dogs eat the crumbs that fall from their masters' table." [28]Then Jesus answered her, "O woman, great is your faith! Be it done for you as you desire." And her daughter was healed instantly.

(6) Origen

He withdrew from Gennesaret, perhaps because the Pharisees ran into a stumbling block when they heard that **It is not what enters in, but what comes out defiles a person**. It seems likely that he departed because they were suspected of plotting against him, as it says, **And when he heard that John was handed over, he withdrew into Galilee** (4:12). Perhaps it is also for this reason that, when he records the events in that place, Mark says, *He rose and went to the regions of Tyre. And, when he entered into the house, he did not want anyone to know about it* (Mark 7:24). Moreover, it seems that he avoided the Pharisees, who were caused to stumble by his teaching, in order to wait for a more fitting and rightly appointed time for his suffering.

He did not come into Tyre and Sidon, but to the regions of Tyre and Sidon, so that some from the Gentiles now believe. Jesus's manner of coming was such that if he had visited all Tyre and Sidon, no unbelieving person would be left in it. But, according to Mark, *Jesus rose and came to the regions of Tyre* (Mark 7:24), the very regions that cause the Gentiles distress, so that those who believe from those regions might also be able to be saved if they would come out from those regions. For, pay close attention to the phrase, **And behold, a Canaanite woman came out from those regions and cried out, saying, "Have mercy on me, Lord, Son of David. My daughter is terribly demon-possessed."** I think that if she had not abandoned those regions, she would have been unable to cry out to Jesus with such great faith (as has been testified). Further, I think that it is according to one's measure of faith that a person is able to come out from those Gentile regions, which, *when the Most High divided the nations, he established according to the number of the children of Israel* (Deut 32:8) and hindered from growing any further.

Here, certain regions are said to belong to Tyre and Sidon. In Exodus, however, they are called the "regions of Pharaoh" (Exod 8:2), where the plagues against the Egyptians took place. Each of us must consider, when he sins, that he is in the regions of Tyre and Sidon, or of Pharaoh and Egypt, or of any of those regions outside the distributed inheritance of God. But, when that person crosses over from malice to virtue, he departs from those evil regions and comes to the regions of God's portion. There is a difference between these regions, and it will be clear to those who are able to affirm the details of the division and inheritance of Israel as an analog with the spiritual law. Pay close attention to the "meeting" between Jesus and the Canaanite woman. Jesus came to the regions of Tyre and Sidon, but she came out from those regions and cried out, **Have mercy on me, Lord, Son of David**.

Gather together from the Gospels some who call him "Son of David," like the Canaanite woman and the blind ones in Jericho (20:30), and some who call him "Son of God," both lacking and including the addition of "truly," like the demon-possessed who said, **What do we have to do with you, Son of God?** (8:29) and those who were worshiping him in the boat, saying, **Truly you are the Son of God** (14:33), respectively. For I think the gathering of these [texts] will help you see the different kinds of people who come to him. Some come to him as to the one who came *from the seed of David according to the flesh* (Rom 1:3), but others come to him as to the one who was *declared to be the Son of God with power according to the spirit of holiness* (Rom 1:4). Of these latter ones, some add "truly," and some do not. Then, notice how the Canaanite woman does not entreat Jesus about a son (which she does not appear to have had to begin with), but concerning a daughter who was terribly demon-possessed. Another mother receives back alive a son that was being carried out dead (Luke 7:12–15). Again, the ruler of the synagogue prays for a twelve-year-old daughter as if she had died (9:18, 23–26), and a royal official prays for a son because he was still sick and about to die (John 4:46–54).

(7) Hilary of Poitiers

Different types of healing produce different effects depending on the situation, but the action and word of healing are similar to what happened earlier. The Lord refuted the unbelief of the Pharisees, reproaching their blind guidance and their superstitious human traditions. Then he came to the regions of Tyre and Sidon, where a Canaanite woman from that place shouted out and begged help for her daughter, while confessing the Lord as the Son of David. The Lord said nothing, but the disciples implored him to do something for her. He responded that he was sent to the lost sheep of the house of Israel. Prostrating herself, she entreated his help, yet the Lord said it is not right to throw the children's bread to dogs. She replied in turn that it is customary for little dogs to eat the crumbs that fall from their master's table. At that point the Lord highly praised her faith, and in that hour the health of the little girl was restored.

In order to follow the underlying principle in these events, we must consider the force of the words of the Canaanite woman. It is certainly true that proselytes belong to the people of Israel. There is a certain confidence that the number of proselytes has existed and remains within the people of Israel; they have passed from paganism to the works of the law. Once proselytes left their former way of life, they were incorporated—like those in a household—in an alien religion and placed under the dominion of law. The Canaanites had lived on the land that is now Judea (Pss 105:11; 135:11–12). They were either absorbed by war, or dispersed throughout local regions, or subjected to slavery as a conquered people (cf. Deut 7:1; Gen 10:18; and Josh 17:13). The result is that they bear only their name, possessing no ancestral land. This people, now mixed with Jews, was originally pagan. Because some of those among the crowd who believed were undoubtedly proselytes, this Canaanite woman should rightly be considered a model of the proselytes, because she left her territory, that is, as one who transferred her identity from the pagans to another people. She who pleads for her daughter is evidently pleading for the pagan peoples. Since she learned of the Lord through the law, she called him the Son of David. For it is written in the law that a sprout comes *from the root of Jesse and that the Son of David* is King of an eternal and heavenly kingdom (Isa 11:1; Jer 23:5).

The one who confessed Christ as Lord and Son of David is not herself in need of healing but pleads on behalf of her daughter, that is, for the people of the pagans who have been weighed down by the domination of unclean spirits. The Lord says nothing, preserving the privileges of salvation for Israel by his silence. And the disciples, feeling pity for her, join in the supplication.

He who realized the mystery of the Father's will (cf. Eph 1:9) responds that he has been sent to the lost sheep of Israel, making it absolutely clear that the daughter of the Canaanite woman represents a figure of the Church. She sought what was offered to others, not because salvation should be denied to the pagans, but because the Lord had come for his own in his own land. He was waiting for the firstfruits of faith from those among whom he had been born (cf. Jer 2:3). The others would later be saved by the apostolic preaching. For this reason he said, **It is not right to take the children's bread and give it to the dogs.** Honor has been accorded to Israel, God's affection for Israel is augmented by his jealousy for it; next to Israel, the pagans received the name "dog." But the Canaanite woman, already saved by faith, and certain of the deeper mysteries of faith, responds by saying that little dogs feed on the crumbs fallen from the table.

So we understand that the Lord's silence was a matter of timing, not a conflict of his will. He said, **O woman, your faith is great**, that is to say, she who was already certain of her own salvation was confident that the time was at hand when the pagans will be freed, as her daughter had been, from all domination of unclean spirits.

(8) John Chrysostom

But Christ said, **I was sent only to the lost sheep of the house of Israel.** What did the woman do when she heard this? Did she fall silent and take her leave or quit entreating the Lord? Not at all, rather, she kept at it. That is not the way with us, however. When we don't get our way, we give up, though we should be all the more insistent. Admittedly, who would not have been discouraged by this reply? While the Lord's silence was enough to drive her to hopelessness, his reply must have confirmed that even more.

When she saw that her supporters had no success and was told that this effort was futile, she could have resigned herself to helplessness. But the woman did not give up. On seeing her advocates defeated, she lost all shame, noble shamelessness. Before this episode, she did not presume to stand out in a crowd, and although you would expect her to go away disappointed, she draws closer at this time and falls down with these words, **Lord, help me (she was crying out after us**, the text says). "What is this, woman, surely you don't have greater confidence than the apostles?" "No," she says, "Rather than having confidence and strength, I am full of shame, but my very shamelessness I put on display for the sake of my petition." Notice how this woman succeeded where the apostles failed and were defeated. Such a wonderful thing is perseverance in prayer.

(9) Augustine

A Canaanite woman who came from that area ventured to ask him to cure her daughter. The Lord wouldn't listen to her; he was giving the impression of ignoring her, so that her faith might show all the brighter. He concealed from her the gift, which he certainly intended to give, in order to wring from her heart the saying that would make her worthy to receive it. Even the disciples, you see, were saying to the Lord, **Send her away, she is crying after us.** But the Lord said, **It is not right to take the children's bread and toss it to the dogs.** (You can see how similar this is to that command, **Do not give what is holy to the dogs, nor toss your pearls in front of pigs.**) **I was sent only to the sheep that were lost of the house of Israel.**

The woman, you see, was a pagan. It was going to happen that the gospel would also be preached to the Gentiles; the Apostle Paul was sent to the Gentiles, he above all was sent to them. But it was after the Lord's passion and resurrection that the preaching of the gospel among the Gentiles was to be undertaken.

The Lord, however, had come in his own personal presence to those sheep that were lost of the house of Israel, because there were many from there too who believed. Of that number, after all, were the apostles; of that number the one hundred and twenty on whom the Holy Spirit came on the day of Pentecost, as the Lord had promised when he said in the Gospel, *I will send you the Spirit of truth* (John 15:26; cf. Acts 1:15; 2:1–4). And everything he promised about the Spirit, he carried out after his passion and ascension on the day of Pentecost. There were a hundred and twenty disciples there on whom the Holy Spirit came, and they were filled with it, and they were of course from among the Jews.

What I am trying to explain is how the sheep that were lost of the house of Israel are among the chosen, the elect. The Apostle Paul also says that the risen Lord was seen by more than five hundred brethren (1 Cor 15:6); they too were of that number. Again, when the Lord was being preached after his ascension, there were many thousands of Jews who believed. The very people who crucified the Lord were made a present of the blood of the Lord. In their rage they shed their own price; they were bought by the very blood they shed (Acts 2:36–41; 4:4; 6:14–15). His words as he hung on the cross were not ineffective: *Father, forgive them, because they do not know what they are doing* (Luke 23:34); and that's why they first shed their price, and afterward drank it.

You know from the Gospel, my dear brothers and sisters, how the Canaanite woman gained by her persistence what she couldn't get by just asking for it one time; and how the Lord, by putting her off, was toning up her desire, not refusing her a favor. You see, he knew what height of perfection her insistent demand would bring to her, because he was himself training her precisely for that. He started by calling her a dog; afterward, **woman, great is your faith**. Upon receiving her request, she departed joyfully. But first she was changed, and only then made joyful. Changed how? From a dog into a woman, so to speak. And into what sort of woman? One whose faith was great. She certainly pushed hard; see what progress she made in a single moment! That's why the Lord put her off; the same Lord who also told us *to pray always, and not lose* heart (Luke 18:1).

This is a statement of the Lord's, urging us to pray. Every day people pray, religious people never miss the times of prayer. As the Apostle too says, *Always rejoicing, praying without ceasing* (1 Thess 5:16–17). That's the same as, *One ought always to pray, and not lose heart.* In another place, the Lord himself says, **Ask, and you will be given; seek, and you will find, knock and it shall be opened to you** (7:7). That's what this Canaanite woman did; she asked, she sought, she knocked, she received.

Matthew 15:29–31

[29]And Jesus went on from there and passed along the Sea of Galilee. And he went up on the mountain, and sat down there. [30]And great crowds came to him, bringing with them the lame, the maimed, the blind, the dumb, and many others, and they put them at his feet, and he healed them, [31]so that the throng wondered, when they saw the dumb speaking, the maimed whole, the lame walking, and the blind seeing; and they glorified the God of Israel.

(10) Origen

And when Jesus crossed over from the regions of Tyre and Sidon (which is clear from what has been said previously), **he came to the Sea of Galilee** (which is usually called Lake Gennesaret), **and he again went up to the mountain and sat down after he ascended.**

It is feasible to say that not only those who are healthy go up to this mountain where Jesus sits. Rather, those who were suffering from various afflictions also went along with those who were healthy. Perhaps this mountain upon which Jesus ascends and sits is more commonly called "the Church," which has been established over the rest of the earth and everyone in it by the word of God. It is not only the disciples who go to the mountain after leaving the crowds behind (as in the Beatitudes, 5:1). Indeed, many crowds who are not categorized as deaf or in poor health also go there, though they include some who are in fact deaf and undergoing suffering. We can see, along with the crowds who come to the mountain where the Son of God sits, some who have become deaf to the promises, others who are blind in soul and who do not see the true light, still others who are crippled and unable to walk reasonably, and yet others who are deformed and unable to work reasonably.

Those who have suffered such things in their soul and who ascend with the crowds to the mountain to be with Jesus are not healed by him as long as they remain distant from his feet. But as soon as those who have suffered such things are thrown by the crowds at his feet or at the extremities of the body of Christ, although not being deserving of these things as far as it depends on themselves, then they are healed by him (15:30).

(11) John Chrysostom

In this instance, the Lord goes away and sits awaiting the diseased; the lame are brought up to the mountain. No longer do they touch so much as his garment, but advance to his feet. By this they showed a twofold faith; first by going up into the mountain though lame, then by wanting nothing else but to be cast at his feet only.

It must have been marvelous and strange to see them that were carried now walking, the blind not needing anyone to lead them by the hand. Both the multitude of the healed and the facility of their cure amazed them.

You may ask why he healed the woman's daughter after delaying for a time (vv. 22–28), yet these he raised immediately. This was not because these are better than she is, but because she is more faithful than they. Therefore, while in her case he defers and delays, to manifest her constancy; on these he grants the gift immediately, stopping the mouths of unbelievers, taking away their every argument.

Matthew 15:32–39

**32 Then Jesus called his disciples to him and said, "I have compassion on the crowd,
because they have been with me now three days, and have nothing to eat; and I am
unwilling to send them away hungry, lest they faint on the way." 33 And the disciples
said to him, "Where are we to get bread enough in the desert to feed so great a crowd?"
34 And Jesus said to them, "How many loaves have you?" They said, "Seven, and a few
small fish." 35 And commanding the crowd to sit down on the ground, 36 he took the seven
loaves and the fish, and having given thanks he broke them and gave them to the dis-
ciples, and the disciples gave them to the crowds. 37 And they all ate and were satisfied;
and they took up seven baskets full of the broken pieces left over. 38 Those who ate were
four thousand men, besides women and children. 39 And sending away the crowds, he
got into the boat and went to the region of Mag'adan.**

(12) Hilary of Poitiers

Many things here are new. The disciples had compassion on five thousand men who had fasted for a single day and wanted to send them away to their villages in order to buy food (14:15). Now they say nothing after three whole days. In the earlier account, the crowd sat on the grass (14:19), taking their place on the ground. There, five loaves are presented; here, it is seven loaves. There, it was two fish; here an indefinite number that seems to indicate a few. There, it was five thousand men; here, four thousand. There, twelve baskets are filled; here, seven baskets are filled. . . .

The pattern of the Lord's word here is that which takes place in the gift of grace. Those who come to baptism first confess that they believe in the Son of God and in his passion and resurrection, and by this sign of profession their faith is proclaimed. So that this verbal promise may follow the truth of these events, they spend the entire time of the Lord's passion in fasting, united to the Lord in a kind of fellowship of shared suffering. Either through the promise of the covenant or in the act of fasting, the whole time of the Lord's passion is passed with the Lord.

The Lord, having compassion on those who possessed this hope and fellowship, namely, the crowd, said that they had been with him for three days. Lest exhaustion should ruin their course of life in the world, that is, completing their path, he wished to feed them with his food and to undergird their strength to carry out the entire journey by power of his bread. . . .

(13) Origen

After the healing of the deaf and everyone else, Jesus takes compassion on the crowd that had already been with him for three days and did not have anything to eat. In the previous story, the disciples petition Jesus about the five thousand (14:15, 21), but here he speaks on his own concerning the four thousand. Also, the five thousand are fed when it is already late, after spending one day with him (14:15), but these four thousand, verified to have remained with him for three days, eat the loaves so that they would not pass out along the way. Again, in the earlier story, the disciples claim to have only five loaves and two fish when Jesus does not even ask (14:17), but here, when Jesus does ask, they reply regarding the seven loaves and a few small fish. There, Jesus commands the crowds to recline (14:19), not to sit, on the grass. Luke also recorded, *Make them recline* (Luke 9:14), and Mark says, *He commanded them all to recline* (Mark 6:39), but here he does not command but **announces to the crowd to sit down**. Moreover, there, the three evangelists say in the same words, **Taking the five loaves and the two fish, he looked up to heaven and blessed them** (14:19; Mark 6:41; Luke 9:16), but here, **Jesus gave thanks and broke them**, as Matthew and Mark recorded (Mark 8:6). Once more, in that earlier account, they recline on the grass (14:19), but here they sit on the ground.

You will find a different account when you look at the variation found in John, who wrote that Jesus said, *Make the men sit down* (John 6:10), and that, having given thanks, he gave of the loaves to them that were seated. However, John did not mention this miracle at all. Considering the variations within the things written about the loaves, I think they are referring to different events. Earlier they are fed on a mountain, but here in a desert place after they had been three days with Jesus, whereas in the first account they were present only for one day and fed that evening.

Matthew 16

Jesus is approached by the Pharisees and Sadducees, who ask him for a sign from heaven. He reprimands them for knowing how to predict weather yet being unable to interpret the spiritual signs of the times. *The sign of Jonah (12:38–42) had been given to them, but* an evil and adulterous generation *is able neither to discern its meaning nor to recognize the divine power in his miracles.*

When Jesus and the disciples came to Caesarea Philippi, he asked them about popular opinion concerning his identity. They answered that people thought of him as either John the Baptist or one of the prophets. When he asked them what they believed, Peter immediately replied, You are the Christ, the Son of the living God. *Jesus commended Peter with the words,* Blessed are you, Simon Bar-Jonah.

Peter's confession was an occasion to explain the relation of the divine and human nature of the incarnate Christ. Hilary notes that, in his words and works, Christ taught the disciples how he should be understood. He presented himself as the eternal Son begotten by the eternal Father, sharing the Father's divinity and eternality. He was also the one who assumed a human body in order to give it the eternal power that brought about our salvation.

Augustine observes that, together, Peter's response and Jesus's question constitute a full confession: Christ refers to himself as the Son of Man, *and Peter calls him* the Christ, the Son of the living God. *The two statements reveal the truth about Christ: "Join them both, and Christ has come in the flesh." One part without the other means not knowing Christ at all. So Leo explains that all that is God's and all that is man's are simultaneously fulfilled by his manhood and his Godhead.*

Instructing the disciples about his future Church, Jesus declared, you are Peter, and on this rock I will build my church. *Peter will also receive the keys of the kingdom of heaven and be authorized to handle earthly and heavenly matters. This led to questions among the ancients about who is the recipient of this unique authority in the Church. Is it Peter alone, all apostles, or everyone who faithfully confesses Christ? For Origen, all who, being instructed by our heavenly Father, confess the true identity of Christ are "derived from the rock." Epiphanius argues that, since Jesus addressed the question about his identity to all the disciples, Peter's response also represented them all. "Because Peter symbolically stood for the Church, what was given to him alone was given to the whole Church" (Augustine).*

From that time on, Jesus began teaching the disciples about his passion (v. 21). This is the first prediction of his death recorded by Matthew (cf. 17:22–23; 20:18–19). Peter, however, tried to persuade Jesus "to postpone his glorious redemptive passion" (Macarius). According to Philoxenus, Satan "incited [Peter] to speak a word against the whole divine plan and bring damage to the whole world." Peter's lack of knowledge is not surprising, explains Philoxenus, because neither demons nor angels knew at that time the mystery of salvation that the Son of God came to fulfill. Jesus recognized and rejected the instigator; it was Satan rather than Peter, calling him a stumbling block[1] *(Hilary). Leo comments on Peter's limited perception of Christ: carried away by a realization of Christ's divinity, he failed to perceive Christ's human nature that would be glorified by his passion. Chrysostom warns, instead of repeating the error of "the chief apostle" and resisting the divine plan by denying "the mystery of the cross," "let no one be ashamed . . . of the royal symbols of our salvation and the summit of good things by which we live and by which we have our being."*

Once he has announced his death, Jesus called the disciples to follow him. He explained that true discipleship involves denying oneself (v. 24) and a readiness to lose one's life (v. 25). Irenaeus notes that Jesus could openly make these challenges to the disciples because he himself was about to undergo a true suffering in a body, not in appearance. Hilary explains that following Christ by taking up one's cross means accompanying him "if not in the circumstances of his passion, then in our will."

Commenting on the paradoxical requirement to lose one's life in order to find it, Hilary explains that wealth and power are worthless for the one whose life has been lost. We must deny earthly riches and "follow Christ by our contempt of everything," and "to gain eternal spiritual benefits entails necessarily the loss of earthly ones." Chrysostom teaches that any lost material possession can be replaced by a similar item, but the loss of the soul is irreplaceable and irreversible, even if the entire world is proposed in exchange. For Leo, denying oneself involves considers the loss of temporal things as a mere trifle in the hope of things eternal.

Matthew 16:1–4

1 And the Pharisees and Sad'ducees came, and to test him they asked him to show them
a sign from heaven. 2 He answered them, "When it is evening, you say, 'It will be fair
weather; for the sky is red.' 3 And in the morning, 'It will be stormy today, for the sky is
red and threatening.' You know how to interpret the appearance of the sky, but you cannot interpret the signs of the times. 4 An evil and adulterous generation seeks for a sign,
but no sign shall be given to it except the sign of Jonah." So he left them and departed.

(1) Origen

We have come to this point in our account where the Pharisees and Sadducees, although they disagreed on matters concerning the resurrection, made an agreement, so to speak, and together approached Jesus in order to test him by showing them a

1. Also rendered "hindrance" or "offense."

sign from heaven. The Pharisees and Sadducees were not satisfied with the miracles he had done consisting of healing of every illness and malady among the people or with his other marvelous acts. Since our Savior had accomplished all these, which were known to many people, they also wanted him to demonstrate a sign from heaven. I suppose they suspected that the signs done on earth might not have come from God. Indeed, they did not hesitate from saying that Jesus *casts out demons by Beelzebub, the ruler of the demons* (Luke 11:15; cf. 12:24). . . . However, they were mistaken concerning both signs on the earth and signs from heaven, because they were neither "approved money-changers"[2] nor did they know how to discern what spirits were sent by God or had revolted against him.

They should have known that many of the miracles leveled against Egypt in Moses's time, though not from heaven, were clearly from God (Exod 7–12). They also should have known that the "fire from heaven" that fell on Job's sheep was not from God (Job 1:16). That fire belonged to the one to whom also belonged those who captured and made three groups of horsemen against Job's cattle. But, just as signs could be demonstrated both from the earth and from heaven (true signs coming from God, but false signs coming *with all power and signs and false wonders* [2 Thess 2:9] from the evil one), I think in Isaiah it is said to Ahaz, *Request for yourself a sign from the Lord your God either in the depths or in the heights* (Isa 7:11). Unless there were some signs in the depths and some in the heights that did not come from the Lord God, he would not have said, *Request for yourself a sign from the Lord your God either in the depths or in the heights.* I well know that such an interpretation of the phrase, *Request for yourself a sign from the Lord your God*, will seem forced to some. So pay attention to what was said by the Apostle about the man of sin, the son of destruction; he will appear *to those who are perishing, with all power and signs and false wonders and every deceit of injustice* (2 Thess 2:9–10), mimicking all of the true wonders. Just as the Egyptian enchanters and magicians mimicked certain powers and signs and genuine wonders by doing false wonders so that genuine wonders would not be believed. Even though they were [even] of lower rank than the man of sin and the son of destruction, I suppose that the man of sin will mimic the signs and powers in the same way.

Perhaps the Pharisees (and I am suggesting the Sadducees as well), being suspicious of these things because of the prophecies about him, asked Jesus to demonstrate a sign from heaven in order to test him. If we do not say they were suspicious of this, then what will we say regarding their reaction with the miraculous things being done by Jesus when they remained stubborn and unashamed? If anyone thinks that we have provided an opportunity for defense to the Pharisees and Sadducees, either in the instance where they say, "In Beelzebub demons are cast out by Jesus" (12:24, 27), or where, along with testing Jesus, they asked him about a sign from heaven, let such a person know that we plausibly claimed that they were dragged away so that they did not believe in Jesus's extraordinary works. But this does not mean that they are deserving of forgiveness, since they did not look into the words of the prophets that were fulfilled in the acts of Jesus and that no such evil power could ever imitate. For example, the return of a departed soul so that the person

2. None of the four Gospels carry this phrase, and it is has been supposed that Origen is citing an agraphon of Jesus. Cf. Clement of Alexandria, *Miscellanies* 1.28, 177.2–3; and Origen, *Commentary on John* 19:7 et passim.

came out from the tomb already stinking on the fourth day (John 11:38–44) was the work of no other entity except the one who heard from the Father, *Let us make man in our image and likeness* (Gen 1:26). Moreover, to command the winds and to calm the turmoil of the sea with a word (8:26) was the act of no other person than that one "through whom all things"—even the sea itself and the winds—have come into being (John 1:3). And again, what did the teaching—harmonious with the law and prophets—that summons people to a love of the Creator, stifles the impulses, and forms ethics in keeping with piety reveal to those who were able to see? Did this teaching not reveal the fact that he who did such great things was truly the Son of God? Concerning these things, Jesus said to the disciples of John, **Go and tell John what you saw and heard; the blind receive back their sight** (11:4–5), and so forth.

Moving on, let us contemplate the way Jesus responded when he was asked regarding one sign and to demonstrate it from heaven for the questioning Pharisees and Sadducees. Jesus said, **An evil and adulterous generation seeks a sign, but a sign will not be given to it except the sign of the prophet Jonah. At this time, Jesus left them and departed** (cf. 16:4). Concerning their question, the sign of Jonah was not simply a sign, but it was also a sign from heaven. To those who were testing him and seeking a sign from heaven, in accord with his own great goodness he did nothing less than give the sign. If the Son of Man spent three days and three nights in the heart of the earth and afterward was raised from it, just as Jonah spent three days and three nights in the belly of the whale, from where else except heaven could we say the sign of the resurrection of Jesus has come? Particularly at the time of the passion, Jesus became a sign to the robber who was favorably granted access into the paradise of God, after which I think he descended into Hades to the dead as *one free among the dead* (Ps 88:5). I think when Jesus does not simply say that a sign similar to the sign of Jonah will be given, but that very sign would be given, the Savior seems to combine the sign that will come from himself with an account of the sign according to Jonah. We should heed the saying, **And a sign will not be given to it except the sign of the prophet Jonah.**

(2) Hilary of Poitiers

The Pharisees and Sadducees were arrogant because of their confidence in the law. Disdaining Jesus's powerful works of faith, they sought a sign from heaven. When they looked on the humble flesh of the body of Christ, they refused to accept his teaching. A human being could not work the great things he did.

The Lord ridicules their arrogance and foolishness in claiming to interpret omens from signs in the heavens, as, for example, a red sky in the morning or a calm and cloudy sky in the evening. Yet they are ignorant of the signs of the times, and are not able to see that his miraculous works were foretold by the law and the prophets. In whatever way the redness of the sky in the morning or the evening betokens the certainty of a storm, so the proofs of his power and works no less reveal that the time is at hand.

The Lord offers them an earthly sign derived from heaven by saying that the sign of Jonah had to be given. He does this to impress on them his bodily humility. The Lord compares himself to this sign of Jonah, who, in the preaching of repentance to Nineveh, had anticipated by an image the Lord's future passion. After Jonah was thrown from the ship because of fierce winds and swallowed by a sea monster, he had come forth alive after three days, not being crushed by the monster. Nor was he chewed as food is chewed, but contrary to the nature of the human body, he escaped, intact and uninjured, to return to the open air as a powerful sign of the Lord. The Lord shows that the sign of his power has plainly been established, as he preaches remission of sins by him through repentance. It was necessary that he be rejected by Jerusalem and the synagogue and not be dominated by unclean spirits, and be delivered over to Pilate's authority, that is, to the judgment of the world. He then had to be swallowed by death, just as the monster does in its environment. After three days, he emerges alive and incorruptible, no longer encumbered by the condition of humanity he had assumed. The qualities of his humanity, taken on at the virginal conception, were full of divine powers; he wanted these to be acknowledged and understood as his own, both by the sign of the prophet and the example of a man.

(3) Chromatius of Aquileia

Jonah was sent to preach to the Ninevites and endured the storm of the sea, while the Son of God was sent from the Father to preach the salvation of the human race and similarly endured the storm of the sea, that is, the persecution of the Church. In the former case, the wind stirs up the sea against Jonah; in the latter, the unclean spirit stirs up the people against the Lord. And then, just as that ship in which Jonah was traveling was being tossed by the threatening tempests as the storm arose, so also the groups among whom the Lord was living were being driven by the hostile unclean spirits to inflict the peril of death.

Just as Jonah, safe in that peril, was both sleeping and snoring in sleep, so also the Lord, in danger of hostile groups, rested in sleep because of the power of his divine nature and was made secure in his passion. Jonah, sent into the depths of the sea, was received by a whale, and similarly the Lord was received by death.

Matthew 16:5–12

5 When the disciples reached the other side, they had forgotten to bring any bread. 6 Jesus
said to them, "Take heed and beware of the leaven of the Pharisees and Sad'ducees."
7 And they discussed it among themselves, saying, "We brought no bread." 8 But Jesus,
aware of this, said, "O men of little faith, why do you discuss among yourselves the
fact that you have no bread? 9 Do you not yet perceive? Do you not remember the five
loaves of the five thousand, and how many baskets you gathered? 10 Or the seven loaves
of the four thousand, and how many baskets you gathered? 11 How is it that you fail to
perceive that I did not speak about bread? Beware of the leaven of the Pharisees and
Sad'ducees." 12 Then they understood that he did not tell them to beware of the leaven
of bread, but of the teaching of the Pharisees and Sad'ducees.

(4) Philoxenus of Hierapolis

Our Lord makes it clear that heretics are cunning and crafty, for he said, **Beware of false prophets, which come to you in sheep's clothing, but inwardly are ravening wolves** (7:15). It is the role of a cunning person to be one thing and appear to be another; the cunning person is the one who teaches the wolves how to display themselves in sheep's clothing. Cunning itself produces two things: it makes wickedness to grow and increase. It also schemes how to teach itself to others: when it is appropriate to hide, it hides, and when it needs to show itself, it shows itself. Wickedness is blind, but it has eyes for cunning.

In another place our Lord taught his disciples to beware of the cunning of the Pharisees and Sadducees, saying, *Beware of the leaven of the Pharisees and of the Sadducees, and of the leaven of Herod* (Mark 8:15). Here he calls cunning and wickedness by the name of *leaven*, because in another passage, when the Pharisees said to him, *Herod wants to kill you* (Luke 13:31), he refers to Herod as a fox because of his cunning: *Go and say to this fox* (Luke 13:32). Since Herod had no power to do what he wanted by legitimate authority, he therefore contrived tricky schemes so that cunning took the place of power, just like a fox. . . . Thus our Lord warned his disciples against the cunning of Herod and the wickedness of the Pharisees, who did one thing while teaching another.

(5) Origen

And when his disciples came to the other side, they realized that they had forgotten to take bread. Because the loaves they had before crossing over were no longer useful to the disciples now that they had crossed over. . . . Here the disciples of Jesus came to the other side, having crossed over from bodily things to spiritual things, and from aesthetic things to intellectual things. Perhaps this occurred to keep those who began in the spirit by crossing over to the other side from running back to the fleshly things, so that Jesus said to those on the other side, **Take heed and beware.**

There was a particular "lump" of teaching and truly ancient "leaven" that the Pharisees and Sadducees offered (16:6–12; cf. 1 Cor 5:7). This lump was not free from malice, because it was based on the bare letter. Jesus did not want his own disciples to eat from that lump any longer, because he had made for them a new and spiritual lump by offering himself, as living bread that came down from heaven and gives life to the world (John 6:33). Jesus offered the new and spiritual lump to any who abandoned the leaven of the Pharisees and Sadducees and came to him. The first step for the person who is no longer using the leaven and lump and teaching of the Pharisees and Sadducees will be to **see**, and the second will be to **beware**, so that no one ever partakes of their hopeless leaven for lack of seeing or paying attention.

Matthew 16:13–17

13 Now when Jesus came into the district of Caesare'a Philip'pi, he asked his disciples,
"Who do men say that the Son of man is?" 14 And they said, "Some say John the Baptist,
others say Eli'jah, and others Jeremiah or one of the prophets." 15 He said to them, "But
who do you say that I am?" 16 Simon Peter replied, "You are the Christ, the Son of the
living God." 17 And Jesus answered him, "Blessed are you, Simon BarJona! For flesh and
blood has not revealed this to you, but my Father who is in heaven."

(6) Origen

Jesus asks his disciples who people say that he is so that from the apostles' responses we will learn the different conceptions held about our Savior at that time among the Jews. Perhaps Jesus also asks so that his disciples might learn to be concerned at all times with what people say about them. Doing so would be beneficial for them since they would be able to remove in every way an occasion for evil if something evil was mentioned, or they would be able to increase an opportunity for good if something good was mentioned.

Given the various opinions among the Jews in their conceptions of Jesus, let us see the ways some people talk about Jesus out of certain unsound beliefs. For, some were saying that Jesus was John the Baptist, similar to Herod the Tetrarch, who said to his servants, **This is John the Baptist; he has been raised from the dead, and for this reason the powers are working within him** (14:2). But others were saying that the one called Jesus was Elijah, who either underwent a second birth, or, being alive in the flesh from that time onward, again appeared in the present. There were those who claimed that Jesus was Jeremiah; not because Jeremiah was simply a type of Christ, but because they were perhaps motivated by the things said about Christ in the beginning of Jeremiah, since these were not then fulfilled in the prophet. Instead, these things began to be fulfilled in Jesus, whom God appointed *to uproot, raze, destroy, rebuild, and replant* the nations and kingdoms (Jer 1:10), because God made him to be a prophet to the Gentiles to whom he preached the word. . . .

Then Peter, being the kind of person who was not a disciple of flesh and blood but who made room for the revelation of the Father in heaven (cf. 16:16), confessed Jesus to be the Christ. What Peter said to the Savior, namely, **You are the Christ** (although the Jews did not know that he was the Christ) was a great confession. What was greater, however, was that Peter knew him not only to be the Christ, but also **the Son of the living God**, who said through the prophets, *I live* (Jer 22:24), and, *They have abandoned me, the spring of living water* (Jer 2:13). And the one who said, *I am the life* (John 14:6) is life as it comes from the spring of life, which is the Father. Consider carefully whether, just as a stream and a river are not the same thing, so also the stream of life and life are not the same thing.

Whereas those mentioned above who declared Jesus to be John the Baptist or any of the other prophets spoke from unsound beliefs, let us also prove this by saying that if they had been near Jesus when he went to John for baptism and near John when he baptized Jesus, or if they had heard about the baptism from anyone, they would not have said that Jesus was John. Also, if they had understood the position from which Jesus said, **If you**

are willing to receive it, he is Elijah who is going to come (11:14), and if they had heard what was said as those who have ears (11:15), some would not have said that he was Elijah. In addition, if those who said that Jesus was Jeremiah would have recognized that most of the prophets adopted certain features symbolic of him, they would not have said that he was Jeremiah. In like manner, none of the others would have said that he was a certain one of the prophets.

Perhaps if we say what Simon Peter replied in the phrase, **You are the Christ, the Son of the living God** (as Peter said it—not by flesh and blood revealing it to us, but by the light from the Father in heaven shining in our heart), we ourselves can become what Peter also became, that is, blessed. The grounds for the blessing applicable to Peter are also applicable to us, because flesh and blood did not reveal to us that Jesus was the Christ, the Son of the living God. So that we might have citizenship in the heavens, the Father in heaven manifested from heaven a revelation that leads up to heaven for those who remove every veil from their heart and who take on the spirit of the wisdom and revelation of God.

(7) Hilary of Poitiers

In the course of his words and works, he gave his disciples certain knowledge of himself, and presented to his disciples a complete self-awareness, and laid down a certain pattern and rationale for how he should be understood. For this is the true and inviolable faith: that from the eternal God—who, because he has always had a Son, always has the right and title of Father; if the Son had not always been [a Son], the Father would not always have been a Father—God the Son has proceeded, to whom belongs eternity from his eternal Father. It was the will of the Father to beget the Son; the Father's power and authority was present in the one who was begotten. The Son of God, therefore, is God from God, one [God] in two, for he received deity (cf. Col 2:9), *deitas* in Latin, of his eternal parent, from whom he proceeded at his birth. He received that which he was, and is born the Word, which was always in the Father. The Son is both eternal and born because there is nothing born in him other than what is eternal.

Accordingly, the whole confession is that he had assumed a body and was made man; just as eternity received a body of our nature, so we should acknowledge that the nature of our body was able to assume the power of eternity. . . . The reason for maintaining this confession is that we may remember that he is both the Son of God and the Son of Man. The one without the other offers no hope for our salvation.

Once it was learned what others thought about him, Jesus inquired what they themselves thought concerning him. Peter responded: **You are the Christ, the Son of the living God.** Peter was aware of the implication of the question when the Lord had said: **Who do men say that I am, the Son of Man?** Of course, his bodily manifestation showed he was a Son of Man. By adding, "Who do they say I am?" Jesus indicated that it was essential to consider another element beyond the obvious fact that he was a Son of Man. What answer did he seek from those thinking about him? It is not, we may suppose, that which he confessed about himself. Rather, it was hidden from anyone who sought it so that the faith of believers was obliged to delve into what he was.

Clearly Peter's confession merits an appropriate reward because he had seen the Son of God in the man. He is blessed and exalted for having directed his view beyond human eyes, regarding not only what was from flesh and blood, but perceiving the Son of God through the revelation of the heavenly Father. And he was judged worthy to be the first one to recognize that what was in Christ was of God. O happy is the foundation of the Church on account of the announcement of his new name. Worthy is the rock upon which the Church is built, against which the laws of hell and the gates of Tartarus and all the prisons of death are broken. O blessed porter of heaven, by whose decree the keys of eternity's entrance are handed over, and whose earthly judgment with heavenly authority has already been decreed. Whatever has been bound or loosed on earth acquires the status of the very same decree in heaven.

(8) Augustine

The heretic[3] hears and proclaims the child-bearing of the Virgin Mary. Does he confess that Christ has come in the flesh? No. How can we prove it? May the Lord assist your understanding, with the greatest of ease. What are we asking? Whether he confesses that Jesus Christ has come in the flesh. How can someone confess that Jesus Christ has come in the flesh, when he denies Christ himself? Who, after all, is Christ? Let us question the blessed Peter. You heard just now, when the Gospel was read, when the Lord Jesus Christ himself had asked who people said he the Son of Man was, how the disciples answered with the opinions of others and said, **Some John the Baptist, others Elijah, others Jeremiah, or one of the prophets.** Those who confessed, or confess, such things, don't know Jesus Christ as more than a man. But if they don't know Jesus Christ as more than a man, quite simply they don't know Jesus Christ. If he's only a man, and nothing further, he isn't the real Jesus Christ. **You therefore**, he says, **who do you say that I am?** Peter answered, one for them all, because representing unity in all, **You are the Christ, the Son of the living God.**

There you have a true confession, a full confession. You must join both things together: what Christ says about himself and what Peter says about Christ. What does Christ say about himself? **Who do people say that I am, the Son of Man?** What does Peter say about Christ? **You are the Christ, the Son of the living God.** Join them both, and Christ has come in the flesh. Christ says about himself that which is the lesser part, and Peter says about Christ that which is the greater part. Lowliness replies about truth, and truth about lowliness; that is, lowliness about the truth of God, and truth about the lowliness of man. "**Who do people say that I am**, he says, **the Son of Man?** I am telling you what I have been made for your sakes; you, Peter, tell us who made you."

So anyone who confesses that Jesus Christ has come in the flesh is actually confessing that the Son of God has come in the flesh. Now let the Arian tell us whether he confesses that Christ has come in the flesh. He confesses that the Son of God has come in the flesh, then he confesses that Christ has come in the flesh. If he denies that Christ is the Son of God, then he doesn't know Christ; he's mixing him up with someone else,

3. Specifically, those called "Arians," who denied that Christ is God in the way that the Father is God.

he isn't really naming him. What, after all, is the Son of God? Just as we were inquiring what Christ is, and we heard that he is the Son of God, so let us inquire what the Son of God is. Here's the Son of God for you: *In the beginning was the Word, and the Word was with God, and the Word was God. This was in the beginning with God* (John 1:1–2). In the beginning was the Word. What do you say, Mr. Arian? *In the beginning,* as Genesis says, *God made heaven and earth* (Gen 1:1). You, though, say, "In the beginning God made the Word." You say the Word was made, you call the Word a creature. You, therefore, say, "In the beginning God made the Word." But the evangelist says, *In the beginning was the Word.* And that's why *in the beginning God made heaven and earth*; it's because the Word was. *All things were made through him* (John 1:3). You say he was made. If you say he was made, you are denying he is the Son.

We are looking for the Son by nature, not by grace; the only Son, the Only-Begotten, not an adopted son. That's the sort of Son we are looking for, such a true Son, that *while he was in the form of God*—they're the apostle's words (Phil 2:6a) . . . we are looking for that Son *who while he was in the form of God,* as the apostle says, *did not reckon it robbery to be equal to God* (Phil 2:6b). It wasn't robbery because it was his nature. If it was his nature, it wasn't an act of robbery. *He did not reckon it robbery to be equal to God.* It wasn't robbery for him, it was nature; that's what he was from eternity, that's how he was coeternal with his Begetter, that's how he was equal to the Father, that's how he was.

He emptied himself so we could confess that Jesus Christ has come in the flesh. *He emptied himself.* How? By losing what he was, or by taking on what he was not? Let the Apostle carry on, let us listen: *He emptied himself, taking the form of a servant* (Phil 2:6–7). That's how he emptied himself, taking the form of a servant, not losing the form of God. The form of a servant was added, not the form of God subtracted. That is to confess that Christ has come in the flesh. The Arian, though, doesn't confess that Christ is equal, doesn't confess that he is the Son. If he doesn't confess he is the Son, he doesn't confess Christ. If he doesn't confess Christ, how can he confess that Christ has come in the flesh?

Matthew 16:18–20

18"And I tell you, you are Peter, and on this rock I will build my church, and the powers of death shall not prevail against it. 19I will give you the keys of the kingdom of heaven, and whatever you bind on earth shall be bound in heaven, and whatever you loose on earth shall be loosed in heaven." 20Then he strictly charged the disciples to tell no one that he was the Christ.

(9) Origen

If you suppose that every individual church is built only upon that one man Peter, then what would you say about John, son of thunder (Mark 3:17), or any of the apostles? Would we really dare to say that **the gates of Hades will not prevail over** Peter, but they will prevail over the rest of the apostles and the mature [believers]? And so, does not what was previously said—that **the gates of hell will not prevail over it** as well as **upon this rock I will build my Church**—apply to all of them or any individual? Are, therefore, the keys **of the kingdom of heaven** given by Christ to Peter alone? Will none other of the blessed receive them? But if the words **I give to you the keys of the kingdom of heaven** apply generally to others, how can both everything said just before this and everything added to Peter not [apply generally]? It indeed seems that in this verse, [the words] **whatever you bind on earth will be bound in heaven** etc. have been said as if to Peter. But in John's Gospel, when the Savior gave the Holy Spirit to the disciples through his breathing, he says, *You all receive the Holy Spirit* etc. (20:22). Accordingly, many will say to the Savior, **You are the Christ, the Son of the living God**, but not all those who affirm this will say it to him: certainly none of those professing this from what **flesh and blood revealed**. But those professing from the Father, **who is in heaven**, who removes the veil laid over their hearts, [will say it], so that after this revelation those who contemplate the glory of the Lord with unveiled face in the Spirit of God might speak, saying about him, "Jesus is Lord," and to him, "**You are the Christ, the Son of the living God**."

And if someone says this to him, not because **flesh and blood reveals** [it] to him, but because **the Father who is in heaven** [does so], then he will obtain what has been said: that the letter of the Gospel speaks to Peter, but that the spirit of the Gospel instructs everyone who becomes like that Peter. For everyone who imitates Christ (cf. 1 Cor 11:1) derives from "a rock," which *spiritual rock follows* those being saved, so that they might *drink a spiritual drink* (1 Cor 10:4). But those derived from the rock are like Christ. And those "derived Christs" are reckoned *members of Christ* (1 Cor 6:15), and from Peter "rocks."[4]

But, receiving an opportunity from these derivations, you say, "The righteous are derived from the righteousness of Christ, and the wise from the wisdom of Christ." And in this way you make derivatives according to the rest of his titles for the saints, and to all such saints the utterance of the Savior might be spoken: **You are Peter** and so on until **they will not prevail over it.** But what is "**it**"? Is it the rock upon which Christ builds the Church? Or is it the Church? It is an ambiguous expression after all. Or are the Church and the rock one and the same?

But I think that this turns out to be the truth: It is neither the rock upon which Christ builds the Church, nor that **the gates of Hades will prevail over** the Church as also "the way of a serpent upon a rock" cannot be found, according to what has been written in Proverbs (Prov 30:19). But if **the gates of Hades will prevail over** someone, such a person could neither be a rock upon which Christ builds the Church, nor could it be the Church built by Christ upon a rock. For that Church is a rock inaccessible to a serpent and stronger than the **gates of Hades** contending against it, since **the gates of Hades** cannot prevail over it because of its strength. But the Church, as a building of Christ, who built it wisely as "a house upon the rock" (7:24), is invulnerable to **the gates of Hades** that prevail over every man outside the rock and the Church, but which have no power over the Church.

Then he commanded his disciples that they tell no one that he is the Christ (16:20). It had been written above that **Jesus sent these twelve, saying to them, Do not depart into**

4. The Greek word for "Peter" means "rock."

the way of the Gentiles (10:5), and whatever Jesus said to them as he sends them on their mission that had been recorded subsequently. Therefore, did he want them, who already were doing the work of apostles, to preach that **he is the Christ**? For if he was intending that, then why is it commanded expressly right here and now to the disciples to seek worthily lest they say that **he is the Christ**? Or if it was not intending that, how can anyone be saved by the mission?

Of course one could also seek out these things at this juncture of the passage: When he sent the twelve, did he not send them thinking that **he is the Christ**? If the twelve were thinking this—as Peter obviously did—then how is he now being called blessed? For the expression clearly indicates by these things that now Peter first acknowledged him as Christ, **the Son of the living God.**

Indeed, Matthew has recorded it, according to some manuscripts, **Then he commanded the disciples that they not tell he is the Christ.** But Mark says, *He strictly charged them so that they would speak about him to no one* (Mark 8:30). And Luke says, *He strictly charged them and commanded them to tell no one this thing* (Luke 9:21). What is *this thing* other than what Peter answered when he said, **You are the Christ of God**, in response to **Who do you say that I am?** To be sure, one must know that some of the manuscripts of Matthew's Gospel have **He strictly charged**. Therefore, the perplexity seems to me to be of the highest order. But let an incontrovertible solution to it be sought. Let the one who discovers it bring it forth, if there might be a more trustworthy solution than what will be laid out by us as a humble opinion.

Therefore, let us begin, if you will, by saying that *believing* Jesus to be the Christ is a lesser thing than *knowing* that which has been believed. But probably there is a difference in knowledge of Jesus as the Christ since not everyone who knows him knows him in the same way. . . . Because there is a difference in knowledge of Jesus as the Christ, among those who know him there is not an equal knowing. And the evident truth would demonstrate the fact to anyone considering it for long enough. For who would confess that Timothy, for example, although knowing Jesus to be the Christ, was illumined with knowledge about him to the same extent that the Apostle Paul was illumined? But again, who would not accept this: that even if the many should say about God, "He himself gave me a trustworthy knowledge of things that exist," despite speaking truly they will say this neither with an equal level of clear understanding and a grasp of what is known, nor accurate knowledge of such things?

And yet, not only according to difference in *knowledge per se* there is also a difference according to the *source* of the knowledge. In this way, he who has known the Son according to revelation from the Father, as we witness Peter to have known him (cf. 16:16), has the greatest blessedness. But if these things were spoken soundly by us, then you will understand whether the Twelve believed earlier, but did not know at first. Then, by believing, they were also grasping the beginnings of knowledge but knew fewer things about him. But later, they were making progress in knowing so that they could receive knowledge from the Father revealing the Son. Peter was in such a state when he was called blessed. For he is called blessed not on the condition of having said, **You are the Christ** only, but with the addition of **the Son of the living God.** Thus, recording Peter having answered saying, **You are the Christ** while not adding what remains according to Matthew, **the Son**

of the living God, Mark and Luke, have not, accordingly, written down the pronouncement of blessedness on Peter upon what was said and the blessing after the pronouncement of blessedness, **You are Peter** and the rest.

(10) Hilary of Poitiers

Clearly Peter's confession merits an appropriate reward because he had seen the Son of God in the man. He is blessed and exalted for having directed his view beyond human eyes, regarding not only that which was from flesh and blood, but perceiving the Son of God through the revelation of the Father. And he was judged worthy to be the first one to recognize that what was in Christ was of God. O happy is the foundation of the Church on account of the announcement of his new name. Worthy is the rock upon which the Church is built, against which the laws of hell[5] and the gates of Tartarus and all the prisons of death are broken. O blessed porter of heaven, by whose decree the keys of eternity's entrance are handed over, and whose earthly judgment with heavenly authority has already been decreed. Whatever has been bound or loosed on earth acquires the status of the very same decree in heaven.

(11) Leo the Great

Beloved, by this rule of faith[6] that we received in the very beginning of the creed through the authority of apostolic instruction, we confess *Jesus Christ our Lord*, whom we declare to *be the one and only Son of God the Father Almighty*, and who *was born of the Virgin Mary through the Holy Spirit*. Nor do we forsake his majesty when we believe in him *crucified* and *dead* and *raised to life on the third day*.[7] For both the humanity and the divinity perfected at the same time all things that are God's and all things that are human's, so that, while the impassible exists in the passible, his power could not be moved by his weakness, nor was his weakness able to overcome in his power.

Deservedly was Peter the blessed Apostle praised for his confession of this union, who, when the Lord was examining what the disciples understood concerning him, quickly anticipating the speech of them all said, **You are the Christ, the Son of the living God.** Surely he saw this not by the revelation of the flesh or blood, which by their opposition could have entangled his interior sight, but by the very Spirit of the Father operating in his believing heart.

You are Peter, and upon this rock I will build my Church, and the gates of hell shall not prevail against her. Therefore, the fortitude of the Christian faith, which, built upon an unbreakable rock, does not fear the gates of death, confesses the Lord Jesus Christ as both truly God and truly man, believing that he is the Son of the Virgin. He was born

5. Latin *infernas.*
6. A brief summary of the creed.
7. Italicized words indicate verbatim citations from the Roman Creed, the basis of the Apostles' Creed.

at the end of the ages (Heb 1:2), who was the Creator of his mother, the Creator of time, and the Lord of all power.

(12) Epiphanius the Latin

Jesus said to them: You, however, who do you say I am? Simon Peter answered: You are Christ, the Son of God (16:15–16). Didn't the Lord know what men said about him? His purpose in asking was to elicit the confession of the Apostle Peter and at the same time leave for us a strong example of faith to come. The Lord was asking not only Peter but also all his apostles when he put the question: **You, however, who do you say I am?** But one responded for all that Christ was the Son of God. As Christ the King, he is going to judge the whole world; as the Son of God, he himself is God; both God and man. . . .

If Christ is the Son of God, he is also God; if he is not God, he is not the Son of God. Because he himself is the Son, having received from the Father all things, like a son, let us hold him inseparably with our heart, because there is no one who escapes his hand (Tobit 13:2). The blessed Peter did not make his confession from what he saw on the outside, a man. Because he confessed on the basis of what was invisible, he merits from the Lord an invisible reward and power when the Lord says: **Blessed are you, Simon Bar-Jonah, because flesh and blood have not revealed this to you, but my Father, who is in heaven** (16:17). . . .

And you are Peter, and upon this rock I will build my Church. The rock is Christ, which is never moved nor worn away. Therefore blessed Peter received his name from Christ to indicate the firm and unshaken faith of the Church. The "gates of hell" signifies the devil, who always instigates storms and scandals and persecutions against the holy Church. Nevertheless, the faith of the apostle, which is established upon the rock of Christ, remains always unconquered and unshaken. To him the keys of the kingdom of heaven have been handed over, so that whomever he has bound on earth might be bound in heaven, and whomever he has loosed on earth might be loosed also in heaven. In light of this, most beloved, let us persevere in the confession of Peter unto the end, so that we might be loosed on earth and in heaven. For the one who has turned aside from this faith and confession binds himself on earth and in heaven. By apostolic authority, the door of heaven is shut forever to someone who has sinned by blasphemies concerning the Son of God, even if this one has received grace. It is loosed for him who, upon having received grace, keeps faith and justice and sanctity. For it profits nothing to save one's soul in this world and to lose it forever.

(13) Augustine

There are many places in Scripture where Peter can stand for or represent the Church, and above all in this particular passage, **To you will I hand over the keys of the kingdom of heaven. Whatever you bind on earth shall also be bound in heaven, and whatever you loose on earth shall also be loosed in heaven.** Did Peter receive these keys, and Paul did not? Did Peter receive them, and John and James and the other apostles did not? Or are these keys not to be found in the Church, where sins are being forgiven every day? Because Peter symbolically stood for the Church, what was given to him alone was given to the whole Church.

So Peter represented the Church; the Church is the body of Christ. Let him receive the pagans who are now made clean, their sins having been forgiven. This is why the pagan Cornelius, along with the others with him, sent for Peter (Acts 10:5). Cornelius's acts of charity had been accepted and had cleansed him in a sense; it only remained for him—like clean food—to be incorporated into the Church, that is, into the Lord's body. Peter was worried about handing the Gospel over to the pagans because of those of the circumcision who opposed the apostles handing over the Christian faith to the uncircumcised. They were saying that pagans shouldn't be admitted to share in the Gospel unless they accepted circumcision, which had been the tradition of their ancestors.

Matthew 16:21–23

21 From that time Jesus began to show his disciples that he must go to Jerusalem and suffer many things from the elders and chief priests and scribes, and be killed, and on the third day be raised. 22 And Peter took him and began to rebuke him, saying, "God forbid, Lord! This shall never happen to you." 23 But he turned and said to Peter, "Get behind me, Satan! You are a hindrance to me; for you are not on the side of God, but of men."

(14) Philoxenus of Hierapolis

Andrew said that he had found the Christ, so why did Jesus give a blessing to Simon Peter on account of his confession? Wouldn't it have been right for the Samaritan woman to have also received this blessing? Didn't Martha, who had a passionate will and heart filled with love for Jesus, deserve the blessing more than Simon? When she was asked by Jesus whether she believed that he could raise the dead, she said to him in a humble and obedient voice, *Yes, Lord, I believe that you are the Christ, the Son of God, he who is coming into the world* (John 11:27). If we observe carefully, we see that the confession of Martha is deeper and more to the point than Simon's. If the offering of the will is most honored before God, the confession of people such as these is more worthy of blessing and honor from God than was Simon. They acknowledged and recognized him as the Christ and Son of God by an act of will rather than by divine revelation as was the case with Simon.

Simon himself didn't grasp what was meant by the revelation that Christ had received from the Father, nor did the disciples recognize it, since the Father who gave it is unseen . . . and for this reason **Blessed are you** etc. was necessary. Even so, all the things that were later spoken and done by the Lord show that Simon did not understand fully what had been said. First, it is true that he was zealous and rash and restrained his Master, saying to him, **God forbid it, Lord; this shall never happen to you**, speaking of the passion. But Jesus rejected these evil words by saying to him **Get behind me, Satan!** to show that Satan had sown this word in Simon's heart. And just as Satan sowed doubt in the soul of Simon and incited him to speak a word against the whole divine plan and bring damage to the whole world, so too Simon received a revelation from the Father and proclaimed Christ as God and natural Son, not knowing fully what he was saying.

Not even the demons knew of this mystery at that time, since it was also hidden from the angels. The mystery was that they should know there is a Son to God by nature and he was going to fulfill in his Being the mystery of the new plan of salvation for men. For men know nothing of spiritual things; the knowledge of the world to come is entirely hidden from us, as the knowledge of this world is hidden from a newborn child. Let us not marvel that a revelation came to Simon and he did not sense its meaning. The truth was made manifest through the revelation that made known that Christ was not a man, but the Son of God, as the Father revealed him.

(15) Macarius of Magnesia

The blessing on Peter was an answer to his words at Caesarea Philippi: **You are the Christ, the Son of the living God.** Christ sees that he has not received this truth from **flesh and blood**, nor even from angels, but as a direct revelation from the Father himself.

For this reason, he says, "you should receive a surname worthy of this grace, and become Peter the Rock-man, showing to all the world a rock that is invincible and unshakeable. The knowledge and the reasoning you possess cannot be moved, and to this day you are a witness that the blessed being cannot be shaken."

It was likely that the evil beast of deceit (the devil), hearing these words and the witness that Peter gave to the Savior, worked cunningly in every way possible to strip Peter of his merit, to overthrow the witness of Christ by the trickery of guile, and to alter the plan that Christ would suffer. For he knew, he clearly knew, that the passion of Christ was a release from the tyranny of his wickedness, and so he was desirous of being a hindrance to the cross. Thus he prompts Peter to say: **Far be it from you, Lord, this shall not happen to you.**

Christ recognizes the real speaker and addresses the devil, and not Peter, when he says: **Get behind me, Satan**. Then he turns to Peter and reprimands him for obeying the prompting of Belial, with the words, **You are an offense to me**, etc. Peter's sudden fall from the highest to the lowest deserved such a rebuke, and at the same time it taught the disciples not to chatter idly about eternal matters. How would the others have responded, if they saw Christ on earth as Peter did, and then heard him persuading Christ to postpone his glorious redemptive passion and remain among earthly things? Peter's great faith had to be severely censured and his fall led to great grief.

(16) Hilary of Poitiers

Get behind me, Satan, you are a stumbling block to me. Just as the gift of God is to know Christ as God in the Spirit, so the work of the devil is not to recognize Christ in a man. The danger is the same whether one denies that the body is without God or that he was

God without a true body. If the eternity of the Spirit God is not incarnate in that flesh, the reason Christ is in a body he assumes from man is for man's salvation.

After Christ announced his passion, the devil seized the opportunity—until the moment when he had withdrawn from Peter—because it seemed completely unbelievable to the apostles that God should suffer in Christ. The devil grasps the occasion of human unbelief to instill in Peter the idea that Christ would not suffer. In short, Peter rejected the passion when he said, **Far be it**, a phrase that conjures up the idea of despising something detestable. But the Lord, knowing that it was inspired by the devil, said to Peter: **Get behind me**; that is, he should follow him in his passion. The Lord also turned against the one who made this suggestion when he added: **Satan, you are a stumbling block to me**. It seems wrong to think that the name of Satan and the offense of a stumbling block should be imputed to Peter after he made so many professions of God's gifts, blessing, and power. Nonetheless, because all unbelief is the work of the devil, the Lord—troubled at Peter's response—rejected the instigator of that unbelief by denouncing him by name.

(17) John Chrysostom

Let everyone ashamed of the suffering of the cross of Christ pay attention. If the chief apostle, even before he had a clear grasp of everything, was called Satan for feeling like this, what excuse would we have who resist the divine plan after the demonstration of so many proofs? When the man who was declared **blessed** for making such a wonderful confession heard this awful rebuke, consider what we would experience who denied the mystery of the cross.

Let no one be ashamed, therefore, of the royal symbols of our salvation and the summit of good things by which we live and by which we have our being (cf. Acts 17:28). Instead, let us bear the cross of Christ like a crown. It is through the cross that everything happens that affects us. If it is a question of rebirth, the cross is there; if nourishment with sacramental food, if ordination or if any other action, that symbol of victory is everywhere presented to us. That is the reason why we inscribe it with great enthusiasm on our houses, on our walls, on our windows, on our foreheads, on our minds. It is the sign of salvation, of our common freedom, and of our Lord's goodness, as *he was like a sheep led to slaughter* (Isa 53:7).

When you make that sign, therefore, consider the meaning of the cross, and quell anger and all the other passions. When you make that sign, fill your forehead with complete confidence, make your soul free. You should make its mark, not idly with your fingers, but deliberately in deep faith.

Matthew 16:24–28

24Then Jesus told his disciples, "If any man would come after me, let him deny himself and take up his cross and follow me. 25For whoever would save his life will lose it, and whoever loses his life for my sake will find it. 26For what will it profit a man, if he gains

the whole world and forfeits his life? Or what shall a man give in return for his life?
27For the Son of man is to come with his angels in the glory of his Father, and then he
will repay every man for what he has done. 28Truly, I say to you, there are some standing
here who will not taste death before they see the Son of man coming in his kingdom."

(18) Irenaeus of Lyons

And the Lord himself made it clear that he suffered. For the disciples asked him about it, **Who do people say the Son of Man is?** (16:13). And Peter answered him, **You are the Christ, the Son of the living God** (16:16). And Jesus praised him, **Flesh and blood did not reveal** this to him, **but the Father who is in heaven, he made it clear that this Son of Man is the Christ of the living God** (cf. 16:17). **From that time**, it also says, **he began to show by his teachings that it was necessary to go to Jerusalem, suffer many things from the priests, be rejected, be crucified, and rise again on the third day** (16:21). The same Christ who was recognized by Peter—the one who blessed Peter since the Father revealed to him the Son of the living God—Christ himself said he must suffer many things and be crucified.

At this point, he rebuked Peter, who thought that he was the Christ and yet recoiled from his suffering—a purely human opinion (16:22–23). Jesus said to his disciples, **If anyone wants to come after me, then he must deny himself, take up his cross, and follow me. For whoever wants to save his soul will lose it, and whoever loses it for my sake will save it** (16:24–25). For in saying these things so clearly, Christ declared himself to be the Savior of those who lost their lives and were handed over to death for confessing him.

Moreover, this same reasoning opposes those who say that he only seemed to suffer. For if he didn't really suffer, then why should we be grateful, since he suffered nothing? And when *we* truly begin to suffer, *he* will appear to be leading us astray by encouraging us to be beaten and **to turn the other cheek** (5:39), if he didn't actually suffer the same thing before us. Just as he deceived people by seeming to be what he wasn't, so he deceives us by urging us to endure what he didn't endure. It will be as if we were **above our teacher** (10:24) when we suffer and put up with those things that the teacher himself neither suffered nor put up with! But since the only true teacher is our Lord, he is truly the good Son of God, and the long-suffering Word of God the Father who became the Son of Man. For he struggled and conquered. He was a man striving for our fathers and redeeming *disobedience through obedience* (cf. Rom 5:19). By destroying sin, **he bound the strong man** (12:29), freed the weak, and gave salvation to his creatures. *He is the most faithful and merciful Lord* (cf. Ps 103:8) because he loves humankind.

(19) Hilary of Poitiers

Then Jesus said to his disciples, If anyone wants to come after me, let him deny himself. O blessed loss and happy sacrifice! The Lord wished for us to grow rich through the loss of soul and body, encouraging us to become as he is. Because he was in the form of God and humbled himself and was obedient unto death, he received the fullness of all God's power (cf. Phil 2:6–7). We must, therefore, follow him by taking up the cross and accompany him, if not in the circumstances of his passion, then in our will. For what do we gain by possessing the world and total domination over earthly power and clinging to worldly riches, if we lose our soul and life is destroyed by death? What will we give in exchange for our soul, once it has been given up? For Christ will come with the angels, rendering to each one what is due. What should we offer for our life (cf. Rom 5:17)? I believe that promised treasures of earthly riches, lofty titles of dignity and glory, the ancient images of our cherished nobility—all these things must be denied so that we may abound in better things. We must follow Christ by our contempt of everything. For us to gain eternal spiritual benefits entails necessarily the loss of earthly ones.

(20) John Chrysostom

Again he dwells on the same point, asking, "Do you have another life to give in place of the one you have?" If you lose money, you can give money . . . likewise for any of your possessions. But if you lose your soul, you have no other soul to give in its place. Even if you owned the universe, even if you were king of the world, even if you were to give a portion of everything in the world along with the world itself, you would not be able to purchase a single soul.

And what is so surprising when it comes to the soul? After all, you can see this happening with respect to the body. You could be wearing innumerable jewels, but if your body is sick or incurably ill, you would not be able to give your whole kingdom in repayment to set this body right, no matter how many persons and cities and possessions you possessed. So consider these things about your soul, or, at least to a greater degree about your soul. Forget everything else; and put your mind on it. Don't neglect your own welfare while attending to others, as those do who work in the mines. They gain no benefit from their work or from the riches they produce. Instead, they suffer great loss because they take risks for no purpose, incurring the risk for others while reaping none of the benefit from their own work and death . . . and yet we are more wretched than they insofar as hell awaits us after our labors. Whereas death brings their efforts to an end, in our case death is just the beginning of endless tribulations.

(21) Leo the Great

In order to confirm that their faith was sound, the Lord asked his own disciples what among the various opinions they believed or perceived about him. The Apostle Peter, through the revelation of the Father on high, overcoming things corporeal and transcending things human, saw, with the eyes of his mind, the Son of the living God and confessed the glory of his divinity. He did not look for the substance of flesh and blood alone. The Lord was so pleased by Peter's sublime faith that he called him **blessed**. He had the firmness of an invincible rock on which the Church would be built. Founded on this rock, the Church would triumph over the gates of hell and the laws of death. For in loosing or binding whatever has been asked, it would be by the judgment of Peter that things will be settled in heaven. But beloved, this loftiness of Peter's praised understanding must be constructed from the mystery of the Lord's inferior substance,[8] lest his apostolic faith, carried away toward the glory of confessing the deity in Christ, should judge his receiving of our infirmity as unworthy of and inconsistent with the impassible God. In this way, he would believe that the human nature in Christ was already glorified, and, as a result, it could neither be affected by punishment, nor dissolved by death.

(22) Leontius of Constantinople

Don't imagine that the Son has two [different] roles, but recognize only one God, the Word with his own flesh. Since the Word in his incarnation was going to cross to the other side, it was not in his capacity as man but his role in the Godhead that he pronounced the teaching with the words: **For the Son of Man is to come in the glory of his Father with his angels, and then he will repay each one according to what he has done.** What kind of Father's glory does he mean? The perpetual kingdom, which cannot be circumscribed, is beyond time and not made by human hands. The glory of the Father is the kingdom of the Son, which is in heaven, not on earth.

And that the Father's glory is the kingdom of the Son you have just heard Christ the Master himself saying: **Truly, I say to you, there are some standing here who will not taste death before they see the Son of Man coming in his kingdom.** Have you seen that the glory of the Father and Son is one? Just before he said: **The Son of Man is to come in the glory of the Father**; now he says: **Before they see the Son of Man coming in his kingdom**, such that the kingdom of Christ is the Father's glory, and the Father's glory is the kingdom of the Son.

Some past interpreters, by reason of what consideration I do not know, understood those words of the Lord as pertaining to his second coming in glory. From this they also stated with certainty that John the Evangelist has not partaken of death, but that he awaits the second coming of the Lord in glory, because the Lord said: **There are some standing here who will not taste death before they see the Son of Man coming in his kingdom.** But the meaning is as follows . . . in this passage, therefore, he does not speak about his second coming in glory, but about the transfiguration on the mountain. It was when he had been transfigured on the mountain that Christ the Master showed in some small way to his disciples the glory of his unseen, divine kingdom.

In this passage, Christ the Master showed his disciples the glory of his unseen kingdom, and did not show them—on one hand, assuring them, on the other, sparing them. To assure them, he showed them the divine glory of the unseen kingdom, not to its full extent, but to the extent that they, with their human eyes, could tolerate it. In sparing them and not begrudging them, he did not show them the full glory of his divine kingdom, lest with the vision they should lose their life.

8. The bodily aspect of the incarnation.

Matthew 17

Jesus promised his disciples that some of them would see him in his glory even before they died (16:21, 27–28). According to Origen, this took place when Jesus was transfigured *before them. On the mountain, Jesus appeared in his glorious divinity, shining as the sun of righteousness (cf. Mal 4:2). Here divinity manifested itself as "ineffable and inaccessible" in the Son's humanity.*

Concerning the appearance of Moses and Elijah, ancient commentators assert that Moses represented the law, and Elijah stood for all the prophets, the two parts of the Hebrew Scripture that pointed to Jesus. In the words of Hilary, the disciples saw "Christ in his kingdom standing among the law and the prophets, with whom he will judge Israel, in whose testimonies he was foretold."

The building of three booths, or shelters, as Peter suggested, would fulfill the typology of the Jewish feast of Tabernacles, which celebrated the forty years of wandering in the desert in the past, as well as indicated the future messianic kingdom under God's reign on earth (cf. Zech 14). Peter, therefore, misinterpreted a glimpse of this kingdom, believing it had arrived permanently, and his response indicates how imperfect the disciples' knowledge was before the crucifixion.

In the voice of God from the cloud, there is the acknowledgement of the Lord's divinity. As the Son of God, he shares the divine nature with the Father, being equal to him in power and eternity. In fact, Leo says, anything that is possible to think about the Father applies also to the Son. This Son, fully sharing in the Father's glory, "brought down his unchangeable divinity all the way to the form of a servant" (cf. Phil 2:7). This episode was the ideal moment for the ancients to stress the double truth of Christ's incarnation—truly God, truly man. In response, the disciples fell to the ground in awe before God and were raised up by the Lord, indicating his death and resurrection; while the disappearance of Moses and Elijah shows that the law and the prophets are no longer needed after his resurrection (Augustine).

Avoiding publicity, Jesus commanded the disciples to be silent about the apocalyptic vision until his resurrection. He explained that Elijah, who, as many believed, would return before the messiah's arrival, had already come as John the Baptist. Yet, as John was rejected by Jewish leaders, so Jesus will be. Marveling at the accuracy of the prophetic language, Chrysostom explains that the "Scriptures speak about two advents of Christ," the past and the future. John the Baptist was the forerunner of the first, and Elijah will be the forerunner of the second.

When Jesus and the three disciples returned from the mountain, they discovered that the rest of the disciples had just failed to heal a boy suffering from epilepsy. Jesus rebuked the disciples for their lack of faith and drove out the demon causing epilepsy, instantly curing the boy. This episode, according to Hilary, shows that the disciples lapsed into the "ancient habit of unbelief," whereas Chrysostom asserts that the initial failure of healing was not caused by the unbelief of any one particular person.

Jesus further revealed himself in handling the payment of the temple tax. "Since he had the form of a servant, he does not pay any different tribute and poll tax from that which his disciple paid." However, unlike earthly kings, he paid it with a coin that he did not own, as the true Son of God, "so that the image of Caesar might never be near the image of the invisible God" (Origen).

(1) Augustine

Before the Lord revealed himself on the mountain, he said, **There are some of those standing around here who will not taste death until they see the Son of Man in his kingdom** (16:28). But all those who were standing around him when he was speaking have fallen asleep. Once the inexorable terms of death overtook them, they are only going to see the Lord as judge in his kingdom when the time of the resurrection comes. So what does he mean?

It's plain that the passage of the Gospel that comes next (17:1–8) has solved the problem. He took three others with him up the mountain, Peter and James and John, and in their presence transfigured himself, so that his face shone like the sun in its splendor. So they were among those standing around, who were not going to taste death until they saw the Lord in his kingdom. Now all of us will be shining splendidly as the sun at the end of the ages, and that is the splendor that the Lord displayed in himself. His members will shine as the head has shone. It is written that he *will transfigure the body of our lowliness to the same form as the body of his glory* (Phil 3:21).

Matthew 17:1–3

1 And after six days Jesus took with him Peter and James and John his brother, and led
them up to a high mountain apart. 2 And he was transfigured before them, and his face
shone as the sun, and his garments became white as light. 3 And behold, there appeared
to them Moses and Eli'jah, talking with him.

(2) John Chrysostom

Matthew says, **After six days Jesus took with him Peter, James, and John**. Though another Gospel writer says, *After eight days* (Luke 9:28), these passages do not stand in contradiction but rather in full agreement, because the latter included the day he spoke and the day when he led them up, whereas the former only the six days in between. Notice how Matthew pursues the truth, not hiding that others were chosen over him. John, in many places, also does the same kind of thing by chronicling the praises of Peter with great accuracy. This group of holy men certainly did not suffer from envy or pride.

Taking the leaders of the disciples, **he led them up a high mountain, by themselves. There he was transfigured before them, and his face shone like the sun, and his clothes became white as light. And Moses and Elijah appeared to them, talking with Jesus.**

Why did he take only these disciples? Because they surpassed the others. Peter demonstrates this with his exceeding love for the Lord, John does so by being loved, and James does it with the answer he and his brother gave, **We are able to drink the cup** (20:22); and not only his answer, but through works, including the fulfillment of what he said as well as everything else he did. For he was so zealous and so troublesome for the Jews that Herod considered his execution of James to be a gift to the Jews (Acts 12:2–3).

But why did he not lead them immediately? Because he did not want the other disciples to suffer any feeling of human weakness. It is for this reason that he also does not announce the names of those who are about to go with him. For the rest would have had a strong desire to follow, ready to witness the image of glory, and they would have been pained if they knew they had been overlooked. For even though he showed his glory in a bodily form, it was still something exceedingly desirable to behold.

Why does he foretell it? So that they might be best prepared to understand its higher meaning, which he had foretold, and so that the disciples might be filled with great desire in the days following, with their minds both alert and prepared.

But why are Moses and Elijah present? There are a number of reasons. The first is that some of the crowd said the Lord was Elijah, others said Jeremiah, and others one of the ancient prophets; therefore, he brought with him the leaders of the disciples in order that they might recognize the difference between the servants—Moses and Elijah—and their Master, and that Peter be commended for calling him the Son of God.

Another reason may be that people were constantly accusing him of breaking the law and calling him a blasphemer who claimed the Father's glory. They would say, *He is not from God because he does not keep the Sabbath* (John 9:16). Or again, *We do not stone you for doing good works but for blaspheming and for making yourself, a man, God* (John 10:33). In order to show that both charges were rooted in envy, that he was innocent of both, and that he neither broke the law nor assumed a glory that only belongs to the Father, the Lord brings forward those who are shining witnesses in these two areas. The Lord chose Moses because he gave the law, and the Jews knew that he would not condone its being trampled upon (which they believed Jesus had done), nor would Moses have shown respect to anyone who transgressed it, for this person is an enemy to the founder of the law. The Lord chose Elijah because he jealously protected the glory of God. For if someone who was an enemy of God claimed to be God himself and made himself equal with the Father even though he was not, Elijah would never stand there and listen to such a man.

And one may mention another reason that has not yet been stated. What is it? It is that he wished to show them that he has power over death and life and has dominion over those above and below. For this reason, he brings forth Moses, who had died, and Elijah, who had not yet suffered in this way.

Now the fifth motive (for it is the fifth of those already mentioned) the evangelist himself reveals. What is it? To show the glory of the cross, to console Peter and the others who were dreading the passion, and to elevate their thoughts on the matter. And when their time had come, they were not silent about this, but, as the Scripture says, *they spoke of the glory that he was about to fulfill in Jerusalem* (Luke 9:31),[1] that is to say, the passion and the cross, for this is what they always call it.

And not only in this way did he encourage them, but he encouraged them also in their virtue, which he consistently sought from them. When he says, **If anyone wants to come after me, he must take up his cross and follow me**, he then brings forth Elijah and Moses, who died countless deaths on behalf of God's decrees and were entrusted with them. Each of these men, having lost his life, found it. And both spoke boldly to tyrants on behalf of ungrateful and disobedient people—one to the Egyptians and the other to Ahab. And the very people these men saved were the people who brought them into extreme danger. And both desired to turn people from idolatry. And both were unlearned, one being of "slow tongue" and with a speech impediment, and the other being uncultivated and even rude. And both were quite poor, for neither had Moses acquired any possessions nor had Elijah anything more than his sheepskin. And all of these things happened under the old law before so great a gift of signs.

And even though Moses was able to part the sea, Peter walked on water, was able to move mountains, cured every kind of bodily disease, drove out uncontrollable demons, and with his shadow alone was able to work extraordinary wonders. In short, he changed the whole world. And even though Elijah raised a man from the dead, the disciples raised thousands—and even before the spirit had been given to them. For this reason too the Lord brings forward Elijah and Moses. For he wanted the disciples to imitate their ability to lead, their strength, and their unflinching steadfastness. He desired for them to be meek like Moses and zealous and judicious like Elijah. For the latter endured a three-year famine for the Jewish people, and the former said, *If you forgive them their sin, forgive; otherwise, blot me out of the book that you have written* (Exod 32:32). And through all these things, he was reminding them through a vision.

(3) Origen

Let us investigate whether Jesus, when he was transfigured before those he led up the high mountain, appeared to them in the form of God in which he anciently existed. If this was the case, then to those below he had the form of a slave (Phil 2:7), but to those who followed him to the high mountain after six days he did not have that form but the form of God.

If you are able, hear these things spiritually while paying close attention; you will notice that [the text] does not simply say **he was transfigured**, but it makes a certain necessary addition. Both Matthew and Mark recorded this necessary addition, since, according to

1. In order to link the glory of the transfiguration to the glory of the death of Christ, Chrysostom here quotes Luke using *doxan*, "glory," which can be found in some ancient manuscripts. Modern scholars, however, prefer *exodon*, "departure," meaning his death.

both, Jesus **was transfigured before them** (17:2; Mark 9:2). Accordingly, we might say that it is possible for Jesus to have been transfigured before some, but at the same time, not to have been transfigured before others.

If any of us desire to be taken along and led up to the high mountain by Jesus and counted worthy to see his transfiguration in isolation, that person must surpass the six days. In other words, that person must no longer look at the things that are seen, must no longer love the world or the things in the world (1 John 2:15), and must no longer lust after any worldly lust, such as the lust of bodily things, of wealth in the body, and of glory in the flesh. They must neither lust after those things that naturally distract and drag the soul away from better and more divine things, drawing it down and affixing it to the deceit of this age, that is, in wealth and glory and the rest of the lusts that are enemies to the truth. Whenever a person exceeds the six days (as we have said), that person will observe a new Sabbath, which he will celebrate on the high mountain because he sees Jesus transfigured before him. For the Word has different forms, and he appears to each person as is advantageous to the one who sees him. But the Word appears to no one who is unable to recognize [him].

It was not only Jesus himself that was transfigured before such disciples. Not only did his face shine like the sun in the course of the transfiguration, but his garments also appeared to be **as white as light** to those who alone were led up to the high mountain by him. Now the garments of Jesus are the sayings and letters of the Gospels with which Jesus also clothed himself. I think that the things clearly indicated about him in the [writings of the] apostles are the garments of Jesus, which become white to those who go up to the high mountain with Jesus.

And if you wish to see the transfiguration of Jesus before those who alone went up to the high mountain with him, look with me at the Jesus in the Gospels. For those who did not ascend the mountain, Jesus was simply understood and known according to the flesh through the works and words that propel people upward to the high mountain of wisdom. This Jesus, however, is no longer known according to the flesh by those who went up the mountain; he is spoken of as divine throughout the Gospels, and he is seen *in the form of God* in accordance with their knowledge (Phil 2:6).

(4) Hilary of Poitiers

After six days, Peter, James, and John were taken apart from the others and brought to the top of a mountain. As they were looking on, the Lord was transfigured and resplendent in all the brilliance of his garments. In this manner, there is preserved an underlying principle, a number, and an example. It was after six days that the Lord was shown in his glory by his clothing; that is, the honor of the heavenly kingdom is prefigured in the unfolding of six thousand years.[2] By the three disciples who were taken apart is shown the future election of the people who were to come from a threefold origin: Shem, Ham, and Japheth. That Moses and Elijah, out of the entire company of saints, were standing by shows Christ in

2. This is the number of the world's duration according to a tradition reflected in Cyprian, *Exhortation to Martyrdom* pref. 2; Lactantius, *Institutes* 7.14.

his kingdom standing among the law and the prophets, with whom he will judge Israel, in whose testimonies he was foretold. So too, the reason that Moses was visibly standing by was to teach that the glory of the resurrection was designated for human bodies. As the Lord became brighter than snow or the sun, he was conspicuous with a splendor that exceeds even our view of the heavenly lights. But to Peter, who offered to make there three tabernacles, he did not respond at all; for it was not yet the time that the Lord should be found in his glory.

(5) Gregory of Nazianzus

Light was also the first commandment given to the first man, since *the commandment of the law is a lamp and a light* (Prov 6:23) and *your judgments are a light on the earth* (Isa 26:9), even if the jealous darkness, bursting in, fashioned evil.[3] But the symbolic light, accommodated to those receiving it, is the written law, which sketches out the truth and the mystery of the great light, by which Moses's face is glorified (cf. Exod 34:29, 30, 35). And, so we might give fuller lights to this discourse, [consider that] there was a light appearing to Moses from the fire, when it was burning the bush without burning it up (Exod 3:2), to demonstrate his nature and make known his power. This was the light that led Israel and tamed the wilderness in the pillar of fire (cf. Exod 13:21). This was the light that caught up Elijah in a chariot of fire yet did not scorch him while taking him up to heaven (2 Kgs 2:11). This was the light that dazzled the shepherds (Luke 2:9), when the atemporal light was brought into contact with the temporal. This is the light of the star moving toward Bethlehem, so that—among other things—it might guide the magi (cf. 2:9) and accompany that light above us when it came to be with us. This light is divinity represented upon the mountain for the disciples (cf. 17:2), almost too real to be seen. This is the light that dazzled Paul in a vision, a wound to his eyes that healed the darkness of his soul (cf. Acts 9:3–18). This is also the light, splendor from heaven to those having been purified here on earth when the righteousness will shine as the sun (Wis 3:7; cf. Mal 4:2), whose God stands in the midst of gods and kings (cf. Ps 82:1), discerning and dividing out those worthy of his blessedness.

(6) Maximus the Confessor

Some of Christ's disciples, because of their persistence in virtue, went along with him up to the mount of his revelation. They saw him transfigured, though they were not able to come near him because of the light in his face. They were awestruck by the brilliance of his clothes, and by the presence of Moses and Elijah they recognized his great majesty. It was there that these disciples moved from flesh to spirit well before their earthly life ended, because the Spirit transformed their senses and tore away the veils of passion from their intellects. Then, when they had had their bodily and spiritual senses cleansed, they learned

3. Gregory means that darkness, not God, is responsible for evil. God provided commandments as a defense against that darkness.

the spiritual truths about the mysteries that were unveiled to them. They were taught mystically that the radiance of his faith shining with truly blessed brilliance, overwhelming the sight of all eyes, was an image of his divinity that surpasses all intelligence, sense, essence, or knowledge.

He had neither *form nor beauty* (Isa 53:2), but they knew him as the Word become flesh, and through it they were enabled to understand that he was *beautiful beyond the sons of men* (Ps 45:2). They were raised to the glory of the Only-Begotten of the Father, *full of grace and truth* (John 1:14), through ineffable theological knowledge that sings of him as wholly without limits.

(7) Leo the Great

Therefore that the apostles might receive the strength of this happy constancy in their own heart and in no way be disturbed by the bitterness of him undertaking the cross, that they might not be ashamed on account of the punishment of Christ, nor believe that this patience, which was about to endure the savagery of his passion, must be shameful for him, that he might not lose the glory of his power, **Jesus took up Peter and James and his brother John**, and, when they had climbed up the towering mountain, he showed to them the brightness of his own glory.

Although they comprehended the majesty of God in him, nevertheless, they did not recognize the power of that body in which his divinity was hidden. Therefore he had promised particularly and distinctly that certain of the disciples **standing by would not taste death before they saw the Son of Man coming in his kingdom** (16:28), that is, in the royal splendor, which specifically pertained to the nature of the manhood he had undertaken. He wanted that [this splendor] would be clearly evident to these three men. For, enclosed by flesh heretofore carnal, they could in no way gaze upon and behold that ineffable and inaccessible vision of his divinity, which is preserved **for the pure of heart** in eternal life (5:8).

Therefore the Lord revealed his own glory before chosen witnesses. He made bright that form of body common to others with so great a splendor that even his face was like **the splendor of the sun** and his clothing was like the whiteness **of snow**. By his transfiguration it was indeed chiefly intended that the scandal of the cross would be removed from the hearts of the apostles, and that the lowliness of his self-willed passion would not disturb their faith, to whom the excellence of his hidden dignity had been revealed.

Matthew 17:4–8

4 Peter said to Jesus, "Lord, it is well that we are here; if you wish, I will make three booths
here, one for you, one for Moses and one for Eli'jah." 5 He was still speaking, when lo, a
bright cloud overshadowed them, and a voice from the cloud said, "This is my beloved
Son, with whom I am pleased; listen to him." 6 When the disciples heard this, they fell on
their faces, and were filled with awe. 7 But Jesus came and touched them, saying, "Rise,
and have no fear." 8 And when they lifted up their eyes, they saw no one but Jesus only.

(8) Augustine

Peter said, **If you like, let us make here three tabernacles—one for you, one for Moses, and one for Elijah.** The Lord made no reply to this, and yet Peter got his answer. While he was speaking and proposing three tabernacles, a shining cloud came and overshadowed them. The heavenly reply showed us that there is only one [divine nature] that a human judgment was ready to divide: the Word of God as Christ, the Word of God in the law, the Word in the prophets. Why are you proposing, Peter, to divide it up? You ought rather to be joining them together. You are proposing three; understand there is really one. As the cloud overshadowed them all, and in a sense made a single tabernacle for them, a voice boomed out from the cloud, saying, **This is my beloved Son**.

Moses was there, and Elijah too. The voice didn't say, "These are my beloved sons." The only Son is one thing, you see, and adopted sons are another. Our attention was being directed to the one who was the boast of the law and the prophets. **This**, he says, **is my beloved Son, with whom I am well pleased; hear you him.** Because you have heard him also in the prophets, and you have heard him in the law, where haven't you heard him?

When they heard this, they fell to the ground. Now we are being shown that the kingdom of God is in the Church. Here is the Lord, here the law and the prophets. But the Lord is present in person as Lord, while the law is present in the person of Moses, prophecy in the person of Elijah. They, however, are there as servants, as attendants. They are like water pots, he is like the spring. Moses and the prophets spoke and wrote, but it was from him they were filled up, when they poured out their message.

At this point, the Lord stretched out his hand and raised them up from where they were lying. Then **they saw nobody but Jesus only.** What does this signify? You heard when the apostle was being read, that *we see now by a mirror in a riddle, but then it will be face to face* (1 Cor 13:12). All tongues will come to nothing (1 Cor 13:8), when what we now hope for and believe will come to pass. So the fact of their falling to the earth signified that we die, because flesh was told, *Earth you are, and into earth shall you go* (Gen 3:19). But when the Lord raised them up, it signified the resurrection. After the resurrection, what use will the law be to you, what use the prophets? That's why Elijah does not appear, and why Moses doesn't appear. What does remain for you is, *In the beginning was the Word, and the Word was with God, and the Word was God* (John 1:1). What remains for you is *that God may be all in all* (1 Cor 15:28).

Moses will be there, of course, but no longer the law. We shall also see Elijah there, but no longer as a prophet. The law and the prophets bore witness to Christ that it was necessary for him to suffer, and on the third day to rise again from the dead, and to enter into his glory (Luke 24:26–27, 44–46). What he promised to those who love him will find its fulfillment there: *Whoever loves me will be loved by my Father, and I too will love him*— and as though he were asked, "What will you give him, seeing that you will love him?"—*and I will show myself to him* (John 14:21).

Let us try to explain the symbolism of this great mystery. Moses and Elijah are talking with the Lord. In Moses we have the law, in Elijah the prophets. When we establish anything from the gospel, we back it up from the law and the prophets. Moses and Elijah are speaking with the Lord, like attendants alongside of the sovereign Lord in the middle. What's the meaning of Moses and Elijah speaking with the Lord? Listen to the Apostle: *Through the law,* he says, *comes knowledge of sin; but now without the law the justice of God has been manifested* (Rom 3:20–21). There you see the Lord together with Moses and Elijah, the law and the prophets bearing witness to him. But when we are resurrected, what need will there be for the law; what need for the prophets? We won't be looking for supporting evidence because we shall see him face to face as he is (1 John 3:2). When will this be? After the resurrection. That's why those disciples who fell down got up again and saw the Lord standing alone.

(9) Origen

Let us look at what Peter understood when he replied and said to Jesus, **Lord, it is good for us to be here; let us make three tabernacles**, and so on. One must examine these words very carefully, because Mark added the phrase, *he did not know what he had answered* (Mark 9:6), and Luke says, *not knowing what he said* (Luke 9:33). We should consider therefore whether Peter spoke these things in an ecstatic trance[4] after he was filled with the spirit who moved him to say these things. The spirit that filled Peter cannot be the Holy Spirit, since, when John said in his Gospel, *The Spirit had not yet come, because Jesus had not yet been glorified* (John 7:39), he taught that no one would have the Holy Spirit before the Savior's resurrection. If the Spirit had not yet come, and if Peter spoke without knowing what he was saying, being moved by some spirit, then the spirit causing him to speak was one of the spirits that had not yet been triumphed over in the cross or been made a show of with those about whom it is written, *Putting off from himself the principalities and authorities, he made an open show of them by triumphing over them in the cross* (Col 2:15). Perhaps this spirit was what Jesus called a "stumbling block" and what was spoken of as "Satan" in the phrase, *Get behind me, Satan; you are a stumbling block to me* (16:23). Now I know all too well that such an understanding may offend many when they read this, particularly those who think that it makes no sense for someone to be spoken poorly of who had just previously been blessed by Jesus in the remark that flesh and blood made no revelation to him, but the Father in heaven had given a revelation to him regarding the Savior, specifically, that he was Jesus and the Christ and the Son of the living God. However, let such a person examine precisely what is said about Peter and the rest of the apostles, who still prayed as though they were yet strangers (17:6–8; Luke 9:34–35) to the one who would redeem them from the enemy and purchase them with his precious blood. Or, let those who claim the disciples were perfected even before Jesus's passion tell us why it happened that when Jesus was transfigured, *Peter and those with him were burdened with sleep* (Luke 9:32).

But the one who has learned to understand the roots of sin as related to the father of sin—the devil—will not say that the apostles stumbled apart from the devil's work, nor that Peter denied Jesus three times before that cock crow without the devil's influence. If this is true, consider whether the devil wanted to cause Jesus to stumble by whatever degree he was able and to turn him away from the arranged plan to suffer willingly and to make salvation possible for humanity. Consider also whether the devil worked toward these aims by attempting to draw Jesus away deceptively, as if it were no longer good for Jesus to make

4. That is, being spiritually inspired.

allowances for mankind and to come and die on their behalf, and as though it were better for him to remain isolated on the high mountain with Moses and Elijah . . . [L]et us investigate the matter, because, just as there is no truth apart from the working of the one who said, *I am the truth* (John 14:6), so also there is no lie apart from the enemy to the truth, as John says, *Whenever he speaks a lie, he speaks of his own, because he is a liar and the father of it* (John 8:44). These opposites therefore were still in Peter, both truth and falsehood.

(10) John Chrysostom

Lord, it is well that we are here. If you wish I will make three booths here, one for you, one for Moses and one for Elijah. What are you saying, Peter? Didn't you just previously distinguish Christ from those who served him [i.e., Moses and Elijah]? Do you now consider him to be one of them? Notice how flawed the disciples' judgment was before the crucifixion. Although the Father had revealed to Peter who Jesus was (16:17), he didn't hold on to this revelation, but was frightened. . . .

Why was there a voice out of the cloud? God always appears that way. *Clouds and thick darkness are around about him* (Ps 97:2); *the Lord is sitting on a light cloud* (Isa 19:1); again, *he makes the clouds his chariot* (Ps 104:3); *a cloud took him out of their sight* (Acts 1:9); and, *as the Son of Man coming upon the clouds of heaven* (Dan 7:13). In order for them to believe that the voice comes from God, it is spoken from a cloud. The cloud is bright because when he threatens, he appears in a dark cloud, as on Mount Sinai (Exod 19:19; 20:21). Here, because he does not want to frighten but to teach them, it is a bright cloud.

(11) Leo the Great

For when the Father said, **This is my beloved Son, in whom I am well pleased, listen to him**, was not **this is my Son** clearly heard as "the one who has existence from me and with me outside of time"? For the Father is not prior to the Son, nor the Son after the Father. **This is my Son**, whom deity does not set apart, nor power divide, nor eternity separate from me. **This is my Son**, not of adoption, but my own, not created by another, but begotten from me, nor made comparable to me from another nature, but born equally from my essence. **This is my Son** *through whom all things were made and without whom nothing was made* (John 1:3), who *does likewise all the things that I do* (cf. John 5:19), and whatever I devote myself to, he inseparably and indiscriminately labors upon (cf. John 5:17).

For the Son is in the Father, and the Father in the Son, and our unity is never divided (cf. John 10:38). Even though I am the one who begat, and he is the one whom I have begotten, nevertheless, for you it is not right to think concerning him anything other than is possible to perceive concerning me. **This is my Son**, who did *not* grasp by *robbery that equality* which he holds with me (Phil 2:6), nor venture it through usurpation. Instead, remaining in the form of my glory, so that he might carry out our common counsel for the restoration of the human race, he brought down his unchangeable divinity all the way to *the form of a servant* (cf. Phil 2:7).

Matthew 17:9

9And as they were coming down the mountain, Jesus commanded them, "Tell no one the vision, until the Son of man is raised from the dead."

(12) Origen

After the episode on the mountain, when the disciples came down to the crowd in order to help the Son of God with the salvation of those people, Jesus commanded the disciples, **Tell no one about this sight until the Son of Man is raised from the dead.** The phrase, **Tell no one about this sight**, resembles the one scrutinized earlier when **he commanded the disciples to tell no one that he is the Christ** (16:20). The things said about that passage can also be useful to us concerning the passage at hand, since Jesus also wishes for nothing to be said about the details of his glory before his post-passion glory comes. Those who heard, and especially the crowds, would have been hurt if they saw him being crucified after having been glorified. Because his glorification via the resurrection would be like his transfiguration when his face appeared like the sun, Jesus wanted the apostles to speak about these things once he was raised from the dead.

Matthew 17:10–13

10And the disciples asked him, "Then why do the scribes say that first Eli'jah must
come?" 11He replied, "Eli'jah does come, and he is to restore all things; 12but I tell you
that Eli'jah has already come, and they did not know him, but did to him whatever
they pleased. So also the Son of man will suffer at their hands." 13Then the disciples
understood that he was speaking to them about John the Baptist.

(13) Origen

I would say that Gabriel, in his words to Zechariah, established what was in Elijah and John as the same substance. For he says, *He will turn many of the children of Israel to the Lord their God, and he will go before him in the spirit and power of Elijah* (Luke 1:16–17). Notice that he did not say "in the soul of Elijah," whereby reincarnation might have had a foothold, but he said, *in the spirit and power of Elijah* (Luke 1:17). The Scripture clearly knows the difference between spirit and soul, as in the phrase, *And may God sanctify you completely, and may your spirit and soul and body be kept complete and blameless in the coming of our Lord Jesus Christ* (1 Thess 5:23). Also, the phrase, as it is in Daniel according to the Septuagint, *Bless, you spirits and souls of the just* (Dan 3:86 [= Song of Azarius] LXX), which supports the difference between spirit and soul. So too, Elijah came to be called John not on account of his soul, but on account of his spirit and power. These qualities, which in no way oppose the Church's teaching, were formerly found in Elijah and are later in John (cf. Mal 3:22–23 LXX; cf. Mal 4:5–6). . . .

We must inquire whether the spirit of Elijah is the same as the spirit of God that is in Elijah, or whether these are different from one another. We must also consider whether the spirit of Elijah that was in him was something supernatural compared to the spirit that is within every person. For the Apostle clearly recognized the Spirit of God to be different from the spirit of and within each person, even though God's Spirit is also within us, when he says, *The Spirit itself testifies with our spirit that we are children of God* (Rom 8:16), and elsewhere, *No person has known the things of a person except the spirit of and in that person; similarly, no one has known the things of God except the Spirit of God* (1 Cor 2:11).

Do not be amazed at what is said about Elijah as if something strange happened to him, unlike any of the other saints who have been recorded, because he was taken up *in a whirlwind to heaven* (2 Kgs 2:11). In the same way, his spirit possessed some remarkable quality, seeing how it rested not only on Elisha, but also descended on John at his birth. And do not be amazed if John was separately filled with the Holy Spirit while still in his mother's womb and came before Christ in the spirit and power of Elijah. Indeed, it is possible for many spirits, both worse and better, to be in the same person. Therefore, David requests to be strengthened by a guiding spirit and to be renewed in his inmost parts with a right spirit (Ps 51:10). . . .

(14) John Chrysostom

The Scriptures speak about two advents of Christ: this one that has already happened, and the one to come in the future. Paul talked about the first one by saying, *For the grace of God has appeared for salvation, training us to renounce irreligion and worldly passions and to live sober, upright, and godly lives in this world* (Tit 2:11–12). Note how he refers to this one, and after it he mentions the other, *awaiting our blessed hope, the appearing of the glory of our great God and Savior Jesus Christ* (Tit 2:13). Indeed the prophets talk about both advents and say of the second that Elijah will be the forerunner. John was the forerunner of the first. Christ called him Elijah because he took up the ministry of that prophet. But the scribes, both misconstruing these events and misleading the people, spoke only about the second advent when they asked whether Elijah had to come before it. That is why the disciples asked the question and also why the Pharisees went to John and asked him, *Are you Elijah* (John 1:21)? They said nothing about the first advent.

What is Christ's answer to the question? "Elijah will come before my second advent, but Elijah has also come now," referring to John. Elijah has come, but if you look for the Tishbite, he will come. That is why he said, **Elijah does come, and he is to restore all things**. What things? Those that the prophet Malachi talks about when he says, *I will send you Elijah the Tishbite, who will restore the heart of the father to the son, lest I come and completely destroy the earth* (Mal 3:22–23 LXX; cf. Mal 4:5–6).

See how accurate the prophetic language is. Christ referred to John as Elijah because of their shared ministry, and thus you might think that Malachi meant John. But the prophet called Elijah a Tishbite, and John was not a Tishbite. Malachi offers a second sign by saying, *lest I come and completely destroy the earth*, which is how he designated Christ's second and fearful advent. For in the first he did not come to destroy the earth. Indeed, he said, *I did not come to judge the world but to save the world* (John 12:47). Malachi said these things to indicate that the Tishbite will come before the second advent.

The reason for saying this is that when the Tishbite comes, he will convince the Jews that Jesus is the Christ and that they may not be destroyed when the Christ returns. That is why Christ recalled this memory with the words **and he is to restore all things**. The statement means that Elijah will correct the unbelief of the Jews who are alive at the time of the second advent.

That is also why, with such remarkable accuracy, Malachi does not say that Elijah "will restore the heart of the son to the father" but "of the father to the son" (cf. Mal 3:23 LXX; Mal 4:6). Because the Jews are the fathers of the apostles, Malachi means that Elijah will restore the hearts of the fathers, that is, the minds of the Jewish people to the teaching of their sons, the apostles.

Christ speaks of Elijah everywhere to indicate his acceptance of the Old Testament and to show that this first advent agrees with prophecy. That is why he adds, **Elijah has already come, and they did not know him, but did to him whatever they pleased.** The last phrase refers to how they threw him in prison, abused him, killed him, and brought his head out on a platter.

So also the Son of Man is about to suffer at their hands. Notice again how at the right time he recalls to their minds his coming death, using John's death as a kind of comfort. He not only soothes them in this way, but also by doing remarkable miracles. Indeed, whenever he mentions his death, he does miraculous acts both before and after such talk. In a number of places he follows that pattern.

Matthew 17:14–20

**14And when they came to the crowd, a man came up to him and kneeling before him
said, 15"Lord, have mercy on my son, for he is an epileptic and he suffers terribly; for
often he falls into the fire, and often into the water. 16And I brought him to your dis-
ciples, but they could not heal him." 17And Jesus answered, "O faithless and perverse
generation, how long am I to be with you? How long am I to bear with you? Bring him
here to me." 18And Jesus rebuked him, and the demon came out of him, and the boy was
cured instantly. 19Then the disciples came to Jesus privately and said, "Why could we
not cast it out?" 20He said to them, "Because of your little faith. For truly, I say to you,
if you have faith as a grain of mustard seed, you will say to this mountain 'Move from
here to there,' and it will move; and nothing will be impossible for you."[5]**

5. Most modern critical Greek editions of the New Testament do not include Matt 17:21: "But this kind does not come out except by prayer and fasting."

(15) Hilary of Poitiers

Though the apostles believed, their faith was not yet perfect. While the Lord was delayed on the mountain, they themselves were sitting with the crowd, a kind of torpor had weakened their faith. This is why he said to them, **Unbelieving and perverse generation, how long will I be with you?** In his absence, their ancient habit of unbelief had stolen upon them. He taught them that they can obtain no healing, just as if, during the time intervening between the Gospels and the second coming, they abandoned their faith as though the Lord were absent.

When the disciples finally asked him why they were not able to drive out the demon, he responded that their lack of faith had rendered them unable to do so. If they had faith like that of a mustard seed, they would have been able to command this mountain with effectual power to move from one place to another. But by this time, he had come down the mountain and was speaking among the crowd. He declared that he himself was like the smallest of all seeds, the mustard seed, referring to the devil as a "mountain" because evil spirits and heavenly powers are found on its heights. . . .

[T]he disciples are surprised that they could not drive out the demon since *all authority had been granted them*, not only to drive out demons, but also for raising the dead (10:8). But because the law was no longer going to apply to them [because they had come down from the mountain and from Moses], the Lord said, **Unbelieving and perverse generation**—it does not seem that he spoke this to those whom he had sanctified—**how long**, he said, **will I be with you?** Those who did not have faith were going to lose the very law that they possessed. If they had maintained faith in him, even if it was a mere mustard seed, the burden of their sins and the heavy weight of their unbelief would have been cast off by the power of the Word, just like the mountain thrown into the sea. They would have been transferred to the ways of the Gentiles and of the age.

(16) John Chrysostom

Scripture indicates that this man has little faith, and this is evident in what Christ says to him: *All things are possible to him who believes*; and also what the man says, *Help my unbelief*. Christ commands the evil spirit to *come out of him and never enter him again*; the man says, *if you can* (Mark 9:22–25). But if the man's disbelief was the cause, why does Christ put the blame on the disciples? He wishes to show that even if those who brought a sick person for healing did not themselves have faith, they may be able to bring about a cure. When the faith of those who bring the sick person is strong, miracles can happen through weak ministers. In a similar way, a miracle can occur when the ministers are strong and the faith of others is weak. . . . In this instance, even the disciples' faith was weak, but not that of every disciple. Those who were called the *pillars* (Gal 2:9) were not there. . . .

Because the man said that the boy had suffered *from childhood* and had said, *if you can do anything*, Christ answered, *If you are able to believe, all things are possible*, turning the man's question back on him (Mark 9:21–23). When the leper said, **If you will, you can make me clean**, testifying to his authority, Christ praised him and agreed with his statement by saying, **I will; be clean** (8:2–3). Because this man's statement did not acknowledge the Lord's power—*if you can do anything*—note how he corrects him for getting things wrong. For Jesus says, if you can believe, *all things are possible to him who believes* (Mark 9:23). What he means is this: "I have enough power to enable others to do miracles. If you truly believe, even you can heal both this one and many others."

(17) Origen

But since an inquiry into the passage only and not every topic is now set before us, let us see what we can say by figuratively interpreting the possessed boy and what his father deemed to be right concerning him. [We want to ask] what it means to experience falling not always but *often* into the fire and into the water, and what it means that Jesus, but not the disciples, were able to heal him. For if every disease and sickness, which our Savior healed in the crowd at that time, refers to different symptoms in sick souls, then it makes sense that paralytics signify the lame who keep their weakened soul lying prostrate on the body; the blind signify those who are blind to the invisible things only the soul can see (and they are blind indeed); the deaf signify those who have been deafened to the reception of the word of salvation. Just like with these cases, we will have to investigate the circumstances surrounding the *epileptic*.

But this episode of epilepsy, which attacks those suffering, occurs in significant intervals. In the times when the afflicted person does not experience an epileptic fit, nothing seems to differ between him and those who are healthy. And you might find such varieties of symptoms in the case of some souls, which people consider to be healthy, possessing moderation and even other virtues. Then, as if by an epileptic fit, they seem to be seized by their passions, are cast down from standing up, and they imbibe lusts stemming from the deception of this age. Therefore, you would not perhaps err if you said that such people are epileptic spiritually (so to speak), having been thrown down by the spirits of evil *in the heavenly places* (Eph 6:12). These people are usually doing evil at the time when the passions lay hold of their soul. When they fall into the fire of fever, they become, according to what is read in Hosea, *those who commit adultery, as a potter's vessel set ablaze for cooking, burnt from the flame* (7:4). At another time they fall into water, when *the king of all dragons in the waters* (Job 41:26 LXX) casts them down from the sphere where they seemed to breathe freely so that they come into the depths of the sea's waves of human life. But the reading in Wisdom about the just man's even temper will draw together the pieces of our interpretation of the epileptic: *The interpretation of a godly man is always wisdom*, but concerning those who have been given over to sin, *the foolish man is as changeable as the moon* (Sir 27:11).[6]

Let us now offer a literal reading and seek in the first place how he who was blinded and cast down by some unclean deaf and dumb spirit is called an epileptic, and why "epileptic" is associated with the great luminary of heaven, second only to the sun, which *God* appointed *to rule over the night* (Gen 1:16).

6. Ancient Greeks described epilepsy as a disease induced by the moon. Origen therefore considers the fool to be a spiritual epileptic who is as changeable as the moon.

Let doctors discuss the physiology of the matter, seeing that they do not consider an unclean spirit to be relevant in the case, but a bodily disease. And let them interpret, inquiring into the nature of things, that the moist things in the head are moved by some affinity with the light of the moon, which itself has a moist nature. But as for us, those trusting in the Gospel, we perceive that an unclean spirit of muteness and blindness produced the disease in those suffering from it. But seeing that some physicians, almost exactly like the Egyptian magicians, are accustomed to proclaim that they have healed such diseased people when they seem to have succeeded among them, we may rather say that perhaps this impure spirit is on the lookout for certain stages of the moon, and in this way he operates in order to make it seem the cause of such evil, so that the suffering of men seems to accord with such and such stage of the moon. Then the suffering is not identified with the mute and blind demon, but the great luminary in heaven. But the moon, appointed to *rule over the night* (Gen 1:16), bears not an ounce of responsibility for such a disease in men. The demons do this for the sake of slandering God's creation, so that *injustice* might be spoken *loftily* and they might *set their mouths against heaven* (Ps 73:8, 9). And they all speak *injustice loftily* (Ps 73:8) when they claim that the cause of all the disorders on earth—whether considered universally or locally—resides in the nature of the stars. And indeed, such men truly *set their own mouths against heaven* (Ps 73:9), declaring that some people do evil and others do good things because of the stars, since not even one star exists apart from the God of the universe. As it has been written according to Jeremiah in Lamentations, *Evil will not proceed from the mouth of the Lord along with good* (Lam 3:38).

But let us pay attention to that passage, This kind does not come out except by prayer and fasting, so that, if we should need to heal such a tough kind of demon, let us neither swear oaths nor make demands of it nor speak to the unclean spirit as if it hears us. Rather, *devoting ourselves to prayer and fasting* (1 Cor 7:5), by praying for the one suffering, let us find success and by our own fasting let us drive away the unclean spirit from him.

Matthew 17:22–23

22 As they were in Galilee, Jesus said to them, "The Son of man is to be delivered into the hands of men, 23 and they will kill him, and he will be raised on the third day." And they were greatly distressed.

(18) Origen

These words seems to have the same effect [on the disciples] as the earlier statement, **Jesus began to show his disciples that he must go unto Jerusalem and suffer many things of the elders and chief priests and scribes** (16:21). And yet there is a difference here since it is one thing **to show to the disciples that he must go unto Jerusalem and suffer many things of the elders and chief priests and scribes**, and, after suffering, **be killed**, and, after being killed, **be raised up on the third day**. It is quite another thing to tell them when they were in Galilee—a fact that we didn't know before—that the Son of Man would be **delivered**

up. The point about being **delivered up** was not mentioned earlier. Moreover, the passage says that he **is to be delivered up into the hands of men**.

Let us consider how he **is to be delivered up into the hands of men**. For we are taught at whose hands he will suffer, and in what place he will suffer, and we also learn that while his suffering takes place at the hands of those previously mentioned, they are not the prime causes of his suffering, even if they are the ones who delivered him up into the hands of men. For someone will note that, in interpreting this, the Apostle says in reference to God that he *spared not his own Son, but delivered him up for us all* (Rom 8:32). Moreover, the Son gave himself to death for us, which is to say that he was delivered up, not only by the Father but also by himself.

Someone else, by gathering scriptural passages together, will observe that the Son is first delivered up by God; then he endures temptation, then he undergoes agony[7] (Luke 4:1–13; 9:44; 22:40–46), then suffers for men, indeed for the whole world that he might take away its sin (John 1:29). But the Son is also delivered to the prince of this age, and to the rest of its rulers, and by them delivered into the hands of men who would kill him.

Let it be, as in the case of Job (cf. Job 1:12), that the Father hands over the Son first to the opposing forces, then these latter betray him into **the hands of men**, among whom also was Judas, into whom *Satan entered after he had taken a morsel* (John 13:27), and he then hands the Son over more properly than Judas. But watch out, lest, by comparing the Father handing over the Son to the opposing forces to their handing over the Savior into **the hands of men**, you think the "handing over" is the same in both cases. But understand that the Father *handed him over for the sake of us all* (Rom 8:32) out of love of humanity. But the opposing powers were not considering that. They did not think that by handing over the Savior into **the hands of men** it would be for the salvation of some. Since none of them knew the wisdom of God that *has been hidden in a mystery* (1 Cor 2:7)—and much less in their case than the men!—they handed him over to be killed, so that his *enemy, death* (1 Cor 15:26), might take him as a captive just like *those who are dying in Adam* (1 Cor 15:22). These men who were appointed killed Jesus by the will of the powers in order to make him a captive to death. But I have deemed it necessary for these things to be scrutinized on account of Jesus being handed over into **the hands of men**, not by men but by the powers to whom the Father *handed over* the Son *for the sake of all* (Rom 8:32). The same Son, who was handed over and who became subject to those to whom he was handed over, destroys *the one having dominion over death* (Heb 2:14). For *by death* he brought to nothing *the one having dominion of death (that is, the devil), and* he set free *these who were subject to bondage all their lifetime by fear of death* (Heb 2:14–15).

Matthew 17:24–27

24When they came to Caper'na-um, the collectors of the half-shekel tax went up to Peter and said, "Does not your teacher pay the tax?" 25He said, "Yes." And when they came home, Jesus spoke to him first, saying, "What do you think, Simon? From whom

7. Origen uses the term "agony" here, which is mentioned in some manuscripts at Luke 22:43–44.

do the kings of the earth take toll or tribute? From their sons or from others?" [26]And when Peter said, "From others," Jesus said to him, "Then the sons are free. [27]However, not to give offense to them, go to the sea and cast a hook, and take the first fish that comes up, and when you open its mouth you will find a shekel; take that and give it to them for me and for yourself."

(19) John Chrysostom

What is this shekel? When God killed the Egyptians' firstborn, he put the tribe of Levi in first place (Num 3:11–13, 41–45). Later, because the tribe numbered less than the Jewish firstborn, God demanded a shekel from those among the firstborn from every tribe who was needed to comprise the larger number (Num 3:46–51). Thus it became customary that the firstborn make a payment.

Christ was firstborn, and Peter was first among the apostles. Thus the tax collectors came to them. I guess because they collected this shekel in every city they approached Christ, because Capernaum was considered his native city. Yet they avoided Christ and cautiously spoke to Peter. They not did accuse but asked, **Does not your teacher pay the tax?** They did not have a proper view of Christ yet, but they evidently felt something about him as a man. They treated him reverently and with honor because of the signs he had done. What did Peter say? **He answered Yes** to the questioners, but he said nothing to Christ, perhaps because he was too embarrassed to talk with him about such things. The Gentle One, knowing everything as he did, did not let Peter ask but instead put to him his own question, **What do you think, Simon? From whom do the kings of the earth demand a tax or tribute? From their sons or from strangers?** And when he said, **From strangers,** Jesus said to him, **Then the sons are free.** . . .

If he were not a son, there would have been no reason to speak of kings. Someone might say, "He is a son, but not truly begotten." In that case, he is not a son, and if not a son, then he is not truly begotten and does not belong to God but to some other. If he belongs to some other, then the comparison in the text doesn't make sense. He is not talking about sons in general terms, but about authentic sons, who share the kingdom with their parents. . . .

Notice too that he confirms the knowledge revealed to Peter. He does not stop there, but in his condescension he states the same truth, an instance of great wisdom. For then he says, **However, not to give offense to them, go to the sea and cast a hook and take the first fish that comes up, and you will find a shekel; take that and give it to them for me and for yourself.**

Consider how he neither refuses the tribute nor orders Peter to pay it. First, having demonstrated that he is not legally obliged to pay it, he offers it in order to offend neither those seeking it nor his circle. He does not give it as payment of a debt but as acting properly in response to their weakness. In other places he does not worry about giving offense, as when he talks about meats (15:11–12). Thus he shows us when to regard something as offensive to others and when not.

In his very manner of paying the tax he again reveals himself. Why didn't he tell Peter to offer the tax collectors money from what they had in hand? He chose this solution to show that he is God of all; even the sea is his dominion. He had already shown this previously when he restrained the winds and called Peter to come to him across the waves (14:22–33). Here he again demonstrates the same thing in a different way, but he still creates utter astonishment. . . . Now as you are staggered by Christ's power, also admire Peter's faith.

(20) Origen

But when they came into Capernaum, those who collected the two-drachma tax went up to Peter (17:24). There are some kings of the earth (cf. Ps 2:2) and their sons who do not pay either tribute or poll tax. There are other sons, who are strangers to the kings of the earth, from whom the kings of the earth take tribute and poll tax. The sons of the kings of the earth are free in the kings' presence, just as all sons are free in the presence of their fathers. But the sons who are strangers to these kings, though free outside the borders of the land, are servants under those who rule over them and enslave them, just as *the Egyptians tyrannized over the sons of Israel, and they embittered their lives* and *caused them to serve with violence* (Exod 1:13–14). For the sake of those servants, as an analogy to the slavery of the Hebrews, the Son of God alone assumed the *form of a servant* (Phil 2:7), even though he did nothing low and servile. Since he had *the form of a servant*, he does not pay any different tribute and poll tax from that which his disciple paid. For the standard coin itself was enough, that is, the single piece of currency given on behalf of Jesus and his disciple. But this piece of currency was not [found] in Jesus's house but happened to be in the sea, and was in the mouth of the fish of the sea, which I think did well for itself when it rose and was caught in the net of Peter, who became a *fisher of men* (Mark 1:17). The fish allegorically represents these men, so that the coin bearing the image of Caesar might both be snatched away from Peter and might take its place among the men caught by those who have learned to fish for men.

Therefore, let the one having the **things of Caesar** render those **things to Caesar**, so that after this he can render **to God the things of God.** But since Jesus, being *the image of the invisible God* (Col 1:15), did not have the image of Caesar, for *the ruler of this age has no claim on him* (John 14:30), he took the image of Caesar from the place close at hand—the sea—so that he might give it to the kings of the earth for himself and for his disciples, so that **those collecting the two-drachma tax** might not suppose that Jesus is in debt to them or to the kings of the earth. He thus paid the debt, neither by seizing it, nor grasping for it, nor procuring it for himself, nor by making it his own possession, so that the image of Caesar might never be near *the image of the invisible God* (Col 1:15).

Matthew 18

In this chapter, Jesus instructs the disciples about the ethical norms of the heavenly kingdom: humility, discipline, and forgiveness. These norms are a reversal of the worldly standards that still govern the disciples' thinking, as their question reveals: Who is the greatest in the kingdom of heaven? *Jesus replied with an object lesson, calling on a child as an example of humility that constitutes the face of greatness.*

Reflecting on the Lord's commandment to be like children, the early theologians point out that Jesus does not encourage infantile behavior. Rather, he calls us to show in our spiritual life the characteristics typical for children, imitating them in simplicity and sincerity, as well as staying away from the preoccupations and vices of adulthood. Chromatius further clarifies that Jesus teaches us to cling to God and the Church, as a child clings to father and mother, reminding us that the greatest example of humility is "the Lord himself, who condescended to becoming a child for our well-being."

Not only do children symbolize humility, they also represent the most vulnerable and neglected people in society. Christians are called to minister to their physical and spiritual needs. So the Lord warns the disciples: it is better to drown with a millstone on the neck than to cause one of these little ones to sin. Causing a believer in Christ to stumble is a much more serious sin than one's infidelity (Chromatius).

Turning to matters of discipline, Jesus stressed the seriousness and the eternal consequences of sin. Hilary offers an elucidation of the Lord's warning against those who create temptations for others: the ugliness of the cross is a stumbling block for many. Jesus's next warning was no less grave. It is better to lose a body part than to stumble and sin because of it. According to Origen, "bodily members" are the people closest to us, that is, our family and friends. These connections ought to be severed if they injure our soul. For Augustine, the stumbling blocks are the "troubles and pressures" that Christians encounter in life's pilgrimage. These pressures act like fire. Depending on our own state, they become either an education or a condemnation, either purifying us like gold, or burning us to ashes like straw.

The parable about the shepherd searching for one lost sheep is of particular interest to the ancient commentators. Chrysostom remarks, "[T]he Lord himself left the ninety-nine sheep and went looking for that other one. He did not let the safety of so many sheep overshadow the importance of saving from death the one that was lost." No matter how weak people may appear to be, none of them is insignificant in the Lord's eyes. For Ambrose and Epiphanius, the lost sheep is the human race, lost in Adam and recovered in Christ.

The ancient fathers find much practical advice in the Lord's teaching about a healthy balance between pardon and reprimand (vv. 15–18). By neither forgiving too easily, nor reproaching too harshly, we should seek to correct the sinner by inspiring shame rather than to punish him, provoking anger or fear (Ambrose). "If you do it out of self-love, you do less than nothing. If you do it out of love for him, you are doing something very good indeed" (Augustine).

Chrysologus directs our attention to the Lord's teaching about prayer. Although Christ does not specify things that he promises to those who pray as a group, it is important to remember that we should ask of God things worthy of God, namely, holy, heavenly gifts, compatible with virtues. The theologian also points out the Lord's preference for corporate prayers over private ones. Those who omit participation in the zeal of the assembled congregation . . . condemn and despise divine arrangements, hindering their own advance in Christlikeness.

Jesus's teaching on forgiveness concludes this chapter. For Hilary, the Lord's directive to forgive seventy times seven *instead of seven teaches us "to offer pardon without measure and without number," as the Lord himself forgave us without measure, according to his favor rather than our own merit. For Augustine,* seventy times seven *symbolizes "a complete whole or total in terms of seven," revealing the Lord's intention to forgive all sins.*

The Lord illustrated his teaching on forgiveness with a parable about a servant who, being forgiven an enormous debt by the king, later refused to forgive a much lesser debt to his fellows (vv. 23–35). Augustine notes that each of us can identify with this forgetful servant in two ways: as being forgiven by God and as having to forgive others. The entire Christian ethical code comes down to only two "works of mercy" Christ sets in the Gospels: "Forgive and you will be forgiven; give and it shall be given you" (Luke 6:37–38). God alone, as the king in the parable, is able to evaluate and judge every human word and act, according to Origen. As Chrysostom points out, the parable teaches that it is easier to forgive others if we remember our own condition as sinners for whom much has been forgiven.

Matthew 18:1–4

1At that time the disciples came to Jesus, saying, "Who is the greatest in the kingdom of heaven?" 2And calling to him a child, he put him in the midst of them, 3and said, "Truly, I say to you, unless you turn and become like children, you will never enter the kingdom of heaven. 4Whoever humbles himself like this child, he is the greatest in the kingdom of heaven."

(1) Origen

A person should **humble himself as the child** whom Jesus called to himself. Haughtiness and conceit of noble birth or wealth, things that some consider beneficial, though in truth they are not, are not present in a child. One can see that toddlers, until they are three or four years old, even if they seem to be of noble birth, are just like the lowborn and do not seem to love rich children any more than poor ones. Therefore, even if children tend to have foolish emotions because of their youth, the disciples of Jesus learned from the Word that one should **humble himself like the child**, as Jesus showed them: neither puffed up because of a little bit of glory, nor becoming disposed toward riches or expensive goods, nor swelling up because of nobility. Above all, the Word proclaimed that those who live as that **child** that **Jesus called to himself** are praised and honored by the name of Jesus, since Christ is especially in these. And for this reason he says, **Whoever receives one such child in my name receives me** (18:5).

But let us consider another interpretation given alongside the simpler one, whether as a teaching or as an exercise. Let us seek what kind of child Jesus called and **made him stand in the midst** of the disciples. Consider whether the child is the Holy Spirit, who humbled himself when he was called by the Savior and was **made to stand in the midst** of the intellect of Jesus's disciples. Or perhaps the Lord wishes us, who turned away from other things, to be turned toward the examples set before us by the Holy Spirit, that in this way we might become like children who also turned and are likened to the Holy Spirit.

Those children are the ones God gave to the Savior, according to what has been said in Isaiah, *Behold, I and the children that God gave to me* (Isa 8:18). One **will never enter into the kingdom of heaven** without being turned away from worldly affairs and made like children who have the Holy Spirit. Therefore, when Jesus **called to himself** the Holy Spirit, the Spirit came down to men from his own perfection, just as Jesus **made the child to stand in the midst** of the disciples. Those who have turned away from worldly lusts must humble themselves, not simply as a **child**, but as this child. Humbling oneself as that child means imitating the Holy Spirit who humbled himself for the salvation of men. But that the Savior and the Holy Spirit were sent by the Father for the salvation of men has been declared by Isaiah in the person of the Savior, *And now the Lord has sent me and his Spirit* (Isa 48:16).

(2) Chromatius of Aquileia

Even now the disciples, not knowing how great the glory of humility was, were arguing about the status of their service or reward, saying to the Lord: **Who do you think is greatest in the kingdom of heaven?** The disciples were in competition about who was greatest in the kingdom of heaven, although there is no doubt that the one who is greatest before God is the most humble, as he himself was saying: **The one who exalts himself will be humbled, and the one who humbles himself will be exalted** (23:12). As a result, not unjustly, in order to halt an unnecessary rivalry of this type between his disciples, it is said: **Jesus called a child and stood him in the midst of them and said: Truly I say to you, unless you are converted and become as children, you will not enter into the kingdom of heaven. Therefore whoever humbles himself like that child, this one is greatest in the kingdom of heaven.** With the child set in their midst as an example of himself, the Lord teaches the disciples by showing that if each does not become like a child, he is not able to enter into the kingdom of heaven. But it was not for this reason that the Lord set forth the example of children, or commanded that we become as children as though we might pretend to be the age of children. For how can one who is older return to infancy? It was rather that we might imitate the simplicity and innocence of children.

The blessed Apostle knows we are commanded by the Lord to be children when he says: *Do not be children in understanding, but be very young children in malice, so that you may be perfected in understanding* (1 Cor 14:20). For a child or a very young person does not know the malice of the world, does not know to sin, does not do evil to a neighbor, does not hold on to anger, hates no one, does not seek riches, does not marvel at the glory of this world, always follows its father, does not withdraw from his mother. For this reason, the Lord wants us to become like children, so that with this example we might live without malice and without deceit in the present world. Let us flee sin, let us not do evil to our neighbor; let us not hold on to anger, let us seek neither after riches nor the glory of the world; let us always follow our father, that is, God, whose sons through adoption we have already begun to be (Rom 8:15; Gal 4:5; Eph 1:5), let us not withdraw from our mother, that is, from the Church, through which we were born spiritually by God. In her bosom, just like very young children who settle down in the lap of their own mother, let us be at peace. From this mother's sound teaching let us feed daily, so that we might grow in the faith and grace of baptism, according to which the Apostle Peter testified in his epistle saying: *As infants, desire milk, so that you may grow by it* (1 Pet 2:2). Holy John shows us also in his epistle that we ought to be like children, when he says: *I write to you, children, because you have known the Father* (1 John 2:14). By these things we are taught to be children so that we may recognize the Father; so that we may live innocent and simple as doves in this world (cf. 10:16). Therefore the Lord, wanting the likeness of children to be in us, rightly says in the present place: **Unless you are converted and become as children you will not enter into the kingdom of heaven. Therefore whoever humbles himself like that child, this one is greatest in the kingdom of heaven.** The Lord makes clear who will be greatest in the kingdom of heaven: whoever has imitated the humility and innocence of a child.

So that he might reveal a perfect example of humility in his person, the Lord also condescended to be made a child by assuming flesh. We learn this from what was written about him: *Seeing that a child is born to us, and a son is given to us, whose rule was made upon his shoulders* (Isa 9:6). By this understanding even the holy patriarchs and prophets and apostles were called children by the Lord. And we also read: *Behold, I and the children whom the Lord has given to me* (Heb 2:13), because they remained like children, without deceit, without malice. Therefore let us imitate the example of children, that is, of all the saints, so that we might be worthy to enter into the kingdom of heaven along with them. Let us imitate the humility of the Lord himself, who condescended to becoming a child for our well-being that we may be able to reign with him.

(3) Epiphanius the Latin

The holy evangelist reports that **in that hour the disciples approached Jesus, saying: Who do you think is greater in the kingdom of heaven?** Earlier our Lord had commanded the blessed Apostle Peter to go to the sea and cast his hook and take the fish that he hooked, and to offer the small coin he had found in the mouth of the fish as a tax payment for the

Lord and for himself (cf. 17:27). Therefore the disciples, upon hearing that he had named Peter alone, and being drawn by suspicion or jealousy, asked the Lord: **Who do you think is greater in the kingdom of heaven?** The Lord, however, seeing the interior of their hearts, confronted their desires and restrained the ambitions of their hearts. For **immediately calling a small child, he placed him in their midst and said: Truly, I say to you, unless you will have converted and become like little children, you will not enter into the kingdom of heaven.** Here the Lord not only opposed the thoughts of the apostles, but he also restrained the ambition of believers throughout the whole world. He who would be the greater must wish to be the least. So he placed a small child as an example, so that what the child is by nature we should become through a holy way of life, free from all sin. For a small child does not know how to be seized by anger or to grow bitter; he does not know how to render evil for evil; he does not contemplate shameful things; he does not commit adultery, nor arson nor homicide; or thefts or quarrels or anything that draw others to sin.

Whatever little children are from infancy, then let us become little children free from sin through a holy life. He who has become a little child in this way will rightly be greater in the kingdom of heaven. And whoever receives such a small child as this will be receiving Christ.

Matthew 18:5–6

5"Whoever receives one such child in my name receives me; 6but whoever causes one of these little ones who believe in me to sin, it would be better for him to have a great millstone fastened round his neck and to be drowned in the depth of the sea."

(4) Maximus of Turin

In the Scriptures, the race of the Gentiles is given the symbol of the ass that, with its eyes closed, is drawn around the millstone of ignorance in a circle of its own error. It toils unwillingly in another's employ while aimlessly going over its own tracks again and again. Does the race of the Gentiles not seem to you to turn a millstone so long as it is circling about in the toil of its own ignorance? It is held in the bonds of nature so that it may grind the word of God and seek the Lord of heaven, and yet so filled with the blindness of a closed mind that it cannot lift up the face of its soul to God or raise the eyes of its heart to heaven.

But since it is true that this stone is a millstone, let us see whether it is also the millstone of the pagans. Without a doubt it is, for the millstone of the pagans is the stony [millstone of] Jupiter and Hercules, around whom they revolve with blind eyes in constant error. I would say, indeed, that the eyes of those are blind who think that they see what they do not see. Looking at a rock, they are sure that they see God. But whoever uses a millstone is sure that sometime he will finish his task, and he hopes to put aside the work that had to be done. Yet the one on whose neck is hung a millstone carries a stone that has refused to bear the yoke of the Lord. The ass, therefore, at the millstone, the blind person at the stone, the pagan at the rock, is the one who adores him whom he neither sees nor knows (Acts 17:23). For God does not dwell in things made by hands (Acts 17:24), nor is he known in metal or stone. When the Gentiles persecute the Christian, they are struck with this punishment so that they, along with their sacrilegious millstone, are drowned in the waters that bring judgment to the world.

(5) Philoxenus of Hierapolis

Once he had rejected the company of wise, cunning, and crafty men and chosen the sinners, the innocent, and the illiterate, our Lord taught them to increase their simplicity, while not remaining in that first grade of their childlikeness. He took a child and set him in their midst, and looking at them all, he said, **unless you become converted and become like this child, you shall not enter into the kingdom of heaven.** Our Lord did this because he saw that the disciples were straying from the mind of simplicity by questioning the position of honor each should be given, even at the expense of the others. Yet the disciples and this question were born of a cunning mind. And our Lord rebuked the outcome of a troublesome question, when he spoke to his disciples, chiding and reproving them, "If you are mine you must become simple; if you seek the kingdom of heaven, you must be like this child; if you wish to receive the life that is to come, you must abide in sincerity; and if you wish to become wise in the word of life, you must abide in your unawareness. I don't want you to become cunning but simple, and it is from being simple that you become wise."

By this command, Jesus our Lord incited us to simplicity, and he warned us to become innocent and upright. For it is not right that we should be ashamed of simplicity; we should not seek to be excused from something that is useless to us in the eyes of the world, nor should simple things be despised in our eyes, nor should we consider them to be good for nothing. Although they may be unnecessary for the world, they are useful and necessary to the kingdom of God.

Matthew 18:7–9

7"Woe to the world for temptations to sin! For it is necessary that temptations come, but woe to the man by whom the temptation comes! 8And if your hand or your foot causes you to sin, cut it off and throw it away; it is better for you to enter life maimed or lame than with two hands or two feet to be thrown into the eternal fire. 9And if your eye causes you to sin, pluck it out and throw it away; it is better for you to enter life with one eye than with two eyes to be thrown into the hell of fire."

(6) Origen

It is possible to apply these words [if your hand or your foot causes you to sin, cut it off and throw it away] also to those near to us, just as we do to our own body parts, because of the closeness of a family member or of some habitual friendship, so to speak. Just as we must not spare those commonly used body parts that harm our soul, let us cast off from ourselves a father or a mother who wants us to act against true worship of God as a hand or foot or eye. Let us cut off the sons or daughters—assuming they can act responsibly for themselves—who cut us off from fellowship with the Church of Christ and his love. But even if *the wife in your bosom or friend who is equal to your soul* (Deut 13:6) become our temptations, let us not spare them. But cutting them off, let us throw them away from ourselves, away from our soul as if they were not our family but hostile to our salvation. For whoever *does not hate father and mother* (Luke 14:26) etc. When the time comes to hate those people as enemies and as threats so that one can gain Christ (cf. Phil 3:8), [the one who fails to do so] is not worthy of the Son of God. And about these persons one can indeed say that as if from misfortune a lame man is saved by having gotten rid of his foot (let us say his "brother"), and he alone inherits the kingdom of God. Likewise, a maimed man is saved even though his father and mother are not saved with him—instead, they are being destroyed at the same time he is separated from them, so that he alone obtains blessings. Similarly, a one-eyed man is saved by cutting out the eye of his own "house," the wife who fornicated, lest with such an eye he might go away into the hell of fire having two eyes.

For a hand that causes one to sin is a sinful action of the soul, a foot the sinful motion of the soul, and an eye the sinful perception of the soul. It is better to throw away and lay aside those things and to enter into life without them as if one is lame or maimed or one-eyed, rather than destroy one's whole soul along with these "body parts." Both the good of the soul and the blessing on its noblest faculties equally furnish its power. But if we are going to be destroyed because of a certain faculty of the soul, then it is more desirable to cast away the use of that which causes sin, so that we might be saved with the remaining faculties of the soul.

(7) Augustine

Let us love the law of God, to escape the words, **Woe to the world because of the stumbling it brings** (18:7). Let us say something now about the stumbling of which the world is full, and how scandals multiply, and afflictions and pressure abound. The world is devastated, the press is trodden down (cf. Luke 6:38; Rev 14:20). Come now, Christians, heavenly seed, strangers on earth who seek a city in heaven, who long to associate with the holy angels, understand that you have come here simply in order to take your departure. You are passing through the world, striving toward him who created the world. Don't let the lovers of the world disturb you, those who wish to remain in the world and willy-nilly are compelled to emigrate from it; don't let them deceive you or lead you astray.

These troubles and pressures are not the stumbling points. Be just, and they will be training exercises. Trouble comes; it will be whichever you wish, your education or your condemnation. Which it will be will depend on what sort of thing it finds you to be. Trouble is like fire; does it find you to be gold? It removes your impurities. Does it find you to be straw? It reduces you to ashes (cf. 1 Cor 3:12–15). If it's not the pressures, which certainly abound, that are the stumbling, what are they? Those little speeches, those words in which we are told, "Look what Christian times are producing," that's where the stumbling is. You see, the point of saying this to you is to make you blaspheme against Christ, if you love the world.

Matthew 18:10–14

[10]"See that you do not despise one of these little ones; for I tell you that in heaven their angels always behold the face of my Father who is in heaven. [12]What do you think? If a man has a hundred sheep, and one of them has gone astray, does he not leave the ninety-nine on the mountains and go in search of the one that went astray? [13]And if he finds it, truly, I say to you, he rejoices over it more than over the ninety-nine that never went astray. [14]So it is not the will of my Father who is in heaven that one of these little ones should perish."

(8) John Chrysostom

If God rejoices so greatly when a little one has been found, how is it possible that you look down upon those whom he seeks so eagerly? Are we not obliged to give up even our own life for these little ones, even it be only one of them? "Even for some weakling and a pauper" you might perhaps say in reply? But that is precisely the reason why you ought to do whatever it takes to make sure that such a person is saved! You see that even the Lord himself left the ninety-nine sheep and went looking for that other one. He did not let the safety of so many sheep overshadow the importance of saving from death the one that was lost.

Let us also imitate the Lord and shun no task that needs to be done for our brothers, no matter how humiliating and inferior that task may appear. Even if the person who needs and receives our services is lowly and poor, even if the labor at hand is exhausting, even if it involves crossing mountains and cliffs, let us endure all these things for the sake of saving our brother. Indeed, God seeks the human soul so eagerly that he did not spare his own Son.

It is for this reason that I urge you, as soon as we step outside at early dawn, let us have in mind this goal only, being earnest about this matter above anything else: to rescue those who are in danger. I am not just speaking about a danger to the body—that, in fact, is no danger at all. I rather mean the danger for the soul that the devil inflicted upon humankind.

A merchant crosses the sea to make his wealth increase. An artisan also does everything in order to add to his possessions. Similarly, let us not be satisfied with our own salvation only, or else we destroy even that.

(9) Ambrose of Milan

We ought to be happy, very happy, that the sheep that was lost in the first Adam is recovered in Christ. Christ's shoulders are the arms of the cross. It is there that I lay down my burden of sins. On the noble neck of Christ's gibbet I rest my head. Though one sheep is spoken of, it represents our race, for *we all form one body* (1 Cor 10:17). It is, of course, a body made up of many members, for as Scripture says: *You are the body of Christ and members of his members* (1 Cor 12:27). For *the Son of Man came to save what was lost* (Luke 19:10), that is to say, since *all died in Adam, so too all come to life in Christ* (1 Cor 15:22).

He must be a very rich shepherd if we form only one percentage of his inheritance.

He possesses innumerable flocks of angels, archangels, dominations, powers, thrones (cf. Col 1:16), and many others. All these he leaves on the heights. Since these are rational beings, they think it right to rejoice over the redemption of the human race. Is it not a further incentive to be good, when you consider that your conversion gives joy to troops of angels? Indeed, we should—each one of us—try to obtain their patronage, and we should dread giving them offense. Let us be a joy to the angels, and then they will surely rejoice when you come home.

(10) Jerome

If someone has a hundred sheep and one of them goes astray, does he not leave the ninety-nine in the mountains and go in search of the one that has gone astray? It is natural that he exhorts mildness in those to whom he had previously said: **See to it that you do not despise one of these little ones**. He adds the parable of the ninety-nine sheep left in the mountains and of the one stray that was unable to walk because of its great weakness. The good shepherd carried it back on his shoulders to the rest of the flock. Some think that this shepherd is he *who while in the form of God did not think it robbery to be equal to God, but he emptied himself, taking the form of a slave, having become obedient to the Father, to the point of death, even death on a cross* (Phil 2:5–7). They think that the reason he came down to the earthly regions was to save the one little sheep that had perished, that is, the human race. But others think that the number of ninety-nine sheep should be understood as the righteous, and the one little sheep should be understood as the number of sinners. This agrees with what he said in another passage: *I have not come to call the just but sinners; for the healthy do not need a physician, but those who are sick* (Luke 5:31). In the Gospel according to Luke, this parable is recorded along with two other parables, that of the ten drachmas and that of the two sons.

(11) Epiphanius the Latin

For no one is the true shepherd but Christ our God. One sheep has wandered away, but it is not the fault of the shepherd but of the sheep that had wandered away from its flock. That one sheep is the man Adam, whom the Lord had formed at the beginning according to his image and likeness. By his deception he wandered away from the way of life with the angels, and through him the whole human race wandered away from God. In most recent times, our Lord came to seek that man whom he had made so that he might recall the whole race of men back from death to life. He approached death for us, so that he might bring us, who were dead, to life. He also rejoiced more concerning the lost and the one-hundredth sheep than over the other ninety-nine. Over a hundred-year period, the patriarch Abraham believed God and was justified through faith. He received his son Isaac and was called through his faith the father of nations and crossed from the left to the right.

The number of a hundredfold is held in the right hand. Therefore, most beloved, the hundredth sheep is the pagans who have so believed and served the Lord, just like Abraham. Thus, they deserve to be placed on the right side, just as the Lord himself said: **Then he will place the sheep on his right, but the goats on his left** (25:33). For the goats are the [unbelieving] Jews or treacherous men and sinners. Those who have been placed on the left, the Lord will say to them: **Depart from me, cursed ones, into the eternal fire, which my Father has prepared for the devil and his angels** (25:41).

Matthew 18:15–18

15"If your brother sins against you, go and tell him his fault, between you and him alone. If he listens to you, you have gained your brother. 16But if he does not listen, take one or two others along with you, that every word may be confirmed by the evidence of two or three witnesses. 17If he refuses to listen to them, tell it to the church; and if he refuses to listen even to the church, let him be to you as a Gentile and a tax collector. 18Truly, I say to you, whatever you bind on earth shall be bound in heaven, and whatever you loose on earth shall be loosed in heaven."

(12) Ambrose of Milan

After telling the parable of the rich man tormented by excruciating sufferings, our Lord wisely recommends us to forgive—I mean, of course, to forgive those who have turned from their wrong-doing. This he does so that no one need feel discouraged, no one need despair of his conversion from sin. Our Lord expresses this with much kindness and moderation, balancing all that he says so that pardon does not become difficult, nor is forgiveness given too lightly. He wants no one to be put off by a harsh reprimand, nor—on the other hand—to be encouraged, by a casual sort of attitude on our part, to continue sinning. He says much the same in another place: **If your brother has sinned against you, go and rebuke him between you and him alone.** For a friendly remonstrance is far better than an angry accusation. The friendly approach inspires shame; the angry attack provokes fury. Hold back your indignation. It is better that the man you are warning should fear it rather than feel it.

I assure you that it is a far better thing that the person whom you are reproaching should consider you more a friend than an enemy. One is readier to listen to advice than to yield to force. This is why the apostle says: *Admonish him as a brother*—so that he will blush—*and do not look on him as an enemy* (2 Thess 3:15). Fear is, in the long run, a poor sort of guardian; but a sense of shame is a good teacher of what is right and what is wrong. The person who fears is reprimanded, not corrected or improved; but one in whom a sense of shame is awoken will return to the right path.

But note the Lord's exact words, **If he sins against you**. For there is a difference between sinning against God and sinning against a fellow human being. So the Apostle, who is an authentic interpreter of the divine oracle says: *Give the heretic one warning, and then avoid him* (Tit 3:10). If someone is false to the faith, then that sin is not to be forgiven the way a fault is forgiven. Yet we have to remember that often it is through our ignorance that error creeps in. That is why the Apostle says we are to give the heretic a warning; a warning may prevent him from growing hardened in heresy, or it may help him to correct his error.

(13) Jerome

But if your brother sins against you, go and correct him between you and him, etc. If our brother sins against us and injures us for any reason, we have the power, or rather the obligation, to forgive. We are commanded to forgive the debts for our debtors (6:12). But if anyone sins against God, it no longer depends on our choice. For the Holy Scripture says: *If a man sins against a man, the priest will pray for him; but if he sins against God, who will pray for him* (1 Sam 2:25)? In contrast with this, we treat lightly an injury to God but are annoyed to the point of hatred about insults to ourselves!

Now our brother ought to be corrected privately, otherwise he may all at once lose his shame and modesty and continue in sin. And if he in fact listens, we have gained his soul, and by the salvation of another we have achieved salvation for ourselves as well. On the other hand, if he is unwilling to listen, another brother should be summoned. And if he does not listen to that one, even a third brother should be summoned. This is done either out of zeal for correcting him or for the purpose of meeting together with witnesses. Next, if he is unwilling to listen to them, then the matter must be told to many. In this way, they formally renounce the one who could not be saved by shame in the hope that he might be saved by their reproaches. Now when it is said, **Let him be to you as a pagan and a tax collector**, it is shown that the one who has the name of believer but who does the works of unbelievers is more accursed than those who are openly pagans. For they are called "tax collectors" as a figure of speech, referring to those who pursue worldly gain and collect taxes by means of business, fraud, theft, crimes, and perjury.

(14) Augustine

Why scold him? Because you are sorry for yourself or because he's sinned against you? God forbid. If you do it out of self-love, you do less than nothing. If you do it out of love for him, you are doing something very good indeed. In any case, notice that the love you show is for him not for yourself: **If he listens to you, he says, you have gained your brother.** So do it for his sake to gain him.

You will see soon enough that which we ought to do at that time, but we aren't sluggishly reluctant to do it. Notice carefully: **If your brother, he says, has sinned against you, reprove him between yourself and him alone.** Why? Because he has sinned against you. What's the meaning, precisely, of **against you**? It means you know he has sinned, because it was something private, not known to other people, when he sinned against you. Look for a chance to do it privately, when you correct him for sinning. After all, if you are the only one who knows that he has sinned against you, and you want to censure him for it in front of everybody, you won't be reproving him, but betraying him.

Look how that just man, Joseph, showed such goodness in sparing the shameful wrong of which he suspected his wife, before he knew how she had conceived. He saw she was pregnant, and he knew he had not known her intimately himself. So there was a suspicion, amounting to a certainty, of adultery. And yet because he was the only one who had noticed it, the only one who knew it, what does the Gospel say about him? **But Joseph, being a just man, and unwilling to disgrace her publicly**. A husband's sense of injury did not look for revenge; he wanted to help the sinner, not punish her. **Being unwilling**, it says, **to disgrace her publicly, wished to divorce her privately.** While he was thinking about this, **behold, the angel of the Lord appeared to him in a dream** (1:19–20) and pointed out the truth of the matter, that she had not dishonored her husband's bed, because she had conceived the Lord of them both, by the Holy Spirit.

Matthew 18:19–20

19"Again I say to you, if two of you agree on earth about anything they ask, it will be done for them by my Father in heaven. 20For where two or three are gathered in my name, there am I in the midst of them."

(15) Jerome

All the above words encourage us to live in harmony. Therefore, a reward is even promised that we might hasten toward peace more zealously since he says that he **will be in the midst of the two or three**. This agrees with that famous example of the tyrant who made prisoners of two men who were friends. One of them left his friend as a hostage in his place and went back to see his mother. By keeping the one man in prison while releasing the other, the tyrant wanted to test them. When the friend returned on the appointed day, the tyrant so admired the fidelity of both men that he begged them to enroll himself as the third partner in their friendship.[1]

We can also interpret the above passage spiritually, where the spirit, soul, and body concur and do not have a war of opposing wills between them, as the flesh lusts against the spirit and the spirit against the flesh. Whatever they may ask for, they will receive it from the Father. No one doubts that when the body wants to have the same things that the spirit wants, it is a desire for good things.

(16) Peter Chrysologus

You have heard how much influence and power there is when we unite in agreement around a holy request. The Lord does not say "either this or that," but promises us *everything*: when he says **whatever they ask for will be done for them**, he means that anything we ask for in

1. Cicero, *On Duties* 3.45.

unity will be supplied. We should, however, ask for such things cautiously and respectfully, seeking from God only those things that are worthy of him. For anyone who asks God for evil things both declares and assumes that God is the author of evil, while whoever begs God for trite and shabby things shows himself to be an unworthy petitioner, oblivious to the unsurpassable might and power of God. So when we come before the giver of gifts, let us always ask for godly things, not wicked ones; for heavenly things, not earthy ones; for things that harmonize with virtue, not vice, for that which promotes peace, not hatred.

And how can anyone dare to regard the assembly of the church with contempt, asserting the superiority of solitary requests to the entreaties of the gathered congregation, when Christ himself tells us that he will be in the midst of the "two or three" gathered together, promising that he will supply everything they have requested? What will he not give, therefore, to *many*? What will he deny to those who make their requests within the gatherings and congregations of the saints?

Matthew 18:21–22

21Then Peter came up and said to him, "Lord, how often shall my brother sin against me, and I forgive him? As many as seven times?" 22Jesus said to him, "I do not say to you seven times, but seventy times seven."

(17) Hilary of Poitiers

We are instructed in every way to be like him in humility and beauty. As a means of softening and lessening the sting from our confused actions, he encourages us by the example of his readiness to forgive by granting pardon through faith to everyone who sins. Since our sinful nature does not deserve his mercy, complete pardon comes from the Lord, who offers mercy even when those who sinned against him returned to their former profession.

Whereas the punishment meted out to Cain was fixed at sevenfold (Gen 4:15), his was a sin against a man. Against his brother Abel, Cain sinned to the point of his brother's death. But in the case of Lamech, the punishment was fixed at seventy times seven (Gen 4:24). In this instance, I do believe, the punishment against the instigators of the Lord's passion has been established. At the same time, the Lord grants pardon for this crime by the confession of those who believe. Through the gift of baptism, he endows with the grace of salvation those who were his detractors and persecutors. He therefore shows how much more fitting it is for us to offer pardon without measure and without number, not keeping count of how many times we forgive. Rather, we should cease from being angry at those [who] sin against us, considering how many times the occasion has arisen for anger to be directed at us! At any rate, being persistent in offering pardon teaches that there is no occasion at all in which it is right for us to be angry, since God bestows his pardon for all of our faults according to his mercy rather than our merit. Nor is it right that we set a limit to the number of pardons that we allow, as if from a legal prescription, since God has given us his favor through the boundless grace of the gospel.

(18) Ambrose of Milan

Is there a fixed number of times that we are to forgive? Or does it mean that God, who rested on the seventh day from all his works, is promising us that after the week of this world there will be lasting rest? In that repose, the evil of this world will go on holiday and work no more; and the rigor of revenge will take a rest. Now, there is a Sabbath not only among days but also among months, and that is why the tenth day of the seventh month is the Sabbath of Sabbaths (cf. Lev 23:15; 25:8, 10); there is also a Sabbath among years, and not only among years, but among all the generations to the end of the world.

This is the image of the great Sabbath, just as in the law there is the seventh week, after which is celebrated the Jubilee Year. It is the mystery that our Lord has chosen to reveal to us, saying: **Not only seven times, but seventy times seven** (18:22). It was in the seventh generation—as you will find in Luke (cf. Luke 3:37)—that Enoch *was snatched away, for fear that evil would change his heart* (Wis 4:11), and he no longer knew sorrow's remorseless sting. So, too, it was in the seventy-seventh generation (cf. Luke 3:23–38) that the Lord was born of Mary; and taking upon himself the sins of the human race, he granted us pardon for all our faults.

(19) Augustine

In the number seventy-seven is contained the mystery of the forgiveness of sins. That's the number of generations we find from Christ back to Adam (Luke 3:23–38). Next interrogate this number a little more thoroughly for its secrets, search out its coverts; knock more insistently, so that it may be opened to you.

Do you want to see how all sins are contained in that number seventy-seven? It's usual to reckon a complete whole or total in terms of seven, because time revolves in seven days, and once you've reached the seventh you go back to the beginning so that it may roll on in the same form. The ages too pass through their revolutions according to the same pattern; there's no departure from the number seven.[2] So he included all sins when he said **seventy-seven times**; because when one multiplies eleven by seven, you get seventy-seven. So he intended all sins to be forgiven, because he pointed to them by the number seventy-seven. Nobody should retain sins against himself by not pardoning them, or his own sins will be held against him when he prays. God says, "Forgive, and you will be forgiven. But I have forgiven you first; at least forgive yourself afterward. Because if you don't forgive, I will summon you back, and whatever I have forgiven you, I will pile on you again."

2. It was taken for granted that the world is destined to last seven aeons or ages. The seventh aeon would be either "the reign of the saints for a thousand years" (Rev 20:4) or the eternal kingdom inaugurated by Christ's return in glory.

Matthew 18:23–35

**23"Therefore the kingdom of heaven may be compared to a king who wished to settle
accounts with his servants. 24When he began the reckoning, one was brought to him
who owed him ten thousand talents; 25and as he could not pay, his lord ordered him to
be sold, with his wife and children and all that he had, and payment to be made. 26So
the servant fell on his knees, imploring him, 'Lord, have patience with me, and I will
pay you everything.' 27And out of pity for him the lord of that servant released him and
forgave him the debt. 28But that same servant, as he went out, came upon one of his
fellow servants who owed him a hundred denarii; and seizing him by the throat he said,
'Pay what you owe.' 29So his fellow servant fell down and besought him, 'Have patience
with me, and I will pay you.' 30He refused and went and put him in prison till he should
pay the debt. 31When his fellow servants saw what had taken place, they were greatly
distressed, and they went and reported to their lord all that had taken place. 32Then
his lord summoned him and said to him, 'You wicked servant! I forgave you all that
debt because you besought me; 33and should not you have had mercy on your fellow
servant, as I had mercy on you?' 34And in anger his lord delivered him to the jailers,
till he should pay all his debt. 35So also my heavenly Father will do to every one of you,
if you do not forgive your brother from your heart."**

(20) Jerome

It is customary in Syria, and even more so in Palestine, to connect parables to all of one's words. By using comparisons and examples hearers can grasp what cannot be grasped simply by commands. And so, the Lord gave a command to Peter by means of this comparison to a king, a master, and a slave who owes ten thousand talents. The slave procures a pardon from his master when he asks for it, that he too might forgive his fellow servants when they sin in lesser amounts. For if that king and lord so easily forgave his slave who owed ten thousand talents, how much more ought slaves forgive lesser amounts to their fellow slaves? Let me try to make this clearer by an example: Suppose one of us commits adultery, murder, blasphemy, and crimes greater than ten thousand talents. Those who ask are forgiven if they themselves forgive lesser amounts to those who sin. But if we refuse to be appeased for an insult that has been made, and if we have continual discord because of a word spoken too bitterly, does it not seem right that we should be led back to prison and that, based on the example of our conduct, no pardon should be granted to us for our great transgressions?

(21) Augustine

Who, I ask, is not in debt to God except the one in whom no sin is found (John 8:46)? On the other hand, who doesn't have a brother in his debt, but someone nobody has sinned against? Do you really imagine anyone can be found in the whole human race who is not under obligation to a brother for sinning against him?

You see, there are two works of mercy that set us free, which the Lord himself set before us briefly in the Gospel: *Forgive, and you will be forgiven; give, and it shall be given you* (Luke 6:37–38). . . . What he says about pardoning: you want your sinning to be pardoned, and you have someone you can pardon yourself. Again, as regards generosity, consider when a beggar asks you for something that you are a beggar too in relation to God. When we pray, we are all beggars before God. We stand in front of the great householder's gate, or rather lying prostrate, and begging with tears, wanting to receive something; and that something is God himself. What do beggars ask you for? Bread. And you, what do you ask God for, if not Christ, who says, *I am the living bread who came down from heaven* (John 6:51)? Do you want to be pardoned? Pardon. *Forgive, and you will be forgiven* (cf. 6:12, 14). Do you want to receive something? *Give, and it shall be given you* (cf. 5:42).

(22) Origen

But you will inquire in these words whether all of the men of this king can be called servants, or whether some are servants *whom he foreknew and predestined* (Rom 8:29), but others are not called servants but bankers who conduct business with the servants. But you will also seek to learn whether there are those besides the servants whom the master of the house professes to tax with interest payments, not only servants who are strangers to devotion to God, but also some of the faithful. But servants alone can be stewards of business accounts.

As he **settled accounts with the servants, the king** demands from those who have borrowed from the servants, whether *one hundred measures of wheat* (Luke 16:7), or *one hundred jugs of olive oil* (Luke 16:6), or whatever those outside the king's household servants have received. For the fellow servant *of the unjust steward* (Luke 16:8) is not found, according to the parable, to be owing *one hundred measures of wheat* and *one hundred jugs of oil*, as is clear from that question, *How much do you owe my master?* (Luke 16:5). But you must comprehend with me that each good or fitting work resembles financial gain and growth, but each rascally deed resembles loss. And just as one financial success yields more money and another less, each with more or less difference, so also with respect to good works, as if a reckoning of greater or lesser gain takes place. But only God understands and is able to search out such things, because he has the perspective to see the disposition, the reasoning, the action, and those attendant circumstances dependent upon us and those that are not. He alone can reckon what sort of work is a great gain, what is lesser, what is least. It is God's prerogative to reckon in **the settling of accounts with the servants** what sort of sin for those hostile to him is discovered to be great loss, what is lesser, and what (if I must talk this way) is the loss of the small copper coin (Luke 21:2) or of the penny (5:26). So, what has been called **the kingdom of heaven** (**compared to a king**) **settles the account** of the whole and each moment of our lives when *we must all present ourselves before the judgment seat of Christ, so that each one might bring those things to him that he did in the body, whether good or evil* (2 Cor 5:10). At the time of the settling of accounts, he will be led into **a settling of accounts** for **every idle word that people might speak** (12:36), and whether he might once have given **a drink of cold water, because he is my disciple** (10:42).

(23) John Chrysostom

First of all I shall set forth God's kindnesses. What are his kindnesses? He made us when we did not exist and created all visible things with us in mind—sky, sea, earth, air, everything in it, animals, plants, seeds—we have to be brief in view of the vastness of his works. Into us alone of the things on earth he breathed such a living soul, he planted a garden, he gave a companion, he set us over all the brute beasts, he crowned us with glory and honor. After this, when he proved ungrateful to his benefactor, the Lord bequeathed to him a greater gift. In other words, you shouldn't consider only the fact that he drove him out of paradise, but think also of the benefit arising from this. After driving him out of paradise, and after working all those countless good deeds and bringing to fruition many different plans, he even sent his own Son for those benificiaries of his goodness who hated him, opened heaven for us, threw open paradise itself and made children of us, foes and ingrates though we were. Hence it would be reasonable to expect us now to exclaim, *O the depth of the riches and wisdom and knowledge of God* (Rom 11:33)! Yet he gave us also a baptism of remission of sins, a deliverance from vengeance and a kingly inheritance. He promised us countless goods for doing what is right, stretched out his hand and poured forth his Spirit into our hearts. Do you see the master's benevolence? Do you see the servant's cruelty?

Matthew 19

Jesus traveled across the Jordan River to Judea and performed healings there. Again he was approached by the Pharisees, who tested him by asking about divorce and remarriage. Their intent was to get Jesus embroiled in the controversy between the two rabbinic schools of Hillel and Shammai, the first of which allowed divorce more freely, while the other one restricted it to cases of adultery. The Pharisees, however, were unable to outwit the very fountain of wisdom, who did not allow the modern laws of men to dismiss the ancient laws of God (Asterius). The Lord answered that, from the time of creation, marriage was established by God as permanent (cf. Gen 1:27; 2:24). It was sin, therefore, to go against God's will and sever the marital union. Moses made provisions for divorce (Deut 24:1–4) because of the hardness of people's hearts, not permitting sin, but rather addressing its consequences. The Lord also made it clear that the requirements of marital fidelity applied equally to men and women. Augustine adds that marriage has a symbolic meaning, for it serves as a metaphor of the union between Christ and his bride, the Church.

The disciples' reaction shows that Christ's teaching about marriage could be misinterpreted. Since marriage appeared to entail many problems, was it not more expedient to remain celibate? Origen points out three types of celibacy: by birth, by alteration, and by choice, and that Jesus was teaching us that absolute chastity is a gift given by God, and not merely the fruit of training. According to Gregory of Nazianzus, despite all the comedy and tragedy of marriage, Christ is not teaching that it should be avoided. Marriage is good for those who seek to bring "into the world more people to please God." Nonetheless, all ancient writers agree that virginity is better.

Explaining the disciples' attempt to prevent children from approaching Jesus, Hilary reminds us that the Gospels often depict present events as prefiguring future ones. In this case, the children "prefigure the pagans to whom salvation was rendered through the hearing of faith" (Rom 10:17). Because Israel was supposed to be saved first of all (cf. Rom 1:16; 2:10; 9:3–5), they (i.e., the children) were prohibited by the disciples to approach. Christ calls us to imitate childlike innocence, but not the innocence that comes from ignorance or inability to sin. "Virtue does not consist in being incapable of sin, but in desiring not to sin and persevering so steadfastly in that resolution to imitate childhood's innocence so that it becomes one's second nature" (Ambrose).

Jesus's response to the rich young man's inquiry about eternal life carries christological and Trinitarian implications, as Ambrose observes in the manner in which the young man addressed Jesus, Good master, *rather than "Good God." This showed the young man's failure to acknowledge the Lord's divinity. God the Father and God the Son share the divine nature and its essential attributes. Even pre-Nicene commentators further reflect on the principle set forward in this account: salvation does not come by keeping the law, as Clement of Alexandria explained. Christ "warmly accepts" the young man's obedience to the law, though it was insufficient to make him perfect. Because he did not recognize Jesus as God, the young man overlooked that Christ himself was the fulfillment of that law (Rom 10:4).*

Concerning Jesus's words, It is easier for a camel to go through the eye of a needle than for a rich man to enter the kingdom of God, *Maximus of Turin draws an interesting parallel: just as the camel cannot pass through a small hole because of the "very crookedness of body," so the "deformity of life" caused by avarice will not permit the rich "to enter through the narrow way of the kingdom." Both riches and poverty can be either used or misused for God.*

The apostles were astonished at Jesus's teaching concerning salvation. They still did not understand the mystery of salvation by grace. But Jesus "freed them from their ignorance and fear, saying, This is impossible with man, but it is possible with God" (Luke 18:27) (Hilary). The Lord promised that, having followed him in the washing of baptism, in the sanctification of faith, in the adoption as heirs, in the resurrection of the dead, the twelve disciples would be blessed by being united with the glory of the twelve patriarchs and by sharing with Christ the rule over the future kingdom.

Matthew 19:1–2

1Now when Jesus had finished these sayings, he went away from Galilee and entered the region of Judea beyond the Jordan; 2and large crowds followed him, and he healed them there.

(1) Gregory of Nazianzus

He visits Galilee for a good reason, so that *the people sitting in darkness* might see *the great light of knowledge* (Isa 9:2). He returns to Judea to persuade the people to rise above the letter and follow the spirit. Now he is teaching on the mountain (5:1); now he reasons on the plains (Luke 6:17); now he crosses over on a boat (Mark 4:36); and now he rebukes the storm (Mark 4:39). He even welcomes sleep (8:24), perhaps to bless sleep; he becomes weary, perhaps to sanctify weariness; he weeps (John 11:35), perhaps to make weeping praiseworthy. He crosses from place to place like a man that no place can contain. He is timeless; he is without a body; and he is incomprehensible.

He was and is. He was beyond time and entered into time. He was invisible and is visible. *He was in the beginning, and he was with God, and he was God* (John 1:1). The third *was* is confirmed by the repetition. He *emptied* himself of what he was (cf. Phil 2:7); he assumed what he was not. He did not become two, but he was sent to become one thing from the two. For God both assumed and was assumed. The two natures coalesced into one Son, not two sons. Let the union not be spoken of falsely!

This Son is so great, so important—but what has happened to me? I have slipped again into using human words! For how can one like Christ be simple? How can something without quantity be so great? But pardon my word, for it is with a limited instrument that I speak about the greatest of matters! For the mighty one, the long-suffering one, the nature without form and without body will accept my words just as those of a body and weaker than the truth. For if he has taken on flesh, he will endure such language.

And a great crowd followed him, and he healed them in that place where there was a larger multitude. If he remained thinking his own thoughts, if he had not condescended to weakness, if he remained what he was, keeping himself unapproachable and incomprehensible, it is likely only a few would have followed him. In fact, maybe not even a few. Perhaps only Moses would have, but he was close enough only to see the back parts of God (Exod 33:23)! For he entered into the cloud (Exod 20:21), being separated from the burden of corporeal existence or drawn away from the senses. But how could he have looked at the immateriality or incorporeity of God? I don't even know what to call it. How could Moses see God, since he had a body and saw with sensible eyes? Because Christ is emptied for our sake, because he comes down—I am speaking of "emptying," a laying aside and lessening of his glory—he becomes comprehensible.

Matthew 19:3–9

3And Pharisees came up to him and tested him by asking, "Is it lawful to divorce one's
wife for any cause?" 4He answered, "Have you not read that he who made them from the
beginning made them male and female, 5and said, 'For this reason a man shall leave his
father and mother and be joined to his wife, and the two shall become one flesh'? 6So they
are no longer two but one flesh. What therefore God has joined together, let not man put
asunder." 7They said to him, "Why then did Moses command one to give a certificate of
divorce, and to put her away?" 8He said to them, "For your hardness of heart Moses al-
lowed you to divorce your wives, but from the beginning it was not so. 9And I say to you:
whoever divorces his wife, except for unchastity, and marries another, commits adultery."

(2) Origen

After this it is said, **The Pharisees came to him and tested him by saying, Is it lawful for a man to divorce his wife for any cause?** (And Mark recorded the same thing [Mark 10:2].) So then, some of those who came to question Jesus were testing him with their questions. And if our mighty Savior is tested, what disciple of his, who is appointed for teaching, would be vexed at being tested by some who also inquire not from a love of learning but from a desire to test?

Now you would find many passages, if you gathered them together, in which the Pharisees and others like them (such as a certain lawyer [22:35; Luke 10:25] and perhaps also scribes [Mark 12:28]) tested our Jesus. If you gathered together the passages concerning those who tested Jesus, you would learn what is appropriate from these kinds of questions.

Even so, the Savior also responds to the testers with instructions of piety. For they were saying, **Is it lawful for a man to divorce his wife for any cause? But he answered, Have you not read that the one who made them from the beginning made them male and female?** (And so forth.) I think that, according to this passage, the Pharisees were posing this question as a pretext, since they were going to pounce on him whatever he might have said. Because if he said, "It is lawful," they would have accused him of dissolving marriages over trifles. But if he said, "It is not lawful," they would have accused him of allowing a man to live with a woman even with sin.

(3) Gregory of Nazianzus

Because he condescended to our weakness, a great crowd was following him. And what should happen then? **And the Pharisees were coming toward him**, it says, **testing him and saying, Is it lawful for a man to divorce his wife for any reason?** Again, the Pharisees are testing him. Once again those who are students of the law do not know the law. And again, those who are interpreters of the law are in need of other teachers. The Sadducees were not satisfied with testing Jesus about the resurrection (cf. 22:23–28), the lawyers with inquiring about perfection (cf. 22:35–36), the Herodians about the poll tax (cf. 22:16–17), and others about his authority (cf. 21:23).

About marriage, someone again questions the one who cannot be tempted; the Creator of matrimony, the one who formed the whole human race from the beginning. **But he answered and said to them, Do you not realize that the Creator created them male and female . . . ?** He knew how to answer some of the questions, in other cases he silenced the questioners. When it is asked, **On what authority do you do these things?** (21:23), Jesus responds with his own question that exposes their ignorance: *Was the baptism of John from heaven or from men* (Luke 20:4)? And he binds those who were questioning him hand and foot!

Therefore, as we imitate Christ, we can sometimes silence those who speak with us in a meddlesome way and resolve the absurdity of questioners with absurd rebuttals. For we who are wise are sometimes foolish, if I may boast about foolish things (cf. 2 Cor 11:16). Yet when Christ sees a sensible question, he does not look down on his questioner and gives a wise answer.

(4) Augustine

Sometimes in the Scriptures Christ is presented in such a way that you are supposed to understand him as the Word equal to the Father, and sometimes in such a way that you are to understand him as the mediator, since *the Word became flesh to dwell among us* (John 1:14), since the only-begotten Son, *through whom all things were made* (John 1:3), *did not consider it robbery to be equal to God, but emptied himself, taking the form of a servant, becoming obedient to the death, even death on the cross* (Phil 2:6–8).

Sometimes, though, Christ is presented in such a way that you are to understand the head and the body, with the Apostle himself expounding as clearly as possible what was said about husband and wife in Genesis: *They will be two*, it says, *in one flesh* (Gen 2:24). Notice his exposition, because I don't want to give the impression of having the nerve to say something I've cobbled up myself. *For they will be two*, he said, *in one flesh*; and he added, *This is a great sacrament.* In case anyone should still think that this [sacrament] is to be found in husband and wife according to the natural joining of the sexes and their bodily joining together, the Apostle continues, *but I mean in Christ and the Church* (Eph 5:31–32). We also take as a reference to Christ and the Church what is said elsewhere: **They shall be two in one flesh; they are not now two, but there is one flesh.**

Just as bridegroom and bride, so also head and body, because *the head of the woman is the man* (1 Cor 11:3). So whether I say head and body, or whether I say bridegroom and bride, you must understand the same thing. That's why the same apostle, while he was still Saul, heard the words, *Saul, Saul, why are you persecuting me?* (Acts 9:4); because the body is joined to the head. And, as a preacher of Christ, he was suffering from others what he had committed as a persecutor, *that I may fill up*, he said, *in my flesh what is lacking from the afflictions of Christ* (Col 1:24), thus emphasizing that his suffering was part and parcel of the *afflictions of Christ*. These words can't be understood in reference to the head, which now in heaven is not suffering any such things, but of the body, that is the Church, the head of which is the one Christ.

Matthew 19:10–12

[10]The disciples said to him, "If such is the case of a man with his wife, it is not expedient to marry." [11]But he said to them, "Not all men can receive this saying, but only those to whom it is given. [12]For there are eunuchs who have been so from birth, and there are eunuchs who have been made eunuchs by men, and there are eunuchs who have made themselves eunuchs for the sake of the kingdom of heaven. He who is able to receive this, let him receive it."

(5) Gregory of Nazianzus

What do the Pharisees say? **If such is the case of a man with his wife, it is better not to marry.** Are you only now, O Pharisee, considering carefully the meaning of **It is better not to marry**? Did you not realize it before when you saw widows and orphans, untimely deaths, mourning following hard upon cheers, funerals after weddings, barrenness, children turning out badly, still-births, being bereft of a mother, and all the tragedy and comedy associated with these states? For both these words are fitting here.

Is it better to marry? For my part, I accept: *Let marriage be held in honor and the marriage bed be undefiled* (Heb 13:4). But it is better for the temperate, not for the immoderate, to regard the flesh more desirously than they ought to. Whenever marriage is only marriage, conjugal union, and a desire for the posterity of children—that marriage is right and good because it brings into the world more people to please God. But whenever it sets flame to the flesh, surrounds it with thorns, and, so to speak, discovers the way of wickedness, then I also say, **It is better not to marry.**

Marriage is good. But I cannot say that it is superior to virginity. Yet virginity would not be something great were it not better than something good. Do not be upset, whichever of you women who are under the yoke of marriage: *It is necessary to obey God rather than men* (Acts 5:29). However, you are bound to one another, both virgins and wives: you are both one in Christ and also one another's adornment. There would be no celibacy, except that marriage exists. For how did you, O virgin, enter into this life in the first place? Marriage would not be holy, except that it bears the virgin as fruit both to God and to life. You must honor your mother, from whom you have been born. Honor, too, the woman who has a mother and is a mother.

The virgin is not a mother, but she is the bride of Christ. Beauty manifest is not hidden; but God sees what is invisible. *All the glory of the king's daughter is within; she is clothed in golden tassels, she has been adorned* (Ps 45:12–13) either with actions or with contemplation. Let the one under the yoke be partly Christ's; let the virgin be fully Christ's. Let the married woman not be completely bound to the world; and let the virgin not belong to the world at all. For whatever is a share for the one under the yoke, it is a totality for the virgin.

You have undertaken a life in the community of the angels. You have taken a vow along with other unmarried women. Do not be seduced into the flesh! Do not be seduced to materiality! Do not be married to materiality! At all events, remain unmarried! A fornicating eye does not guard virginity; a fornicating tongue comes in contact with evil. Feet walking in an undisciplined way invite disease or danger to the mind. Let your thinking be celibate! Let it neither wander, nor be led astray, nor carry about the marks of evil deeds in itself—and that mark is a participation in sexual immorality. And do not let it make what is hated into idols within the soul.

(6) Ephrem of Nisibis

They came and asked him, **"Is it allowed for a man to divorce his wife?"** (19:3). He responded and said, "This is not allowed." And they began to tell him, "Moses has allowed us" (Mark 10:4). But if Moses allowed this, why did he say it was not lawful? It is because of the hardness of your heart that Moses allowed this; **but from the beginning it was not so** (19:8). It therefore follows from this particular commandment that the things established by Moses, because of the hardness of the people's heart, were supposed to be abrogated; and *a stiff-necked people* (Exod 32:9; 33:3) had to be replaced by a people who loved the faith of Abraham.

You shall not kill and *You shall not commit adultery* (Exod 20:13–14) and other commandments were observed even before the law, but they were issued in the law and perfected in the gospel. All of the law's commandments that were introduced by the original reason have ceased, not because the former order was abolished, but so that it may be affirmed by the new order.

Matthew 19:13–15

[13]Then children were brought to him that he might lay his hands on them and pray. The disciples rebuked the people; [14]but Jesus said, "Let the children come to me, and do not hinder them; for to such belongs the kingdom of heaven." [15]And he laid his hands on them and went away.

(7) Hilary of Poitiers

It is strange that the disciples had forbidden the small children to come to Christ, who were brought to him so that he might lay his hands on them and pray for them. The substance of the gospel is realized in the present and in the future, a kind of equilibrium that adapts one to the other as an image of the future conforms. It is certainly true that little children had been brought forward, but it is also true that they were dissuaded from doing so. But these children also prefigure the pagans to whom salvation was rendered through the hearing of faith (Rom 10:17). The Jews were to be saved first (cf. Rom 1:16; 2:10; 9:3–5), and the disciples prohibited the children from approaching. Of course the notion that they should be prohibited stands in contrast to the desire of the apostles. The point is that the children are a fulfillment of a type. The Lord said that they should not be prohibited because **to such is the kingdom of heaven.** And now the gift and the offering of the Holy Spirit through the laying-on of hands and prayer (cf. Acts 8:14–17) are bestowed on the pagans because the works of the law are ended.

(8) Ambrose of Milan

A little child is not physically strong; its character is not formed; its will is not mature. Our Lord cannot mean that one age is preferable to another; if so, it would make growing up a detrimental thing. How could I want to reach a mature age if it meant losing my claim to the heavenly kingdom? Am I to believe that God allows us to develop to full maturity only so that our vices could grow greater? If it comes to that, why didn't he choose little children, rather than grown men, to be his apostles? Why does he say of children that theirs is the **kingdom of heaven**? Perhaps the answer is that they are unacquainted with vice; they haven't learned to deceive; they are afraid to strike back; they know nothing about the pursuit of wealth; they have neither the desire for honors nor the goad of ambition.

But virtue consists not so much in ignorance of all these things as it is a kind of contempt for them. If we are innocent simply because we are powerless, there is no great cause for praise. So the childhood to which our Lord refers is a pure goodness that imitates the simplicity of children. Virtue does not consist in being incapable of sin, but in desiring not to sin and persevering so steadfastly in that resolution to imitate childhood's innocence so that it becomes one's second nature. This is how our Lord puts it: **Unless you change and become like this child; you shall not enter the kingdom of heaven** (18:3).

Who is this child that Christ's apostles are supposed to imitate? It can't simply be one of these little ones? Are the virtue and valor of an apostle to be found in one of them? Again, who is this child? I think that it must be the Child of whom Isaiah speaks: *For a Child is born to us, a Son is given to us* (Isa 9:6). Now learn how you can recognize this Child: *When he was reviled, he did not revile in return. When he suffered, he did not threaten* (1 Pet 2:23). You see, his virtue was perfect.

Therefore you can have, even in tender childhood, a true maturity of conduct. And in old age you can have an innocence such as children might have. For, as Scripture says: *Venerable old age is not a matter of long life. It is not counted by the number of your years. White hair is wisdom, and a spotless life is old age* (Wis 4:8–9). It is also written: *Children, praise the Lord; praise the name of the Lord* (Ps 113:1 [Latin Ps 112:1])—for none can praise the Lord unless he is perfect, and *none can say that Jesus is Lord except by the Holy Spirit* (1 Cor 12:3).

(9) Epiphanius the Latin

When our Lord was preaching in Judea and was instructing his disciples concerning the divine mystery . . . **children were presented to him, so that he might place his hands on them. However, the disciples were keeping them back.** Why were they keeping them back? Not because they were wicked, but because of a lack of propriety, so that our Lord would not become tired on account of such a huge crowd. But he said to them: **Allow the little children, and do not keep them from coming to me. For of such ones is the kingdom of heaven.**

Little children are ignorant of wickedness, nor do they know how to render evil for evil; they don't know how to commit injustice, or lust, or fornicate, or covet. What the child hears, he believes, and he loves his parents with complete affection. Therefore, most beloved, the Lord has commanded that we should have regard for that which excels in them. That is, we are to have the fear of the Lord and a transformed life, with a love of the kingdom of heaven that should make us like children. Unless we will pull ourselves away from every sin, like little children, we cannot approach the Savior.

Matthew 19:16–18a

16And behold, one came up to him, saying, "Teacher, what good deed must I do, to have eternal life?" 17And he said to him, "Why do you ask me about what is good? One there is who is good. If you would enter life, keep the commandments." 18He said to him, "Which?"

(10) Ambrose of Milan

And he said to him, Why do you ask me about what is good? There is only one who is good. We should believe that God is good, perfect, omnipotent, and true, as we find in the Law and the Prophets and the rest of the divine Scriptures. Without such attributes there is no God. It is impossible that he who is God could not be good, since the fullness of goodness is in his nature as God. It is impossible that God, who made time, should be a product of time. Nor is it possible that God be imperfect; for he who is less is certainly imperfect, whose lack of something could be compared to greatness. This is the faith we preach: God is not evil; with God there is nothing impossible, God does not exist in time, God is not a lesser being. If I am wrong, let it be refuted.

Since Christ is God then, he is certainly good, omnipotent, eternal, perfect, and true. For these are the marks of divinity. Let them rather deny the divine nature in Christ, since they cannot deny to God those properties that belong to the divine nature.

Lest anyone fall into error, let us follow after these things that are in Holy Scripture so that we might understand how it pertains to the Son: He is called the Word, he is called the Son, he is called the Power of God, he is called the Son of God, the Wisdom of God (1 Cor 1:24; Col 2:3). He is the Word because he is immaculate, he is the Power because he is perfect, he is the Son because he is begotten of the Father, he is Wisdom because he is one with the Father, one in eternity, one in divinity. But the Father is not himself the Son, because between the Father and the Son there is the distinction of being generated; the Son is God from God, Immutable from Immutable, Fullness of Fullness (Col 1:19; 2:9).

He said to him: Why do you call me good? No one is good but God alone.

A clever answer to a clever question. This ruler, who was actually testing Jesus and trying him out, called him *Good master* when he should have called him "Good God." Goodness lies in the divinity, and the divinity lies in goodness—for **no one is good but God alone**, whereas *every man is a liar* (Rom 3:4), and it is certainly not a good thing to be a liar. However, in adding *Good master*, the ruler is making out our Lord to be only partially good, and not totally good. Only God is totally good, while humanity is only partially good. This explains why the Lord says, "why do you call me good, you who deny that I am God. Why call me good when only God is good?" He is not denying that he is good, but he is pointing out that he is God.

But you will recall that it is written: *There is no one who does good. No, not one* (Ps 14:3 [Latin Ps 13:3]). Here it can plainly be seen that the Lord was speaking of humankind, not of God. For God is one, one in nature but not in number of persons. So the Son of God is set apart as being unique. He is not of the common crowd. He is the Only-Begotten, he is not one of a crowd that have been begotten. In saying **no one is good**, there is no intention of denying that Christ is good, for no one can judge Christ. **No one** is said in a general manner of the human species, but Christ is not of the common multitude.

If someone has difficulties with these words, **no one is good but God alone**, he should be equally disturbed that no one is good but God. If the Son is not excluded from the divinity, then Christ is surely not excluded from goodness. While being in God, the Son remains a distinct person, though one with the Father in power. *There is but one God, of whom are all things, and one Lord, by whom are all things* (1 Cor 8:6), since God and Lord are not two gods, but one single God, for *The Lord your God is one Lord* (Deut 6:4). If by his majesty there is but one God in each person, then in the two persons—Father and Son—there is only one goodness. For how could he, who is begotten of the one who is good, fail to be himself good? **A good tree produces good fruit** (7:17). How could he be other than good, since the substance of goodness drawn from the Father has not become less in the Son? Nor has it become less in the Spirit. Therefore we read: *Your good spirit shall guide me on the right way* (Ps 143:10 [Latin Ps 142:10]). If therefore the Spirit is good, and the Spirit has received from the Son (cf. John 16:14), then he who gave to the Spirit is surely good also. And if the Father is good, he who received all from the Father (cf. John 17:10) is most certainly good. In short, if you deny that the Son possesses goodness, you deny it of the Father too.

(11) John Chrysostom

The young man showed no little zeal at that moment. He had such a great desire and, while some of the others were putting Jesus to the test, and others coming forward about illness, whether their own or that of others, he came to speak about eternal life. We see how his "*soil*," was fertile and rich, but a great number of thorns choked the seed (13:7). Notice how the young man was ready to obey the commandments by asking, **What must I do to inherit eternal life?** At least he showed readiness to do whatever might be asked of him. . . . If he had come forward to put Jesus to the test, he would certainly have **gone away sorrowful** (19:22) at what he heard. This was not the reaction of the Pharisees, who were indignant at having their mouths stopped.

No, the young man was not like that: he went off downcast, clearly a sign that he had come forward with a proper but weak disposition, and while he had a desire for life, he was in the grip of another and grievous passion. Notice the great force of his passion. As soon as Christ told him to get rid of his possessions it overwhelmed and depressed him—he who had come forward in joy and zeal. The result was that he made no reply: he left saying nothing, downcast and sullen.

Matthew 19:18b–22

And Jesus said, "You shall not kill, You shall not commit adultery, You shall not steal,
You shall not bear false witness,
19Honor your father and mother, and, You shall love
your neighbor as yourself."
20The young man said to him, "All these I have observed;
what do I still lack?"
21Jesus said to him, "If you would be perfect, go, sell what you
possess and give to the poor, and you will have treasure in heaven; and come, follow me."
22When the young man heard this he went away sorrowful; for he had great possessions.

(12) Origen

If that young man is perfect, we might ask, why did he say in response to Jesus: **all these things I have observed from the time of my youth; what do I still lack?** The Savior agreed with his statement. **All these things I have observed**, but despite **all these things** he was not perfect: **If you would be perfect, go, sell what you possess and give to the poor,**

and you will have treasure in heaven; and come, follow me. What is the reason for this seeming contradiction?

It may well have been that the words **You shall love your neighbor as yourself** may not have been part of the Savior's original words at the time, but added by someone who did not fully grasp the precise meaning of the passage. It is my suspicion, therefore, that the words **You shall love your neighbor as yourself** are a later addition, which is confirmed by the account of the incident in Mark (10:21) and in Luke (18:22). Neither of these texts mention the clause, **You shall love your neighbor as yourself**, within the list of commandments mentioned by Jesus in this place.[1] For the reader who believes that the commandment **You shall love your neighbor as yourself** is an inappropriate amplification, we might also comment that even if the same things were recorded in the three Gospels with different words, still, Jesus would have said, *One thing you are lacking* (Mark 10:21) or *yet you need one more thing* (Luke 18:22), to a person who claimed to have fulfilled all the commandments.

According to Mark, Jesus, upon seeing this rich man, who said, **All these I have observed**, *loved him*. It seems that Jesus did agree that the man had kept all that he claimed to have kept. Jesus read his heart and saw that he was a man who claimed with a good conscience to have fulfilled the commandments he names.

Had the words **You shall love your neighbor as yourself** been also spoken along with the other commandments, Mark and Luke would not have omitted so central and comprehensive a commandment. It may be that someone will argue that the passages do have a resemblance but that they do not refer to the same incident. Yet how could Jesus have said to one who was not yet perfect, **If you will indeed be perfect, go, sell what you possess and give to the poor**, etc., to a man who claimed to have fulfilled all the commandments, including **You shall love your neighbor as yourself**?

We are not irreverently suggesting that because the passage in Matthew was an addition, the Savior never really mentioned it to the young man. However, there are many other details that differ in our copies, such that the texts of Matthew do not all agree, nor do all other Gospels. It is recognized that there is much diversity in our copies, whether by the carelessness of certain scribes, or by someone who too rashly made a text correction, or by some others making arbitrary additions or omissions in their corrections. Concerning the copies of the Old Testament, we discovered with God's help a method for curing the problem of differences. We compared other versions to determine a measure. Where a point was uncertain in the Septuagint because of the differences in our copies, we made a decision by looking at other versions. What agrees with them is the reading we have used.[2]

Someone might want to think of the commandment, **You shall love your neighbor as yourself**, not as an addition to this passage but as something the Lord originally said. Such a person can argue that our Savior wanted gently and directly to show the young man that he was not correct in stating that he had kept the commandment, **You shall love your**

1. The manuscripts of the Gospels bear out Origen's remarks. All the extant texts of Mark and Luke omit the suspected text.

2. Origen is talking about how he made judgments about the text of the Old Testament in his *Hexapla*, a huge book that printed out the original Hebrew, the Hebrew in Greek letters so it could be pronounced, and four Greek versions.

neighbor as yourself. So the Lord said to him, **If you would be perfect, go, sell what you possess and give to the poor.** In that way, he could confirm the truth of the man's claim to have kept the commandments.

(13) Clement of Alexandria

Jesus doesn't correct the young man because he has not fulfilled every detail of the law; rather he loves him and warmly accepts the obedience he has learned. But Jesus says he is not perfect in regard to eternal life, because he has not reached full maturity. Although he was a doer of the law, he has not achieved the true life. What he has done is good (and who says that is not so, for *the commandment is holy* [Rom 7:12]), but he has had a kind of training with fear and discipline that prepares him for the goal to which the law points and also for grace (Gal 3:24). For Christ is the fulfillment *of the law for righteousness to everyone who believes* (Rom 10:4; cf. 13:10), not making slaves, but making sons and brothers and co-heirs who carry out the Father's will (Rom 8:14–17). . . .

Because he did not understand these things properly, the very wealthy man who kept the law could not see how the same person can be both poor and rich, have possessions and not have them, make use of the world and not make use of it (1 Cor 7:31). He went away sad and downcast (Mark 10:22), abandoning the kind of life he could only desire but not attain, thereby making the difficult impossible. It is hard for the soul not to be seduced and destroyed by the splendid things and brilliant charms that come with much wealth. Even so it is not impossible to take hold of salvation, provided one removes himself from material wealth and holds fast to that which is grasped by the mind and taught by God and learns to make good and proper use of what is neither good nor bad. In that way he can strive for eternal life.

(14) Augustine

Some rich man was seeking advice from the good master about how to obtain eternal life. He was in love with a great thing, but he was unwilling to let go of a cheap thing that had no value. Because it was with a contrary heart that he heard what the **good master**—as he called him—had to say, he forfeited his dearest possession through his greater love for his cheapest. And yet, unless he had been genuinely interested in eternal life, he wouldn't have sought advice about acquiring eternal life.

So why, brothers and sisters, did the man reject the words of the one he had called good master; words of sound, reliable teaching that were offered him? If the Lord was a good master before he gave his teaching, was he a bad one after giving it? Before he gave his advice, he was called **good**. The man didn't hear what he wanted to, but he heard what he needed to. He had come with all eagerness and enthusiasm, but he went away sorrowful. What if he had been told, "Destroy everything you own"? Would he have gone away sorrowful if he were told, "Take good care of everything you own"?

Nobody should be afraid of spending money on the poor. Nobody should imagine that the one who receives it is the one whose hand is outstretched to accept it, since the one who receives is the Lord who ordered you to give it. And this isn't just my own idea, I'm not saying this as a piece of merely human guesswork; listen to him as he both gives you a warning and writes you out a guarantee. **I was hungry**, he says, **and you gave me to eat**. And when, after he has mentioned several other forms of kindness, they answer, **When did we see you hungry?** He in turn replies, **When you did it to one of the least of mine, you did it to me** (25:35–40).

[The Lord says:] "I received earth, I will give heaven; I received temporal things, I will return eternal things; I received bread, I will give life." Or rather, we can say this: "I received bread, I will give bread; I received a drink, I will give a drink; I received hospitality, I will give a home; I was visited in sickness, I will give health; I was visited in prison, I will give freedom. The bread that you gave to my poor has been eaten up; the bread that I will give both fills and never fails." May he give us bread, being himself the bread that came down from heaven (John 6:33, 41, 51). When he gives bread, he will be giving himself.

Matthew 19:23–24

23 And Jesus said to his disciples, "Truly, I say to you, it will be hard for a rich man to enter the kingdom of heaven. 24 Again I tell you, it is easier for a camel to go through the eye of a needle than for a rich man to enter the kingdom of God."

(15) Augustine

The rich man departed saddened, and the Lord said, *How difficult it is for anyone who has riches to enter the kingdom of heaven!* (Mark 10:23). He showed just how difficult it would be by offering a comparison that makes it so difficult as to be altogether impossible. I mean, everything impossible is difficult, but not everything difficult is impossible. How difficult is it? Look at the comparison: **Truly I tell you, it is easier for a camel to pass through the eye of a needle than for a rich person to enter into the kingdom of heaven.** For a camel to enter through the eye of a needle it would be impossible; if he had said a flea, it would be possible.

In any case, **when they heard this, the disciples were saddened and said, If that is so, who ever can be saved?** (19:25). Who among the rich? You that are poor, listen to Christ. I'm speaking to the people of God. Most of you are poor; you at least must try to understand. Any of you inclined to boast about your poverty, beware of pride, or you may be beaten to the punch by the rich who are humble; beware of irreverence, or the rich who are religious may beat you to it; beware of drunkenness, or the rich who are sober will beat you to it. Don't boast about your poverty, if they shouldn't boast about their riches. He doesn't suffer this experience as a result of wealth, but because of his own baseness. The same is true of a man who improperly persists in a praiseworthy account of his poverty. Many are poor; they are not all praiseworthy, but each is considered on account of his own experience. It is not his wealth that harms the rich man, but his unseemly course of life that shows the wealth to be useless and unbeneficial. Neither does his poverty lead the poor man up to heaven, but his bent of mind makes him think his poverty is profitable to his soul. For in rich and poor alike, it is the nature of upright conduct and the disposition toward it that gives excellence to right action.

Just as the same medicine will affect various people differently, so both riches and poverty may make a man either good or bad. In any case, no one is put to shame in the life eternal because he has lost his wealth through love of the kingdom of heaven, nor has he missed the mark by creating distance between himself and his possessions. By giving what he has, he has received what he had not. By setting aside the earthly burdens that are hardships to bear, he has received a fame that is light and not burdensome.

(16) Maximus of Turin

The Lord Jesus Christ says in the holy Gospel: **Truly, I say to you: It is easier for a camel to pass through the eye of a needle than for one who is rich to enter the kingdom of heaven.** I fear that these words may not suit you—you who either have or seek after the riches of this world. Like the camel, which is twisted and deformed and whose very crookedness of body does not permit it to pass through the extremely narrow hole of a needle, their deformity of life does not permit the rich, weighed down by avarice and polluted by desire, to enter through the narrow way of the kingdom. For the same Lord says: **Strait and narrow is the way that leads to life** (7:14). In the case of the camel, it is the construction of its body that makes the passage difficult, but in the one who is rich, it is the burden of his sins that causes the blockage.

Rightly, then, is a rich person compared to a camel, since bodily ungainliness prevents the one from passing through a needle, while concern for his property hinders the other from entering the Church. And just as a small needle cannot receive the one, which is hampered by the grossness of its body, so also the sacred portal cannot take in the other, who is encumbered by the weight of his offenses. Each has his own burden: the one is weighed down by his physiognomy, the other by his sins. And just as the one cannot pass through the needle's tiny eye, so the other is unfit for the most blessed kingdom of God, except that the camel's body is disordered by nature, and it is the will of the rich man that makes him evil.

Matthew 19:25–30

**25When the disciples heard this they were greatly astonished, saying, "Who then can be
saved?" 26But Jesus looked at them and said to them, "With men this is impossible, but
with God all things are possible." 27Then Peter said in reply, "Lo, we have left everything
and followed you. What then shall we have?" 28Jesus said to them, "Truly, I say to you,
in the new world, when the Son of man shall sit on his glorious throne, you who have
followed me will also sit on twelve thrones, judging the twelve tribes of Israel. 29And
every one who has left houses or brothers or sisters or father or mother or children or**

lands, for my name's sake, will receive a hundredfold, and inherit eternal life. [30]But many that are first will be last, and the last first."

(17) Clement of Alexandria

And after hearing what Jesus said to the rich young man, the disciples themselves became alarmed and amazed. Why exactly? Was it because they had also acquired many possessions? But their only possessions were their nets and fish hooks and boats that they had left long ago. Why then are they so disconcerted and say, **Who can be saved?** As disciples, they listened carefully to what was spoken in parables and in hidden ways by the Lord, and they sensed the depth of his words. They were confident of salvation because they lacked possessions; but because they knew they had not fully put away their passions (for they were beginners and only lately chosen by the Savior), *they were exceedingly astounded* (Mark 10:26), and they despaired of themselves no less than that very wealthy man who clung tenaciously to his property, which he preferred to eternal life.

We must not reject, then, possessions that can help our neighbors. For they are possessions in that they are possessed, and benefits in that they are beneficial and provided by God for human benefit. Like materials and instruments, they lie at hand and can be put to good use by those who know how to use them. The tool, if you use it skillfully, is skillful; if you lack the skill, it displays your ignorance. It is not at fault.

Wealth is such a tool. You can use it justly so that it serves justice. Or one can use it unjustly, so that it becomes a servant of injustice. For its nature is to be subservient, not master. So we must not fault what is of itself neither good nor bad, since it is not at fault. The fault lies in the one who has the power to use it well or ill, because he has freedom of choice. For the mind and judgment of man is free and able to determine how to use what is given to him. For this reason, let no one do away with wealth; rather do away with the passions of the soul that stand in the way of using one's possessions rightly. If one becomes good and virtuous, one can make good use of wealth. So then, renouncing and selling one's possessions (Luke 14:33) must be understood to be speaking of the passions of the soul.

(18) Hilary of Poitiers

When the apostles heard that no one can be saved by the law, they understood its spiritual meaning even though they were still under the law. They retained a love of the law and were favorably disposed toward it. They were not yet fully convinced of the evangelical mystery, fearing that no one could be saved without the law. At that time, they still based their salvation entirely on the law. But with straightforward and clear reasons, the Lord freed them from their ignorance and fear, saying, *This is impossible with man, but it is possible with God* (Luke 18:27). . . . But what is more unreasonable than to be saved by faith (cf. 9:22), to regenerate through water, to conquer through the cross, to adopt on account of the gospel, and to raise to life what was dead through the resurrection?

(19) Epiphanius the Latin

When the young man turned down the Lord's invitation, he possessed nothing on earth or in heaven. So the Lord said to his disciples, "A rich man will enter with difficulty into the kingdom of heaven; and he will enter with so much difficulty, that a camel would more easily pass through the eye of a needle than a rich man into the kingdom of heaven." What profit do riches bring if they separate us not only from God and from the kingdom of heaven, but also deliver us to eternal punishment?

Then Peter, responding: Behold, we have left behind everything and have followed you. How much did they leave behind? Wasn't it just a net and a boat? But the Lord requires more than surrendering material things. He who renounces the devil and his vices leaves everything behind; he who despises the love of the world and the desires of the flesh and the pomp of the world (1 John 2:15–16) leaves everything behind; he who denies himself and follows Christ has left everything behind.

And so, most beloved, while our apostles were still on earth, the Lord promised them honors and the kingdom of heaven, saying: **Truly, I say to you, that you, who have followed me, when the Son of Man will be seated in his majesty, you also will be seated on twelve thrones judging the twelve tribes of Israel.** And he added, saying: **And everyone, whoever has left home or brothers or sisters or mother or father or fields or vineyards, will receive a hundredfold and will possess eternal life.**

Even now the results of the Lord's sowing are sprouting (13:37). But we bear the weight of responsibility if they never sprout. **Many indeed have been called, but few chosen** (20:16; 22:14). So let us give attention to faith and obeying the gospel of our Lord, so that when he comes to judge the entire race of humanity, we will not be punished with all sinners but will be led into rest with the few and the chosen.

Matthew 20

The chapter begins with the story of the laborers hired to work in a vineyard at different times during the day. Some commentators take the movement of the day from morning to the eleventh hour as the historical time span from Adam to the Lord's coming. The workers who worked all day represent the Hebrew people, to whom the law was given (Hilary) and who in the persons of "the elect . . . eagerly worshiped God with right faith from the very beginning of the world" (Gregory the Great). The workers hired at the eleventh hour are the Gentiles, "who neglected to work for the whole of their lives, while so much of the world's history passed by" (Gregory the Great). Though they began working late, they were the first to obtain the payment as determined by a whole day's work (Hilary), receiving wages that were not earned but given a gift that signified salvation by grace. For Chrysostom, the day of laboring is a human lifetime, and the hours at which one is hired correspond to different ages when people come to God.

Despite variation in the meaning of particular elements of the parable, the ancient writers agree on its central teaching. God does not reward by human standards, because his grace cannot be earned by one's labors. Those who came to God "last"—either late in life or, like the Gentiles, late in history—are justified by grace through faith.

On the way to Jerusalem, Jesus announced to the disciples that he was going to die. Chrysostom comments, the Lord "constantly reminds them of it in order to train their minds and to undercut its pain," carefully choosing the timing for the announcement. It was only after he had given them sufficient proof of his miraculous power and instruction about eternal life that he spoke of his death. Christ promised the disciples that after his death he would return in three days, to let them know that his death would be followed by resurrection. However, they still did not understand the mystery, unable to accept that the one who healed others would himself have to suffer.

In the next episode, the mother of the sons of Zebedee, James and John, asked Jesus to sit her sons to the right and left of the Lord in his kingdom. In Hilary's interpretation, the mother represents the law that granted special privileges. But the apostles "had already come to faith on the basis of the law," by which they "attained the freedom and resolve of a martyr" and could suffer with the Lord and drink "the sacramental cup of his passion." According to Chrysostom, the disciples "were not asking for anything spiritual" but thinking in terms of God's earthly reign that they expected to appear immediately (Luke 19:11). They saw themselves as "more honorable than the others."

In the final scene of the chapter, Jesus restores the sight of two blind men. Because they called Jesus Lord and the Son of David, their minds "were illumined, God in man was proclaimed" (Hilary). They are a figure of the pagans who will believe, and, given spiritual sight, that is, the knowledge of God, they will follow the Lord. For Augustine, the two blind men are two people, the Jews and the Gentiles, whom Jesus came to heal. Chrysostom calls us to imitate the blind men, who, by their earnest prayer, exemplify "a persistent soul."

Matthew 20:1–16

1“For the kingdom of heaven is like a householder who went out early in the morning
to hire laborers for his vineyard. 2After agreeing with the laborers for a denarius a day,
he sent them into his vineyard. 3And going out about the third hour he saw others
standing idle in the market place; 4and to them he said, ‘You go into the vineyard too,
and whatever is right I will give you.’ So they went. 5Going out again about the sixth
hour and the ninth hour, he did the same. 6And about the eleventh hour he went out
and found others standing; and he said to them, ‘Why do you stand here idle all day?’
7They said to him, ‘Because no one has hired us.’ He said to them, ‘You go into the
vineyard too.’ 8And when evening came, the owner of the vineyard said to his steward,
‘Call the laborers and pay them their wages, beginning with the last, up to the first.’
9And when those hired about the eleventh hour came, each of them received a denarius.
10Now when the first came, they thought they would receive more; but each of them also
received a denarius. 11And on receiving it they grumbled at the householder, 12saying,
‘These last worked only one hour, and you have made them equal to us who have borne
the burden of the day and the scorching heat.’ 13But he replied to one of them, ‘Friend, I
am doing you no wrong; did you not agree with me for a denarius? 14Take what belongs
to you, and go; I choose to give to this last as I give to you. 15Am I not allowed to do
what I choose with what belongs to me? Or do you begrudge my generosity?’ 16So the
last will be first, and the first last.”

(1) Pseudo-Athanasius

Let us carefully inquire and learn who these laborers are, and what this vineyard is, and who the master is. In the first place, the master in this vineyard is God the Father, who has governed his creatures from the beginning. He has spoken to them through the prophet who told us that the vineyard of the Lord of Hosts is the house of Israel. The laborers whom he hired in the beginning are Moses, and Aaron and Joshua, son of Nun. . . . Those whom he hired at the third hour were the judges, whom he appointed overseers of his people. Those who were hired at the sixth hour and at the ninth hour were Samuel, and David, and all the prophets. Samuel worked in the vineyard with a horn (1 Sam 16:13). David transplanted a sprout of the vine from the land of Egypt, and he cultivated it with the psaltery. Hosea found Israel to be like a vine in the desert, for he said, *Israel is a branch of a vine that is good, and its fruit abundant* (Hos 10:1). Those who were hired at the eleventh hour were the apostles, who had been idle the whole day. They were idle in respect to the works of sin of every kind, because no one had hired them, and the devil could not hire them for the service of idols. . . . So, no one on earth could hire them to work and give wages according to what they were worth.

These words enable us to know that it is the Father who hires laborers for his vineyard. Who is this steward? I say it is the Lord Jesus, the Christ, the Son of God, in whose hands in a mysterious way are all the things of God. His power is in Israel and in the other nations, for he himself said, *The Father loves the Son and has given everything into his hand* (John 3:35).

(2) John Chrysostom

What does this parable mean? We must clarify its meaning before speaking of other matters. The vineyard is God's commandments and laws; the period of working is one's lifespan; the laborers are those who, at different times, are called to do what God commands; the early morning and the third, ninth, and eleventh hours are those who, at differing times in their lives, have come and become just.

But the question is this: why were the first laborers who had acquitted themselves well and were well-pleasing to God, and worked throughout the whole day with great toil, ultimately gripped by evil passion, envy, and jealousy? When they saw that the others had enjoyed the same rewards, they said, **These last ones worked but one hour, and you have made them equal to us who endured the burden of the day and the scorching heat.** They show by these words that, although they were not wronged and their wages were not reduced, they were indignant and upset at the good fortune of the others, certain evidence of their envy and jealousy. Moreover, the householder, in justifying and defending himself against those who said these things, accuses them of wickedness and envy, saying, **Didn't you agree with me for a denarius? Take what belongs to you and go; I choose to give to the last as much as I gave to you. Are you envious because I am generous?**

So why did he not hire all of them from the outset? As far as the householder was concerned, all were present even if not all responded at the same time; the difference was the readiness of those who were called. This is the reason why some are called early in the morning, some at the third hour, some at the sixth, some at the ninth, and some at the eleventh—at the times when they were ready to respond.

Paul clearly says this too: *When God, who separated me from my mother's womb, was pleased* (Gal 1:15). When did it please him? When Paul was ready to respond. God himself willed it from the beginning, but since Paul would not have yielded, God was pleased when Paul also was ready to be persuaded. God called the thief in a similar way (Luke 23:42). Even though he could have called him before, he would not have responded. For if Paul would not have responded at the beginning, much less so the thief.

By all accounts, it is clear to us that the parable is meant for those who pursue virtue from earliest childhood and those who do so later in old age—for the former that they might not be proud and reproach those who come at the eleventh hour; for the latter that they may learn that it is possible to recover everything even in a short time.

(3) Augustine

Just now you heard a parable from the holy Gospel: The **kingdom of heaven is like a householder, who went out to hire laborers for his vineyard** (20:1). He went out early and hired those he found, and he agreed with them on a daily wage of ten dollars. He went out again at nine in the morning and found others, and he brought them to work in the vineyard. He did the same also at noon, and again at three in the afternoon. He went out too even at five o'clock, almost at the end of the day, and found some people standing around idle. And he said to them, "Why are you lounging around here? Why aren't you working in the vineyard"? They answered, "Because no one has hired us." "You come as well," he said, "and I will give you what is fair." A wage of ten dollars was agreed upon.

When would these men, who were only going to work for one hour, ever have dared to promise themselves ten dollars? They were pleased to think they were going to get anything, being hired for one hour. At the end of the day, he ordered them all to be paid their wages, from the last comers to the first. He began paying from those who had come at five o'clock and ordered them to be given ten dollars. When those who had come at seven o'clock in the morning saw these fellows getting ten dollars each, which they themselves had agreed upon, they hoped they would get rather more; it came to their turn—and they received ten dollars. They grumbled against the householder and said, "Look, here are we who have borne the heat and the bustle of the day, and you have put us on the same level as these fellows who have worked only one hour in the vineyard."

And the householder gave one of them the fairest possible reply and said, "Friend, I haven't done you any wrong; that is to say, I haven't cheated you. I've paid you what I agreed to. I haven't cheated you, because I've paid what I stipulated. As for this man, my wish is not to pay him but to give him a present. Am I not allowed to do what I like with my own? Or are your eyes envious because I am generous? If I had robbed someone else's money to give to someone else, I would be rightly blamed for it as a cheat and as unjust; if I hadn't paid someone what I owed them, I would be rightly blamed as a cheat and as refusing their rights. But when I pay what I owe, and also make a present to anyone I like, the one to whom I owed money can't blame me, while the one I made a present to has all the more reason to rejoice."

No answer was possible; they had all been treated as equals, and the last had become first and the first last (20:16) by putting them on the same level; not by turning them back to front. What's the meaning of "The last have become first and the first last"? That both the first and the last have received exactly the same.

So why did he begin paying out starting with the last? Weren't they all, as we read, going to receive together at the same time? You see, we read in another place in the Gospel that he is going to say to those he places on his right hand, **Come, blessed of my Father, receive the kingdom that has been prepared for you from the beginning of the world** (25:34). So if all are going to receive together, how are we to understand it here that those who worked from five o'clock were the first to receive their wages, while those who worked from seven o'clock in the morning were the last? If I can explain in such a way as to make you understand, then God be thanked. He, after all, is the one you ought to thank, because he is the one paying out to you through me; I mean, I'm not paying out to you out of my own assets.

If you were to ask two of these men, for example, who were the first to receive their wages, first the one who received his wages after one hour, and then the other after his twelfth hour of working, everyone would answer that the one who had worked one hour received before the one who had worked twelve. Although they all received their wages at the same time, some received them after one hour, others after twelve, and the ones who received them after working a short time are said to have received them first.

The first righteous men, like Abel and Noah, were called—so to speak—at the beginning of the day, and they are going to receive the happiness of the resurrection along with us. Other righteous men, Moses and Aaron (and others of their time), were called, you could say about noon, and they are going to receive the happiness of the resurrection along with us. After them, the holy prophets were called, as it were, in the afternoon to receive the same happiness along with us. At the end of the world, all Christians, who are called at the equivalent of five o'clock, are going to receive the happiness of this resurrection along with these. We are all going to receive it together. But notice after how long a time those first people are going to receive it. If those first people receive it after a long time and we after a short time, although we all receive it together, still we seem to have received it first, because our reward hasn't been so long in coming.

(4) Gregory the Great

The householder hired workmen to cultivate his vineyard in the morning, and at the third, sixth, ninth, and eleventh hours. . . . The morning was, in fact, from Adam to the time of Noah, the third hour from the time of Noah to the time of Abraham, the sixth from the time of Abraham to the time of Moses, the ninth from the time of Moses to the coming of the Lord; and the eleventh is from the coming of the Lord to the end of the world. In this period, the holy apostles, who received a full reward even though they came late, have been sent as preachers. At no time, then, did the Lord cease sending his people workmen to instruct them, to cultivate his vineyard, as it were. When he first cultivated his people through the patriarchs, and later through the teachers of the law, and then through the prophets, and at last through the apostles, he worked at cultivating his vineyard through his workmen. Everyone who had the right faith with good works, in whatever capacity or measure, was a workman in his vineyard. And so the Hebrew people are meant by the workmen who came to the vineyard in the morning and during the third, sixth, and ninth hours. As the elect, they eagerly worshiped God with right faith from the very beginning of the world, and they did not cease from cultivating his vineyard.

The Gentiles were called at the eleventh hour, and it was said to them: **Why do you stand here the whole day idle?** Those who neglected to work for the whole of their lives, while so much of the world's history passed by, were like those standing the whole day. But consider, my friends, what they answered when they were questioned. They said: **Because no one has hired us.** In truth, no patriarch and no prophet had come to them. When they said, "No one has hired us to work," was that the same thing as saying, "No one has preached to us the ways of life"? What, then, are we to say, to excuse ourselves for our having ceased to do good works? We have come to the faith almost from our mothers' wombs, we have heard the words of life from our cradles; we have received divine preaching from the breasts of the holy Church together with our mothers' milk!

But we can also apply these same hourly periods to each individual person's life. Morning is the childhood of our understanding. The third hour can be interpreted as our youth, because the sun is advancing on high, as the impetuosity of age increases. The sixth hour is that of young adulthood, because we reach our full strength, just as the sun is in the center of the heavens. The ninth hour we take to be old age, because like the sun descending from its zenith, this age lacks the warmth of youth. The eleventh hour is the age that is called infirm or old, and so the Greeks call people who are very old to indicate that they are very advanced in age. . . .

Since then one person is brought to a good life in childhood, another in youth, another in young adulthood, another in old age, another at the age of infirmity, it is as if workmen are being called to the vineyard at different hours. Look at your conduct, my friends, and see whether you are still God's workmen. Let everyone reflect on what he is doing, and consider whether he is laboring in the Lord's vineyard.

Matthew 20:17–19

17And as Jesus was going up to Jerusalem, he took the twelve disciples aside, and on
the way he said to them, 18"Behold, we are going up to Jerusalem; and the Son of man
will be delivered to the chief priests and scribes, and they will condemn him to death,
19and deliver him to the Gentiles to be mocked and scourged and crucified, and he will
be raised on the third day."

(5) John Chrysostom

Jesus did not immediately go up to Jerusalem from Galilee. First, he performed miracles, silenced the Pharisees, and spoke with the disciples about the virtue of poverty . . . virginity . . . humility . . . giving up the things of this present world . . . and receiving the rewards of the next. Finally, approaching Jerusalem, and just before entering into the city, he once again spoke of his suffering. Since it was likely the disciples would forget about it—because they were unwilling to accept it—he constantly reminds them of it in order to train their minds and to undercut its pain.

He necessarily spoke to them in private in order to prevent rumors with any of this circulating publicly. Nor could he speak plainly because that would have been useless. For if the disciples were bewildered listening to the Lord's speaking about his suffering, how much more would the masses be disturbed by it.

But one might ask, "Why is it so? Didn't he speak to the masses?" He did speak to the masses but not as clearly. Addressing the public, he said, *Destroy this temple, and in three days I will raise it up* (John 2:19), and **This generation seeks after a sign, but no sign shall be given to it except the sign of Jonah** (12:39), and again, *I will be with you a little while longer, and you will seek me, but you will not find me* (John 7:33–34). But he did not speak this way with the disciples; instead, just as he spoke openly about other matters, so he also explained this with openness too. Why then did the Lord speak to the people at all, if they did not understand the power of his words? The reason was so that afterward they would come to realize that he had foreknown his suffering, and that he went to it willingly, not in ignorance or under compulsion.

This, however, was not the only reason why Jesus predicted his suffering to the disciples. As I have already said, his purpose was that they might be prepared to endure this suffering, and so be trained to expect it, rather than be cast into severe turmoil by it. This is why, early on, he spoke only about dying. But here, after they had spent time meditating upon it and getting accustomed to the idea, he adds other details: that he will be **given up to the Gentiles and will be mocked and flogged**. Because of this, when the disciples see these mournful predictions come to pass, they will also expect the resurrection shortly after. The Lord, because he did not hide that which was painful and seemingly disgraceful, must surely be trusted when he speaks about that which is pleasing—that is, his resurrection.

But consider with me how wisely he chooses the timing for this conversation with the disciples. Neither did he speak with them from the beginning, so that they would not be utterly confused, nor did he speak about it right before his passion, so that they might not cause an uproar. Only after they had received sufficient proof of his power, and he had given them the great promise of eternal life, does he introduce the idea that he will suffer. He does this once, then twice, and even several times, interweaving it with miracles and teachings.

(6) Peter Chrysologus

Adversities are evil if they come upon us unaware; but less so if we walk in them knowingly. But the Lord suffered *willingly*; he voluntarily "went up" to the place where he would suffer. Death rules over the reluctant but serves those who welcome it. When Christ willed to die, therefore, he was not falling under the dominion of decay, but unveiling the reality of his power. *I have the power*, he says, *to lay down my life . . . and I have the power*, he clarifies, *to take it up again. No one can snatch it from me* (John 10:18). Think about it: if he has the power both to "lay down" his life and "take it up again," in what sense was his death inevitable? It wasn't. Instead it was voluntary. Remember, he tells us that *No one can snatch it from me.* No one, not even death.

Death was unable to destroy him, hell unable to hold him. Trembling at his decree, it let slip even those souls it had once cowed by its power: **And the tombs**, we are told, **were split asunder; and the bodies of many saints arose** (27:52). Christ's arrival in this world had set everything off kilter; his conception broke all natural laws, his birth flouted all custom. Now at his death, Tartarus lost its power over its denizens, the ancient jurisdiction of hell was wrenched aside, and death itself was forced to relinquish its time-honored prerogatives in the face of the new order.

But let us return to the text. **Behold**, he says, **we are going up to Jerusalem, and the Son of Man will be handed over to the chief priests. They will condemn him to death, and they will hand him over to the Gentiles**. God knows everything that will happen, because he has foreseen the future. He was aware of the scandal of the cross, the tumult of the passion. He knew that the earth would tremble at the injustice done its author; that the heavens would flinch in horror, that the sun would hide itself and its light would turn to shadow, that hell would bristle, that all of creation would stand aghast, would fall into confusion.

And after three days he will rise. Is there really time for sorrow if he returns so swiftly? **After three days**, his leaving and return was of such a sort that we could fairly say he was never absent. Even when God departs, he is nevertheless present—and since he is always present, he is never truly gone. Christ withdrew from his apostles, but he never left them; the Lord approached death, but he never abandoned life. His descent into hell was not an emigration from heaven, as he assures us when he says, *No one can ascend into heaven except for him who has first descended from heaven—that is, the Son of Man who is in heaven* (John 3:13).

It is a mark of our humanity that we do not wish to die, that we fear death, because to die and rise again is a mark of God alone. **And after three days**. Why not four? Why not five? What's so important about three? I'll tell you why: so that the participation of the whole Trinity might be revealed in the passion of the Son. The "three days" symbolically refer to the Trinity. The same triune God who originally formed humanity through the work of Christ in the beginning now renews humanity through his passion at the end. The same one who said, *Let us make man* (Gen 1:26), now says, **Baptize all nations in the name of the Father, the Son, and the Holy Spirit** for the forgiveness of sins (28:19). Think about it: if the Trinity is united in its merciful forgiveness of sins, how could it fail to be of one will regarding the passion of the Son?

Christ told us that **Just as Jonah was in the belly of the whale for three days and three nights, so will the Son of Man be in the heart of the earth** (12:40). Notice that he said **in the heart of the earth**; he most certainly did *not* say "within the power of the earth." In other words, the earth recognized its author, and it trembled since it was not able to hold him. Rather than engulfing him in decay, it received him in humble submission. For the earth did not assume that it had a claim to the body of its Lord; instead, it received it as an ambassador from the realms of glory.

The founder of everything! The author of the universe! Why would he will to be born, unless he was willing to die? Why would God clothe himself in the fragility of flesh, unless he was willing to experience its affliction? Why would the Lord of all creation take on the appearance of a slave, unless he meant to undergo a slave's humiliation? The judge allows himself to be judged, the advocate is condemned, surrendering himself to the sentence of the depraved. Why? Why should he suffer if he retains both the power and the inclination to save? Why must he die if he possesses both the strength and the means to give life?

Behold, we are going up to Jerusalem, and the Son of Man will be handed over to the chief priests. They will condemn him to death, and they will hand him over to the Gentiles. They will mock him, they will spit on him and after three days, he will rise. We are going up to Jerusalem: and on the day of the Passover! Why? So that the Jewish city in its entirety may view the passion on display, the death-show, the scandal of the cross. Ordinary suffering, private demise, a simple death, a death like any other death—this will not suffice. To fit the singularity of the sufferer, the city must see a passion unparalleled.

And so it happened in such a way that the world's author would die with the world as his witness; the Lord of the earth would be unveiled in condemnation rather than glory. The peace of heaven would be delivered up by a treacherous kiss. He who holds the world in his hands is held, he who bounded the universe is bound, and the one who draws all to himself is drawn forth. Truth is accused by false witnesses, he for whom the world stands now stands at the dock. The Jews hand him over to the Gentiles, and the Gentiles return the favor. Pilate pawns him off on Herod, and Herod shifts him back to Pilate. Piety is reimbursed by impiety, holiness led to the auction block of cruelty. Now forgiveness is flogged, kindness condemned, majesty mocked, and honor humiliated. Now he who lavishly gives rain is bathed in spit, the spreader of the sky is fixed by spikes of iron. The designer of honey is offered gall; the fount of all springs chokes on vinegar. Finally, though there is nothing left to punish, death is wary, death delays its onslaught, since it knows that it has no claim to what lies there.

Matthew 20:20–23

20Then the mother of the sons of Zeb'edee came up to him, with her sons, and kneeling
before him she asked him for something. 21And he said to her, "What do you want?" She
said to him, "Command that these two sons of mine may sit, one at your right hand and
one at your left, in your kingdom." 22But Jesus answered, "You do not know what you
are asking. Are you able to drink the cup that I am to drink?" They said to him, "We are
able." 23He said to them, "You will drink my cup, but to sit at my right hand and at my
left is not mine to grant, but it is for those for whom it has been prepared by my Father."

(7) Hilary of Poitiers

We should understand that this request of the mother of the sons of Zebedee was no small thing. Didn't her sons know what she was seeking? But this happened so that the events foretold in the past would come to be.

The apostles had already come to faith on the basis of the law that made them ready to believe in the gospel. The mother of the sons of Zebedee should be understood as the law, because the law, confident of its privileged status, was an advocate for those whose faith was drawn only from the law. When earlier she had heard that **the first shall be last, and last shall be first** (19:30), she asked that her sons be given preference in the Lord's kingdom so that one may **sit at his right hand and the other on his left**. The Lord responded that she did not know what she was asking (for his earlier words left no doubt concerning the glory of the apostles and that they were going to be judges) (19:28). In the midst of the discussion, the Lord asked whether they were able to drink his cup. He was certainly not speaking of the type of commonly used cup, since drinking from it requires no effort. Rather, he was asking about the sacramental cup of his passion. For it was promised to those who already attained the freedom and resolve of a martyr that they would drink of this cup. Extolling their faith, the Lord says that they are able to suffer with him in martyrdom, but to sit at his left or right had been prepared for others by God the Father.

The Lord teaches that they should not exercise preeminence as the pagans do. Glory and great honor are shown by ministers and servants (cf. 20:26–27), not by those who have been served. Such was the example of the patriarchs and the prophets who served, as well as by the apostles who ministered, and also by the example of the Lord, who yielded his life for the redemption of our salvation (cf. 20:28).

In light of the glory of his humility, Jesus instructs them by means of a meal or a banquet, reminding them not to recline at the more eminent places of the table, lest someone who is more distinguished come along and they suffer the insult of being humiliated when the master of the meal asks them to give up their place (cf. Luke 14:8–11). If they recline at a modest place at the table to begin with, they might be moved up to the prominence of a more elevated place when more lowly guests come along. And thus, it is not right to presume upon any honor, but to merit it by one's works of humility.

(8) John Chrysostom

Let us first learn, what were they asking for? What was behind their request? And what was their true motivation? Believing themselves to be more honorable than the others, they expected to be granted this request. But for what are they asking? Listen to another Gospel writer who clarifies this issue. He says that they were asking these things *because they were near Jerusalem, and because they thought that the kingdom of God was about to appear* (Luke 19:11).

They believed that the kingdom of God was at hand, that they could sense it, and that once they received the benefits they were asking for, they would face no hardship. They were seeking the kingdom of God not for its own sake, but to be free of hardship. For this reason, Christ quickly leads them away from this kind of thinking and urges them to expect slaughter, danger, and the most dreadful horrors. He even says, **Are you able to drink the cup that I am to drink?**

But do not be troubled if the apostles are imperfect. For the cross had not yet been accomplished, nor had the grace of the Spirit been given. If, however, you wish to know the virtue of the disciples, you should closely examine their later life, and you will see them overcoming every passion. It is for this reason that the Lord reveals their flaws, in order that you might know what kind of people they became by grace.

That they were not asking for anything spiritual and that they did not have any idea about the kingdom above is evident from what follows. Let us examine how they approach him and what they say. *We want you to do for us whatever we ask of you* (Mark 10:35). Christ replies to them, *What do you want?* (Mark 10:36), not because he does not know, but to force them to answer, thereby exposing the wound so that he might apply the medicine.

Now they had taken him aside from the other disciples and made their request in private because they were embarrassed and ashamed that they were driven by human desire. For the text says that they had gone ahead of others in order not to be discovered and told him exactly what they wanted. What they wanted no doubt came from what they had already heard: **You will sit on twelve thrones** (19:28). They wanted the most privileged positions on these thrones. Though they knew they had an advantage over the others, they were anxious about Peter. This is why they say, **Command that one may sit at your right hand and one at your left**. They even pressure him by saying, **command**.

What does Jesus say? By his reply, he shows that they were not asking for anything spiritual, and if they had realized what they were asking for, they would not have dared to ask for it. Thus he says, **You do not know what you are asking.** This request is too great, too wonderful, and beyond what is appropriate even for the powers above.

Then he adds, *Are you able to drink the cup that I am about to drink, or to be baptized with the baptism with which I am baptized?* (Mark 10:38). Do you see how he leads them away from their way of thinking by approaching the matter from a completely different angle? He says, "You are talking to me about honor and crowns, while I am talking to you about struggles and toils. Now is not the time to talk of rewards. Nor is it time to reveal my glory. On the contrary, the present is the time of death, wars, and all kinds of danger."

Also notice how, by the way he phrases the question, he both reprimands and encourages them at the same time. For he did not say, "Are you capable of being killed? Are you capable of shedding your blood?" How did he ask the question? **Are you able to drink the cup?** To encourage them, he adds, **that I am about to drink**, in order that through their communion with him, they might be made ready. And he again calls these things a "baptism," indicating just how much cleansing this world requires given its present state.

(9) Gregory the Great

When the sons of Zebedee, through their mother, asked that one should sit at God's right hand and the other at his left, they heard the Lord say: **Can you drink the cup that I am going to drink?** They were seeking a place of eminence. Truth called them back to the way by which they could come to it, in the way he says: "You're delighted by this place of eminence for now, but first you must follow the way of suffering. The cup is the way to greatness. If your heart seeks what it longs for, first drink what causes it pain. Only through bitter drink prepared for you will your heart reach the joy of salvation."

Matthew 20:24–28

**24 And when the ten heard it, they were indignant at the two brothers. 25 But Jesus called
them to him and said, "You know that the rulers of the Gentiles lord it over them, and
their great men exercise authority over them. 26 It shall not be so among you; but who-
ever would be great among you must be your servant, 27 and whoever would be first
among you must be your slave; 28 even as the Son of man came not to be served but to
serve, and to give his life as a ransom for many."**

(10) Jerome

The ten apostles are not indignant at the mother of the sons of Zebedee, nor do they think she was being audacious. They know the request came from her sons because their unreasonable ambition had exceeded their station. It is to them that he had said: Even the Lord had said to them: **You do not know what you are asking.** From the Lord's response, as well as the indignation of the other apostles, it is clear that it was the sons who had sent their mother to ask for something so great.

However, the humble and meek Master neither convicts the two who made a request that sprang from inordinate ambition, nor does he rebuke the remaining ten for their indignation and jealousy. Instead, he offers an example to teach them that the greatest is the one who becomes least, and he who is the servant of all is the one who becomes lord. In vain, therefore, the two brothers had sought things that were beyond their measure, and in vain are the others offended by the desire of some to be the greatest. For the summit of virtue is reached not by a display of power but by humility.

(11) John Chrysostom

When the ten were filled with anger, what did Christ say? **Calling them he said, The rulers of the Gentiles lord it over them**. Since they were disturbed and troubled, he soothes them by calling out to them and drawing them near before ever speaking a word. Because the two who separated themselves from the other ten had been standing nearer to him, pleading their own interests, he calls the others to come near. In this way, by exposing what was said and then leading the others closer to him, he disarms the emotions of both parties.

But unlike earlier occasions, here he reprimands them. Previously he had brought little children into their midst and told the disciples to imitate their simplicity and meekness. Here he reproves them in a different way that cuts deeply, saying, **The rulers of the Gentiles lord it over them, and their great ones exercise authority over them. It shall not be so among you; but whoever wishes to be great among you must be a servant of all, and whoever wishes to be first must be last of all.** He states that to love ruling over others is the sort of thing the Gentiles do. And to love such things is tyrannical and acts as a hindrance even to great men. This is the reason for a harsh critique. The Lord severely reproves the disciples by comparing them with the Gentiles. In doing so, he is trying to transform their festering souls and cut off the root of their envy and quarreling.

It is as if he is saying, "Don't be angry or insulted. Those who seek to be first bring harm and disgrace upon themselves, for they are truly among the last. But we do not do things the way they do. Even though **the rulers of the Gentiles lord it over them**, with me the last is first. As proof that I'm not just flippantly saying these things, consider all I've done and suffered. And there's even more than that! Though I was King of the heavenly powers, I was willing to become a man and to be despised and insulted. But even this was not enough! I gave myself over to death." **Just as the Son of Man came not to be served but to serve, and to give his life as a ransom for many.** "Nor did I stop at this," he says, "but I gave my life as a ransom, and for whom? For my enemies. When you are humbled, then, it is beneficial to you. And when I humbled myself, this too is for your benefit."

The humble person is not conquered by passion. He is not troubled by anger, nor the love of glory, nor envy, nor jealousy. What is more glorious than a soul set free from these things? But the arrogant is held sway by them all. He is like a worm crawling in the mud, and jealousy, envy, and anger are an ever-present plague on his soul.

Matthew 20:29–34

**29 And as they went out of Jericho, a great crowd followed him. 30 And behold, two blind
men sitting by the roadside, when they heard that Jesus was passing by, cried out, "Have
mercy on us, Son of David!" 31 The crowd rebuked them, telling them to be silent; but
they cried out the more, "Lord, have mercy on us, Son of David!" 32 And Jesus stopped
and called them, saying, "What do you want me to do for you?" 33 They said to him,
"Lord, let our eyes be opened." 34 And Jesus in pity touched their eyes, and immediately
they received their sight and followed him.**

(12) Hilary of Poitiers

It is appropriate that the two blind men who were sitting along the road represent the two peoples of the pagans originating from Ham and Japheth,[1] who observed the Lord's route of departure and asked that their sight be restored. The crowd ridiculed them because of their cries and harshly told them to be silent. This was not because the crowd regarded silence itself as a sign of respect, but because they heard bitterly from blind men what they denied, namely, that the Lord is the Son of David. When the minds of the blind were illumined, God in man was proclaimed, So it was true what the Lord said: *For judgment I have come into this world, that they who do not see may see, and they who see might be made blind* (John 9:39).

Although they were hindered by the people of the law, **they cried even more**, bearing witness to the fervor of their faith ever more strenuously. Then the Lord took pity and asked them what they wanted. They asked that their eyes be opened. Having pity, he touched their eyes and restored their vision, which is the knowledge of God. In order that a figure of the pagans who was called to believe would find fulfillment and receive the knowledge of heavenly grace, those who had been blind saw the Lord and followed him.

1. Cf. Gen 9:20–28. Ham was cursed by his father Noah and became ancestor to the Egyptians and the Canaanites (Gen 10:6), the eventual enemies of Israel. And Japheth was the ancestor of the "people of the coastlands," which is a phrase used in the Old Testament for the Gentiles. Abram was a descendent of Shem.

(13) John Chrysostom

Let us listen to these blind men who were better off than many who have sight. They had no one to lead them, nor could they see him as he approached, yet they came to him, crying out in a loud voice, and when told to be quiet, they cried out even louder. This is what a persistent soul is like: it is lifted up by the obstacles it meets. And yet Christ allows them to be scolded so their zeal would be even more intense, and for you to learn that they deserved the joy by being healed. This is why he does not ask, as usual, "Do you believe?" By crying out and coming to him, they made their faith clear to everyone. Learn from this, dearly beloved, that though we might be of a very low station and an outcast, when we approach God with all our heart we shall obtain what we ask. Observe, moreover, how these men had none of the apostles as an ally. Rather, they had many people to scold them, yet they succeeded in overcoming these obstacles and came to Jesus on their own.

Let us, then, imitate them. If God delays his giving, don't hold back; don't stop asking, for this is the way to win God over. Observe here too how nothing was too big an obstacle to their enthusiasm—not poverty, not blindness, not failing to be heard, not the scorn of the crowd. This is the nature of a fervent and living soul.

(14) Augustine

What are the two blind men beside the road if not the two peoples for whose healing Jesus has come? Let us discover these two peoples in the Holy Scriptures. It is written in the Gospel, *I have other sheep who are not of this fold; and them too I must bring along, that there may be one flock and one shepherd* (John 10:16). So who are the two peoples? One is the Jews, the other the Gentiles. **I was only sent, he says, to the sheep that were lost of the house of Israel** (15:24). Whom did he say this to? It was to the disciples when that Canaanite woman was crying out and confessing she was a dog in order to earn the crumbs from the table of her masters. Because she earned these crumbs, he now shows that there are two peoples to whom he had come, namely, the Jewish people, of whom he said, **I was sent only to the sheep that were lost of the house of Israel**; and the Gentile people whose role was played out in advance by this woman (15:26–28).

Representing the latter was also that centurion, of whom the Lord said, **Truly I tell you, I have not found such great faith in Israel.** This was because the centurion had said, **I am not worthy that you should come in under my roof; but just speak the word, and my boy will be healed** (8:10). Even before his passion and glorification the Lord was already indicating the two peoples: one that he had come to because of the promises made to the ancestors; the other that in his mercy he did not turn away in order to fulfill what Abraham had been promised, **In your seed shall all the nations find a blessing** (Gen 12:3; 18:18; 22:18).

Christ is also called the cornerstone that made both one (Eph 2:20, 14). A corner joins two walls coming from different directions. What could be more different than circumcised and uncircumcised, meaning one wall from Judea and another wall from the Gentiles? But they are joined together by the cornerstone. For the stone that the builders rejected, this has become the head of the corner (21:42; Ps 118:22). You don't find corners in buildings except where two walls coming from different directions converge on them and are joined together with a kind of unity. So symbolically speaking, the two blind men crying out to the Lord were these two walls.

The crowd that was with the Lord tried to suppress the clamor of those who were seeking to be healed. Brothers and sisters, do you see what I'm trying to say? The fact is, I don't know how to say it, and yet, I don't know how to keep quiet about it. I will say it, and say it openly. You see, I'm terrified of Jesus passing by, and stopping; and that's why I can't keep quiet. Good Christians, really earnest Christians who want to carry out the commandments of God written in the Gospel, are told not to be bad or lukewarm Christians. The crowd with the Lord tells them to stop crying out; they tell them, in effect, to stop doing good in case they should persevere with it and be healed.

We must go on crying out and not give up, nor be influenced by the bogus authority of crowds, nor imitate those who may have become Christians earlier, but who lead bad lives and resent people doing good works. We mustn't say, "Let us live in the same way as the great majority lives." Why not rather live as the Gospel tells you? Why do you want to live according to the reproaches of the crowd trying to shut you up, instead of according to the footsteps of the Lord passing by?

Matthew 21

Ancient Christian commentators offer a wide range of interpretations of Jesus's triumphal entry into Jerusalem on a donkey. The untying of the donkey and the colt by the two disciples is taken as a symbol of the liberation of humanity from the bondage of sin. Hilary sees in the action a prefiguring of the conversion of the Gentiles, whom God will use, as the Lord used the colt, "young, defiant . . . and ferocious in spirit," as his vehicle. Likewise, Ambrose says that the animals were set free "by command of the Lord," and this points to those who were "expelled by death" and "recalled by life." He also says that riding on a donkey has "a deep and mysterious meaning," because it is a figure of the Lord's desire "to 'ride' our minds and direct our steps," as well as "to accustom the pagans to his loving control."

The Lord's action of turning over the tables of the money changers is directed against those "who put the gift of the Holy Spirit up for sale . . . overturning the seats by which ministry given by God is transacted," and it is "a future prefiguration . . . that the sins of the Church have to be purified at the very advent of the Lord's glory." Ambrose suggests that, by chasing the vendors out of the temple, Jesus warned us "that those who traffic in the grace of the Holy Spirit should have no place in the Church of God." The cursing of the fig tree (vv. 18–22) was not a sign of the Lord's anger, but a manifestation of his power to the disciples so that they would be strengthened before his approaching passion (Chrysostom). Eusebius of Emesa says that it was "a demonstration of power" that showed the Lord was not constrained by the authority of others, nor was he being led to death against his will.

Jesus answered the Pharisees' inquiry about the source of his authority (vv. 23–32) by asking them about the authority of John the Baptist. Since they could not answer, the Lord reproved them with a parable about two sons. As Chrysostom interprets it, the obedient son exemplifies the Gentiles who, though not being "recipients of the law, gave evidence of obedience by their actions." The other son represents the Jewish leaders who failed to keep their promises to obey God's commands (Exod 19:8).

In the interpretation of the parable of the wicked tenants (vv. 33–46), Hilary says that God the Father (the landowner), in expectation of fruit from his people of Israel (the vineyard), sent the prophets (the servants), and, eventually, his Son. Neither the messengers nor the Son were acknowledged. The return of the landowner symbolizes God's future judgment. The Son is the stone rejected by the builders, who will become the cornerstone of a new edifice (Ps 118:22–23) that unites the Gentiles and those who kept the law.

Matthew 21:1–5

[1]And when they drew near to Jerusalem and came to Beth'phage, to the Mount of Ol-
ives, then Jesus sent two disciples, [2]saying to them, "Go into the village opposite you,
and immediately you will find an ass tied, and a colt with her; untie them and bring
them to me. [3]If any one says anything to you, you shall say, 'The Lord has need of them,'
and he will send them immediately." [4]This took place to fulfill what was spoken by the
prophet, saying,

> **[5]"Tell the daughter of Zion,**
> **Behold, your king is coming to you,**
> **humble, and mounted on an ass,**
> **and on a colt, the foal of an ass."**

(1) Origen

Note that Matthew did not cite the text as it is found in the prophet. For in place of "Rejoice greatly, daughter of Zion, proclaim it, daughter of Jerusalem," he wrote, **Say to the daughter of Zion**, abbreviating the prophecy. Then he omits the words "just and saving, he" and says, as it is written, **humble and mounted** instead of "upon an ass and a colt, the foal of a beast of burden. . . ."

Furthermore, I do not think the statement **If anyone says anything to you, you shall say, The Lord has need of them, and immediately he will send them**, is worthy of the greatness of the divinity of the Son of God. For it suggests that a nature as great as that of the Son of God needs an ass to be untied along with a colt. For everything the Son of God needs must be great and worthy of his goodness.

The meaning of these passages is given only to those who have a true understanding of things and can say, "*But we have the mind of Christ* (1 Cor 2:16b) and are able to see the things given to us by God." Now Jesus is the Word of God (John 1:1–14) who enters the soul, which is called Jerusalem, riding on an ass that has been untied by the disciples. Now by the ass I mean the plain letters of the Old Testament, which are explained by the two disciples who unloosed them. One of these disciples interprets these passages allegorically using them to heal the soul, whereas the other disciple discerns the things that are to come by means of what is found in shadow.[1]

Next he rides the young colt, which is the New Testament. It is possible to find in both Testaments the word of truth, which cleanses us and drives out all the thoughts that are taken up with buying and selling in us (Mark 11:5). The Lord does not enter the soul, which is Jerusalem, alone; neither does he enter with only a few. For there must be many qualities present before the Word of God who perfects us enters in, and many others that follow him. All the people praise and glorify him, placing their clothing and garments under him so that his colt would not touch the ground, since it carries the one who has come down from heaven.

1. That is, whatever compromises spiritual truth.

So that the old and new words of the Scriptures that carry him should be higher than the ground, branches had to be cut from the trees to allow them to tread on a foundation of sound expositions. The crowds that go before and follow him signify the angels who prepare the way for him within our souls.

(2) Ambrose of Milan

In the little town, there was a she-ass tied up with its foal. It could be set free only by command of the Lord. The apostles untied it. What a deed, what life, what grace! Imitate the apostles, and you too will set the captives free.

Let us now consider those people who were caught in sin, exiled from paradise and held captive in a fortress. Then you will see how those who expelled by death (Gen 3:15) have been recalled by life. In Matthew, we read that there was a she-donkey and a foal. As the two people expelled from paradise were male and female, so the two animals remind us of both sexes. The she-donkey represents Eve, mother of error, and her foal represents the Gentile people. This is why Jesus chooses the foal to be his mount.

Appropriately, on this foal *no one has ever sat* (Luke 19:30) because no one before Christ had ever called the pagans to enter the Church. So, too, in Mark we read: *upon which no man has yet sat* (Mark 11:2). This creature was held captive by the bonds of unbelief. He had been delivered to the wicked master to whom his own sinfulness had made him subservient, but he could no longer reclaim him. It was not by right of nature that the devil had mastery over him, but by reason of his sin.

In saying, *The Lord has need of it* (Luke 19:31), Jesus is showing us that there is but one Master. While there are many gods and many masters in a general sense, there is only one God and one Master. In giving himself no name, our Lord is making himself known not as an individual person, but in his nature as Lord of all.

In setting the donkey free, did the disciples use words of their own? No, they used the exact words that Jesus had given them. We should learn from this that it was not by their own preaching, but by the word of God that they poured faith into the pagan people in Christ's name. And it was by that word of God that the hostile powers, which had held sway over the nations until then, fell down before the power of God.

The apostles spread their own garments before the feet of Christ (cf. Luke 19:36), as if to highlight the splendor of so great an event as the preaching of the Gospel. In Scripture, as you know, garments often symbolize virtues. Also, these robes would, by their virtue, soften the harshness of the Gentile people. At the same time, by spreading these robes out of love and zeal, they were smoothing the way for Jesus.

For we must not imagine that it was to please himself that the Lord of the world chose to be seen riding on the foal of a she-donkey. No, there lies here a deep and mysterious meaning. He wished to saddle the inmost recesses of our heart. Like a mystic rider, he wished to seat himself in the depths of our soul. As a rider might ride his mount, he wished, in his divinity, to "ride" our minds and direct our steps, reining in the lascivious desires of the flesh. He wishes to accustom the pagans to his loving control, and so to tame their savage impulses. Happy, happy indeed, are those who inwardly submit their back to such a rider as this! Truly, truly happy are those whose mouth is held in check from idle chatter, restrained by the bridle of the heavenly Word!

Matthew 21:6–11

[6]The disciples went and did as Jesus had directed them; [7]they brought the ass and the colt, and put their garments on them, and he sat thereon. [8]Most of the crowd spread their garments on the road, and others cut branches from the trees and spread them on the road. [9]And the crowds that went before him and that followed him shouted, "Hosanna to the Son of David! Blessed is he who comes in the name of the Lord! Hosanna in the highest!" [10]And when he entered Jerusalem, all the city was stirred, saying, "Who is this?" [11]And the crowds said, "This is the prophet Jesus from Nazareth of Galilee."

(3) Cyril of Alexandria

The colt is brought by two disciples sent by Christ. It follows that two groups serve him, prophets and apostles, through whom the Gentiles were drawn together with the Jews to faith. And the colt was brought from a certain village to show the crude thinking of the pagans, who were not brought up in the law but lived carelessly and savagely. However, he transferred them to what is more civilized through Christ, who taught these things. Young people ran before him lifting up *branches of palm trees* (John 12:13), joining the apostles in praise so that through them we might see the new people, as it has been written in the Scriptures: *And the people who will be created will praise the Lord* (Ps 102:18).

(4) Eusebius of Emesa

The Lord sent two disciples—confirming the word by two witnesses—to bring the colt of a donkey for him to sit upon it; a colt on which no other person had ever sat. When it is said that *the Lord has need of it*, the reference is to his human body, not because the only-begotten Lord of heaven and earth needed to be carried by a donkey. It's true that the Gospel says earlier that, when he had grown fatigued from his journey, he sat above a well, reviving his body (John 4:6). Yet it is not that his indefatigable power had grown weary, but that he was truly man as well as truly God. . . .

The Lord, therefore, was walking because he was obliged to fulfill every prophecy; when he had come near to Jerusalem, he procured the colt of a donkey, which was led into the city to fulfill the prophets. Consequently, the colt led to resentment on the part of the unbelieving Jews; for they were angry that he was called the Son of David and seated on the colt of a donkey in accord with the prophecy. . . .

The Lord was sitting on a colt, and the bones were softened, that is to say, the severity of the people [was appeased]. For those who had never spread a tunic under the feet for someone walking by now did so under the feet of a colt, and because of the power of the prophecy, they spread out their garments. Some others cut off branches and tossed them onto the ground, while yet others were raising their branches to heaven. All the children were shouting loudly—how unexpected was this testimony—**Hosanna, blessed is he who comes in the name of the Lord**, blessed is the King of Israel.

At the same time, the Jews who were disturbed over the episode of the two blind men (9:27–30) were now bursting with envy because of the shouting multitude. And their jealousy soon spread. To be sure, envy is the worst evil; just like some spark of a fire. From the smallest of beginnings, it goes on to engulf a forest as the fire builds up, blazing to the highest degree. And so this most bitter flame of envy and jealousy, although it might be set off by some insignificant issue, immediately inflames and burns up the mind of him who is possessed by this evil. Because envy had seized them since the healing of the blind men, and in accordance with the prophecy, they see the colt and hear the children's voices that testified to the effective power of the Lord. They did not anticipate what was happening, nor did they expect to hear the things that were being proclaimed. Instead, they were spurred on by a jealous rivalry.

The Lord Jesus, then, was entering the stubborn city of Jerusalem, and Scripture says that the whole city was stirred up. It would have been better to say that the whole city was joyful; but being stubborn, it says, **it was stirred** up, and much like a barren city—which had never given birth—it was rejoicing. As he ascended to his home,[2] the Son of the Father fulfilled the prophecy and received praises from the mouths of children, while the fathers voiced condemnation. Thus, the little ones were shouting, and the fathers were grieving, and the Lord was being glorified, and the prophecies were being fulfilled by word and deed.

And the Lord said, "Do you not hear what they are here proclaiming? Even now if these ones here had remained silent, the rocks would have cried out. If your little ones," he said, "were to be silent, having been suppressed by your wickedness, all creation, in recognition of its Creator, would confess these things." The words of the prophets, therefore, were being fulfilled: on the one hand, by means of a colt: *Behold your king comes, sitting on the colt of a donkey* (Zech 9:9; Matt 21:5); on the other hand, by means of children: *Out of the mouths of infants and nursing babies, you have prepared praise* (Ps. 8:2; Matt 21:16).

(5) Augustine

Hosanna to the Son of David; blessed is he who comes in the name of the Lord. Then the Pharisees said to him, "Make the children hush, don't let them shout such things to you." He replied, *If these keep quiet, the stones will cry out* (Luke 19:40).

He had us in mind when he said, *If these keep quiet, the stones will cry out*. Who are the stones but those who worship stones? If the Jewish children keep quiet, the elders and the minors of the nations will cry out. Who are the stones but the very ones about whom John spoke, who came *to bear witness to the light* (John 1:7)? I mean, when he saw the Jews being so proud of their descent from Abraham, he said to them, *Brood of vipers* (Luke 3:7).

2. Jerusalem was located on a hill.

They were calling themselves children of Abraham, and he was calling them a brood of vipers. Was he insulting Abraham? Not at all! Because of their habits and behavior, he was giving a name to people who would have imitated Abraham if they had really been children of Abraham. As Jesus himself also says to the ones who tell him, *We are free and have never been slaves to anyone; we have Abraham as our father*; he says, *If you were children of Abraham, you would do the deeds of Abraham. You wish to kill me, because I tell you the truth. This, Abraham did not do* (John 8:33, 39–40). That's where you trace your generations back to, but you have degenerated.

So what does John say? *Brood of vipers, who has shown you to flee from the wrath to come?* This happened as they were coming to be baptized with John's baptism for repentance. *Who has shown you to flee from the wrath to come? So bear fruit worthy of repentance, and do not say to yourselves, We have Abraham as our Father. God is able from these stones to raise up children to Abraham* (Luke 3:7–8). From these stones, which he could see in spirit, *God is able*— he was speaking to them and foreseeing us—*God is able from these stones to raise up children to Abraham.*

It's about such stones; *if these keep quiet, the stones will cry out.* You've heard it only this moment, and you are crying out. It's fulfilled, it has come true, *the stones will cry out.* After all, we come from the nations. In our parents, we worshiped stones. That's why we are also called dogs. Remember what that woman heard who was crying out after the Lord. She was a Canaanite, a worshiper of idols, a handmaid of demons. So what did Jesus say? *It is not good to take the children's food and throw it to the dogs* (Mark 7:27). Have you never noticed how dogs lick stones that have had oil poured on them? Well, that's what all worshipers of images are like.

But grace has come to you. *But as many as did receive him, he gave them power to become children of God.* Whom did he give it to? *To those who believe in his name* (John 1:12).

Matthew 21:12–13

12 And Jesus entered the temple of God and drove out all who sold and bought in the temple, and he overturned the tables of the money-changers and the seats of those who sold pigeons. 13 He said to them, "It is written, 'My house shall be called a house of prayer'; but you make it a den of robbers."

(6) Ambrose of Milan

He drove out those that were selling and buying in the temple; and overturned the money-changers' tables and the chairs of the sellers of doves. Earlier he taught us in a general way that business should not be carried on in God's temple (cf. John 2:14–16). But he makes a particular point here of driving out the money-changers. Who are these money-changers? They are surely those profiteers who want to make themselves rich at the expense of the Lord's treasury, and are unable to distinguish between good and bad.

Our Lord's silver and gold is divine Scripture. In the parable, the master, upon taking his departure, distributed gold and silver coins among his servants (Matt 25:14–30), and in another parable, the nobleman divided the talents (cf. 25:14; Luke 19:13). The good Samaritan gave the innkeeper two coins to look after the wounded man (cf. Luke 10:35); for it is by the two Testaments that our wounds are healed.

As good money-changers, let us treasure *the words of the Lord, chaste words, silver proved and tested in the fire* (Ps 12:6). These are words purified by the sevenfold gifts of the Spirit. Never accept in exchange coins stamped with a false image of the King. For *even Satan can change himself into the likeness of an angel of light* (2 Cor 11:14). . . .

Do not tempt your listeners by jingling coins, for the tinkling sounds of silver could prevent them from listening devoutly to the Scriptures. The desire to parade one's wealth could seep into the hearts of the devout. I do not condemn all money-changers, for some are good. In our Lord's parable in the Gospel, we hear the master say: *You should have given my money to the money-changers, and on my return I could have reclaimed it with interest* (25:27). If it is true to say that Scripture is a form of currency, then it has a right to claim interest.

As for the literal sense of turning over the chairs of the sellers of doves, I am at a loss to understand why our Lord should do this. The chairs occupied by people who sell birds in the market place can hardly be looked upon as conferring any dignity on the holder! Do the doves, then, confer some sort of respect? One wouldn't think so. However, if you consider the Lord's baptism—when the Holy Spirit descended in the form of a Dove—you will learn something: we are being warned by the example of these vendors chased from the temple that those who traffic in the grace of the Holy Spirit should have no place in the Church of God. Since **you have freely received**, says our Lord, **and freely you should give** (10:8). Simon (of Samaria) thought he could buy the gift of sanctification with money. Peter replied to him: *Keep your money to yourself to perish with you, because you thought God's gift could be purchased with money* (Acts 8:9–24).

(7) Jerome

Accompanied by the crowd of believers that had spread their garments in order that the colt might enter with an unhurt foot, Jesus goes into the temple. He expels all who were selling and buying in the temple, and he overturns the tables of the money-changers. He scatters the seats of those selling doves and brings forth a testimony from the Holy Scriptures, that his **Father's house must be a house of prayer, not a den of thieves**, or as is written in another evangelist, a house of business (cf. John 2:16).

In the first place, we need to know that in accordance with the commandments of the law, especially on feast days, innumerable sacrifices of bulls, rams, and goats were offered in the temple of the Lord, the most venerated in the whole world. This took place when the Jewish people gathered there from nearly all countries. The poor offered the chicks of doves and turtle-doves, lest they should be without a sacrifice. Very often it happened that those who had come from afar did not have victims to sacrifice. Therefore, the priests thought out how they could plunder the people. They sold all kinds of sacrificial animals to anyone who needed them, so that these people in turn could sell to those who did not have any. The Lord, seeing this kind of business, or rather thievery, going on in the Father's house, was stirred up by the ardor of his spirit in accordance with what was written in the sixty-eighth Psalm: *The zeal of your house has consumed me* (Ps. 69:9). He made a whip for himself from cords, and he ejected from the temple a very great multitude of men, saying: **It is written: My house shall be called a house of prayer, but you have made it a den of thieves.** For a man is a thief, and converts the temple of God into a den of thieves, who seeks after financial gain from religion. His worship is not so much the worship of God as a pretext for business.

The foregoing has been said about the historical narrative. But according to the mystical understanding, Jesus daily enters the temple of the Father and expels from his own Church all such bishops, priests, and deacons, as well as laymen and the whole crowd. He holds them all guilty of a single crime, namely, of selling and buying. For it is written: **Freely you have received, freely give** (10:8).

Matthew 21:14–17

**14And the blind and the lame came to him in the temple, and he healed them. 15But
when the chief priests and the scribes saw the wonderful things that he did, and the
children crying out in the temple, "Hosanna to the Son of David!" they were indignant;
16and they said to him, "Do you hear what these are saying?" And Jesus said to them,
"Yes; have you never read,**

> **'Out of the mouth of babes and sucklings**
> **thou hast brought perfect praise'?"**
> **17And leaving them, he went out of the city to Bethany and lodged there.**

(8) John Chrysostom

The chief priests and the scribes were not even persuaded by his miracles. Instead, they were indignant, even though they had heard the prophet's proclamation and children—young though they were—singing praises to the Lord (21:15). This is why Christ also counters them, using Isaiah as their accuser, and quoting, **My house shall be called a house of prayer** (Isa 56:7).

However, this was not the only way for Christ to demonstrate his authority; he shows it forth also by healing a variety of severe diseases. We are told, **The blind and the lame came unto him, and he healed them.** Here he displays both his power and authority.

The officials were not persuaded even by this, however. Instead, in the midst of the last miracles and listening to the children singing praises to the Lord, they were overcome with anger, saying, **Don't you hear what these are saying?** Yet, in truth, it was Christ who should have addressed this question to them, **Don't you hear what these are saying?** The children were singing to him as to God.

What did Christ say? Since the leaders were contradicting the obvious, he censures them more directly and corrects them, saying, **Have you never read, Out of the mouth**

of babes and sucklings you have brought perfect praise? Indeed, he said it rightly, **out of the mouth**, because, in truth, their words were not produced by their minds. It was the Lord's power that enabled their imperfect tongues to speak distinctly.

The singing of the children was also a symbol of the Gentiles who, though inarticulate, suddenly began uttering great things with understanding and faith. And even to the apostles it brought much consolation. So they may not lose heart wondering how they with no skill would become capable of proclaiming the gospel, the children removed all their anguish. They assured the apostles in advance that the one who gave the children the ability to sing praises would give them ability to speak to the apostles as well.

Matthew 21:18–22

18In the morning, as he was returning to the city, he was hungry. 19And seeing a fig tree by the wayside he went to it, and found nothing on it but leaves only. And he said to it, "May no fruit ever come from you again!" And the fig tree withered at once. 20When the disciples saw it they marveled, saying, "How did the fig tree wither at once?" 21And Jesus answered them, "Truly, I say to you, if you have faith and never doubt, you will not only do what has been done to the fig tree, but even if you say to this mountain, 'Be taken up and cast into the sea,' it will be done. 22And whatever you ask in prayer, you will receive, if you have faith."

(9) Eusebius of Emesa

What does that fig tree signify? We have often heard that that tree is a symbol for Jerusalem, and I have nothing against this. But . . . let me pose this question: since the Lord came to Jerusalem out of season and beyond the time that such a tree bore fruit, how could he find fault with the tree? If it wasn't the season for figs to appear, certainly both the old and young knew this. Do you suppose then that men and boys knew as much, whereas the Creator of all things and of this very tree did not know that it was not the season for a fig tree to bear fruit?

But why did he want fruit from a tree out of season? Or what could the tree have done wrong? There is an explanation to this question and a proof for the explanation. For the Lord desired to show, in anticipation of what was to come, that he is powerful inasmuch as he moistens that which is dry and dries out that which is moist. All the moisture of the tree was separated from itself, as it were. As a result, the green vegetation vanished, and the fig tree was suddenly withered and dry, leaving the disciples astounded at the eminence of his power. Since the Lord was in the process of being betrayed and hunted down, he especially wanted the disciples to possess faith. If they believed, even though they might dissuade their adversaries, they would be freed from those who held power. For this reason, the Lord gave them a sign in the form of the fig tree before his passion so that he could show them that he was voluntarily delivering himself to the authorities and would be willfully affixed to the cross. By means of this sign, he gave a certain confidence to the disciples, convicted all others, and strengthened us in our faith.

These words of the Lord that followed show clearly that his act was done neither out of rage nor anger; it was done on account of showing a sign. As the disciples were marveling at the sign of his power and how the tree had immediately withered upon his command—just as the eyes of the blind men had been opened immediately when the Lord wished it (21:14)—the Lord said to them: **If you shall believe and have faith, not only will you say to this fig tree, but also even to the mountain, which bore this tree, not just that it should wither, but also that it should lift itself from here and throw itself into the sea**. The sea was located far from this place in which these words were said; nevertheless he said, **it will obey you**.

So why did the Lord merely dry up the fig tree, while he told the disciples—to whom he granted authority (10:1)—that one could move mountains? For elsewhere he said also, *he who believes in me, and the works that I do, he will do even greater things* (John 14:12). When he was present in the world, he did lesser things while saving the greater for his disciples. Let us learn, therefore, the mysterious things of wisdom.

The disciples are heralds of the Lord's resurrection; they proclaim this extraordinary event. The Lord was not seen by the Jewish leaders after the resurrection, nor did the pagans see him. Although the eyes of the enemy saw the crucifixion, the eyes of the faithful saw the resurrection. The resurrection was unbelievable at the time, and even though it was unbelievable, he would do greater signs through them. Because the disciples were heralds of the resurrection, the Lord reserved these signs for them so that, while proclaiming his death, they could announce the living Christ.

Certainly the parable that explains how the Lord sent servants and a son to the Jews shows that he sent them in his allotted time (21:33–42). It says that the kingdom of heaven is similar to the man who planted his vineyard and arranged everything. **But when the time of harvest came, he sent his servants**. If the parable indicates that the Lord sent those servants at the properly allotted time, why did he seek fruit from the fig tree out of season? Can the two parables be posed as corresponding to one another? Indeed, it might. Again the Apostle says, *but when the fullness of time had come, God sent his Son* (Gal 4:4). He condemned Jerusalem in conformity with the proper season. For he had come to Jerusalem in its allotted time and at the right moment, which was in keeping with a certain day, as the Lord himself shows when he says to Jerusalem: "*if you knew*" that [coming] day (cf. 23:37–39). Although the time of the Lord's coming was prepared down to the day, Jerusalem completely failed to recognize its allotted time. For that reason, we do not accept the view that the fig tree is Jerusalem. If he demanded from these same ones (i.e., the Jews) their "fruit" out of season, then they would not have sinned at all, since their time was not yet come.

The Lord himself, then, showed that the action against the fruitless fig tree was neither out of rage nor anger. A demonstration of power was made so that it would be evident that the Lord was not constrained by the authority of others, nor that he was being led to death against his will. He was able to shrivel up anyone he might wish (for a human becomes more easily dried out than a fig tree). When they had come to arrest him (cf. 26:48–50), they sought a watchword (for they were eagerly wishing to learn secret things), and he who was sought said to them, *whom are you seeking?* (John 18:4). It certainly was not out of ignorance that he asked, but so that he might show his perseverance to those searching for him. We see here that he had anticipated the event and said, *whom are you seeking?* They said, *Jesus of Nazareth.* They were indeed ignorant of the heavenly one. He says to them, *I am he.* This was not a mark of fear, but of exclamation. When they heard *I am he*, they immediately fell as though they were lifeless (John 18:6). If they did not have the strength to bear the power of his voice and fell as though lifeless, how much more would they have been overcome if the Lord told them to "shrivel up"! Although he had the power to do this, he did not want to, so that the efficacy of the Lord's true power would be known and the patience of the Lord would be manifest. He said, therefore, to the seekers, *I am he* whom you seek, which is even more apparent in his earlier words: *the cup that the Father has given to me, shall I not drink it?*

Predictably the disciples were restraining him from ascending to Jerusalem. He, on the other hand, was hurrying to go, knowing that death could do nothing to him. His passion was for the sake of humanity. He wasn't going to perish; rather, he was going to save those who had been destroyed by death. It was on account of this that he was indicted.

(10) John Chrysostom

In the morning, as he was returning to the city, he was hungry. Why is he hungry in the morning? He yields to his human body and shows that he has feelings. **And, seeing a fig tree by the road, he approached it, and found nothing on it but leaves only.** Another evangelist says, *It was not yet the season [for figs]* (Mark 11:13). But if it was not yet the season, how can this other evangelist say, "He came in order that perhaps he might find some fruit on it"? This suggests that the disciples, who were not yet mature in faith, were wondering why the tree was cursed. And, in fact, there are many places where the evangelists report that the disciples lacked faith.

Here the Lord does not hint at any of these things. Rather, as I said, in this case [of cursing the fig tree] he gives a sampling of the power of his punishment. This he shows by his words, *For it was not yet the season [for figs]*, revealing that his primary purpose in approaching the tree was not his hunger. He did it for the sake of the disciples, who were greatly astonished, even though he had already performed many wonders of a greater importance. As I said, this miracle appeared strange to the disciples, because in this instance the Lord displayed his power to exact just punishment for the first time. For this reason, the Lord performed this wonder not with any tree, but upon a green and healthy tree, so that, in consequence, the sign could appear even greater.

In order that you may understand that the miracle was for the disciples' sake—to strengthen their confidence—listen to the words that Christ says next. What does he say? **You yourselves will perform greater miracles, if you believe and have confidence in prayer.** Do you see that he did all this for their sake, so that they might neither be afraid nor tremble with fear from the plots formed against them? On their account, he repeats this, in order to strengthen them in their devotion to prayer and faith. And not only these things will you do, since you will even move mountains and perform many more things, being confident in faith and prayer.

Matthew 21:23–32

[23]And when he entered the temple, the chief priests and the elders of the people came up to him as he was teaching, and said, "By what authority are you doing these things, and who gave you this authority?" [24]Jesus answered them, "I also will ask you a question; and if you tell me the answer, then I also will tell you by what authority I do these things. [25]The baptism of John, whence was it? From heaven or from men?" And they argued with one another, "If we say, 'From heaven,' he will say to us, 'Why then did you not believe him?' [26]But if we say, 'From men,' we are afraid of the multitude; for all hold that John was a prophet." [27]So they answered Jesus, "We do not know." And he said to them, "Neither will I tell you by what authority I do these things.

[28]"What do you think? A man had two sons; and he went to the first and said, 'Son, go and work in the vineyard today.' [29]And he answered, 'I will not'; but afterward he repented and went. [30]And he went to the second and said the same; and he answered, 'I go, sir,' but did not go. [31]Which of the two did the will of his father?" They said, "The first." Jesus said to them, "Truly, I say to you, the tax collectors and the harlots go into the kingdom of God before you. [32]For John came to you in the way of righteousness, and you did not believe him, but the tax collectors and the harlots believed him; and even when you saw it, you did not afterward repent and believe him."

(11) Hilary of Poitiers

The response of the Pharisees bears a kind of prophetic truth. They recognized, though unwillingly, who had done the father's will, namely, the first son who acted in obedience even though he did not profess it at the time. The point is that faith alone justifies. For this reason, **publicans and prostitutes will be first in the kingdom of heaven.** Because they believed John, they were baptized for the remission of sins; they confessed what Christ had done, offered praise for his works of healing, embraced the mystery of his passion, and acknowledged the power of his resurrection (cf. Phil 3:10).

(12) John Chrysostom

The arrogant and conceited Pharisees, who were anxious to undermine his teaching, came to him with the question: **By what authority do you do these things?** Once again he levels an accusation at them through parables, hinting both at their ingratitude and at the response of those whom they severely condemned. These two sons, in fact, exemplify what happened in the case of the Gentiles and the Jews. The former, you see, though not promising to respond, nor being recipients of the law, gave evidence of obedience by their actions; the latter, though having promised, *We shall perform and attend to all God says* (Exod 19:8), were disobedient in their actions. Lest they think the law is of any benefit to them, the Lord shows that it is the law itself that condemns them, as Paul also says, *It is not the hearers of the law that are righteous in God's sight: the doers of the law will be made righteous* (Rom 2:13). To bring them to the point of condemning themselves, he makes certain that the verdict is delivered to them, as he does in the following parable of the vineyard. In anticipation, he gives the accusation a preliminary trial in the mouth of another person. Since they were unwilling to make an admission directly, he then induced them to do as he wished by a parable. When they did not grasp his point and delivered the verdict, then he unfolded what was obscured, saying, **Tax collectors and prostitutes go into the kingdom of heaven ahead of you.**

(13) Peter Chrysologus

The Pharisees asked **by whose power** he was doing those mighty works that he performed on his own authority. In that way, if he said "God's," they could fan the hatred of the crowds, and if he refused to respond, they could denounce him as a magician. For they said: **He is able to cast out demons by the power of Beelzebub, leader of the demons.** And just as we read today, they both denounced the famous teacher in the presence of his disciples for having associated with tax collectors and accused the disciples in the presence of their teacher of being totally unaware of the virtues of fasting, utter slaves to their stomachs. Animated by envy, they sought to drive a wedge of hatred between the disciples and their teacher and sow seeds of discord between the teacher and his disciples.

Matthew 21:33–46

33"Hear another parable. There was a householder who planted a vineyard, and set a
hedge around it, and dug a wine press in it, and built a tower, and let it out to tenants,
and went into another country. 34When the season of fruit drew near, he sent his ser-
vants to the tenants, to get his fruit; 35and the tenants took his servants and beat one,
killed another, and stoned another. 36Again he sent other servants, more than the first;
and they did the same to them. 37Afterward he sent his son to them, saying, 'They will
respect my son.' 38But when the tenants saw the son, they said to themselves, 'This is the
heir; come, let us kill him and have his inheritance.' 39And they took him and cast him
out of the vineyard, and killed him. 40When therefore the owner of the vineyard comes,
what will he do to those tenants?" 41They said to him, "He will put those wretches to a
miserable death, and let out the vineyard to other tenants who will give him the fruits
in their seasons." 42Jesus said to them, "Have you never read in the scriptures:

> **'The very stone which the builders rejected**
> **has become the head of the corner;**
> **this was the Lord's doing,**
> **and it is marvelous in our eyes'?**

43Therefore I tell you, the kingdom of God will be taken away from you and given to a
nation producing the fruits of it."

45When the chief priests and the Pharisees heard his parables, they perceived
that he was speaking about them. 46But when they tried to arrest him, they feared the
multitudes, because they held him to be a prophet.

(14) Hilary of Poitiers

Here we understand that God the Father is the landowner who has planted his people Israel in anticipation of an excellent harvest (Jer 2:21). He enclosed them within his wall, sanctified by the name of the fathers, that is, by the nobility of Abraham, Isaac, and Jacob, as someone who is surrounded and protected in a distinctive way. He also equipped the prophets, a kind of winepress into which he pours the fruitfulness of the Holy Spirit, who creates fermentation of a new wine (Acts 2:13–17). The tower is the nobility of the law (cf. 2 Cor 3:10), which lifts us to the height of heaven and enables us to fathom Christ's advent. The tenants are an image of the chief priests and Pharisees to whom the authority of teaching has been granted.

The servants, who were sent to gather the fruit, signify the advance of the prophets who had often and in various ways called the people to repentance. Later, as time passed, the preaching of a few gave way to a great number of prophets. Some were beaten, stoned, and killed because they attempted to harvest fruit from the people they had formed and instructed. Finally, when he sent the son, by which we understand the advent and passion of our Lord, he was driven out of Jerusalem as a vine from a branch and was condemned. The tenants believed that once they had killed the heir they could claim the inheritance. But it was a vain hope to think that the glory of the law could be preserved after Christ has been slain. In the return of the landowner, we have an image of the glory of the Father's majesty appearing in the Son at the time of judgment (16:27). The response of the chief priests and Pharisees indicates that the inheritance of the law is more worthily handed over to the apostles. Finally, the Son himself is the stone that has been rejected by the builders and becomes the cornerstone that is marvelous in the eyes of all (1 Pet 2:6–7). The cornerstone unites two sides of the building, that is, the law and the Gentiles.

Matthew 22

The parable of the wedding feast (vv. 1–14) has deep and rich significance for the church fathers. God (the king), according to Gregory the Great, "sent his servants twice with the invitation because he said through the prophets that his only Son's incarnation would come about, and it was proclaimed through the apostles that it had." This second invitation signifies the expansion of the kingdom to the Gentiles.

For Gregory, the feast represents the marriage between Christ and the Church joined "through the mystery of his incarnation" in the bridal chamber of the Virgin's womb. The presence of the good and the bad at the banquet (v. 10) is a figure of the Church that admits both types of people "now without distinguishing them but separates them later when they leave this life."

The banquet table also signifies the Eucharist, where Christians are admonished to approach worthily (cf. 1 Cor 11:29) wearing the wedding garment of "love from a pure heart, and from a good conscience and sincere faith" (1 Tim 1:5), as Augustine observes. The one who arrives at the wedding in suitable clothes of "faith and love" will avoid being cast out into the outer darkness, as happened to one of the guests in the parable.

In the next part of the chapter, Jesus is approached by representatives of different Jewish groups and asked provocative questions. First, the Herodians sent by the Pharisees asked Jesus whether it is lawful to pay taxes to Caesar (vv. 15–22), wishing to trap him by causing him to side either with the Romans or with the Jews on what was a sensitive issue of taxation. In reply, the Lord asked them to show him a coin with Caesar's image engraved on it. His answer, Render therefore to Caesar the things that are Caesar's, and to God the things that are God's *(v. 21), implies that "the image of Caesar on the coin is Caesar's, and the image of God in man is God's," that is, ourselves (Tertullian). According to Hilary, it is appropriate that we render to God what belongs to him: body, soul and will, "seeing that we owe to him our origin and development." Augustine adds that we are Christ's currency, and we pay him with his own proper coin, namely, by sculpting and renewing the image in which we were created.*

Jesus was then confronted by the Sadducees, a religious group who denied the resurrection (vv. 23–33). Their question was based on the law of levirate marriage, which required the male to marry the widow of his deceased brother. Proposing an exaggerated example of a woman who outlived seven husbands, they ask Jesus whose wife she would be in the resurrection. Jesus rebuked them for their ignorance of both the Scripture and the power of God (v. 29). Chrysostom explains that the Lord's reply "proves . . . that there will be a resurrection, though it will not be a resurrection as they suspect" because they assume that "the order of the things present is like that to come." By stating that God is not God of the dead, but of the living, *Jesus affirmed God's unchanging power over death.*

The religious leaders also asked him about the greatest commandment in the law (vv. 34–40). Hilary says that they asked him this question, "not realizing that the practice of the law had been perfected in Christ." Augustine likewise points out that just as the Ten Commandments of the Decalogue summarize countless commandments, so Jesus quotes the two chief commandments that encapsulate the Ten Commandments. The first three commandments of the Decalogue define our relationship to God, and the remaining seven teach us to love our neighbor. Loving God wholeheartedly means that "with the whole of what is alive in you, you shall love the fountain of life." Augustine makes an interesting observation that "there are two commandments, and yet three things to be loved": God, your neighbor, and yourself. So Jesus also gives the rule how to love yourself: "Love God with the whole of yourself; there, you see, you will find yourself, or else in yourself you might lose yourself."

Finally, Jesus himself posed a question to the religious leaders. If Christ is the Son of David, how is it that David calls him "Lord"? (vv. 41–45). Since the leaders considered him to be a mere man, he presents David proclaiming his Godhead. . . . And he shows the Father himself taking vengeance upon them on his behalf, for he says, Until I make your enemies your footstool. *Augustine explains that, because of the incarnation, Christ is both "David's Lord and David's Son" and "in one person he is both man and God." "We must hold on to both things," he says, "true man, true God; God and man, the whole Christ. This is the catholic faith."*

Matthew 22:1–14

**[1]And again Jesus spoke to them in parables, saying, [2]"The kingdom of heaven may be
compared to a king who gave a marriage feast for his son, [3]and sent his servants to call
those who were invited to the marriage feast; but they would not come. [4]Again he sent
other servants, saying, 'Tell those who are invited, Behold, I have made ready my dinner,
my oxen and my fat calves are killed, and everything is ready; come to the marriage
feast.' [5]But they made light of it and went off, one to his farm, another to his business,
[6]while the rest seized his servants, treated them shamefully, and killed them. [7]The king
was angry, and he sent his troops and destroyed those murderers and burned their city.
[8]Then he said to his servants, 'The wedding is ready, but those invited were not worthy.
[9]Go therefore to the thoroughfares, and invite to the marriage feast as many as you find.'
[10]And those servants went out into the streets and gathered all whom they found, both
bad and good; so the wedding hall was filled with guests.**

**[11]"But when the king came in to look at the guests, he saw there a man who had
no wedding garment; [12]and he said to him, 'Friend, how did you get in here without a
wedding garment?' And he was speechless. [13]Then the king said to the attendants, 'Bind
him hand and foot, and cast him into the outer darkness; there men will weep and gnash
their teeth.' [14]For many are called, but few are chosen."**

(1) John Chrysostom

Listen, all you who are partakers of the mysteries and are coming to the wedding: you have clothed your soul with filthy works. Listen to where you were called from: the streets. What kind of person were you? Lame and blind in your soul, which is far worse than a bodily blindness. You should stand in awe of the grace of the one who called you and let no one be dressed in filthy garments. Rather, let each one of us be concerned with how his soul is clothed.

Listen you women, listen you men. You have no need for weaving gold into your garments, which adorn our outer selves, but for adorning those things on the inside. Until we uphold the latter it is difficult to be clothed with other. We cannot adorn the soul and the body at the same time. In no way can we serve mammon and obey Christ, as if the two were the same. Let us therefore throw off this heavy tyranny. For no one adorns his house with tapestries of gold and then is ordered to sit naked in torn rags—would you personally endure such a thing? But you now are doing this injury to yourself, since you adorn the house of your soul, that is, the body, with countless tapestries, whereas you allow the soul to sit in tattered rags. Are you not aware that a king should be decorated more than the city? For this reason, the city is decorated with flags made from linen, but purple and a crown are bestowed on the king. So too, the body should be clothed in worthless garments, whereas the soul decorated with purple, crowned, and its throne established on high. And yet you act in a contrary way; while you are decorating the city in multiple colors, you nevertheless permit the king—or your reason—to be dragged around in a sordid condition. Don't you know that you have been called to the wedding, the wedding of God? Don't you know how the soul, which is called, should enter into these wedding chambers decked out in gold-leaf and adorned with an assortment of colors (Ps 45:13; Eph 3:10)?

(2) Ambrose of Milan

The Lord, despised and disdained by the rich, turned to the Gentiles. He made good and bad alike come in [to the marriage feast] so that he might increase the goodness of the good and change for the better the dispositions of the bad. So we find that text we read today is fulfilled: *Then shall the wolves and the lambs feed together* (Isa 65:25). He invites the poor, the infirm, and the blind. This shows us that physical infirmity excludes no one from the kingdom. The very infirmity of these people lessens their temptation to sin, and so their sins are fewer. Or, we can interpret the text to mean that the infirmity of sin is forgiven by the mercy of the Lord. And so, having been redeemed from sin, not by works but by faith, one can glory only in the Lord (cf. Rom 9:32; 1 Cor 1:31).

The king sends out his servants into the streets to fetch the poor and the lame, *for wisdom preaches abroad and utters her voice in the streets* (Prov 1:20). He sends his servants out into streets and public places to call sinners from the broad and easy way into the narrow way that leads to life (cf. 7:13–14). He sends them along the highways and hedges. These people are ready for the kingdom of heaven. They are not encumbered by insatiable desires for riches. They hasten toward those riches that belong to the next world. They are hastening along the road of virtue and good will. Just as a hedge separates cultivated fields from land that is uncultivated and protects those fields from the incursions of wild animals, so too such people know how to distinguish between good and evil. They know how to protect themselves with the ramparts of faith against the assaults of the evil spirits.

Then to show how carefully he protected his vineyard, he says: *I surrounded it with a hedge and a ditch* (21:33). The Apostle speaks of the wall running through the hedge that breaks up the enclosure, and he tells us that that dividing wall was removed (cf. Eph 2:14). So faith and reason seek each other out, and they are found in the streets—that is to say, in the wandering passages of our heart and mind. For as it is written: *May water flow abundantly in your streets* (Prov 5:16).

It is not enough, however, simply to come when invited to the wedding feast. You have to have clothes suitable for a wedding, that is to say, you must have faith and love. Those who approach the altars of God without wearing faith and love will be seized, hand and foot, and thrown out into exterior darkness: **Where there shall be weeping and grinding of teeth.**

What darkness is this? Does it mean that, in that other world, there will be dungeons and quarries? No, no. But whoever is shut out from the promises of the heavenly commandments is in outer darkness, because God's commandments are light (cf. John 12:35). Whoever is outside of Christ is in the dark, because Christ is the light of the soul.

(3) Augustine

All the faithful know about the wedding of the king's son and that the banquet of celebration and that the food of the Lord's table is offered to all present here. However, it makes a difference how you approach when access to the table is open. In fact, the Holy Scriptures teach us that the Lord provides two banquets, one to which both good and bad people come, the other to which the bad do not approach.

So the Lord's banquet, about which we just now heard when the Gospel was read, clearly had good and bad people on the invitation list. All who excused themselves from attending this banquet are bad, but not all who came are good. So I am addressing my remarks to all you good people who sit down to this banquet, those of you who take to heart the words: *Whoever eats and drinks unworthily eats and drinks judgment upon himself* (1 Cor 11:29); all of you who are of that sort, I am reminding you not to look for good people outside, and also to put up with bad people inside.

The householder went in to observe the guests at table, and he found a man who did not have on a wedding garment. And he said to him, Friend, how did you get in here not having a wedding garment? But he was speechless. When the householder questioned him, there was no way he could be excused. The garment, in fact, was being observed on the heart, not on the body. If it had been the sort of clothing you put on over the body, its absence would have passed unnoticed even by the servants. You can recognize where the wedding garment is to be worn from the text that says, *May your priests be clothed with justice* (Ps 132:9). It is about that garment that the Apostle says, *Provided we be found clothed, and not naked* (2 Cor 5:3).

So a man was discovered by the Lord who had escaped the notice of the servants. When questioned, he is speechless; he's tied up, he's cast out, he is condemned, one out of many. . . . Recall with me the words you have heard, and in a moment you will discover that that one man was many, and you will see this for yourselves. Certainly, the Lord had questioned one man, **Friend, how did you get in here?** One man had been speechless, and about that one man it had been said, **Bind him hand and foot, and cast him into the outer darkness; that is where there shall be weeping and gnashing of teeth.** Why all this? **For many are called, but few are chosen.**

Who could oppose this demonstration of the truth? **Cast him**, he says, **into the outer darkness**. That man is the one about whom the Lord says, **For many are called, but few are chosen.** So a few are not cast outside. Sure, that was just one man who didn't have on a wedding garment. **Cast him out**. Why is he to be cast out? **For many are called, but few are chosen.** Leave the few, cast out the many. Certainly it was just one man, but insofar as he is many, the many like him definitely surpass the number of the good. We should say that the good are also many; but in comparison with the bad, the good are few.

So what's going on here? All of you who approach the Lord's table before us should not be among the many who will be separated, but among the few who are included. How can you be sure of this? Receive the wedding garment. "Explain the wedding garment to us," you will say. There is no doubt at all that it is a garment that only the good have, those who are included in the banquet—preserved for the banquet to which no bad person has access—brought to it by the grace of the Lord. They are the ones who have on the wedding garment.

So what is that wedding garment? Here's your answer: *But the goal of the commandment*, says the apostle, *is love from a pure heart, and from a good conscience and [from] sincere faith* (1 Tim 1:5). That is the wedding garment. Not any sort of love; even people, after all, who are companions in a bad conscience are often enough seen to love each other. Those who commit armed robberies together, who engage together in witchcraft, who share their devotion to play-actors, who yell encouragement to their favorite charioteers and huntsmen, they all, very often, love each other. But you don't find in them *love from a pure heart, and from a good conscience and from sincere faith*. It's only such love that is the wedding garment.

Clothe yourselves in the wedding garment—I'm addressing you, you people who don't yet have it on. Now you are already inside, you have already come in to the banquet, and you are still not wearing a garment in honor of the bridegroom. You are still seeking your own advantage, not that of Jesus Christ (Phil 2:21). A wedding garment, after all, is accepted in honor of the couple, that is, of the bride and bridegroom. You know who the bridegroom is: Christ. You know who the bride is: the Church. Show respect to them both as they get married. If you show proper respect to these two who are getting married, you yourselves will be sons and daughters. So, make progress in this regard. Love the Lord, and in so doing learn how to love yourselves, so that when, by loving the Lord, you genuinely love yourselves, you may have no hesitation about loving your neighbors as yourselves.

(4) Gregory the Great

We must ask whether this lesson in Matthew is what Luke (Luke 14:16–24) describes, since some details appear inconsistent. Here in Matthew it is a midday meal, there in Luke it is a dinner; here the one who came into the marriage feast improperly dressed was cast out, and there none of those who entered were cast out. From this we can infer that, in this passage, the marriage feast represents the Church of the present time, and the dinner in Luke represents the final and eternal banquet. Some who enter the one will leave it, but no one who has once entered the other will later go out. But if anyone argues that it is the same lesson, I think it better to save the faith and yield to another's interpretation than to give in to heated argument. Perhaps we can reasonably take it that Luke kept silent about the man who Matthew said came without a marriage garment and was thrown out. That one called it a dinner and the other a midday meal does not stand in the way of my interpretation, because when the ancients took their daily midday meal at the ninth hour it was also called a dinner.

Who made a marriage feast for his son. God the Father made a marriage feast for God the Son when he united him to a human nature in the Virgin's womb, when he desired him, who was God before the ages, to become a human being at the end of the ages. Because such a union customarily takes place between two persons, we must keep ourselves from believing that the person God-and-man, our Redeemer Jesus Christ, is the union of two persons. We do indeed say that he exists from and in two natures, but we avoid as sinful the belief that he has been made up of two persons.

A clearer and safer thing to say is that the Father made a marriage feast for his Son by joining the Church to him through the mystery of his incarnation. The womb of the Virgin who bore him was the bridal chamber of this bridegroom, and so the psalmist says: *He has set his tent in the sun, and he is like a bridegroom coming forth from his bridal chamber* (Ps 19:4–5). He truly came forth like a bridegroom from his bridal chamber who, as God incarnate, left the inviolate womb of the Virgin to unite the Church to himself.

And so he sent his servants to invite his friends to the marriage feast. He sent once, and he sent again, because first he made the prophets, and later the apostles, preachers of the Lord's incarnation. He sent his servants twice with the invitation because he said through the prophets that his only Son's incarnation would come about, and it was proclaimed through the apostles that it had.

Because those who were first invited to the marriage banquet refused to come, he said in his second invitation: **See, I have prepared my meal; my oxen and fatlings have been slain, and everything is ready.** What do we understand the oxen and fatlings to be but the fathers of the Old and New Testaments? Since I am speaking to everyone, I must also explain these words of the Gospel reading.

His servants went out into the roads and gathered all whom they found, bad and good, and so the marriage feast was filled with guests. The character of those at the banquet reveals clearly that the king's marriage feast represents the Church of this time, in which the bad are present along with the good. The Church is a thorough mix of a variety of offspring. She brings them all forth to the faith, but she does not lead them all to the liberty of spiritual grace successfully by changes in their lives, because their sins prevent it. As long as we are living in this world, we have to proceed along the road of the present age thoroughly mixed together. We shall be separated when we reach our goal. Only the good are in heaven, and only the bad are in hell. This present life is situated between heaven and hell. It exists in the middle, so to speak, and takes in the citizens of both parts. The Church admits them now without distinguishing them but separates them later when they leave this life.

If you are good, bear patiently with the bad as long as you remain alive. Anyone who does not bear with the bad is a witness against himself through his intolerance that he himself is not good. The person not schooled by Cain in evil is declining to be Abel. On the threshing floor, the grains of wheat are pressed down beneath the straw. Flowers spring up amidst briers. The fragrant rose grows along with piercing thorns.

The first man had two sons: one was chosen, the other rejected (Gen 4:1–5). The ark held three sons (Gen 6:10); of these, two were chosen and one rejected (Gen 9:24–27). Abraham had two sons: one was chosen, the other rejected (Gen 21:10–12). Isaac had two sons: one was chosen, the other rejected (Gen 27:27–37). Jacob had twelve sons: one of them was sold on account of his innocence, while the others on account of their wickedness sold their brother (Gen 37:27–28). Twelve apostles were chosen: mixed together was one who would test, and eleven who would be tested (10:2–4; 26:47–56). Seven deacons were ordained by the apostles (Acts 6:5–6): six of them remained orthodox in their faith, one became a source of error (Rev 2:6).[1] In the Church, then, there can be no bad without good, nor good without bad.

What do we think is meant by the wedding garment, dearly beloved? If we say it is baptism or faith, is there anyone who entered this marriage feast without them? A person is outside because he has not yet come to believe. What then should we understand by the wedding garment if it is not love? That person enters the marriage feast, but without wearing a wedding garment; it is one who is present in the holy Church and has faith but does not have love. We are correct when we say that love is the wedding garment, because this is what our Creator himself possessed when he came to the marriage feast to join the Church to himself. Only God's love brought it about that his only-begotten Son united the hearts of his chosen ones to himself. John says that *God so loved the world that he gave his only-begotten Son* for us (John 3:16).

The one who came to us out of love made known that this love is the wedding garment. Every one of you who belongs to the Church, who has believed in God, has already come in to the marriage feast; but he has not come in a wedding garment unless he preserves the gift of love. And surely, my friends, if anyone of you was invited to a marriage feast, he would change his clothing and show by his dress how he rejoices with the bridegroom and bride; he would be ashamed to appear in contemptible clothing among those rejoicing and celebrating the festive occasion. We come to God's marriage feast and do not care to change the clothing our hearts wear. The angels rejoice, the chosen are taken up to heaven! In what frame of mind do we look upon this spiritual feast, if we don't possess the wedding garment of love that is alone beautiful?

1. It is most unlikely that the Nicolaitians in Ephesus, who are condemned in Revelation, stemmed from the Nicolaus who was appointed a deacon in Jerusalem (Acts 6:5).

Matthew 22:15–22

15 Then the Pharisees went and took counsel how to entangle him in his talk. 16 And they
sent their disciples to him, along with the Hero'dians, saying, "Teacher, we know that you
are true, and teach the way of God truthfully, and care for no man; for you do not regard
the position of men. 17 Tell us, then, what you think. Is it lawful to pay taxes to Caesar, or
not?" 18 But Jesus, aware of their malice, said, "Why put me to the test, you hypocrites?
19 Show me the money for the tax." And they brought him a coin. 20 And Jesus said to them,
"Whose likeness and inscription is this?" 21 They said, "Caesar's." Then he said to them,
"Render therefore to Caesar the things that are Caesar's, and to God the things that are
God's." 22 When they heard it, they marveled; and they left him and went away.

(5) Tertullian

The things that are Caesar's are to be rendered to Caesar. To set the contrast, he added, **and to God the things that are God's.** What things are Caesar's? Specifically he had in mind those things about which he was questioned, whether tax should be paid to Caesar. When the Lord asked to see the money, he asked whose image was on it. When he heard it was Caesar's, he said, **Render to Caesar what are Caesar's, and what are God's to God**, that is, the image of Caesar on the coin is Caesar's, and the image of God in man is God's. Thus, we render our money to Caesar and ourselves to God. Otherwise, what would be God's if everything was Caesar's?

We are God's, paid for in blood, and so owe no money for our head, because Christ is our head. It is inappropriate that Christ would charge us a fee. How could martyrdoms, for example, give glory to the Lord, if we were supposed to pay a tax for the freedom to follow our way of life? Whoever, therefore, demands this at a price, is opposed to the divine order of things. . . .

How shall I render **to God the things that are God's**? By bearing his image and stamp, inscribed with his own name, namely, the one who wears the name Christian. What do I owe God as I owe a *denarius* to Caesar, except the blood that his Son poured out for me? If I do indeed owe anything to God, it is my life as a man and my own blood. But I am now in such a position that, if a demand is made upon me for the payment of that debt, I am guilty of cheating God by not giving what I owe. Have I properly kept the commandment by rendering to Caesar what belongs to Caesar, when I am denying to God what belongs to God?

(6) Athanasius of Alexandria

Cease doing these things,[2] I entreat you, and remember that you happen to be a mortal human. Fear the day of judgment; keep yourself pure until it[s arrival]. Do not insert your-

2. That is, banishing bishops, arbitrating in ecclesial trials, compelling Church officials to accuse others.

self in ecclesiastical matters nor give us advice about them. Instead, learn of them from us. To you God has given a kingdom; to us he has entrusted the things of the Church. Just as someone who robs authority out from under you is contradicting the commands of God who ordained it, so you too should fear lest you also forcibly compel the Church's matters to yourself, becoming liable to a great charge. **Render**, it is written, **the things of Caesar to Caesar, and the things of God to God.** Neither therefore is it permissible for us to rule over the earth, nor do you, emperor, have authority to offer incense. I write these things out of a concern for your salvation.

(7) Hilary of Poitiers

O wholly miraculous response and perfect clarity of heavenly words! The entire matter has to do with negotiating between contempt for the world and the affront of opposing Caesar. When the Lord declared which things should be rendered to Caesar, he freed hearts devoted to God from every worry and human need. If there is nothing left for us to render to Caesar, we will not be bound by the limitation of surrendering to him what is his. If we have a possessive attitude toward the things that are Caesar's and acknowledge his right of authority, and, if we behave like mercenaries who claim the right of another's inheritance, then we can make no complaint about rendering to Caesar what is Caesar's and rendering to God what belongs to God: our body, soul, and will. It is from God that we possess these [three], which grow and increase. As a result, we are completely justified in rendering to him everything, seeing that we owe to him our origin and development.

(8) Ambrose of Milan

The command was given, "Hand over the basilica." I answered, "It is not lawful for me to hand it over, nor is it expedient for you, O emperor, to receive it. If you cannot rightly violate the house of a private individual, do you think that the house of God can be appropriated?" It is alleged that all things are permitted to the emperor, that everything is his. To which I reply, "Do not burden yourself with thinking that you have imperial power over things that are divine. Do not exalt yourself, but, if you wish to be emperor for a long time, be subject to God. The Scripture says, **what things belong to God are God's, what things belong to Caesar are Caesar's.** Palaces belong to the emperor, churches to the bishop. You have been given authority over public buildings, not over sacred ones.

(9) Augustine

The image of God, by which we were created, should be progressively sculpted afresh. You see, by sinning it was defaced, worn down. How did it get worn down, get defaced? By being rubbed on the earth. What's that, rubbed on the earth? It is rubbed by earthly desires. *Although man walks in the image*, you see, *yet he is troubled in vain* (Ps 39:6). What one looks for in an image is for it to be true, not faulty. It's by loving the truth that the image of God by which we were created is sculpted anew, and his very own coin is paid back to Caesar.

Do you remember the reply of the Lord to the Jews who were trying to trap him, when he said, **Why are you trying to test me, you hypocrites? Show me the coin of the tax**, that is, the image stamped on it and the inscription. "Show me what you pay, what you prepare, what is demanded of you. Show it to me." They showed him a **denarius.** And he asked whose image and inscription it had on it. They answered, **Caesar's.**

Caesar too requires his image. He doesn't want to lose what he has levied, nor does God want to lose what he has made. Caesar, my dear brothers and sisters, didn't make the coin, the imperial mint made it. An order was given to the craftsmen after he instructed his ministers. An image was stamped on the coin: the image of Caesar. And yet he is demanding what other people have stamped, he is collecting it, and he won't be denied. As human beings, we are Christ's currency. That's where Christ's image is, Christ's name, Christ's style and titles.

Matthew 22:23–33

23 The same day Sad'ducees came to him, who say that there is no resurrection; and they
asked him a question, 24 saying, "Teacher, Moses said, 'If a man dies, having no children,
his brother must marry the widow, and raise up children for his brother.' 25 Now there
were seven brothers among us; the first married, and died, and having no children left
his wife to his brother. 26 So too the second and third, down to the seventh. 27 After them
all, the woman died. 28 In the resurrection, therefore, to which of the seven will she be
wife? For they all had her."

29 But Jesus answered them, "You are wrong, because you know neither the scrip-
tures nor the power of God. 30 For in the resurrection they neither marry nor are given
in marriage, but are like angels in heaven. 31 And as for the resurrection of the dead,
have you not read what was said to you by God, 32 'I am the God of Abraham, and the
God of Isaac, and the God of Jacob'? He is not God of the dead, but of the living." 33 And
when the crowd heard it, they were astonished at his teaching.

(10) John Chrysostom

Why didn't they assert two or three brothers instead of seven? Was it to heap more ridicule on the resurrection in asserting this? They then said, "they all had her," which was supposed to put the Lord in a tight spot.

What did Christ say? He responds to both points, considering not their words but their attitudes, by which he exposes their hidden intentions. At one moment he exposes their intentions, at another moment he leaves the refutation of those who are asking the questions to their own minds. See here how he proves both points, as well that there will be a resurrection, though it will not be a resurrection as they suspect.

What did he say? **You are in error, not knowing the Scriptures, nor the power of**

God. Because they refer to Moses and the law, as if they knew them, the Lord shows that this is precisely the question that betrays their ignorance of the Scriptures. And because of their ignorance of the Scriptures, and their lack of the right understanding of God's power, they also tried to test him.

"It is not so amazing," the Lord says, "that you test me, since I am still unknown to you. But neither are you acquainted with the power of God of which you [claim to] have so much experience. And yet you possess neither common understanding of it from the Scriptures, nor have become acquainted with it." After all, even by means of common sense, we can know that for God everything is possible.

In the first instance, Christ answers the question asked. Since the cause of their denial of the resurrection was their belief that the order of the things present is like that to come, he cures this problem. Then, he also cures the symptom (from which arose the disease) and shows the manner of the resurrection. **For in the resurrection**, he said, **they neither marry, nor are given in marriage, but are as angels of God in heaven.**

After answering their question, he did not stop, but continued by answering their thoughts. Thus, when they ask out of ignorance, and not out of an evil intention, he teaches them beyond what their question asked for. However, when they ask solely out of wickedness, he does not even address the question.

A second time, he reduced them to silence by invoking Moses, since they had brought the example of Moses forward. He said, **But as touching the resurrection of the dead, have you not read, I am the God of Abraham, and the God of Isaac, and the God of Jacob? He is not the God of the dead, but of the living.** By "the dead" the Lord does not mean "those who no longer live, who have vanished once and for all, who will rise no more." He did not say, "I was," but, **I am**; of them that are, and of them that live. For like Adam, although he lived on the day that he ate of the tree, he died in the sentence passed upon him. It is likewise with Abraham, Isaac, and Jacob; although they had died, they lived in the promise of the resurrection.

How then does he say elsewhere, *That he might be Lord both of the dead and of the living*? (Rom 14:9). There is no contradiction here, since he is speaking of the dead, who will also come to life. But there is also a difference between the statements, **I am the God of Abraham**, and *That he might be Lord both of the dead and of the living.* He knows of another death too, about which he said, **Let the dead bury their dead** (8:22).

And when the multitudes heard this, they were astonished at his doctrine. Yet not even in these circumstances are the Sadducees astonished. They go away defeated, while the impartial crowd reaps the benefit. What did Christ say? He replies to both points, taking his stand not against the words, but their intention, revealing the secrets of their hearts. On the one hand, he exposes them, on the other, he leaves the refutation of those that question him to their consciences.

(11) Augustine

After some angels in wicked pride had deserted God and been cast down into the deep darkness of the air, the remaining angels stayed in eternal happiness with God. There was not one fallen and condemned angel who had engendered the others so that the original evil might bind them in the chains of harmful succession and drag them all to their deserved punishment. Instead, after the one who became the devil was exalted with his companions in wickedness and was laid low with them because of this exaltation, the rest remained with the Lord in loyal obedience and also received what the others did not have, a sure knowledge to make them secure concerning their own everlasting stability, from which they were never to fall. . . .

As for the other part of the rational creation, that is, humankind, since they had totally perished by reason of their sins and punishments, both original and each person's own, some of them were to be restored to fill the gap left in the company of the angels by the devil's fall. For this is the promise made to the saints when they rise again: that they will be equal to the angels of God. So, the Jerusalem that is above, our mother, the city of God (cf. Gal 4:26; Rev 21:2), will not be cheated of the due number of her citizens, or perhaps will reign with an even greater number. For we do not know the number either of holy men and women or of the impure demons into whose place will succeed the children of that holy mother who appeared barren (cf. Isa 54:1; quoted in Gal 4:27) on earth, to live unendingly in the peace from which they fell. But the number that there will be of those citizens, either now or in the future, is in the contemplation of the *maker who calls into existence the things that do not exist* (Rom 4:17) and arranges *all things by measure and number and weight* (Wis 2:20).

Matthew 22:34–40

34But when the Pharisees heard that he had silenced the Sad'ducees, they came together.
35And one of them, a lawyer, asked him a question, to test him. 36"Teacher, which is the
great commandment in the law?" 37And he said to him, "You shall love the Lord your
God with all your heart, and with all your soul, and with all your mind. 38This is the
great and first commandment. 39And a second is like it, You shall love your neighbor
as yourself. 40On these two commandments depend all the law and the prophets."

(12) Clement of Alexandria

When asked what is the greatest of the commandments, the teacher says, *You shall love the Lord your God with all your soul and with all your might* and *no commandment is greater than this one* (Mark 12:30–31)—and quite reasonably. For it was in fact prescribed regarding both the first and the greatest: God himself, our Father, through whom everything was both made and exists, and to whom what is restored returns again. Indeed, because we were loved beforehand by him and obtained our existence from him, it is impious to hold something else as more honored or respected. Since we have nothing else whatsoever to conceive as compensation for a God who is perfect and without need, we render only this small gratitude for the greatest gains: by the very act of loving the Father to the limit of our own strength and might, we reap incorruptibility. For the more we love God, the more we progress deep within God.

So Jesus brings love into both commandments, but he has divided it by rank. The first duties of love he attaches to God, but the second duties he assigns to our neighbor. But who else is this neighbor except the Savior himself? Or who more than he has compassion on us, who has almost been put to death by the *worldly powers of darkness* (Eph 6:12) with many wounds, fears, lusts, angers, afflictions, deceptions, and pleasures? Now Jesus is the only doctor for these wounds because he wholly cuts off the passions by the roots; not like the law that produces bare results by cutting off the fruits of bad trees, but by bringing up his own axe against the roots of depravity (cf. 3:10; Luke 3:9). He is the one who poured out the wine, the blood of the vine of David, over our wounded souls; he is the one who lavishes us with oil, the compassion from the Father's affection; he is the one who shows that the indestructible bonds of health and salvation are love, faith, and hope; he is the one who commanded the angels and rulers and authorities to serve us for a great reward, since they too will be set free from the emptiness of the world at the revelation of the glory of the children of God (cf. 1 Cor 15:24; Rom 8:19–21). Thus we must love him equally with God. And the one who loves Christ Jesus does his will and keeps his commandments (cf. John 14:15). For *not everyone who says to me "Lord, Lord" will enter the kingdom of heaven, but the one who does the will of my Father* (7:21); and *why do you call me "Lord, Lord" and do not do what I say?* (Luke 6:46); and blessed are you who see and hear what neither the righteous nor the prophets have seen or heard, if you do what I say (cf. 3:16–17; John 13:17).

(13) Hilary of Poitiers

The Pharisees asked him what was the most important commandment in the law, not realizing that the practice of the law had been perfected in Christ. He responded to their arrogant ignorance with the words from the law itself, a response that included in itself all the teaching of the truth. For it is the very mission of our Lord Jesus Christ to introduce the knowledge of God and to reveal an understanding of his name and authority. He has come as the one who was sent, and as the one who proceeded from eternity, he accomplished what was pleasing to God. And so he responded that the first command is: **Love the Lord your God with all your heart, with all your soul, and with all your mind**. There is nothing here other than what the law contains, because the precepts of the law represent a prefiguration of that which he will accomplish. He reminded them that instead of glorifying themselves with their legal knowledge, they should love God Almighty with every affection of the mind, heart, and soul (cf. Deut 6:5) so that his teaching would be confirmed by what was given in the law.

Then he added: This is the great and first commandment. And the second is similar to this one: Love your neighbor as yourself. By saying that the second commandment follows the first and is like it means that the obligation is worth the same as with the first. For the love of God has no value without Christ, nor is the love of Christ of value without God. The one without the other offers no benefit for our salvation. For that reason, he says, **On these two commandments hang all the law and the prophets.** All of the law and the prophets have their full measure in Christ's coming, through which we receive knowledge of God.

(14) Leo the Great

Thus says the Lord: **You shall love the Lord your God with your whole heart and your whole mind, and you shall love your neighbor as yourself.** Let the faithful soul undertake the unfading charity of her own Creator and Ruler. Let her submit her entire self to his will, in whose works and judgments nothing exists without the truth of justice, nothing without the compassion of mercy. Even if anyone should be fatigued by great labors and many misfortunes, there is good reason for the one to endure who understands that he is either being corrected or proved by trials.

But the piety of this charity will not be perfect unless the neighbor also is loved. This name [i.e., neighbor] must not only be understood as those who are joined to us in friendship or nearness, but surely all men, with whom we share a common nature, whether they might be enemies, comrades, free, or slave. For one maker fashioned us, one Creator gave us life. We all enjoy the same sky and air, the same days and nights. Although some are good, some bad, some just, some unjust, nevertheless God is a liberal giver to all. He is kind to all. It is just as the apostles Paul and Barnabas said to the Lycaonians concerning the providence of God: *In past generations he let all the nations go their own ways. But indeed he did not leave them behind without a testimony, doing good to them, giving rain and fruitful seasons from heaven, filling our hearts with food and joy* (Acts 14:16–17).

But the breadth of Christian grace, which extends to all parts of the entire world, has given to us greater reasons for loving our neighbors. It despairs of no man, since it teaches that no one must be neglected. And rightly so does he enjoin us **to love our enemies and pray for our persecutors** (cf. 5:44). Daily *grafting* from all the nations the shoot of a *wild olive tree* into the holy branches of his own olive tree (cf. Rom 11:17), he makes those of his enemies reconciled, strangers he makes his adopted sons, wicked men he makes just, *so that every knee might bow of those in heaven, in earth, and in hell, and that every tongue might confess that Jesus Christ is Lord to the glory of God the Father* (Phil 2:10–11).

(15) Augustine

The law contains many commandments, and the particular law that is called the Decalogue has Ten Commandments. But the Ten Commandments are, so to speak, general laws, to which all the countless other ones may be referred. To show how the other commandments, which seem to be innumerable, may be reduced to this small number of ten would mean an infinite amount of discussion. What we can at least demonstrate now, to the extent that the Lord helps us, is that just as the other commandments are all referred to these ten, which I said would be an enormous labor to discuss, so these ten can be referred to two.

The ten, of course, are these: About worshiping the one God, not worshiping any other, there is one commandment there, *You shall not make yourself an idol, nor the likeness of anything, neither of the things in heaven above, nor of the things on earth beneath* (Exod 20:4). *The Lord your God is one Lord* (Deut 6:4). The second commandment is, *You shall not take in vain the name of the Lord your God* (Exod 20:7). The third commandment is, *Observe the day of the Sabbath* (Deut 5:12). These commandments refer to God.

To teach a Christian anything about the observance of the Sabbath would seem to be rather superfluous. On the contrary, not only is it not superfluous, but it is in fact basic, bedrock doctrine, because it is a shadow of things to come. The people, you see, are forbidden to perform servile works on the Sabbath. Now I ask you, are we not forbidden to perform servile works? Listen to the Lord: *Everyone who commits sin is the slave of sin* (John 8:34). And yet to hope to receive from God this very thing, of not committing sin, that is to celebrate the Sabbath, that's why it is written, *God rested on the seventh day from all his works* (Gen 2:2). God rested: God causes you to rest. Does God himself need to rest? When did he tire himself out working, seeing that he created all things with a word?

So these three refer to God; the seven others refer to man. *Honor father and mother; you shall not commit adultery; you shall not kill; you shall not bear false witness; you shall not steal; you shall not covet your neighbor's wife; you shall not covet your neighbor's property* (Exod 20:12–17). If you love God, you neither worship any other, nor take his name in vain, and you keep the Sabbath for him, so that he may rest in you, when he causes you to rest. If you love your neighbor, you honor your parents, and don't commit adultery, and don't kill, and don't harm anybody with false witness, and don't steal from anybody, and don't covet anyone's wife, and don't covet anyone's property. And in this way, **You shall love the Lord your God with your whole heart, and with your whole soul, and with your whole mind**; and **You shall love your neighbor as yourself. In these two commandments is fulfilled the whole law, and the prophets.**

Listen also to the Apostle: *The fullness of the law*, he says, *is charity* (Rom 13:10). He didn't send you off to carry out many things, not even ten, not even two; one charity fulfills everything. However, this charity is twofold: toward God, and toward your neighbor. Toward God, how much? With the whole. The whole what? I mean, not the whole ear, and nose, and hand, and foot. He can be loved with the whole of what? With the whole heart, with the whole soul, with the whole mind; with the whole of what is alive in you, you shall love the fountain of life. So if I have to love God with the whole of what is alive in me, what will I leave myself to love my neighbor with? You see, when you were instructed about loving your neighbor, you weren't told "with the whole heart, and the whole soul, and the whole mind," but **as yourself.** God with the whole of you, because he is better than you are; your neighbor as yourself, because he is the same as you are yourself.

So there are two commandments, and yet three things to be loved. Two commandments given: love God and love your neighbor; and three things to be loved. After all, it wouldn't say **and your neighbor as yourself** unless you were also to love yourself. So if there are three things to be loved, why are there only two commandments? Why? Here's the answer. God didn't consider that you had to be admonished to love yourself; there are no people, after all, who don't love themselves. But because there are many who suffer the loss of themselves by loving themselves in the wrong way, by being told to love God with the whole of yourself, you were also given a rule there on how you should love yourself. Do you want to love yourself? Love God with the whole of yourself; there, you see, you will find yourself, or else in yourself you might lose yourself. If you love yourself in yourself, you are bound to fall away even from yourself, and go looking for many things besides yourself.

Which is why the Apostle traced all evil back to that one source, where he says, *For people will be loving themselves.* There you are; you've chosen to love yourself. Let's see whether you even manage to remain in yourself. It's not true, you can't remain there; fallen away from God, you've also fallen away from yourself. There, after all, is where firm ground is; that's where you should have stuck fast, that's where you should have made yourself a fortress and a house of refuge. Now, though, you have slackened off the connecting rope of your love, or you've even cut it between him and you; you can't even remain in yourself. Listen, anyway, to the Apostle himself: After saying, *For people will be in love with themselves*, he immediately added, *lovers of money* (2 Tim 3:2).

Didn't I say that you weren't going to remain even in yourself? Are you money? Just look, you've even become lost to yourself, once you have withdrawn from God. What's left for you, but to squander the inheritance of your mind, living recklessly with harlots, that is to say, with lusts and various greedy desires, and to be compelled by this need to feed pigs? That is, because unclean avarice has taken possession of you, unclean demons are to be fed from what you have. But that son, after enduring extremes of want, and being worn down by hunger, *returned to himself and said*. He returned to himself because he had been lost to himself, and in himself he found himself in great need. He looked for gratification everywhere and found it nowhere. He returned to himself, and what did he say? *I will arise and go.* Go where? *To my father* (Luke 15:17–18). He had already returned to himself, but he was still lying there; *I will arise and go*; "I won't lie here, I won't remain any longer."

So a rule has been laid down for you about how you should love yourself: love the one who is better than you, and you have already loved yourself. I mean one better by nature, not by will. After all, many people can be found who are better than you by will, but only God is so by nature: Creator, Establisher, Maker, himself made by none. Fix yourself firmly there. Come to your senses some time or other and say, *But for me*. But for you, what? *To attach myself to God is good.* Why so? Notice what he had said just before: *You have lost everyone who goes whoring away from you* (Ps 73:27–28). So because he has lost everyone who goes whoring away from him, you have found yourself; *but for me to attach myself to God is good*, that is, not to go whoring away from God, not to remove myself from God. Do you wish to see what is being promised you in this connection? *But whoever attaches himself to God is one spirit* (1 Cor 6:17).

So this is what it means to love yourself, that is, the love you love yourself with: to love God. Now I can also entrust your neighbor to you, whom you are to love as yourself, because I can see that you have begun to love yourself. I mean, if you loved gold and possessed gold, and loved your neighbor as yourself, in loving him you would be dividing what you possessed and making him a sharer in your gold. But by this division you would each have less. So why not possess the one in whom you will experience no diminution of property with your coheir? However many people you can persuade, however many you can invite, summon, and compel to love God, he is wholly there for all of them, and wholly there for each of them.

(16) Augustine

So what is this summary and short few words about? **You shall love the Lord your God with your whole heart, and with your whole soul, and with your whole mind; and you**

shall love your neighbor as yourself: On these two commandments depends the whole law, and the prophets. There you are, that's what's learned in the house of discipline; to love God, to love your neighbor; God as God, your neighbor as yourself. You won't find God's peer, after all, so that you could be told, "Love God as you love that other one." About your neighbor a standard has been found for you, because you yourself are found to be your neighbor's peer. You ask how you are to love your neighbor. Look at yourself, and at how you love yourself, and love your neighbor like that. No room for any mistake there. So I wish to commit your neighbor to you on those terms that you love him as yourself; that's what I wish, but I still have my qualms about it.

I want to tell you, **Love your neighbor as you love yourself**, and I have my qualms; I still wish, you see, to examine how you love yourself. So don't take it badly; you yourself are not to be lightly dismissed, since your neighbor is to be committed to your care. We mustn't deal with you in an offhand manner. You are one person, your neighbors are many. In the first place, you see, you shouldn't understand your neighbor as just being your brother, or relative, or one of your in-laws. A neighbor to every person is every single other person. Father and son, father-in-law and son-in-law are said to be neighbors. Nothing is so near, so much a neighbor, as one human being to another. But if we assume that only those born of the same parents are neighbors, let's turn our attention to Adam and Eve, and we are all brothers and sisters. Brothers and sisters, indeed, insofar as we are human, so how much more so in that we are Christians? As regards your being human, your one father was Adam, your one mother Eve. As regards your being a Christian, your one father is God, your one mother the Church.

You will be telling me next, "I do love my neighbor as myself." I hear you, certainly I hear you; you want to get drunk with this man whom you love as yourself. "Let's have a good time today, let's drink as much as we can." Notice that that's how you love yourself, and that you are drawing him to yourself, and inviting him to what you love. Loving him as you love yourself, you are bound to draw him there to what you also love. All too human, a man—or rather bestial man—loves the same sort of things as the beasts! God, you see, made the beasts prone in form, with their faces to the ground, looking for their food from the ground, whereas you he set on your two feet, upright from the ground. He wanted your face to be looking upward. Don't let your heart contradict your face.

Don't have your face turned upward and your heart turned downward. On the contrary, hear what is true, and do what is true: "Lift up your hearts"; don't lie in the house of discipline. After all, when you hear this, you answer; but let what you answer be true. Love yourself in that way, and you will really love your neighbor as yourself. What, after all, does it mean to have your heart lifted up, but what you were told first: **You shall love the Lord your God with all your heart, and with all your soul, and with all your mind**?

So while there are two commandments, wouldn't it have been enough if he had just given one? Yes, even one is enough, if rightly understood. Because Scripture sometimes speaks in this fashion, like the Apostle Paul: *You shall not commit adultery, you shall not commit murder, you shall not lust, and any other commandment there may be is summed up in this saying: You shall love your neighbor as yourself. Love of neighbor does not work any evil. So charity is the fulfillment of the law* (Rom 13:9–10). What is charity? It's love. He appears to have said nothing about the love of God, but he said that love of neighbor alone was enough to fulfill the law. *Whatever other commandment there may be is summed up in this saying*, is fulfilled in this saying. In which one? **You shall love your neighbor as yourself.** There you have one. But certainly there are two commandments on which the whole law depends, and the prophets.

Matthew 22:41–46

41Now while the Pharisees were gathered together, Jesus asked them a question, 42say-
ing, "What do you think of the Christ? Whose son is he?" They said to him, "The son of David." 43He said to them, "How is it then that David, inspired by the Spirit, calls him Lord, saying,
44'The Lord said to my Lord,
Sit at my right hand,
till I put thy enemies under thy feet'?
45If David thus calls him Lord, how is he his son?" 46And no one was able to answer him
a word, nor from that day did any one dare to ask him any more questions.

(17) John Chrysostom

Since he had given them an answer, he asked in turn, **What do you think of Christ, whose son is he? They said to him, the son of David.** After that, after many miracles, after many signs, after many questions, after a great demonstration of his unity with the Father in deed as well as in words, after having commended the one who said, *God is one*, he asks this question so that, after knowing what he did, they could not claim he was an enemy of the law and a foe of God. . . .

Since he was about to go to his passion, he finally sets forth the prophecy that plainly proclaims him to be Lord. For good reason he did not address this matter openly or earlier. When he had posed this question before, they did not respond with the truth concerning him. In fact, they said he was a mere man. For this reason he introduces David as proclaiming his divinity and refutes their mistaken opinion. For the disciples really supposed that he was a mere man, which is why they called him **the son of David** (cf. Acts 9:20). However, the Lord corrects this opinion by bringing in the prophet as a witness of his lordship and of the truth of his sonship, as well as of his equality in honor with his Father.

But he doesn't stop at this point. In order to move them to reverence, he adds what follows, **until I make your enemies your footstool**, so that at least in this way he might win them over. That they may not say that he called [on David] in self-flattery and that this was a human judgment, see what he says, **How then does David in spirit call him Lord?** See how humbly he introduces the sentence and judgment concerning himself. First, he had said, **What do you think? Whose son is he?** By a question he brings them to an answer. . . .

That is why he now presents his teaching in form of questions and answers. However, in this way he also obscurely intimates his dignity. For it was not as much to be called Lord of the Jews as son of David.

Observe also how timely this is. For when he had said, "There is one Lord," then he said of himself that he is Lord, no longer showing it only by his works, but also by the prophecy. And he shows the Father himself judging them on his behalf, for he says, **Until I make your enemies your footstool**. By this he also shows the great unanimity and honor toward himself on the part of the Father that begot him. These are the words by which the Lord provides a powerful and convincing conclusion of his reasoning with the Pharisees, one that shut their mouths tightly.

(18) Augustine

Only what they, the Pharisees, could see did they know about the Lord. What they saw was the Son of Man; what was hidden from them was the Son of God. That's why they thought they could defeat him, and why they mocked him as he hung on the cross, with the words: **If he is the Son of God, let him come down from the cross, and we will believe in him** (27:40, 42). They saw one thing about him, they did not know the other. For if they had known, *they would never have crucified the Lord of glory* (1 Cor 2:8).

It is therefore a great thing to know the mystery of how he is both David's Lord and David's Son (1:1); how in one person he is both man and God; how in the form of man he is less than the Father, in the form of God equal to the Father. How can he say both *the Father is greater than I* (John 14:28) and *I and the Father are one* (John 10:30)? Because it is a great mystery, our minds and hearts have to be prepared, if we will be capable of grasping it. It is closed, you see, to the unworthy, opened to the deserving.

If you recognize him as David's Lord, Lord of heaven and earth, Lord of the angels, if you recognize him as equal to God in the form of God (Phil 2:6), how is he David's son? Pay attention to how it goes on. The Apostle has shown you David's Lord by saying, *Who since he was in the form of God did not consider it robbery to be equal to God.* How does he show him as David's son? *But he emptied himself, taking the form of a servant, being made in the likeness of men; and being found in condition as a man, he humbled himself, becoming obedient unto death, the death indeed of the cross. Wherefore God has also exalted him* (Phil 2:6–9).

Christ rose again from the seed of David as the Son of David because he had emptied himself. How did he empty himself? By taking what he was not, not by losing what he was. He emptied himself, he humbled himself. Though he was God, he made himself known as a man. He was despised as he walked the earth, though he made the sky. He was despised as a mere man, as though he had no power. Not only despised, but on top of that he was also killed. He was a stone lying flat; the Jews stumbled over him and were shaken. And what does he say about that himself? **Whoever stumbles over this stone will be shaken; but as for anyone upon whom this stone comes, it will crush him** (21:44; Luke 20:18; Isa 8:14–15). First he lay flat, and they stumbled; he will come from above and crush them, after they have been shaken.

You have grasped that he is both David's Son and David's Lord. He is David's Lord always, and also David's Son from a point in time. As David's Lord, he was born of the substance of the Father; as David's Son, he was born of Mary the virgin, conceived by the

Holy Spirit. We must hold on to both things. One of them will be our eternal dwelling place, the other one is our liberation from exile. If our Lord Jesus Christ had not been prepared to become human, humanity would have perished. He became what he made, that what he made might not perish. True man, true God; God and man, the whole Christ. This is the catholic faith.

So the Lord says to the Jews, **Whose son do you say the Christ is? They answered, David's.** They knew that perfectly well; they could gather it easily enough from the preaching of the prophets. And indeed he was *from the seed of David*, but *according to the flesh* (Rom 1:3), through the Virgin Mary, married to Joseph. So when they answered that Christ was the Son of David, Jesus said to them, **So how does David in the spirit call him Lord, saying: The Lord said to my lord, Sit at my right hand until I place your enemies under your feet? So if David in the spirit calls him Lord, how is he his son?** (cf. Ps 110:1). And the Jews couldn't answer. That's what we have in the Gospel. He did not deny he was the Son of David, even though they were unaware that he was the Lord of David. What they held to about the Christ was that he came to be in time; what they did not understand about him was that he is in eternity! So therefore, wishing to teach them about his divinity, he put a problem to them about his humanity, as though to say, "You know that the Christ is the Son of David; answer and tell me how he can also be the Lord of David." But to prevent them saying "He isn't David's Lord," he quoted David himself as a witness. And what does *he* say? He says the truth, of course. On the one hand, you have that place in the Psalms where he says to David, *I will place of the fruit of your body upon your throne* (Ps 132:11). There you have "Son of David." And how is the one who is the Son of David also "Lord of David"? *The Lord said to my lord*, he says, *Sit at my right* (Ps 110:1). Are you surprised at David having his Son as his Lord, when you see Mary has given birth to her Lord? David's Lord, because he's God; David's Lord, because he's everyone's; but David's Son, on the other hand, because he's the Son of Man. One and the same person who is Lord and who is Son: David's Lord, because *since he was in the form of God, he did not think it robbery to be equal to God*; David's Son, because *he emptied himself, taking the form of a servant* (Phil 2:6–7).

Matthew 23

After refuting verbal attacks made against him in the previous chapter, Jesus charges the religious leaders with legalism, hypocrisy, and external righteousness; and he also pronounces judgment over the nation of Israel for rejecting him.

Hilary explains that Christ called the people to obey the law that the Pharisees preach, because every precept of the law points to his advent. However, the Pharisees themselves break this law. They impose the burden of the law on others and fail to recognize, in Christ, the Lord about whom the law speaks. For this reason, their outer displays of religiosity (for example, wearing phylacteries[1]) and their claims to be called teachers (rabbis) are meaningless (vv. 1–7). Chrysostom cautions that pride is especially dangerous for teachers.

Jesus pronounced several condemnations against the chief priests, each beginning with the word "woe." As Hilary explains, not only do they disobey the law themselves, they also conceal its true meaning from others, thus preventing them from entering the kingdom of heaven (v. 13). They infect new converts with their own legalism (v. 15). The tricky wording of their oaths allows the Pharisees an easy escape from fulfilling the law.

Not only do the scribes and Pharisees deny their own need for correction and guidance, they also claim that they can guide others. By "doing everything for show," Chrysostom remarks, they lead others to follow their ritualistic external purity, while neglecting the true purity of the soul and transgressing the commandments that consist in "justice and mercy and faith in God" (Cyril). Reflecting on the metaphor of whitewashed tombs, *beautiful on the outside, but full of dead bones within, Chrysostom reminds his hearers that a born-again person is God's temple where the Holy Spirit dwells.*

The chapter ends with a scene of Jesus weeping over Jerusalem as the holy city of the Jewish nation. He had instructed the people and desired to gather them as a hen gathers her brood under her wings, *but they gave him no heed. Hilary explains: "Just as a hen gathers her young, so he wished to hold them under his wings (23:37). Just as if he had become an earthly and domesticated bird having wings as a bodily covering, the Lord granted to his young the warmth of eternal life and was teaching them to fly into the sky of a new birth." So the Lord predicted that their house would be* forsaken and desolate *(v. 38). Eusebius of Caesarea describes the fulfillment of this prophecy: "The people of Jerusalem suffered after*

1. Small leather containers with verses from the Hebrew Scriptures, attached to the arm and the forehead.

the Romans attacked their city. Some of the inhabitants were slaughtered by the rights of war; some they led away as captives; some died from famine; and others were driven out and scattered every which way. The Romans burned their house and temple and enveloped them in utter desolation."

Matthew 23:1–7

1Then said Jesus to the crowds and to his disciples, 2"The scribes and the Pharisees sit on Moses' seat; 3so practice and observe whatever they tell you, but not what they do; for they preach, but do not practice. 4They bind heavy burdens, hard to bear, and lay them on men's shoulders; but they themselves will not move them with their finger. 5They do all their deeds to be seen by men; for they make their phylacteries broad and their fringes long, 6and they love the place of honor at feasts and the best seats in the synagogues, 7and salutations in the market places, and being called rabbi by men."

(1) Hilary of Poitiers

Jesus showed that the glory of the law bears witness to himself; the law was an image of the truth to come. In all its details, it prepared the way for Christ's coming, for whatever was contained in the law pointed to the revelation of knowledge of Christ. For this reason, he told the disciples to obey the precepts of the Pharisees (19:19). Because they sit in the seat of Moses, he commanded them to obey all the commandments of the law. At the same time, he told them not to follow the deeds and their works, lest human customs and unbelief nullify the teaching of the law. For the Pharisees impose heavy burdens of the law on the people who follow them. And yet, the Pharisees do not lift a finger to help them. Though they say that we should love the Lord with all of our heart and love our neighbor as oneself (19:19), in matters that concern them, they oppose the testimony of the law—even though it is known to them—and attack God in Christ because of his sufferings.

They inflate the glory of their words by wearing phylacteries, though they do not see that the author of eternal life is in Christ. They magnify themselves as emissaries who honor the law, with tassels hanging from their garments, though they are unfamiliar with the whole law and recognize neither its works nor its power. They love to sit at the head table at banquets. But their destiny is eternal fire rather than banquets, while Gentiles will sit with Abraham. They love the important seats in the synagogues but do not know who their teacher is according to the testimonies of the law and the prophets. They love to be greeted in the marketplace, forgetting that humility of heart and service required of everyone. They desire to be called "teacher" by men, though they are unfamiliar with the teaching of the law and reject the teacher of eternal salvation. All such profane and perverse things are condemned as pretentious. What is required is that one listens to the law and observes its words, because they bear witness to Christ.

(2) John Chrysostom

It brings me to tears even now when I hear mention of **best seats** and **salutations**, and when I think of the great troubles that have arisen from this for the churches of God. It is not necessary to go into details for you now, or, at least, any elderly people do not need to be informed of it by us. For your part, however, take note of where the vice of pride was in force: in the synagogues, the place where they were told not to be arrogant, a place where they went to perform service for others. I mean, to display this vice to a certain degree at feasts does not seem so dreadful, though even there the teacher should be above reproach, not only in church but everywhere. Just as human beings, wherever they be, are clearly different from brute beasts, so too are teachers; be they speaking or remaining silent, dining or doing anything at all, they should be recognizable by deportment and appearance, by garb and other things. The scribes and Pharisees, by contrast, were in all respects ridiculous and consistently disgraced themselves, getting involved in what they should have avoided. **They love it**, the text says: and if loving it was a fault, how bad was doing it? It is awful to have a vice that compels one to go hunting and chasing after something until it is obtained. So while Jesus went no further than to accuse them of other vices, these being small and insignificant, and the disciples did not need to be corrected on these matters, the Lord focused on these, correcting and lecturing others and usurping the role of teacher about ambition, itself the cause of all the vices.

Matthew 23:8–13

8"But you are not to be called rabbi, for you have one teacher, and you are all breth-
ren. 9And call no man your father on earth, for you have one Father, who is in heaven.
10Neither be called masters, for you have one master, the Christ. 11He who is greatest
among you shall be your servant; 12whoever exalts himself will be humbled, and who-
ever humbles himself will be exalted.

13"But woe to you, scribes and Pharisees, hypocrites! because you shut the kingdom of heaven against men; for you neither enter yourselves, nor allow those who would enter to go in."

(3) John Chrysostom

The humble **will be exalted.** Where shall we find this humility? Are you prepared to go again to the city of virtue, the tents of the saints—the mountains and the glens? In fact, it is there that we shall see the height of humility: people famous for secular dignities in some cases, and for wealth in others, have in all cases become self-effacing in matters of diet, of dwelling, of those to whom they serve, and in every respect they leave a record of humility as though it were written down. The things that are a spur to pride—fine clothing, lavish accommodation, having many servants—things that frequently impel people involuntarily into pride—are all eliminated there. They do the lighting of fires, they chop wood, they do the cooking, they serve visitors. You don't hear anyone giving insults there or see anyone insulted, no one being given orders or giving orders: everyone is involved in ministering, each washes the feet of visitors, and there is great rivalry about this. Each one performs the service, not inquiring who it is, slave or free, simply discharging the same service to everyone. No one there is important or unimportant. Is the result confusion? Far from it; there is first-class orderliness. Should someone be of no importance, the important do not see it; instead they regard themselves as lowlier than the other and so become greater.

(4) Hilary of Poitiers

For those who know they are indeed his disciples, the Lord sets forth his teaching on a truly humble life so that they may remember that they are all brothers, the children of one parent. Through the generation of a new birth, they put behind themselves their earthly origins and now embrace one teacher of heavenly truth for all. Through awareness of their lowliness, they assume they take up the glory of eternal honor, for God will humble the proud and exalt the humble with glory. **Woe to you, scribes and Pharisees, you hypocrites, who close off the kingdom of heaven**. The Lord condemns their pretentiousness by pointing to their punishment; **woe** is an expression of misery. He says that they **close off the kingdom of heaven** because they mask within the law the anticipations of Christ. By their pretentious teaching, they disguise that he came in bodily form as the prophets proclaimed. They hide the fact of his bodily advent preached by the prophets. They do not enter the way leading to eternity, nor do they allow others to find the way.

Matthew 23:15–22

15 "Woe to you, scribes and Pharisees, hypocrites! for you traverse sea and land to make a single proselyte, and when he becomes a proselyte, you make him twice as much a child of hell as yourselves.

16 "Woe to you, blind guides, who say, 'If any one swears by the temple, it is nothing; but if any one swears by the gold of the temple, he is bound by his oath.' 17 You blind fools! For which is greater, the gold or the temple that has made the gold sacred? 18 And you say, 'If any one swears by the altar, it is nothing; but if any one swears by the gift that is on the altar, he is bound by his oath.' 19 You blind men! For which is greater, the gift or the altar that makes the gift sacred? 20 So he who swears by the altar, swears by it and by everything on it; 21 and he who swears by the temple, swears by it and by him who dwells in it; 22 and he who swears by heaven, swears by the throne of God and by him who sits upon it."

(5) John Chrysostom

Vice is always harmful, but particularly when someone thinks only others need correction, not himself. For this reason, Christ calls them **blind guides**. If it is a calamity and misfortune for blind people to think that they have no need of a guide, see what a deep hole they will fall in were they to guide others. Now, the Lord said this to say that in all things they lust for glory and their extreme frenzy to acquire this malady. The cause of all their vices was that they were doing everything for show. This led them away from true belief, caused them to neglect genuine virtue, and persuaded them to occupy themselves with bodily purification alone, while neglecting the cleansing of the soul.

Matthew 23:23–25

23"Woe to you, scribes and Pharisees, hypocrites! for you tithe mint and dill and cumin, and have neglected the weightier matters of the law, justice and mercy and faith; these you ought to have done, without neglecting the others. 24You blind guides, straining out a gnat and swallowing a camel!

25"Woe to you, scribes and Pharisees, hypocrites! for you cleanse the outside of the cup and of the plate, but inside they are full of extortion and rapacity."

(6) Cyril of Alexandria

O Pharisees, the text says, you demand tithes wherever possible, even the smallest garden herbs, while neglecting the commandments, a far greater transgression. And what is the nature of these commandments? **Justice**; this means to judge upright and blamelessly; and with **mercy**; which means to be born truly, to be born of God. For justice and mercy and faith in God are better than tithes and firstfruits. Therefore also, the God of all things says through the prophet, *And now, Israel, what does the Lord God seek from you but to do justice and love and to seek mercy and to be prepared to walk with the Lord your God* (Mic 6:8).

Matthew 23:26–27

26"You blind Pharisee! first cleanse the inside of the cup and of the plate, that the outside also may be clean.

27"Woe to you, scribes and Pharisees, hypocrites! for you are like whitewashed tombs, which outwardly appear beautiful, but within they are full of dead men's bones and all uncleanness."

(7) John Chrysostom

It is not such a dreadful thing for the scribes and Pharisees to be seen in this light—though it is surely dreadful—but that you, who have been deemed worthy to become temples of God, should all of a sudden become tombs—with their foul odors—is worst of all! What terrible wretchedness for the person in whom Christ dwells and in whom the Holy Spirit and the holy sacraments are at work to be called a tomb. What weeping and wailing when the limbs of Christ (1 Cor 6:15) have become a tomb full of uncleanness! Consider how you came to birth, with what gifts you have been blessed, what a garment you have received, how you have been fashioned as a temple without fault, how lovely in your adornment, not with gold or pearls but with the Spirit that is more precious than these. . . .

You would be scorned by everyone if you are carrying about a soul that is dead. If someone were to carry around the figure of a corpse, would he not be shunned and everyone would take to their heels? Would they not all flee? Think likewise in this case: you are going around with a sight that is much more alarming, a soul deadened by sin, a soul paralyzed. So who will pity such a one? After all, when you do not pity your own soul, how will someone else pity a person who is cruel and hostile to himself? How do you even dare to set foot in the churches of God and the holy temples, giving out a stench from such an abomination?

Matthew 23:28–39

28"So you also outwardly appear righteous to men, but within you are full of hypocrisy
and iniquity.

29"Woe to you, scribes and Pharisees, hypocrites! for you build the tombs of the
prophets and adorn the monuments of the righteous, 30saying, 'If we had lived in the
days of our fathers, we would not have taken part with them in shedding the blood of
the prophets.' 31Thus you witness against yourselves, that you are sons of those who
murdered the prophets. 32Fill up, then, the measure of your fathers. 33You serpents, you
brood of vipers, how are you to escape being sentenced to hell? 34Therefore I send you
prophets and wise men and scribes, some of whom you will kill and crucify, and some
you will scourge in your synagogues and persecute from town to town, 35that upon you
may come all the righteous blood shed on earth, from the blood of innocent Abel to the
blood of Zechari'ah the son of Barachi'ah, whom you murdered between the sanctuary
and the altar. 36Truly, I say to you, all this will come upon this generation.

37"O Jerusalem, Jerusalem, killing the prophets and stoning those who are sent
to you! How often would I have gathered your children together as a hen gathers her
brood under her wings, and you would not! 38Behold, your house is forsaken and des-
olate. 39For I tell you, you will not see me again, until you say, 'Blessed is he who comes
in the name of the Lord.'"

(8) Eusebius of Caesarea

The people of Jerusalem suffered after the Romans attacked their city. Some of the inhabitants were slaughtered by the rights of war; some they led away as captives; some died from famine; and others were driven out and scattered every which way. The Romans burned their house and temple and enveloped them in utter desolation. But even though this took place later, the Savior anticipated what was coming by his foreknowledge as God the Word and predicted what would happen in the words we are now considering (that is, vv. 37–39).

He refers to the whole nation of Jews as the city's **children** (cf. 23:37) and calls the temple their **house** (cf. 23:38). Then he testifies that, because of their guilt, gloom will pursue them, though he had often desired to gather their children under the yoke of piety (cf. 23:37). For Christ was before all—from eternity—and showed concern for them, attempting to persuade them and appealing to them in the prophets, generation after generation. But they would not heed his call. So he uttered this judgment against them: **Look, your house is left to you desolate** (23:38). Now he is very careful not to say that the city will be desolate, but the **house** in the city, clearly meaning the temple, which he no longer wishes to call his house or God's house, but their house. But he prophesies that it will be desolate only in that it will be bereft of the care that it once enjoyed. Hence he said, **Look, your house is left to you desolate.**

And indeed one might wonder about how his words were fulfilled. Never before did the place suffer such desolation, not even when the Jews were conquered by the Babylonians on account of their excessive impiety, idolatry, and bloodthirstiness against the prophets. For at that time, seventy years was the period of the place's desolation.[2] Thus it would not have been proper to say to them then, **Look, your house is left to you desolate.** For it was not left desolate, but the place was regained after not much time, at which point it was deemed worthy of a restoration greater than its former state, just as one of the prophets foretold: surely *the latter glory of this house will surpass the former glory* (Hag 2:9). But to those who visit these places, the sight itself best demonstrates the fulfillment of our Savior's pronouncement, that the inhabitants were forsaken and their house fell into utter desolation through the judgment of God. And the period has grown long and reached many years—not only double the seventy years of desolation that occurred in the time of Babylon, but even beyond quadruple, confirming the judgment that our Savior predicted.

And again on another occasion, when the Savior was walking around the aforementioned temple, his disciples were greatly admiring the construction of the outer walls and pointed out to him the grandeur and beauty of the temple itself. **But in response, he said to them, You see all these, do you not? I tell you, not one stone here shall be left on another that will not be torn down** (24:2). Indeed, that every part of the structure and ornamentation of that temple was well worth seeing is made clear by the ancient accounts. As further proof, some remains have been preserved even up to today, through which traces of the ancient decorations are detectable. But what is most remarkable of all is our Savior's divine statement of foreknowledge, which was declared to those who were astonished at

2. Eusebius draws this number from Dan 9:2, which is based on Jer 25:11–12.

the structure. In that very place where they stood amazed, every stone that remained was going to be brought down (cf. 24:2).

(9) Hilary of Poitiers

Even though he spoke these words in the flesh, *found as a man* (Phil 2:7), offering to all people his help, he often wished to gather them, the Jews, according to the preaching of the prophets (Isa 54:7; Jer 23:3). As it happened, he showered this affection in vain and to no purpose. Just as a hen gathers her young, so he wished to hold them under his wings (23:37). Just as if he had become an earthly and domesticated bird having wings as a bodily covering, the Lord granted to his young the warmth of eternal life and was teaching them to fly into the sky of a new birth. Among birds there is one reason for being born, and another to have a life. First, they are enclosed in the shell of the egg, which is like a barrier around the body. Then after they have been kept warm by the care of the parent, they take flight. In the manner of this familiar and almost earth-bound bird [viz., the hen], the Lord wished to gather them together under him so that after they had been brought forth through physical birth, they would be reborn by the birth of another kind of generation. By his warmth they would be reborn in the heavenly kingdom, just as if they were taking flight on wings.

(10) Augustine

We must see what the Apostle most truthfully said of God: *Who wills everyone to be saved* (1 Tim 2:4). Since not all are saved, but many more are not saved, it seems that what God wills to happen does not happen because a human will frustrates the will of God. When it is asked why not all are saved, the reply usually given is that it is because they themselves do not wish to be saved. This cannot be said of infants, who cannot yet either will or not will. If we thought we could attribute to their own will the childish movements they make when they are baptized, we should say that they do not wish to be saved, since they resist as much as they can.

The words of the Lord in the Gospel make the matter even clearer when he rebukes a wicked city with the words: *How often have I desired to gather your children together as a hen gathers her brood under her wings, and you were not willing!* (23:37). It is as if God's will had been overcome by the will of men, and the Most Mighty was not able to do as he willed because the very weak[3] prevented him by being unwilling. What happened to that omnipotence that has done *whatever it willed in heaven and on earth if he willed* (Ps 135:6) by gathering together the children of Jerusalem, and yet it did not happen? Or was it rather that the city did not want her children to be gathered together by him? But he gathered together the children he willed to gather together despite the city's unwillingness, for in heaven and on earth he does not will some things and [then] do them, nor does he will others but not do them; rather, he does everything he willed.

3. A purposeful contrast between the will of God and will of man.

(11) John Chrysostom

I shall ask them, "Did he send prophets and wise men? Did they kill them in the synagogues? Was their house left desolate? Did all the effects of retribution fall upon them?" Obviously, no one denies it. Hence, let us also, while there is time, practice what is good.

As long as we are sick, let us therefore summon physicians, spend money, and be constant in taking the trouble to recover from the ailment and thus go off in good health. You ask, "How are we to do it? Show our ailing soul to Paul; bring in Matthew; get John to sit in." Hear from them what the patient in this condition must do; they will be frank and hide nothing. They are not really dead, you see, they are alive and have something to say. But does the soul take any heed when it is in the grip of the fever? Let us bring pressure to bear on it and arouse its faculties. Bring in the prophets, although there is no need to pay these physicians; they require no payment for their services, and for the medicines they prepare they do not oblige you to pay anything except almsgiving. In all other respects, they even make a contribution; for example, in requiring you to exercise restraint, they rid you of untimely and inappropriate expenditures; in advising you to abstain from intoxication, they make you more affluent. Do you see the skill of physicians who provide you with money along with good health? Get them to come, and learn from them the nature of your ailment.

Matthew 24

This chapter is the first of the two chapters devoted to Jesus's discourse on the Mount of Olives, also known as the Olivet Discourse. Here he outlines the events known as the "tribulation" (vv. 4–14), which will precede his second coming (vv. 15–28). Upon leaving the temple, he foretold its complete destruction (vv. 1–2), and the disciples inquired when this destruction would take place and what would be the signs of the Lord's coming at the end of the age. Instead of giving them a specific date, Jesus outlined the events of the tribulation, cautioning them to be alert: even in their lifetime, imposters would come and claim to be the Christ, leading many astray (vv. 3–5). There will be wars, not only among nations, but also within the human heart, described by Ambrose as combats against lust, passion, and ambition. The world will show signs of sickness (birth-pangs)*: famine, plague, and persecution (vv. 6–9); and the Lord promises to deliver those who would persevere to the end (v. 13). Hilary interprets Jesus to mean that the end would not come until the gospel "has spread to all humanity" (v. 14).*

Turning to the signs of his coming, Jesus forewarns the disciples against believing false Christs and false prophets *who will perform miracles and lead many astray (vv. 23–25). The devil "directed all his cunning and deceit into various attempts to confuse and deceive by using his own son and assistant, the antichrist" (Victorinus of Poetovio). And Chrysostom declared that the Lord admonished the disciples* to not go out *(v. 26), in order that they might not be deceived by the miracles performed by the antichrist in his attempt to imitate Christ.*

Victorinus reflects on the signs that will appear in the sky. The sun, the moon, and the stars "will be loosed from their functions. . . . because time has ceased. . . . Their power is no longer necessary since now the true day shines" (v. 29). The Lord will appear in his glory, gleaming "with the heavenly power," and "the cross will appear in the sky like a trophy of victory over death." Thus, the Lord's presence will be made known to "the entire universe," and "the whole order and structure of sin and crime will be no more" (Ambrose).

The angels will gather the elect with a trumpet call (v. 31). Just as the leaves on a fig tree signify that the summer is near, so the signs of the times show that the Lord's advent is approaching. It was the right time for God to send Christ "in the world's old age in order to put you together again when everything else was going to pieces," Augustine concludes.

According to the church fathers, Jesus's presumed ignorance of the exact day of the end of the age (v. 36) cannot mean he does not know the hours. His aim is to prevent us from the vain attempt of calculating the exact day. However, Jesus also conveys urgency and warns us that this day will come unexpectedly and we should be ready: "As it was at the time of the flood, that great day will burst into the course of our lives, into the midst of all our business and misery" (Hilary) (vv. 37–38). Chrysostom suggests, "the reason he does not tell them when that day will come is that he wants them to be on the lookout, always to be ready," in the hope that they would always look forward to his coming, "in order that they may exert themselves at all times." While God may appear unjust saving one person and leaving the other, "when our last moment comes," Ambrose declares, "the Lord will judge us not by our exterior actions, but by our interior attitudes" (vv. 40–41).

Matthew 24:1–2

[1]Jesus left the temple and was going away, when his disciples came to point out to him the buildings of the temple. [2]But he answered them, "You see all these, do you not? Truly, I say to you, there will not be left here one stone upon another, that will not be thrown down."

(1) Hilary of Poitiers

As he was walking away from the temple, his disciples approached and beckoned him to look at the edifice of the temple. After threatening that Jerusalem would be forsaken (23:38), he is shown the grandeur of the temple, as though he would be impressed by its grandeur. But he said that it would be entirely destroyed and turned into ruins as all the stones of its structure are knocked to the ground. An eternal temple is one that is consecrated as a dwelling place of the Holy Spirit, that is, a person who through knowledge of the Son, believing in the Father, and obedience to the commandment, is worthy to become a habitation for God (cf. 1 Cor 6:19; 2 Cor 6:16).

(2) John Chrysostom

His disciples pointed out to him the beauty of the temple and were perplexed that so much beauty, such costly materials, and unspeakable variety of workmanship could be destroyed. At this point, however, the Lord was not merely speaking to them about its desolation, but he foretells its complete destruction. He said, **You see all these things, do you not?** But do not marvel or be amazed.[1] **There shall not remain one stone upon another**. We might wonder, "Why did some of it remain intact? What happened?"[2] But his prediction was not wrong. He said these things to indicate either its total desolation or its destruction at that very spot where he was speaking, since there are parts of the temple that were destroyed all the way down to the foundation.

1. This last statement is not found in Matthew or any parallel account.
2. The western wall, for example, remained.

Matthew 24:3–14

**3As he sat on the Mount of Olives, the disciples came to him privately, saying, "Tell us,
when will this be, and what will be the sign of your coming and of the close of the age?"
4And Jesus answered them, "Take heed that no one leads you astray. 5For many will
come in my name, saying, 'I am the Christ,' and they will lead many astray. 6And you
will hear of wars and rumors of wars; see that you are not alarmed; for this must take
place, but the end is not yet. 7For nation will rise against nation, and kingdom against
kingdom, and there will be famines and earthquakes in various places: 8all this is but
the beginning of the birthpangs.**

**9"Then they will deliver you up to tribulation, and put you to death; and you will
be hated by all nations for my name's sake. 10And then many will fall away, and betray
one another, and hate one another. 11And many false prophets will arise and lead many
astray. 12And because wickedness is multiplied, most men's love will grow cold. 13But he
who endures to the end will be saved. 14And this gospel of the kingdom will be preached
throughout the whole world, as a testimony to all nations; and then the end will come."**

(3) Hilary of Poitiers

Once the Lord had withdrawn to the mountain, his disciples came and asked him privately when this would happen [to the temple] and by what sign would they recognize his coming, and about the end of the age. Here, we have three questions in one; he separates them by chronology and meaning. First he addresses the question about the destruction of the city Jerusalem. He confirms the truth of his teaching so that a deceiver might not be able to disturb the ignorant; for there would come a time when some come claiming to speak in the name of Christ. Therefore he warns them that their faith could be undermined by a pernicious lie. In fact, it happened that Simon the Samaritan, bolstered with diabolical works and words, led many astray by his miracles (Acts 8:9–11). And because this took place during the time of the apostles, the Lord said, **the end is not yet. The end is not yet** until nations and kingdoms attack one another, and **famines and earthquakes** occur. This is not the dissolution of all things, but the **beginning of sorrows** (24:8), from which all evils would originate. He encouraged them to endure suffering: flight, scourging, death, and the pagan's public hatred toward them on account of his name. Because of these troubles, many will be shaken and will stumble in the face of increasing wickedness and will be incited to hate one another. There will be **false prophets** like Nicolaus, one of the seven deacons (Acts 6:5; Rev 2:6, 15), who will pervert many by falsifying the truth. And because of mass wickedness, love will grow cold (24:12). But for those **who persevere to the end**, salvation is assured (24:13).

As apostolic men are scattered throughout all parts of the world, the truth of the gospel will be preached. Once the knowledge of the heavenly sacrament that is the gospel has spread to all humanity, the fall and end of Jerusalem is imminent.

(4) Origen

Since God is *fire* (Heb 12:29; Deut 4:24) and the angels *a flame of fire* (Heb 1:7; Ps 104:4) and the saints are all *fervent in spirit* (Rom 12:11), those who have fallen away from the love of God, on the contrary, have undoubtedly cooled in their affection for him and have become cold. For the Lord also says, **Because sin has multiplied, the love of many will grow cold.** Furthermore, all those things, whatever they may be, which Holy Scripture compares to opposing power, you will invariably find to be cold. Hence, the devil is called a "serpent" and a "dragon"(Rev 12:9; 20:2), and what can be found colder than these? Again, a dragon—an allusion certainly to one of the wicked spirits—is said to rule in the waters, while the prophet declares it to live in the sea (Ezek 29:3; 32:2). . . . Another prophet says that evil will be kindled from the north upon all who live on the earth (cf. Jer 1:14). Now the north wind is described in the Scriptures as cold, as it is written in Wisdom as *the cold north wind* (Sir 43:20). This must undoubtedly be understood of the devil.

Things that are holy are called "fire" and "light" and "fervent," while their opposites are called "cold," and the love of sinners is said to grow cold. We should ask whether perhaps the word "soul," which in Greek is called *psyche*, . . . could have the sense of growing cold after a better and more divine condition, because the soul seems to have grown cold by the loss of its first natural and divine warmth. . . .

(5) Ambrose of Milan

They asked the Lord when the destruction of the temple would take place and about the sign of his coming. He spoke to them about the signs, and yet he doesn't think it important that the time should be made known. He then explains to the disciples when the temple would be destroyed, what was to be the sign of his coming, and how the world was going to end.

No one can give better witness to the Lord's words than we ourselves, since we have seen the end of the world come upon us! What wars we have witnessed, what rumors of wars we have heard! The Huns rise up against the Alani, the Alani against the Goths; the Goths rise against the Taifali and the Sarmatians,[3] who force us[4] from Illyria,[5] our own native land. And that is not all. Everywhere there is famine; everywhere there is plague—plague among cattle; plague among people; plague among livestock of every kind. It has been so deadly that even where there are no wars, the land has been devastated as if by hostile forces. Since we are at the end of the world, we see the world in decline. This decline begins with the sicknesses of the world: famine is one sickness of the world, plague is another sickness of the world, and persecution is yet another sickness.

At the same time, the valiant Christian has other wars to face. There is combat against lust; there are conflicts with desire—the enemy within is worse than the enemy without.

3. Names of major tribal peoples in what is now eastern Europe.

4. The Romans.

5. What is approximately today Hungary and part of Croatia.

At one moment, lust excites us; at another moment, passion inflames us. At one moment, fear makes our blood run cold; at another moment, anger drives us mad. At one moment, ambition sorely tries us; on another occasion, it is demons, wicked spirits that dwell in the air (cf. Eph 6:12), who attempt to taunt us. Our passions are easily swayed, our minds are easily agitated, and so these wars throw us down, and these earthquakes—so to speak—cause us to tremble.

But the brave of heart says: *Though an army may encamp against me, my heart shall not fear. Though war break out against me, even then will I hope* (Ps 27:3). Bravely he stands in the line of battle and faces the enemy. Even if some Goliath rises up, ferocious and gigantic, and even though others are filled with fear, our hero will withstand him. He will cast off the weapons offered him by the kings of this earth (cf. 1 Sam 17:39) and take up instead the lighter weapons of faith. With his sling, woven from three stout cords, he will hurl the missile of pure faith and fatally wound his mocking persecutor. He will despise the giant's threats. He does not tremble before the great and powerful ones of this world, because Christ lives within him.

Matthew 24:15–19

15"So when you see the desolating sacrilege spoken of by the prophet Daniel, standing in the holy place (let the reader understand), 16then let those who are in Judea flee to the mountains; 17let him who is on the housetop not go down to take what is in his house; 18and let him who is in the field not turn back to take his mantle. 19And alas for those who are with child and for those who give suck in those days!"

(6) Hilary of Poitiers

Next there follows a sign of his future advent. When they see the **abomination of desolation . . . standing in the holy place**, it should be understood as a sign of his glorious return. Concerning this matter, I think that our comment is superfluous, given the teaching of the most blessed Daniel (Dan 9:27) and Paul (2 Thess 2:4). What each says concerns the time of the antichrist. He is an **abomination** because he rises up against God, claiming for himself the honor due to God. As for the phrase **abomination of desolation**, it means the antichrist will render the earth desolate by war and bloodshed and bring about a sacrilege (see Isa 34:10; 62:4; Jer 12:11; Ezek 6:14). Because the antichrist was received by the Jews, he will stand in the holy place (24:15; Dan 11:31–32), where God used to be invoked by the prayers of his saints and where the antichrist is received by unbelievers with the same honor with which they venerated God.

When he says, **And those who are on the rooftops should not come down to pick up anything in their houses**, we have here a statement that defies explanation in word or action. Humans cannot understand. The one on the rooftop who is supposed to leave Judea cannot leave that place until he comes down. Moreover, what is the purpose of staying on the roof, as opposed to remaining in the house? We are often reminded, however, that the significance of words and places requires reflective thought if we want to find the meaning of its heavenly teaching.

The roof is the summit of the house and the lofty perfection of the whole dwelling. A house without a roof is not a house. The one who stands on the top of his house, that is, in the perfection of his heart—renewed by regeneration, elevated in the spirit, perfected by the divine gift of absolution—will not have to descend to the lower desires of the things of this age. Nor will he have to abandon the height of his rooftop because he was seduced by the passions of the body inside.

And that whoever is in the field should not go back to pick up his cloak. He who has obediently followed the commandment should not return to former cares of life (cf. Eph 4:22). He should not desire any clothing for the body (cf. Col 3:10), lest he return to the cloak of his former sin with which he once covered himself.

Woe to pregnant women and nursing mothers. This verse can be understood simply as pertaining to the delay of their flight. Hampered by the weight of the womb, it is difficult for them to flee from the imminent destruction of that time. But in what way did their gender and capacity to bear children deserve this? Perhaps that phase in a woman's life is to be especially cursed. But that cannot be right! In no way can anything evil befall a person except through his own fault. We should not believe that the Lord was speaking literally about the burden of the woman's womb when he says, **Woe to pregnant women**. Rather, he was directing us to souls burdened with the weight of sin (2 Tim 3:6).

By remaining on the rooftop or in the field, they cannot escape the storm of wrath that is reserved for them (cf. 1 Thess 1:10). Indeed, suffering is a natural consequence of pregnancy, and the womb cannot give birth without bodily pain. In like manner, souls that are found in that situation will be burdened with a burden of grief.

Matthew 24:20–22

[20]"Pray that your flight may not be in winter or on a Sabbath. [21]For then there will be great tribulation, such as has not been from the beginning of the world until now, no, and never will be. [22]And if those days had not been shortened, no human being would be saved; but for the sake of the elect those days will be shortened."

(7) Hilary of Poitiers

[W]e are urged to pray that our flight be neither in the winter nor on the Sabbath. That is, we should not be found in the coldness of our sins (cf. Rom 5:12) or indifferent to good works. The heavy burden of affliction weighs upon everyone. For the sake of God's elect, those days will be shortened so that the swift passing of time will lessen the overwhelming calamities.

(8) Ephrem of Nisibis

Pray that you may be worthy to escape from all those things that are to be.[6] There was a terrible sound of the voice of the Lord when he was raised on the cross (cf. 27:50), and fear, dread, persecution, and sorrow came upon the disciples for their Lord. When that likeness comes again, there will be tribulation because that terrible voice will sound again, along with the dread and fear, agitation and persecutions, grief and sorrow for our Lord. As for the disciples, the dawn of the morning was about to break, bringing the good news of the joy of their Lord. If a day like that happens to us, the dawn of the morning will break at the good news and joy of our Lord, just as our Savior also said, **For the sake of the elect those days will be shortened.**

(9) Cyril of Alexandria

These words also contain a riddle. They mean that we should not leave the body while we are seeking rest from doing good works, which is what **the Sabbath** indicates, or on account of evil deeds from unfruitfulness, which **winter** clearly means. We should note that God did not make **winter** from evil things; rather, we experience **winter** when the desires of the flesh rule in us.

Matthew 24:23–28

23"Then if any one says to you, 'Lo, here is the Christ!' or 'There he is!' do not believe
it. 24For false Christs and false prophets will arise and show great signs and wonders,
so as to lead astray, if possible, even the elect. 25Lo, I have told you beforehand. 26So, if
they say to you, 'Lo, he is in the wilderness,' do not go out; if they say, 'Lo, he is in the
inner rooms,' do not believe it. 27For as the lightning comes from the east and shines as
far as the west, so will be the coming of the Son of man. 28Wherever the body is, there
the eagles will be gathered together."

(10) Ambrose of Milan

Many will fall into error and abandon true religion. Then the Lord's Day will come. The Apostle makes this very clear when he warns us to be on our guard: . . . *as if the day of the Lord were at hand. Let no one deceive you by any means. First there shall come the apostasy, and the man of sin shall be revealed, the son of perdition who opposes man and who is lifted up above all that is called God or that is worshiped. He goes so far as to sit in God's temple as though he were God* (2 Thess 2:2–4), and so on.

After false prophets will come famines. Think back to the days of Elijah (1 Kgs 18),

6. A Syriac version of the Greek text.

and you will find that at that time there were prophets who spread confusion; then there was Jezebel; then famine; then drought. Why? Because wickedness had overflowed, and love had grown cold (cf. 24:12). As a result, the innocent went to live in the desert, and the unjust sat on royal thrones.

There is another antichrist, father of the first one. I refer to the devil. He tries with his armies and legions (cf. Luke 8:30) to besiege my own Jerusalem—that is, my soul—because a soul truly belonging to God is a soul at peace. *For it is not against flesh and blood that we have to struggle, but against princes and powers, against the rulers of the world of darkness* (Eph 6:12). There is apostasy when the soul abandons itself; when she (the soul) thinks about our Lord, she trembles and is troubled. As long as this antichrist *prevails, until the time comes when he is taken out of the way* (2 Thess 2:7), justice and innocence are in exile. Iniquity reigns.

Because faith will become rare, the Lord says, as though doubtful, *When the Son of Man comes, shall he find any faith on earth?* (Luke 18:8). *On earth* means, of course, the whole world. So, too, in another place, we read: *The Lord has looked down upon the children of men to see whether any of them understand and seek God* (Ps 14:2). This does not mean that God has doubts, but that faith had become so rare that, humanly speaking, there were grounds for doubting.

(11) Victorinus of Poetovio

The Lord says to watch for the time when there will be persecutions and anxieties. Do not believe it when you hear people say, "Look, this one is the Messiah." For pseudo-Christs and false prophets will rise up. They will offer great signs and portents in an attempt to win over the elect. I have predicted this for you. The devil was tossed down from heaven to earth because of his pride. Knowing that he had only a short time to conquer the earth, he directed all his cunning and deceit into various attempts to confuse and deceive by using his own son and assistant, the antichrist. Because he didn't wish to die alone, he hoped to enlist many allies.

The devil wished to be described, even for the short time he ruled the earth, as a deity, so that he could sit in the church, that is, the Lord's temple, and present himself as a god. Even though he was doomed to die, he wished to enjoy this ruse for as long as possible. He didn't want to die before he had finished what he started. Blinded by furor and rage, he could not acknowledge what he knew to be the truth. He didn't act like someone already defeated, nor did he seem to accept his defeat. Rather, he led himself to believe that he was a conqueror as long as he did not deviate from what had been predetermined. He might have endured, had he willingly submitted, but destruction was his punishment.

In order to protect his servants, the Savior predicted and warned that all these future events were meant to seduce them, and that they must endure with the hope of reward. He told them that he was not going to appear in one place, as opposed to another, but that his return would be seen universally and that all things hidden would become apparent to everyone at the same time. **Just as the lightning comes from the east and shines as far as the west, so will be the coming of the Son of Man.** In this way, every one of the devil's tricks and snares, just like the lie about Christ appearing in an inner room or in the desert, can be rejected. For the Savior will not appear as an embodied man who is seen in one place and not another, but as the Son of God, so that he may fill the world with the splendor of his majesty. As in his first coming, God was seen in man, and in the second, the man will be seen [to be] in God, namely, the Son of God, radiant in spiritual power. At this sight, the righteous will delight in life, whereas all others will lose life and be left to endure fear with its torture.

Those saints who by their strong faith have overcome the hazards and perils of the relentless antichrist will be snatched up together with (cf. vv. 37–41) the saints accompanying the Lord's return. **Where the body has been, there the eagles will be gathered together**, so that after trials and tribulations they may rest with the Lord and their brothers. The **body** signifies the saints of the Lord, because *we are members of his body* (Eph 5:30). The Lord also spoke about them as **eagles**, because Christians are a royal race, and for this reason, they are equated to eagles, as the Apostle Peter called them, *a royal nation* (1 Pet 2:9).

(12) John Chrysostom

Once he finished his remarks concerning Jerusalem, he moved on to the subject of his second coming and explains the signs that portend it. He does this not only for their benefit, but for ours also and for all those who come after us.

Then. When is this? Here, as I have often said, the word **then** doesn't connect chronologically with the things previously mentioned. When he wishes to express an element of time, he says, **Immediately after the tribulation of those days**, that is, not here and now, but **then**. The timing of this passage does not follow immediately after what precedes it; rather, it refers to what will happen in that time when these things are supposed to happen, of which he was about to speak. It is the same when Matthew says, **In those days, John the Baptist appeared** (3:1). He is not speaking of the time immediately after what has just been said, but many years down the road at a time he was about to explain. Having just spoken about the birth of Jesus, the coming of the magi, and the death of Herod, Matthew immediately says, **In those days, John the Baptist appeared**, even though thirty years had come and gone. This kind of story-telling device is quite typical in Scripture. Here in our passage, then, Jesus skips over the large span of time between the destruction of Jerusalem and the beginning of the consummation, and he speaks about something that takes place just before the consummation. Therefore, he says, **Then if anyone says to you, "Look, here is the Christ!" or "There he is!" do not believe it**.

He is not coming as he first came in Bethlehem, a small corner of the world where no one initially knew him. He is coming openly and with great splendor, and there will be no need to spread the word. The sign of his coming is no small thing, because his coming will not be in secret.

Notice, however, that he says nothing about war here (since he is clearly talking about his second coming); he speaks only about those who attempt to deceive. There were some in the days of the apostles who were deceiving many people. For Jesus said that **some**

would come and deceive many (24:5). Others, however, will do so just before his second coming, and they will be even worse than the former. **For they shall show**, he says, **signs and wonders, so as to deceive, if possible, even the elect.** Here he speaks of the antichrist and indicates that some will serve him. Paul also speaks about him. He calls him the *man of sin*[7] and the *son of perdition* (2 Thess 2:3), and he adds, *His coming is in accord with the work of Satan, with all power and false signs and wonders and with all wicked deception for those who are perishing* (2 Thess 2:9–10).

Take notice how the Lord comforts the disciples: **Do not go out into the desert** and **do not enter into the secret chambers** in search of Christ's second coming. He did not say, "You may go, just don't believe." He said don't even go out there and don't enter in. For many will be deceived because of the deceptive miracles.

Having first told them how the antichrist will come and his location, he then explains how he himself will come. So how will he appear? **As the lightning comes from the east and shines as far as the west, so will be the coming of the Son of Man. For wherever the carcass is, there also will be the eagles.**

In what way does lightning shine? It needs no one to spread the word, and it does not require a herald. For those sitting in their houses, even in their inner rooms, lightning reveals itself in an instant of time throughout the whole world. So also Christ's coming will be like that. He will shine immediately and everywhere because of the magnificence of his glory. He speaks of another sign: **Wherever the carcass is, there also will be the eagles.** This is a reference to the multitude of angels, martyrs, and all the saints.

Matthew 24:29–30

[29]"Immediately after the tribulation of those days the sun will be darkened, and the moon will not give its light, and the stars will fall from heaven, and the powers of the heavens will be shaken; [30]then will appear the sign of the Son of man in heaven, and then all the tribes of the earth will mourn, and they will see the Son of man coming on the clouds of heaven with power and great glory; . . ."

(13) Victorinus of Poetovio

Among all the other things written, we have to account for those days of tribulation when the sun and the moon will be loosed from their functions. The clarity of light has now passed because time has ceased. So it is written in the book of the Apocalypse that time will be no more once the seventh angel has blown the trumpet (Rev 11:15). Once the Lord returns in glory, the faithful ones will be left without light. How then, after the tribulation, will the Lord be seen by those who have survived? All these things will transpire quickly when he appears in the heavens in the light of his glory. Earthly suffering will cease because everyone will be unchained. At the same moment, the sign of the Lord will shine

7. Actually, Paul calls him the *man of lawlessness*.

in the sky. If it is true that tombs were broken open and that the rocks quaked during the Lord's passion (27:52), how much more majestically will he come to deliver the faithful ones from their fears of oppression and sorrow? Once the tribulation has ended, the sun and moon will immediately go dark. . . . Their power is no longer necessary since now the true day shines—a day not followed by night and whose brilliance touches the whole world.

When the Lord returns, the sun and the moon will immediately stop working and give up their task of dispensing light. After the days of the tribulation, the Lord says that **the sun will be blotted out and the moon will no longer give light. The stars will fall from the sky**, and even heaven's strongholds **will be shaken. Then the Son of Man will appear in the sky**. It will be very evident to everyone when the Lord comes down from heaven—the place from which the devil was cast—and thus the Lord appears and makes the earth shine with his glory.

Some powers[8] fall down now that they are aware of the sickness brought about by their own sin. Others, in humbled reverence at the return of the Lord, throw themselves on the ground before their Creator. At this time, the sign of the Lord will be seen in the sky. The cross will appear in the sky like a trophy of victory over death. Death now seems to be foolishness and is shameful for the sinful. His return lights the whole earth, and his sign will be seen in the sky to let everyone know who he is.

They will see the Lord coming, just as he said, **in the clouds and with great power and majesty**. This occurs so that, when they see him coming in the clouds, they will believe him to be the Lord. Even the clouds in the sky will appear to give the Lord his due reverence. He returns with mighty power in the company of countless legions of angels. And when he speaks, he speaks with distinction. His entire army gleams with the heavenly power that is expected of an almighty King.

Given all these things, shining together from on high, the Lord will be recognized. This is the Lord who was first mocked and scorned as a frail man (cf. Isa 53:4; Mark 14:65). No one would imagine that he was either a usurper or the thief of a kingdom. On his return he will come **in the clouds with great power and majesty**. Why else would everyone focus on him unless they recognized him to be their Creator?

(14) Hilary of Poitiers

Immediately after the tribulation of those days, the sun will be darkened, etc. He indicates his glorious advent and majestic return by the *darkening of the sun, the eclipse of the moon, the falling of stars* (cf. Isa 13:10), the shaking of the heavenly bodies, the display of portentous signs, the lamentation of the pagans when they recognize the Son of Man in the glory of God, and the appointing of the angels with trumpets for the gathering of the saints—the opening of freedom for all; it so happens that a huge tree comes from a mustard seed (cf. Luke 13:19; Dan 4:10–11); it so happens that a statue taken from the stone of a mountain covers the whole earth (cf. Dan 2:35); it so

8. A term for celestial beings. See, for example, Eph 6:12.

happens that the city will be made visible to all (5:14–15; Rev 21:2–4); it so happens that there will be a light from the world that illuminates the universe (cf. John 3:19–21); and it so happens that from the humility of death comes the glory of God. Through the revelation of these many events, the Lord wants us to know about the time of our redemption, when we will be transferred from the corruption of the body to the honor of the spiritual substance (1 Cor 15:44).

(15) Ambrose of Milan

We await our Lord's coming when his presence will be known throughout the entire universe by all creatures. Indeed, his presence is known in each of us if we receive Christ with all our heart. So too the powers or virtues of heaven will experience an increase of grace at the coming and return of the Lord of salvation—for remember that he is *Lord of the virtues* (Ps 24:10). Feeling the power of God so close to them, they will be, so to speak, **shaken**.

There also exist powers or virtues of the heavens that make known the glory of God (cf. Ps 19:1); and these too are now shaken by a fuller outpouring of Christ. These are the spiritual powers that see Christ. David teaches us how these powers are moved, when he says: *Come close to me, and be enlightened* (Ps 34:11).

Paul also teaches us how to see Christ, when he says: *After you have been converted to the Lord, the veil shall be removed* (2 Cor 3:16). In other words, you will see Christ. You will see him in the clouds. I do not imagine the Lord coming in dark and threatening rain clouds. There are different sorts of clouds: some blot out the light of heaven, covering it over with gloom and darkness. How could we say, *He has set his tent in the sun* (Ps 19:4), if he comes in a downpour of rain?

There are other clouds that cast a veil, but this is a veil to shield us from the blazing light of the heavenly mystery. There are clouds wet with the dew of spiritual grace. Think of that cloud in the Old Testament: *To them he spoke in a pillar of cloud* (Ps 99:7). Yes, he spoke through Moses; and through Jesus (Joshua), son of Nun, who stopped the sun so that daylight could last longer (cf. Josh 10:12). So Moses and Jesus (Joshua), son of Nun, are clouds. Just see how the saints are clouds: *They fly like clouds, like doves with their fledglings* (Isa 60:8).

Then there are the lofty clouds, Isaiah and Ezekiel. Through the cherubim and seraphim, they reveal to me the holiness of the divine Trinity (cf. Isa 37:16; Ezek 10:1). All are clouds. It is in clouds such as these that Christ will come. He comes on a cloud in the Song of Songs (Song 3:6, 11); on a serene cloud—a bridegroom radiant with joy. He comes, too, on *a light cloud* (Isa 19:1), when he takes flesh from the Virgin. The prophet saw a cloud coming from the east and said, expressively, *a light cloud*— for it is not weighed down by the vices of the earth. See the cloud on which the Holy Spirit rested and that the power of the Most High covered with his shadow (cf. Luke 1:35).

When Christ appears on the clouds, *all the tribes of the earth shall prostrate themselves* (Rev 1:7). By Christ's coming, the whole order and structure of sin and crime will be no more.

Matthew 24:31–35

31". . . and he will send out his angels with a loud trumpet call, and they will gather his
elect from the four winds, from one end of heaven to the other.
32"From the fig tree learn its lesson: as soon as its branch becomes tender and
puts forth its leaves, you know that summer is near. 33So also, when you see all these
things, you know that he is near, at the very gates. 34Truly, I say to you, this generation
will not pass away till all these things take place. 35Heaven and earth will pass away, but
my words will not pass away."

(16) Hilary of Poitiers

The sign of the times, which we are supposed to know, the Lord compared to the fig tree. When its branches become tender and blossom, we are made to understand that **summer is near**. But the time of a tree's blossoming is wholly different from the time of the summer season. For there is a sizable interval between the beginning of spring, when the branches of the tree swell with buds, and the summer, when the branches become green in foliage. By this we should recognize that the verse is not speaking about this tree. In fact, we already dealt with the property of the fig tree at an early point. We read that Adam clothed himself with the foliage of this tree (Gen 3:7), covering his shameful conscience; that is to say, he clothed himself under the law as if with a garment of his sin.

The branch of the fig tree should be understood as the antichrist, the son of the devil, the doorway to sin, an advocate of the law. When the branch begins to green and blossom, then summer is close at hand—the day of judgment will take place. The blossoming of the branch is recognized as a kind of overflow of sins for those who rejoice in them (cf. Prov 2:14; Sir 11:16). Indeed, there will be then a flowering of evildoers, an honoring of the wicked, and delight in sacrilege. For then it is obvious that the scorching heat (cf. Rev 7:16) of summer, that is, the heat of eternal fire, is near at hand (24:33).

In order that there would be complete assurance about these future events, and by saying **amen** in declaring the truth, the Lord adds that our generation will not pass away until every one of these things has happened. Those things that are thought to be firmly in place, namely, heaven and earth, will be no more, whereas his words are not able to be void. That is to say, heaven and earth were created out of nothing, and because they were created, it is possible for them no longer to exist, but his words that are brought into being from eternity have in themselves the power to endure.

(17) Augustine

Why, after all this, are you upset (24:26–31)? Your heart is upset by the pressures of the world in the same way as was that boat in which Christ was asleep (Luke 8:23; Mark 4:37). This boat in which Christ slept is the heart, in which faith is asleep. I mean, is anything really new being said to you, Christian? In these Christian times, the world is being laid to waste, the world is going to pieces.[9] Didn't your Lord tell you, "The world will be laid waste"? Didn't your Lord tell you, "The world will go to pieces"? Why did you believe it when it was foretold but now become upset when it is being fulfilled? That's why the storm is raging in your heart. Beware of shipwreck, rouse up Christ!

Let your faith wake up, and Christ immediately starts talking to you. Are you astonished at the world going to pieces? You might as well be astonished that the world has grown old. The world is like a man; he's born, he grows old. Old age is full of complaints: coughing, phlegm, bleary eyes, aches and pains, weariness—it's all there—the world has grown old; it's full of troubles and pressures. Has God, in fact, provided for you too little too late by sending you Christ in the world's old age in order to put you together again when everything else is going to pieces?

"There it is," they say, "we're living in the Christian times, and Rome is destroyed." Perhaps Rome isn't destroyed; perhaps it has been scoured but not put to death, punished perhaps, not obliterated. What is Rome, after all, but the Romans? I mean, we are not concerned with brick and mortar, with apartment blocks and extensive city walls. All this was put up in such a way that it would one day fall into ruin. When men build, they put stone upon stone; when they destroy it, they take the stones apart. Men put it up. Men pulled it down.

Is it an insult to Rome to say that it's falling down? "Not to Rome," they say, "but perhaps to its builder." So do we really insult its founder when we say Rome, which Romulus founded, is in ruins? The whole world is going to burn up (2 Pet 3:7), and that was founded by God. But anything put up by men only collapses when God wishes. So if the works of men don't fall down unless God wills, can the works of God collapse at the will of men?

It is the people who are the pride of a city, the people who inhabit, plan, and govern a city; and they come just to go, are born just to die, come in just to pass on. **Heaven and earth will pass away**; so why be surprised if a city sometimes comes to an end?

(18) John Chrysostom

Alas for that fearsome day! Though we should rejoice on hearing of it, we are distressed, we are downcast, our faces fall. Or am I the only one to feel this way, while you rejoice to hear of it? On me, at any rate, there comes a kind of trembling at these words, I lament bitterly and groan from the depths of my heart; in these words, there is nothing for me, only in what is said afterward to the virgins, to the man burying the talent he received, to the wicked servant (cf. 25:1–30). I weep on this account: for the great glory we are due to lose, the great blessings hoped for—and this forever without end, just to spare ourselves a little effort. I mean, if the effort had been great and the law demanding, there would then have been grounds for doing so; but even if many of the slothful seemed to have some excuse—a slight one, admittedly, but they seemed to have one, the burden of the commandments, that the effort was great, the time unending, the weight unbearable—yet now we cannot allege any such excuse.

9. A reference to the sack of Rome in 410 by Alaric and the Visigoths.

This is likely to gnaw at our vitals at that time no less than the terrors of hell, when for the sake of a slight effort and little toil we have lost heaven and its ineffable goods. The time in fact is brief, the effort slight, and yet we fail and give up. The contest is on earth, the crown in heaven; punishment is from men, honor from God; you run the course for two days, the prize lasts for ages without end; the bout is fought in a corruptible body, the title bestowed on an incorruptible one.

In order to verify that his coming will certainly happen, the Lord speaks about **the fig tree**. Whenever he intends to speak of those things that will definitely happen, he uses examples from the normal course of nature—both he and the blessed Paul who imitates him. For instance, when speaking about his resurrection, he says, *If a grain of wheat falls to the earth, unless it dies, it remains a single seed; but if it dies, it brings forth much fruit* (John 12:24). In this way, the blessed Paul, being instructed, uses the same illustration when speaking to the Corinthians about the resurrection. *You fool*, he says, *what you sow will not come to life unless it dies* (1 Cor 15:36).

In order that those listening might not immediately ask, "When," the Lord returns to what he had been saying, **Truly, I say unto you, This generation will not pass away until all these things have happened.** Tell me, what are **all these things**? They are the matters concerning Jerusalem, the wars, the famines, the disease, the earthquakes, the false christs, the false prophets, the sowing of the gospel everywhere, the seditions, the tumults, and all the other things we said would occur prior to his coming. Why then, one might ask, did he say, **this generation**? He was speaking not simply of the generation then living, but of believers in any time. He understands that a generation is not only measured by time, but also by its form of worship and its ultimate citizenship, as when he says, *This is the generation of them that seek the Lord* (Ps 24:6).

Just as it was said above, **All these must come to pass,** and again, **The gospel shall be preached** (24:14), it is reiterated here also that all these things will happen, and the generation of the faithful will endure and not be cut off by anything here mentioned. And though Jerusalem will be destroyed, and many of the Jews will be led astray, nothing will prevail over this generation—not famine, not disease, not earthquakes, nor the chaos of wars, not false christs, not false prophets, not deceivers, not traitors, not the wicked, not false brother or sisters, nor any similar trial.

Leading them into a yet deeper faith, he says, **Heaven and earth will pass away, but my words will not pass away.** That is, it is easier for these fixed and immovable bodies to be blotted out than for any of his words to fail. Whoever would contradict these things, let him put Jesus's sayings to the test. When he has found his statements regarding past events to be true—and, without doubt, this is how he will find them—let him also believe the things yet to come. And let him diligently search everything, and he will see how the actual events bear witness to the truth of the prophecy. For Jesus makes mention of the elements of the cosmos in order simultaneously to show that the Church has greater honor than heaven and earth and to indicate that he is the Creator of all things. Since the Lord was referring to the end—a point disbelieved by many—he brings forth heaven and earth to demonstrate his unspeakable power. And with great authority, he shows that he is Lord of all and that what he says is trustworthy, even to those who wish to dispute it.

Matthew 24:36

36"But of that day and hour no one knows, not even the angels of heaven, nor the Son, but the Father only."

(19) Hilary of Poitiers

Concerning the end of that time, the Lord removed the weight of our anxiety by saying that no one knows that day. Not only are the angels ignorant of it, but he himself does not know (24:36). O inestimable mercy of the divine goodness! Has God the Father denied the Son knowledge of that day by hiding his intentions, even though the Son said, **All things have been committed to me by my Father** (11:27)? How could everything be committed to him if there is something denied to him? But he delivered to us everything that he received from the Father (John 15:15). The Word possesses in himself the certainty, not so much of future events that will happen, as of the events that have happened. For this reason, the day has been set but without further qualification. Even though God permits a generous amount of time for our repentance, he recognizes our anxiety, always a fear of the unknown. By telling no one about his will when it comes to setting this day, he prevents any further qualification of his words. As it was at the time of the flood, that great day will burst into the course of our lives, into the midst of all our business and misery (24:37–39).

(20) Cyril of Alexandria

If the Son is the wisdom of the Father (1 Cor 1:30) and does not know God's wisdom—which he does know—then he is ignorant. Or, if the Son's human nature defines him more than his divine wisdom, then God possesses within himself composite and dissimilar natures. However, God does not make not knowing and knowing the measure of his Being, not even before men. Rather, overruling desire is the chief factor behind ignorance, something that the Son does not have. God is not capable of experiencing such divisive desires within his nature. And if all things that belong to the Son are the Father's and all things that belong to the Father are the Son's, then they are both ignorant, or the Father knows, and the Son knows, because he has all things of the Father according to the divine nature that is in him. . . . Whenever Scripture names the Father, it signifies the whole of the divine Being who is comprehended and worshiped in the holy Trinity.

Matthew 24:37–51

37"As were the days of Noah, so will be the coming of the Son of man. 38For as in those
days before the flood they were eating and drinking, marrying and giving in marriage,
until the day when Noah entered the ark, 39and they did not know until the flood came
and swept them all away, so will be the coming of the Son of man. 40Then two men will

be in the field; one is taken and one is left. [41]Two women will be grinding at the mill; one is taken and one is left. [42]Watch therefore, for you do not know on what day your Lord is coming. [43]But know this, that if the householder had known in what part of the night the thief was coming, he would have watched and would not have let his house be broken into. [44]Therefore you also must be ready; for the Son of man is coming at an hour you do not expect.

[45]"Who then is the faithful and wise servant, whom his master has set over his household, to give them their food at the proper time? [46]Blessed is that servant whom his master when he comes will find so doing. [47]Truly, I say to you, he will set him over all his possessions. [48]But if that wicked servant says to himself, 'My master is delayed,' [49]and begins to beat his fellow servants, and eats and drinks with the drunken, [50]the master of that servant will come on a day when he hoes not expect him and at an hour he does not know, [51]and will punish him, and put him with the hypocrites; there men will weep and gnash their teeth."

(21) Ambrose of Milan

The night is the antichrist, the time is shrouded in darkness—it is the time of shadows that spreads over the human heart, as this wicked one claims to be the Christ. False prophets will arise to say that Jesus is at hand, or that he is in the desert. They do this to trick and confuse people by spreading abroad their falsehoods and erroneous opinions. On another occasion, they say that he is here in a house, so that those who hear them are seized with terror. For even to hear the name of one possessed of such controlling powers strikes fear.[10]

But Christ, when he comes, will be like lightning that shines from one end of the sky to the other, filling the entire world with its dazzling splendor. He is not in the desert, nor is he enclosed in any place, because, *I fill the heavens and the earth, says the Lord* (Jer 23:24). Dazzling in light and glory, Jesus shines upon us so that in the darkness of this night, we may see the glory of the resurrection.

What is the significance of these words: *There shall be two men in one bed; there shall be two women grinding together; two men shall be in the field. One shall be taken and the other shall be left* (Luke 17:34–35)? It appears as if God is unjust. It looks as though he makes distinctions among people, although their occupations are the same and they live together without any difference between them on the basis of what other things they do. But that is not so, since the reward corresponds to each one's actions. Simply because we live together does not mean that our merits are equal. Zeal for religion can turn father against son and son against father (Luke 12:53). Not all finish what they have undertaken. **It is the one who perseveres to the end that shall be saved** (10:22). When our last moment comes, the Lord will judge us not by our exterior actions, but by our interior attitudes. Even if you offer your sacrifice correctly, but do not divide it justly, that sacrifice will not please God (cf. Gen 4:7).

One is taken from a bed, and another is left. The bed represents human infirmity, as

10. The antichrist.

Scripture says: *You have turned his bed in his sickness* (Ps 41:3). The one who is taken is lifted up into the air to meet Christ (cf. 1 Thess 4:16), but the one who is left is found unworthy.

(22) John Chrysostom

The reason he does not tell them when that day will come is that he wants them to be on the lookout, always to be ready. In effect, he says that he will come when they are not expecting it because he wants them to be prepared and virtuous in every aspect of life. What he means is something like this: If most people knew when they would die, they would exert themselves in that hour. But in order that they may exert themselves at all times, he does not specify either a general time or the particular time. He wants them vigilant in their readiness and to be always striving. For this reason, he also leaves the end of each person's life uncertain.

In the passage that follows, he clearly and plainly calls himself Lord, something he nowhere else says so openly. At this point, he seems to me to be targeting the carefree who take less interest in their own soul than people care about their money when they expect a thief. When someone expects a thief, they stay awake and allow nothing within their house to be stolen. But you, he is saying, though you know that he will come—and he will come indeed!—you do not stay awake and are not prepared lest you be carried away. The result is that the day dawns to the ruin of those asleep. Just as that person would have escaped if aware of it, so too you will escape if you are ready.

(23) Cyril of Alexandria

Take care because the Word divides men into two groups, those who are saved and those perishing. He says that those who are saved are the ones taken, but those who perish are left behind, that is to say, they are rejected. We should understand **field** here as the world, where *the one who sows in the Spirit reaps eternal life*, but *the one who sows in the flesh reaps corruption* (Gal 6:8). But those who speak the truth he compares to teachers who explain the Scriptures in a way that their thoughts are easily received and the divine words easily understood.

Matthew 25

In their interpretation of the parable of the ten virgins, the church fathers perceive the five wise virgins to be faithful Christians who are good stewards of what they have been given and persevere to the end. What of the five foolish virgins? There was widespread interest in understanding their symbolic identity. Augustine emphasizes that the five wise and five foolish virgins are "all, without exception, Christian souls," but the foolish ones fall short of their calling. Gregory the Great reflects this understanding when he writes that "in the Church the wicked are mingled with the good." More specifically, Gregory (with Augustine) declares that the foolish virgins are those who do good works for the sake of human praise and flattery. Caesarius says that the "five prudent virgins" are the "five senses," and he regards the "five foolish virgins" as those who engage in sinfulness through their senses. Regarding the oil for the lamps, the interpretations also vary. Some say they signify good works (Hilary and Caesarius), others charity (Augustine), and yet others mercy, or prayers for sin (Victorinus). However, there is general agreement that the sleeping of the virgins is the short sleep of death until the thunderous cry of the coming bridegroom awakens them for judgment.

The sellers of oil likewise yield very different interpretations. Hilary and Victorinus say the oil sellers are the needy who offer Christians the opportunity to serve them in Christ's name, and thus they "are selling to us a conscience of good works" (Hilary). However, Gregory and Caesarius interpret them as obsequious flatterers who offer meaningless praises for those who seek to receive human glory.

Concerning the parable of the talents, the emphasis is placed on human responsibility. As Gregory the Great says, with the increase of gifts from God, "the responsibility of accounting for them also grows greater."

In response to the division of the sheep and the goats, Valerian asks, "Who are these brethren?" *Is the Lord requiring service to all people or to the specific brethren known as Christians? Valerian answers that we are called to serve "all those related to us, on account of their having been born." We are to feed, clothe, welcome, and visit all people, regardless of religion or nationality. Chrysologus similarly directs us to serve the poor, as does Augustine, but the latter adds that "when you feed a Christian, you're feeding Christ."*

Matthew 25:1–5

[1]"Then the kingdom of heaven shall be compared to ten maidens who took their lamps and went to meet the bridegroom. [2]Five of them were foolish, and five were wise. [3]For when the foolish took their lamps, they took no oil with them; [4]but the wise took flasks of oil with their lamps. [5]As the bridegroom was delayed, they all slumbered and slept."

(1) Hilary of Poitiers

The bridegroom and the bride is our Lord God in the body. As the Spirit is wedded to the flesh, so the flesh is to the Spirit. When the trumpet finally sounds the alert, we will go out to meet only one spouse: the two have become one now that the humility of the flesh had passed over to spiritual glory. . . . The lamps are the light of shining souls radiant from the sacrament of baptism. The oil is the fruit of good works. The jars are human bodies in whose inward parts the treasure of a good conscience should be stored (1 Tim 1:5, 19). But the sellers (of the oil), who need the mercy of believers, are the ones providing the good that is sought from them. For the satiety of their own need, they are selling to us a conscience of good works. This is the abundant fuel of an inextinguishable light, which we should buy and store up by the fruits of mercy.

The marriage is the reception of immortality, the joining of corruption and incorruption into a new alliance (cf. 1 Cor 15:53–54). The delay of the bridegroom is the time of repentance. The falling asleep of those waiting is the rest of the believers and temporary death of everyone who comes to the time of their penitence. The shout in the middle of the night for all who are unaware is *the sound of the trumpet* that precedes the coming of the Lord and that arouses everyone to go out to meet the bridegroom (1 Thess 4:16). The taking up of the lamps is the return of the souls to their bodies, and the light is the shining conscience of good works, within the confines of their bodies.

(2) Augustine

So, dearly beloved, let us take this parable as referring to all of us, that is, to the whole Church, not only to its leaders, whom we were talking about yesterday, nor only to the people, but absolutely to all of us. So why two lots of five virgins? These five and five virgins are all, without exception, Christian souls. But to give you my own opinion, which I have formed under God's inspiration, these are not any sort of Christians, but only those souls that have the catholic faith and seem to have good works to their credit in the Church of God; and yet of these, five are wise and five foolish.

Even with these virgins and lamp-carriers, he called some wise, others foolish. How do we tell which is which, how do we tell the difference? By the oil. The oil stands for something tremendous, something tremendously important. Don't you think it is charity? The Apostle says, *I now show you a yet more excellent way.* What is the more excellent way he shows them? *If I speak with the tongues of men and of angels, but do not have charity, I have become booming bronze, or clashing cymbals* (1 Cor 12:31–13:1). That is the more excellent way, namely, charity, which is deservedly signified by oil. Oil, after all, excels all other fluids. Pour in water, pour oil on top, the oil excels by staying on top. Pour in oil, pour water on top, the oil excels by coming to the top. If you keep the right order, it wins; if you reverse the order, it wins. *Charity never falls away* (1 Cor 13:8).

So what then, brothers and sisters? So now we can discuss the difference between the five wise virgins and the five foolish ones. They wanted to go and meet the bridegroom. What does going to meet the bridegroom mean? To go in spirit, to look forward to his coming. But he was late. While he is taking his time, **they all went to sleep.** All of them? Yes, both wise and foolish, **they all felt sleepy and went to sleep.**

Are we to suppose this is a good sleep? What is this sleep? Possibly, while the bridegroom is taking his time, iniquity abounds and the charity of many grows cold. Is that how we are to understand this sleep? I don't agree with that, and I'll tell you why. Because the wise ones are included; and when the Lord said, **Because iniquity has abounded, the charity of many grows cold**, he went on to add, **But whoever perseveres to the end, that person shall be saved** (24:12–13). Where do you want to place these wise ones? Surely, among those who persevere to the end. For no other reason, brothers and sisters, for no other reason at all would they be allowed in, unless they had persevered to the end. So the chilling of charity hasn't crept over them, charity has not grown cold in them, but it remains piping hot till the end. It's because it remains piping hot till the end that the bridegroom's doors are open wide; it's for that reason they are told to enter, like that other excellent servant: **Enter into the joy of your Lord.** So what's the meaning of **they all went to sleep**? There's another sort of sleep, which no one can avoid. Don't you remember the apostle saying, *But about those who have fallen asleep, I would not have you ignorant, brothers* (1 Thess 4:13), meaning about those who have died? Why should they be said to be sleeping? Surely because in their own time they are to be raised up. So they all went to sleep. You don't imagine, do you, that just because they are wise they don't have to die? Be the virgins foolish or be they wise, they all undergo the sleep of death. I mean, look at these foolish virgins who didn't carry oil with them; by their self-denial that earns them the name of virgins, and by their good works represented by the lamps they bring, they are intent on pleasing other people. And if they are intent on pleasing other people, and that's why they do these admirable things, they are not carrying oil with them. So you, then, mind you, carry it with you, carry it inside, where God can see; carry the testimony of your conscience there. But if your manner of life depends on other people's testimony, you are not carrying oil with you. So if you refrain from unlawful things and perform good works in order to be admired by other people, there is no oil inside you.

In any case, as soon as people begin not to admire you, the lamps start going out. Would your graces please pay close attention! Before those virgins went to sleep, it doesn't say that their lamps were going out. The wise ones' lamps were burning from the oil inside them, from the assurance of their consciences, from their inner boast, from their deepest charity. But those of the foolish ones were also burning. Why were they burning then? Because there was no lack of admiration from other people.

(3) Caesarius of Arles

Now those five prudent virgins signify all the saints who are destined to reign with Christ. Those five foolish virgins, on the contrary, seem to prefigure wicked Christians who glory only in the title of Christian but are completely without good works. Moreover, they are called the five foolish and wise virgins because there are shown to be the five senses in all men: sight, hearing, taste, smell, and touch. Now through these senses, like certain kinds of doors or windows, either death or life approaches our soul, and concerning them the prophet also said, *Death has come up through our windows* (Jer 9:21). For this reason, then, five virgins are called wise, since they use their senses well, and five are called foolish, because through those five senses, they receive more death than life.

(4) Gregory the Great

We must first ask what the kingdom of heaven is, and why it is compared to ten virgins, some of whom are called wise and some foolish. We know that none of the condemned enters the kingdom of heaven, and so why is it likened to the foolish virgins as well? We must be aware that often in the sacred Scriptures the Church of the present time is called the kingdom of heaven. In another place, the Lord says: **The angels will come and gather out all causes of sin from the kingdom of my Father** (13:41), although in that kingdom of blessedness, in which there is the greatest peace, there will be no causes of sin to be gathered in. Again it is said: **But whoever breaks one of the least of these commandments, and so teaches others, will be called least in the kingdom of heaven; but whoever observes and teaches [them] will be called great in the kingdom of heaven** (5:19). In fact, anyone who preaches in words what he does not fulfill in his life is breaking a commandment and so teaching others.

Everyone exists by the five senses of the body, and twice five is ten; and because the entire number of the faithful is gathered in from the two sexes, the holy Church is said to be like ten virgins. And because in the Church the wicked are mingled with the good, the condemned with the elect, it is likened to wise and foolish virgins. There are many who are chaste and keep themselves from worldly desires, and others drawn by hope to inner things. They mortify their bodies; with their whole desire they pursue their homeland on high, they seek eternal rewards, they decline to receive human praise for their labors. Surely these do not put their glory in the mouths of other persons, but they conceal it within their own consciences. But there are others who afflict their bodies through abstinence, but in this abstinence they are seeking for human approval. They are devoted to teaching, they bestow much on the needy; but they are foolish virgins, because they seek only the recompense of fleeting praise.

Matthew 25:6–9

6"But at midnight there was a cry, 'Behold, the bridegroom! Come out to meet him.'
7Then all those maidens rose and trimmed their lamps. 8And the foolish said to the

wise, 'Give us some of your oil, for our lamps are going out.' [9]But the wise replied, 'Perhaps there will not be enough for us and for you; go rather to the dealers and buy for yourselves.'"

(5) Victorinus of Poetovio

Although the bridegroom was delayed, the wise virgins are those who remain steadfast in prayer and look forward to the kingdom of God. And when certain signs of God's coming appear in heaven, the foolish virgins are those who seek prayers for their sins from the wise. This is why the wise responded to the foolish, saying in effect, "because we have our own sins, we fear that perhaps our prayers will not be enough to suffice for you and us. You go, rather, and buy for yourselves from those who sell it."

Who are those who sell that oil of mercy? Recognize that it is the blind, the crippled, the enfeebled, the poor, widows, orphans, strangers and exiles, those in the mines, prisoners, the sick, and others like these. The impoverished ones, therefore, are those who watched for their salvation too late; they delayed rather than seek the forgiveness of their sins, and on the day of judgment, they will find the door shut. Thus the Lord said, **while the bridegroom was delayed, they all fell asleep**—that is, they died.

(6) Caesarius of Arles

When the foolish virgins said to the wise virgins, **give us some of your oil**, and the wise responded, **lest there may not be enough for us and you**, this is fearfully and humbly said. This is because so great will be the fear and examination on the day of judgment, that even for those who know themselves to have prepared abundantly the oil of mercy, fear will not be enough when it comes to the purpose of redeeming all their sins. Indeed, what is said, **rather go to the merchant and buy some for yourselves**, can be understood to refer to the poor. For they themselves are the merchants who sell the necessary oil for the lamps of souls. Through the poor, Christ accustomed himself to operate this business affair. In them, he receives earthly goods so that he may return heavenly ones. He accepts fleeting things, repaying with eternal goods. Lastly, he himself said: **as long as you have done to one of the least of these, you have done to me** (25:40).

Therefore, the lamps are understood to be souls, and the vessels where the oil is reserved signify good consciences. What does it mean to have oil in vessels, unless it is to store away good works within one's conscience? Because some men do good works for the love of God, while others do so for the desire of human praise. The foolish virgins, though they were in community and occupied themselves with vigils, psalms, readings, or prayers, all that was done for human praise, not for God or eternal blessedness. Therefore, at the moment when death intervened and the praise of men ceased from the foolish virgins, the oil also gave out. What is said to them, **rather go to the merchant and buy some for yourselves**, can likewise be accepted differently, so that the merchants may be understood as adulators who exalt with false praises those who seem to do good works for human glory.

Lastly, he who does something good for human praise does not do it at all if no one praises him. From this, it is understood that all who desire to receive human praises sell to human adulation what they seem to employ in the work of God. They are receiving vain praise and are squandering their eternal rewards. Those virgins, however, who have had oil in their vessels, have put every good work within their conscience. They do this not for human praise but for divine mercy.

(7) Gregory the Great

At midnight a cry arose: See, the bridegroom is coming; go forth to meet him. A cry that the bridegroom was coming arose at midnight because the day of judgment approaches so silently that its coming cannot be foreseen. Hence it is written: *The day of the Lord will come like a thief in the night* (1 Thess 5:2). Then all the virgins arise, because the elect and the condemned are awakened from their sleep of death; they trim their lamps, because they count the works for which they expect to receive eternal blessedness. The lamps of the foolish virgins go out, because their works, which appeared outwardly evident to people at the judge's coming, are hidden within; and they find no recompense from God, because they have received from men the praises that they loved. What does it mean that they then request oil from the wise, except that at the judge's coming they seek external testimony when they find that they are empty within.

The wise virgins add here by way of rebuke: **Go rather to those who sell, and buy some for yourselves.** Those who sell oil are people who are obsequious. When they receive any kind of favor, by their meaningless praises they offer a show of glory as if they were selling oil. The psalmist says of this oil: *But let not the oil of a sinner anoint my head* (Ps 141:5). Our head is our ruling member, and by speaking of the head he means the mind that rules the body. The oil of a sinner anoints the head when the good will of an obsequious person flatters the mind.

You see how he himself calls, how he calls by the patriarchs, the prophets, the apostles, by pastors, and even by me; often he calls by miracles, often by calamities; sometimes he calls by prosperity in this world, sometimes by adversity. Let no one treat this lightly: if he has excused himself when he was called, when he wants to come in, he may not be able to. Listen to what Wisdom tells us in the words of Solomon, *Then they will call upon me, and I will not hear; they will rise up in the morning, and will not find me* (Prov 1:28). It is because of this that the foolish virgins who came late cried out: **Lord, Lord, open to us.** But as they sought an entrance, they were told, **Truly, I say to you, I do not know you.**

What should we do in this case, dearly beloved, but abandon everything, lay aside the cares of the world, and attend to our eternal desires alone? But this is given to few. I want to advise you to abandon everything, but I do not venture to do so. If you cannot abandon every worldly thing, then hold on to the things of this world so that you are not held in the world by them; so that you possess earthly things and they do not possess you; so that your heart controls your possessions. If your heart is overcome by the love of earthly things, it may be possessed by its own possessions.

Matthew 25:10–13

[10]"And while they went to buy, the bridegroom came, and those who were ready went in with him to the marriage feast; and the door was shut. [11]Afterward the other maidens came also, saying, 'Lord, lord, open to us.' [12]But he replied, 'Truly, I say to you, I do not know you.' [13]Watch therefore, for you know neither the day nor the hour."

(8) Augustine

Although the Lord is not at this vigil of ours,[1] he is being awaited as though he was still going to rise again. Yet, the memory of his resurrection is being renewed in this annual solemnity, and in the same way, when we celebrate it, we symbolize what living by faith is all about. You see, in this age, representing night, as it's running its course, the Church is keeping vigil: the eyes of her faith fixed upon the Holy Scriptures as upon lamps lit at night until the Lord comes. So you have what the Apostle Peter says, *We have the more certain prophetic word, to which you do well to pay attention, as to a lamp in a dark place, until the day dawns, and the morning star rises in your hearts* (2 Pet 1:19). That's why the Savior himself also enjoins upon us a spiritual vigil, when he is speaking of the suddenness of his coming: **Watch**, he says, **because you do not know the day or the hour.**

So just as now, when I came to you in the name of the Lord, I found you awake and watching in his name; so too the Lord himself, in whose honor this solemnity is being celebrated, will find his Church awake and watching with mind alight and alert, when he comes to rouse her even from her bodily sleep in the tombs.

Matthew 25:14–30

[14]"For it will be as when a man going on a journey called his servants and entrusted to them his property; [15]to one he gave five talents, to another two, to another one, to each according to his ability. Then he went away. [16]He who had received the five talents went at once and traded with them; and he made five talents more. [17]So also, he who had the two talents made two talents more. [18]But he who had received the one talent went and dug in the ground and hid his master's money. [19]Now after a long time the master of those servants came and settled accounts with them. [20]And he who had received the five talents came forward, bringing five talents more, saying, 'Master, you delivered to me five talents; here I have made five talents more.' [21]His master said to him, 'Well done, good and faithful servant; you have been faithful over a little, I will set you over much; enter into the joy of your master.' [22]And he also who had the two talents came forward, saying, 'Master, you delivered to me two talents; here I have made two talents more.' [23]His master said to him, 'Well done, good and faithful servant; you have been faithful over a little, I will set you over much; enter into the joy of your master.' [24]He also who

1. The Paschal Vigil celebrated on Saturday evening of Easter.

had received the one talent came forward, saying, 'Master, I knew you to be a hard man, reaping where you did not sow, and gathering where you did not winnow; [25]so I was afraid, and I went and hid your talent in the ground. Here you have what is yours.' [26]But his master answered him, 'You wicked and slothful servant! You knew that I reap where I have not sowed, and gather where I have not winnowed? [27]Then you ought to have invested my money with the bankers, and at my coming I should have received what was my own with interest. [28]So take the talent from him, and give it to him who has the ten talents. [29]For to every one who has will more be given, and he will have abundance; but from him who has not, even what he has will be taken away. [30]And cast the worthless servant into the outer darkness; there men will weep and gnash their teeth.'"

(9) John Chrysostom

Let us, then, listen to these words. As opportunity offers, let us make efforts for our salvation, let us get oil for the lamps, let our talents grow in value. If we hang back and spend our time in idleness in this life, no one then will have pity on us in the life to come, no matter how much we lament. The person with soiled garments likewise condemned himself and gained nothing. The person with the one talent restored the deposit with which he was entrusted, and he was thus condemned; the virgins made their appeal, came forward and knocked, all to no avail.

If we are aware of these things, let us contribute money, effort, support, and everything for the neighbors' welfare: talents in this case are each person's resources, be it in support, in money, in teaching, in anything at all of this kind. Let no one claim, I have one talent, and I can do nothing: even with one you are capable of measuring up. I mean, you are not poorer than that widow, you are not more unlettered than Peter and John, who were simple and unschooled, yet by giving evidence of zeal and doing everything for the common good, they attained to heaven. Nothing, in fact, is so pleasing to God as living for the benefit of all. For this reason, God gave us speech, hands and feet, bodily strength, a mind and understanding, so that we might use them all for our own salvation and the neighbors' benefit.

(10) Gregory the Great

The reading from the holy Gospel advises us, dearly beloved, to bear in mind that we who have received something more than others in this world may be judged more severely by the world's Creator. When his gifts increase, the responsibility of accounting for them also grows greater. Everyone must be more humble, then, and readier to serve, as a result of his gifts, the more he sees that he will be constrained to render an account of them.

The man setting out for foreign parts entrusted his goods to his servants, granting his spiritual gifts to those who believed in him. To one he entrusted five talents, to another two, to another one. There are five bodily senses, sight, hearing, taste, smell and touch. The five talents represent the gift of the five senses, that is, knowledge of external things;

the two talents signify understanding and devotion [to spiritual practice], the one talent signifies understanding alone.

The person who received five talents gained another five. There are some who, even without knowing how to probe into inward and mystical matters, use the natural gifts they have received to teach correctly those they can reach, in order to strive for their heavenly home. While guarding themselves from physical wantonness, from striving after earthly things, and from taking pleasure in things they can see, they restrain others too from these things by their counsel.

And there are some endowed with two talents, so to speak, who comprehend both understanding and devotion. They understand the fine points of internal matters and accomplish astonishing things outwardly. When they preach to others by both theory and practice, their business venture, so to call it, yields a twofold gain. It is good that another five and another two are said to have been gained, since the response to preaching is given to both sexes by means of the talents received and doubled so to speak.

But the person who received one talent went away, dug in the earth, and hid his master's money. Hiding a talent in the earth means employing one's abilities in earthly affairs, failing to seek spiritual profit, never raising one's heart from earthly thoughts. There are some who have received the gift of understanding but have a taste only for things that pertain to the body. The prophet says of them: *They are wise in doing evil, but they do not know how to do good* (Jer 4:22).

But let us listen to the penalty his master imposes on the lazy servant: **Take the talent from him, and give it to the one who has ten talents.** It would seem more appropriate to take the one talent from the wicked servant and give it to the one who received two talents rather than to the one who received five. It should have been given to the one who had less rather than to the one who had more. But, as I said above, the five talents represent the five senses, that is, knowledge of external things; and the two talents signify understanding and devotion [to the spiritual practice]. Therefore the one who received two had more than the one who had received five, because the one who was found worthy of the direction of externals through his five talents still lacked the knowledge of inner things. And so the one talent, which, as I said, signifies theory, was bound to be given to the one who attended so well to the external things he had received. We see this daily in the Church. Many attend very well to external things as they receive them, and are brought by additional grace to mystical understanding as well. Thus those who faithfully attend to externals may also be strong in their inner understanding.

And immediately a general thought is added: **For to everyone who has, more will be given, and he will have more than enough; but from everyone who has not, even what he seems to have will be taken away from him.** To the one who has, more will be given, and he will have more than enough. Whoever has love receives other gifts as well. Whoever does not have love loses even the gifts he appeared to have received. Hence it is necessary, my friends, that in everything you do, you should be vigilant about guarding love. True love is to love your friend in God, and your enemy for the sake of God. Whoever does not have this loses every good that he has; he is deprived of the talent he received, and according to the Lord's sentence he is cast into outer darkness. Outer darkness comes as a punishment to one who has fallen voluntarily into internal darkness through his own sin. The one who freely enjoyed pleasurable darkness in this world will be constrained to suffer punishing darkness in the next.

We must be certain that no slothful person is safe from the consequences of receiving a talent. No one can truly say, "I have not received a talent, and there is no reason I should be compelled to give an account." Even the very little that any poor person has received will be counted as his talent. One person has received understanding and owes the office of preaching to his talent. Another has received earthly possessions and is under obligation to distribute alms from his properties. Another has received neither understanding of inner things nor many possessions, but has learned a skill that sustains him; in his case, his skill is counted as a talent. Another has acquired none of these things, but perhaps he has merited acquaintance with a rich person and has received the talent of acquaintance: if he tells him nothing on behalf of the poor, he is condemned for keeping back his talent. Therefore the one with understanding must take care not to remain silent, the one with an abundance of possessions must watch that he is not slow in showing mercy, the one with a skill must be especially zealous to share his craft and usefulness with his neighbor, the one with an opportunity to speak with a rich person should fear to be condemned for keeping back his talent if he does not intercede with him on behalf of the poor when he can.

(11) Peter Chrysologus

The rich man was deliberately glossing over the fact that the Lord (who may have walked in poverty on earth but ascended into heaven with great wealth) *lent* rather than received the talents that he then passed on to his servants: five to one, two to another, to a third one. Indeed, he even declares that he will *demand* rather than deliver interest on those talents, when he castigates his servant, saying: **You good for nothing sluggard! If you had at least lent out my money, I would have come and collected the interest!** The rich man is therefore doubly damned: he did *not* act on behalf of his neighbor, and the good things in life that came his way were not the result of good actions, but wicked ones.

But now let's turn our attention to the poor man Lazarus, and see whether we can't tease out the meaning of the following passage: *But Lazarus, on the other hand, received bad things* (Luke 16:25). Even if he didn't accomplish good things, it is to his credit—indeed, to his honor—that he accepted bad ones. Truly, brothers, if you faithfully trust in God's goodness toward you when you're undergoing trials, you're blessed! You're blessed if you keep in mind your debt to God, blessed if you repay that debt. If you can't, then at least weep in utter humility over the magnitude of your debt to God so that you may be forgiven, just as the Lord himself urges you: **Forgive us our debts** (6:12). And you are blessed if you repay even those debts you were unaware of contracting, those debts that the prophet alludes to in his profound words: *I restored what I had not stolen* (Ps 69:4).

Ultimately, this is how it works: you must accuse yourself before God at all times, so that God may forgive you at all times. Scripture puts it this way: *the righteous man accuses himself from the beginning* (Prov 18:17). But if he is righteous, why should he accuse himself?

Because, in fact, *No one living is righteous in your sight* (Ps 142:2 LXX; 143:2). Yes, humans often brag about their "righteousness," their "innocence," their "worth" when they're around other people—but if they tried blustering on about such things in the presence of God, they would lose their essential humanity. They would become like the Pharisee of old, who, instead of praying, sat there enumerating his "worth," describing his "innocence," belching out his "righteousness"—and all the while paling beside the tax collector, who truly *became* so (cf. Luke 18:9–14).

Matthew 25:31–40

31"When the Son of man comes in his glory, and all the angels with him, then he will sit on his glorious throne. 32Before him will be gathered all the nations, and he will separate them one from another as a shepherd separates the sheep from the goats, 33and he will place the sheep at his right hand, but the goats at the left. 34Then the King will say to those at his right hand, 'Come, O blessed of my Father, inherit the kingdom prepared for you from the foundation of the world; 35for I was hungry and you gave me food, I was thirsty and you gave me drink, I was a stranger and you welcomed me, 36I was naked and you clothed me, I was sick and you visited me, I was in prison and you came to me.' 37Then the righteous will answer him, 'Lord, when did we see thee hungry and feed thee, or thirsty and give thee drink? 38And when did we see thee a stranger and welcome thee, or naked and clothe thee? 39And when did we see thee sick or in prison and visit thee?' 40And the King will answer them, 'Truly, I say to you, as you did it to one of the least of these my brethren, you did it to me.'"

(12) Valerian of Cimelium

Who are these **brethren**? Of necessity, all those related to us are brethren on account of their having been born. Why should any person be excluded from our offerings? Why is no distinction of persons to be made? The reason is that something that is necessary does not require an order to carry it out. Why must you ask whether the one who makes a request is Christian or Jew, heretic or pagan, Roman or foreigner, free man or slave? If the matter is pressing, you don't have to discuss the identity of the person. Otherwise, in separating out those unworthy of your mercy, you may likewise lose the Son of God. How can we know in what region of earth Christ dwells? He who is known to possess everything should be believed to be everywhere.

If we compare heavenly things with earthly, it is evident that something very valuable is for sale at a rather low price. How great are your alms in proportion to all the things that the Lord has clearly promised to mortal men? Look, we give earthly goods; he bequeaths those of heaven. We offer goods that last a while; he, those that endure forever.

(13) Augustine

A man full of sores was lying at the gate, but the rich man ignored him. He longed to appease his hunger on the scraps that fell from the other's table. He himself fed the dogs with his sores, and he wasn't fed by the rich man. Take notice, brothers and sisters, of the destitution of the poor. *Blessed is he*, it says, *who is understanding about the needy and the poor* (Ps 41:1); take notice, and don't ignore, so to say, disease-ridden Lazarus lying at your gate. Give to the poor, because the one who receives what you give is the one who wishes to go in need on earth and to enrich from heaven. The Lord did say, after all, **I was hungry and you gave me to eat; I was thirsty and you gave me to drink; I was a stranger and you took me in**, and so on. And they answered, **When did we see you hungry or thirsty or naked or a stranger?** And he said, **When you did it to one of the least of mine, you did it to me.** In the least of his followers, laboring under severe affliction on earth, he wished somehow to be mercifully present in person, thus bringing support from heaven.

So you are giving to Christ when you give to a needy person—or are you afraid that such a keeper may lose some of what you give, or that such a rich person may not be able to pay you back? God is almighty, Christ is almighty; you can't possibly lose any of it. When do you entrust it to him? Whenever you give to the poor. Such riches don't pass away when flesh passes away like grass, and the splendor of man like flowers in the grass.

And so, brothers and sisters, if we were terrified that we may suffer such pains and torments after this life as that proud and callous rich man endured, now, now, while there is still time, let us reform. For then, you see, there will be no chance of getting help, because there will be no chance of reforming. Help comes to you, I mean, when you reform. This life is the time for reform, this life is the time for getting help and comfort.

(14) Peter Chrysologus

But what are we to make of these words that you yourself, O Lord, have said to us? You have told us that *The Father judges no one, but has given all judgment over to the Son* (John 5:22). But then you said: *Who made me an arbiter between you?* (Luke 12:14). So who is going to cleave the righteous from the wicked, **as a shepherd separates the sheep from the goats**? If you are the one responsible for the judgment of humanity—if it's by your hand that the whole world is to be divided, then why did you say, *Who made me a judge or arbiter between you?*

We must consider the context. Yes, Christ will preside over all judgment that ever was, is, or will be, but at that particular time he had not come to judge, but to be judged—not to condemn sinners, but to be condemned by them, though innocent. Even though he was God, he comported himself as a human; even though he was Lord, his actions were those of a servant. The judge of the world "went native," so to speak, inhabiting the temporal plane he himself had made. And that is why he rightly answered, *Who has made me the judge or arbiter between you?*

That the one who shrouds the heavens may be found threadbare among the poor; that abundance itself starves among the hungry; that the fount of fountains gasps with the thirsty: is this not a high and blessed thing to grasp? That he whom the heavens cannot contain is enveloped by poverty; that he who enriches the world is found destitute among the needy, that the giver of all gifts begs for a crumb of bread, a sip of water—that God himself in his love for the poor so abases himself that he not only draws near them, but becomes one of them.

But I'll let him tell us in his own words how it is that he can transfigure the poor into himself and merge himself with the needy: **I was hungry**, he says, **and you gave me something to eat**. He did not say, "the *poor* were hungry, and you gave *them* something to eat," but rather "*I* was hungry, and you gave *me* something to eat." Notice: he's claiming that he is given what the poor receive, that he chews what they eat, that he swallows what they drink! Is there anything that love for the poor cannot do? The very things that humiliate the poor on earth are counted glorious by God in heaven; what they see as insults here he counts as honors there.

He could have just said, **You gave me something to eat** and **something to drink**—but instead, he precedes these words with **I was hungry . . . I was thirsty**. Why? Because it's a poor facsimile of love that merely offers handouts to the needy without first experiencing their suffering: true love simply cannot be demonstrated without suffering. Indeed, true love works itself out in making the hardships of others our own. How incredible that God has partaken of the table scraps of the poor! How inconceivable that he who needs no created good has prophesied from his heavenly realm, in the presence of all his angels and the assembly of the resurrected, that he was nourished by the fare of the needy!

Hear the words of the Apostle: *If we suffer with him, we will also reign with him* (2 Tim 2:12). He who was born for us will certainly, when he comes, present the kingdom to us, a promise he himself swears by when he says: **Come, you who are blessed by my Father, and take hold of the kingdom that has been prepared for you from the beginning of the world.** Notice: he says "for you," not "for me." When he comes, he will be with us always: he who is now so dear to our hearts will be visible to our eyes. When he comes, he who is now the glory of those who will share the kingdom will become the safeguard of their affection.

And his kingdom shall have no end (Luke 1:33). You who trust in his return, rejoice! He has promised you a kingdom without end, a kingdom in which your service will never be terminated and your honors are everlasting. Why then do people dash this way and that after fleeting shadows, and not after unfading realities? Why, I ask you, are they willing to spend all their wealth on crumbling honors but expect to receive eternal ones for nothing?

Matthew 25:41–43

[41]"Then he will say to those at his left hand, 'Depart from me, you cursed, into the eternal fire prepared for the devil and his angels; [42]for I was hungry and you gave me no food, I was thirsty and you gave me no drink, [43]I was a stranger and you did not welcome me, naked and you did not clothe me, sick and in prison and you did not visit me.'"

(15) Caesarius of Arles

Consider further, brethren, the reason why they will be cast into eternal fire. It is not going to be said: "Because you committed murder, because you committed adultery, because you seized the property of another," but they are going to hear only this: **For I was hungry, and you did not give me to eat**. I urge you, brethren, do not think of this as a small matter. . . .

Believe most firmly that Christians and catholics are going to hear it, if they persevere in evil deeds. Neither pagans nor heretics nor Jews are coming to judgment, because it is written of them, *He who does not believe is already judged* (John 3:18). Now among those who will be sent to the left hand will not be only the laity, but also many bishops, and what is worse, wicked clerics, even avaricious or proud monks, as well as angry, haughty, or covetous pious widows. If fruitful repentance does not come to their assistance, they are going to hear that dreadful, irrevocable sentence: **Depart from me, accursed ones, into the everlasting fire**. If we are willing to listen to this sentence devoutly and with great concern, it will be able to recall us from every evil deed.

(16) Augustine

But a plunderer of other people's property says to me, "I'm not like that rich man. I provide 'agape meals' (cf. Jude 12). I send food to those chained up in prison; I clothe the naked; I welcome strangers." Do you really imagine you're giving? Stop grabbing, and then you have really given. The person to whom you've given something rejoices; the one from whom you've snatched something is crying; which of these two is the Lord going to listen to? You say to the one to whom you've given something, "You should thank me for what you've received." But the other person says to you from the other side, "I'm wringing my hands for what you've taken from me; and anyway, you've taken practically everything and given him the merest fraction."

So even if you had given the needy the whole of that which you took off that other person, God does not like such works, since he says to you, "Fool, I commanded you to give, but not from what belongs to someone else. If you have property, give from what is yours. If you have nothing to give from what is yours, you would do better not to give anything to anyone than to despoil other people."

The Lord Christ is going to say, when he takes his seat at his great assize and separates some to the right and others to the left, he's going to say to those who do good, **Come, blessed of my Father, receive the kingdom**; to the unprofitable ones, however, who have done nothing good for the poor, **Go into everlasting fire**. And what's he going to say to the good? **For I was hungry, and you gave me to eat**, etc. And they will answer him. **Lord, when did we see you hungry?** And he will tell them, **When you did it for one of the least of mine, you did it for me.** So understand, you fool you, wishing to give alms with stolen property, that when you feed a Christian, you're feeding Christ; when you strip a Christian, you're stripping Christ. Just notice what he said to those on the left: **Go into everlasting fire**. Why? **For I was hungry, and you did not give me to eat; I was naked, and you did not clothe me** (25:31–46). Go. Where to? **Into everlasting fire**; straightaway, go. Why? **I**

was naked, and you did not clothe me. So if the person to whom Christ is going to say, **I was naked and you did not clothe me**, is going into eternal fire, what place in the eternal fire, do you think, will that person have to whom he is going to say, "I was clothed, and you stripped me"?

Matthew 25:44–46

44"Then they also will answer, 'Lord, when did we see thee hungry or thirsty or a stranger
or naked or sick or in prison, and did not minister to thee?' 45Then he will answer them,
'Truly, I say to you, as you did it not to one of the least of these, you did it not to me.'
46And they will go away into eternal punishment, but the righteous into eternal life."

(17) John Chrysostom

Note how simple are his requirements: He did not say, "I was in prison and you freed me, I was sick and you put me on my feet," but **you visited me . . . you came to me.** Not even in the case of hunger, in fact, are the instructions demanding: he was not requesting a lavish banquet, only what is necessary, basic nourishment, and he requested it as a suppliant.

The result was that everything was enough to bring punishment on them who are on the left hand: the ease of fulfilling the request, bread alone; the pitiable condition of the beggar, poor as he was; natural fellow-feeling, since he was a man; the desirableness of the promise, the kingdom being promised; the fearsome character of the punishment, hell being threatened; the dignity of the recipient, God receiving the gift in the person of the poor; the high degree of the honor, since he deigned to be so considerate; the justice of the return, since he received what was his. Yet in the face of all this, covetousness once and for all blinded those in its grip, despite such an awful threat hanging over them. Earlier on, remember, he said that those who do not receive such people would suffer a worse fate than the inhabitants of Sodom, and here he says, **Just as you did not do it to one of the least of my brethren, you did not do it to me.** Why do you say **my brethren**? How is it you call them **least**?

They are **brethren** because they are lowly, they are poor; they are outcast. Such people in particular he invites to brotherhood: such as the unknown and the contemptible, referring not just to the monks and those that occupy the mountains, but to every believer, secular or not, as long as they are hungry and thirsty, naked and a stranger. He wants them to receive this care in every way. For baptism and participation in the divine Eucharist render them brothers.

(18) Valerian of Cimelium

There are two kinds of riches: the one leads to death, the other to life. Here are ones that lead to death: to brood like a miser upon another's wealth; to take in money amid the tears of the unfortunate, and stack it up, and count it day by day as something to swell the legacies of this world. The sound and genuine riches are those by which souls are redeemed and sins purged. God finds acceptable the riches of that man by whose generosity the poor man is fed, the naked man clothed, the captive ransomed, the imprisoned man freed, and the inheritance of the heavenly kingdom acquired. I do not want those riches that by their daily growth increase a hunger for them, and then, eventually stripped of their attraction and beauty, allow their lovers to remain hungry.

Matthew 26

The reality of Jesus's passion was certain evidence of his full humanity. In order to show the extent of his suffering, the ancient commentators carefully observe the details surrounding the Last Supper, Jesus's arrest, and trials. In preparation for his passion, his body is anointed by the woman with perfume, a figurative act that carries several meanings: "the aroma of good morals and the perfume of honest deeds" (Ambrose) or "the fruit of good works" (Hilary). At the Last Supper, Jesus said that he will be betrayed this very night (by Peter and Judas), and this shows that we "profit nothing from grace from on high if good will is lacking" (Chrysostom).

That Jesus said his soul was sorrowful and that he would have preferred not to drink the cup of suffering presented a problem for ancient writers, because these words seemed to compromise the Son's divinity. How could God, with an eternal nature, truly experience sorrow or doubt? Surely the Son was not sorrowful or doubtful in any literal sense. According to Hilary, Jesus did not fear the cross or death but was expressing what the disciples felt so that they would themselves be prepared for the trials that lay ahead. Indeed, Ambrose asserts that God the Word could not have been arrested, as if he were "arrested in spite of himself, arrested because he was powerless." The issue at stake, says Augustine, is that we must recognize the Son's dual nature: "he was God with the Father," but he was also "in the form of a servant" (Phil 2:5–7). As God the Son would know, the cup could not pass by him, but he utters these words so as to demonstrate for us how to deal with temptation when it comes.

Matthew 26:1–2

1When Jesus had finished all these sayings, he said to his disciples, 2"You know that after two days the Passover is coming, and the Son of man will be delivered up to be crucified."

(1) Leo the Great

When the merciful and almighty Savior became man, through the veil of our infirmity he hid the power of his deity, which is inseparable from his manhood. In this way, he foiled the wiles of his cunning foe. For he thought that the birth of this boy was begotten for the salvation of the human race, was as subject to him as all others who are born. For he saw him wailing and crying; he saw him *wrapped in swaddling clothes*, presented *for circumcision* and offering *the sacrifice prescribed by the law* (cf. Luke 2:21); he saw in him the usual *growth of a boy* and assumed he would reach maturity in the natural way (cf. Luke 2:22–24).

In the course of the stages of his life, the enemy introduced insults, multiplied injuries, and brought curses, reproaches, blasphemies, and outcries upon him. Finally, he poured out on him every violence of his fury, making him pass through all kinds of temptations. Knowing the poison by which he had corrupted human nature, he did not believe that Christ was exempt from transgression, because there were so many things that gave proof of his mortality. Therefore, this wicked robber and greedy thief persisted in opposing him who had nothing of his own. And as the devil pursued him as one corrupted by sin, Christ destroyed the *bond*[1] (Col 2:14) that held us and exacted from one who had not faulted the penalty for sin.

Matthew 26:3–13

3Then the chief priests and the elders of the people gathered in the palace of the high
priest, who was called Ca'iaphas, 4and took counsel together in order to arrest Jesus by
stealth and kill him. 5But they said, "Not during the feast, lest there be a tumult among
the people."
6Now when Jesus was at Bethany in the house of Simon the leper, 7a woman came
up to him with an alabaster flask of very expensive ointment, and she poured it on his
head, as he sat at table. 8But when the disciples saw it, they were indignant, saying,
"Why this waste? 9For this ointment might have been sold for a large sum, and given
to the poor." 10But Jesus, aware of this, said to them, "Why do you trouble the woman?
For she has done a beautiful thing to me. 11For you always have the poor with you, but
you will not always have me. 12In pouring this ointment on my body she has done it
to prepare me for burial. 13Truly, I say to you, wherever this gospel is preached in the
whole world, what she has done will be told in memory of her."

(2) Ambrose of Milan

The Lord Jesus came into the house of Simon the leper. You can see clearly what he has in mind. He does not avoid the leper. He does not shun him as someone contaminated, since he came to wipe away the ugly marks on the human body. The leper's house was at Bethany, a name interpreted to mean "House of Obedience." The region all around was called Bethany, and Simon's place formed part of that region. Don't you think that Bethany

1. The "bond" (Latin *chirographum*) literally means a handwritten document, though Leo probably has in mind Paul's description of Christ's action in Col 2:14: *erasing the record* [or "bond"] *that stood against us with its legal demands. He set this aside, nailing it to the cross* (NRSV).

stands for the world in which we are all detained to undergo a service of obedience; and the house of Simon the leper is the earth that forms part of the universe? The prince of this world is, in a manner of speaking, a kind of Simon the leper. The Lord Jesus, leaving the higher regions, came into this world and descended to earth. He was not in this world, but—with loving obedience on his part—he was sent into this world. He says it himself: *Since you have sent me into this world* (John 6:57).

This woman learned that Christ had come, and she entered into Simon's house. For this woman could never have been cured unless Christ had come on earth. And, if she entered into Simon's house, is she not perhaps a sign or figure of a very elevated soul, or of the Church itself—which has descended on earth to draw people about her by the sweetness of her perfume?

So Matthew writes that this woman who entered pours perfume on Christ's head. Perhaps it is for that reason that he did not like to call her a sinner. Luke, on the other hand, calls her a sinner and says that she poured her perfume on the *feet* of Jesus. Possibly they are not speaking of the same woman, in which case it cannot be said that the evangelists seem to contradict each other. Or again, it may be that it has to do with the sequence of events and the woman's spiritual growth. In the first instance, the woman is still a sinner; in the other, she has attained a higher degree of perfection.

Although the Church, or the soul, does not change personality, it changes in that it makes progress. Take, for instance, a soul that approaches God with faith. Free from shameful and frightful sins, she serves the Word of God with utmost devotion. Her chastity is without stain. You can surely see that such a soul ascends to the very head of Christ—*And Christ's head is God* (1 Cor 11:3). There she pours out the fragrance of her merits, for *we are Christ's incense to God* (2 Cor 2:15). God is indeed honored by good people whose life breathes out a most delicious fragrance.

If you understand things in this way, you will see how truly happy this woman is. Her fame will never be forgotten, because: **Wherever this gospel is preached** her story will be told. Never shall her memory be forgotten, for she poured over Christ's head the aroma of good morals and the perfume of honest deeds.

Still, the apostles do not yet understand God's plan, because he has hidden it within himself from all eternity (cf. Eph 3:9). For, *who has known the mind of God?* (Rom 11:34). The disciples grumbled because this woman had poured perfume over his head, and they complained: **Why this waste? The perfume could have been sold for a good price, and the money given to the poor.** To understand our Lord's displeasure, you have to be able to recognize the mystery. After all, it is only men of luxury who use perfume—in fact men do not usually use it—and even those who do use it generally rub it on. They do not pour it out. Why then is our Lord seriously displeased when the disciples object, **This could have been sold for a good price, and the money given to the poor**? In fact, Jesus himself had earlier said: **Whatever you did to one of these little ones, you did it to me** (25:40). But he was offering himself for these poor, these little ones.

Understand that you have to delve beneath the surface of the text when he says: **In pouring this ointment upon my body, she has done it for my burial** (26:12). So it was not the perfume that Jesus cared about, but her love. He welcomed her faith and approved her humility.

You too, if you want to gain favor, increase your love. Pour over the body of Jesus your faith in his resurrection. Pour the perfume of the Church, the fragrance of love of the community. In doing these things, you will be giving to the poor. That money will mean more if, instead of giving of your plenty, you pour out in the name of Christ and give to the poor as you would an offering to Christ—money that might have been very useful to you. So do not take, in a literal sense only, this perfume poured on his head—for *the letter kills*. Take it in the spiritual sense, for *the Spirit gives life* (2 Cor 3:6).

(3) Hilary of Poitiers

This woman is a symbol of the pagan peoples who offered glory to God in the passion of Christ. She anointed his head—for the head of Christ is God (1 Cor 11:3). The perfume is the fruit of good works. For the purpose of caring for the body is especially pleasing to the feminine sex. In honor and praise of God, she lavished meticulous care upon his body and the full affection of a devoted heart. But the disciples, as often is the case, are concerned for the salvation of Israel; this perfume should have been sold and used for the poor. Yet this woman was not going to sell this perfume, whereas the term **poor**, according to prophetic inspiration, signifies those lacking faith (cf. Pss 68:6; 109:22; Rev 3:17). The faith of the pagans had to be purchased by the salvation of the poor.

The Lord said to the disciples that there are many opportunities when they may care for the poor, but that salvation can be extended to the pagans only by his command; they have been buried together with him (Rom 6:5) through the pouring out of this woman's perfume. Regeneration is not accorded until we die together with him in the profession of faith at baptism (Rom 6:4; Col 2:12).

(4) Leontius of Constantinople

Did you see the woman's act? Every tongue is too paltry to praise her. She surpassed Abraham: Abraham washed the Lord's feet (Gen 18:3–4);[2] she anointed the Lord's head.

The woman is incomparable: she touched the head of the Lord; she performed (the tasks of) a priest's rank; she imitated an altar; she filled the place of the cherubim; she emulated the powers above. If someone were to call her a spiritual dove, he would not be wrong. Truly she flew around in the heavens; truly she ran with the sun, using her hands like wings. The woman surpassed all people—not only women, but men too. And let none of the men present glower at a woman when he realizes that she is preferred above a man, for the gain is one, whether a woman or a man be lauded. The leaven is one, and the dough is one and the same. Blessed Paul is witness to this when he says: *The head cannot say to the feet, I have no need of you* (1 Cor 12:21). If, therefore, the head needs the feet, and the feet are in want of the head, the head needs a rib much more (cf. Gen 2:21), for being and sharing are one.

2. It was a commonplace in patristic exegesis to consider theophanies in the Old Testament as manifestations of the preincarnate Son.

Have you seen that the woman had the Lord as her advocate? She obtained a good lawyer. She fell silent, and the Lord pleaded her case before his disciples in these words: **Why do you trouble the woman?** She wasn't doing anything unsuitable; she depicts the Church in advance and discloses the resurrection in advance; she grieves the devil in advance; she observes the salvation of the world in advance; she punishes Judas in advance; she makes the women rejoice in advance. **Why do you trouble the woman?** She knows what she has done; she has acknowledged the mystery before you acknowledged it. Judas is going to sell me, and she anoints me. You flee from my suffering, and she summons it. She knows what is expedient for humanity.

Matthew 26:14–16

[14]Then one of the twelve, who was called Judas Iscariot, went to the chief priests [15]and said, "What will you give me if I deliver him to you?" And they paid him thirty pieces of silver. [16]And from that moment he sought an opportunity to betray him.

(5) John Chrysostom

What awful folly! How covetousness finally blinded him! The man who had often seen Jesus moving about in their midst without being apprehended and giving proof of his divinity and power looked for an opportunity to lay hold of him. Even then, the Lord used words that were both frightening and persuasive to charm Judas in hopes that he would abandon his wicked intent. Not even at the supper, in fact, did the Lord not care for him; to the last day he kept talking of these things to him, but to no avail. The Lord did not give up trying.

Knowing this, let us not cease doing everything for those who are sinful and indifferent: teaching, exhorting, urging, encouraging, even if we get nowhere. Christ, you will remember, knew that the traitor was incorrigible, yet he did not cease using all his power, advising, threatening, bewailing—never blatantly or openly, but with subtlety. At the very moment of betrayal, he even allowed him to kiss him, though this did the fellow no good. Such is the great evil of covetousness: it made him both traitor and temple thief.

Listen up, all you who are covetous, who suffer from the malady of Judas; listen up, and ward off this passion. After all, if one who was familiar with Christ and who did wonders and heard his marvelous teaching yet descended to such depths because he had not rid himself of this ailment, how much more will you, who do not even pay heed to the Scriptures and who are always attached to things of the present, become an easy victim of this passion, unless you give it your full attention.

Matthew 26:17–19

[17]Now on the first day of Unleavened Bread the disciples came to Jesus, saying, "Where will you have us prepare for you to eat the passover?" [18]He said, "Go into the city to a

certain one, and say to him, 'The Teacher says, My time is at hand; I will keep the passover at your house with my disciples.'" [19]And the disciples did as Jesus had directed them, and they prepared the passover.

(6) Ambrose of Milan

It is important to note where the Lord keeps the Pasch. In Matthew we read: **Go into the city to a certain man**. Just consider his divine majesty as he speaks to his disciples: He knows in advance what is going to happen. Consider also his humility. He does not choose someone rich or powerful. No, he wants someone who is poor. He prefers the simple hospitality of the poor to the palatial houses of the nobility. **Go**, he says, **to a certain man**. Lord, you knew his name. You must have, since you knew he was at your service. You knew he was at your service, since you knew he was about to be present. But purposely you give him no name, just to show that he was someone unknown. Nothing here was prearranged. We are not told who the person is, all we are told is the business on hand.

Matthew 26:20–25

[20]When it was evening, he sat at table with the twelve disciples; [21]and as they were eating,
he said, "Truly, I say to you, one of you will betray me." [22]And they were very sorrow-
ful, and began to say to him one after another, "Is it I, Lord?" [23]He answered, "He who
has dipped his hand in the dish with me, will betray me. [24]The Son of man goes as it is
written of him, but woe to that man by whom the Son of man is betrayed! It would have
been better for that man if he had not been born." [25]Judas, who betrayed him, said, "Is
it I, Master?" He said to him, "You have said so."

(7) Caelius Sedulius

Then he celebrated the traditional Passover festival
By means of the sacred duties of the annual meal; he humbled himself,
Though he was the Master, and leaving his disciples a clear example
He got up and gladly served his servants; equipped
With a linen cloth he paid them every honor,
So much so that while voluntarily washing the feet of all disciples,
He did not even exclude Judas, although he knew he was planning
A wicked betrayal. But that honor, cruel traitor,
Did not allow you to remain with clean feet,
For you were polluted by your thoughts, like every tomb
On the outside covered with a coating of whitewash
While the inside is filled with filth and rotting corpses.

The Lord was well aware of his treachery and exposed
The one planning the future crime by handing him the bread—
He who was himself the bread that would be handed over. For then
The Lord blessed the two gifts of his own body and blood
As he distributed the food and drink that signifies that never
For eternity, will faithful and pure souls experience thirst and hunger.

(8) Leo the Great

But Jesus, sure of his own counsel and undaunted in carrying out his Father's plan, fulfilled the Old Testament and established a new Passover. For while **his disciples were reclining** with him **to eat** the mystical **supper**, Caiaphas's house plans were being laid how to kill him. Christ therefore ordained the sacrament of his body and blood and taught how the sacrifice should be offered to God. Nor was the traitor barred from this mystery to show that Christ was not provoked by any injury, although he had known before of his wicked intentions.

The traitor was the cause of his own ruin for himself and of his own faithlessness by following his leader, the devil; he did not wish to have Christ as his guide. When he said, **Truly I say unto you that one of you is about to betray me**, the Lord showed that the mind of his betrayer was known to him. He does not confound him with a harsh or open rebuke of his wickedness, but addresses him with a gentle and hidden admonition, so that penitence might correct him more easily than the disgrace of rejection.

(9) Leontius of Constantinople

You have just heard the evangelist saying: **When it was evening Jesus reclined at table with his twelve disciples.** What marvelous actions! What philanthropy of the Lord! And he made Judas recline with him. Shouldn't he have thrust the traitor away? He reclined with him. Why? So that Judas would not find a pretext for betraying him. Unless Jesus had made him recline with the rest of the disciples, Judas could have said: "I have been rejected, I have become an object of contempt, and because of that, I have gone on to sell the Lord." In order to remove any excuse on Judas's part, he made him also recline with the disciples. In this the Lord also revealed his prescience as God to all reclining with him, when he said to the disciples: **Truly, I say to you, one of you will betray me.**

Judas heard this. He should have fallen to his knees in supplication, confessed, and been repentant; he did none of this but approached the Lord as if the latter were ignorant, saying, as you have just heard: **Is it I, Rabbi?** The Lord replied to him: "If you are unaware, ask. If you don't know, inquire. If you don't dip your **hand in the dish**, test me. You are carrying my price, and you ask: **Is it I, Rabbi?** You're not comparing me with the prophet Elisha either? Elisha the prophet questioned his own servant Gehazi on his return from Naaman, when Gehazi had taken payment for the healing, and Gehazi, thinking that he could mislead the man, said to him: *Your servant did not go this way or that* (2 Kgs 5:25).

Showing him up, Elisha said: *Wasn't my heart with you when you went down to Naaman?* (2 Kgs 5:26). If Elisha's heart was not misled, will my divine knowledge[3] be wrong?"

Matthew 26:26–30

26 Now as they were eating, Jesus took bread, and blessed, and broke it, and gave it to the disciples and said, "Take, eat; this is my body." 27 And he took a cup, and when he had given thanks he gave it to them, saying, "Drink of it, all of you; 28 for this is my blood of the covenant, which is poured out for many for the forgiveness of sins. 29 I tell you I shall not drink again of this fruit of the vine until that day when I drink it new with you in my Father's kingdom."

30 And when they had sung a hymn, they went out to the Mount of Olives.

(10) John Chrysostom

By the sacrament of the Eucharist he reminds the disciples once more of his being slain, and during the meal he speaks of the cross, making it possible to grasp that he would suffer by repeating the prediction of his passion. **While they were eating, he took bread and broke it**. Why on earth did he perform this sacrament at the time of Passover? So they could learn from everything: both that he is the lawgiver of the old dispensation and that what is foreshadowed there refers to this moment. He was introducing the new reality in fulfillment of the type.

The evening was a sign of the fullness of time, and now events had reached their actual fulfillment. He also gives thanks in order to teach us how this sacrament should be celebrated, emphasizing that he does not go to the passion unwillingly, and thus gives us a lesson to bear with thanksgiving whatever we suffer which instills hope. For if the type of the Old Testament resulted in deliverance from such the heavy burden of slavery, how much more will the reality set the world free? It is for the benefit of our nature that he is delivered up. This surely is the reason why he did not institute the sacrament before this time when the provisions of the law had come to an end. The central feast comes to an end and is transferred to another and most awesome table, in the words, **Take, eat; this is my body, broken for many**.

(11) Augustine

Therefore receive and eat the body of Christ, yes, you that have become members of Christ in the body of Christ; receive and drink the blood of Christ. In order not to be scattered and separated, eat what binds you together; in order not to seem cheap in your own estimation, drink the price that was paid for you. Just as this [sacrament] turns into you when you eat

3. Lit., divinity.

and drink it, so you for your part turn into the body of Christ when you live devout and obedient lives. He himself, you see, as his passion drew near, while he was keeping the passover with his disciples, took bread and blessed it, and said, *This is my body that will be handed over for you* (1 Cor 11:24). Likewise he gave them the cup he had blessed and said, **This is my blood of the new covenant, which will be shed for many for the forgiveness of sins** (26:28).

You were able to read or to hear this in the Gospel before, but you were unaware that this Eucharist is the Son. But now, your hearts sprinkled with a pure conscience, and your bodies washed with pure water, *approach him and be enlightened, and your faces will not blush for shame* (Ps 34:5). Because if you receive this worthily, which means belonging to the new covenant by which you hope for an eternal inheritance, and if you keep the new commandment to love one another, then you have life in yourselves. You are then, after all, receiving that flesh about which Life itself says, *The bread that I shall give is my flesh for the life of the world*; and *unless people eat my flesh and drink my blood, they will not have life in themselves* (John 6:51, 53).

Matthew 26:31–35

**31Then Jesus said to them, "You will all fall away because of me this night; for it is writ-
ten, 'I will strike the shepherd, and the sheep of the flock will be scattered.' 32But after
I am raised up, I will go before you to Galilee." 33Peter declared to him, "Though they
all fall away because of you, I will never fall away." 34Jesus said to him, "Truly, I say to
you, this very night, before the cock crows, you will deny me three times." 35Peter said
to him, "Even if I must die with you, I will not deny you." And so said all the disciples.**

(12) John Chrysostom

From this passage we are taught an important doctrine, that people's good will is not enough if they are not in receipt of grace from on high, and correlatively that we profit nothing from grace from on high if good will is lacking. Both these truths Judas and Peter demonstrate: though one enjoyed much assistance, it did him no good, because he lacked good will and contributed nothing of his own; whereas the latter, though full of good will, came to grief because he received no assistance. Virtue, you see, is woven from these two things. Hence I urge you not to leave it all up to God and fall asleep, nor in a flurry of zeal to think you achieve the whole thing by your own efforts. In fact, God does not want us to be lethargic, hence he does not do everything himself; nor is he presumptuous; for that reason, he does not leave it all up to us. Instead, he removed the harmful element in each option and left to us the beneficial part. This is why he allowed even the chief apostle to fall, to render him less presumptuous and to prompt him to stronger love in the future; Scripture says, "The person to whom more is forgiven will love more" (cf. Luke 7:47). Let us therefore believe God in everything and offer no opposition, even if what is said seems to be at variance with our thoughts and senses. Rather, let his word carry greater authority than both thoughts and senses. Let this be true of us in respect also of the Eucharist, not just using our eyes in what lies before us, but holding also to his words: while his word is proof against deception, our senses are easily led astray, the former never failing, whereas the latter are generally wrong. Since the Word says, then, "This is my body," let us be convinced and believe, gazing upon it with the eyes of our mind.

(13) Augustine

Such is that Peter, a denier and lover; a denier out of human weakness, a lover by divine grace. When Peter made his denials, you see, he was being shown up to himself. He had, after all, been so cocksure, and had after a fashion given his own strength a puff with his proud boast, *Lord, I am with you to the death* (Luke 22:33), relying presumptuously on his own strength. And then, indeed, he heard who and what he really was. The sick man, you see, was so cocksure of himself, and the doctor was taking the pulse of his heart. He found him sick in his innermost self, and like a true and truthful doctor, he predicted what was going to happen, as though to say, "Yes, you think you're better. You don't realize the fever's still there, but it will reveal itself to you in no time. You will be dismayed when the crisis comes."

So when he was questioned by the serving maid, what the doctor had predicted, and not what the patient had self-confidently presumed, came true: that before the cock crowed, three times would such a fine servant deny his Lord. What's written in the Gospel after he has made his three denials? *The Lord looked round at him, and he wept bitterly* (Luke 22:61–62). He would never have wept if the Lord hadn't looked round. Finally, to help you understand in what sense it says *he looked round at him*, examine the Gospel, and notice that, when Peter denied him, the Lord was in a place where he couldn't look round at him with his bodily eyes; his case was being tried, you see, by the leaders of the Jews in the interior of the house, while Peter denied him in the courtyard. But where can he not look round to, the one who is everywhere?

(14) Juvencus

That evening, as soon as the twelve disciples sat down together,
Their Master spoke to them in these words of things to come.
"Now the time is almost upon us when one of you
is wickedly planning to hand Christ over to death."
At once they all asked him who would dare do such a thing.
Who was mad enough to conceive such a poisonous idea?
Then Christ replied, "He is now eating this meal with me.
But the Son of Man will undergo those sufferings for a short while,
As laid down long ago, while he who betrays the one who is just
Will be in torment forever. How much happier would he have been
If he had never experienced the light of life on earth!"

Then Judas, whose guilty conscience was causing him deep anguish,
Said, "Surely it is not Judas whom you suspect?"
The Lord replied, "It is you whom I see saying this."
When he had spoken thus he broke the bread with his hands,
And divided it up, solemnly blessed it and handed it around,
Telling his disciples that they were thereby eating his own body.
Then the Lord took the cup and filled it with wine,
Consecrated it with words of thanksgiving and handed round the drink,
Telling them that he was sharing out his own blood.
He said, "This blood has paid for the sins of the people.
Drink this—it is mine. For you must believe the truth of my words;
After this I will never again taste the juice of the vine
Until it is granted me through the gift of a better life
To rise again and drink new wines in my Father's kingdom."
Next, when they had sung a hymn in sacred harmony,
Together they all climbed up the Mount of Olives.
Then Christ poured out these words from his heart,
All of you, during this present night, will be driven by fear
To scatter far and wide, wretchedly deserting your leader.
For thus it is written: as a result of the shepherd's misfortune,
All the sheep will scatter across the fields in different directions.
Peter answered, "If we must believe you, everyone else
May have doubts and refuse to obey your commands,
But no danger will ever make me change my allegiance.
Then Christ replied, "This night that draws the light shining
Over the earth to be concealed, and now broods upon the waves,
Will hear how you, in fear, three times will tell a lie.
For all your courage, Peter, you will yet deny Christ
Before the rooftops echo with the crowing of the cock."

Matthew 26:36–41

36 Then Jesus went with them to a place called Gethsem'ane, and he said to his disciples,
"Sit here, while I go yonder and pray." 37 And taking with him Peter and the two sons
of Zeb'edee, he began to be sorrowful and troubled. 38 Then he said to them, "My soul
is very sorrowful, even to death; remain here, and watch with me." 39 And going a little
farther he fell on his face and prayed, "My Father, if it be possible, let this cup pass
from me; nevertheless, not as I will, but as thou wilt." 40 And he came to the disciples
and found them sleeping; and he said to Peter, "So, could you not watch with me one
hour? 41 Watch and pray that you may not enter into temptation; the spirit indeed is
willing, but the flesh is weak."

(15) Hilary of Poitiers

Some are of the opinion that his grief reached to his divinity and that fear of the approaching passion had broken him, because he said, **My soul is sorrowful unto death** and **Father, if it be possible, let this cup pass from me** and again, **the spirit is willing but the flesh is weak**, and yet again, **if this cannot pass unless I drink it, thy will be done.** They wish, because of the weakness of the flesh, to attach his grief to the Spirit, as though taking on of flesh with its feeble condition corrupted the power of his incorruptible substance. Eternity was engulfed in a fragile nature. If he is sorrowful to the point of fear, if weak to the point of pain, if anxious to the point of death, eternity will be subjected to corruption, and thus it will fall into corruption because of its many weaknesses. Eternity will become what it was not: sorrowful because of anguish, anxious because of fear, shocked because of grief, and eternity will be changed through fear. If it could in fact become something that it was not, it would not continue to be what it once was.

God, however, cannot be measured by time and always is; God is eternal. Eternity remains in its infinity . . . always complete, incorruptible, perfect. Apart from God nothing exists. Eternity is not bound to a particular place, but everything within it is capable of conferring upon us that which is its own, lacking nothing in itself that it has given.

Then the Lord said, **My soul is sorrowful unto death**. Did he say, "My soul is sorrowful because of death"? Certainly not. Had he been afraid of death, he would have addressed death itself, not his feelings. For it is one thing to fear something **unto death**, another to be afraid of the thing itself. The end does not produce the cause, because things turn out differently from the way in which they began.

The Lord had said earlier, **You will fall away this very night on account of me**. He knew that his disciples were going to be terrified and put to flight, and would deny him. Because blasphemy against the Spirit is not forgiven either in this world or in the one to come (cf. 12:31), the Lord was afraid that they would deny God once they observed him being killed, spat upon, and crucified. This is the reason that Peter, who was going to deny him, said: **I do not know the man**, since any word against the Son of Man will be forgiven. The Lord is, therefore, **sorrowful unto death**. It is not the fear of death but the moment of death that brings fear. Later on, the faith of believers will be confirmed by the power of resurrection.

He says, **if it be possible**, because flesh and blood shrink in terror from these things, and it is hard for human bodies not to be overwhelmed by their fears. When he says, **Not as I will, but as you will**, it means that he would rather they not suffer, lest they despair in suffering and lose faith but merit the glory of Christ's inheritance without the hardship of suffering. He did not ask that they not suffer; as he said, **Not as I will**, but what the Father wills, so that the strength of drinking the cup may pass from him to them. It was the will of the Father that the devil must be conquered, not only by Christ but also by his disciples.

(16) Ambrose of Milan

Father, if it is possible, take this chalice from me (Luke 22:42). Some people would like to twist the true sense of these words. They exploit this passage and the Lord's sadness, pretending that such sadness gives proof of innate weakness while, in fact, it was something assumed by the Lord for the time. For myself, not only do I see no need to make excuses on the matter, but it makes me admire all the more the tenderness and majesty of the Lord. His kindness to me would have been less had he not shared my sense of suffering.

It was for *me* that he was afflicted; as regards himself, there was no need for him to suffer affliction. But he put to one side his enjoyment of eternal divinity and let himself be attacked by the lassitude of my infirmity. He took on himself my sadness, my depression, so that he might lavish on me his own joy. In our footsteps he followed all the way down to the anguish of death. In this way, he chose that we should follow upward in his footsteps and be restored to life.

I am not ashamed to speak of his sadness, since I preach the cross. The point is that he did not take merely the appearance of incarnation, but the reality. That meant that he must also take suffering and thereby triumph over sadness. To escape it did not serve his purpose. How can one be praised for his courage if he has been anesthetized—so to speak—in order not to feel the pain of his wounds?

A man of sorrows and acquainted with sufferings (Isa 53:3), he wanted to be a lesson to us. Joseph had already taught us not to fear prison (cf. Gen 39:20); in Christ we learn how to overcome death. Better still, we learn how to overcome the anguish of eternal death. How could we imitate you, Lord Jesus, unless we followed you as man, unless we believed that you died, unless we saw your wounds? How could the disciples have believed that he was on the point of death, unless they had seen for themselves the agony of one who is about to die?

The disciples slept on, ignoring the grief of Christ—who suffered that grief for them. It is as we read in Scripture: *He has borne our sins and carried our infirmities* (Isa 53:4). So, Lord, you suffer. But it is my wounds, not yours, that cause you pain. You suffer, not because of your death but because of our infirmities. We looked on you as one who suffered, when all the time it was not for yourself that you suffered, but for me. You were wounded, but it was for our sins (cf. Isa 53:4). This state of being wounded was not something you received from your Father; it was something you assumed for my sake. It was good for me that *the chastisement that was to bring us peace lay on him; and that by his bruises we were healed* (Isa 53:5).

Is it so strange that he should suffer to save the world, when he wept for one single person? When, at the moment of raising Lazarus to life (cf. John 11:33–35), he shed tears? A sister's love moved him to tears, for those tears touched his human soul; and here he is stirred to action by the profound consideration that he, in his own flesh, was about to abolish sin. And so, the dreadful anguish of our soul would be dissolved by the bitter anguish of his own soul.

Perhaps, too, his sadness stems from the fact that, since Adam's fall, the only way we can get out of this world is through death. God did not make death, and he finds no joy in the death of the living (cf. Wis 1:13). For him, it is repugnant to have to undergo something that he did not create.

In the same way that as a man he was weak, so as a man he grieved, and we believe he was a man of sorrows (Isa 53:3). Because he was a conqueror over weakness for our sake, he was not conquered by weaknesses. He did not grieve for himself or suffer weakness on his own account, but because of our sins, he was bruised that we might be cleansed (Isa 53:5).

Who is the man with wounds, and *who knows how to bear our weakness* (Isa 53:3b LXX) unless it is because he had compassion on our wounds? But how would he know to bear our weakness if he were closed off to the experience of weakness? Since we bear the weight of this burden that we embraced, he therefore accepted our sins so that he may bear what he accepted for the purpose of removing them. Since it is written, *and he himself removed their sins. He will therefore possess many as his inheritance and will divide the spoils of the strong* (Isa 53:11b–12a) . . .

And so he said, *Will not my soul be subject to God?* (Ps 61:2 LXX). He said his soul was subject, not his divinity; it was his soul, not the power of God, that was subject (cf. 1 Cor 1:20). For the power of God in its strength cannot be subject; Christ makes use of his union and fellowship with this strength in his suffering. The human condition that is fragile and lesser is changed, not what cannot change. His precious human soul that suffers was joined with God in fellowship. It was subject to sadness insofar as he was human, for it is written, **My soul is sorrowful unto death**. He was subject to that which was assumed, not what was born from God the Father. But the subject is not only apparent in his weakness . . . it is more like carrying out a temporary plan than being sold into lifelong servitude. And that is why he says, *Will not my soul be subject to God?* (Ps 61:2 LXX)

(17) Leo the Great

After the Lord warned his disciples that they should strive against the power of present temptation by vigilant prayer, he says in supplication: **Father, if it is possible let this cup depart from me. But nevertheless, not as I will but as you will.** The first is a petition of weakness, the second of power. In the former, he willed from our resources; in the latter, he chose from his own character.

For the Son, being equal to his Father, knew that all things are possible for God. He had descended to this world to undertake the cross apart from his own wishing,[4] so that he might endure this conflict of variant feelings since his judgment was disturbed in a certain measure. But in order that there might be a manifest difference between the nature assumed and the nature of the one assuming it, what was of man longed for the power of God, what was of God had regard for the human condition. Therefore, his lesser yielded to its superior.

Therefore, beloved, when the Son of God says, **Father, if it is possible, let this cup depart from me**, he uses the voice of our nature and pleads the case of human weakness and trepidation, so that in these things that he must suffer, his endurance would be strengthened and his fear driven away. At length, ceasing to ask even this, since his fear from our weakness was excused to a certain extent—though it is not expedient for us to abide in this fear—he changes to another mindset and says, **But nevertheless not as I will, but as you will**, and again, **If this cup cannot depart from me unless I drink of it, let your will be done.**

This cry of our head is salutary for the whole body. This cry has instructed all the faithful. It has kindled all the confessors and has crowned all the martyrs. For who of

4. That is, according to the will of his human nature.

this world could overcome hatred, who the whirlwind of temptations, who the terrors of persecutions, if Christ did not say in all and for all to the Father, **Let your will be done**? Therefore, let all the sons of the Church learn this saying, *You were redeemed at great cost* (cf. 1 Cor 6:20), *justified by his grace* (Rom 3:24). And when the adversity of some violent temptation presses upon them, let them use the stronghold of this most mighty conviction (cf. Heb 2:18). When once the quaking of fear has been overcome, they receive endurance for suffering (cf. 2 Cor 1:6).

(18) Maximus the Confessor

The Lord has by nature a human will, just as he has an essentially divine will. The Word himself shows clearly, when, in the course of the economy that took place for our sake, he humanly begged to be spared from death, saying, **Father, if it be possible, let the cup pass from me**, in order to manifest the weakness of his own flesh. So, his flesh was acknowledged by those who saw him not to be a phantom deceiving the senses, but he was in truth and properly a human being. To this his natural will bears witness in his plea to be spared from the death that took place in accordance with the economy. And again, that the human will is wholly deified—in its agreement with the divine will itself, the former is eternally moved and shaped by the latter, and in accordance with it—is clear when he shows that all that matters is a perfect verification of the will of the Father, in his saying as a human being, **Not mine, but your will be done.** In this way, he provides himself as a type and example of setting aside our own will by the perfect fulfillment of the divine, even when we find ourselves face to face with death. For unless he became a human being by nature, and possessed a natural human will, and submitted this in accordance with the economy and constrained it to union with the Father's will, and said to the Father himself, **Not my will be done, but yours**, then clearly he said this as God by nature, and this would show that he did not possess a will identical with and equal to that of the Father, but another one, different by nature. When he submits, he is asking to become only the Father's.

Again it appears that as God, being also a human being in essence, he wills to fulfill the economy of the Father and work the salvation of us all. It is made clear then that as man, being by nature God, he acts humanly, willingly accepting the experience of suffering for our sake. And it is again made clear that as God, who is human by nature, he acts divinely and naturally exhibits the evidence of his divinity. From which the same one is recognized as being at the same time God and man by the natures, out of which and in which he exists, possessing naturally the same number of wills and the same number of energies,[5] for the confirmation of the perfect existence of those [natures with their natural properties] that he properly is.

It does not seem that Christ is naked God, or again a mere human being—neither God acting in his own nature without the body, nor a human being doing in his own nature whatever he thinks—but God enfleshed and for our sake perfectly incarnate, the same acting at once divinely and humanly . . . he makes haste to associate with himself the holy flesh

5. Or "powers."

as a coworker. God, with his almighty command, gives life by the touch of his holy flesh, hypostatically united to himself. It is to this flesh that properly belong touch, voice, and the rest, which has the ability to give life through its essential energy. Then, as he showed that the natural energies[6] of Christ the God, who is composed of both, are perfectly preserved, that of his Godhead through the almighty command, and that of his humanity through the touch, he proves them to be thoroughly united by their mutual coming together and interpenetration, showing that the energy is one through the union of the Word himself to his holy flesh, and not naturally or hypostatically. For the teacher did not say any such thing. But kinship exists through the parts, through them, as he said, in accordance with his almighty command and the touch of his hand.

Matthew 26:42–46

**42Again, for the second time, he went away and prayed, "My Father, if this cannot pass
unless I drink it, thy will be done." 43And again he came and found them sleeping, for
their eyes were heavy. 44So, leaving them again, he went away and prayed for the third
time, saying the same words. 45Then he came to the disciples and said to them, "Are you
still sleeping and taking your rest? Behold, the hour is at hand, and the Son of man is
betrayed into the hands of sinners. 46Rise, let us be going; see, my betrayer is at hand."**

(19) John Chrysostom

He makes the remark to them all by accusing them of weakness. Having wished to die with him, they could not stay awake at that time to share his agony; sleep got the better of them. He, however, is praying fervently lest it all seem to be an act on his part. His sweat likewise flows for the same reason: that the heretics cannot claim even here that he is pretending to be in agony.[7] This is the reason for sweating drops of blood: an angel appeared for the purpose of strengthening him (4:11), along with countless other signs of dread, lest anyone claim the words are a pretense.

This is the purpose for his prayer: on the one hand, by saying, **If it be possible, let it pass**, he brings out the humanity, whereas by saying, **But not as I will**, he makes clear his power (lit., virtue) and sound values, instructing us to follow God even when nature resists. Since, you see, the ignorant would not be convinced if he only showed his face, he went on to provide words as well. Likewise, words alone did not suffice, since actions also were required. He associated these with the words so that extremely contentious people might also believe that he became man and died. After all, if there is disbelief, even when these steps were taken, how much more disbelief would there be if they had not been taken? Do you see how many methods he uses to bring out the reality of the incarnation?

6. That is, the interpenetration of the divine power and human power in one incarnate Christ.

7. Chrysostom is likely referring to Marcionites, who denied the reality of Christ's humanity. Marcionite churches continued to be a viable threat in the east throughout the fourth and fifth centuries.

(20) Augustine

Pick up your cross and follow the Lord. He too, your savior, though God in the flesh, though God with flesh, still gave you a demonstration of purely human feelings, when he said, **Father, if it is possible, let this cup pass from me** (26:39). He knew that this cup could not pass from him, that it had come in him in order to be drunk. That cup was to be drunk willingly, not out of necessity. He was almighty; if he wished, it would most certainly pass from him, because he was God with the Father, and he and God the Father were one God. But in the form of a servant, in the form he took from you for you, he uttered those words in the voice of a man with the voice of the flesh. He stooped to transposing you into himself, so that you in him might utter words of weakness, so that you in him might take a grip on decisive strength. He showed you the will through which you could be tempted; and straightaway he taught you which will you should prefer to which. **Father**, he said, **if it can be so, let this cup pass from me**. This is a human wish; I am wearing a man, I am speaking from the form of a servant. **Father, if it can be so, let this cup pass**. It's the voice of the flesh, not of the spirit, the voice of infirmity, not of divinity. **If it can be so, let this cup pass**.

This is the wish about which Peter is told, *But when you get old, another will gird you, and take you away, and bring you where you do not wish* (John 21:18). So how did the martyrs likewise overcome? They put the wishes of the spirit before the wishes of the flesh. They loved this life, and they weighed it up and played it down. From it they considered how much eternal life should be loved, if this perishable life is loved like that. The man about to die doesn't want to die; and yet he will of necessity be dying some time, even though he is reluctant to die immediately. You can do nothing by just not wanting to die, achieve nothing, extort nothing, you have no power or authority to eliminate the necessity of death. It will come: what you are afraid of, even though you don't want it; it will present itself: what you are putting off, even though you refuse it. Yes, you can take steps to put death off; you can't take any to eliminate it. So if such efforts are made by the lovers of this life to delay death, how great the pains that should be taken to eliminate it! Certainly, you don't want to die. Change your kind of love, and you will be shown, not a death that will present itself to you against your will, but a death that will, if you so will, absent itself altogether.

Matthew 26:47–50a

**47 While he was still speaking, Judas came, one of the twelve, and with him a great crowd
with swords and clubs, from the chief priests and the elders of the people. 48 Now the
betrayer had given them a sign, saying, "The one I shall kiss is the man; seize him."
49 And he came up to Jesus at once and said, "Hail, Master!" And he kissed him. 50 Jesus
said to him, "Friend, why are you here?"**

(21) Ambrose of Milan

Here we have a fine manifestation of the divine power and a great lesson in virtue. The traitor is unmasked, but our Lord is still sweet and ready to forgive. Lord, you have made manifest his secret, and at the same time, you have revealed who has been betrayed. You have shown this in saying: **Son of Man**. For it is in the flesh, not in the divinity, that Christ is to be arrested. Yet, what a terrible reproach for the ungrateful Judas to be told he has betrayed one who, though Son of God, had out of love for us been willing to be Son of Man!

It is as if our Lord is saying: "It is for you, ungrateful one, that I took upon myself the flesh that you betray." What hypocrisy on the part of Judas! In my opinion, we must read Christ's words as though they were a challenge; as though, with tender love, he was reproaching the traitor: *Judas, is it with a kiss that you betray the Son of Man?* (Luke 22:48). To put it in other words, Jesus is saying: "Is it by the pledge of love that you inflict this wound? Is it by a mark of affection that you spill my blood? Is it by the sign of peace that you do me to death? Is it by a kiss that you, a servant, betray your Lord; that you, a disciple, betray your Master; that you, a chosen one, betray your Creator?" How truly it is said: *Better the wounds given by a friend than the calculating kisses of an enemy* (Prov 27:6). So much for the traitor; but for the person of peace we have: *Let him kiss me with the kisses of his mouth* (Song 1:2).

Then Jesus kisses him, though not in order to teach us dissimulation, but to show that he does not fly from the traitor's embrace. At the same time, by accepting the traitor's kisses, he heaps upon him reproaches. For it is written: *With the enemies of peace, I was peaceful* (Ps 120:7).

(22) Leo the Great

You, Judas, whom penitence did not call back to the Lord, proved to be more wicked and more unhappy than anyone. Despair dragged you to the noose. If you had awaited the consummation of your crime until the blood of Christ was shed for all sinners, you would have postponed your hideous death by hanging. When so many miracles and so many gifts of the Lord turned your conscience, those mysteries at least would have recalled you from your headlong fall, those same mysteries that you had received at the Passover meal when already your faithlessness was revealed by a sign of divine knowledge.

Why are you distrustful of his goodness, who did not reject you from the communion of his body and blood, who did not deny to you your kiss of peace when you came to arrest him with a crowd and a cohort of armed men? But you are an unchangeable man, *a wind that wanders and comes not again* (Ps 78:39), and you followed the madness of your own heart. And *since the devil stands at your right hand* (Ps 109:6), you have returned upon your own head the iniquity that you marshaled against the head of all the saints. Because your crime has exceeded the entire measure of revenge, your wickedness considers you as a judge, your punishment is extended to you as executioner.

Matthew 26:50b–56

Then they came up and laid hands on Jesus and seized him. 51And behold, one of those who were with Jesus stretched out his hand and drew his sword, and struck the slave of the high priest, and cut off his ear. 52Then Jesus said to him, "Put your sword back into its place; for all who take the sword will perish by the sword. 53Do you think that I cannot appeal to my Father, and he will at once send me more than twelve legions of angels? 54But how then should the scriptures be fulfilled, that it must be so?" 55At that hour Jesus said to the crowds, "Have you come out as against a robber, with swords and clubs to capture me? Day after day I sat in the temple teaching, and you did not seize me. 56But all this has taken place, that the scriptures of the prophets might be fulfilled." Then all the disciples forsook him and fled.

(23) Ambrose of Milan

We have seen that Peter cuts off the ear. Why Peter? Because he was given the keys of the kingdom of heaven. He condemns, and he absolves, because he has received the power to bind and to set free. He cuts the ear off the servant who knew not how to listen; and with his spiritual sword he cuts off the inner ear of those who willfully misunderstand.

Let no one cut off your ear. Be on your guard. We read the passion of the Lord, but if we apply to his divinity the infirmity and suffering of his physical body, our ear is cut off. It is cut off by Peter, who does not stand for people making out that Christ is but a prophet. No, no. Peter has taught us, by his proclamation of faith, that Christ is Son of God (cf. 16:16). So when we read that Christ was arrested, let us beware of believing those who would tell us that as God he was arrested, arrested in spite of himself, arrested because he was powerless. True, in his physical body he was apprehended and tied up—we have John's witness for this (cf. John 18:12). But woe to those who would fetter the Word! We tie up Christ in chains when we see him as being merely a man. We bind him up when we do not believe that he knew all things in advance, or when we do not recognize that he is all-powerful. But these chains used by the Jews are poor chains. They do not tie up Christ; on the contrary they bind fast those who use them. Now, Christ is not chained up in the house of some good, devout person, but in the house of Caiaphas (cf. Matt 26:57). That is to say, in a wicked house. That was the very house where it was prophesied that he should die for all (cf. Matt 26:57; John 18:24). People must be mad to recognize the good that Christ does, and yet they persecute the very author of those good deeds!

So they lose their ear, because they have lost the purpose of their ear. There are many who think they have an ear, but have none. In the Church, all have an ear; outside the Church, they do not have an ear. Perhaps, too, Peter cut off the ear to prevent them sinning still more by hearing what they were incapable of carrying out in practice. It reminds me of what the Lord did long ago. He confounded the tongues of those who were building the tower (cf. Gen 11:7), to prevent them from understanding each other and from bringing to a conclusion their impious work.

(24) John Chrysostom

See all the things he does that are capable of bringing them to their senses? He sent them sprawling, he healed the servant's ear, he threatened them with a violent death: **Those who draw a sword will perish by a sword.** By his healing of the ear he gave credence also to this fact; by every action, from the present to the future, he displayed his power, showing that getting the better of him was not in their power. . . . Working these things was, in fact, more marvelous than coming down from the cross. If they thought he was responsible for it, they should have believed and been afraid, if not of him, but the Father; they should also have felt compunction at the darkness (27:45) coming due to his wrath at their crimes. Clearly it was not an eclipse but anger and displeasure, not just for this reason but also for reason of the duration, lasting three hours, whereas an eclipse is over in a flash, as eyewitnesses know, since one happened in our generation as well. How is it, you ask, that they were not all amazed and did not believe him to be God? Because the human race at that time was caught up in deep indifference and vice.

In order to avoid sounding as though he is boasting, he does not bring up the miracles and speaks only about teaching. "While I was teaching you, you did not capture me. Yet you attacked me only as soon as I stopped talking. No one restrained me when I was in the temple. How come you show up to get me now, armed with daggers and clubs, so suddenly and untimely, even in the middle of the night? What need is there for these arms against the one who was there with you all this time?"

By these words, Jesus makes it clear that they would have never been able to take hold of him, unless he had given himself up willingly. Just as their earlier attempts to arrest Christ had failed when he was still in their hands, just as they were never able to catch him when he walking in their midst, their present attempts of overpowering him would not have been any more successful, had he not willed so. He even further clarified the misunderstanding about why now he himself willed to be arrested: **All this has taken place so that the Scriptures of the prophets might be fulfilled.**

(25) Cyril of Alexandria

Does Christ ask the Jewish leaders why they did not prepare the trap of death for him at an earlier point? He does not indicate this directly but observes that he restrained them from seizing him, despite the fact that he taught daily in the temple, because he was the one who controlled the proper time of his suffering. Christ, therefore, does not impute these charges to the Jews, and neither does he reprove their slowness in seizing him although he had been present and already among them. Little does he engage in this debate since the task of the Lord's seizure and arrest is a work beyond his opponents' strength. What was not possible for them is possible for the work of his will, the one who accepted the involuntary suffering of the incarnation, carrying out the will of God in this way. Even though it was not good to suffer, he was about to restore the things that happened to human nature since their beginning. His seizure, therefore, was the work of his consent.

Matthew 26:57–68

**[57]Then those who had seized Jesus led him to Ca'iaphas the high priest, where the
scribes and the elders had gathered. [58]But Peter followed him at a distance, as far as
the courtyard of the high priest, and going inside he sat with the guards to see the end.
[59]Now the chief priests and the whole council sought false testimony against Jesus that
they might put him to death, [60]but they found none, though many false witnesses came
forward. At last two came forward [61]and said, "This fellow said, 'I am able to destroy
the temple of God, and to build it in three days.'" [62]And the high priest stood up and
said, "Have you no answer to make? What is it that these men testify against you?"
[63]But Jesus was silent. And the high priest said to him, "I adjure you by the living God,
tell us if you are the Christ, the Son of God." [64]Jesus said to him, "You have said so. But
I tell you, hereafter you will see the Son of man seated at the right hand of Power, and
coming on the clouds of heaven." [65]Then the high priest tore his robes, and said, "He has
uttered blasphemy. Why do we still need witnesses? You have now heard his blasphemy.
[66]What is your judgment?" They answered, "He deserves death." [67]Then they spat in
his face, and struck him; and some slapped him, [68]saying, "Prophesy to us, you Christ!
Who is it that struck you?"**

(26) Hilary of Poitiers

The rest of the events follow a pattern: false witnesses were procured, and the priest was ignorant of the very law about which he boasted. He wished confirmation with an oath that he was the Christ as testified by the law and the prophets, as though they spoke covertly of him. In fact, the priest himself confessed Christ unwillingly when the Lord said to him, **You have said it.** As soon as he heard of his majesty, the priest tore his own clothes; that is, he tore the veil that covered the law (cf. 27:51). With fists and spitting, every kind of insult was inflicted on Christ in order to consummate the debasement of his humanity.

(27) John Chrysostom

Why did they do these things while they were putting him to death? What was the need of this mockery? So that you should learn of their deranged spirit, and that having taken him like a prey, they thus showed their intoxication and gave full measure to their madness—making this a festival, and assaulting him with pleasure, and showing forth their murderous disposition.

What could equal this great arrogance? When it beheld the Lord's face, the sea gave reverence (8:26), and when the sun contemplated it upon the cross, the shining rays turned away (27:45). Yet the soldiers and people spit and struck his face with the palms of their hands, and some upon the head, giving full swing in every way to their own madness. For indeed they inflicted the blows that are most insulting of all, buffeting, smiting with the palms of their hands, and to these blows adding the insult of spitting at him. They spoke words teeming with great derision, saying, **prophesy unto us, thou Christ, which of us hit you?** The reason was that the crowd called him a prophet.

Let us always read about these things, let us rightly remember them, let us write these things on our minds, because they bring honor to us. In these things I take a pride, not only in the thousands of dead that he raised, but also in the sufferings that he endured. These things Paul puts forward in every way, the cross, the death, the sufferings, the abuses, the insults, the scorn: *let us go forth unto him bearing his reproach* (Heb 13:13) and now, *who for the joy that was set before him endured the cross, despising the shame* (Heb 12:2).

Matthew 26:69–75

69Now Peter was sitting outside in the courtyard. And a maid came up to him, and
said, "You also were with Jesus the Galilean." 70But he denied it before them all, say-
ing, "I do not know what you mean." 71And when he went out to the porch, another
maid saw him, and she said to the bystanders, "This man was with Jesus of Nazareth."
72And again he denied it with an oath, "I do not know the man." 73After a little while
the bystanders came up and said to Peter, "Certainly you are also one of them, for your
accent betrays you." 74Then he began to invoke a curse on himself and to swear, "I do
not know the man." And immediately the cock crowed. 75And Peter remembered the
saying of Jesus, "Before the cock crows, you will deny me three times." And he went
out and wept bitterly.

(28) Hilary of Poitiers

We must carefully consider in what context Peter made his denial. . . . At first, he says that he did not understand what she, the servant, was saying. Then he denied that he belonged to Jesus's followers (cf. Mark 14:69–70). And the third time, he declared he did not know the man. It is true that Peter denied the Lord, though this was not sacrilege because he had been the first to recognize him as the Son of God (16:16). Nevertheless, he had doubts because of the weakness of his flesh and wept bitterly. Knowing that he had already been warned, Peter could not evade the weight of his guilt.

(29) Ambrose of Milan

It is true that Peter denied Jesus, because the Lord himself said: **You will deny me three times** (26:34) . . . What did he deny? He denied the promise that he had imprudently given. At the time he made it, he was thinking of his devotion to the Lord but was forgetting his own human condition. Peter was punished for saying that he would lay down his life, a thing that is beyond the power of human weakness. Only the Lord has power to do this. But if Peter had to pay so dearly for a thoughtless word, what will be the punishment of those who refuse to believe!

(30) Leo the Great

When the Son of God offered himself to receive judgment for our iniquity, the blessed Apostle Peter, whose faith was burning with such devotion that he was prepared to suffer and die with the Lord, was terrified by the accusing maidservant of the priest and because of his weakness denied him. . . .

Happy are your tears, holy apostle, which had the power of holy baptism for washing off the sin of denial. For the right hand of the Lord Jesus Christ was present, which took hold of you as you were slipping before you could fall and brought back strength so that you could stand in the very peril of falling. The Lord saw in you not that your faith had been conquered, not that your love had been turned away, but that your constancy had been shaken. When affection has not failed, tears abound and the spring of charity washes away the words of fear. Nor is the remedy of amnesty hindered when there is no judgment of the will. Therefore, the Rock quickly returned to its own solidity, receiving a strength so great that what he then had feared during the passion of Christ he later did not fear in his own suffering.

(31) John Chrysostom

From this passage learn an important doctrine, that people's good will is not enough if they are not in receipt of grace from on high, and correlatively, that we profit nothing from grace on high if a good will is lacking. Both these truths Judas and Peter demonstrate: though one enjoyed much assistance, it did him no good because he lacked good will and contributed nothing of his own, whereas the latter, though full of good will, came to grief because he received no assistance. Virtue, you see, is woven from these two things. Hence I urge you not to leave it all up to God and fall asleep, nor in a flurry of zeal to think you achieve everything by your own efforts. God does not want us to be lethargic, leaving everything to him; nor does he want us to be presumptuous, depending solely on ourselves. Instead, he removed what is harmful in either possibility, leaving to us what helps us. That is why he allowed even the chief apostle to fall, so that he would be less presumptuous and to encourage him to love more fully in the future. Scripture says, *The person to whom more is forgiven will love more* (cf. Luke 7:47).

Matthew 27

Having seen Jesus sentenced to death and taken to Pontius Pilate (27:1–2), a remorseful Judas tries to return thirty silver coins to the chief priests. Left to deal with it on his own, Judas hanged himself (27:3–5). Ancient commentators are unanimous in their judgment of Judas's deeds and suicide. Leo the Great does not hesitate to associate Judas with the adversary in Ps 109:6 [108:6 LXX], a figure sometimes identified as the devil himself. As Leo describes him, Judas had had his fair chance but deprived himself of it by diving into his "headlong fall."

Ambrose comments that, when questioned by Pilate, the Lord remained silent and willingly suspended his power because he did not need to defend himself, for his cause was right. "He, the salvation of all, sacrifices his own safety so that he might win the salvation of all" (vv. 11–13).

Following a common custom to release a prisoner on a holiday, Pilate asked the crowds whom he should release (v. 15). Leo the Great observes that this inquiry betrays Pilate's cowardice, his inward assurance of Christ's innocence, and lack of "constancy in his own opinion." The crowds demanded Christ to be crucified and Barabbas, a notorious prisoner, *to be released. Pilate washed his hands, but this gesture purged neither the blood of a just man (v. 24) from the governor's hands nor his "polluted spirit" and "impious intention." Augustine points out that among the Jews who shouted,* His blood be on us and on our children! *(v. 25), there were future believers intended to be cleansed by this blood "in mercy," as well as unbelievers who were "to be destroyed [by this blood], in justice." Augustine further explains that God "didn't choose good people, but people he wished to make good," by healing the inborn: the Adamic infection of some of those who are "all in the shadow of death . . . bundled together in the lump of sin."*

Hilary of Poitiers ponders the significance of the scarlet robe in which Jesus was redressed: "by assuming all the weaknesses of our body, the Lord was being steeped in the scarlet-colored blood of all the martyrs who will follow." This Latin exegete associates the thorns "from which the crown of Christ's victory is woven" with the sins of those who pierced him, so that glory would be derived from "pernicious and worthless things that encircled the head of God" (vv. 27–31). John Chrysostom underscores the liturgical function of these passages relating Jesus's beating and mockery: "at the great vigil on Easter eve, this whole account is read aloud" so that "even if you were made of stone, you would become softer than any wax and expel all haughtiness from your soul."

The Matthean Gospel portrays Simon from Cyrene carrying the cross of Christ on the way to Golgotha (v. 32). Aware of a different account in the Gospel of John where Christ carries the cross himself (John 19:17), Ambrose resolves the discrepancy christologically, seeing in it a glimpse of the mystery of the divine humanity of Christ. Christ the man carries the cross, yet his humanness is indwelled by his divinity in such a way that Christ the God can be said to have carried his cross himself. The cross thus becomes a trophy of a victor who then "passed it on to the martyrs for them to lift it up." Leo the Great sees the cross as a sign of "a future glory" of "the faith of the Gentiles." The transfer of the cross from the Lord to a stranger signifies the transfer of the "propitiation of the spotless lamb" to the uncircumcised, a replacement of the old sacrificial system with a new sacrifice that "would be placed upon a new altar, and the cross of Christ would be the altar not of the temple, but of the world" (Ambrose).

Reflecting on the theological significance of the cross, ancient writers underscore that Christ's death was freely chosen by him as an act of his will surrendered to the will of the Father. When tempted to save himself in light of his claims of divinity (vv. 39–44), Jesus "certainly was able to come down from the cross, but he did not because he wished to carry out the will of his Father" (Eusebius of Emesa). It would have been much easier "to come down from the cross" than "to make the dead rise after four days" (cf. John 11:17). Naming a number of pairs of mutually exclusive characteristics of the human-divine Christ, Gregory of Nazianzus says that, on the cross, "He was both sacrifice and high priest, the one who offered the sacrifice, yet God who received it." Leo the Great comments that Jesus's last cry, My God, my God, why have you forsaken me? *(v. 46), is "a teaching, not a grievance." It is the voice of the flesh in the fear of death, that is, the voice of those whom the divine Christ, inseparably united in one person to the human nature, was redeeming. He died willingly, not only by the will of the Father, but also his own: "not only did the Father abandon him, but also the Lord even deserted himself in a certain way, not by a timorous withdrawal, but by an intentional surrender," in his "eternal obedience to the Father for the reconciliation of the world" (2 Cor 5:19).*

The death of Jesus was accompanied with several phenomena that the ancients emphasize. "The elements were granted the right to look upon this face. . . . [A]s the light shone forth / At the time of the Lord's birth, so at his death it withdrew" (Caelius Sedulius). A sudden three-hour darkness (v. 45) is presented by Chrysostom as a fulfillment of an Old Testament figure: the three-day thick darkness that overtook Egypt (Exod 10:21–22) preceding the last plague, and the Passover is now fulfilled in the three-hour darkness eventually leading to Easter morning. Ambrose interprets the phenomena apocalyptically: "The Lord's passion gives us sure signs that things present will crumble away to make room for that which is to come." Rocks split (v. 51), pointing out that "in time to come the force of the Word would penetrate the hardest of hearts." The veil of the temple was torn because it could no longer conceal its mysteries, as "Truth was removing its types and the messages [formerly] announced until they became superfluous" (Leo the Great). The risen dead who appear in the holy city prefigure the eschatological resurrection of the dead and their dwelling in the heavenly Jerusalem (vv. 52–53). The natural course of things was subverted as "supernatural life killed death" (Ephrem of Nisibis). It is the God-Man Christ who suffers and dies: "even in the midst of these punishments his inviolable deity and his suffering nature preserved his own character as well as his unity" (Leo the Great). Having seen this, the centurion and his soldiers exclaimed, Truly this was the Son of God!

Having obtained Pilate's permission, Joseph, a rich man from Arimathea, wrapped Jesus in a clean linen cloth and buried him in a new tomb cut out in the rock (vv. 57–60). Following Pilate's order, the grave was secured with a seal and guards (vv. 62–66). "Since nothing except Christ ought to enter our hearts, a stone was rolled in front of the entrance" (Hilary of Poitiers).

Matthew 27:1–5

1When morning came, all the chief priests and the elders of the people took counsel against Jesus to put him to death; 2and they bound him and led him away and delivered him to Pilate the governor.

3When Judas, his betrayer, saw that he was condemned, he repented and brought back the thirty pieces of silver to the chief priests and the elders, 4saying, "I have sinned in betraying innocent blood." They said, "What is that to us? See to it yourself." 5And throwing down the pieces of silver in the temple, he departed; and he went and hanged himself.

(1) Leo the Great

Since he was the *son of perdition* (John 17:12) *at whose right hand stood the devil* (Ps 109:6), the traitor Judas could not reach this remission [of those who called for the crucifixion]. He passed into desperation before Christ fulfilled the mystery for general redemption. Because the Lord died for all the wicked, even Judas could have attained this strong cure, if he had not hastened to the noose. But because of his wicked heart, now given over to the plots of crime, now occupied with parricidal fellowship, he had never in any way adhered to the proofs of the Savior's mercy. Nor had he received the words of the Lord speaking to pious ears, *I have not come to call the just, but the sinners*, and *the Son of Man came to seek and to save what was lost* (Luke 5:32 and 19:10). Nor had he understood the mercy of Christ, who not only was healing bodily infirmities, but was even curing the wounds of the poor in spirit, speaking to the healed paralytic, *Stand firm, O son, for your sins have been forgiven you* (Mark 2:5), and to the adulteress presented to him, *Nor will I condemn you, go and sin no more* (John 8:11). He said these things so that he might show through all his works that he came by this arrival as the Savior of the world, not as its judge. Having been estranged from this understanding, the wicked traitor rose up against himself, not in the decision of one repenting, but in the fury of one perishing. As a result, he who sold the author of life to murderers, by dying was sinning for the increase of his own damnation.

Matthew 27:6–10

6But the chief priests, taking the pieces of silver, said, "It is not lawful to put them into the treasury, since they are blood money." 7So they took counsel, and bought with them the potter's field, to bury strangers in. 8Therefore that field has been called the Field of

Blood to this day. [9]Then was fulfilled what had been spoken by the prophet Jeremiah, saying, "And they took the thirty pieces of silver, the price of him on whom a price had been set by some of the sons of Israel, [10]and they gave them for the potter's field, as the Lord directed me."

(2) Ambrose of Milan

This money was the price of blood and is not put in the sacred treasury of the Jews. Instead, the potter's field was purchased with the pieces of silver for which Christ was sold. When this plot of land had been consecrated as a burial place for strangers, the prophetic oracle was clearly fulfilled, and the mystery of the Church that was coming into being was revealed.

The field, according to divine Scripture, is the whole world (cf. 13:38). The potter is he who fashioned us from clay. As you have read in the Old Testament, *God fashioned man from the slime of the earth* (cf. Gen 2:7). It was in his power to form us from earth and to reform us through grace. For even if we should fall because of our own vices, his mercy will nonetheless restore the breath of life to us and build us up again (cf. Jer 18:2).

The price of blood is the price of our Lord's passion. Christ bought the world at the cost of his own blood. He came so that *the world might be saved through him* (John 3:17), and so that the world might be his, both as its author and as its rightful Redeemer. He came to bring eternal happiness to those who, through baptism, would die and be buried with Christ (cf. Rom 6:4, 8; Col 2:12).

Matthew 27:11–14

[11]Now Jesus stood before the governor; and the governor asked him, "Are you the King of the Jews?" Jesus said, "You have said so." [12]But when he was accused by the chief priests and elders, he made no answer. [13]Then Pilate said to him, "Do you not hear how many things they testify against you?" [14]But he gave him no answer, not even to a single charge; so that the governor wondered greatly.

(3) Ambrose of Milan

This is a wonderful passage that pours into our hearts a disposition to bear with patience every insult that comes our way. The Lord is accused, and he is silent. He is right to be silent, for he has no need to defend himself. To defend oneself is all very well for people who are afraid of being defeated. His silence does not confirm their accusation; by not answering his accusers, he shows his contempt. Why should he fear, seeing that he does not wish to be saved? He, the salvation of all, sacrifices his own safety so that he might win the salvation of all.

But why do I speak of God's silence? Susannah was silent and won (cf. Dan 13:35; Sus

42–43); when the cause is just, there is no need of defense. In this case, too, Pilate dismisses [the Lord]. By his judgment he absolves; but because of the divine mystery, he crucifies. But this is the mystery of Christ. . . .

Herod wanted to meet Jesus, hoping to see some miracles. Jesus was silent (cf. Luke 23:8), and he worked no wonders. The cruel man standing before him did not deserve to see divine wonders. Moreover, the Lord did not want to flaunt his power. Perhaps Herod is a figure and emblem of all impious people; if they believe neither in the law nor in the prophets, they would not be able to see the marvelous miracles of Christ in the gospel.

Matthew 27:15–26

**15Now at the feast the governor was accustomed to release for the crowd any one pris-
oner whom they wanted. 16And they had then a notorious prisoner, called Barab'bas.
17So when they had gathered, Pilate said to them, "Whom do you want me to release
for you, Barab'bas or Jesus who is called Christ?" 18For he knew that it was out of envy
that they had delivered him up. 19Besides, while he was sitting on the judgment seat, his
wife sent word to him, "Have nothing to do with that righteous man, for I have suffered
much over him today in a dream." 20Now the chief priests and the elders persuaded
the people to ask for Barab'bas and destroy Jesus. 21The governor again said to them,
"Which of the two do you want me to release for you?" And they said, "Barab'bas." 22Pi-
late said to them, "Then what shall I do with Jesus who is called Christ?" They all said,
"Let him be crucified." 23And he said, "Why, what evil has he done?" But they shouted
all the more, "Let him be crucified."**

**24So when Pilate saw that he was gaining nothing, but rather that a riot was begin-
ning, he took water and washed his hands before the crowd, saying, "I am innocent of
this man's blood; see to it yourselves." 25And all the people answered, "His blood be on
us and on our children!" 26Then he released for them Barab'bas, and having scourged
Jesus, delivered him to be crucified.**

(4) Augustine

Some people saw the resurrection of the Lord; others did not believe it when told about it; and they were chided by the Lord, now present among them, because they had not believed those who saw it and brought them the news. What a stupendous favor done to the nations and to those born long afterward! What has God granted those who now fill the churches of Christ? The holy apostles had gone round with the Lord, heard the word of truth from his mouth, seen him raise the dead; and they didn't believe that the Lord had risen. We though, born long afterward, have never seen his bodily presence, never heard a word from the mouth of his flesh, never observed with these eyes any miracle performed by him; and yet we have come to believe, on hearing what was written by those who at the time refused to believe. They didn't believe a most recent event when news of it was brought them; they wrote something for us to read, we heard it, and we believe.

That the Lord Jesus, though, declined to appear to the Jews is because he did not judge them worthy to see the Lord Christ after the resurrection; he showed himself to his own people, not to strangers. And while his own people were preaching, strangers came to believe; and those who had been strangers became his own. I mean, many of those, as you can read in the Acts of the Apostles; many of those who crucified the Lord, who defiled themselves by shedding his blood; many of those who said, **His blood be upon us and upon our children** (27:25), later on came to believe the apostles bringing them the good news of the resurrection. His blood was indeed upon them, but it was to wash them, not to destroy them; it was upon some to destroy them, upon others to cleanse them; upon those to be destroyed, in justice; upon those to be cleansed, in mercy.

And now too, do all have faith? Just as at that time some of the Jews themselves believed, others did not, so too now with the nations; some have come to believe, others don't believe. *Not everyone has faith* (2 Thess 3:2). Those who do have faith, though, believe by God's grace; they mustn't pride themselves on it. It's a gift from God. Is the reason God chose us, do you suppose, that we were good? He didn't choose good people, but people he wished to make good. We were all in the shadow of death, we were all being held, bundled together in the lump of sin coming from Adam. With the root infected, what sort of fruit could be born of the tree of the human race? But the one who would heal the infection came without infection, and the one who came to clean up sins came without sin.

(5) Leo the Great

Therefore, allowing whatever the fury of the people was daring to bring upon him by the incitement of the priests, Christ is led to Annas, the father-in-law of Caiaphas, and then Annas passes him to Caiaphas himself (cf. John 18:13, 24). After the raving objections of slanderers, after the devised falsehoods of suborned witnesses, he is transferred by a delegation of priests to an audience with Pilate. These, having broken the divine law, were clamoring that they had no king except Caesar, as if they were devoted to the Roman laws. They would reserve the entire judgment for the power of the governor. They sought after an executor of their savagery rather than a judge for their case. For they were presenting Jesus, bound by harsh ropes, flayed by frequent buffets and blows (cf. Isa 53:4–5), besmeared with spit, and condemned already by their shouts, so that in the midst of so many preceding judgments, Pilate would not dare absolve one whom all wanted to perish. In fact, the inquiry itself informs that he neither found fault with the one accused nor held constancy in his own opinion. The judge condemns one whom he pronounces innocent, adding **the blood of a just man** to an unjust people (27:24). He had perceived in his own understanding and he had recognized in the dream **of his wife** (27:19) that he ought to have abstained from this judgment. **Hands that are washed** do not cleanse a polluted spirit (27:24), nor is this crime purged by the water on his cruel hands, since it was committed by his impious intention.

Matthew 27:27–31

[27]Then the soldiers of the governor took Jesus into the praetorium, and they gathered the whole battalion before him. [28]And they stripped him and put a scarlet robe upon him, [29]and plaiting a crown of thorns they put it on his head, and put a reed in his right hand. And kneeling before him they mocked him, saying, "Hail, King of the Jews!"
[30]And they spat upon him, and took the reed and struck him on the head. [31]And when they had mocked him, they stripped him of the robe, and put his own clothes on him, and led him away to crucify him.

(6) Hilary of Poitiers

After the Lord was beaten, a scarlet robe, a purple cloak[1] were put on him, and a crown of thorns. With a reed in his right hand, he was mocked as they knelt and worshiped him. It is clear that by assuming all the weaknesses of our body, the Lord was being steeped in the scarlet-colored blood of all the martyrs who will follow and to whom belongs the kingdom with him (cf. Rev 6:9; 7:13–17; 18:24). With honor worthy of the prophets and the patriarchs, the Lord is clothed in purple. He also is crowned with thorns, that is, the sins of the pagans who pierced him. In this way, glory could be derived from pernicious and worthless things that encircled the head of God. The points of the thorns are the sins from which the crown of Christ's victory is woven (cf. 1 Cor 15:54–55). By the reed held in his hand we understand the strengthening of the weakness and frailty of the same pagans.

(7) John Chrysostom

What could be worse than this? What is more abusive? What happened surpasses all telling. It is read out in our presence when everyone has assembled. In case pagans should claim, "That which is splendid and illustrious, like the signs and the miracles, you broadcast to the crowds and the nations, but what is shameful you conceal," the grace of the Spirit so ordered things that it be read on a public festival when men and women are present in great numbers. For when everyone is present at the great vigil on Easter eve, this whole account is read aloud. . . . When it is heard by everyone, Christ is professed as God; for besides the other reasons he is worshiped, here we learn that for our sake he suffered these things and instructs us in every virtue. Let us always read them, then, for their value is great, and we receive much benefit from them. When you see him jeered in words and in deeds, the knee bent in mockery, abused, and subjected to extreme suffering, even if you were made of stone, you would become softer than any wax and expel all haughtiness from your soul.

1. Matt 27:28 (scarlet robe); Mark 15:17 (purple cloak).

Matthew 27:32–34

[32]As they went out, they came upon a man of Cyre'ne, Simon by name; this man they compelled to carry his cross. [33]And when they came to a place called Gol'gotha (which means the place of a skull), [34]they offered him wine to drink, mingled with gall; but when he tasted it, he would not drink it.

(8) Ambrose of Milan

It is time for the victor to erect his trophy: the cross. Christ's trophy is placed on his shoulders; whether it is he or Simon (cf. Luke 23:26) who carries it, Christ carried it as man, and man carried it in Christ. There is no disagreement between the evangelists, for in presenting the mystery, they are in total harmony.

All this is told in proper order: first he himself took up the trophy of the cross (cf. John 19:17), and then he passed it on to the martyrs for them to lift it up . . . for it is written: *Take up your cross and follow me* (Luke 9:23). It is our cross that Christ mounted, not his own. And he died not in his divinity but as man. This is why he says: **O God, look at me! Why have You forsaken me?** (27:46).

(9) Leo the Great

But when the crowds were going with Jesus to the place of his punishment, a certain Simon of Cyrene was found. The cross of punishment was transferred from the Lord to him, so that even by such a deed, the faith of the Gentiles would be signified beforehand to whom the cross of Christ was not a shame but a future glory. Consequently, it was not by chance, but a figured and mystical thing that the stranger ran to suffer for Christ while the Jews were raging against him. So the Apostle says, *If we suffer with him, we will also reign with him* (2 Tim 2:12). . . . For through this transfer, the propitiation of the spotless lamb and the fulfillment of all mysteries will pass over from the circumcision to the uncircumcised, from the sons of the flesh to the sons of the spirit. Just as the Apostle says, *Christ was sacrificed as our Passover [lamb]* (1 Cor 5:7), who offered himself to the Father as a new and true sacrifice of reconciliation (cf. Heb 2:17). He was crucified not in the temple, whose place of honor had now come to an end, nor within the walls of the city, fit to be cast down on account of the merit of its wickedness, but *outside beyond the camp* (Lev 17:3). This took place so that, with the mystery of the old victims ceasing, a new sacrifice would be placed upon a new altar, and the cross of Christ would be the altar not of the temple, but of the world.

Matthew 27:35–37

[35]And when they had crucified him, they divided his garments among them by casting lots; [36]then they sat down and kept watch over him there. [37]And over his head they put the charge against him, which read, "This is Jesus the King of the Jews."

(10) Caelius Sedulius

Then at once he was hung high on the spreading cross,
Transforming the anger of the crisis by means of loving devotion.
He himself was the peace of the cross, and illuminating the violent
Forces with his own limbs, he clothed the punishment with honor,
Giving a sign that it was not a punishment but salvation,
And sanctifying the tortures he suffered, he blessed them.
Everyone should know that the shape of the cross is to be revered,
For it bore our Lord in his triumph and by a powerful logic
It brings together the four corners of the world.
The radiant East shines forth from the Creator's head,
His holy feet are licked by the sun setting in the West,
His right hand holds the North, his left supports the center of the sky;
The whole of Nature lives from the Creator's limbs,
And Christ rules throughout the world, encompassed by the cross.
On it a heading also was inscribed: This is the King of the Jews,
So that nothing would lack divinity; for heaven arranged
That this was recorded in Hebrew, in Latin, and in Greek.
Thus the one faith teaches us to call on the one King three times.[2]

(11) Augustine

The leaders of the Jews urged Pilate not to write without qualification that he is the King of the Jews, but that he himself said he was the King of the Jews (John 19:21). [In his decision] Pilate was representing the wild olive to be grafted on in place of the broken branches (Rom 11:19–20), because he was a man from the nations, writing for the nations their confession of faith, so that the Lord himself rightly said about them, **The kingdom shall be taken away from you and given to a nation that does justice** (21:43). That does not mean, however, that he is not the King of the Jews. The root, after all, carries the wild olive, not the wild olive the root. And although those branches were broken off for unbelief, that does not mean that God has repudiated his people, whom he foreknew; *I too*, he says, *am an Israelite* (Rom 11:1). And although the sons of the kingdom, who did not wish the Son of God to reign over them, go off into the outer darkness; all the same, many shall come from east

2. An allusion to the Trinity.

and west and sit down, not with Plato and Cicero, but *with Abraham and Isaac and Jacob in the kingdom of heaven* (8:11–12).

Pilate, certainly, wrote **King of the Jews**, not "King of the Greeks or the Latins," even though the Lord is going to reign over the nations. And what he has written he has written, and he didn't change it at the urging of unbelievers. He had been told not to do this a very long time before in the Psalms: *Do not corrupt the inscription of the title.*[3] All the nations believe in the King of the Jews, he reigns over all the nations, but he is still the King of the Jews. Such was the worth and potency of that root, that it could change the engrafted wild olive into itself, while the wild olive could not eliminate the name of the olive.

Matthew 27:38–44

38Then two robbers were crucified with him, one on the right and one on the left. 39And those who passed by derided him, wagging their heads 40and saying, "You who would destroy the temple and build it in three days, save yourself! If you are the Son of God, come down from the cross." 41So also the chief priests, with the scribes and elders, mocked him, saying, 42"He saved others; he cannot save himself. He is the King of Israel; let him come down now from the cross, and we will believe in him. 43He trusts in God; let God deliver him now, if he desires him; for he said, 'I am the Son of God.'" 44And the robbers who were crucified with him also reviled him in the same way.

(12) Hilary of Poitiers

And so it was that the salvation and life of all was hung on the tree of life.[4] To [Christ's] left and right, two thieves were crucified, showing that the whole human race everywhere is called to the sacrament of the Lord's passion. But because there is a difference between believers and unbelievers, there is an overall division between those on the right and those on the left (cf. 25:32–33). The thief placed to the right was saved by the justification of faith.

(13) Eusebius of Emesa

The hostile crowd said, **Come down now from the cross, and we shall believe in you.** Do you suppose he was unable to come down? He did not want to obey those spiteful ones. Just as when the devil proposed, **tell these stones to become loaves of bread** (4:3; Luke 4:3), the Savior could have turned stones into bread; but under no circumstances would he obey the devil. Therefore, that which he was able to do he did not do, so that he would not seem to yield to the wicked.

3. A conflated reading of LXX Ps 56:1 (57:1), which supplies chapter headings with the following: *Do not destroy . . . a stele inscription.*

4. A reference to two trees of life, one in Paradise (Gen 2:9) and one the cross on which Christ died.

He certainly was able to come down from the cross, but he did not because he wished to carry out the will of his Father. It is not that the Father was acting against the Jews, but that he was showing favor to the Gentiles. For the Father did not kill the Son; rather the wicked greed of the Jewish leaders was roused against him. Though it was prophesied that they would do this, they did not do it because of the prophecy. It was prophesied because they were going to do it. But even if he had come down from the cross, they certainly would not have been persuaded to believe. Think then, what is easier, to come down from the cross or to make the dead rise after four days (John 11:17)? If they were not persuaded when Lazarus was resurrected—whose odor caused them to hold their nostrils and whose appearance they saw before their eyes—must we say that something else was necessary? And if another sign had been done, they might have said that it was not enough and that something more should be done. . . .

To be sure, we have greater admiration for what the Lord did on the cross than if he had come down from the cross. The dead have also been raised by the prophets, but no one ever voluntarily, either by artifice or the love [for others], arose from the body. Instead, we mortals lie under the constraints of the laws of nature; we depart from life either because of age or the sword or fire or travel or invasions by hostile races. Being mortals and men according to nature, we are subject to the misfortunes of death. But the Lord of life and humanity, the one and only-begotten Son of the Father, who had the power to become man from a virgin—something that is contrary to nature—had the power to surrender to death against his nature. And thus two thieves were affixed to a cross along with him, so that by seeing him along with other mortals he would demonstrate his power.

(14) Gregory of Nazianzus

Christ, a physician who descended into the world of foul-smelling passions, stripped off none of his divinity in bringing my salvation. He was mortal, yet God, of the seed of David, but still the one who gave form to Adam. He bore flesh, yet had an existence outside a body. He is son of a mother, yet she is a virgin. He was subject to limitation, yet he was beyond measure. A manger received him, and magi, led by a star, came bringing gifts and bending their knees in worship. As a mortal man he faced temptation, yet he prevailed undefeated over the tempter in the threefold conflict (4:3–7). Food was laid before him, yet it was he who fed thousands and turned water into wine. He was baptized, but himself cleansed sins and was proclaimed Son of the Eternal by the thundering voice of the Spirit. As a human being he needed sleep, while as God he lulled the sea to sleep. He bent his knees in weariness, but he restored strength to the knees of the palsied. He prayed, yet it was he who heard the supplications of the weak. He was both sacrifice and high priest, the one who offered the sacrifice, yet God who received it. He offered his blood to God and cleansed the whole world. When a cross raised him up, its nails put an end to sin.

Matthew 27:45

45Now from the sixth hour there was darkness over all the land until the ninth hour.

(15) Caelius Sedulius

Then suddenly a horrendous darkness fell,
Taking possession of the whole sky, covering the shadowy daylight
With gloomy mourning; the sun buried
Its glistening rays in a cloud, veiled in a dark mantle,
And withdrew, darkening the sad world with its grief.
The elements were granted the right to look upon this face;
Deprived of their father's support, they showed joy at his rising,
Grief at his setting. For as the light shone forth
At the time of the Lord's birth, so at his death it withdrew,
Not remaining absent for long, but providing by this period of time
A hidden spiritual meaning; for just as for three hours
The darkened stars hid in the unilluminated sky, so for three days
The Lord endured imprisonment in the cave that was his tomb.

(16) John Chrysostom

It was much more marvelous for these things to happen when he was nailed to the cross than when walking on the earth. Yet it was not only in this respect that it was a wonder. What they were seeking from heaven now took place all over the world. Once it had happened in Egypt at the time of the Passover.[5] The events of ancient time are a figure of events that are now fulfilled. Notice also when it took place: at midday so that every inhabitant of the world might know of it. That it was daylight across the world was enough to convert them, not by the magnitude of the portent, but when it occurred. So it happened after their drunken behavior and wicked mockery. When they had ceased their rage, when they stopped jeering, when they had had enough of jeering and said whatever they wished, then he brings on the darkness, so that finally, after venting their anger, they might benefit from the wonder they beheld. Bringing about something so marvelous was far greater than coming down from the cross. Whether they thought he was able to do it or not, they should have believed and been afraid. If not he, then the Father, and they should also have felt remorse because the darkness was due to his anger at their crimes. Clearly it was not an eclipse, but anger and disapproval. . . . How is it, you ask, that they were not all astounded and did not believe him to be God? Because the human race at that time was caught up in deep indifference and vice.

5. That is, when darkness covered the land of Egypt (Exod 10:21).

Matthew 27:46–50

46 And about the ninth hour Jesus cried with a loud voice, "Eli, Eli, la'ma sabachtha'ni?"
that is, "My God, my God, why hast thou forsaken me?" 47 And some of the bystanders
hearing it said, "This man is calling Eli'jah." 48 And one of them at once ran and took a
sponge, filled it with vinegar, and put it on a reed, and gave it to him to drink. 49 But the
others said, "Wait, let us see whether Eli'jah will come to save him." 50 And Jesus cried
again with a loud voice and yielded up his spirit.

(17) Leo the Great

Our head, the Lord Jesus Christ, transforming all the members of his own body into himself, in the punishment of the cross within the voice of his own, whom he redeemed, was crying aloud that which he had once uttered in the psalm: *My God, my God, look upon me, why have you forsaken me?* (Ps 22:1; cf. Matt 27:46 and Mark 15:34). This utterance, beloved, is a teaching, not a grievance. For since there is the one person in Christ, of God and man, he could not be abandoned by the one from whom he could not be separated. For us, we who are anxious and weak, he asks why the flesh, fearing to suffer, has not been heard.

For as his passion was taking place, in order to cure and correct the fear stemming from our frailty, he had said, **Father, if it is possible, let this cup depart from me. But nevertheless not as I will, but as you will**, and again, **Father, if this cup cannot depart unless I drink of it, let your will be done** (26:39). Therefore, once he conquered the trepidation of his flesh, he surrendered to the will of his Father, and when he had spurned the whole terror of death, he continued to fulfill the work of his command. Why is it that, when he was exalted in the very triumph of so great a victory (cf. John 12:32 and Col 2:15), he asked for the cause and reason by which he was abandoned, which question is not heeded? It was to show that this one feeling that he received to excuse human fear was different from that feeling to which he had bound himself in his eternal obedience to the Father *for the reconciliation of the world* (2 Cor 5:19). Therefore, the fact that his cry was not heard is the explanation of this great mystery, for the power of the Redeemer would not bestow anything upon the human race if our infirmity should obtain what it was seeking.

Therefore, **Jesus was crying out with a great voice, Why have you forsaken me?** [He said this] in order to make known to all how it was right that he neither be rescued nor protected, but that he be abandoned to the hands of savage men. That is, he could become the Savior of the world and the Redeemer of all men not through misery, but through mercy, nor by a loss of help, but by a decision to die. But what must be thought in this matter about this cutting off of life, when his soul was let forth *by* his own *power* and called back *by* his own *power* (cf. John 10:17–18)? Indeed, the blessed Apostle says, *The Father did not spare his own Son, but gave him up for all of us* (Rom 8:32). Again he says, *Because Christ loved the Church and gave himself up for her, so that he might sanctify her* (Eph 5:25–26). Therefore, it was as much the will of the Father as it was his own will for the Lord to be given over to his passion. As a result, not only did the Father abandon him, but also the Lord even deserted himself in a certain way, not by a timorous withdrawal, but by an intentional surrender.

(18) Peter Chrysologus

Notice that Jonah was the engineer of his own submersion, as he tells us himself: *Pick me up and throw me into the sea* (cf. Jonah 1:12). This is a foreshadowing of the Lord's own voluntary ordeal.[6] Think about it: why would the sailors wait for him to say this when the gravity of their situation would have naturally led them to suggest it on their own? When the safety of the many depends on the death of the one, you can bet that the choice will quickly be offered to the unlucky person, who, if he consents, may yet be able to delay or even avert the danger of destruction.

But we know that this story is in reality a prefigurement of the Lord's passion; therefore we *expect* to see Jonah taking responsibility for his own death. His death, like the Lord's, was not brought about by blind fate; it is instead a demonstration of his power. Hear the voice of the Lord: *I have the power to lay down my life, and I have the power to take it up again. No one can snatch it from me* (John 10:17–18). How can he assert this? Because Christ deliberately **gave up his spirit**—it did not slip away from him. If he holds the lives of every creature in his hand, how could he lose his own? Hear the voice of the prophet: *My life is always in your hands* (Ps 119[LXX 118]:109)—or again: *Into your hands I commit my spirit* (Ps 30:6 LXX; 31:5).

(19) Ephrem of Nisibis

Our Lord subjected his might, and they seized him,
So that through his living death he might give life to Adam.
He gave his hands to be pierced by nails,
To make up for the hand that plucked the fruit (Gen 3);
He was struck on his cheek in the judgment room (cf. John 18:22)
To make up for the mouth that ate in Eden;
And while Adam's foot was free, his feet were pierced;
Our Lord was stripped that we might be clothed;
With gall and vinegar, he sweetened the poison of the serpent that had bitten man.

(20) Venantius Fortunatus

The blessed cross shines bright on which the Lord incarnate hung,
And with his blood he washes our wounds,
Becoming for us a sacrificial offering, gentle in his devoted love.
The holy Lamb snatched the sheep from the wolf's jaws
When with hands transfixed he redeemed the world from disaster;
Blocking death's path by his own death.

6. In Matt 12:39, the prophet Jonah is said to be a sign (of the resurrection). In this case, Jonah is presented as a figure of the Lord's voluntary choosing of his suffering.

Here was that hand pierced by the bloody nails,
The hand that snatched Paul from sin, Peter from death.
O sweet and noble tree, powerful in your fruitfulness,
Since you bear such fresh fruit on your branches.
This tree's[7] new fragrance makes the corpses of the dead rise up,
And those who were deprived of the day return to life.
Summer's heat will not burn beneath the leaves of this tree
Neither will the moon by night nor the sun at noon.
Planted beside the rushing waters you shine forth,
Spreading your leafy locks, adorned with fresh blossoms.
Between your arms, a vine is hung from which
There flow sweet wines, colored red as blood.

Matthew 27:51–53

**51 And behold, the curtain of the temple was torn in two, from top to bottom; and the
earth shook, and the rocks were split; 52 the tombs also were opened, and many bodies
of the saints who had fallen asleep were raised, 53 and coming out of the tombs after his
resurrection they went into the holy city and appeared to many.**

(21) Ambrose of Milan

The Lord's passion gives us sure signs that things present will crumble away to make room for that which is to come. Darkness poured down on the eyes of the unbelievers (cf. Luke 23:44), so that the light of faith might reappear; the sun set, or hid itself from the sight of sacrilege, and thereby drew a veil over the ghastly spectacle of sin; rocks split apart and, by the rents caused in them, made manifest that in time to come the force of the Word would penetrate the hardest of hearts. . . . As for the open tombs, these surely foretell the bursting open of the prisons of death and the resurrection of the dead; for the sight of the dead made those who saw them believe, and their apparition prefigured resurrection. These dead who arose went through the holy city announcing, by their presence and their aspect, that the heavenly Jerusalem will be the meeting place of those who rise again. So, too, the temple veil is torn in two, proclaiming either the separation of the two peoples or the profanation of the mysteries of the synagogue. The ancient curtain is torn down so that the freshness and beauty of the faith may be hung aloft. The veil of the synagogue is removed so that, with the eyes of our soul, we might gaze steadfastly at the secret mysteries of religion (cf. 2 Cor 3:14).

7. The cross.

(22) Leo the Great

For Jesus says, *Truly I say to you, today you will be with me in paradise* (Luke 23:43). This promise excels the human condition, nor is it set forth as much from the wood of the cross as from the throne of power. From that loftiness is the reward of faith given, by which *the bond* of human transgression is abolished; for the *form of God* does not cut itself off from *the form of a servant* (Phil 2:6–7), while even in the midst of these punishments his inviolable deity and his suffering nature preserved his own character as well as his unity.

The witness of the whole creation is added to confirm our hope. When Christ sent forth his spirit, all the elements trembled. As the splendor of the sun was swallowed up by heavy shadows, in an extraordinary way, it yielded the day over to night. As the earth tottered from the deep shaking, it did not keep stable, and the firmness of the rocks burst asunder when their solidity was shattered. The veil of the temple, in which mysteries were no longer fit to be concealed as before, was torn, and, as the bodies of many saints were roused, their tombs were opened to secure the faith for the imminent resurrection.

But it was demonstrated that the exalted Jesus had drawn all things to himself (cf. John 12:32), not only by suffering in our nature, but also by the commotion of the entire world. For while the Creator hung on the gibbet, the whole creation groaned, and all the elements at the same time felt the nails of the cross. Nothing was free from that punishment. By this he drew both heaven and earth into communion with himself, by this he destroyed the rocks, he opened tombs, he unlocked hell, and he hid the rays of the sun in the bristling of thick shadows (cf. 27:45). For the world owed this testimony to its author, that in the death of its Creator all things would wish to come to an end. But God's patience preserves his own order for events and for seasons. He invites us to that better affection that we might seek the salvation of those whose crime we abhor.

O the wonderful power of the cross! O the ineffable glory of his passion! In this was the tribunal of the Lord, the judgment of the world, and the power of the crucified. For you drew all things to yourself, Lord, and *when you had stretched out your hands the whole day to an unbelieving people* (Isa 65:2) who spoke against you, the whole world received a sense of your majesty . . . when the lights of heaven were darkened and the day was turned to night. The earth also was shaken by unwonted motions, and the entire creation refused itself for the use of the wicked. You drew, Lord, all things to yourself. For, when the veil of the temple was torn, the holy of holies withdrew from those unworthy priests, so that the figure would turn into its reality, prophecy into its manifestation, law into gospel. You drew, Lord, all things to yourself, so that what [once] was done in the one temple of the Jews in darkened signs, prayer [now] celebrates in the full and open gospel revelation of all nations everywhere. For now there is a more honorable order of Levites, a greater dignity of elders, and a holier anointing of priests, since your cross is the spring of all blessings, the cause of every grace, and through it believers are given power instead of weakness, glory instead of shame, and life instead of death. Now indeed, since the variety of fleshly sacrifices has ceased, one offering of your body and blood fulfills every kind of sacrifice. For you are the true *Lamb of God who takes away the sins of the world* (John 1:29), and thus you complete all mysteries in yourself. As a result, just as there is one sacrifice for every victim, so there is one kingdom over and above every nation.

(23) Ephrem of Nisibis

Our Lord was trampled by death, and he treaded a path beyond death. He is the one who submitted and endured death, as it was willed, in order to overthrow death, contrary to (death's) will. Our Lord carried his cross (John 19:17) and went forth as death willed. But on the cross, he called out and brought the dead out of Sheol, contrary to death's will. With the very weapon that death had used to kill him, he gained the victory over death. Divinity[8] disguised itself in humanity and approached (death), which killed, then was killed: death killed natural life, but supernatural life killed death.

Yet the medicine of life flew down from above and joined himself to that mortal fruit, the body. And when death came as usual to feed, life swallowed death instead. This is the food that hungered to eat the one who eats it. Therefore, death vomited up the many lives that it had greedily swallowed, because of a single fruit that it had ravenously swallowed. The hunger that drove it after one was the undoing of the voracious appetite that had driven it after many. Death succeeded in eating the one (fruit), but it quickly vomited out the many. As the one fruit was dying on the cross, many of the buried came forth from Sheol at the sound of his voice.

This is the fruit that escaped death, which had swallowed it, and brought the living out of Sheol, to whom it had been sent. Sheol stored up all that it had devoured. But because of one thing that it could not eat, it gave back everything it had eaten. When a person's stomach is upset, he vomits out what agrees with him as well as what disagrees with him. Death's stomach became upset, so when it vomited out the medicine of life that had soured it, it vomited out with him the living as well, whom it had been pleased to swallow.

This is the Son of the skillful carpenter, who set up his cross over all-consuming Sheol and led humanity to the place of life. Since humanity fell into Sheol because of a tree (Gen 3:3), it passed over to the place of life upon a tree. And so, on the tree where bitterness was tasted, sweetness has been tasted, so that we might learn who it is who has no rival among his creatures. Praise to you who suspended your cross over death so that souls could pass over on it from the place of the dead to the place of life.

Matthew 27:54–56

54When the centurion and those who were with him, keeping watch over Jesus, saw the earthquake and what took place, they were filled with awe, and said, "Truly this was the Son of God!"

55There were also many women there, looking on from afar, who had followed Jesus from Galilee, ministering to him; 56among whom were Mary Mag'dalene, and Mary the mother of James and Joseph, and the mother of the sons of Zeb'edee.

8. In Syriac *alahuta*, here used as an abstraction for the Son.

(24) Pseudo-Lactantius

As you come, whoever you may be, entering the gates in the midst of the temple,
stop for a while and look upon me, the innocent one who suffered for your crime;
Ponder me in your soul, keep me in your heart.
I am the one who pitied the bitter death of men.
To this place I come as the mediator of a promised peace, and with a full
pardon for the guilt of all. Here the brightest from on high
has returned to the earth; here is the nourishing image of salvation;
Here I am, your rest, the right way, true redemption,
And the banner of God, a sign and a remarkable destiny.

For your sake and your life, I entered the womb of the Virgin,
I am made man and suffered a terrible death;
Nor did I find rest in any corner of the earth,
But everywhere there are threats, everywhere there are labors;
In the first place, a pitiful dwelling in the land of the Jews
housed me at birth and was for my parent mother.
Here, amidst the irrational beasts scattered about, I was first given
hay as a bed in a narrow manger.
I lived my earliest years in the Pharian regions,[9]
having fled from Herod's reign and later returned
to Judea; always fasting, and always in the very extremes of poverty,
and found in the most lowly of circumstances.

Always encouraging human character, through beneficial and wholesome teaching,
To embrace uprightness, by revealing goodness,
by enjoining the many miracles to teaching, on account of which
the unfaithful, agitated by its twisted burden
of envy, and cruel hatred, and blinded fury,
dared to seek against me—one who was innocent—
deadly punishments, a cruel death on the terrible cross.
If you yourself want to discern [these events] more fully, and if
it helps you to review all my groaning and experience my sorrows,
then piece together the plots and jealousies and the wicked price
of my innocent blood, as well as the pretended kisses of a friend,
and the insults, and the abuses of a cruel mob.

Moreover, there are the lashes of the whip,
and testimonies prompted to lay blame.
Consider in your mind both the witnesses and
the abominable judgment of Pilate made blind,

9. That is, in Egypt.

and a heavy weight of the cross pressing on my shoulders and wearied back,
and burdened steps toward a painful death.

Now look upon me, as one also deserted, at the limit of suffering,
and raised up at a distance from my sweet mother.
Examine me from head to foot and notice
how my hair is clotted with blood and
how my neck under the scalp is bloodstained,
and my head put upon by cruel thorns,
fresh blood flowing down everywhere on my divine face.

Look upon my eyes squinted and dimmed,
and my beaten cheeks; see my tongue parched, poisoned with gall,
and my visage paled with death.
Peruse my hands pierced by nails,
and my shoulders dislocated,
as well as a huge wound in my side, see how the blood flows,
and my feet that are cut open, and my bloodstained limbs.

Bend your knee, and with tears revere the venerable wood of the cross,
Dripping innocent blood on the ground,
praying with humbled face, tears freely flowing,
and be reminded at times of my teaching as you are devoted to me in heart.

(25) Leo the Great

Therefore the reproaches of an empty scoffing were spurned. No jeers drove away the mercy of the Lord from the path of his purpose, that mercy that was restoring the lost and fallen from any indignity. For a singular sacrifice was offered to God for the salvation of the world. The killing of the true Lamb, prophesied for so many generations, brought the sons of the promise to the liberty of faith. The new covenant was also being confirmed, and by the blood of Christ, the heirs of the eternal kingdom were being recorded. The highest priest was entering the holy of holies, and the spotless priest was entering *through the veil of his own flesh* (Heb 10:20) in order to appease God. Finally, at this point, an evident transition was made from the law to the gospel, from the synagogue to the church, and from many sacrifices to one. When the Lord let forth his spirit, that mystical veil that used to close off the holy and secret place **was torn all the way from top to bottom** by a sudden force. Truth was removing its types and the messages [formerly] announced until they became superfluous. A commotion to be feared of all the elements was added to these things, and nature withdrew herself from the authors of Christ's crucifixion. When the centurion, the overseer of this punishment, was terrified by the things that he had seen, he said, **Truly this man was the Son of God.**

Matthew 27:57–61

57 When it was evening, there came a rich man from Arimathe'a, named Joseph, who also was a disciple of Jesus. 58 He went to Pilate and asked for the body of Jesus. Then Pilate ordered it to be given to him. 59 And Joseph took the body, and wrapped it in a clean linen shroud, 60 and laid it in his own new tomb, which he had hewn in the rock; and he rolled a great stone to the door of the tomb, and departed. 61 Mary Mag'dalene and the other Mary were there, sitting opposite the sepulchre.

(26) Hilary of Poitiers

There are the facts that Joseph (of Arimathea) asked Pilate to turn the body over to him, and he wrapped it in a linen sheet and placed it in a new tomb that had been cut out of rock, and a huge stone was rolled in front of the entrance to the tomb. Provided that this is the right order of events and that it was necessary to bury him who would soon be resurrected from the dead, still, every one of the acts would not have been described unless there was some importance to them.

Joseph presents a figure of the apostles, which is the reason (though he was not numbered among the twelve apostles) why he is declared as the Lord's disciple. It was Joseph who wrapped the body in a clean linen sheet, the same linen sheet on which every kind of animal was let down from heaven to Peter (Acts 10:11–12). From this, it is perhaps not superfluous to understand from the representation of this linen sheet that the Church is buried together with Christ, because in this sheet (cf. Rom 6:4; Col 2:12), just as in the Church's confession, the diversity of clean and unclean creatures has been assembled. Thus, the Lord's body is laid to rest in an empty and new chamber, hewn out of stone, just as through the apostolic teaching Christ is conveyed into the hard heart of the pagans hewn out by the labor of teaching, making a rough and new chamber where fear of God had never entered before. Since nothing except Christ ought to enter our hearts, a stone was rolled in front of the entrance. Just as no author before him had conveyed to us divine knowledge, so nothing would be conveyed after him.

Matthew 27:62–66

62 Next day, that is, after the day of Preparation, the chief priests and the Pharisees gathered before Pilate 63 and said, "Sir, we remember how that impostor said, while he was still alive, 'After three days I will rise again.' 64 Therefore order the sepulchre to be made secure until the third day, lest his disciples go and steal him away, and tell the people, 'He has risen from the dead,' and the last fraud will be worse than the first."
65 Pilate said to them, "You have a guard of soldiers; go, make it as secure as you can."
66 So they went and made the sepulchre secure by sealing the stone and setting a guard.

(27) Ambrose of Milan

A just man (Joseph of Arimathea) wraps Christ's body in a linen cloth (cf. Luke 23:53); and one who is innocent of heart embalms him with perfume. Each of these two actions has its own distinct significance: for justice is the vestment of the Church, and innocence is her beauty. You too, my friends, should clothe Christ's body in glory, and then you too will be just. Even if you think him dead, clothe him with the fullness of his divinity. Anoint him with myrrh and aloes, so that you may be the sweet fragrance of Christ (cf. 2 Cor 2:15). Joseph, that good and just man, provided a fine linen cloth. It was, perhaps, the linen cloth that Peter saw descending from heaven, and on it were *all manner of four-footed beasts, and creeping things of the earth, and birds of the air* (Acts 10:11). These prefigured the Gentile nations. So the Church is buried with this mysterious and precious perfume, having first gathered together all manner of people in the community of faith.

With regard to Joseph, it is only in John (cf. John 19:38) that I find that he went secretly to Pilate for fear of the Jews. Why should a just person want secrecy? Why should he fear danger? I think that he asked in secret in order to obtain the body, not to avoid danger. In any case, would it be so surprising for a just person to hide himself when even the apostles were hiding?

Come, my friend. Yes, I mean you. Even if you come late; even if you come at night. Come any time at all, and you will find Jesus very happy to welcome you. He will not reward you any less because you come late. Even the one who came at the sixth hour was not deprived of his reward; and the one who came at the eleventh hour was given a full amount (cf. 20:9). Besides, Nicodemus came by night (cf. John 3:2). It was night because it was not yet the resurrection. But once Christ is risen, the just person says: *The night is passed, and the day is at hand* (Rom 13:12).

Luke calls Joseph just (cf. Luke 23:50), and Matthew calls him rich (cf. 27:57). It is quite true that he was rich, for he had obtained the body of Christ. In receiving him who is rich, Joseph could not possibly be poor in faith. One is rich, therefore, when one is just. So Joseph wraps Jesus in a linen cloth. But the Israelite mixes different fragrances of virtues and pours in about a hundred pounds of aloes (cf. John 19:39–40): that is to say, the perfect measure of faith. And they swathed the body of Jesus, according to the custom of the Jews. I mean Jews in the truly spiritual sense. They did not tie him with knots of unbelief, but with the winding sheets of faith. Then they laid him in a garden. Often the Church is compared to a garden (cf. John 19:41), for in it you find, in rich variety, the fruits of merit and the flowers of virtue.

It is significant that one evangelist speaks of a new tomb (cf. Luke 23:53), and another calls it Joseph's tomb (cf. 27:60). So Christ had no tomb of his own. Tombs are prepared for those subject to the laws of death; the conqueror of death has no tomb of his own. What could God have in common with a tomb? That is why Ecclesiastes says of one who meditates on what is good: *There is no burial for him* (Eccl 6:3).

We see that Christ's death has a character all its own, different from the death common to the rest of us. Also, he is not buried along with other people, but shut up alone in a tomb. So too it is with the incarnation of the Lord. It resembled in every way our humanity, but even while resembling our humanity, there were differences. There was resemblance in his birth from a virgin, but a difference in his conception; he healed the sick, but did so by his command; John baptized with water, but he baptized with the Holy Spirit (cf. Luke 3:16). In the same way, Christ's death is like ours as regards his physical nature, but not like ours with regard to his power.

Matthew 28

In discussing Christ's death and resurrection, John Chrysostom divides what took place into public and private signs. The darkness (27:45) was a public sign for the world, while private or local signs included the appearance of the angel and the earthquake (v. 2). In his resurrection, Christ is the way of "ascent to incorruption" for us who follow after him (Cyril of Alexandria).

Peter Chrysologus says that faithlessness had put the stone before the tomb, but "now, it is rolled away to make room for faith." After Christ's resurrection, much is inverted, and he notes that the tomb, normally an abode of death, has become a new type of womb "that conceives death but brings forth life!" He adds that the heart in which Christ lives is like heaven, while the heart in which Christ is believed to be dead and buried is itself a tomb.

The angel is described as having an appearance like lightning and clothes as white as snow (v. 3). Peter Chrysologus says that this is because lightning comes from heaven and snow from the earth. Gregory the Great gives a different explanation, saying that lightning holds dread and fear, while there is a soothing whiteness in snow. Thus, the angel of God is able both to "frighten the condemned and reassure the devout." Peter Chrysologus finds irony in the fear of the guards in the presence of the angel, remarking how they were "pierced by the fear of death at the very moment of life's return!"

John Chrysostom heaps scorn on the claim of the chief priests that the disciples stole Jesus's body from the tomb. Among the many difficulties in carrying out such a complicated task, he wonders what would be the motivation for the disciples to do that. Why would the disciples want to risk their lives to feign a resurrection, especially since they had been content to hide in fear from authorities in order to protect their lives?

At the very end of the Gospel, Jesus says, All authority in heaven and on earth has been given to me. *Both Cyril of Alexandria and Peter Chrysologus say authority had been conferred on Jesus in his humanity but that, as God, he already possessed it. Jesus goes on to command his followers to make disciples of all nations and to baptize them in the name of the Father, Son, and Holy Spirit (v. 19). Eusebius of Caesarea remarks that the ability of the rustic disciples to succeed in making Christianity known throughout creation, including the greatest of cities like Rome, could not have happened without the divine assistance that Jesus promises. As Gregory of Nazianzus puts it in relation to the power of the crucifixion, "A few drops of blood formed anew the whole cosmos."*

Matthew 28:1–4

[1]Now after the sabbath, toward the dawn of the first day of the week, Mary Mag'dalene and the other Mary went to see the sepulchre. [2]And behold, there was a great earthquake; for an angel of the Lord descended from heaven and came and rolled back the stone, and sat upon it. [3]His appearance was like lightning, and his raiment white as snow. [4]And for fear of him the guards trembled and became like dead men.

(1) Peter Chrysologus

The *Lex Tartari*[1] has rightly run its course: the court of the grave has withdrawn, the rule of death repealed in punishment for its temerity. Because of the injustice suffered by their advocate, souls are recalled, bodies are renewed (cf. 27:52–53), humanity is restored, life is revived. All things are now under the new law of forgiveness, because their judge is the author of life.

O blessed stone that both veils and reveals Christ! Blessed are you, I say, for your witness to the rising of the flesh resurrects our own faith! Here the natural order has changed; here the tomb devours *death*, not the dead! The house of the dead has become the headquarters of life; what a strange womb it is that conceives death but brings forth life!

(2) Augustine

That period of three days, during which Lord died and was resurrected, cannot be rightly understood unless, in a manner of expression, we say the part is regarded as the whole. Thus the Lord himself spoke, **Just as Jonah was three days and three nights in the whale's belly, so the Son of Man will be in the heart of the earth for three days and three nights** (12:40). However we calculate the time, whether from the point when he surrendered the spirit, or from the point when he was buried, it does not work out smoothly unless we accept the intermediate day, that is, the Sabbath, as a complete day, that is, a full day along with its night. And we should understand those other days—that is, the day of the preparation and the first day of the week, which we call the Lord's Day—as the part regarded as the whole.

It remains, therefore, in keeping with that manner of expression . . . in which a part is comprehended as the whole that we find the day of preparation at one end of the three-day period during which the Lord was crucified and buried, and from that first day, we understand it is part of the whole day, now having been completed with its night. In this way, too, we must take the intermediate member, that is to say, the day of the Sabbath, not as calculated simply from the part, but as a really complete day. The third day, again, must be computed from its first part; that is to say, calculating from the night, we must look upon it as making up a whole day when its day portion is connected with it.

1. Law of the underworld.

(3) Peter Chrysologus

Wretched men, pierced by the fear of death at the very moment of life's return! And yet they were agents of savagery, enforcers of the treachery of their ringleaders; how could they ever accept such a supernatural event? Thus they blockaded the tomb, barricaded the path of the resurrection, striving to keep death from dying, life from breaking out. Rightly, then, were they laid low when the angel appeared, utterly demoralized at his coming. They were so worried about dying, these miserable men, ever enemies to themselves—and yet they preferred to fight against the resurrection! Why didn't they rather open the tomb themselves, smoothing the way for the risen Christ, facilitating the miracle of his appearance, the hope of his example, the truth of his return, the assuredness of life never-ending? Only the deepest abyss of madness could have led them to deny what Christ was doing before their very eyes.

But an angel descended and **rolled the stone away**. He didn't do this in order to make a way for the Lord to escape, but rather to unveil his resurrection to the world. He offered a helping hand, not to the rising of his Lord, but to the faltering faith of his fellow servants.

He rolled the stone away. Faithlessness had put it there; now, it is rolled away to make room for faith. **He rolled the stone away**, so that what had once been a guardian of death might become a monument to life.

Now let us pray, brothers, that the angel may descend today and roll away all hardness from our heart, that he may uncover the hidden recesses of our inner lives, that he may bear witness to Christ rising out of the tomb of our minds—for just as our hearts may be compared to heaven, where Christ is living and reigning, so too our souls are like tombs, in which Christ has lain dead and buried until now. But just as we believe that Christ's death really happened, so must we also believe that it was a one-time event. Christ, as a human, did indeed suffer, die, and was buried; but now he reigns, endures, and will continue forever as God. Listen to the voice of the Apostle! *Even if we once knew Christ according to the flesh, we do not know him in that way any longer* (2 Cor 5:16). And again: *He died once, dying to sin, but now he lives for God* (Rom 6:10)—that is, he lives *as* God.

His appearance, so it says, **was like lightning, but his garments were like snow.** The brilliance of his face is distinguished from the radiance of his clothes, for the appearance of the angel, we are told, was like lightning, but his clothes were like snow. Why mention this? Because lightning ought to remind us of heaven, and snow of earth. Listen to the voice of the prophet: *Praise the Lord from the earth, O fire, hail, and snow!* (Ps 148:7–8). Therefore, in the angel's face we may perceive the brilliance of heavenly beings, while his clothes represent the grace of his communion with humanity. The appearance of the angel who is speaking in this passage thus blends these two realities, granting our earth-bound eyes the ability to see not merely the gentle radiance of his clothes but also the flashing fire of his face—a face that makes us tremble in wonder before this envoy of our Creator.

Matthew 28:5–7

5But the angel said to the women, "Do not be afraid; for I know that you seek Jesus who was crucified. 6He is not here; for he has risen, as he said. Come, see the place where he

lay. [7]Then go quickly and tell his disciples that he has risen from the dead, and behold, he is going before you to Galilee; there you will see him. Lo, I have told you."

(4) Peter Chrysologus

Do not fear. Fear has dominion over the evil, just as love possesses the good. Fear, in fact, terrifies the wicked in the same way that affection comforts the righteous. **Do not fear**: in other words, fear is for those who delivered Christ over to death; for Pilate, who sentenced him, for the soldiers, who mocked him, for the wicked, who crucified him. The cruel should fear, who forced him to swallow a bitter drink, and the brutish, who guarded his grave. So too should the treacherous, who traded in lies and profited from trust, and the pitiless, who deplored not the Lord's death but his resurrection. But you, you have gathered together in joy, not fear! He whom you have searched for has risen from the dead! He whose murder you have mourned is alive!

Come, see the place where the Lord was laid. Come, women, come! See where you laid Adam, where you buried humanity itself, where you cast down a man by your council, since it was for the sake of his servants that your Lord lay there in death. Know that as great as your offense was, the forgiveness of the Lord is greater. **Come, see the place where the Lord was laid.** An angelic power proclaims that this is the Lord who was crucified; how then can human weakness wonder whether it is the same Lord who was raised? Certainly Christ underwent his trials according to his humanity, but not in such a way that he lost any part of his divinity.

(5) Cyril of Alexandria

After the Lord had endured the suffering on the cross for our sake and he had given his own body in exchange for the life of all, he was in a tomb like someone *unmourned, forsaken among the dead* (Ps 88:5), according to the hymn in the Psalms. The women ran carrying the things for the care of the body and bringing many spices.

There is no reason to be amazed. The women did not know that God, who is life, would destroy the power of corruption and that, as God, Christ would come back to life. Even the apostles themselves thought the message about his resurrection was nonsense, that it was simply a claim that is untrue, because they did not know the divinely inspired Scripture. So, the women came to the tomb, and instead of finding the body of Christ, they saw a holy angel. . . . In truth, an evangelist and herald of the resurrection had come to them. He said, "Do not seek *the one who* always *lives*—for his nature is life—*with the dead*, for *he is not here*" (Luke 24:5–6). He is not dead, and even in a tomb, he has been raised and opens the ascent to incorruption, not for himself, but for us.

It was for this reason that he lowered himself and became empty, assuming our likeness (Phil 2:5–11), so that *by the grace of God*, as the blessed Paul says, *he might taste death on behalf of everyone* (Heb 2:9). He becomes the death of death and the abolition of the curse inflicted on the first-formed man. For the Lord prepared the way for faith to be within us when he said, "Truly I say to you, *the one who believes in me, even if he dies, will live*" (John 11:25). Just as angels announced the birth to the shepherds in Bethlehem, so too the spiritual powers[2] proclaimed the resurrection.

(6) Gregory the Great

Let us hear what the angel said to the women: **Do not be terrified.** This is as much as to say: "Let them be frightened who do not love the coming of those who live on high, let those be afraid who are weighed down by bodily desires and despair of being able to belong to their fellowship." But why do we see our fellow citizens afraid? Matthew, describing the apparition of the angel, said: **Its appearance was like lightning, and its clothing like snow.** In lightning, indeed, are dread and fear, but in snow there is the soothing quality of whiteness. Because almighty God is both fearful to sinners and soothing to the righteous, the angel who witnessed his resurrection was aptly described as looking like lightning and as being white in dress. By its very sight, the angel would frighten the condemned and reassure the devout.

Matthew 28:8–10

**8So they departed quickly from the tomb with fear and great joy, and ran to tell his
disciples. 9And behold, Jesus met them and said, "Hail!" And they came up and took
hold of his feet and worshiped him. 10Then Jesus said to them, "Do not be afraid; go
and tell my brethren to go to Galilee, and there they will see me."**

(7) John Chrysostom

The women saw an astonishing thing that was unheard of, the tomb where they had previously seen him placed was empty. They wanted to see him that they might become witnesses to both the empty tomb and the resurrection. They did not entertain the idea that someone had taken him, since there were so many soldiers on duty; they thought he had raised himself. So they are filled with joy and astonishment at the same time, and they receive the reward of their patience: to be the first to see and announce the good news, not only of what was said (28:5–6), but also of what was seen. So they left in fear and joy, and **Behold, Jesus met them and said, Greetings. They clasped his feet**, running to him with surpassing joy, and receiving by that touch a sign and assurance of the resurrection.

Do any of you want to become like those women and clasp the feet of Jesus? You can even now, if you want to, clasping not only the feet and hands, but also that sacred head, by enjoying the awesome sacrament of the Eucharist with a clear conscience. Not here only, though, you will also see him on that day when he comes in ineffable glory and with the

2. That is, angels.

ranks of angels, provided you are ready to be merciful. You will hear not only this word, **Greetings**, but also those others, **Come, you that are blessed by my Father, inherit the kingdom prepared for you before the foundation of the world** (25:34). Become merciful, then, so as to hear these words.

(8) Leo the Great

The death of Christ had greatly disturbed the hearts of the disciples. From the punishment of the cross, from the departure of his spirit, from the burial of his lifeless body, a kind of torpor of unbelief had stolen upon their minds, which were heavy with sadness. When the holy women, just as the Gospel account reveals, proclaimed that the stone was rolled back from the tomb, that the tomb was devoid of any body, and that angels were witnesses of the living Lord, their words seemed to the apostles and other disciples like absurdities (cf. Luke 24:1–11).

Although their uncertainty faltered in human weakness, by no means would the Spirit of truth have allowed this unbelief to enter the hearts of his own preachers if this anxious disquiet and curious delay had not laid the foundations of our faith. Accordingly, this faith of the apostles was to help our confusion and our fears: We are taught by these men to defend against the slanders of the wicked and against the arguments of earthly wisdom. Their seeing has instructed us, their hearing has educated us, and their touching has made us strong. Let us give thanks for this divine provision and for the necessary slowness of the holy fathers. Others doubted so that we might not fall into doubt ourselves.

Matthew 28:11–15

**11While they were going, behold, some of the guard went into the city and told the chief
priests all that had taken place. 12And when they had assembled with the elders and
taken counsel, they gave a sum of money to the soldiers 13and said, "Tell people, 'His
disciples came by night and stole him away while we were asleep.' 14And if this comes
to the governor's ears, we will satisfy him and keep you out of trouble." 15So they took
the money and did as they were directed; and this story has been spread among the
Jews to this day.**

(9) Gregory of Nazianzus

I will stand on my watch, says the excellent Habakkuk (Hab 2:1). And with him today—with the authority and vision given to me by the Spirit—I will watch and learn what will appear and be spoken to me. I stood and watched. Behold, a man was riding on the clouds; and this man was exceedingly lofty. His appearance was like the appearance of an angel. His robe was like the radiance of lightning shooting through the sky (cf. 28:3). He raised his hand toward the east, and he called out with a great voice (cf. Rev 19:17). His voice was like the voice of a trumpet (cf. Rev 4:1). Those around him were like the multitude of the heavenly host (cf. Rev 7:9). And he said, "Today the world has salvation, both the visible and the invisible. Christ is risen from the dead: you all are risen with him (cf. Col 2:12). Christ is being restored to himself: you all are restored. Christ is released from the grave: you all are set free from the chains of sin. The gates of Hades are opened and death is destroyed. The old Adam is done away with and the new is being completed. If anyone is *a new creation in Christ* (2 Cor 5:17), *you all are made new*." He said these things. But others surrounding him were offering praise as before when Christ was made manifest to us through his birth here below: *Glory to God in the highest, and upon earth peace, goodwill to men* (Luke 2:14). With them also, I proclaim these wonders among you. And may it be that I receive a voice worthy of the angels, which would resound to all the ends of the earth.

In this way and for these reasons (i.e., the law gradually educating us and causing us to turn away from idols and toward the living God), the written law entered in, moving us toward Christ. And this is the logic of the sacrifices insofar as my logic can express it. So that you might not be ignorant of the depths of wisdom and the richness of his unsearchable judgments (cf. Rom 11:33), he did not completely abandon these sacrifices as unholy or as useless or as having been derived from mere blood. But the great and unsacrificed sacrifice—if I may speak this way—so far as in his first nature, has been mixed with the customary sacrifices. And it is purifying, not merely for small portions of the world, nor for a little while, but for everyone in the world and throughout the ages (cf. Heb 9:23–10:18).

A sheep is taken, therefore (Exod 12:5), for its innocence and the original clothing of nakedness (Gen 3:7). For the offering on our behalf is so great that it is both in name and in actuality an incorruptible garment. He is a perfect offering, not only because of his divinity, which is more perfect than anything, but also because of the humanity he assumed, which was anointed with divinity. Since he became like that which anointed him,[3] I even make bold to say he is equal to God.

But he is male, presented on Adam's behalf, the stronger rather than the strong (the first man who fell under sin). While he certainly resembles nothing female, there being no effeminacy in himself, he cried out at birth from the bonds, simultaneously virginal and maternal, according to his great authority, and he was born a male from the prophetess,[4] as Isaiah preaches (Isa 8:3). But he is a one-year-old like the sun of righteousness[5] (Mal 4:2): originating from above, he was then circumscribed by his visible nature, but finally he returned into himself. He is both a crown blessed with goodness (cf. Ps 65:4, 11) and in every way equal and like to himself. And not only that, but he is also the giver of life to the sphere of virtues, which are being gently added and united to one another by the law of friendship and order. He is unblemished and unadulterated, as the healer of faults and also of the defects and damage caused by evil. Even though he assumed our sins and endured our diseases (cf. Isa 53:4), he did not himself suffer something that

3. "That which anointed him" refers to the Holy Spirit.

4. Isa 8:3 reads: *And I went to the prophetess, and she conceived and bore a son.* Gregory applies this passage to Mary and Jesus.

5. Gregory's reference to Christ as a "one-year-old" arises from the "leaping calves" of the second half of Mal 4:2, *You shall go out leaping like calves from the stall* when the *sun of righteousness* appears. Christ is the first of the calves to rejoice.

needed to be healed. *For he was tempted by all things, according to our likeness, but without sin* (Heb 4:15). And the devil who was pursuing the *light made manifest in darkness* (John 1:5) did not catch it!

Clearly, there were many wonders at that moment: God being crucified, the sun being darkened and again inflamed (it was necessary for created things to sympathize with the Creator), the curtains [of the temple] being torn, the blood and water of his side being poured out (the one of a man, but the other surpassing humanity), the earth quaking, rocks being shattered because of the Rock, the dead being raised for belief in the last and final resurrection, and the signs at the tomb, and those after it. Could anyone worthily praise these signs? But none of these wonders is as great as my salvation. A few drops of blood formed anew the whole cosmos, and they came to be just like a binding agent to all men, joining us and gathering us into one.

(10) John Chrysostom

The earthquake drove the soldiers to panic, and because of what they had seen, they bore witness. This happened to these soldiers to drive them to panic and to bear witness. Their report is certainly trustworthy, because it came from the guards themselves. Of the signs, some were displayed to the whole world, while others were shown to those by the tomb. The darkness, for example, was a sign for the whole world; the signs of the angel and of the earthquake were for those by the tomb.

When these witnesses returned with their report—for the truth shines when proclaimed by its enemies—they were given money in exchange for saying that Christ's disciples came and stole his body. But how in the world could they steal him? Oh, what fools they were. The light of truth is so bright that it even makes them incapable of lying. Indeed, their words were so unpersuasive that their lies had no weight.

Tell me, then, how the disciples, men without any means or skills and lacking courage to come out in the daylight, could steal him. Do you suppose there was no seal on the door of the tomb? Were there not guards and soldiers and Jews everywhere? Were they not suspecting that very thing, watching closely and anxiously, remaining constantly on alert?

We must also ask: why in the world would the disciples steal him? In order to create some sort of teaching about resurrection? And how could such an idea have crossed the mind of those who were living in hiding? What's more, how could they have lifted up the stone placed firmly at the entrance? Had they done all these extremely difficult things, how would they ever get away with it? Even if they didn't care about dying, they would not have taken the risk of going intentionally against so many guards with little chance of success.

On the contrary, their earlier behavior showed that they lacked courage. For example, when they saw the Lord being arrested, every one of them fled in great haste. Then, if they did not have the courage to stand firm when he was still alive, how could they not be terrified by such a huge crowd of soldiers after his death? Moreover, in order to steal the body, wouldn't they have had to break through the entrance of the tomb? Was it possible for someone to sneak in there alone and do it unnoticed? Not a chance. The stone blocking the entrance was huge, and it required many hands to remove it.

Matthew 28:16–20

[16]Now the eleven disciples went to Galilee, to the mountain to which Jesus had directed them. [17]And when they saw him they worshiped him; but some doubted. [18]And Jesus came and said to them, "All authority in heaven and on earth has been given to me. [19]Go therefore and make disciples of all nations, baptizing them in the name of the Father and of the Son and of the Holy Spirit, [20]teaching them to observe all that I have commanded you; and lo, I am with you always, to the close of the age."

(11) Eusebius of Caesarea

When Jesus handed down these teachings for all people to keep, both Greeks and barbarians, he made clear exactly what Christianity is, who we are, and the kind of person he wanted to produce through his sayings and teachings like these. Jesus, our Lord and Savior, the Christ of God, established this new and most excellent way of life throughout the whole world, so that not only men but also women, both the rich and the poor, and slaves together with their masters, learn to study these teachings.

And yet the herald of this new legislation was acknowledged to have followed everything according to the law of Moses. This is itself something of wonder. For although he was to become the legislator of a new way of life—the new covenant according to his gospel—he did not reject the teachings of Moses, nor did he malign them or disparage them. For if it were truly his custom to command what was opposed to Moses, he would have given impious heretics a pretext to slander Moses and the prophets;[6] and to those of the circumcision, he would have given just and reasonable cause for their plot against him. In any case, they had already contrived to kill him as a transgressor and deserter of the law.

Now when I examine the message in and of itself, I find it has no persuasive power, nor anything uplifting or credible, nor with enough plausibility to convince a simple person, much less the wise and reasonable. But when I turn my attention to the power of the word—the myriads of people it has persuaded, and the great many churches that came together under those simple and rustic disciples of Jesus, established not in obscure or hidden places, but in the most distinguished cities: I mean, in the imperial city of Rome itself, in Alexandria and Antioch, throughout the whole of Egypt and Libya, Europe and Asia, in villages and country places and in every kind of nation—I am again compelled to seek out the cause. I must confess that this could only have happened by a divine power beyond human capability and with the cooperation of the one who said to them, **Make disciples of all nations in my name**. For when he said this, he appended a promise by which they would take courage and readily dedicate themselves to what was commanded. He said to them, **And behold, I am with you always, to the end of the age.**

6. Probable reference to the Marcionites.

(12) John Chrysostom

This seems to be his last appearance in Galilee, when he sent forth the disciples to baptize. Even if **some doubted,**[7] . . . yet they were assured by what they saw. So what does he say as he looks at them? **All authority in heaven and on earth is given to me.** Again he speaks to them in human fashion, for they had not yet received the Spirit, who would be able to raise them to a higher level. **Go and make disciples of all nations, baptizing them in the name of the Father and of the Son and of the Holy Spirit, teaching them to observe all I have commanded you.** He makes one announcement in regard to teaching, the other in regard to what they are to do. He . . . does not focus on the past, delivers no reproach to Peter for his denial or to any of the others for their flight; instead, he bids them go throughout the world entrusted with that teaching of baptism.

Lo! I am with you always, even to the end of the world. Do you see his power once again? Do you see how those other things also were spoken so we could understand? And he made the promise not only to the disciples, but also to all who will believe after them. Plainly the apostles were not to remain at this place **to the end of the world**; so he speaks to the believers as to one body. Therefore, do not tell me, says he, about the difficulty of these things, for **I am with you** and will make all things easy. This he also said often to the prophets in the Old Testament, to Jeremiah, who said he was but a youth (Jer 1:6, 8), to Moses (Exod 4:10, 12) and Ezekiel (Ezek 2–3), who [all] shrank from the office: **I am with you.** And notice, I beg you, the excellence of these disciples; others when they were sent to one nation often made excuses, but these said nothing of the sort even though they were sent forth to the world. And he reminds them also of the consummation to draw them all the more and that they should not look at the present dangers only, but at the good things without end that are to come.

(13) Cyril of Alexandria

Incarnate and human, he said: **All authority [is] given to me.** He wanted it understood that he has authority in all things like God. And quitting the measure of emptiness in his natural state, he also returned to the glory that had always belonged to him. Though in flesh, he was God of all things and Lord who commands. So when he says, **All authority is given to me,** it was not as though he was receiving it for the first time, but as one who receives it as human and from a human perspective. Because he is from the Father, and God by nature, he had always possessed it.

(14) Peter Chrysologus

But when he tells us, **All power has been given to me, whether in heaven or on earth**, he's actually saying that *he* has given it *to himself*! For proof, we may turn to the Apostle's

7. Thomas in John 20:24–27.

own words: *In Christ, God was reconciling the world to himself* (2 Cor 5:19). The Son of God offered to the Son of the Virgin—or better, God granted to a human, divinity to flesh—what he had *always* held alongside the Father and the Spirit. That's why when he tells us, **Go, baptize all nations in the name of the Father, and the Son, and the Holy Spirit**, he's actually saying that he will restore all nations to their salvation, using the exact same power through which he had created them in the first place.

And behold, I am with you always, even until the end of the age. So he who is always with the Father is now always with *us*, and he will come for us in that body that he received from us. What more can I say, brothers? The fact that he was born, that he suffered, that he rose, that he is now waiting to receive us—these are not things that were brought about by blind chance or fate. They were intentional deeds, and they were accomplished for our salvation.

(15) Augustine

Now listen and learn how this great and single Trinity has been indicated from the very origins of the human race. Hear about it in the Law and the Prophets, in the Psalms and in the Gospel, hear it plainly stated without a shadow of doubt in the Apostle. Hear about it, I say, in Genesis: *God made man in the image of God* (Gen 1:27). To show at the same time how the Trinity is inseparable, he says in the same book, *And the Spirit of God was being moved over the waters* (Gen 1:2). Listen to the prophet, saying in the person of Christ, *The Spirit of the Lord is upon me, which is why he has anointed me, has sent me to proclaim good news to the poor* (Isa 61:1). Listen to it in the Psalms: *By the word of the Lord were the heavens fixed firm, and by the breath of his mouth all their might* (Ps 33:6); and again, *Give me back the joy of your salvation, and confirm me with the sovereign spirit* (Ps 51:12). Listen to the same thing confirmed in the Gospel: The Lord Christ says to the apostles, **All authority has been given to me in heaven and on earth; go and baptize all nations in the name of the Father and of the Son and of the Holy Spirit**. Listen to the Apostle: *Oh, the depths of the riches of the wisdom and knowledge of God! How inscrutable are his judgments, and unsearchable his ways! For who has ever known the mind of the Lord, or who has ever been his counselor? Or who ever first gave [a gift] to him and was repaid? Since from him and through him and in him are all things; to him be glory forever and ever* (Rom 11:33–36).

Thus it has been sufficiently and clearly proven from the Scriptures of the Old and New Testaments that the divine unity is an inseparable Trinity; let us therefore utterly reject the heretics, following what the Apostle says: *Shun a heretic after one correction* (Tit 3:10), and let us now confirm our faithful congregations in this catholic faith. There are indeed no greater riches or treasures or honors, no greater wealth of this world than the catholic faith, which saves sinners, gives light to the blind, heals the sick, baptizes catechumens, justifies the faithful, restores the penitent, helps the just to grow in justice, crowns the martyrs, preserves virgins, widows, and married couples in a chaste way of life, ordains clergy, consecrates bishops, prepares us all for the kingdom of heaven, has a share with the holy angels in the eternal inheritance.

There is one substance of Godhead in the Trinity, one power, one might, one majesty, one name of divinity; just as he himself said to his disciples when he had risen from the dead: **Go, baptize the nations**, not in several names, but **in the one name of the Father and the Son and the Holy Spirit**. So, believing then in the divine Trinity and the threefold unity, take care, dearly beloved, that no one seduces you from the faith and truth of the catholic Church. Because, *whoever preaches to you another gospel besides the one you have received, let him be anathema*. Listen to the Apostle, not me, saying, *But even if we ourselves or an angel from heaven should preach to you another gospel besides the one you have received, let him be anathema* (Gal 1:8–9).

You can certainly see, my dear friends, even in the very words of the holy symbol,[8] how at the conclusion of all the articles that belong to the mystery of faith, a kind of supplement is added, which says, *through the holy Church*.[9] So, shun as best you can the many and various deceivers, the multitude of whose sects and names it would take far too long to explain now. You see, we have many things to say to you, but you cannot bear them now. One thing only I urge you to take to heart, and that is by every means possible to turn your minds and your ears away from the person who is not a catholic, so that you may be able to lay hold of *the forgiveness of sins* and *the resurrection of the flesh* and *life everlasting* through the one, true, and holy catholic Church, in which we learn of the Father and the Son and the Holy Spirit, one God, to whom is honor and glory forever and ever.

(16) Leo the Great

Therefore, beloved, throughout this time that passed between the Lord's resurrection and his ascension, the providence of God attended to this, taught this, and recommended this to the eyes of his own: that the Lord Jesus Christ should be acknowledged as resurrected, who truly was born, suffered, and died. The blessed apostles and all the disciples, who had been anxious because of his death on the cross and uncertain in their belief of his resurrection, were thus strengthened by the manifest truth that when the Lord went to the heights of heaven, not only were they not affected by any sadness, but they were even filled with a great joy. Truly and unspeakably great was their cause for rejoicing, since in the sight of the holy multitude, the nature of the human race ascended above the dignity of all celestial creatures. It was about to pass beyond the angelic orders, elevated beyond the heights of the archangels. Human nature was not going to have a limit to its promotion or be limited by any sublime beings until it had been received at the assembly of the eternal Father. Human nature is joined with the throne of that glory to whose nature it is bound together in the Son.

Therefore, since Christ's ascension is our advancement even where the glory of the head has led the way, in that place also is the hope of the body. Let us exult, beloved, in worthy joys, and let us rejoice through pious thanksgiving. For today, not only are we proved to be possessors of paradise, but in Christ we have also entered the heights of heaven. We

8. The baptismal creed.

9. The phrase is puzzling. In the creed the words are "in the holy Church."

have secured more through the ineffable grace of Christ than we had lost through the devil's hatred. For those whom the virulent enemy had driven out from the happiness of our first habitation the Son of God has now placed at the right hand of the Father, united with him in one body, who lives and reigns with God the Father Almighty and the Holy Spirit forever and ever. Amen.

Appendix 1: Authors of Works Excerpted

Ambrose (ca. 339–97), a powerful bishop of Milan, the capital of the western Roman Empire, exerted much influence on the emperors of his time. He was a defender of Nicene orthodoxy against Homoian teaching, and he was also partly responsible for the conversion of Augustine. He is one of the four "doctors" (i.e., teachers) of the Latin Church. Fluent in Greek, he was acquainted with the biblical commentaries of Origen and other Greek fathers. Ambrose wrote several thematic treatises on Old Testament figures, but also a commentary on the Gospel of Luke.

Apollinaris (ca. 315–ca. 390) was a close associate of Athanasius of Alexandria and supporter of the Council of Nicaea. He was chosen bishop of Laodicea about 360. Apollinaris developed an understanding of the union of divine and human in Christ, according to which the human mind and will were replaced by the divine. He also wrote treatises against Greek philosophers and extensive commentaries on Scripture, most of which has been lost. Only fragments are extant from his commentary on Matthew.

Arnobius the Younger (d. after 450). A native of North Africa, he came to Rome and lived there as a monk until his death. He authored a dialogical work against Monophysitism and two biblical commentaries: the first on the Psalms, in which he defends a pro-Nicene theology of the Trinity, and a second called *Expositiunculae* (notes) on the Gospels of John, Matthew, and Luke. It is possible Arnobius wrote the so-called *Praedestinatus*, which lacks the name of the author but shares similar characteristics in content and vocabulary with the commentary on the Psalms. Ironically, it heavily depends on Augustine's *De haeresibus* and yet refutes Augustine's teaching on grace and predestination.

Augustine (354–430), the preeminent Western theologian of the patristic period, was trained in rhetoric in North Africa and Rome and taught it in Milan. He was a follower of Platonic philosophy and then of Manicheanism before his conversion to Christianity and his baptism by Ambrose in 387. Forcibly ordained priest of Hippo (in modern Algiers) and shortly thereafter bishop, he spent much of his time defending the catholic faith in opposition to Manicheans, Donatists, and Pelagians. His vast surviving output embraces exegesis (sermons and commentaries), theology, dogma (e.g., *On the Trinity*), apologetics (*City of God*), and autobiography (*Confessions*). Among the central themes of his work are God as the supreme object of human desire, evil as a purely negative privation of the good, the radical dependence of man upon the grace of God, and the doctrine of original sin.

Basil of Caesarea or Basil "the Great" (ca. 330–79) was bishop of Caesarea in Cappadocia (in modern Turkey) and founder of a monastery and charitable institutions. One of the three Cappadocian fathers, he was the brother of Gregory of Nyssa and close friend of Gregory of Nazianzus. His rules for monks, published in several different forms, are still influential in Eastern churches. Basil defended the Christology of Nicaea against the Neo-Arians, who denied the full divinity of Christ. His treatise *On the Holy Spirit* is concerned to defend the divinity of the Spirit.

Caelius Sedulius (5th c.), a Christian poet known for his *Paschale Carmen*, an account in five books of the miracles in the Old and New Testaments. The poem is addressed not only to Christian readers, but pagan as well, thus paving the way of presenting the Christian faith to the latter. In the early Middle Ages, the *Paschale* was regarded as one of the most successful biblical poems of Late Antiquity.

Caesarius of Arles (ca. 470–542) was initially a member of the monastic community in Lérins but later left for reasons of health. After his recovery, he was named abbot of a monastery near Arles, where he remained until being appointed bishop of Arles in 514 by Symmachus, bishop of Rome. Soon after his installment, Caesarius founded the convent of St. John for women, for which he composed a *Regula virginum*. As bishop, his chief concern was pastoral formation and moral education for the Church and ascetic communities. A popular preacher, his largest work is a collection of sermons on diverse scriptural themes and figures, as well as the annual cycle of feast days. Some of these sermons are material edited from earlier writers, especially Augustine. Toward the end of his life, he prepared a Rule for Monks that shows signs of dependency on the Augustinian Rule.

Chromatius of Aquileia (ca. 335/340–408). A member of the clergy of Aquileia by 370, Chromatius participated in the council of Aquileia (381), a council where Ambrose of Milan had two major proponents of Homoian theology condemned. Several collections of Chromatius's sermons have been discovered, which include sixty-one tractates on Matthew's Gospel, as well as seventeen other sermons on Matthew, a sermon on the Beatitudes, and a short preface to the Lord's Prayer. As bishop (in 388), Chromatius became a patron to Jerome and Rufinus and spoke out against the deportation of Chrysostom.

Clement of Alexandria (ca. 150–ca. 215), a Christian apologist, philosopher, and polymath, was the first Christian to attempt a thoroughgoing synthesis of the Bible and Greek philosophy. He is known primarily for a trilogy that consists of the *Exhortation*, an invitation to the Christian faith directed at educated Greeks, the *Pedagogue*, a moral treatise that focuses on the elementary stages of the Christian life, and the *Stromateis* or *Miscellanies*, an enigmatic, diffuse work in seven books that discusses various theological and moral topics.

Cyprian of Carthage (d. 258). Thascius Caecilianus Cyprianus, like Tertullian, whom he called "the teacher," was a rhetorician by profession. Converted to Christianity, he was chosen bishop of Carthage in 249, just months before the beginning of the Decian persecution, during which he governed the Carthaginian church from exile, and after which he showed himself a decisive leader of all the African churches in a period when disagreements and schisms were occasioned by differences over the treatment of the many Christians who had fallen away during the persecution. When persecution was renewed under Emperor Valerian, Cyprian himself was martyred.

Cyril of Alexandria (d. 444) was patriarch of Alexandria and an influential theologian who played an important role in the formulation of the classic doctrine of the person of Christ. He led opposition to the teaching of the Antiochene Nestorius, bishop of Constantinople. His writings include theological treatises, letters, and many commentaries, including one on Matthew.

Didache ("The Teaching"). A manual of Christian and church practices compiled around the end of the first century, though earlier versions may be much earlier. Its contents betray a period when the liturgical institutions of Christianity were still developing and not familiar to all churches. The document's opening with the "Two Ways" is the earliest use of this standard pattern of Jewish moral instruction, indicating a dependency on Jewish teaching (e.g., as found in Deuteronomy and Qumran's *Rule of the Community*).

Ephrem (306–73), Syriac writer and poet, native of Nisibis in southeastern Turkey. He is the author of many hymns and verse homilies dealing with biblical persons and events, ascetical topics, and theological themes, as well as biblical commentaries. He is the only Syriac writer recognized by the Catholic Church as "Doctor of the Universal Church" and is celebrated in the Eastern Church as "The Lyre of the Holy Spirit."

Epiphanius the Latin (sixth century). Almost nothing is known about this writer except for the attribution, in medieval manuscripts, of the *Interpretation of the Gospels* to a certain "Epiphanius Latinus." Presumably the designation of this Epiphanius as "the Latin" is meant to distinguish him from the Greek heresiologist, Epiphanius of Salamis. The commentary focuses primarily on texts from the Gospel of Matthew, using a literal method of interpretation.

Eusebius of Caesarea (260–339), bishop of Caesarea in Palestine, prolific and learned Christian scholar and father of church history. He wrote the first history of the church and other historical works, a Life of Constantine, theological and apologetic writings, and various works on the Bible, including a complete commentary on Isaiah.

Eusebius of Emesa (ca. 300–ca. 359), educated in Antioch and Alexandria, was also a student of Eusebius of Caesarea. Most of his works, polemical and biblical commentary, survive only in fragments, but a Latin translation of twenty-two homilies on various topics of biblical exegesis has been preserved.

Gregory of Nazianzus (329–89), known as "the Theologian," was bishop of Sasima in Cappadocia (in modern Turkey) and a prominent preacher in Constantinople. Along with the other two Cappadocian fathers (Basil of Caesarea and Gregory of Nyssa), he was a strong supporter of the creed formulated at Nicaea in 325 and a contributor to the resolution of the Arian controversies at the Council of Constantinople in 381. Well educated in Greek culture and rhetoric, he was known for his eloquence, evident, for example, in his *Five Theological Orations* and his many poems.

Gregory of Nyssa (ca. 330–ca. 395), bishop of Nyssa and an important theologian, was the brother of Basil of Caesarea and one of the three Cappadocian fathers. He championed the creed of Nicaea (325) against followers of Arius, who denied the full divinity of Christ (see his polemical work *Against Eunomius*). Among his many works are the *Great Catechesis*, an introduction to the Christian faith and sacraments; *On Virginity*, which recommends the ascetic life; the *Life of Moses*; and homilies on the Beatitudes, the Lord's Prayer, and the Song of Songs. His exegesis, influenced by Origen, emphasizes the mystical sense of Scripture.

Gregory the Great (ca. 540–604; bishop of Rome, 590–604). Gregory was the offspring of a Roman Christian family of senatorial rank. After a brief public career and the death of his father, he disposed of his inheritance by founding and endowing six monasteries in Sicily and one in Rome, the latter on the site of his family home, where he himself became a monk. Popes Benedict I and Pelagius II employed him, now a deacon, as their representative to the imperial court in Constantinople. He succeeded Pelagius II as Pope in 590, to become an energetic, practical, and thoughtful administrator of his see and a principal guide of his posterity—medieval Latin Christianity.

Hilary of Poitiers (317–67), Latin theologian, biblical commentator, and hymn writer. His most important work, *The Trinity*, is a defense of the teaching of the Council of Nicea. He is also the author of a commentary on the Gospel of Matthew as well as one on the Psalms.

Irenaeus (ca. 130–ca. 200), bishop of Lugdunum in Gaul (modern Lyon), wrote *Against the Heresies* to oppose Gnostic teachers such as the followers of Valentinus. He defends the Christian use of the Old Testament and argues for its unity with the New Testament, of which he is an important early interpreter. His theology emphasizes God's providential direction of history and the central biblical themes of creation, redemption through the incarnation, and eschatological fulfillment.

Jerome (ca. 345–420), an influential biblical scholar and ascetic, was educated in Rome and then devoted himself to the ascetic life, spending several years as a hermit in the Syrian desert and serving as head of a monastery in Bethlehem. He is best known for the Vulgate, his translation of the Bible from Hebrew and Greek into Latin, and for his many biblical commentaries (including works on the Prophets, Matthew, Galatians, Ephesians, and Philemon). He was much influenced by Origen, some of whose works he translated into Latin, but later in life he denounced some of Origen's ideas. His *On Illustrious Men*, a catalogue of Christian writers, contains a brief biography of the Apostle Paul and a description of his letters.

John Chrysostom (ca. 347–407) studied rhetoric under the pagan orator Libanius and theology under Diodore of Tarsus, head of the Christian school in Antioch. As a priest in Antioch and later bishop at Constantinople, he was known especially for his uncompromising morality, his courage in difficult political circumstances, and his eloquence. His honorific title "Chrysostom" means "golden tongued" and reflects his great reputation as a preacher. He preached extended series of sermons on many biblical books, including a complete collection on the gospel of Matthew.

Juvencus (early fourth century). According to Jerome, Gaius Vettius Iuvencus composed the first Christian poem around 330. Described as a priest from a prominent family in Spain, Juvencus transcribed the four Gospels (in four books) into 3,219 hexameters. In the *Evangeliorum libri*, the author expressed great admiration for Homer and Virgil.

Leo the Great (Leo I, d. 461) became pope in 440. During an unstable time, he greatly enhanced the authority of the see of Rome over all the western provinces. His many letters and sermons are forcefully written.

Leontius of Constantinople (ca. mid-sixth century). As a presbyter in Constantinople, Leontius did much preaching, with some of his homilies having survived. Their main concern is with holy days, as well as one on the birth of Christ, one on Pentecost, and another on Christ's transfiguration.

Macarius of Magnesia (ca. late fourth and early fifth centuries) was the author of an anti-pagan apologetic treatise, *Apokritikos ē monogenēs pros Hellēnas* (*Response of the Only-Begotten to the Greeks*), commonly called the *Apocriticus*. Of the original five books, only portions of it survive. In a fictitious dialogue, Macarius refutes a pagan critic who finds inconsistencies in the New Testament. The writer is familiar with and responds to Porphyry's *Against the Christians*.

Maximus of Turin (d. 408/423) wrote more than a hundred sermons, some of which were widely read in the Middle Ages.

Maximus the Confessor (580–662) was an Eastern theologian who wrote on theological, cosmological, and ascetic topics. He is most noted for his critique of monotheletism, the teaching that Christ had only a divine will, and for his brilliant interpretation of the double will of Christ. He was imprisoned, his tongue was cut out and his right hand cut off, and he died in exile. For his faithfulness, he was honored with the name "confessor."

Origen of Alexandria (ca. 185–ca. 254) was a leading third-century theologian and exegete who lived in Alexandria and later in Caesarea in Palestine. He wrote many commentaries and homilies on Old and New Testament books (e.g., on Genesis, Exodus, Leviticus, Jeremiah, Matthew, Luke, and John) and apparently commented on all the Pauline epistles (of these only the commentary on Romans survives in substantial quantity). His other works include *Against Celsus*, a defense of Christianity against the attack of the Platonic philosopher Celsus, and *On First Principles*, a compendium of Christian theology.

Peter Chrysologus (d. ca. 451) was bishop of Ravenna and reputed author of nearly 200 sermons of which 183 are most likely Peter's own. For the most part, the sermons are about the Gospels, Psalms, and letters of Paul. The others take up liturgical themes, providing a sketch of the liturgical year.

Philoxenus of Hierapolis (or Mabbug) (ca. 440–523) was born in Persia and educated at the School of Edessa. He was consecrated bishop of Hierapolis in Syria, where he vigorously defended Monophysite Christology. Writing in Syriac, his works include homilies on the virtues and commentaries on Matthew and Luke, of which only fragments survive.

Tertullian (ca. 160–ca. 225), from Carthage in North Africa, the first to write theological treatises in Latin, also wrote apologetic, anti-heretical, and moral works, all of which display great rhetorical skill. While he wrote no biblical commentaries, the use and interpretation of Scripture heavily imbue nearly everything he wrote. Later in life, Tertullian was attracted to the New Prophecy (Montanism), in part by the rigorous moralism of this movement.

Theodore of Heraclea (d. 355). Also known as Theodorus, this bishop was among the Eastern delegation that condemned Athanasius and Marcellus at the counter-council of Philippopolis (343). He was regarded as a learned interpreter of the Gospels. There remain fragments of commentaries on Matthew, Luke, and John, as well as on Psalms, Isaiah, and other biblical texts.

Theodore of Mopsuestia (ca. 350–428), a friend of John Chrysostom and bishop of Mopsuestia in Cilicia, was a representative of Antiochene exegesis and theology. In his biblical commentaries, surviving only in fragments, Theodore emphasizes philological and historical questions and avoids Alexandrian allegorical interpretation.

Valerian of Cimelium (Cimiez) (d. ca. 460). Very little is known about this Gallic bishop's life, despite mention of him in Leo (I)'s letters. Twenty homilies have come down from his pen, in which he preaches on the goals of the Christian life.

Venantius Fortunatus (530–610), a Latin poet and hymn writer, was the author of two hymns sung during Holy Week, "Pange lingua gloriosi" (Sing, My Tongue) and "Vexilla regis prodeunt" (The Royal Banners Forward Go). He was best known for writing the *Life of Hilary* (of Poitiers).

Victorinus of Poetovio (Pettau) (b. ca. 230) is the author of the earliest expositions of Scripture in Latin. Later patristic writers tell of his works on many Old Testament books, as well as a commentary on Matthew, which Jerome copied and sent to his female patrons in Rome. This commentary has not been preserved, but it is likely that the extant *De decem virginibus* (Matt 25:1–13) is taken from it. Also surviving are several short explanations on the Apocalypse, on the creation of the world, and a work entitled, *Against All Heresies*, often identified as Tertullian's.

Appendix 2: Sources of Texts Translated

1. Abbreviations of Source Titles

ACW	Ancient Christian Writers. New York: Newman, 1946–.
CCSL	Corpus Christianorum: Series latina. Turnhout (Belgium): Brepols, 1953–.
CSCO	Corpus Scriptorum Christianorum orientalium. Paris, 1903–.
CSEL	Corpus scriptorum ecclesiasticorum latinorum. Vienna, 1866–.
CSS	Cistercian Studies Series. Kalamazoo, MI: Cistercian Publications, 1969–.
FOC	Fathers of the Church. Washington, DC: Catholic University of America Press, 1948–.
GCS	Die griechischen christlichen Schriftsteller der ersten drei Jahrhunderte. Berlin: Akademie Verlag, 1901–.
GNO	Werner Jaeger et al., ed., Gregorii Nysseni opera. Leiden: Brill, 1960–72.
MKGK	Matthäus-Kommentare aus der griechischen Kirche. Berlin: Akademie-Verlag, 1957.
PG	J.-P. Migne, ed., Patrologiae cursus completus: Series graeca. 161 vols. Paris, 1857–66.
PL	J.-P. Migne, ed., Patrologiae cursus completus: Series latina. 221 vols. Paris, 1844–64.
PLS	A. Hamann, ed., Patrologiae latinae supplementum. Paris, 1957–.
SC	Sources chrétiennes. Paris: Éditions du Cerf, 1948–.
WSA	Works of Saint Augustine. Brooklyn, N.Y.: New City, 1990–.

2. Sources of Individual Excerpts

Preface to Matthew

(1) John Chrysostom, *Homily* 1, PG 57:15, 23.
(2) Irenaeus of Lyons, *Against the Heresies* 3.11.8, SC 211:160–64.
(3) Origen, *Homilies on Luke* 1.1–2, GCS 9.3–4; *Commentary on John* 1.7, GCS 10:10–11, *Origenes Werke* 4. *Commentarius in Johannem* (1903: Erwin Preuschen); *Commentary on Matthew*

cited in Eusebius of Caesarea, *Ecclesiastical History* 6.25.4, SC 41:126, trans. Lawlor and Oulton, 197–98.
(4) Eusebius of Caesarea, *Theophania* 5.37–38, GCS 3/2:34–35, 245–46.
(5) Chromatius of Aquileia, prologus, *Tractatus lxi in euangelium Matthei* 1, 3–4, 9, 11; CCSL 9A:185–87, 189–91.
(6) Augustine, *On the Consensus of the Gospels: De consensu Evangelistarum libri quattuor* 1.1; 2.4, CSEL 43:1–2, 4.

Matthew 1

(1) Eusebius of Caesarea, *Ecclesiastical History* 1.7.1–17, SC 31:25–29, trans. Lawlor and Oulton, 19–22.
(2) Hilary of Poitiers, *On Matthew* 1.1, SC 254:90.
(3) Augustine, *Sermon* 51.12–13, 29–31, PL 38:339–40, 350–52, WSA III/3:27–28.
(4) Jerome, *Commentary on St. Matthew* 1.1.1, SC 242:72–76.
(5) Peter Chrysologus, *Sermon* 146.2–6, CCSL 24B:901–5.
(6) Leo the Great, *Sermon* 22.3, 2, CCSL 138:93–95.
(7) Peter Chrysologus, *Sermon* 145.1, CCSL 24B:889–91.
(8) Ephrem of Nisibis, *Homily on Our Lord* 1.2.4, CSCO 270:2, 4.
(9) John Chrysostom, *Homily* 2, PG 57:25.
(10) Augustine, *Sermon* 51.3, 20, PL 38:334–35, WSA III/3:20–21, 32–33.
(11) Hilary of Poitiers, *On Matthew* 1.3, SC 254:94.
(12) Jerome, *Commentary on St. Matthew* 1.1.1, SC 242:76–78.
(13) John Chrysostom, *Homily* 2, PG 57:26.
(14) Augustine, *Sermon* 51.30, PL 38:350–51, WSA III/3:40.

Matthew 2

(1) John Chrysostom, *Homily* 6.4–5, PG 57:63–67; *In natalem Christi diem*, PG 56:392.
(2) Leo the Great, *Sermon* 33.1–2, CCSL 138:170–72.
(3) Epiphanius the Latin, *On the Interpretation of the Gospels* 3, PLS 3:836.
(4) Origen, *Contra Celsum* 1.60, *Origen: Contra Celsum*, trans. H. Chadwick (Cambridge: Cambridge University Press, 1953), 54–55.
(5) Gregory of Nazianzus, *On the Testaments and the Coming of Christ*, PG 36:461–63, trans. D. A. Sykes, *St. Gregory of Nazianzus: Poemata Arcana*, ed., C. Moreschini (Oxford University Press, 1997).
(6) Leo the Great, *Sermon* 31.2, CCSL 138:162.
(7) Epiphanius the Latin, *On the Interpretation of the Gospels* 5, PLS 3:837.
(8) Leo the Great, *Sermon* 33.2–4; 34.3, CCSL 138:171–72, 181–83.
(9) Hilary of Poitiers, *On Matthew* 1.5, SC 254:98.
(10) Basil of Caesarea, *Homilia in sanctam Christi generationem* 6, PG 31:1472–73.
(11) John Chrysostom, *Homily* 7.4–6, PG 57:77–78.
(12) Gregory the Great, *Homily* 10.1, 7, CCLS 141:66–67, 71–72, CSS 123:54–55, 59–60.
(13) Hilary of Poitiers, *On Matthew* 1.7, SC 254:100.
(14) Leo the Great, *Sermon* 31.3, CCSL 138:163.

(15) Peter Chrysologus, *Sermon* 152.2–4, CCSL 24B:948–51.
(16) John Chrysostom, *Homily* 9.1–3, PG 57:175–79.
(17) Jerome, *Commentary on St. Matthew* 1.2.17–18, SC 242:86.
(18) Jerome, *Commentary on St. Matthew* 1.2.22, SC 242:86–88.
(19) Gregory of Nazianzus, *Sermon* 38.1–2, 17–18, PG 36:312a–313b, 331a–c, trans. Charles Kannengiesser, *Early Christianity Spirituality* (Minneapolis: Fortress, 1986), 78–81 (slightly adapted).
(20) Hilary of Poitiers, *On Matthew* 2.1, SC 254:100–102.
(21) Epiphanius the Latin, *On the Interpretation of the Gospels* 5, PLS 3:837.
(22) Jerome, *Commentary on St. Matthew* 1.2.23, SC 242:88.
(23) Augustine, *On the Consensus of the Gospels: De consensu Evangelistarum libri quattuor* 2.5.16; 2.9.21–22, CSEL 43:98–99, 188–89.

Matthew 3

(1) John Chrysostom, *Homily* 10, PG 57:185–87.
(2) Hilary of Poitiers, *On Matthew* 2.2, SC 254:102.
(3) Jerome, *Commentary on St. Matthew* 1.3.11, SC 242:92.
(4) Theodore of Heraclea, *Commentary on Matthew: Fragment* 18, MKGK 61–62.
(5) Epiphanius the Latin, *On the Interpretation of the Gospels* 11, PLS 3:838–39.
(6) Gregory of Nazianzus, *Oration* 39.14–15, SC 358:178–84.
(7) Chromatius of Aquileia, *Seventeen Tractates* 1.1.1–5; 3.1–3, CCSL 9:391–92.
(8) Theodore of Mopsuestia, *Commentary on Matthew: Fragment* 14, MKGK 101.
(9) Hilary of Poitiers, *On Matthew* 2.5, 6, SC 254:108, 10.
(10) Philoxenus of Hierapolis, *Fragments* 11 and 13, CSCO 392:11–12, 19, trans. CSCO 393:9–10, 16–17.
(11) Chromatius of Aquileia, *Seventeen Tractates* 2.1.1–3.2, CCSL 9:393–94.
(12) Augustine, *Sermon* 52.1–2, 4, 7–8, 14–15, PL 38:354–57, 359–60, WSA III/3:51–53, 56–57.
(13) Gregory of Nazianzus, *On the Spirit; Poemata Arcana*, ed. Claudio Moreschini, trans. Donald F. Sykes (Oxford: Oxford University Press, 1996), 10–15.

Matthew 4

(1) John Chrysostom, *Homily* 13, PG 57:207–9.
(2) Hilary of Poitiers, *On Matthew* 3.1, SC 254:110, 112.
(3) Epiphanius the Latin, *On the Interpretation of the Gospels* 13, PLS 3:840.
(4) Gregory the Great, *Homily* 16:3–4, CCSL 141:112–13, CSS 123:103–4.
(5) Hilary of Poitiers, *On Matthew* 3.2, SC 254:114, 116.
(6) Jerome, *Commentary on St. Matthew* 1.4.6–7, SC 242:98, 100.
(7) Peter Chrysologus, *Sermon* 11.6, CCSL 24:75.
(8) Epiphanius the Latin, *On the Interpretation of the Gospels* 15, PLS 3:841.
(9) John Chrysostom, *Homily* 13, PG 57:213.
(10) Hilary of Poitiers, *On Matthew* 3.5, SC 254:116, 118.
(11) Leo the Great, *Sermon* 40.3, CCSL 138A:225–27 (alpha text).
(12) Gregory the Great, *Homily* 16.1–3, CCSL 141:109–12, CSS 123:101–3 (modified).

(13) Epiphanius the Latin, *On the Interpretation of the Gospels* 18, PLS 3:844–45.
(14) Gregory of Nazianzus, *Oration* 37.1, SC 318:270, 272.
(15) Gregory the Great, *Homily* 5.2–3, CCSL 141:34–36, CSS 123:10–11 (modified).
(16) Hilary of Poitiers, *On Matthew* 3.6, SC 254:118, 120.
(17) Epiphanius the Latin, *On the Interpretation of the Gospels* 16, PLS 3:842.
(18) Gregory the Great, *Homily* 2, 10–13, PL 76:1096, CSS 123:12.

Matthew 5

(1) Augustine, *Sermon on the Mount* 1.1.1, CCSL 35:1–2.
(2) Gregory of Nyssa, *Beatitudes* 1–2, GNO 7/2:79–81, 89–90, ACW 18:87–88, 97.
(3) Leo the Great, *Sermon* 95.1, CCSL 138A:582–83.

---

(1) Jerome, *Commentary on St. Matthew* 1.5.1, SC 242:104.
(2) Chromatius of Aquileia, *Seventeen Tractates* 3.1.1–5, CCSL 9:394–95.
(3) John Chrysostom, *Homily* 15, PG 57:223.
(4) Chromatius of Aquileia, *Seventeen Tractates* 3.2.1–6, CCSL 9:395–96.
(5) Gregory of Nyssa, *Beatitudes* 1, GNO 7/2:82–84, 88, ACW 18:89–90, 91, 94–95.
(6) John Chrysostom, *Homily* 15, PG 57:224.
(7) Augustine, *Sermon on the Mount* 1.2.5, CCSL 35:5; *Sermon* 53A.8, WSA III/3:81.
(8) Chromatius of Aquileia, *Sermon on the Eight Beatitudes* 2.4–6, CCSL 9:384; *Seventeen Tractates* 3.3.1–5, CCSL 9:396–97.
(9) Gregory of Nyssa, *Beatitudes* 2, GNO 7/2:94–95, 97, ACW 18:101–2, 104.
(10) Augustine, *Sermon on the Mount* 1.2.4; 1.4.12, CCSL 35:4–5, 11; *Sermon* 53A.7, WSA III/3:81.
(11) Chromatius of Aquileia, *Seventeen Tractates* 3.4.1–2, 4, CCSL 9:397–98; *Sermon on the Eight Beatitudes* 2.5–6, CCSL 9:384.
(12) Origen, *Commentary on John* 13.4, SC 222:44.
(13) Gregory of Nyssa, *Beatitudes* 4, GNO 7/2:119–22, ACW 18:126–29.
(14) Augustine, *Sermon on the Mount* 1.2.6, CCSL 35:5; *Sermon* 53A.9, WSA III/3:81.
(15) Chromatius of Aquileia, *Seventeen Tractates* 3.5.1–4, CCSL 9:398–99.
(16) Gregory of Nyssa, *Beatitudes* 5, GNO 7/2:126–27, ACW 18:132–33.
(17) Augustine, *Sermon* 53.5, PL 38:366, WSA III/3:67–68; *Sermon* 53A.10, WSA III/3:82.
(18) Leo the Great, *Sermon* 10.2, CCSL 138:41–42.
(19) Irenaeus of Lyons, *Against the Heresies* 4.20.5–7, SC 100:636–48.
(20) Gregory of Nyssa, *Beatitudes* 6, GNO 7/2:137–48, ACW 18:143–48, 153.
(21) Apollinaris of Laodicea, *Commentary on Matthew: Fragment* 12–13, MKGK 4–5.
(22) Augustine, *Sermon* 53.6–7, 10–11, PL 38:366–69, WSA III/3:69, 70–71.
(23) Origen, *Commentary on Matthew* 2, PG 13:832; *Philocalia* 6.
(24) Epiphanius the Latin, *On the Interpretation of the Gospels* 18, PLS 3:847–48.
(25) Chromatius of Aquileia, *Seventeen Tractates* 3.7.1–6, CCSL 9:400–401.
(26) Augustine, *Sermon on the Mount* 1.3.10, CCSL 35:7–9.
(27) Chromatius of Aquileia, *Seventeen Tractates* 3.8.1–2; 9.2–3, CCSL 9:401–2.
(28) Epiphanius the Latin, *On the Interpretation of the Gospels* 18, PLS 3:848.
(29) Chromatius of Aquileia, *Sermon on the Eight Beatitudes* 9.1–3, CCSL 9:387.
(30) John Chrysostom, *Homily* 15, PG 57:228.
(31) Augustine, *Sermon on the Mount* 1.4.11–12, CCSL 35:9–12.

(32) Chromatius of Aquileia, *Seventeen Tractates* 4.1.1–3; 2.1–5; 3.3–4; 4.1–2, CCSL 9:402–5.
(33) Epiphanius the Latin, *On the Interpretation of the Gospels* 19, 16, PLS 3:851, 842.
(34) Gregory the Great, *Homily* 19.11–13, 22–23, CCSL 141:123–24, 131, CSS 123:140–41, 147.
(35) Origen, *Commentary on John* 1.25.162–66, SC 120:140–42.
(36) Hilary of Poitiers, *On Matthew* 4.11–13, SC 254:128–32.
(37) Augustine, *Sermon on the Mount* 1.6.17, CCSL 35:16–18; *Sermon* 54.1, 3, PL 38:372–74, WSA III/3:87–88.
(38) Chromatius of Aquileia, *Seventeen Tractates* 5.1.1–3; 2.1, 3; 5.1–5, CCSL 9:405–6, 408–9.
(39) Origen, *Commentary on Matthew* frag 99, GCS 41:1, 56.
(40) Hilary of Poitiers, *On Matthew* 4.14–15, SC 254:132–34.
(41) Chromatius of Aquileia, *Seventeen Tractates* 6.1.1–4, CCSL 9:409–10.
(42) Jerome, *Commentary on St. Matthew* 1.5.19, SC 242:112.
(43) Hilary of Poitiers, *On Matthew* 4.16, SC 254:134.
(44) Augustine, *Sermon on the Mount* 1.9.21, CCSL 35:23; *Sermon* 55.1–2, PL 38:375, WSA III/3:91–92.
(45) John Chrysostom, *Homily* 16, PG 57:248.
(46) Chromatius of Aquileia, *Seventeen Tractates* 7.2.1–5, CCSL 9:412–13.
(47) Augustine, *Sermon on the Mount* 1.10.27, CCSL 35:28–29.
(48) Tertullian, *On Prayer* 11.1–3, CCSL 1:263–64.
(49) Hilary of Poitiers, *On Matthew* 4.18–19, SC 254:136–38.
(50) Caesarius of Arles, *Sermon* 145.1, 3, CCSL 104:597–98.
(51) Hilary of Poitiers, *On Matthew* 4.21, SC 254:138–40.
(52) Chromatius of Aquileia, *Seventeen Tractates* 9.2.1–3; 1.1–2, 6–7, CCSL 9:416–18.
(53) Augustine, *Sermon on the Mount* 1.12.33–34, CCSL 35:36–37.
(54) Hilary of Poitiers, *On Matthew* 4.22, SC 254:140–42.
(55) Augustine, *Sermon on the Mount* 1.14.39, CCSL 35:41–42.
(56) Chromatius of Aquileia, *Seventeen Tractates* 10.1.1–5, CCSL 9:419–20.
(57) Hilary of Poitiers, *On Matthew* 4.23–24, SC 254:142–44.
(58) Augustine, *Sermon* 180.1–3; PL 38:972–74, WSA III/5:314–16.
(59) Augustine, *Sermon on the Mount* 1.19.57, 59, CCSL 35:65, 67.
(60) Chromatius of Aquileia, *Seventeen Tractates* 11.3.1–2; 4.1–2, CCSL 9:423–24.
(61) Hilary of Poitiers, *On Matthew* 4.27, SC 254:146–48.
(62) John Chrysostom, *Homily* 18, PG 57:268.
(63) Jerome, *Commentary on St. Matthew* 1.5.44, SC 242:124–26.

Matthew 6

(1) Augustine, *Sermon on the Mount* 2.1.1, CCSL 35:91–92.
(2) Jerome, *Commentary on St. Matthew* 1.6.2, SC 242:126.
(3) John Chrysostom, *Homily* 19.1–3, PG 57:273–76.
(4) Augustine, *Sermon* 149.11–14, PL 38:803–5, WSA III/3:23–25 (slightly revised).
(5) Origen, *On Prayer* 19.2, GCS 2:341–42, trans. Greer, *Origen*, 119.
(6) Hilary of Poitiers, *On Matthew* 4.28, SC 254:148–50.
(7) Chromatius of Aquileia, *Preface to the Lord's Prayer*, CCSL 9:445–46.
(8) Hilary of Poitiers, *On Matthew* 5.1, SC 254:150.
(9) Augustine, *Sermon on the Mount* 2.3.10–11, CCSL 35:101–2.

(10) Origen, *On Prayer* 21.1–2, GCS 2:345–46, trans. Greer, *Origen*, 123.
(11) Jerome, *Commentary on St. Matthew* 1.6.8, SC 242:128–30.
(12) Origen, *On Prayer* 18.1–3, GCS 2:340–41, trans. Greer, *Origen*, 119.
(13) Chromatius of Aquileia, *Seventeen Tractates* 14.7.6–7, CCSL 9:434; *Preface to the Lord's Prayer*, CCSL 9:445–47.
(14) Tertullian, *On Prayer* 2.1–3, CCSL 1:258.
(15) Cyprian, *On the Lord's Prayer* 1–3, 8, CCSL 3A:90–91, 93.
(16) Gregory of Nyssa, *Lord's Prayer* 2, GNO 7/2:20–21, 26–28, ACW 18:35–36, 41–42.
(17) Origen, *On Prayer* 22.1, 3, 5, GCS 2:346–49, trans. Greer, *Origen*, 123–25.
(18) Origen, *On Prayer* 24.1–5, GCS 2:353–56, trans. Greer, *Origen*, 129–31.
(19) John Chrysostom, *Homily* 19.7, PG 57:279.
(20) Tertullian, *On Prayer* 4.1–3, CCSL 1:259–60.
(21) Cyprian, *On the Lord's Prayer* 13, CCSL 3A:97.
(22) Origen, *On Prayer* 25.1; 26.3, 6, GCS 2:356–57, 360–61, 362–63, trans. Greer, *Origen*, 132, 134–35.
(23) Gregory of Nyssa, *Lord's Prayer* 3, GNO 7/2:34–35, 37–38, ACW 18:48, 51.
(24) Tertullian, *On Prayer* 6.1–4, CCSL 1:260–61.
(25) Origen, *On Prayer* 27.1–2, 4, 9, 12–13, GCS 2:363–65, 369–72, trans. Greer, *Origen*, 137–39, 141–42, 143–44.
(26) Augustine, *Sermon on the Mount* 2.7.25–27, CCSL 35:113–16.
(27) Cyprian, *On the Lord's Prayer* 22, CCSL 3A:103–4.
(28) Origen, *On Prayer* 28.1, 6–7, GCS 2:375–76, 378–79, trans. Greer, *Origen*, 147, 149–50.
(29) Gregory of Nyssa, *Lord's Prayer* 5, GNO 7/2:59, ACW 18:71–72.
(30) Augustine, *Sermon* 181.4, 6, PL 38:981–82, WSA III/5:326–27 (slightly revised).
(31) Origen, *On Prayer* 29.1, 9, 11, 17, GCS 2:381–82, 385–86, 391–92, trans. Greer, *Origen*, 152, 155–56, 160–61.
(32) Chromatius of Aquileia, *Preface to the Lord's Prayer*, CCSL 9:447.
(33) John Chrysostom, *Homily* 19.10, PG 57:282.
(34) Augustine, *Sermon* 58.12, PL 38:399, WSA III/3:124.
(35) Tertullian, *On Prayer* 9.1–3, CCSL 1:262–63.
(36) Cyprian, *On the Lord's Prayer* 23, CCSL 3A:104–5.
(37) Augustine, *Sermon on the Mount* 2.11.38–39, CCSL 35:128–30.
(38) Hilary of Poitiers, *On Matthew* 5.2, SC 254:150–52.
(39) Chromatius of Aquileia, *Seventeen Tractates* 15.2–3, CCSL 9:436–37.
(40) Theodore of Heraclea, *Commentary on Matthew: Fragment* 45, MKGK 69.
(41) Augustine, *Sermon on the Mount* 2.13.45–46, CCSL 35:136–38.
(42) Philoxenus of Hierapolis, *Homilies* 8.223–27, SC 44.222–24.
(43) Chromatius of Aquileia, *Seventeen Tractates* 17.4.1–3, CCSL 9:441–42.
(44) Hilary of Poitiers, *On Matthew* 5.6, SC 254:154–56.
(45) Jerome, *Commentary on St. Matthew* 1.6.26, SC 242:138.
(46) John Chrysostom, *Homily* 21.6, PG 57:299–300.
(47) Hilary of Poitiers, *On Matthew* 5.12–13, SC 254:162–66.
(48) John Chrysostom, *Homily* 22.3–4, PG 57:302–3.
(49) Augustine, *Sermon on the Mount* 2.17.56, CCSL 35:147–48.

Matthew 7

(1) Hilary of Poitiers, *On Matthew* 5.14–15, SC 254:166–70.
(2) John Chrysostom, *Homily* 23.1–2, PG 57:307–10.
(3) Augustine, *Sermon on the Mount* 2.18.61–62, CCSL 35:156–58.
(4) Caesarius of Arles, *Sermon* 148.2, CCSL 104:607.
(5) Jerome, *Commentary on St. Matthew* 1.7.6, SC 242:142.
(6) John Chrysostom, *Homily* 23.3, PG 57:310–11.
(7) Augustine, *Sermon on the Mount* 2.20.68–70, CCSL 35:164–66.
(8) Augustine, *Sermon* 61A.2–5, WSA III/3:150–54.
(9) John Chrysostom, *Homily* 23.4–5, PG 57:311–12.
(10) Augustine, *Sermon on the Mount* 2.22.74, 76, CCSL 35:171–72, 174–75.
(11) John Chrysostom, *Homily* 23.5, PG 57:312–13.
(12) Jerome, *Commentary on St. Matthew* 1.7.13, SC 242:144.
(13) Valerian of Cimelium, *Homily* 2.1, 4, PL 52:696, 698, FOC 17:309, 312–13.
(14) Caesarius of Arles, *Sermon* 151.2, CCSL 104:618.
(15) Jerome, *Commentary on St. Matthew* 1.7.18, SC 242:144–46.
(16) Augustine, *Sermon on the Mount* 2.24.78, 80–81, CCSL 35:174–77, 179–81.
(17) Hilary of Poitiers, *On Matthew* 6.5, SC 254:174–76.
(18) Jerome, *Commentary on St. Matthew* 1.7.22–23, SC 242:148.
(19) Gregory the Great, *Homily* 29.4, CCSL 141:248–49, CSS 123:230.
(20) Jerome, *Commentary on St. Matthew* 1.7.25–26, SC 242:150–52.
(21) Hilary of Poitiers, *On Matthew* 6.6–7, SC 254:176–78.
(22) Augustine, *Sermon* 179.8, PL 38:970–71, WSA III/5:303.
(23) John Chrysostom, *Homily* 25.1–2, 5, PG 57:327–29, 334.

Matthew 8

(1) Jerome, *Commentary on St. Matthew* 1.8.2, CCSL 77:47–48.
(2) Epiphanius the Latin, *On the Interpretation of the Gospels* 22, PLS 3:856.
(3) Augustine, *Sermon* 62.1, 4, PL 38:414–16, WSA III/3:156–57; *Sermon* 77.12, PL 38:488, WSA III/3:323.
(4) Epiphanius the Latin, *On the Interpretation of the Gospels* 22, PLS 3:857.
(5) Gregory the Great, *Homily* 28.2, CCSL 141:240–42, CSS 123:222–23.
(6) Hilary of Poitiers, *On Matthew* 7.4–5, SC 254:182–84.
(7) Augustine, *Sermon* 77.12, PL 38:488, WSA III/3:323; *Sermon* 62.6, PL 38:417, WSA III/3:158–59.
(8) Epiphanius the Latin, *On the Interpretation of the Gospels* 22, PLS 3:858.
(9) Augustine, *Sermon* 62A.2–3, *Miscellanea Agostiniana*, ed. G. Morin (Rome, 1930), 1:609–10, WSA III/3:171 (slightly modified).
(10) Hilary of Poitiers, *On Matthew* 7.6, SC 254:184–86.
(11) John Chrysostom, *Homily* 27.1, PG 57:344–45.
(12) Chromatius of Aquileia, *Tractatus in Matthaeum* 40.1–3, CCSL 9A:386–87.
(13) Hilary of Poitiers, *On Matthew* 7.8, 11, SC 254:186–92.
(14) Jerome, *Commentary on St. Matthew* 1.8.20, CCSL 77:51.
(15) John Chrysostom, *Homily* 27.6, PG 57:347–48.
(16) Hilary of Poitiers, *On Matthew* 8.1–2, SC 254:192–94.

(17) John Chrysostom, *Homily* 28.1, PG 57:351.
(18) Ephrem of Nisibis, *Hymn on Virginity* 33.9–11, CSCO.S 223:122, trans. Sebastian P. Brock, *The Harp of the Spirit: Eighteen Poems of Saint Ephrem* (San Bernardino, CA: Borgo, 1983), 54–55.
(19) Peter Chrysologus, *Sermon* 20.1–3, CCSL 24:117–19.
(20) John Chrysostom, *Homily* 28.2, PG 57:352–53.
(21) Chromatius of Aquileia, *Tractatus in Matthaeum* 43–44, CCSL 9A:407–8.
(22) John Chrysostom, *Homily* 28.4, PG 57:354–55.

Matthew 9

(1) Jerome, *Commentary on St. Matthew* 1.9.1–2, SC 242:166.
(2) John Chrysostom, *Homily* 29.1, PG 57:358–59.
(3) Hilary of Poitiers, *On Matthew* 8.6–7, SC 254:200–202.
(4) Chromatius of Aquileia, *Tractatus in Matthaeum* 44.1, 4, CCSL 9A:412–15.
(5) John Chrysostom, *Homily* 30, PG 57:361–63.
(6) Epiphanius the Latin, *On the Interpretation of the Gospels* 23, PLS 3:858–59.
(7) Gregory the Great, *Homily* 24.1, CCSL 141:197, CSS 123:180 (modified).
(8) Hilary of Poitiers, *On Matthew* 9.2, SC 254:204–6.
(9) Epiphanius the Latin, *On the Interpretation of the Gospels* 23, PLS 3:859–60.
(10) Philoxenus of Hierapolis, *Homilies* 1.18–19, SC 44.38–39.
(11) Tertullian, *Against Marcion* 4.20.7–10, 12, CCSL 1:595–96, trans. Evans, 367–69.
(12) Augustine, *Sermon* 63B.2–3, *Miscellanea Agostiniana*, ed. G. Morin (Rome, 1930), 1:611–12.
(13) John Chrysostom, *Homily* 31.2, PG 57:372–73.
(14) Eusebius of Caesarea, *Ecclesiastical History* 7.18.1–3, SC 41:191–92, trans. Lawlor and Oulton, 231.
(15) John Chrysostom, *Homily* 31.3–4, PG 57:373–74.
(16) Hilary of Poitiers, *On Matthew* 9.9, SC 254:212–14.
(17) John Chrysostom, *Homily* 32.1, PG 57:377.
(18) Chromatius of Aquileia, *Tractatus in Matthaeum* 48.1–2, CCSL 9A:436–37.
(19) Hilary of Poitiers, *On Matthew* 9.10, SC 254:214.
(20) John Chrysostom, *Homily* 32.2, PG 57:378.
(21) Theodore of Heraclea, *Commentary on Matthew: Fragment* 59, MKGK 73.
(22) Hilary of Poitiers, *On Matthew* 10.2, SC 254:216–18.
(23) John Chrysostom, *Homily* 32.4, PG 57:379–80.

Matthew 10

(1) Tertullian, *Against Marcion* 4.13.3–5, CCSL 1:572–73, trans. Evans, 320–31.
(2) Jerome, *Commentary on St. Matthew* 1.10.2, SC 242:186.
(3) John Chrysostom, *Homily* 32.5, PG 57:380–81.
(4) Hilary of Poitiers, *On Matthew* 10.3, 5, SC 254:218–20.
(5) John Chrysostom, *Homily* 32.6–7, PG 57:382.
(6) Gregory the Great, *Homily* 4.2–3, CCSL 141:28–30, CSS 123:122–23.
(7) Hilary of Poitiers, *On Matthew* 10.4, SC 254:218–20.

(8) John Chrysostom, *Homily* 32.8, PG 57:383–84.
(9) Tertullian, *Against the Valentinians* 2–3, CCSL 2:754–55.
(10) Augustine, *Sermon* 64.2–3, PL 38:425–26; *Sermon* 64A.3, *Miscellanea Agostiniana*, ed. G. Morin (Rome, 1930), 1:312–13 (slightly revised).
(11) Tertullian, *On Flight during Persecution* 4–6, CCSL 2:1140–43.
(12) Hilary of Poitiers, *On Matthew* 10.12–13, SC 254:230–32.
(13) John Chrysostom, *Homily* 34.1, PG 57:397–98.
(14) Tertullian, *Scorpiace* 9, CCSL 2:1084–85.
(15) Eusebius of Emesa, *Sermon* 27.1–4, Buytaert 2:195–96.
(16) John Chrysostom, *Homily* 33.5–6, PG 57:394–95.
(17) Eusebius of Emesa, *Sermon* 27.5–7, Buytaert 2:197–99.
(18) Hilary of Poitiers, *On Matthew* 10.17, SC 254:234–36.
(19) Philoxenus of Hierapolis, *Homilies* 6.169–71, SC 44:172–73.
(20) Augustine, *Sermon* 65.8, PL 38:430, WSA III/3:196.
(21) Jerome, *Commentary on St. Matthew* 1.10.29–31, SC 242:204–6.
(22) Hilary of Poitiers, *On Matthew* 10.23–24, SC 254:242–46.
(23) Eusebius of Emesa, *Sermon* 26.21–24, Buytaert 2:187–89.
(24) Ambrose of Milan, *Commentary on the Gospel of Luke* 7.135–36, CCSL 14:260–61, trans. Ní Riain, 286–87.
(25) Augustine, *Sermon* 65A.1, 5, 8; *RB* 86 (1976), 41, 43, 45–46; *Sermon* 159.8, PL 38:872, WSA III/5:126; *Sermon* 344.6, PL 39:1516, WSA III/10:54–55.
(26) *Didache* 11.1–6; 12.1–5, M. Holmes, ed. and rev. *The Apostolic Fathers* (Baker, 1999), 263–65.
(27) Clement of Alexandria, *Who Is the Rich Man That Will Be Saved?* 30–31, GCS 17/2: 179–81.
(28) John Chrysostom, *Homily* 35.4, PG 57:408–9.

Matthew 11

(1) Hilary of Poitiers, *On Matthew* 11.1–2, SC 254:252–54.
(2) Theodore of Mopsuestia, *Commentary on Matthew: Fragment* 57, MKGK 115.
(3) Gregory the Great, *Homily* 5.1–3, CCSL 141:38–40, CSS 123:28–30.
(4) Ambrose of Milan, *Commentary on the Gospel of Luke* 5.104, 108–9, CCSL 14:169, 171–72, trans. Ní Riain, 185, 187–88.
(5) Augustine, *Sermon* 379.1–3, PL 39:1674–75, WSA III/10:355–56.
(6) Philoxenus of Hierapolis, *Fragment* 25, CSCO 392:22–23, trans. in CSCO 393:20.
(7) Gregory the Great, *Homily* 5.4–6, CCSL 141:40–42, CSS 123:30–31.
(8) Ambrose of Milan, *Commentary on the Gospel of Luke* 8.1, CCSL 14:298–99, trans. Ní Riain, 331.
(9) Clement of Alexandria, *Miscellanies* 5.3.5–7, Staehlin, 336; *Who Is the Rich Man That Will Be Saved?* 21, GCS 17/2:173.
(10) Tertullian, *On the Soul* 35.5–6, CCSL 2:837–38.
(11) John Chrysostom, *Homily* 37.5, PG 57:423.
(12) Cyril of Alexandria, *Commentary on Matthew: Fragment* 143–44, MKGK 198–99.
(13) Ambrose of Milan, *Commentary on the Gospel of Luke* 6.2–3, 6–7, CCSL 14:175–77, trans. Ní Riain, 193–95.
(14) John Chrysostom, *Homily* 37.6, PG 57:424–25.
(15) Irenaeus of Lyons, *Against the Heresies* 4.6.7, SC 100:452–54.

(16) Origen, *Commentary on John* 32.355–59, GCS 10:473–75.
(17) Augustine, *Sermon* 67.8, PL 38:436–37, WSA III/3:219; *Sermon* 68.7, PLS 2:506–7, WSA III/3:227.
(18) John Chrysostom, *Homily* 38.5, PG 57:433–34.
(19) Augustine, *Sermon* 69.2–3, PL 38:441, WSA III/3:235–36.
(20) Epiphanius the Latin, *On the Interpretation of the Gospels* 26, PLS 3:865–66.
(21) Caesarius of Arles, *Sermon* 70.3, CCSL 103:299.

Matthew 12

(1) Irenaeus of Lyons, *Against the Heresies* 4.8.3; 4.9.2; 4.17.4, SC 100:470–76, 480–82, 590.
(2) Ambrose of Milan, *Commentary on the Gospel of Luke* 5.28, 32–34, CCSL 14:145–48, trans. Ní Riain, 157–58, 160.
(3) Hilary of Poitiers, *On Matthew* 12.4–5, SC 254:272.
(4) Hilary of Poitiers, *On Matthew* 12.6–8, SC 254:272–74.
(5) Ambrose of Milan, *Commentary on the Gospel of Luke* 5.39–40, CCSL 14:148–49, trans. Ní Riain, 161–62.
(6) John Chrysostom, *Homily* 40.2, PG 57:441.
(7) Chromatius of Aquileia, *Tractatus in Matthaeum* 49.2–4, CCSL 9A:441–43.
(8) Epiphanius the Latin, *On the Interpretation of the Gospels* 24, PLS 3:861–62.
(9) Augustine, *Sermon* 71.1–2, WSA III/3:246–47.
(10) Hilary of Poitiers, *On Matthew* 12.16, SC 254:281.
(11) Ambrose of Milan, *Commentary on the Gospel of Luke* 7.92, CCSL 14:244–45, trans. Ní Riain, 269.
(12) Augustine, *Sermon* 71.7, 9, 18–21, PL 38:448–49, 455–56, WSA III/3:250–51, 256–59.
(13) Clement of Alexandria, *Who Is the Rich Man That Will Be Saved?* 17, GCS 17/2:170.
(14) Origen, *Commentary on Romans* 8.11.4; *Der Römerbriefkommentar des Origenes*, 639.
(15) Hilary of Poitiers, *On Matthew* 12.17–18, SC 254:282–86.
(16) Epiphanius the Latin, *On the Interpretation of the Gospels* 21, PLS 3:854–55.
(17) John Chrysostom, *Homily* 43.3, PG 57:459.
(18) Theodore of Heraclea, *Commentary on Matthew: Fragment* 90, MKGK 81–82.
(19) Eusebius of Emesa, *De Incorporali et Invisibli Deo* 11, Buytaert 2:86–87.
(20) Augustine, *Sermon* 72A.2, WSA III/3:282.
(21) Macarius of Magnesia, *Response of the Only-Begotten* 19.1–3, Goulet, II.19–20, trans. Crafer, *Apocriticus*, 33–34.
(22) Ambrose of Milan, *Commentary on the Gospel of Luke* 6.36, 38, CCSL 14:187–88, trans. Ní Riain, 206–7.
(23) Augustine, *Sermon* 72A.4, WSA III/3:284.

Matthew 13

(1) Gregory of Nyssa, *Commentary on the Song of Songs*, GNO 6:384–86.
(2) Peter Chrysologus, *Sermon* 47.1, CCSL 24:260.
(3) Hilary of Poitiers, *On Matthew* 13.1, SC 254:294–96.
(4) Jerome, *Commentary on St. Matthew* 2.13.3, FOC 117:152.

(5) Augustine, *Sermon* 165.5, PL 38:905, WSA III/5:204.
(6) Cyril of Alexandria, *Commentary on Matthew: Fragment* 165, MKGK 206–7.
(7) John Chrysostom, *Homily* 45.1–2, PG 58:472–73.
(8) Peter Chrysologus, *Sermon* 96.1, CCSL 24A:592.
(9) Philoxenus of Hierapolis, *Fragment* 26, CSCO 392:23–24, trans. CSCO 393:20–21.
(10) Jerome, *Commentary on St. Matthew* 2.13.22–23, FOC 117:155–56.
(11) John Chrysostom, *Homily* 45.2–3, PG 58:474–75.
(12) Cyril of Alexandria, *Commentary on Matthew: Fragment* 168–69, MKGK 207–8.
(13) Gregory the Great, *Homily* 12 (15).2, 5, CCSL 141:104, 106–7, CSS 123:88, 90.
(14) Epiphanius the Latin, *On the Interpretation of the Gospels* 24, PLS 3:860–61.
(15) Augustine, *Sermon* 73A.2–3, PL 2:422–23, WSA III/3:296–97.
(16) Peter Chrysologus, *Sermon* 96.6, CCSL 24A:594–95.
(17) Eusebius of Emesa, *Sermon* 11.6, Buytaert 1:259.
(18) Clement of Alexandria, Fragments from *Catena on Matthew*, PG 9:744.
(19) Ambrose of Milan, *Commentary on the Gospel of Luke* 7.176–81, CCSL 14:275–77, trans. Ní Riain, 303–4.
(20) Ephrem of Nisibis, *Exposition of the Gospel* 29, CSCO.Ar 291:21–22.
(21) Ambrose of Milan, *Commentary on the Gospel of Luke* 7.187–90, CCSL 14:279–81, trans. Ní Riain, 307–9.
(22) Ephrem of Nisibis, *Exposition of the Gospel* 30, CSCO.Ar 291:22–23.
(23) Origen, *Commentary on Matthew* 10.2, GCS 40:2–3.
(24) Chromatius of Aquileia, *Tractatus in Matthaeum* 51.1–2, CCSL 9A:450–51.
(25) Irenaeus of Lyons, *Against the Heresies* 4.26.1, SC 100:712–16.
(26) Origen, *Commentary on Matthew* 10.5, 9–10, GCS 40:5–6, 10–11.
(27) John Chrysostom, *Homily* 47.2, PG 58:483–84.
(28) Ephrem of Nisibis, *Exposition of the Gospel* 86, CSCO.Ar 291:69–70.
(29) Origen, *Commentary on Matthew* 10.12, GCS 40:13–14.
(30) Augustine, *Psalmus contra partem Donati* 3–14, CSEL 51, trans. Carolinne White, *Early Christian Latin Poets* (London: Routledge, 2000); *Sermon* 362.3, PL 39:1612–13, WSA III/10:242.
(31) Peter Chrysologus, *Sermon* 47.3–5, CCSL 24:261–62.
(32) Gregory the Great, *Homily* 9 (11).4, CCSL 141:76, CSS 123:64–65.
(33) Irenaeus of Lyons, *Against the Heresies* 4.9.1, SC 100:476–80.
(34) Origen, *Commentary on Matthew* 10.15, GCS 40:19–20.
(35) Gregory the Great, *Homily* 9 (11).5, CCSL 141:78–79, CSS 123:66.
(36) Origen, *Commentary on Matthew* 10.19, GCS 40:25–26.
(37) Hilary of Poitiers, *On Matthew* 14.2, SC 258:10–12.

Matthew 14

(1) Origen, *Commentary on Matthew* 10.23, GCS 40:31–32.
(2) Hilary of Poitiers, *On Matthew* 14.3, 7–8, SC 258:12–14, 16–20.
(3) Ambrose of Milan, *Commentary on the Gospel of Luke* 6.69, CCSL 14:198–99, trans. Ni Riain, 177.
(4) Jerome, *Commentary on St. Matthew* 2.14.11, SC 242:300–302, FOC 117:169.
(5) Peter Chrysologus, *Sermon* 127.6–7, 9, CCSL 24B:784–86.

(6) Origen, *Commentary on Matthew* 11.1–2, GCS 40:34–36.
(7) Hilary of Poitiers, *On Matthew* 14.10–12, SC 258:20–26.
(8) Eusebius of Emesa, *Sermon* 8.1, 6, 9, 19, 16, Buytaert 1:196, 199–200, 202–3, 210, 207–8.
(9) John Chrysostom, *Homily* 49.3, PG 58:499.
(10) Hilary of Poitiers, *On Matthew* 14.14–16, SC 258:28–30.
(11) Augustine, *Sermon* 75.3–4, PL 38:475–76, WSA III/3:305.
(12) Macarius of Magnesia, *Response of the Only-Begotten* 3.13, 8–30; Goulet, II.121–29, trans. Crafer, *Apocriticus*, 74–75.
(13) Arnobius the Younger, *Expositiunculae in Evangelium*, CCSL 25A:287.
(14) Eusebius of Emesa, *Sermon* 8.22, 24, Buytaert 1:211–13.
(15) Jerome, *Commentary on St. Matthew* 2.14.28, SC 242:314–16, FOC 117:175.
(16) Augustine, *Sermon* 76.1, 4–5, 8, PL 38:479–82, WSA III/3:311, 313, 315; *Sermon* 75.10, PL 38:478, WSA III/3:308–9.
(17) Chromatius of Aquileia, *Tractatus in Matthaeum* 52.6–8, CCSL 9A:458–59.
(18) Hilary of Poitiers, *On Matthew* 14.19, SC 258:32.
(19) John Chrysostom, *Homily* 50.2–3, PG 58:507.
(20) Eusebius of Emesa, *Sermon* 8.25–26, Buytaert 1:213–14.

Matthew 15

(1) John Chrysostom, *Homily* 51.1–2, PG 58:509–12.
(2) Cyril of Alexandria, *Commentary on Matthew: Fragment* 182–83, MKGK 212–13.
(3) Clement of Alexandria, *Instructor* 1.3, GCS 12/1:95.
(4) Origen, *Commentary on Matthew* 11.13–14, GCS 40:54–56.
(5) John Chrysostom, *Homily* 51.5–6, PG 58:515–18.
(6) Origen, *Commentary on Matthew* 11.16–17, GCS 40:59–62.
(7) Hilary of Poitiers, *On Matthew* 15.2–5, SC 258:34–40.
(8) John Chrysostom, *Homily* 52.2–3, PG 58:520–21.
(9) Augustine, *Sermon* 60A.2, WSA III/3:139; *Sermon* 77B.1, WSA III/3:332–33.
(10) Origen, *Commentary on Matthew* 11.18, GCS 40:65.
(11) John Chrysostom, *Homily* 52, 4, PG 58:222.
(12) Hilary of Poitiers, *On Matthew* 15.7–10, SC 258:42–46.
(13) Origen, *Commentary on Matthew* 11.19, GCS 40:67–68.

Matthew 16

(1) Origen, *Commentary on Matthew* 12.2–3, GCS 40:70–73.
(2) Hilary of Poitiers, *On Matthew* 16.1–2, SC 258:48–50.
(3) Chromatius of Aquileia, *Tractatus in Matthaeum* 54.1–2, CCSL 9A:469–70.
(4) Philoxenus of Hierapolis, *Homilies* 4.113, SC 44:123.
(5) Origen, *Commentary on Matthew* 12.5, GCS 40:75–76.
(6) Origen, *Commentary on Matthew* 12.9–10, GCS 40:80–86.
(7) Hilary of Poitiers, *On Matthew* 16.4–7, SC 258:50–54.
(8) Augustine, *Sermon* 183.3–5, PL 38:989–90, WSA III/5:338–39.
(9) Origen, *Commentary on Matthew* 12.11, 15, GCS 40:86–88, 101–5.

(10) Hilary of Poitiers, *On Matthew* 16.4–7, SC 258:54.
(11) Leo the Great, *Sermon* 62.2, CCSL 138A:377–78.
(12) Epiphanius the Latin, *On the Interpretation of the Gospels* 28, PLS 3:869–70.
(13) Augustine, *Sermon* 149.7, PL 38:802, WSA III/5:21–22.
(14) Philoxenus of Hierapolis, *Fragment* 27, CSCO 392:26–28, trans. CSCO 393:23–24.
(15) Macarius of Magnesia, *Response of the Only-Begotten* 3.27, 4–6, Goulet, II.172–74, trans. Crafer, *Apocriticus*, 93–94.
(16) Hilary of Poitiers, *On Matthew* 16.9–10, SC 258:56–58.
(17) John Chrysostom, *Homily* 54.6–7, PG 58:536–37.
(18) Irenaeus of Lyons, *Against the Heresies* 3.18.4, 6, SC 211:352–55, 360–65.
(19) Hilary of Poitiers, *On Matthew* 16.11, SC 258:58–60.
(20) John Chrysostom, *Homily* 55.4, PG 58:544.
(21) Leo the Great, *Sermon* 51.1–2, CCSL 138A:297–98.
(22) Leontius of Constantinople, *Homily* 14.18–19, 21–23, CCSG 17:440–45, *Leontius, Presbyter of Constantinople*, 189–90.

Matthew 17

(1) Augustine, *Sermon* 79A.1, PLS 2:808, WSA III/3:347.
(2) John Chrysostom, *Homily* 56.2–3, PG 58:549–51.
(3) Origen, *Commentary on Matthew* 12.37, GCS 40:152; 12.36, GCS 40:151–52.
(4) Hilary of Poitiers, *On Matthew* 17.2, SC 258:62–64.
(5) Gregory of Nazianzus, *Oration* 40.6, SC 358:206–8.
(6) Maximus the Confessor, *Ambigua* 10, PG 91:1125–28, trans. Andrew Louth, *Maximus the Confessor* (London: Routledge, 1996), 109.
(7) Leo the Great, *Sermon* 51.2–3, CCSL 138A:298–99.
(8) Augustine, *Sermon* 78.3–5, PL 38:491–92, WSA III/3:341–42; *Sermon* 79A.3, PLS 2:809, WSA III/3:348–49.
(9) Origen, *Commentary on Matthew* 12.40, GCS 40:157–61.
(10) John Chrysostom, *Homily* 56.4–5, PG 58:552–53.
(11) Leo the Great, *Sermon* 51.6, CCSL 138A:300–302.
(12) Origen, *Commentary on Matthew* 12.43, GCS 40:169–70.
(13) Origen, *Commentary on Matthew* 13.2, GCS 40:182.
(14) John Chrysostom, *Homily* 57.1–2, PG 58:557–60.
(15) Hilary of Poitiers, *On Matthew* 17.6–8, SC 258:66–68.
(16) John Chrysostom, *Homily* 57.3, PG 58:561–62.
(17) Origen, *Commentary on Matthew* 13.4, GCS 40:187–88; 13.6, GCS 40:193–94; 13.7, GCS 40:198.
(18) Origen, *Commentary on Matthew* 13.8, GCS 40:202–4.
(19) John Chrysostom, *Homily* 58.1–2, PG 58:566–68.
(20) Origen, *Commentary on Matthew* 13.10, GCS 40:207–8.

Matthew 18

(1) Origen, *Commentary on Matthew* 13.16, 18, GCS 40:222, 226–27.
(2) Chromatius of Aquileia, *Tractatus in Matthaeum* 55.1–2, CCSL 9A:472–74.
(3) Epiphanius the Latin, *On the Interpretation of the Gospels* 27, PLS 3:866–67.
(4) Maximus of Turin, *Sermon* 48.4, CCSL 23:189–90, ACW 50:114.
(5) Philoxenus of Hierapolis, *Homilies* 5.133–34, SC 44.138–39.
(6) Origen, *Commentary on Matthew* 13.25, GCS 40:247–48.
(7) Augustine, *Sermon* 81.7, PL 38:503–4, WSA III/3:363–64.
(8) John Chrysostom, *Homily* 59.5, PG 58:579–80.
(9) Ambrose of Milan, *Commentary on the Gospel of Luke* 7.209–10, CCSL 14:287, trans. Ní Riain, 320–21.
(10) Jerome, *Commentary on St. Matthew* 3.18.12, FOC 117:210.
(11) Epiphanius the Latin, *On the Interpretation of the Gospels* 27, PLS 3:867–68.
(12) Ambrose of Milan, *Commentary on the Gospel of Luke* 8.21–22, CCSL 14:305, trans. Ní Riain, 342–43.
(13) Jerome, *Commentary on St. Matthew* 3.18.15–17, FOC 117:211.
(14) Augustine, *Sermon* 82.4, 10, PL 38:507, 510–11, WSA III/3:369–70, 374–75.
(15) Jerome, *Commentary on St. Matthew* 3.18.19–20, FOC 117:212.
(16) Peter Chrysologus, *Sermon* 132.3–4, CCSL 24B:811–12.
(17) Hilary of Poitiers, *On Matthew* 18.10, SC 258:84–86.
(18) Ambrose of Milan, *Commentary on the Gospel of Luke* 8.23, CCSL 14:305–6, trans. Ní Riain, 343.
(19) Augustine, *Sermon* 83.6, 7, PL 38:517–18, WSA III/3:384–85.
(20) Jerome, *Commentary on St. Matthew* 3.18.23, FOC 117:213.
(21) Augustine, *Sermon* 83.2, PL 38:515, WSA III/3:382.
(22) Origen, *Commentary on Matthew* 14.8, GCS 40:293–95.
(23) John Chrysostom, *Homily* 61.5, PG 58:590.

Matthew 19

(1) Gregory of Nazianzus, *Oration* 37.2–3, SC 318:272–76.
(2) Origen, *Commentary on Matthew* 14.16, GCS 40:318–20.
(3) Gregory of Nazianzus, *Oration* 37.5, SC 318:280–82.
(4) Augustine, *Sermon* 341.12, PL 39:1500, WSA III/10:26–27.
(5) Gregory of Nazianzus, *Oration* 37.9–10, SC 318:288–92.
(6) Ephrem of Nisibis, *Commentary on the Gospel Harmony* 14.18, CSCO.Ar 137:196–97, SC 121:253–54.
(7) Hilary of Poitiers, *On Matthew* 19.3, SC 258:90–92.
(8) Ambrose of Milan, *Commentary on the Gospel of Luke* 8.57–58, CCSL 14:319–20, trans. Ní Riain, 289–90.
(9) Epiphanius the Latin, *On the Interpretation of the Gospels* 25, PLS 3:862.
(10) Ambrose of Milan, *On the Faith* 1.2.14–16, CSEL 78:9–10; *Commentary on the Gospel of Luke* 8.65–66, CCSL 14:322–23, trans. Ní Riain, 292–93.
(11) John Chrysostom, *Homily* 63.1–2, PG 58:604–5.
(12) Origen, *Commentary on Matthew* 15.14, GCS 40:385–90.

(13) Clement of Alexandria, *Who Is the Rich Man That Will Be Saved?* 9, 20, GCS 17/2:165, 172.
(14) Augustine, *Sermon* 86.2–3, 5, PL 38:524–25, WSA III/3:396–98 (modified).
(15) Augustine, *Sermon* 85.2, PL 38:521, WSA III/3:392.
(16) Maximus of Turin, *Sermon* 32.1, CCSL 23:125–26, ACW 50:77–78 (modified).
(17) Clement of Alexandria, *Who Is the Rich Man That Will Be Saved?* 20, 14, GCS 17/2:172–73, 168–69.
(18) Hilary of Poitiers, *On Matthew* 20.3–4, SC 258:104–6.
(19) Epiphanius the Latin, *On the Interpretation of the Gospels* 25, PLS 3:863–64.

Matthew 20

(1) Pseudo-Athanasius, *On the Laborers in the Vineyard, Coptic Homilies in the Dialect of Upper Egypt*, in *Coptic Texts*, vol. 1, ed. and trans. E. A. W. Budge (New York: AMS, 1977), 226–29.
(2) John Chrysostom, *Homily* 64.3–4, PG 58:612–13.
(3) Augustine, *Sermon* 87.4, PL 38:531–32, WSA III/3:408–9.
(4) Gregory the Great, *Homily* 19.1–2, CCSL 141:143–45, CSS 123:78–79.
(5) John Chrysostom, *Homily* 65.1–2, PG 58:617–19.
(6) Peter Chrysologus, *Sermon* 72A.1–2, 4, CCSL 24A:435–38; *Sermon* 72B.1–2, CCSL 24A:440–41.
(7) Hilary of Poitiers, *On Matthew* 20.9–12, SC 258:112–18.
(8) John Chrysostom, *Homily* 65.2, PG 58:618–19.
(9) Gregory the Great, *Homily* 27.4, CCSL 141:232, CSS 123:214.
(10) Jerome, *Commentary on St. Matthew* 3.20.24–25, FOC 117:228.
(11) John Chrysostom, *Homily* 65.4–5, PG 58:622–24.
(12) Hilary of Poitiers, *On Matthew* 20.13, SC 258:118–20.
(13) John Chrysostom, *Homily* 66.1, PG 58:625–26.
(14) Augustine, *Sermon* 88.10, 13, PL 38:544–46, WSA III/3:425–28.

Matthew 21

(1) Origen, *Commentary on John* 10.162, 165, 172, 174–77, 185–89, SC 157:482, 484, 488–90, 494–96.
(2) Ambrose of Milan, *Commentary on the Gospel of Luke* 9.3–5, 8–9, CCSL 14:333–35, trans. Ní Riain, 304–6.
(3) Cyril of Alexandria, *Commentary on Matthew: Fragment* 230–31, MKGK 231–32.
(4) Eusebius of Emesa, *Sermon* 11.12–14, Buytaert 1:263–66.
(5) Augustine, *Sermon* 121.3, PL 38:678–79, WSA III/4:235.
(6) Ambrose of Milan, *Commentary on the Gospel of Luke* 9.18–19, CCSL 14:337–38, trans. Ní Riain, 308–9.
(7) Jerome, *Commentary on St. Matthew* 3.21.12–13, FOC 117:235–37.
(8) John Chrysostom, *Homily* 67.1, PG 58:632–33.
(9) Eusebius of Emesa, *Sermon* 11.7, 16–23, Buytaert 1:260, 267–72.
(10) John Chrysostom, *Homily* 67.1–2, PG 58:633–34.
(11) Hilary of Poitiers, *On Matthew* 21.15, SC 258:140.
(12) John Chrysostom, *Homily* 67.2–3, PG 58:634–35.
(13) Peter Chrysologus, *Sermon* 31.1, CCSL 24:178–79.
(14) Hilary of Poitiers, *On Matthew* 22.1–2, SC 258:142–44.

Matthew 22

(1) John Chrysostom, *Homily* 69.2, PG 58:651.
(2) Ambrose of Milan, *Commentary on the Gospel of Luke* 7.202–4, CCSL 14:284–85, trans. Ní Riain, 314–15.
(3) Augustine, *Sermon* 90.1, 4–6, PL 38:559–63, WSA III/3:449–52 (revised).
(4) Gregory the Great, *Homily* 38.1–4, 6–7, 9, CCSL 141:360–62, 365–66, 368–69, CSS 123:339–42.
(5) Tertullian, *On Idolatry* 15.3, CCSL 2:1115–16; *On Flight in Persecution* 12.8, 10, CCSL 2:1152–53.
(6) Athanasius of Alexandria, *History of the Arians* 44, PG 25b:744d–748a.
(7) Hilary of Poitiers, *On Matthew* 23.2, SC 258:152–54.
(8) Ambrose of Milan, *Epistle* 76.19, CSEL 82:2, 118–19, FC 26:371.
(9) Augustine, *Sermon* 90.10, PL 38:566, WSA III/3:455–56.
(10) John Chrysostom, *Homily* 70.2, PG 58:657–58.
(11) Augustine, *Enchiridion* 9.28–29, CCSL 46:64–65, WSA I/8:291–92 (modified).
(12) Clement of Alexandria, *Who Is the Rich Man That Will Be Saved?* 27, 29, GCS 17/2:178–79.
(13) Hilary of Poitiers, *On Matthew* 23.6–7, SC 258:158–60.
(14) Leo the Great, *Sermon* 12.2, CCSL 138:49–51.
(15) Augustine, *Sermon* 179A.3–4, PLS 2:709–12, WSA III/5:308–9.
(16) Augustine, *Sermon* 399.3, 5, PL 40:670–72, WSA III/10:459–61.
(17) John Chrysostom, *Homily* 71.1, PG 58:663–64.
(18) Augustine, *Sermon* 91.1, 3, PL 38:567–68, WSA III/3:459; *Sermon* 92.2–3, PL 38:572–73, WSA III/3:467–68; *Sermon* 51.20, PL 38:344, WSA III/3:32–33.

Matthew 23

(1) Hilary of Poitiers, *On Matthew* 24.1, SC 258:164–66.
(2) John Chrysostom, *Homily* 72.2–3, PG 58:669–70.
(3) John Chrysostom, *Homily* 72.3, PG 58:671.
(4) Hilary of Poitiers, *On Matthew* 24.2–3, SC 258:166–68.
(5) John Chrysostom, *Homily* 73.2, PG 58:674–75.
(6) Cyril of Alexandria, *Commentary on Matthew: Fragment* 258, MKGK 240.
(7) John Chrysostom, *Homily* 73.3, PG 58:676.
(8) Eusebius of Caesarea, *Theophania* 4.18, GCS 11/2:27–28, 192–93.
(9) Hilary of Poitiers, *On Matthew* 24.11, SC 258:176–78.
(10) Augustine, *Enchiridion* 24.97, CCSL 46:100, WSA I/8:328–29 (modified).
(11) John Chrysostom, *Homily* 74.3, 4, PG 58:683–84.

Matthew 24

(1) Hilary of Poitiers, *On Matthew* 25.1, SC 258:180.
(2) John Chrysostom, *Homily* 75.1, PG 58:685–86.
(3) Hilary of Poitiers, *On Matthew* 25.2, SC 258:180–84.
(4) Origen, *On First Principles* 2.8.3, GCS 22:156–58, *Origenes Werke* 5, trans. G. W. Butterworth (Gloucester, MA: Peter Smith, 1973), 123–24 (modified).

(5) Ambrose of Milan, *Commentary on the Gospel of Luke* 10.9–12, CCSL 14:348–49, trans. Ní Riain, 319–20 (modified).
(6) Hilary of Poitiers, *On Matthew* 25.3, 5–6, SC 258:184–86.
(7) Hilary of Poitiers, *On Matthew* 25.7, SC 258:190.
(8) Ephrem of Nisibis, *Exposition of the Gospel* 91, CSCO.Ar 291:74; CSCO.Ar 292:68.
(9) Cyril of Alexandria, *Commentary on Matthew: Fragment* 269, MKGK 244.
(10) Ambrose of Milan, *Commentary on the Gospel of Luke* 10.16–19, CCSL 14:350–51, trans. Ní Riain, 321–22 (modified).
(11) Victorinus of Poetovio, *Incipit de Matheo evange* 3–5, 228–30.
(12) John Chrysostom, *Homily* 76.2–3, PG 58:696–97.
(13) Victorinus of Poetovio, *Incipit de Matheo evange* 9, 6–7, 232, 230–31.
(14) Hilary of Poitiers, *On Matthew* 26.1, SC 258:192–94.
(15) Ambrose of Milan, *Commentary on the Gospel of Luke* 10.39–43, CCSL 14:356–57, trans. Ní Riain, 327–28.
(16) Hilary of Poitiers, *On Matthew* 26.2–3, SC 258:194–96.
(17) Augustine, *Sermon* 81.8, 9, PL 38:504–5, WSA III/3:364–65.
(18) John Chrysostom, *Homily* 76.5, PG 58:699; *Homily* 77.1, PG 58:701–2.
(19) Hilary of Poitiers, *On Matthew* 26.4, SC 258:196–98.
(20) Cyril of Alexandria, *Commentary on Matthew: Fragment* 274, MKGK 246–47.
(21) Ambrose of Milan, *Commentary on the Gospel of Luke* 8.46–47, CCSL 14:314, trans. Ní Riain, 285.
(22) John Chrysostom, *Homily* 77.2–3, PG 58:705.
(23) Cyril of Alexandria, *Commentary on Matthew: Fragment* 275, MKGK 247.

Matthew 25

(1) Hilary of Poitiers, *On Matthew* 27.4, SC 258:204–6.
(2) Augustine, *Sermon* 93.2, 5–6, 10, PL 38:574–77, WSA III/3:469, 471–73.
(3) Caesarius of Arles, *Sermon* 155.1, CCSL 104:632–33.
(4) Gregory the Great, *Homily* 12.1, CCSL 141:81–82, CSS 123:69–70.
(5) Victorinus of Poetovio, *On the Ten Virgins*, PLS 1:174.
(6) Caesarius of Arles, *Sermon* 156.3, CCSL 104:637–38.
(7) Gregory the Great, *Homily* 12.3, CCSL 141:83–84; *Homily* 36.10–11, CCSL 141:342, CSS 123:69–71, 322.
(8) Augustine, *Sermon* 223D.3, PLS 2:718, WSA III/6:225.
(9) John Chrysostom, *Homily* 78, PG 58:714–15.
(10) Gregory the Great, *Homily* 9.1, 4–7, CCSL 141:58–60, 62–64, CSS 123:127–28, 130–32 (modified).
(11) Peter Chrysologus, *Sermon* 123.4–5, CCSL 24A:740–41.
(12) Valerian of Cimelium, *Homily* 7.4, 6, PL 52:715–16, FOC 17:348, 350.
(13) Augustine, *Sermon* 113B.4, WSA III/4:186.
(14) Peter Chrysologus, *Sermon* 162.6–7, CCSL 24B:1002; *Sermon* 14.3–4, CCSL 24:89; *Sermon* 144.8–9, CCSL 24B:884–85.
(15) Caesarius of Arles, *Sermon* 157.4, CCSL 104:643.
(16) Augustine, *Sermon* 178.4, PL 38:962–63, WSA III/5:291–92.
(17) John Chrysostom, *Homily* 79.1, PG 58:717–18.

(18) Valerian of Cimelium, *Homily* 8.4, PL 52:718–19, FOC 17:355.

Matthew 26

(1) Leo the Great, *Sermon* 22.4, CCSL 138:96–97.
(2) Ambrose of Milan, *Commentary on the Gospel of Luke* 6.13–15, 27–29, CCSL 14:179–80, 183–84, trans. Ní Riain, 160–61, 164–65 (modified).
(3) Hilary of Poitiers, *On Matthew* 29.2, SC 258:220–21.
(4) Leontius of Constantinople, *Homily* 6.10–11, 13, CCSG 17.236–37, *Leontius, Presbyter of Constantinople*, 84–86.
(5) John Chrysostom, *Homily* 80, PG 58:727.
(6) Ambrose of Milan, *Commentary on the Gospel of Luke* 10.46, CCSL 14:358, trans. Ní Riain, 328.
(7) Caelius Sedulius, *Carmen Paschale* 5.20–37, CSEL 10:115–17, trans. White, *Early Christian Latin Poets*, 108.
(8) Leo the Great, *Sermon* 58.3, CCSL 138A:342–43.
(9) Leontius of Constantinople, *Homily* 6.5, 7, CCSG 17.232–33, *Leontius, Presbyter of Constantinople*, 82–83.
(10) John Chrysostom, *Homily* 82, PG 58:737–38.
(11) Augustine, *Sermon* 228B.3, WSA III/6:262.
(12) John Chrysostom, *Homily* 82, PG 58:742–43.
(13) Augustine, *Sermon* 229P.3–4, WSA III/6:328–29.
(14) Juvencus, *Poem on the Gospels* 4.433–74, CSEL 24:130–31, trans. White, *Early Christian Latin Poets*, 37–38.
(15) Hilary of Poitiers, *On Matthew* 31.2, 5, 8, SC 258:226–29, 231–33, 235.
(16) Ambrose of Milan, *Commentary on the Gospel of Luke* 10.56–58, trans. Ní Riain, 332–33; *Explanatio Psalmorum XII* 61.6, CSEL 64:381.
(17) Leo the Great, *Sermon* 56.2; 58.5.
(18) Maximus the Confessor, *Opuscule* 7.80c–81a, trans. Louth, *Maximus the Confessor*, 188–89.
(19) John Chrysostom, *Homily* 83, PG 58:745–46.
(20) Augustine, *Sermon* 344.3, WSA III/10:50–51.
(21) Ambrose of Milan, *Commentary on the Gospel of Luke* 10.63–64, CCSL 14:364, trans. Ní Riain, 334.
(22) Leo the Great, *Sermon* 54.3, CCSL 138A:319.
(23) Ambrose of Milan, *Commentary on the Gospel of Luke* 10.67–69, CCSL 14:365–66, trans. Ní Riain, 35–36.
(24) John Chrysostom, *Homily* 88, PG 58:775; *Homily* 84.2, PG 58:753.
(25) Cyril of Alexandria, *Commentary on Matthew: Fragment* 299, MKGK 260.
(26) Hilary of Poitiers, *On Matthew* 32.3, SC 258:243.
(27) John Chrysostom, *Homily* 85.1, PG 58:757–58.
(28) Hilary of Poitiers, *On Matthew* 32.4, SC 258:243–44.
(29) Ambrose of Milan, *Commentary on the Gospel of Luke* 10.74–75, 78–79, CCSL 14:367–68, 368–69, trans. Ní Riain, 337–38.
(30) Leo the Great, *Sermon* 60.4, CCSL 138A:367–68.
(31) John Chrysostom, *Homily* 82, PG 58:742–43.

Matthew 27

(1) Leo the Great, *Sermon* 62.4; 54.3, CCSL 138A:379–80; 319.
(2) Ambrose of Milan, *Commentary on the Gospel of Luke* 10.95–96, CCSL 14:373, trans. Ní Riain, 342.
(3) Ambrose of Milan, *Commentary on the Gospel of Luke* 10.97–99, CCSL 14:373–74, trans. Ní Riain, 343.
(4) Augustine, *Sermon* 229F.1, *Miscellanea Agostiniana* 1:471–72, WSA III/6:285–86.
(5) Leo the Great, *Sermon* 59.2, CCSL 138A:350–51 (beta text).
(6) Hilary of Poitiers, *On Matthew* 33.3, SC 258:250–52.
(7) John Chrysostom, *Homily* 87.1, PG 58:769–70.
(8) Ambrose of Milan, *Commentary on the Gospel of Luke* 10.107, CCSL 14:376, trans. Ní Riain, 345.
(9) Leo the Great, *Sermon* 59.5, CCSL 138A:355–56.
(10) Caelius Sedulius, *Carmen Paschale* 5.182–99, PL 19:724a–727a, trans. White, *Early Christian Latin Poets*, 110.
(11) Augustine, *Sermon* 218.7, PL 38:1085–86, WSA III/6:184–85 (modified).
(12) Hilary of Poitiers, *On Matthew* 33.5, SC 258:252–54.
(13) Eusebius of Emesa, *Sermon* 11.24–25, Buytaert 1:272–74.
(14) Gregory of Nazianzus, *On the Son*, PG 406a–407a, trans. Sykes, *Poemata Arcana*, 8–9.
(15) Caelius Sedulius, *Carmen Paschale* 5.234–46, PL 19:730a–731a, trans. White, *Early Christian Latin Poets*, 111–12.
(16) John Chrysostom, *Homily* 88.1, PG 58:775.
(17) Leo the Great, *Sermon* 67.7; 68.2, CCSL 138A:412–13, 415–16.
(18) Peter Chrysologus, *Sermon* 37.3, CCSL 24:213.
(19) Ephrem of Nisibis, *Nisibene Hymns* 36.1, CSCO.S 240:8–9, trans. *Hymn* 7.1 by Brock, *Harp of the Spirit*, 40.
(20) Venantius Fortunatus, *Poem* 2.1, "The Lord's Cross," PL 88:87b–c, trans. White, *Early Christian Latin Poets*, 165–66.
(21) Ambrose of Milan, *Commentary on the Gospel of Luke* 10.128, CCSL 14:382, trans. Ní Riain, 351.
(22) Leo the Great, *Sermon* 53.1–2; 57.4; 59.7, CCSL 138A:314, 336–37, 357–59.
(23) Ephrem of Nisibis, *Homily on Our Lord* 3.1, 3, 4–4.1, CSCO.S 270:3–4, FOC 91:277–80.
(24) Pseudo-Lactantius, *Carmen de Passione Domini*, PL 7:283d–286a.
(25) Leo the Great, *Sermon* 68.3, CCSL 138A:417.
(26) Hilary of Poitiers, *On Matthew* 33.8, SC 258:256–58.
(27) Ambrose of Milan, *Commentary on the Gospel of Luke* 10.136–40, CCSL 14:384–86, trans. Ní Riain, 354–55.

Matthew 28

(1) Peter Chrysologus, *Sermon* 74.3–5, CCSL 24A:452–54.
(2) Augustine, *On the Consensus of the Gospels: De consensu Evangelistarum libri quattuor* 3.24.66.
(3) Peter Chrysologus, *Sermon* 74.7, CCSL 24A:455–56; *Sermon* 75.4, 6, CCSL 24A:460–62.
(4) Peter Chrysologus, *Sermon* 80.2–3, CCSL 24A:491–93.

(5) Cyril of Alexandria, *Commentary on Matthew: Fragment* 317, MKGK 267–68.
(6) Gregory the Great, *Homily* 21.3, CCSL 141:175, CSS 123:159.
(7) John Chrysostom, *Homily* 89, PG 58:784.
(8) Leo the Great, *Sermon* 73.1, CCSL 138A:450–51.
(9) Gregory of Nazianzus, *Oration* 45.1, 13, 29, PG 36:624a–b, 640c–641b, 661d–663a.
(10) John Chrysostom, *Homily* 90.1, PG 58:787–88.
(11) Eusebius of Caesarea, *Demonstratio evangelica* 3.7.21–23; 1.6.75–76, *Eusebius Werke*, vol. 6, ed. Ivar A. Heikel (GCS 23; Leipzig: J. C. Hinrichs, 1913), 144, 34–35; *Laus Constantini* 16.8–9, *Eusebius Werke*, vol. 1, ed. Ivar A. Heikel (GCS 7; Leipzig: J. C. Hinrichs, 1902), 250–51.
(12) John Chrysostom, *Homily* 90.2, PG 58:789–90.
(13) Cyril of Alexandria, *Commentary on Matthew: Fragment* 321, MKGK 269.
(14) Peter Chrysologus, *Sermon* 80.9–10, CCSL 24A:495–96.
(15) Augustine, *Sermon* 384.3, PL 39:1690, WSA III/10:384–85; *Sermon* 215.8–9, PL 38:1076; WSA III/6:164–65.
(16) Leo the Great, *Sermon* 73.4, CCSL 138A:452–54.

Index of Names

Index of Subjects

Index of Scripture References